RICE

The Management of Election Campaigns

Consulting Editor

John C. Bollens

University of California,
Los Angeles

The Management of Election Campaigns

Robert Agranoff

Northern Illinois University

Holbrook Press, Inc.   Boston

Library of Congress Cataloging in Publication Data

Agranoff, Robert,
  The management of election campaigns.

  Bibliography: p.
  Includes index,
    1. Campaigns management—United States.
2. Electioneering—United States. I. Title.
JK2281.A59   329'.01   76-883
ISBN 0-205-05039-5

To the memory of my parents,
Phillip and Rose

Contents

Preface

This book is devoted to the principle that political science does have something to contribute to those who are interested in practical politics. Too often the practitioner has ignored the academic as unconcerned with the real experiences and problems that politicians confront on a day-to-day basis. The academic, in turn, has dismissed the practitioner as concerned only with parochial and peripheral matters. My personal involvement in both worlds—as a course and field-work instructor, campaign manager, campaign staffer, political party official, paid consultant and unpaid advisor—demonstrated that there was no convenient means of bringing basic political science understanding of campaigns and voting processes to those who need it. There was no readily available conceptual base to "take off" from, helping students and campaigners understand the basic situation, assess a candidacy, plan a strategy, establish an organization, or select appropriate media. To bridge this gap it seemed necessary to compile, for the campaigner, that which is relevant from the past quarter-century of research into campaigns, elections, voting, political parties, communications, and other socio-political processes, a work that would be useful in understanding and operating within election campaigns. Hopefully, this book, which does not require a prior political science background, will help comprehend the processes while broadening outlooks and encourage involvement in and management of election campaigns.

One need not be a formal campaign manager to be concerned with the administration of campaigns. Like so many other activities, campaigning involves a considerable amount of problem solving, and it is ordinarily useful to have the benefit of an information base when approaching such a situation. Everyone who studies, observes, or is in some way actively involved in a campaign, must utilize information to reach a solution. Most of our information is based on experiences and observations. In campaigning, many come from "outside" endeavors and life experiences. This book is predicated on raising the level of "inside" or election-campaign information so that it can be combined with experience to assist one in making the numerous judgmental decisions required in campaigning.

The reader will quickly note the infant state of managerial technology revealed herein; it is an *accurate* reflection of the state of the art. No mystical systems, magical campaign-management formulas, or secret weapons are revealed; nor are there any quick and easy recipes for victory. That few of the studies cited are of elections held long ago is an unfortunate result of little or no subsequent research on these topics. They are cited for the concepts they illustrate, rather than the relevance of time and setting. These dormant concepts and other conceptual gaps discovered by the reader should intimate the future directions of campaign research. I have tried to develop as much relevant professional literature, managerial insights, case experiences, and hints as are possible to include within the covers of a single book. For those who wish to investigate various subjects in a more detailed and technical fashion, ample references and bibliographic citations are provided at the conclusion of each chapter.

However, the key to campaign management is not necessarily technical knowledge, but *understanding* of the situation and the process. One must know what campaigning is all about as well as know how to apply that knowledge. It will become abundantly clear that I am as equally concerned with creating an outlook on management as I am with transmitting specialized information.

I have made a conscious decision to err by de-emphasizing the crucial political dimension of campaigning. Needless to say, I have observed and experienced many strategic decisions made on the basis of factional pressures or to allay the fears and jealousies of major supporters or simply to please volunteer workers. A major event, such as a national or local crisis, war, or recession, can have a profound impact on a campaign. The "character" of the 1974 campaigns, with demands for disclosures of candidate personal income tax returns, eschewal of large contributions, unostentatious electioneering, and tones of personal sincerity, was shaped by the Watergate imbroglio. Yet, it is my opinion that there are numerous, descriptive, political campaign books, and too few deal with concepts, managerial approaches, and concrete mechanisms for the operation of a campaign. Thus, the error of commission.

Space, organization, and other considerations make it necessary to neglect some important dimensions of campaigning. It is difficult to deal with primary elections separately because of an unfortunate lack of significant, comparable literature. However, the management considerations of setting are designed to be applicable to all situations, from the small community election to national office elections, high- or low-visibility contests, small and large budgets, primary or general elections. Another important dimension, unfortunately undeveloped, is the role, in a theoretical sense, of campaigns in the American political system. This important subject is better left to separate works. An additional neglected concern, here and elsewhere, is the systematic treatment of election administration. Electoral reform has engendered a renewed interest in this important subject, and, in the future, the complexity of election codes may make it increasingly necessary for the campaigner and the political scientist, as well as the administrator of elections, to become familiar with election administration.

This book is organized in a braidlike fashion. First, an introduction to the nature of campaigns, voting, and participation and communication processes is developed (Chapters 1, 2, and 3, respectively). Next, the approaches and techniques of studying these processes are revealed (Chapters 4 and 5), so that the particular situation can be investigated. The use of these tools for strategic planning is then discussed (Chapter 6). Next, the more specific aspects of organization (Chapter 7), finance (Chapters 8 and 9), public relations (Chapter 10), the media (Chapters 11 to 14), and direct voter contact (Chapter 15) are discussed as they relate to previous sections of the book. Within these latter topics, the approach, again, is to begin by presenting basic concepts and findings, and then, practical applications. Therefore, it became necessary to introduce a topic, then weave new topics into the braid, only to bring topics presented earlier back into the body of the book, at a later stage, as they apply in research, planning, or practical contexts.

The acknowledgements for this book proved most difficult to write, because so many have contributed. Needless to say, the approach taken here would not be possible without the research of the many authors cited throughout the text. Moreover, hundreds of students, candidates, and campaigners whom I have consulted or served, in addition to professional exchanges, have helped to shape the perspectives contained herein. In particular, Dale Enoch of the Institute of Politics in Arkansas was helpful in reading portions of the manuscript and reacting to many ideas. Robert D. Cantor, Paul H. Conn, Douglas Dobson, Frederick H. Damaske, Edward C. Dreyer, George Goodwin and George J. Graham, Jr. read the manuscript and tried to keep me on the political science straight and narrow. Charles Backstrom pored over the early chapters with a fine tooth comb and again demonstrated how much one can learn from him about blending political science and politics. Henry Fisher, now State Chairman of the Minnesota Democratic-Farmer-Labor (Democratic) Party helped by opening up campaign files to me, by reacting to my original outline, by a detailed sharing of his experiences in campaign management, and by giving me hours of free consultation. Several people contributed to the manuscript preparation, including: Rodney Christie, William Denham, Lisa Parts, Dianne McDaniel and Alex Pattakos. John Servideo of Holbrook Press did an outstanding job of managing the production of the book. My wife Zola, who somehow has found a way to endure both involvement and living in a household with this project, typed more than two drafts of the manuscript. Our children, Karen and David, endured considerable parental inattention in the interest of this book. Finally, Paul Conway, senior editor at Holbrook Press, deserves much credit. Paul and others at Holbrook encouraged me to write this book. I find working with Paul to be relaxed yet professional, and I admire his patience with tardy authors.

Each year the number of persons concerned with the problems of campaign management reaches the hundreds of thousands. The link between political science and these active and concerned citizens has been tenuous. Hopefully this will be the beginning of a new direction.

Robert Agranoff

The Nature
of Election Campaigns

Election campaigns are among the most significant but perhaps the most neglected enterprises in the United States. The events surrounding the Watergate break-in before the 1972 presidential election, the subsequent cover-up, the alleged campaign-funding abuses, campaign intelligence tactics, and the enormous sums of money spent have sustained public interest in that campaign long after the votes were counted. Yet, the 1972 presidential campaign is not typical. In a four-year cycle of general elections, more than 500,000 officials are elected to office: 537 to national offices, more than 13,000 to state offices, more than 56,000 to special district offices, more than 74,000 to county offices, more than 108,000 to school board offices, more than 129,000 to township offices, and more than 144,000 to municipal offices. The officers elected to these positions make numerous, significant decisions: they levy taxes, determine pollution control policies, zone land, control our educational system, organize and supervise the delivery of most public services, and administer state and federal programs. In spite of the importance and ubiquity of these offices, too little attention is paid to the process by which people reach them.

Many fields of endeavor have long traditions of study and management of their enterprise; business, marketing, labor, education, and military science are but a few. Election campaigns have been part of our lives for a long time yet there exists no such tradition of management. In the past, any attention given to campaigns has been anecdotal, journalistic, or the cookbook approach—providing a recipe for easy victory. Systematic attention given to campaigns and campain management is a recent phenomenon.

A number of reasons have led to this situation. First, many assumed that party organizations were the exclusive agents for election campaigns, and, since more voters previously were staunch party supporters, the greater emphasis in electioneering was the mobilization of the "faithful" behind a party ticket—a tactic well suited to party organization effort. Second, campaigns are short-term operations. Ordinarily the efforts expended to elect a candidate range in time from a few weeks to several months. This inevitably has meant that campaigning is rarely a continuous or evolving process. Third, campaign personnel (party workers, volunteers, managers, and candidates) change from campaign to campaign. Such constant turnover promotes inexperience and discontinuity—few records are kept, procedures are rarely codified, and techniques are passed on haphazardly. Fourth, campaigns are usually characterized by an aura of secrecy and self-interest because it is thought advantageous to keep one's strategy and techniques within the organization. The idea of exchanging information is often considered detrimental to the cause so campaigners have a long tradition of guarding against strategic leaks. Fifth, until recently a functional body of scientific knowledge for the purpose of gaining insights and making useful inferences for planning campaigns did not exist. And sixth, the development and application of technology in the form of television, computers, and opinion polls is a recent innovation. In short, campaign management has more closely resembled a cottage industry rather than a business availing itself of modern technology.

Several factors have contributed to a significant reversal of these trends. Voting is less party oriented, requiring candidates to mobilize their own electorates. In search of more diverse electorates they increasingly find that they must put their own campaigns operation together. The contemporary candidate and campaigner is less likely to rise up through party organization ranks. The newer breed is more likely to come from outside traditional political ranks and brings diverse experiences to the campaign—often in a more systematic or managerial fashion than their earlier couterparts. The increased output of research into the political process, in general, and elections, in particular, have made it possible to speak of a body of knowledge, from which strategic principles, useful guidelines, and *caveats* can be gleaned for the campaigner. The advent of campaign technology has produced a corps of new technologists concerned with the art and science of campaigning. These new campaign specialists are developing a new technical field of applied campaign management. Thus, new political forces and advances in knowledge and technology are contributing to an emerging tradition of campaign management.

The intent of this book is to bring together political trends, knowledge, and experience, into a work on campaign management. Similar to its counterparts in other fields of management, it contains both art and science. It is predicated on the following assumptions: (1) that one must understand campaigns and attendant political processes before one can manage them; (2) that management of campaigns involves a blend of the best information obtainable *and* the wisest judgment about that information; (3) that campaign strategies and tactics are situational—one must understand the situation and apply relevant knowledge; (4) at present, campaigns are among America's most poorly managed enterprises; and (5) they can be better managed with information and insight. Whether the reader is a student involved in a campaign as part of an academic experience, a campaign worker, a campaign manager, or a candidate, all are campaigners and must understand as much as possible about campaigns before they can operate with them in a meaningful capacity.

WHAT ARE CAMPAIGNS?

A campaign is a coordinated effort to achieve some objective, such as electing a candidate to office, connecting various operations that organize and use environmental, human, social, and material resources. We hear "campaign" used often in connection with other efforts, particularly with military battles and advertising programs. The military campaign for Italy in World War II was a series of connected military operations, forming a distinct stage of the war. So too are the combined efforts of a business firm, an advertising agency, and the media to capture a share of the market.

Perhaps because they are open to public scrutiny, election, military, and advertising campaigns all share the "'distinction" of being subject to public examination and the criticism of armchair strategists. Yet, until recently election campaigns did not benefit from a body of knowledge or a corps of professionals. Indeed, the "first wave" of attention focused on election campaigns borrowed much from other types of campaigns. Hence words like "counterattack," "intelligence," "footsoldiers," "lieutenants," and "frontal assault" became part of the lexicon of campaigning. One book about campaigning was entitled *Politics Battle Plan*.[1] Election campaign advertising plans looked strikingly similar to those written for product advertising,[2] often working toward capturing a "share of the market," discussing "impact and reach" or "selling the candidate."[3]

Election campaigns, however, are connecting operations that use different types and mixtures of environmental, human, social, and material factors than do military battles or product-advertising campaigns. In election campaigns the campaigner tries to win by connecting operations that deal with idiomorphic forces: basic premises about the nature of the constituency, political resources, assets and liabilities, and advantages.

Premises about the Constituency

At all levels of organization and planning, candidates or campaigners establish their campaigns on the basis of some thoughts about the constituency: values, its geography, major social and economic arrangements, previous political behavior, and many other aspects.

One very important premise that campaigners often have about their constituencies concerns the level of potential and actual political activism of the citizenry. Some campaigners undoubtedly underestimate the potential for political activity, but most overestimate it. Political activists themselves and very often having activist associates, campaigners often assume that their entire constituency is composed of an involved citizenry willing to act through the same channels as themselves. The evidence is to the contrary. Table 1.1 summarizes the reports of citizens concerning their political activity. Voting in presidential elections is the only political activity engaged in by the majority of Americans. More than 25 percent do not even vote. Only about one-third of the citizenry is ever involved in any political activity other than voting. Political activity involving a minor investment of time is engaged in by about 18 to 23 percent, about one-sixth of the population. Most of the activities that involve greater investments of time and energy have been engaged in by less than 15 percent of the voting-age population.[4] Even more surprising to those who are used to our organized system of politics is that few Americans would use the

Table 1.1   Percentage of Citizens Engaging in Twelve Different Acts of Political Participation

Type of Political Participation	Percentage
1. Report regularly voting in Presidential elections.	72
2. Report always voting in local elections.	47
3. Active in at least one organization involved in community problems.	32
4. Have worked with others in trying to solve some community problems.	30
5. Have attempted to persuade others to vote as they were.	28
6. Have ever actively worked for a party or candidates during an election.	26
7. Have ever contacted a local government official about some issue or problem	20
8. Have attended at least one political meeting or rally in last three years.	19
9. Have even contacted a state or national government official about some issue or problem.	18
10. Have ever formed a group or organization to attempt to solve some local community problem.	14
11. Have ever given money to a party or candidate during an election campaign.	13
12. Presently a member of a political club or organization.	8
Number of Cases: weighted 3,095	
unweighted 2,549	

Source: Sidney Verba and Norman H. Nie, *Participation in America* (New York: Harper and Row, 1972), p. 31.

same channels that political activists use to try to influence local government. A study indicated that only 1 percent of the respondents would work through a political party, and only 4 percent through an interest group whereas 56 percent would organize an informal group to activate their friends and neighbors.[5] These findings, substantiated by research,[6] give some indication of the political activity of Americans—it is minimal and marginal.

Campaigners are often unaware of statistics such as these, even though they must consider the political activity of citizens. They plan their campaigns as if everyone were knowledgeable, interested, and active in organized groups. This is the reason so many candidates spend the bulk of their time and effort discussing complex issues before organized groups. However faulty, inaccurate, or incomplete the information, campaigners do think about their constituency and its people, and the resulting conclusions, however explicit, are formulated into theories of campaigning.

What sorts of premises do campaigners have concerning constituencies? In an interesting study of candidates' beliefs about voters, John Kingdon found that a close relationship exists between a politician's beliefs about the importance of various political influences and what he perceives those of voters to be. For example, when asked to rate the importance of candidate, party, and issue influences on the campaign, those who believed party to be most important tended to rank it first in importance to voters. Candidates who believed certain issues most important thought voters rated the same issues highest. Of course, many who win attribute victory to candidate factors. Also, those candidates with a high estimate of voter information tend to believe voters are interested in the campaign, and vice versa. Although there are obvious differences between winners and losers, Kingdon concludes that:

> [there is. . .] some degree of cognitive consistency among politicians beliefs about voters. There is apparently a general tendency to praise voters: to estimate high levels of interest, information and issue awareness among voters, quite apart from the effect that winning or losing has on the candidate's beliefs. Other candidates, however, have a general tendency to depreciate the voters' interest, information and issue awareness—again apart from whether they won or lost.[7]

Kingdon's work suggests that candidates probably have an explicit or implicit theory of voting behavior and that these notions are part of a complex of beliefs that form premises about the constituency. .

Other kinds of beliefs campaigners are likely to have about their constituencies relate to the political norms of the people, their beliefs and expectations, the type of people in the constituency, the size and physical makeup of the district, and their religious, political, and economic loyalties. These beliefs are normally formulated through experience and reflection such as the following assessments by state legislators:

In my opinion, the great majority of my constituents feel that I'm their voice and vote in the legislature, and are willing to delegate the responsibility to me that I'm willing to accept. We are all common folks, living in a common habitat, having the same desires and needs.

They are pitifully ignorant of how you spend state money. People often fight for legislation, like education, that would hurt the county tax-wise. Thirty PTA women once came to see me about education. I explained to them my position, but they don't know and don't care.

My constituents think like I do, mainly because they too are small businessmen and farmers.

My constituents are in accord with my ideas. We are a remote county and have the lowest percentage of college educated.

The general public is too little informed as a whole on the way the government operates. They know the broad principles, but the general citizenry judges on results. Of course, this doesn't apply to those who are informed and active. Elections, though, are often determined by the pleasant smile—someone in the small counties who "talks" to the people and in the cities by a "name . . . ."[8]

These legislators indicate that they have formulated some premises about the habits, needs, and expectations of the voters of their districts. That their methods of campaigning are based on these premises is more than likely.

Resources

Every election campaign, regardless of the extent of commitment made by campaigners, is based on the organization and use of resources. Even if the candidate merely files for office and conducts no campaign, the candidate's known personal attributes and, very often, his party affiliation are resources—reserves, supplies, supports, available means, skills—that have an effect on the outcome. Indeed, one researcher concluded that effective resources are the *sine qua non* of campaigns. David Leuthold maintains that "from the standpoint of the candidates, an election campaign can be considered as the *process of acquiring and using the political resources that can secure votes.*"[9]

To Leuthold the resources that a campaign is able to acquire and the uses made of them will determine the success of the campaign. Closely following the major classification trends of elections research, Leuthold lists the following resources that are important to acquire:

1. The candidate and a corresponding candidacy. Acquisition involves candidate selection and the development and presentation of personal characteristics that are regarded highly by voters.

2. Party, which is usually acquired by winning the nomination of a major

party, but gaining the support of party leaders and party organizations is also important.

3. Issues, which then requires that information be secured about the attitudes of the public in order to calculate the effect of advertising particular issue positions, as well as securing information about the content of issues in order to support the stands they adopt.

4. The support of primarily nonpolitical groups, such as farmers, labor unions, business, and veterans groups.

5. Money and people are two more resources that must be acquired. In order to disseminate the information to influence public attitudes, and to insure that voters so influenced cast their ballots campaign workers are also needed.[10]

After the resources are acquired, candidates use them to secure votes, Leuthold explains, by resource expenditure on activities (advertisements, mailings, personal contacts and appeals to influence voters).[11]

Interestingly, Leuthold concludes that the problems of acquisition of resources are far more significant than the problems of using them.[12] But, whether acquisition or distribution of campaign resources is more problematical depends on the situation. We will see (in Chapter 6) that each resource category poses a different problem for each candidate. Some resources are readily available and useful to the campaigner while others are more difficult to obtain and control.

Assets and Liabilities

Although all candidates do not weigh resources in exactly this fashion, each campaigner must face up to a sort of personal balance sheet of assets and liabilities that notes as many credits and debits as possible. Probably no campaigner has a complete ledger with all items entered in red and black, but surely they think in terms of relative political position, in a similar fashion to an individual's assessment before undertaking a financial venture.

Resources are the primary factors which make up assets and liabilities. Money is the most obvious one. In fact, some would argue that it is only money that counts—an argument that we will find misleading. In 1968, Nixon's campaign committee had 24 million dollars available to spend on his campaign while Humphrey's committees were able to raise and borrow only about 10 million dollars,[13] a liability commonly associated with Humphrey's narrow loss. Fourteen-million-dollar liabilities in a campaign are uncommon but 2.4-to-1 ratios, or higher, are not. It is not unusual for one congressional candidate to spend over $100,000 and his opponent to spend 15 to 20,000 dollars.[14] In local races, some candidates appear even more disadvantaged; it is not uncommon for a candidate to match less than one hundred dollars against thousands of dollars.

Other assets and liabilities have to be considered in addition to money. Lewis Froman has suggested that group support and voter support can be mobilized into key campaign assets. No candidate can begin his campaign as though his potential support is the same from all sources. Many groups, through past performance and overlapping participation in parties, lean toward the candidates of one party. This is true, for example, of most labor unions and Democratic candidates. Other groups are impossible to woo into one's camp. Voters are similarly predisposed, most often because of their party identification, and as Froman maintains, within any election candidates must work with an already committed pool of voters.[15] If a campaigner begins a campaign with group and voter support he has a significant asset. Consider a Democratic candidate for alderman from a heavily Democratic working-class district in a Northern city. Many residents are likely to be union families who have a habit of giving their support to almost any Democrat who runs for office. Two important assets, then, are key group and party support. His Republican opponent, no matter how great his financial assets, begins with these two key liabilities.

The effectiveness of the organization is another factor that may be an asset or a liability. Campaign organizations are quite mutable and their strength is related to the acquisition of other resources, particularly money, group, and appeal of the candidate. Party organizations are ostensibly ongoing structures that the campaigner must calculate as an asset or a liability. Sorauf found that county party organizations in Pennsylvania exist on a continuum from the well organized and active in campaigns to the inactive, "paper" organizations.[16] In a study of Congressional campaigns, Huckshorn and Spencer found that 64 percent of losing candidates from marginal districts cited lack of local party support as a significant contributor to their defeat. Lack of support, reported these candidates, was a combination of organizational unwillingness to help congressional candidates and organizational inability to do so.[17] Campaigners in some way have to take stock of how much of an asset or liability the party organization will be.

Many do not take adequate stock of campaign assets and liabilities. Huckshorn and Spencer report that many candidates were well into their campaigns before they realized the general weakness of ward and precinct organizations.[18] However, candidates often overestimate their opponents' assets, even when they can be objectified. A Democratic candidate for county office in northern Illinois related to the author in 1970 that his campaign was hopeless because the Republicans had a three-to-one advantage in party support and that no Democrat had won in the county for 100 years. He was correct only on the latter. If he had taken the time to examine the records he would have found the Democratic proportion steadily increasing in the county. The party average was about 45 percent in 1968 and Lyndon Johnson carried the county in 1964. Two other Democratic candidates for county office may well have examined these records and operated with a different attitude. They campaigned hard and barely won, becoming the first Democrats to be elected in 100 years.

Advantages and Disadvantages

Some factors that we have not classified as resources exist in relationship between one candidate and another, in the context of the particular campaign, in a particular election, in a particular constituency. They can be either an advantage or disadvantage for the candidate. There are many such factors that can be listed in each situation: age, issue positions, incumbency or non-incumbency, occupation, ethnicity, religion, residence, and so on. Candidates older than seventy years often find younger opponents pitting youth and vigor against their advanced age, sometimes by invidious comparison. Generally, these factors are immutable in the context of the campaign—they cannot be altered by campaign efforts. They are important because campaigners may have to deal with them, by integrating favorable factors into advantages and ignoring the unfavorable.

Incumbency is generally considered to be an advantage, although it is conceivable that if large blocs of voters are antagonistic to "ins" and are disposed to throw the rascals out it could be disadvantageous. One study estimated the actual vote advantage of incumbent Congressmen at from 2 to 3 percent of the vote,[19] which could be the margin of victory in a closely competitive district. Incumbency generally gives the candidate earlier and more frequent opportunities to campaign. As a government official he is asked to speak before many groups and to appear at many events. Even if uninvited, somehow it is easier for a known official to appear at church suppers, club picnics, and twenty-fifth anniversary celebrations. These activities can be carried on before the campaign officially starts. Incumbents receive other political advantages. It has been estimated that the franking, or free-mail privilege that Congressmen receive, is worth about $7200.[20] Other officials such as state legislators do not have as large a mailing budget, but it is generally sizeable. Incumbents already have been through the experience of building a successful campaign and putting together a winning coalition. Previous campaigns plus performance in office mean that the incumbent is well known to the electorate. Another study indicated that twice as many voters know the incumbent Congressman as know the challenger.[21] Thus, the nonincumbent usually suffers from many disadvantages.

The length of time a candidate has resided in a constituency also appears to be an advantage. It gives the candidate knowledge of the area, and active people in the community knowledge of the candidate. In a study of congressional candidates, it was found that 83 percent of successful candidates had lived in their states all their lives.[22] Moreover, since most candidates are long time residents of their constituencies, one would suspect that the selection process screens out shorter-term residents. Even in states experiencing rapid growth, most successful candidates are recruited from among the long-term residents.[23]

Previous experience in elected office is often used by candidates to an advantage, and most often provides the training and launching position for higher office. Most Presidential candidates are governors or U.S. Senators. Governors, Attorneys General, State Treasurers, and Congressmen often serve "apprenticeships" in state legislatures.[24] Candidates stress previous experience and accomplishments, and if significantly greater than their opponents', this too is made known. Candidates with previous elective office experience usually are more successful at the polls. Even if they lose they are likely to come closer to victory than inexperienced losers.[25] Previous office is advantageous for two reasons: first, the candidate has experienced a campaign and has some voter exposure; secondly, the candidate has a public record and can claim experience that can be turned into campaign advantages by being paraded before voters.

Positions on well-known issues can also be used to advantage, but, if voter sentiment on a particular issue is moving in the opposite direction, it can be a disadvantage. In the 1964 campaign Senator Goldwater's well-known positions on the war in Vietnam and welfare policies were different from that of most Americans.[26] His opponent, Lyndon Johnson, turned this to his advantage by stressing a centrist position on domestic policy and identifying himself with peace and nuclear responsibility. Key issues are not often well known to the entire voting population, but even if a small, interested public is aware of an issue, a candidate can turn this to an advantage. Candidates for local office may see a junkyard in a neighborhood, a zoning problem or a sewer problem and identify with these issues. They may not be as global as war and peace, but they affect people directly and arouse attention. A suburban legislative candidate once found in a candidate's poll that in one ward of the constituency, respondents considered trash removal "the single most pressing problem facing the state government." Recognizing that voters do not delineate federal, state, and local responsibility as neatly as constitutional lawyers, the candidate stressed trash removal—he would work through his good friend, fellow parishoner, and fellow partisan, the mayor—in a state legislative campaign. We do not know whether his position concerning trash removal elected him (a Democrat in a 61-percent Republican district), or whether it has had anything to do with re-election two more times before he went on to the county board; but he did turn an issue position into an advantage.

CHARTING A PATH: STRATEGY

The aim of this chapter is to explain what campaigns are all about. We have reached the point where we can say that it takes more than connected operations to mobilize human, social, environmental, and material forces. Election campaigns deal with the specific forces we have discussed: premises about constituencies, resources, assets, liabilities, advantages, and disadvantages. These operations are connected by the campaigner who charts a path based on the most reliable and most complete information available, in order to wisely acquire and distribute resources, maximize assets, reduce liabilities, make the best use of advantages, and play down disadvantages. The connections and pathways are imperfect: premises do not square with reality, resources are difficult to maximize, there are liabilities as well as assets, advantages are sometimes unknown, and disadvantages exist. Campaigners do their best with what they have, marshalling the best information and maximizing resources, assets, and advantages through utilization of concepts, theories, and techniques. As they chart these pathways they are developing a campaign strategy.

To paraphrase a dictionary definition, strategy is the science or art of employing the organized (armed) strength of a contestant (belligerent) to secure the objects of an election contest (war), especially the large scale planning and directing of operations in adjustment to the electoral arena (combat area), possible opponent (enemy) action, political alignments, and so on.[27] The military analogy now becomes clear. Campaigns and military leaders face similar situations. As Ranney and Kendall explain:

> The leaders—the men who direct our parties' campaigns—face problems in 'strategy' and 'tactics' no less urgent than those our military leaders are called upon to solve in directing our military campaigns when the nation is at war. In deciding what steps to take and what order to take them in, party leaders, like generals, try to rely as little as possible on intuition (hunches) and coin flipping and as much as possible on cool calculation based on the results of reflective analysis of past experience—i.e., *theory*. And the first step toward understanding the kind of campaigns they conduct is to come to grips with the theory on which they proceed.[28]

Generals and campaigners reflect on the past mobilization of human, environmental, social, and material forces into situational premises, resource distribution, assets and advantages. They use information to theorize about campaign strategies.

PLANNING IN CAMPAIGNS

How Campaigns are Managed

Many popular accounts of campaigns like to depict the campaign organization as a well-trained and highly disciplined army of campaign workers efficiently implementing a carefully researched plan toward a well defined set of goals. Although not explicit, these accounts imply that candidates have superior information, a vast storehouse of resources, and assets and advantages are exploited to the fullest. Most such accounts are attributed particularly to winning candidates, especially those whose financial resources outstrip their opponent's. Few such campaigns operate with the neat precision to which they are ascribed and for every one of these "neatly" executed campaigns we hear about, there are literally hundreds of campaigns that are unplanned, disorganized, and lacking in sound information.

A very typical example of this point will suffice. In a mayoral campaign in a city of 35,000, the campaign chairman and the candidate decide they ought to have some door-to-door work conducted in the precincts. About four weeks before the election they begin the search for a chairman and one week later the tenth person contacted accepts. He is given no instructions except that they would like to have some voter registration, voter turnout, and distribution of literature. The new chairman finds that no plans have been made and since registration closes in two days that activity must be dropped. He begins to recruit ward chairmen but finds people do not readily accept. Of those who do accept, some recruit precinct and block captains. He plans to distribute literature throughout the city but at this late stage only twenty-five workers are available. Regardless of how important areas might be for the candidate, might as well let them work in their own neighborhoods. As it turns out, the literature is not back from the printers on the first distribution night so the volunteers are asked to report to headquarters to stuff envelopes for mailing. Three of them do, the rest go home. The get-out-the-vote campaign is worse. Only six volunteers agree to call before election day but the chairman discovers that there are no lists of supporters to call—only the list of all 15,400 registered voters supplied by city hall. Someone suggests that since the turnout is generally low in city elections, the callers should telephone those persons who had not voted by late afternoon and urge them to vote. Two problems immediately arise. First, since there is no record of supporters anywhere the telephoners would have to call every non-voter, some of whom would vote for the opponent. Secondly, no arrangements have been made to have poll watchers at the polling places to check off those who voted.

The point of this true story is obvious. Lack of planning, coordination, and timing led to chaos, inactivity, and poor management. Proper planning, management, and integration of this category of activities requires some rather intricate steps. The various activities (precinct work, telephoning, watching polls, literature distribution, voter registration, voter turnout) and supervision of them should have been planned months in advance, shortly after the candidate decided to run for office and selected his campaign manager. Timetables are important because campaigns must end at specified points. In this case registration could not be conducted because someone failed to take notice of the deadline, volunteers went home because literature was not ready, and voters never were identified because someone neglected to follow through the initial planning. During these activities management did not realize that volunteer chairpersons, captains, and workers would be difficult to secure, or if fewer than needed were available, where they would have the greatest impact. Integrated planning of these activities might have indicated that the researcher could have established priorities among precincts so that the twenty-five volunteers would have been deployed in areas of strength. Such a lack of planning, management, and coordination is critical if one assumes that campaigning does indeed mobilize votes—and votes are requisite to victory.

To those who follow politics and campaigns, one of the most striking phenomena is that in a society priding itself on efficient management of enterprises, most American campaigns are poorly run. They lack managerial experience and ability, with low levels of reason or little application of a body of knowledge. Candidates and campaigners rush into their campaigns, trying to duplicate activities they have observed, without the slightest knowledge of why or how it should be done. One political consultant calls this the "why don't we" mode of planning. If victory is achieved it is assumed that those activities contributed to victory.

Campaigns very often are so void of *reasonable* planning, management, and coordination that they would have to be ranked below family financial management in efficiency. That is, the average family probably does a better job of managing its financial affairs than the average campaign manager does managing a campaign. When the family embarks on a major financial undertaking—going into a small business, the purchase of stocks or insurance, the purchase of real estate, or the purchase of a major applicance—one tries to avoid impulse buying by consulting consumer information and considering alternatives. For example, think of the questions buyers must consider when purchasing a home. (Can we afford it? How much are the mortgage payments? What will these payment do to our budget? Is the title clear? How much insurance will we need? How much will the insurance cost? What are the hidden costs beyond the purchase price? How much additional money will we have to spend for improvements? What are our financing options? How much interest will we be paying? How much are the property taxes? Will this be offset by tax deductions?) In other words, the purchasers chart a path by bringing premises into a "field" that blends information assessment, resource assessment, and alternatives into a plan. Campaigns are generally devoid of such activities; they are too frequently characterized by "impulse buying."

The Professionalism of Campaigns

Some campaigns are well planned and well executed. Presidential and other campaigns for high visibility office, with multi-million dollar budgets, often use media consultants, advancemen, field organizers, pollsters, advertising men, and other specialists. But the use of professional campaign consultants, or the size of the budget, or the level of the office does not necessarily guarantee a well-run or effective campaign. Most campaigns are faced with factionalism, intra-organizational jealousies, and problems dealing with volunteers. No office level appears to have a monopoly operating efficient or inefficient campaigns.

However, the candidate for lower level or small-constituency office tends to be extremely disadvantaged regarding knowledge, access to professional help, and experience. Huckshorn and Spencer found that about half of the Congressional candidates they studied were new to politics and campaigns:

> However personally well qualified or professionally competent these newcomers were, they were forced to learn their politics during their campaigns by intensive on-the-job training, with little supervision. The only staging area for their candidacies was in private life—not in public office.[29]

This situation is more typical of candidates for alderman, state legislator, or school board who simply do not have the means to professionally plan and run campaigns. They do not have ready access to campaign information systems, volunteers are difficult to secure, and money is difficult to raise. Rather than working toward realistic plans and techniques, too often the campaigner is daunted by the thought that approaches used in other campaigns are beyond his or her reach.

Maximized Information Plus Judgment

Even well planned and organized campaigns are not based on 100 percent complete information. The 1960 campaign of John F. Kennedy was noted as one of the best researched of its time. Not only was Louis Harris polling, but a group performed a computerized simulation that attempted to account for the voter impact of certain campaign events.[30] Those who conducted the simulation were able, for example, to tell Kennedy's manager approximately how many votes (or states) he would gain or lose by being a Catholic. Harris could tell the managers what people thought of both Kennedy and Nixon and which issues were important in the campaign. The television people could estimate accurately the audience of any time slot purchased. But there were many information gaps. No poll or simulation information could tell them how to deal with the Catholic issue, nor could they tell the campaigners exactly how to present candidate images, nor could the media marketing information tell media planners which type of appeal would best motivate viewers. The planners had to fill in their information gaps with reasoned hunches. The data told them what was happening, but the campaign planners still had to decide what to do.

Faulty Information

To the manager of any enterprise faulty information is worse than incomplete information, particularly when it is unnecessary. One piece of faulty information that misleads candidates for local office while campaigning door-to-door is to assume that the response they receive constitutes a poll. One legislative candidate knocked on the doors of a large segment of his district and was sure he would win because 80 percent of the people he spoke to said they would vote for him. He got only 40 percent of the vote. Some of the people he visited were not registered, some did not go to the polls, some did not bother to vote at all in the legislative contest, some forgot the candidate's name, some got to the polls and found out that the candidate they promised their vote to was running on the other party's ticket, and others simply promised a vote to the candidate while intending to vote for his opponent. The candidate was so sure of the accuracy of his "poll" that he returned to his law practice for the final month of the campaign. In many cases, faulty information can be so easily avoided, yet campaigners do not take the time and effort to do so. Registration and voting figures are easily obtainable from public source, yet campaigners guess about them, and then act on wrong assumptions.

Contingency Based Planning

Campaigns must be planned, but sufficient leeway must also be allowed for contingency situations. Campaigners must not only consider what they will do, but also what an opponent is likely to do. New events might occur, creating new issues and situations, perhaps necessitating the abandonment of plans or major portions of them. The amount of money raised might be less than budgeted. Less volunteers than expected are available. The campaigner cannot plan for these situations but he can be ready to meet them.

An interesting case of an attempt to live up to an idealized or extremely comprehensive (militarylike model) was notably unsuccessful. Lamb and Smith studied the 1964 campaign organization styles of Lyndon Johnson and Barry Goldwater. They labelled Goldwater's a Comprehensive Ideal model (based on Goldwater's identification with the military) in which rational decisions would be made at the top of a pyramid, with each decision-maker cognizant of their role, rank, and responsibility. Each move was to be carefully planned and researched, and once plans were made, they were to be precisely executed, in a fashion similar to a coordinated attack of air power, landing force, infantry, and armored vehicles.[31] The authors conclude that this type of planning is difficult to apply to a campaign. The rigidity of the model in the actual operation of the campaign meant that decisions were difficult to reach, the focus of attention was narrowed to exclude data that the original plan did not include, and decisions were hard to enforce.[32] Lamb and Smith concluded that the perceived military analogy locked them into campaign plans that they were unwilling to change.

> But Barry Goldwater and his close advisers, devoted to presumptions of clear authority and delegated responsibility, limited their foci of attention to exclude much crucial information. As Admiral Yomomoto, speeding toward Midway Island, ignored the possibility that his code had been cracked, Barry Goldwater's policy group ignored or discounted the opinion polls. The isolation of the policy group from other elements of the organization caused its members to remain ignorant of the early stages of discontent in their own organization and to disregard the potential harm of well developed dissent in the party at large.[33]

Thus, although fairly comprehensive planning is necessary, it must not be so rigid that the events and conditions of the campaign are ignored.

CANDIDATE ORGANIZATION AND PARTY ORGANIZATION

Many readers by now must have asked themselves why the candidate should be concerned about these matters when the two major political party organizations are available to manage and conduct a candidate's campaign? Only in the rarest circumstances can the campaigner rely exclusively on the party effort. There are four possible reasons for this, and most campaigners face at least one of the four.

First, it is a well-known fact to those who have observed American parties that they are extremely fractionalized. Our parties are organized at national, state, and local levels. There are township, legislative district, ward, city, county, Congressional district, state, and national party organizations. These organization levels reflect the constituencies of the bulk of offices that party operatives generally try to capture. There is no guarantee that parties at all these levels agree on candidates or issues. But there is more complexity. Parties are broad based coalitions reflecting divergent views on current issues and consisting of many interests, organized and unorganized. The two major parties encompass members who are at the center and at the extremes of the political spectrum as well as many who are between the fringes and the center. Both parties have agricultural, business, labor, civil rights, environmental, foreign policy, and many other interests, only to varying degrees and with varying emphasis. Still another factor contributing to fractionalism is intraparty feuding. Parties tend to divide by various warring groups or leaders, often cutting across levels of organization or ideological concerns—often to serve the ambitions or interests of those within the party structure. The factors that contribute to fractionalizing our parties may make it difficult for the "party" to unite behind every candidate who is running for office on a party ticket.

Second, of the thousands of offices to be filled by elections not all candidates are elected on a partisan ballot. Although it varies from state to state, every state has some nonpartisan elective offices. Among the most nonpartisan of the states is Minnesota where until 1974 less than ten offices (all but president, congress, and state officers) were elected on a nonpartisan basis. Parties then tend to concentrate on those races that are partisan, only occasionally supporting nonpartisan candidates. In Minnesota, for example, the parties took interest in the nonpartisan legislature, big city mayoral contests, and city council races in the larger cities. Other partisans running for offices were left to their own devices.

Third, even if the contest is partisan, there is no guarantee that the party organization will be concerned with it. In many primary election contests, when all candidates are of the same party, party organizations often adopt a neutral stance until a candidate is nominated. In primary or general elections, party organizations rarely give equal treatment to all candidates running for office on the party ticket. In a study of state party chairmen it was found, not surprisingly, that the gubernatorial contest was by far the most important contest to state organizations.[34] Congressional candidates often find that their campaigns fall "between the stools" of state party organization and local organizations; with neither taking a great deal of interest in them.[35] In many local parties one would assume [incorrectly] that it is local candidates that interest activists. Very often it is the most visible candidate at the top of the ticket that local partisans are interested in aiding. That those who flood the precinct caucuses for a particular presidential candidate and take control of the party organization are interested, for the most part, in using the party organization to further the interests of that candidate, often to the exclusion of services to all other candidates has been true in most states.[36] Similarly, the regular Democratic organization in Cook County, Illinois usually gives inordinate attention to the state attorney race, a contest party leaders apparently consider to be of prime importance, and which is elected at the same time as the president and the governor of Illinois.

Fourth, and most important, party organizations are rarely able to help candidates in the manner necessary to conduct a modern campaign. Money, an important campaign resource, now tends to flow to the candidate rather than to the party, diminishing the party's contribution to the campaign. And, although many retain the image of the party organization "machine" able to mobilize massive blocs of loyal voters in urban elections, in reality, few such efficient "machines" existed. Even in Chicago, such tactics did not work always.[37] In a study of political parties in a more typical setting, Eldersveld found that electioneering activities by party workers in Detroit do not fit these popular conceptions.[38] (See Chapter 15.) Furthermore, even if willing to perform campaign services, it is not clear whether political parties, as they are now constituted, are able to fully assist candidates in campaigns. At a time when campaigns rely increasingly on systematic vote analysis, polls, advertising, and print and broadcast media, political parties do not have all the important skills to offer the candidate.[39]

This indicates that if one ever could, the contemporary campaign operation can no longer rely exclusively on the political party to do its campaigning. The candidate, with a group of campaigners around him, must build his own campaign organization, organized to cover the entire constituency and able to perform all strategic tasks. In a sense, each campaign group is similar to a "nuclear party" group centered around the candidate and key campaigners,[40] extensive enough in size and complexity to perform that which is necessary to plan and implement the strategy for a single candidate contesting a single office in a single election year, rather than a party that has many strategies for many candidates for many offices in many election years.

Notes to Chapter 1

1. Herbert M. Baus and William B. Ross, *Politics Battle Plan* (New York: Macmillan, 1968).

2. Few written campaign plans are ever made public. The campaign plan for the 1952 Eisenhower presidential campaign was subsequently published in Harold Lavine, *Smoke-Filled Rooms* (Englewood Cliffs, N.J.: Prentice-Hall, 1970), pp. 33-71.

3. The most famous is, of course, Joe McGinniss, *The Selling of the President 1968* (New York: Trident Press, 1969).

4. Sidney Verba and Norman H. Nie, *Participation in America* (New York: Harper and Row, 1972) pp. 3-32.

5. Gabriel A. Almond and Sidney Verba, *The Civic Culture* (Boston: Little, Brown, 1965), p. 148.

6. Robert E. Lane, *Political Life: Why Peopl Get Involved in Politics* Glencoe, Illinois: The Free Press, 1959); Lester W. Milbrath, *Political Participation* (Chicago: Rand McNally, 1965).

7. John W. Kingdon, *Candidates for Office: Beliefs and Strategies* (New York: Random House, 1968), p. 28.

8. John C. Wahlke, Heinz Eulau, William Buchanan and LeRoy C. Ferguson, *The Legislative System* (New York: John Wiley, 1962), pp. 296, 298, 299, 303.

9. David A. Leuthold, *Electioneering in a Democracy* (New York: John Wiley, 1968), p. 1.

10. Ibid., p. 2.

11. Ibid., pp. 2-3.

12. Ibid., p. 3.

13. Herbert E. Alexander, *Financing the 1968 Election* (Lexington, Mass.: D.C. Heath, 1971), pp. 81-85.

14. David W. Adamany, *Campaign Finance in America* (North Scituate, Mass.: Duxbury Press, 1972), pp. 44-45.

15. Lewis A. Froman, Jr., "A Realistic Approach to Campaign Strategies and Tactics," in M. Kent Jennings and L. Harmon Zeigler, eds., *The Electoral Process*, (Englewood Cliffs, N.J.: Prentice-Hall, 1966), pp. 4-6.

16. Frank J. Sorauf, *Party and Representation* (New York: Atherton Press, 1963), pp. 46-52.

17. Robert J. Huckshorn and Robert C. Spencer, *The Politics of Defeat* (Amherst, Mass.: Univ. of Massachusetts Press, 1971), pp. 150-51.

18. Ibid., p. 151.

19. Robert S. Erickson, "The Advantage of Incumbency in Congressional Elections," *Polity* 3 (1971): 395-405.

20. The Twentieth Century Fund, *Electing Congress*, Report of the Twentieth Century Fund Task Force on Financing Congressional Campaigns (New York: The Twentieth Century Fund, 1970), p. 36.

21. Donald E. Stokes and Warren E. Miller, "Party Government and the Saliency of Congress," *Public Opinion Quarterly* 26 (1962): 540.

22. Huckshorn and Spencer, *The Politics of Defeat*, p. 33.

23. Ibid., p. 35.

24. Joseph A Schlesigner, *Ambition and Politics* (Chicago: Rand McNally, 1966), ch. 5.

25. Huckshorn and Spencer, *The Politics of Defeat*, p. 39.

26. Phillip E. Converse, Aage R. Clausen and Warren E. Miller, "Electoral Myth and Reality: The 1964 Election," *American Political Science Review* 59 (1965): 334.

27. *Webster's New Collegiate Dictionary* 2nd. ed. (Springfield, Mass.: G. & C. Merriam, 1956), p. 837.

28. Austin Ranney and Willmoore Kendall, *Democracy and the American Party System* (New York: Harcourt, Brace, 1956), p. 340.

29. Huckshorn and Spencer, *The Politics of Defeat*, p. 39.

30. Ithiel de Sola Pool, Robert P. Abelson and Samuel Popkin, *Candidates, Issues and Strategies: A Computer Simulation of the 1960 and 1964 Presidental Elections* (Cambridge, Mass.: M.I.T. Press, 1965).

31. Karl A. Lamb and Paul A. Smith, *Campaign Decision-Making* (Belmont, Ca.: Wadsworth, 1968), p. 20-21.

32. Ibid., p. 37.

33. Ibid., p. 133.

34. Robert Agranoff and Edward F. Cooke, *Political Profile of State Party Chairmen* (Pittsburgh, Pa.: Center for Politics, Univ. of Pittsburgh, 1965), p. 12.

35. Huckshorn and Spencer, *The Politics of Defeat*, pp. 144-50.

36. cf., David Lebedoff, *Ward Number Six* (New York: Charles Scribner's, 1972).

37. Harold F. Gosnell, *Machine Politics: Chicago Model* 2nd ed. (Chicago: Univ. of Chicago Press, 1968), ch. 5.

38. Samuel J. Eldersveld, *Political Parties: A Behavioral Analysis* (Chicago: Rand McNally, 1964), p. 350.

39. Robert Agranoff, *The New Style in Election Campaigns* (Boston: Holbrook Press, 1962), pp. 15-20.

40. Joseph A. Schlesinger, "Political Party Organization" in *Handbook of Organizations*, ed. James G. March (Chicago: Rand McNally, 1965), pp. 774-75.

For Further Reading and Research

Agranoff, Robert. *The New Style in Election Campaigns*, 2d ed. Boston: Holbrook Press, 1976.

Anderson, Walt. *Campaigns: Cases in Political Conflict*. Pacific Palisades, California: Goodyear, 1970.

Barber, James David, ed. *Choosing the President*. Englewood Cliffs, N.J.: Prentice-Hall, 1974.

Broder, David S. *The Party's Over: The Failure of Politics in America*. New York: Harper and Row, 1972.

Cotter, Cornelius P., ed. *Practical Politics in the United States*. Boston: Allyn and Bacon, 1969.

Davis, James W. *Presidential Primaries: Road to the White House*. New York: Thomas Y. Crowell, 1967.

Hershey, Marjorie Randon. *The Making of Campaign Strategy*. Lexington, Mass.: D.C. Heath, 1974.

Hess, Stephen. *The Presidential Campaign*. Washington: Brookings, 1974.

Huckshorn, Robert J., and Spencer, Robert C. *The Politics of Defeat: Campaigning for Congress*. Amherst: U. of Massachusetts Press, 1971.

Kessel, John H. *The Goldwater Coalition: Republican Strategies in 1964*. Indianapolis: Bobbs–Merrill, 1968.

Kingdon, John W. *Candidates for Office: Beliefs and Strategies*. New York: Random House, 1968.

Leuthold, David A. *Electioneering in a Democracy: Campaigns for Congress*. New York: John Wiley, 1968.

Mileur, Jerome M. and Sulzner, George T. *Campaigning for the Massachusetts Senate*. Amherst: U. of Massachusetts Press, 1974.

Polsby, Nelson W. and Wildavsky, Aaron W. *Presidential Elections*. 3d ed. New York: Scribner's, 1971.

Pomper, Gerald M. *Elections in America*. New York: Dodd, Mead, 1968.

Saloma III, John S., and Sontag, Fredrick H. *Parties: The Real Opportunity for Effective Citizen Politics*. New York: Random House, 1973.

Weisbord, Marvin R. *Campaigning for President*. New York: Washington Square Press, 1966.

What Election Studies
Can Tell Us
about Campaigns

Many readers are familiar with the work of the public pollsters, such as Gallup or Harris, particularly during the campaign period when they publish "trial heats" between candidates in the most visible races. Some newspapers also publish the "horse race" results between a gubernatorial, senatorial or other large constituency candidates, although with varying degrees of reliability. Less familiar but occasionally mentioned are the private pollsters, 200 or so small operators[1] who sell their wares to those candidates able to afford their high-priced services. The information gathered is usually peculiar to the given campaign and constituency—images of the candidate, key issues, local media habits—and the results are the private property of the candidate. Almost unknown to most people is the corps of academic survey researchers, who study the behavior of electorates by survey methods similar to the pollsters. Their work is less concerned with the "here and now" of campaigns, but rather with explaining phenomena such as who votes and who does not vote, why voters vote as they do, and what effect this voting has on the system. This chapter, and the next will be concerned primarily with the third group of election followers.

Modern voting behavior research has been in existence for three decades,[2] and it butresses other types of information campaigners bring to campaigns. For example, the belief that many have about voters in a democracy, according to classical democratic theory, has been proven inaccurate. Normative democratic theorists expected the citizen to be interested and participative in political affairs. Moreover, he was expected to be well informed and to have arrived at his principles by reason after carefully considering the implications and alleged consequences of the alternative proposals, and to cast his vote on the basis of principle—not fortuitously or frivolously or impulsively or habitually, but with reference to standards not only of his own good but of the common good as

well.[3] Research has indicated that the general interest, information, and participation level of American voters is generally low. A classic study of presidential
elections in the 1950s, *The American Voter*, indicated that a little less than one-
third of the citizenry was "not much interested" in presidential campaigns, a
little more than one-third was "somewhat interested" and a little less than one-
third were "very much interested."[4] It is a well known fact that only 55 to 65
percent of the eligible electorate votes in presidential elections and fewer vote
in other elections—less than 20 percent in some local elections. *The American
Voter* revealed that few voters knew much about many issues (generally they
were familiar with only one to three of sixteen national issues they were presented with) and even fewer used their issue information as a basis for voting.[5]
Rather, the authors found that parties play a particularly important role in
organizing voters' thoughts about issues into meaningful choices, serving as a
filter through which opinions are formed, acting as a basis for identification
with political objects, and serving as a guide to voting in the absence of other
stimuli.[6] Thus, survey research has altered the reality of the theory of the
classical democratic voter.

It is important for the campaigner to bear in mind such information when
planning and implementing a campaign. A reasonable understanding of how
electorates actually behave will help formulate more accurate campaign premises and will assist the campaigner in avoiding some rather elementary pitfalls
such as ignoring party-committed voters or discussing complicated issues with
uninterested people. However, the survey data related in this chapter is not in any
way intended as campaign advice from the authors, but are solely inferences
drawn from research.

PARTISANSHIP AND PARTY VOTING

Since the earliest days of political parties, it must have been clear to those who
contacted voters directly that there existed a group who, out of personal loyalty
to the party worker, or for historical, economic, or social reasons always (or
almost always) supported the candidates of one party. Together these loyalists
became the party faithful or the party-in-the-electorate—those voters who if
properly stimulated could be counted on to support the candidates of a party.

Survey research has not only confirmed that many voters associate themselves with political parties but also that such associations are important means
by which a great number of voters conceptualize politics. This association with
political parties is similar to identification with an ethnic group or the identification of a laborer with the union movement; it does not require any formal
participation or membership. According to the authors of *The American Voter*,
party identification "is a psychological identification, which can persist without
legal recognition or evidence of formal membership and even without a consistent record of formal support. Most Americans have this sense of attachment
with one party or the other. And for the individual who does, the strength

and direction of party identification are facts of central importance in accounting for attitude and behavior."[7] Party identification is generally measured in a survey by self-classification of respondents, often by asking a question such as, "In politics do you consider yourself to be a Republican, a Democrat, or something else?"

Although most Americans identify with one of the two major parties, they do so with varying degrees of attachment. That is, a continuum of intensities exists to which people identify with the parties ranging from strongly Republican to strongly Democratic.[8] This continuum is usually measured by having people place themselves at certain points by asking (after choosing one of the parties), "Do you consider yourself to be a strong or not so strong Democrat (Republican)?" Persons who consider themselves independents are asked which of the parties they generally lean toward.

While these measures somewhat artificially force people into categories, they offer a general picture of where voters stand in terms of their likely predisposition toward a party. Table 2.1 depicts the distribution and strength of party identification in the United States in the twenty-year period from 1952 to 1972. Notice the relative stability over time of the various categories.[9] It is also noteworthy that while there is much talk about increased independence in voting, the number of citizens who are actually giving up their party identifications for professed independence has risen very gradually—a point we will return to later. These figures are for the entire country and, for each constituency they will differ significantly. In some election districts, party identifiers are distributed more equally and in others the members of one party can outnumber the identifiers of other parties by ratios of ten to one.

Not surprisingly, there is a considerable amount of consistency between one's party identification and one's vote. Even in presidential elections, which uncover massive amounts of information about the candidates and the issues, party identification is closely associated with presidential voting. Table 2.2 demonstrates the relation between the strength of party identification and party voting in the 1972 presidential election. Despite notable defections, each party's presidential candidate is the recipient of the votes of a large block of party identifiers. Table 2.3 examines this relationship over a two-decade span. Over 80 percent of the strong partisans regularly vote for the party they identify with. Weaker party identifiers are less consistent in their support, with around 60 percent voting consistently with their party. As one would expect, independents support parties even less consistently, although surprisingly some independents do regularly vote for one of the two parties. About four in ten independents who lean to a party, vote mostly for the same party. Generally, four-fifths of the independents do not regularly support a party. Thus, direction plus the strength of party identification have a bearing on the consistency of the vote for one party. The stronger one identifies with a party the more likely the vote is in that direction.

The loyalty of voters to their party helps explain why any candidate running on a party ticket always seems to get at least some of the vote. As

Table 2.1   Distribution of Party Identification in the United States, 1952-1972

	Oct. 1952	Sept. 1953	Oct. 1954	Oct. 1956	Nov. 1957	Oct. 1958	Oct. 1960	Oct. 1961	Aug. 1962	May 1964	Oct. 1964	Nov. 1966	Oct. 1968	Nov. 1970	Oct. 1972
Strong Democrat	22%	22%	22%	21%	21%	23%	21%	26%	23%	24%	27%	18%	20%	20%	15%
Weak Democrat	25	23	25	23	26	24	25	21	24	22	25	28	25	24	26
Independent Democrat	10	8	9	7	7	7	8	9	7	7	9	9	10	10	11
Independent	5	4	7	9	8	8	8	10	11	10	8	12	10	13	13
Independent Republican	7	6	6	8	6	4	7	5	5	5	6	7	9	8	11
Weak Republican	14	15	14	14	16	16	13	13	16	17	13	15	15	15	13
Strong Republican	13	15	13	15	10	13	14	11	11	11	11	10	10	9	10
Apolitical (do not know)	4	7	4	3	6	5	4	5	3	4	1	1	1	1	1
Total	100%	100%	100%	100%	100%	100%	100%	100%	100%	100%	100%	100%	100%	100%	100%
No. of Cases	1614	1023	1139	1772	1488	1269	3021	1474	1317	1465	1550	1278	1553	1501	2697

Source: Angus Campbell, Phillip E. Converse, Warren E. Miller and Donald E. Stokes, Elections and the Political Order (New York: John Wiley, 1966), p. 13; 1966-1972 data from Survey Research Center, University of Michigan. Made available through the Inter-University Consortium for Political Research.

Table 2.2   Vote for President by Partisans and Independents in 1972

Category of Partisanship	Nixon	McGovern	VOTE Schmidt	Others	Non Voters	Total	N
Strong Democrat	17%	47%	0%	0%	36%	100%	396
Democrat	30	28	0	0	42	100	689
Independent	34	17	1	0	48	100	927
Republican	64	6	1	0	29	100	352
Strong Republican	74	3	0	0	23	100	275

Source: Survey Research Center, University of Michigan. Made available through the Inter-University Consortium for Political Research.

Table 2.3   Proportion Reporting Voting Always or Mostly
for Same Party by Strength of Party Identification, 1952-1972

	1952	1956	1960	1964	1968	1972
Strong Party Indentifiers	87%	82%	81%	82%	82%	85%
Weak Party Indentifiers	72	60	55	56	53	63
Independents Leaning to Party	46	36	29	35	39	39
Independents	19	16	17	16	17	24

Source: Survey Research Center, University of Michigan. Made available through the Inter-University Consortium for Political Research.

soundly as Sen. Barry Goldwater was defeated by Lyndon Johnson (1964) he did receive 27 million votes, including over 80 percent of the votes of strong Republicans, 50 percent of the votes of the weaker Republicans and more than 25 percent of the Independents' votes.[10] A former state legislator once filed for Congress in a Midwestern district at the urging of party leaders just to have a Democratic candidate on the ballot against a very popular Republican incumbent. The Democrat did absolutely no campaigning except to wave to the camera duing a statewide televised rally. He received 38 percent of the two-candidate vote (almost the exact proportion the Democrat running in that district received two years earlier) due, undoubtedly, to consistent partisan support.

Party identification, then, is a very important ingredient in making up the vote. Yet, with all of the appeals made by candidates and with all of the issues being mentioned in a campaign, some obviously counter to the voter's partisanship, how does the voter maintain this partisan consistency? Some partisan voters do not face the problem because they do not follow politics very much and their partisanship is all they bring into the contest, even in a highly visible presidential race.[11] A larger group of voters think about candidates and issues to a certain extent, but they receive campaign messages within the context of their partisanship.

It has been asserted that partisan attitudes are supported in a campaign through one of two means. If a partisan identifier has formed attitudes that are consistent with his party allegiance, that is if his views and his party's views are very similar, then that allegiance will serve as an attitude-supporting mechanism as campaign messages are received by the individual. The voter, therefore, receives messages confirming or reinforcing his party-consistent views. Partisan attitudes can, for other persons, serve as a defense mechanism in the individual's fixed partisan commitment as competing messages are received.[12] As Donald Stokes asserts:

> But for most people the tie between party identification and voting behavior involves subtle processes of perceptual adjustment by which the individual assembles an image of current politics consistent with his partisan allegiance. With normal luck, the partisan voter will carry to the polls attitudes toward newer elements of politics that support his long-standing bias.[13]

Partisanship consistency has led voting researchers to seek some means of measuring the stable partisanship component of various constituencies over time. They have developed the analytic device known to political scientists as the "normal vote"[14] or "expected division of the vote."[15] The normal and expected vote is based on the distribution of party identification in a constituency, and is predicated on the likelihood that persons will not deviate from their partisanship. That is, for analytic purposes, researchers assume that all voters vote on the basis of their party identification. Independents are distributed equally. That the attraction of candidates or key issues will not pull people across party lines is assumed for the sake of analysis. Of course, this does not happen, but it affords the researcher the opportunity to interpret elections by looking at how, in a given election, voters behaved regarding other elections. The normal or expected vote distribution is often approximated by campaign researchers through surveying voters' partisan habits or by aggregate election data base party race indicators. Each constituency contains something like a normal vote distribution, based largely on the party loyalties of its voters.

Some contests become less visible, and there ordinarily is less information about other forces (candidates, issues, and so on). Therefore, the voter is more likely to rely on party. The available research is scant, but a significant study of 1970 Congressional voting by Freedman illuminates the point. When respondents were asked if they could remember the names of their congressional candidates only 43 percent claimed they could. Of these, 29 percent incorrectly named the candidates. Table 2.4, from the Freedman study, reports the relationship between awareness of the candidates and the likelihood of voting for one's party or crossing over. An individual was considered aware of a candidate if he correctly named him, not if he named his party. The candidates' party was then determined, and the "own party/other party" correspondence was made with the respondent's party identification. Table 2.4 makes it clear that as knowledge of the other party's candidate increased so did the tendency to vote for him. Since this study was in part a replication of a 1958 study, Freedman tried to make comparisons over time. He found that there was more overall partisan vote shift in 1970 than in 1958. Also, in 1970 a majority of partisans abandoned their party when their knowledge was limited to the other party's candidate, whereas in 1958, a majority of voters in this category remained loyal to their party. But, the general trends were the same in both years. If the voter has no information (the largest group) it is almost certain he will vote for the candidate

Table 2.4 Voter Awareness of Candidates and Party Voting.
Percentage Voting for Own Party and Other Party Candidate for
House, by Saliency of Candidates in Contested Race, in 1970

Voted for Candidate	Both Candidates (N=150)	Own Party Candidate Only (N=128)	Other Party Candidate Only (N=60)	Neither Candidate (N=228)
Of own party	75	99	43	84
Of other party	25	1	57	17
Total	100	100	100	101

Source: Stanley R. Freedman, "The Salience of Party and Candidate in Congressional Elections: A Comparison of 1958 and 1970," in Public Opinion and Public Policy, Norman R. Luttbeg, ed., (Homewood, Ill.: Dorsey, 1974), p. 130.

of his party identification. To a greater degree, if the voter knows only the candidate of his party, he will vote according to his party loyalty. Only if partisan identifiers know something about the opposition candidate is there any likelihood that he will vote in that direction.[16] What is important is that even in this "high on the ticket" race (congress is generally placed below president and senator, and above governor) a substantial body of voters were unaware of candidates and they relied on party choice for voting, probably as a residual cue. In the absence of any other cues, they relied on the best bet—party.

If this paucity of candidate information exists at the Congressional contest level it is likely that candidate (and issue) cues are even more absent in races that receive less attention. Indeed, Gerald Kline's research indicates that the information flow that voters receive in most non-presidential contests is so low that he refers to these elections as "party elections."[17] A campaign for University of Illinois Trustee, clerk of state district court, county surveyor, local dog catcher or Minnesota Public Service Commissioner ordinarily does not reach voters and, thus, the proportion of voters having no information about the candidates is even larger. For those who vote in these contests, party identification undoubtedly looms large. While low visibility and high partisanship generally go together, this phenomenon is not always true. Often contestants for alderman, a mayoral contest, county board, or other local contests generate a certain degree of visibility. Incumbent state constitutional officers are often visible by means of their activities in office, particularly secretaries of state with their omnipresent names on drivers licenses, license plates, and other state forms. There is a point, however, at which any race becomes invisible to some voters and if they choose to vote in that race, party is often an important motivator.

There are other characteristics of the party identifier that are of interest to the campaigner. Generally, strong party identifiers tend to be more interested in political matters than are those with weaker identifications or independents; they tend to be more interested in the campaign and they are more concerned about the outcome of the campaign.[18] Unlike the political activist, most partisans have a modest level of awareness of their party's position regarding the issues. Depending on the issue, only about 40 to 60 percent of the more informed segment of the population perceives party differences on those issues they are aware of. For less informed partisans the proportion is significantly reduced.[19] The stronger the party identification the more likely the citizen is to turn out to vote.[20] In general, research has indicated that partisans, through their identification with the important political object of party, and the fact that so many political stimuli emanate from that object, makes them a more stable and regular part of the political system.

PARTY IMPLICATIONS FOR CAMPAIGNS

The implications of party identification for the campaigner are numerous. First, for most races in most constituencies there is likely to be a pool of previously committed voters. These voters are often the "base" that campaigners build on. The reason why so many congressional seats are "safe" (from 66 to 75 percent are won consistently by 55% percent or more of the same party) is due to the high concentration of habitual party supporters within a given district. Realizing that voters would not have the usual, all-important party cue in nonpartisan ballot legislative elections until 1974, both parties in Minnesota took steps to identify the party affiliation of voters and emphasize party affiliation of candidates. Until that time such information was disseminated by propaganda techniques. In most contests there is a pool of party-committed voters whose numbers can be estimated and who can be mobilized.

Second, this means that those strongly committed to the opposition party are unlikely to be automatically motivated to vote for the opposition candidate. In every contest there are some who will vote for the candidates regardless of who runs because they strongly identify with their party and they almost consider it a breach of faith to cross party lines. It is obviously a waste of time to appeal to or campaign among such people. Every campaigner must acknowledge the fact that he will not receive every vote, and thus must "write off" certain categories. Third, it also suggests that the partisans most likely to vote for an opposition party candidate are those whose party loyalty is weak. As indicated in Table 2.3 (page 26), the weaker the party support, the higher the degree of support for candidates of the other party over time. Likewise, in any given election it is the weaker partisans who are among the largest group of ticket splitters or cross-over voters. Thus, the weak partisans of the opposition party, if identified, may be a fruitful field to win voters over by candidate and issue appeals. This of course includes independents who lean to one party or the other. It must also be noted that a campaigner's own weaker partisans are also fruitful territory for the opponent and that steps may have to be taken to hold them for the candidate.

A fourth and related consideration is that party identification, particularly when strong, does not appear to be something that voters just bring into a specific election; it is developed over time. It begins in early childhood and is based on the voter's reaction to family, group, social, economic, and political events.[21] Also, it appears to be relatively stable for the individual over a long period of time. For some voters, party identification means enough to them personally that they will retain it even though they have a very poor image of the party[22] and regularly vote against the party's candidates.[23] Matthews and Prothro found this to be the case among many white Southerners, who for historical and personal developmental reasons still considered themselves to be Democrats but had a poor "image" of the party due primarily to its civil rights stance. These types voted against Democratic presidential candidates while hanging on to their party identification.[24] The message is clear. The campaigner cannot get involved in partisan conversion; it is a long and difficult process that is nearly impossible to achieve in the short course of a campaign. As we will see, the only conversion ordinarily possible is in the context of the campaign—for a vote rather than for a party. Too often campaigners use the campaign as a vehicle to convert party supporters or party organizations ask campaigners to use the campaign to enlist the consistent loyalties of voters rather than to elect specific candidates. It is a nearly impossible task.

That there are many partisans in a constituency who will not receive any campaign messages is a fifth consideration of partisanship for the campaigner. Either the messages will not get to the voter or they will not be received because he or she "tunes out" politics. But some of these persons will go to the polls and vote. When faced with a contest in which no candidate or issue cues are received, the partisan will rely on the party—the best bet or only cue. It is difficult for the campaigner to plan or account for these voters, yet they are a part of vote totals and the campaigner should be aware of their existence.

INDEPENDENT VOTERS

According to classical democratic theory all voters were assumed to be some sort of independent—attentive to politics, weighing conflicting viewpoints in a campaign, and reaching a judgment without any sort of partisan prejudice. As we have already indicated, fewer voters than commonly believed are truly independent of the political parties, in terms of their views and making voting decisions. In fact, some professed independents even vote habitually for the same party, raising the suspicion they are actually partisans who profess nonpartisanship because they believe it to be civically virtuous. Yet, the independent is a force to reckoned with in American politics and thus, is a target group for the campaigner.

One type of independent is the citizen who knows and cares little for politics, knows little about the political parties, and feels that "independent" is the right thing to be. The authors of *The American Voter* first identified this group, finding that those who did not choose to identify themselves with a party were:

> . . .as a group somewhat less involved in politics [than partisans]. They
> have a somewhat poorer knowledge of the issues, their image of the
> candidates is fainter, their interest in the campaign is less, their concern
> over the outcome is relatively slight, and their choice between competing
> candidates, although it is made later in the campaign, seems much less to
> spring from discoverable evaluations of the elements of national poli-
> tics.[25]

Undoubtedly great numbers of professed independents do fit into this category
of the uninterested, but Flanigan cautions us that party clashes might not
interest these voters but that they actually have an interest in politics. He also
points out that the relationship could be artifactual because so much of the research is channeled through party concepts.[26]

In all probability, another type of independents exist who fit more closely
the democratic ideal. These voters are interested and informed, weigh the information about candidates and issues, and vote by linking their perception of
what is desirable to the candidates. Above all, to fit into this "classical independent" category, the voter would have to do so independent of party. In his
research, V.O. Key found a group of vote switchers who were more informed
and interested than previous research indicated, although not exactly independents. The switch in party support from one election to the next for this
group appeared to be more related to examination of the issues than to other
factors, suggesting a modification of the first type of independent as the only
one.[27] More to the point, David RePass actually discovered a group of self-
identified independents who were well-informed about the issues although issue
information was not sought by asking reactions to party issues—a usual technique for gathering issue information until that time. When asked to identify
important issues (exclusive of party concerns), about one-third of the independents rated highest in issue information and almost half were in the middle
category. This level of issue information compared favorably with partisan
identifiers, even exceeding strong Democrats by a two-to-one ratio.[28] Repass'
work gives strong evidence to the notion that a portion of the Independents are
closer to the classical model than voting researchers earlier believed.

Yet still another type of independent is the voter who is in a transitional
stage between identification with one party and another. Matthews and Prothro
first found this relationship among Southern whites who had forsaken the
Democratic party, primarily because of its stance on civil rights and social-wel-
fare policy. They were voting Republican but could not bring themselves to
identify with the party of their historical enemy.[29] Thus, they called themselves Independents, but were probably in transition between the two parties.
In all likelihood these Independents still voted for some Democrats on the
state or local level, a category once called presidential Republicans. Former
partisans of all types are the largest contributors to the growing group of

independents.[30] Although this group of voters is probably small, the campaigner should be aware of their existence. Some who call themselves independents are in the process of switching their allegiance from one party to the other.

No matter which type of independent is involved, the number of professed independents is increasing in the United States. Slowly but steadily the numbers doubled from 15 to 30 percent from 1937 to 1968.[31] By 1974, that figure increased to one-third of the voting-age population.[32] Even more impressive are the rates of independence from the parties among various subgroups of the population. Most prominent is the tendency for the younger voter and college student to reject party labels. As the Gallup data in Table 2.5 illustrates, more than half of all college students and more than four out of ten young persons

Table 2.5   Independence of Voters

	24 Years and Over	Under 24	College Students
Democrats	45%	38%	30%
Republicans	27	18	18
Independents	28	42	52

Source: Gallup Opinion Index, no. 68, February, 1971, *Newsweek*, October 25, 1971.

consider themselves to be independents; whereas fewer than three out of ten older voters are independents. Some of these younger voters surely will adopt a party identification as they get older, just as many older partisans developed their partisanship a little later in their adult lives.[33] But, the increasing aggregate figures suggest that more and more of the younger independents will not adopt a party label. In fact, 26 percent of the voters who were in their twenties in the 1960s were independents then, but the proportion of that age cohort is 40 percent independent ten years later (when that group was in their thirties).[34] Among older citizens, independence from the Democratic party—voters who were formerly Democrats and now are independents is greatest among Catholic voters. Their proportion rose from 18 to 30 percent from 1960 to 1970. Most Republican losses to the independents are in the suburbs, among the college educated and among voters who consider themselves middle class. Geographically, the movement from Republicanism to independence is distributed equally across all regions, but it is heaviest in the Northeast.[35] Richard Merelman suggests that such factors as less cohesive family structures (since family is a major transmitter of partisan identification) and increased education (since independence increases with college level education) will continue and perhaps accelerate the proportion of independents.[36]

CAMPAIGN IMPLICATIONS
OF INDEPENDENT VOTERS

The campaigner must be aware of the fact that independents are not equally distributed in all districts. Independents of the first type who are barely interested in politics are probably in all political districts, but there may be significant pockets of them in the poorer social and economic districts, assuming a strong party organization does not have a hold on them through the various techniques used. The more informed independent may be concentrated in wealthier districts or in areas that have a high proportion of college-educated persons. A district may on occasion have both, such as when a university campus is located in the heart of a poor area. Campaigners on college campuses or in residential areas near colleges should be aware of the likelihood that fewer students affiliate with parties. In sum, the campaigner should be on the lookout for areas where independents of all types are likely to be concentrated.

It is obvious that where independents have been individually identified or where concentrations exist, appeals to party loyalty will not work. The campaigner will have to base his or her approach to this group either on issues or the candidate, or perhaps both. The more informed independent, in particular, may expect candidate-issue messages; they want to know what the candidate's stand on the issues are. Less informed independents, if they truly are independent of party, may be motivated by various candiate appeals alone, since they rarely follow issues. We actually know very little about these forces, but it is logical to assume that party appeals will not work on those who refuse to accept party labels.

The independent voter can be underestimated or overestimated in a campaign. Some believe all voters to be like the informed independent and approach voters that way, spending the entire campaign discussing numerous and complicated issue appeals. Others neglect the independent completely, never getting beyond the few committed voters at party meetings, never mentioning issues or not even getting across the personal qualities of the candidates. As for so many other facets of campaigning, finding the right balance is critical.

CANDIDATE VOTING
AND CANDIDATE IMAGE

The reader must be wondering by now, after reconsidering Table 2.1 and the other findings presented, how President Eisenhower and President Nixon could have won by such landslides in 1956 and 1972 respectively, when over half of all party identifiers were Democrats. In 1956, all of the Republicans and all of the Independents did not equal Eisenhower's landslide; obviously some Democratic identifiers also voted for him. In practically every election a group of voters (including identifiers of the other party) supports a candidate because of his personal appeal. Such voting behavior is based on candidate image or candidate appeal and it is increasingly important in many contests. Moreover, in some local, nonpartisan elections where parties or local groups do not contest elections, or in primary elections where all candidates are of the same party, candidate appeal usually is the single most important factor.

The importance of the candidate dimension in voting first became obvious during the 1950s in *The Voter Decides*, a study of the Presidential election of 1952. Eisenhower's victory was attributed, in considerable measure, to Democratic identifiers who generally supported Democratic issue positions. Indeed, 12 percent of the strong Democrats, 26 percent of the weak Democrats and 28 percent of the Independent leaning Democrats voted for Eisenhower.[37] The authors attribute this crossover to the more favorable image Eisenhower had over Stevenson. They summarized candidate factors into the concept of candidate orientation, "the structuring of political events in terms of a personal attraction to the major personalities involved."[38] Respondents were asked to answer in a free association manner the questions, "What in particular do you like about Eisenhower (Stevenson)," and, "What in particular do you dislike about Eisenhower (Stevenson)?" The responses to these questions were then placed into a reasonable number of categories and an approximate picture of the candidates emerged. Briefly, the picture that emerged was one of Eisenhower as the man with the qualities of leadership; in particular he was seen as a man who could handle the foreign (Korean) situation.[39] Fewer respondents made any comments at all about Stevenson, confirming that he was less well known, and of those that did comment, the fact that he was a Democrat was most important.[40] In this case, the unfavorable reactions did not add much to the candidate orientation, although 20 percent considered Stevenson to be "Truman's man."[41] Not surprisingly, the greater the personal attraction to the candidate, the more likely one was to vote for that candidate (in this election Eisenhower), even when one identified with the opposite party.[42]

As researchers became aware of the increasing importance of candidate factors they began to see that it had more complex dimensions than merely personal qualities. In the 1960 campaign, Kennedy's Catholicism was the reason that some voters deviated from their normally expected vote—some in favor and some against Kennedy. His Catholicism accounted for an estimated net loss of 2.2 percent of the total vote.[43] Research of the 1964 campaign made it clearer that candidates have an issue or *policy* dimension to their images as well as a *personality* dimension. Personal and policy references to Johnson and Goldwater were separated. It was found that Johnson received a net favorable margin of 80 to 20 on his policies while Goldwater's policy image was 30 to 70. Personality relationships were quite different; Johnson's advantage declined owing to his wheeler-dealer style and the aura of conflict of interest, whereas Goldwater's personal integrity and sincerity drew considerable praise. Goldwater's image was thus unfavorable because of his policies, particularly his social welfare, domestic, and foreign policy positions, which were appealing only to hardcore Republicans.[44]

Goldwater's failure to capture the Republican party's advantage in foreign policy capability suggests that a "prospective job performance" dimension exists in candidate voting. Only 12 percent of American voters saw Goldwater as the candidate more likely to keep the United States out of war, the only time a Republican candidate has not held such an advantage since presidential elections have been systematically studied.[45] Walter DeVries has categorized this dimension as "ability to handle the job," for the office under consideration. DeVries polled for Governor Milliken of Michigan and in a postelection poll he found that to those voters who were either undecided at the later stages of the campaign, or those who switched from the Democrat Levin to Milliken, candidate factors were the most important in their decisions, and that ability to handle the job far outweighed personality as a candidate factor.[46] For the entire sample, the DeVries study finds candidate oriented factors to be the most important of all factors, and of those respondents who claim that candidate factors are the "most important in deciding political matters," 48 percent cited the candidate's personality and background, 28 percent the ability to do the job, and 19 percent the candidate's stand on the issues.[47] Despite George McGovern's "peace stance" in relation to Nixon, in the 1972 campaign, more people thought Nixon would be more capable of achieving peace in Vietnam, including over one third of the Democratic identifiers.[48] Voters also had scant confidence in McGovern's ability to manage the economy—an advantage that most Democratic candidates have enjoyed. A candidate's image among voters as to how he can handle the job of the office sought can work as either a positive or a negative force.

Researchers often try to combine the candidate's personality, the candidate's partisanship, the candidate's issue positions and perception of his ability to do the job by asking voters to give some overall feeling for a candidate. One method is called the semantic differential. Voters are asked to rate the candidate on a scale, usually containing seven points, in reaction to several opposing terms such as liberal-conservative, active-passive, strong-weak, slow-fast, decisive-indecisive. Then they are asked to mark the point closest to their feelings.[49] The composite of these ratings gives an overall image of the candidate. Such devices have indicated to candidates that their images were either of a passive, indecisive, weak, or liberal politician when they featured themselves as middle-of-the-road, decisive, or activist. One incumbent U.S. Senator found that he was much "colder" and "impersonal" in the eyes of his constituents than either he or his staff had thought. Weisberg and Rusk also report the use of a candidate "feeling thermometer" that asks respondents to indicate, on a 0- to -100-degree temperature scale, how "warm" or "cold" they feel toward candidates. A score of 50 degrees indicates neither a warm nor a cold feeling about the candidate. Respondents are given a card listing corresponding verbal meanings.[50] Such a technique can give a general indication of voters relative "feelings" toward candidates and how various subgroups rate the candidates. When there are a number of candidates, such as in a primary election, the ratings could be a valuable indicator of choice. If the candidate survives the primary, his rating takes on

Figure 2.1   Feeling Thermometer Used by Survey Research
Center for 1968 Presidential and Vice Presidential Candidates

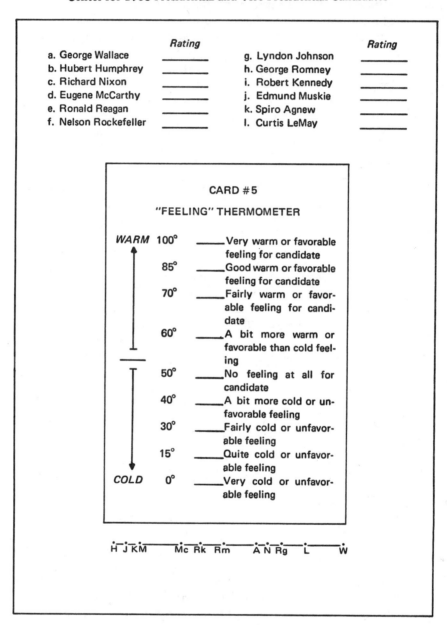

Source: Herbert F. Weisberg and Jerrold S. Rusk, "Dimensions of Candidate Evaluation," *American Political Science Review,* 64 (December 1970), 1175.

a new light as opponents are eliminated; he now has second and third choice information.

Candidate voting is definitely rising in the United States for many reasons. In brief, candidates now offer more information through mass media or through their own personal campaigns; parties campaign less for candidates; and voters are showing more independence of party cues at the polls.[51] More and more voters seem to be shifting their votes and evidence indicates that these shifting votes are primarily due to candidate appeals.[52] In the 1968 presidential election, a full third of all white voters switched their vote from one party's candidate in 1964 to the other party's in 1968. Almost one Goldwater voter in five switched to Humphrey or Wallace (3 to 1 for Wallace). Three out of every ten white, Johnson voters switched to Nixon or Wallace (4 to 1 for Nixon). Forty percent of Nixon's votes came from voters who had supported Johnson in 1964.[53] Congressional candidates are increasingly being insulated from the tides of presidential politics. More and more Congressmen carry or lose their districts independent of the vote for president in that district. By the late 1960s one third of the Congressional districts showed split results between Congress and the president whereas the number of split outcomes was 3.4 percent of the districts in 1900.[54] In 1948, 72 percent of American voters claimed to have voted a straight ticket in state and local races; by 1966 that figure had dropped to 50 percent of all voters.[55] The number of victors from different parties in senatorial and gubernatorial contests at the same election has steadily increased from less than one fourth to one half of all such elections.[56] Split control of state government between governors of one party and state legislatures controlled by the opposition is also increasing.[57] Moreover, there seems to be less congruence between the totals of each candidate on a party ticket. It is not unusual anymore to find results where Republican and Democratic candidates receive large margins in the same election.

All of these trends are due to the ticket splitter, according to DeVries and Tarrance, an emerging type of voter who is largely a candidate voter. Instead of measuring how persons identify themselves with parties, the authors argue that one should examine how voters actually behave. An increasing number of "party identifiers" actually split their tickets regularly.[58] Ticket splitters make up one fourth of the electorate. They are more politically interested, tend to be in the middle income bracket, are likely to be professional and technical persons, and are well educated.[59] The ticket splitter is more likely to make up his mind on the basis of candidates, issues, party identification and group identification in that order.[60] Indeed, more and more voters claim to split their tickets—as high as one half of all voters, according to a Gallup Poll.[61] We actually know very little about the habitual ticket splitter. The DeVries and Tarrance work is only a beginning; it really only identified and crystallized the concept, leaving many unanswered questions as to the nature and conditions of ticket splitting.

CANDIDATE
IMPLICATIONS FOR CAMPAIGNS

As candidate-oriented concerns become more important in voting, they obviously must become a more central part of the campaign. No matter how strongly partisan a constituency is—and fewer constituencies seem to be safe for the candidates of one party—campaigners are finding it difficult to rely on party appeals alone. For example, in the 1972 election for Cook County state's attorney the regular Democratic organization found that appeals to party loyalty were not enough to carry many black precincts for party nominee Edward Hanrahan. His association with the Black Panther apartment raid, and candidate appeals by Republican Bernard Carey made an organized black voter ticket splitting campaign possible. Precincts that normally vote eight to one and nine to one Democratic split almost even between the candidates, contributing to Carey's surprise victory.

Many elections are both formally and informally nonpartisan, such as for village trustee, mayor of a small city, or county offices. By convention, the candidates do not use their party affiliation if they have one.[62] In these cases, party as a factor is irrelevant; candidate and issue concerns are paramount. In most such contests candidate factors generally are, undoubtedly, most important since few issues are visible to people and interest in the campaign is generally low. This helps explain why electioneering in many of these small constituency campaigns consists primarily of handshaking, attending meetings, suppers, weddings, and anniversaries. Such elections are often called "popularity contests."

Unlike party appeal, which is largely a pre-existing sentiment, and which the candidate can expect, to some extent, from the party, the candidate and his campaigners must create candidate sentiment. The candidate organization cannot merely associate itself with the party label or party organization but must formulate appeals that stimulate candidate voting. Whether projecting personality, issue positions, or ability to do the job, the candidate group has to "manufacture" sentiment. Harking back to all the good programs the party has brought to the people in the past will not convey what the candidate plans to do for the people in the future. In 1972, George McGovern had the problem of demonstrating personally that he was as competent in foreign policy as Richard Nixon, because voters place their confidence *in a leader*. As will be demonstrated throughout this book, the manufacture of candidate sentiment is one of the major products of a campaign organization.

If the goal of the campaigner is to win the support of those who generally support the other party, then candidate appeals are a must. Recall the information offered in Table 2.4 (page 28) concerning voter awareness of candidates and party. The more information a partisan had about an opposition party candidate the more likely he was to vote for him or her. Party, in that context, was labelled as a residual (in the absence of other cues the party voter would rely on his party). Thus, if campaigners want to avoid having their candidates fall into this residual situation, some appeals will have to be made. As we will see in the next section, issue appeals are often not received by voters. Candidate information is the best alternative. Even if the campaigner is trying to woo his partisans, it is useful to offer partisan-oriented candidate cues. Party affiliation, political attitudes toward the issues, and candidate choice very often run together.[63]

Another inference about candidate voting is the apparant modal or a set of essential expectations voters have about the office sought by the candidate. This factor refers primarily to the "ability to handle the job," but refers to issues and personality also. Modern presidential aspirants are expected to be competent managers of prosperity, have experience, and be able to establish a feeling of security in foreign policy. In fact, there is some evidence that competent handling of foreign policy may be more important than any directional position on the issues of foreign policy.[64] Research on modal voter expectations for other offices is almost nonexistent, but voters undoubtedly have such thoughts. Other chief executives, such as mayors and governors, are no doubt expected to be astute fiscal managers and should possess the capacity to govern.[65] Legislature candidates are likely to be expected to perform a mixed representative role combining service, representation, and leadership.[66]

A final set of inferences relates to a candidate's recognition level and total image. When respondents are asked to volunteer candidate image information, the more responses received, the better known the candidate appears to be. In a poll taken for a lieutenant governor hoping to become governor, 40 percent of those sampled offered evaluations of him—a remarkably high rate for a lieutenant governor. On the other hand, the governor received responses from twice as many respondents, indicating that the governor was far better known, suggesting that the lieutenant governor would have to do more to make himself known. In addition, the responses to candidate image have to be considered at some point in a net fashion. If the minuses exceed the pluses, the candidate possibly has image problems. Consider, for example, some facets of McGovern's net personal minus in 1972 among Democrats. Sixty percent said McGovern handled the Eagleton affair badly, more Democrats than Republicans named Nixon as having the more appropriate personality to be president, and equal number of Democrats "trusted" Nixon as "trusted" McGovern, over one-third of the Democrats thought Nixon was more likely to achieve peace in Vietnam. These are the components of a net image—in this case, a negative one. Finally, a composite image of the candidate, such as the leadership, foreign policy, and trust image of Eisenhower is a useful organizing concept for campaign planning, in formulating candidate appeals, issue positions, and advertising.

ISSUE VOTING AND ISSUE VOTERS

One of the greatest controversies among those who study and are involved in elections is the role of issues. The controversey centers around the critical question of the extent to which American voters adhere to the democratic ideal by using issue concerns as a basis for making voting decisions.

Challenges to the democratic ideal came with the earliest voting studies. In *Voting,* a study of the 1948 election, issue positions were considered to be conceptualized in terms of social groupings, and that Truman's last minute rally to victory was in large part due to a switch back on the part of some voters to the New Deal-Fair Deal on the group basis of Truman's issue appeals.[67] In *The American Voter,* it was stated that reasonably high consistency exists between the party's position on an issue and the party identifier's attitude toward issues. The authors claim, "The fact that without exception these attitude forces become steadily more pro-Republican as we move from the Democratic to the Republican end of the party dimension suggests the extent of the party's impact on the electorate's evaluations of the elements of politics."[68] But the authors generally found low levels of issue information on the sixteen issues presented. Only one-third of the electorate had opinions on fourteen of the sixteen issues. Another one-fourth had opinions on issues but did not know what the government was doing about the issues.[69] More importantly, it was found that varying with the issue, only about one-half of the public that holds an opinion on an issue perceives party differences on those issues, and thus can locate one or the other party as closer to their position. The lesson is clear, they maintain, that "even when 'political' attitudes are held, there is no guarantee that partisan implications are drawn."[70] In spite of the fact that there is congruence between issue positions and the party position, it is not very important to the voter's decision. They conclude that the impact of issues is probably overstated, "If our findings suggest only a modest articulation between party policy and voter response, they raise questions as well concerning the issue significance that may be ascribed to national elections, at least at the level of the relatively specific policy matters under consideration here."[71]

The relatively low place of issues both in terms of the individual voting decisions and as a factor in electoral change triggered a debate. V.O. Key, Jr. in *The Responsible Electorate* argued that "voters are not fools"; the electorate is moved by "concern about central and relevant questions of public policy, of governmental performance, and of executive personality."[72] Key looked at voting changes from one election to the next by organizing the electorate into three groups: "standpatters," switchers, and new voters. He found a general congruence between the issue preferences of the standpatters and the party in power, whereas the switchers tended to disagree with existing policies. New voters also tended to distribute their votes in terms of their policy preferences. While the switchers are a smaller group (20 to 30%) than the standpatters, Key suggests they are a notable, significant, and often a decisive force in an election.[73]

Key's work seemed to trigger other work on the issue question. Walter Dean Burnham argues that the controversies and tensions over important issues are key elements in party realignments and thus must be important in voting.[74]

RePass, analyzing issues both exclusive of and including party identification, found a substantial effect for issues in the 1964 election. After controlling for the various reciprocal influences of party, candidate, and issue on each other, he found candidate factors to be the single most influential factor of the three, but issues and party were nearly the same in relative influence. He concluded that while candidate image was undoubtedly the most important factor in that election, issues had a strong independent effect; in fact, "salient issues had almost as much weight as party identification in predicting voting choice."[75]

The SRC (Survey Research Center) study of the 1968 election was used as a means to refine the earlier position of *The American Voter* in the debate. Stating that Key's general thesis was a welcome corrective to the earlier thesis of low issue content in voting, they used the Wallace vote as the basis of their refinement. They found substantial correlations between Wallace's issue positions on law and order, civil rights, Vietnam, and the voters' issue positions, whereas party identification was insignificant to these voters. The public reacted to the Wallace candidacy, they assert, as an issue candidacy. But when it came to issue and party relationships relating to the Humphrey and Nixon candidacies, it was "party that towers over other predictors, and the central 1968 issues tend to give rather diminutive relationships."[76] They conclude that the pattern of Wallace support shows the kind of strong issue orientation Key sought to demonstrate, whereas evaluations of Humphrey and Nixon show strong party allegiance suffocating most issue concerns.[77] The Wallace findings show that, as Key argued, the public can relate policy controversies to its own estimates of the world and vote accordingly, but one of "the cardinal limiting conditions is the 'drag' or inertia represented by habitual party loyalties: as soon as features of the situation limit or neutralize the relevance of such a factor, issue evaluations play a more vital role."[78]

The debate continues on. Pomper analyzed the issues used by SRC and found that in the 1956 election period issue differences between the parties and, thus, issue voting may not have been as evident. But 1964 was a critical point at which there was a clarification of the parties' issue positions, particularly in the area of civil rights, and votes began to shift accordingly. He presents evidence that there is an increasing correlation between a voter's party identification and a "liberal" or "conservative" position on five issues: aid to education, medical care, job guarantees, fair employment, and school integration. Pomper hastens to add that it still remains to be demonstrated that votes are actually cast *because* of issue preferences.[79] In a similar vein, Richard Boyd argues that the 1956 election, on which *The American Voter* was based, was a relatively quiescent political year, but in other election years issues can effect the vote. Using the "normal vote" concept, Boyd found that beliefs about Vietnam, race, and urban unrest in the 1968 election did indeed change the normal or expected vote based on party affiliation.[80] Other researchers have questioned these attempts to elevate the role of issues in voting, by charging that these studies have not adequately untangled the relationship between attitudes and voting[81]

Table 2.6 Correlation* Between Issue Positions, Partisanship and
Ratings of the Major Candidates, 1968 Presidential Election
(Whites Only)[a]

ISSUE DOMAIN	NON-SOUTH			SOUTH		
	Humphrey	Nixon	Wallace	Humphrey	Nixon	Wallace
A. Civil Rights (6 or 7 items)[b]	.17	.09	.27	.24	.08	.41
B. Law and Order (2 items)	.25	.05	.27	.19	.01	.35
C. Vietnam (2 items)	.05	.03	.23	.14	.02	.26
D. Cold War (4 items)	.12	.11	.15	.16	.05	.28
E. Social Welfare (2 or 3 items)[b]	.22	.20	.09	.26	.13	.10
F. Federal Gov't Too Powerful? (1 item)	.37	.18	.17	.49	.13	.15
SUM: 18 issue items	.19	.10	.20	.22	.07	.31
SUM: Three Major 1968 Issue Domains (A,B,C)	.16	.07	.26	.22	.07	.37
PARTISANSHIP: (3 items)	.47	.47	.04	.39	.36	.03

[a]Cell entries are average absolute values of gamma ordinal correlations between items of the types listed in the rows and affective ratings of the candidates noted in the columns.

[b]An item having to do with the role of the federal government in aid to local education was considered a social welfare item outside the South, but a civil rights issue within that region.

*Values range from no relationship between the stated issue concerns and a candidate choice (0.00) and a perfect relationship between issue concerns and a candidate choice (1.00).

Source: Philip E. Converse, Warren E. Miller, Jerrold G. Rusk, and Arthur C. Wolfe, "Continuity and Change in American Politics: Parties and Issues in the 1968 Election," *American Political Science Review* 63 (December 1969), 1098.

nor have they fully accounted for the role of candidate and other short term forces.[82]

This summary of the ongoing debate over the role of issues in elections indicates that the web is yet to be completely untangled. What is clear is that for partisans, issues seem to be in some way involved in partisanship, but that there are cases in which issues pull people away from their normal partisanship. Also, under some conditions for some voters issues can become the single most important factor in voting decisions.

In order for issues to become an important determinant of the vote certain conditions must be met. To parphrase the authors of *The American Voter:*

- The voter must be aware of the issue and he must have an opinion in some direction about it.
- The issue must arouse some minimal intensity of feeling—the voter must attach some importance to the issue.
- The voter must be able to perceive a difference between the candidates or parties on the issue—usually that one candidate or party will handle the issue better than the other.[83]

These conditions are not often easy to meet for voters in a campaign, especially those with lower levels of interest and knowledge, or when it is difficult for issue messages to get through in a campaign. Also, of the large number of issues that are presented in a campaign, only a few break through and become important for voters. As the debate over issue voting demonstrated, we have yet to pin down the exact relationships of the conditions stated between issue awareness, intensity, perceived differences, and the vote.

When issues are important to a voter, they usually have been organized in their minds through the framework of parties or candidates. Issue partisanship is the tendency for partisan voters to place or accept issues as they receive messages about them within the context of their own party orientation. The party identifier who sees his party espouse issues is likely to be influenced by that issue,[84] and the more sensitive the partisan is to party differences the more of an issue partisan he is.[85] Envision a strong Republican from Michigan who had previously heard nothing about government financing of medical care, who hears Senator Robert Griffin, campaigning in 1976, assert in a short television news report that the National Health Insurance bill would destroy the present, free medical system, bankrupt social security, and make more citizens wards of the state. The citizen forms an opinion against federal health insurance and assumes the Republicans are against it on the basis of Griffin's message—a case of issue partisanship. Issues can also be linked through candidate orientation. While excluding this dimension from their analysis of candidate factors, the authors of *The Voter Decides* refer to its existence.[86] In *The American Voter* there was some mention that references to candidates often were through issue positions.[87] Brody and Page say that linkage of a voter's position with the candidate's and with a corresponding evaluation, is a necessary and sufficient condition of policy voting.[88] Although he does not control for party identification, DeVries offers actual evidence of voters claiming that the issue position of the candidate was the reason for voting,[89] and the reason for a shift from undecided to a vote or for a vote switch.[90]

There is some evidence, however, that issue candidacies and issue-candidate voting, independent of parties, is increasing in presidential elections.[91] Undoubtedly, some voters do link up their voting decisions for candidates on the basis of issues, exclusive of any partisan considerations. Issues are then linked through both parties and candidates, both of which, incidentally, are usually identified on the ballot. There are no known ballot forms in existence that list issue positions beside the candidate's name and party.

ISSUE IMPLICATIONS FOR THE CAMPAIGN

Regardless of the exact proportion of issue voters, it is important for the campaigner to recognize that there is an issue-voter component in every electorate. Some of it is pre-existing (voters are seeking out issue messages). The remainder is flexible, it expands as issues are discussed in the context of the campaign. When the campaign is truly nonpartisan in orientation, the issue component of the electorate for that contest, while not over whelmingly large, in all probability expands. With party eliminated as a major concern, the dialogue shifts to candidates and issues. To avoid the "personality contest" onus, candidates usually turn to issues. Moreover, it is likely that the issue electorate is a larger portion of the total electorate in nonpresidential elections, because the electorate in these elections is usually reduced in size and quality through smaller turnouts and non-voting. In sum, the issue component of the electorate is flexible and mutable, and the campaigner must turn attention to these people.

The debate over issue voting also suggests that for partisans (or for that matter persons predisposed to candidates for personality reasons) certain issues—if the voter is aware of the issue, feels strong enough about it, and is aware of the candidates position on the issue—can pull people away from the preferences they bring into a campaign. The message to the campaigner is that he must discover issues and how groups feel about these issues. If he agrees with the direction, he must make appeals on the basis of those issues. The key is to discover the right issues, the right groups, and make the right appeals so that they can supercede the "drag" or inertia of partisan or candidate predisposition.

Even for the committed partisan, issue appeals can be used to consolidate or retain the support of those who are predisposed. Rather than assuming that the partisan will automatically march to the polls and pull the lever for each and every party candidate, the campaigner should assume that a group of voters might support the candidate if given a reason. Partisanship is there, anyway, due to long term development, the party organization, and labelling on the ballot. Moreover, it has been demonstrated that many partisans who receive issue messages use them to reinforce their partisanship. Why not use every available weapon to support party predisposition? Partisan oriented issue appeals can be an important part of the arsenal.

For those voters who do not have a party orientation, or even for those whose orientation is so weak that it is virtually nonexistent, issues may be the important device for linkage with candidates. Here the reference is to the issue-candidate orientation facet of candidate voting. A notable proportion of those who base their voting decision on the basis of candidates do so because of issue stands—as opposed to personality and ability to do the job. Campaigners should be prepared to take measures to link the voter to the candidate on the basis of issues as well as job preformance and personal demeanor.

Just as the campaigner has to create sentiment for the candidate, one must also produce issue appeals. The need is perhaps less critical since issues and partisan positions are to a certain extent linked in the minds of voters. But voters increasingly vote for candidates not parties, and if they are to do so on the basis of issues the candidate organization is then responsible for issue production. Also, impressive evidence indicates that it is key issues and the linkage of them with candidates, not the issue appeal of the opposition party that engenders switch votes. Voters obviously are not in a position to switch or select votes for a candidate unless the message is transmitted and received. Parties have the problem of producing more general issue appeals. The individual campaigner must produce the means for linking issue and candidate.

GROUPS AND THE VOTE

The very earliest studies of voting behavior characterized social groups as being all-important factors in determining the vote. They presented evidence that most voters tended to vote for the same party as their fathers; husbands and wives ordinarily voted for the same candidate; social friends, and to a lesser extent co-workers, tended to agree on parties and candidates; and people of the same social, economic, and religious groupings tended to vote alike.[91] They concluded that social environments were generally homogenous and therefore most individuals are not exposed to the opposite views, since most discussed politics with members of their own social groups. It was theorized in *Voting* that:

> usually high rates of interaction, permitting rapid culmination of successive influence or simultaneous multiple-person influence on an individual, rebuild majorities in social groups beyond the specific political reasons involved. Alternation of high with low rates of such influences must produce a "pulsating system" of greater or lesser social differentiation in politics, accompanying greater or lesser social discussions of politics over recurrent phases in the cycle.

The social analysis of political votes, then, arrives back at the starting point. The solid foundations of American political parties are in distinctive social groups that not only have 'interests' involved but have sufficient social differentiation from other groups, sufficient closed or in-group contact in successive generations to transform these initial political interests into persistant and durable social traditions.[93]

The more these various social characteristics were found together, the more likely the individual's vote conformed to the direction of his grouping. Thus, a Protestant son of a Republican who was a high income businessman living in a small town was highly disposed to and almost certainly would vote Republican. Because they assumed the environment was homogenous, they merged these factors into a index of political predisposition, combining social and economic status (SES), religion, and place of residence. Thus, in contrast to the Republican, a person predisposed to vote Democratic would be low in SES, Catholic, and urban.[94] These early researchers obviously believed that social groupings caused the vote, and that political forces in the campaign were secondary factors placed in the context of the voter's social relationships.

A close examination of these works reveals that not all voters of a social category did vote according to their social predispositions, and people did think about the political objects in the campaign. Moreover, the authors could not prove that such social groupings led to the vote, or even that people considered themselves to be members of the group, merely that there were tendencies for people in groups to act similarly. It might be surmised by now that the approach taken by this book, as well as most of the voting studies previously cited, in effect reverses that order by stating that it is political forces such as parties, candidates, and issues that "cause" the vote. What, then, is the role of such social groupings? Simply stated, our model of voting assumes that only some of the social-grouping relationships discussed here are important to the individual when he thinks about politics and elections during the campaign. When family, friendship group, or organization is a factor in political thinking, it is ordinarily placed in a context of parties, issues, and candidates.[95] Take the example of the strong Democrat, regular church-going, fundamentalist Protestant, who thought a great deal of John F. Kennedy and didn't dislike what he had to say. To be sure he considered Kennedy's Catholicism, and what had been said at church over the years. He might have even discussed it with his wife, church friends or coworkers. But at some point he had to think about candidate Kennedy, the Democratic party, maybe one or two issue positions, perhaps how he would perform as president, Nixon, the opponent, and the thought of voting Republican. The closer he got to the point of decision, and the more heated the campaign became, the more he had to consider any such social considerations in terms of candidates, issues, and parties. Thus, social groups and social factors are not being relegated to unimportance. They are viewed as antecedent to the political.

Within this conceptualization there are two types of groups that can play an important role in campaigns. Primary groups—family, friends, coworkers, and so on, operate by mediating and interpreting interpersonal messages in the campaign. Members of the group sometimes discuss politics and there is evidence that people get some of their political information through these groups. As will be demonstrated later, some mass media messages are transmitted by opinion leaders, and certain key people in small groups are important in transmitting these messages to group members. The group can either serve as a force to confirm a member's political choice or serve as an agent of change. It depends on the complex nature of the individual's relationship with the group, the importance of politics to the individual and the group and, whether the group tries to enforce conformity in political matters.[96] Obviously, the more important the group is to the individual, the more important politics is to the group, and if the group takes steps to enforce conformity, the more likely the primary group is to have an effect on confirming or changing a person's political views.

Secondary groups, such as one's race, religion, organization memberships, ethnicity, are more distant from the individual but can have an important effect on voting. The key factor is the degree to which the individual identifies with, or sees himself as a part of the group. In *The American Voter,* it was found that union members, Catholics, Negroes, and Jews tended to be more Democratic in their voting among those members of the group who were most closely associated with their respective groups.[97] Keech found that voting among Southern blacks, a group that has a very high degree of group identification, was highly cohesive when organized groups operated to mobilize votes in a certain direction.[98] Blacks throughout the South indicate a willingness to support a candidate if he has the support of a black organization or most other blacks.[99] Wolfinger reports that ethnicity is more important in the absence of other plain cues to guide voters' decisions, particularly in nonpartisan elections where voters cannot rely on party labels. He also asserts that many strong ethnic identifiers retain their earlier voting habits when their SES changes.[100]

When the individual does identify with a particular group it becomes a reference point for the formation of attitudes and political behavior. Of course, such reference behavior depends on the group maintaining a political posture and transmitting it in some way to its identifiers.

The distribution of votes by groups in presidential elections depicted in Table 2.7 indicates that groups rarely vote exclusively for a party's candidate. Rather, there are only tendencies for groups to vote in certain directions. The only exception to this is the nonwhite group, particularly blacks who increasingly have voted for Democratic presidential candidates in near unanimous proportions.

The campaigner should be aware of the tendencies of groups to vote in certain directions, but he or she should also note that they are only tendencies. Some voters stray from the central tendencies presumably because small group networks lead them away or group identification is weak and thus, cue-taking is nonexistent or a conflicting identification prevails. For example, Wolfinger

Table 2.7 Vote by Groups in Presidential Elections since 1952
(Based on Gallup Poll Survey Data)

	1952 Stev. %	1952 Ike %	1956 Stev. %	1956 Ike %	1960 JFK %	1960 Nixon %	1964 LBJ %	1964 Gold. %	1968 HHH %	1968 Nixon %	1968 Wallace %	1972 McG. %	1972 Nixon %
NATIONAL	44.6	55.4	42.2	57.8	50.1	49.9	61.3	38.7	43.0	43.4	13.6	38	62
SEX													
Men	47	53	45	55	52	48	60	40	41	43	16	37	63
Women	42	58	39	61	49	51	62	38	45	43	12	38	62
RACE													
White	43	57	41	59	49	51	59	41	38	47	15	32	68
Non-white	79	21	61	39	68	32	94	6	85	12	3	87	13
EDUCATION													
College	34	66	31	69	39	61	52	48	37	54	9	37	63
High School	45	55	42	58	52	48	62	38	42	43	15	34	66
Grade School	52	48	50	50	55	45	66	34	52	33	15	49	51
OCCUPATION													
Prof. & Business	36	64	32	68	42	58	54	46	34	56	10	31	69
White Collar	40	60	37	63	48	52	57	43	41	47	12	36	64
Manual	55	45	50	50	60	40	71	29	50	35	15	43	57
AGE													
Under 30 years	51	49	43	57	54	46	64	36	47	38	15	48	52
30-49 years	47	53	45	55	54	46	63	37	44	41	15	33	67
50 years & older	39	61	39	61	46	54	59	41	41	47	12	36	64
RELIGION													
Protestants	37	63	37	63	38	62	55	45	35	49	16	30	70
Catholics	56	44	51	49	78	22	76	24	59	33	8	48	52
POLITICS													
Republicans	8	92	4	96	5	95	20	80	9	86	5	5	95
Democrats	77	23	85	15	84	16	87	13	74	12	14	67	33
Independents	35	65	30	70	43	57	56	44	31	44	25	31	69
REGION													
East	45	55	40	60	53	47	68	32	50	43	7	42	58
Midwest	42	58	41	59	48	52	61	39	44	47	9	40	60
South	51	49	49	51	51	49	52	48	31	36	33	29	71
West	42	58	43	57	49	51	60	40	44	49	7	41	59
Members of Labor Union Families	61	39	57	43	65	35	73	27	56	29	15	46	54

suggests that wealthy ethnics who remain in their old, ethnic neighborhoods are less likely to change their voting than those who move to the suburbs, because they retain stronger identifications. Their suburban counterparts move to economically homogeneous and ethnically diverse neighborhoods. Such conditions diminish ethnic consciousness.[101]

In a campaign, these forces are more difficult to deal with than candidates, issues, and parties. In many cases the campaigner has to use judgment to determine when the appropriate channels for group identification are useful and when they are not.

DEMOGRAPHIC DYNAMICS AND THEIR CAMPAIGN IMPLICATIONS

Until now it has been assumed that the electorate a campaigner faces is static— voters do not change from election to election. In practice, the campaigner must add changes in the demography of voters to considerations of parties, candidates, issues, and groups. The primary influences on demographic electoral changes are the migration of voters and fluctuations of the electorate by reason of those becoming eligible to vote, and the demise of older voters.

Migration

As voters move from place to place the composition of the electorate changes. The Census Bureau estimates that about one in every five families moves each year. Sometimes these changes are very obvious, such as in the case of a rapid influx of suburbanites to a previously rural township. In other cases, the change may be less obvious, such as in the case of the slower migration of rural residents to urban areas. These cases obviously refer to potential changes in the size of the electorate. The campaigner should be aware of the fact that the district he faces is likely to be reduced or expanded in size through such population movements.

Aside from questions of size, the political effects of such movements are interesting. There are at least three important kinds of political changes that can occur as a result of migration. First, there is the aggregate change in the political composition of the area. As people move out of Congressional districts, cities, and states, they may change the partisan composition of the constituency. There is evidence, for example, that much of the Democratic composition of the mountain states is due to the Western migration of Southern Democrats.[102] Some suburbs adjacent to cities that were slightly Republican in the 1940s gradually became Democratic as working-class Democrats began to move across the city limits. By the 1960s their massive influx made the suburbs relatively safe Democratic territory. Likewise, other suburbs were changed in a Republican direction, or their Republican nature has been accentuated. DuPage County,

Illinois is a former rural, small town county that has been transformed by suburban migration into the second largest county in the state. Although the population increases by 20 percent each decade, it remains almost as Republican, in ratio, as it was four decades ago. Presumably, because the same kind of people move into the area as are already there, there are few individual changes in voter allegiance.

A second kind of effect due to migration can occur when individuals undergo political change. In some cases it is social, economic, and residential changes that occur at approximately the same time, that lead to political changes. Consider, for example, the Democrat who achieves financial success through a new and more prestigious occupation, moves to a wealthy suburb, and acquires a new group of friends. Under these circumstances he may become less partisan, or even become a Republican. However, the change may not necessarily be partisan, it may be in political values and expectations only. The individual may shift his interest from concerns for economic security to efficiency in government and lower taxes. A third and related type of effect is that the political effect is singular—it comes as a result of moving. After arriving in the new locale, the individual responds to the new environment by adopting the political values of his new neighbors. The limited evidence available indicates that few individuals actually change politically to conform to their new environment.[103] Many more people take their political views with them when they change residence. There is some evidence, however, to support the second type of change mentioned. People do change their political outlooks as they move up and down the social scale. But interestingly, it is not enjoyed exclusively by people who move physically when their status changes. Those who stay behind are likely to adjust their political outlooks also.[104]

The campaigner must be on the lookout for such political changes. It is not only important to note political migrations, but one must note *who* is moving. Many related questions can be asked—

- Are the new residents upwardly mobile or are they people whose status is basically the same, yet have sought a new location?
- How are the new development tracts and the new residents going to affect the partisanship of the district?
- What measures must be taken to see that the new apartment dwellers register and vote?
- Are those remaining in an area of migration the same, or are they older or different citizens?
- What happens to the electorate if a large industry closes down in a small town area and employees begin to move on?

In short, the campaigner must examine the constituency before each election to see if population movement has significantly altered the composition of the electorate.

Replacement of the Electorate

In each election there is a change in the structure of the electorate due to deaths, the eligibility of new voters, and the politicization of those who have never previously voted. Key estimated that each presidential electorate from 1940 to 1960 was made up of from 15 to 20 percent first-time voters.[105] In 1972, due to the Twenty-sixth Amendment and the coming of age of other young citizens, there were 23 million potential new voters. The actual number of new voters in 1972 was closer to 10 million. Traditionally, new voters show the lowest turnout in an election, thus diminishing their potential impact.[106]

Some eligible voters do not vote in every election. The most prevalent drop in numbers is not between presidential elections, but between presidential elections and state and local elections. There are many such "off and on" voters, due chiefly to a lack of interest in the elections. Others do not vote because they are not legal residents, because they are away from home, because they are ill, or for some reason could not get to the polls. All of these non-voters are potential voters in another election.

At the same time new voters are becoming part of the electorate of a given election, other voters are dropping out of the electorate, chiefly because of old age or death. Not surprisingly, voter participation tapers off about age sixty-five and decreases sharply among voters in their seventies.[107] As voters die or no longer vote, the composition of the electorate changes. Butler and Stokes found, for example, that during the 1960s the British electorate had a net gain of Labor Party-oriented young voters becoming part of the electorate while more Conservative Party-oriented older voters "left" the electorate.[108] During the 1950s the Democratic party's advantage in loyalists was solidified as more and more New Deal-oriented voters came of age and more older Republican voters died off.[109]

These forces obviously can lead to political change. It is unlikely that an even number of Democrats and Republicans (or any other voter category, party notwithstanding), enter and leave the electorate simultaneously. Butler and Stokes estimate that the net change due to such replacement of the electorate in each British national election is between one and two percent.[110] That does not sound like a huge proportion, but many elections are decided by small margins and the absolute number of voters can be in the thousands or millions. This figure is of course an overall figure for an entire nation. In a particular constituency the net effect of such changes can be great. For example, now that eighteen year olds who live in growing college communities are eligible to vote in those communities, the number of young voters entering the electorate probably exceeds older voters leaving the electorate by substantial margins. In these areas the electorate is expanding and becoming younger—and probably becoming less partisan.

The campaigner must be on the lookout for both qualitative and quantitative changes in the electorate. Sometimes he or she must account merely for an increase or decrease in numbers of voters. A new housing development may, for example, attract large numbers of young families to a district. It is perilous, however, to assume that replacements will equal previous electorates. A campaigner in the South who assumes that equal proportions of Democratic votes or Democratic identifications means that no change has occurred is mistaken. Actually, whites have changed their partisanship, migrated, or died and have been replaced by new black voters. A change in campaign strategies based on the new Democrats would obviously be in order. Less dramatic but equally important replacements regularly occur as voters exposed to earlier political eras and life experiences are substituted for products of other eras. Partisan references to the New Deal are less likely to work for younger Democrats. If a relatively static community is suddenly faced by a large housing development for moderate-income, young families, issues must shift from senior citizens to schools, property taxes, and parks. As the qualitative characteristics of the people change, so too will the nature of the campaigning.

VOTER TURNOUT

Voting requires more than the decision to mark a ballot for one candidate or the other. It requires the previous decision of whether to vote at all. Although the study of voting has given increasingly more attention to the factors behind the direction in which votes are cast, many elections are probably decided by the all-important rate of voter turnout. Campaigners often base a part of their efforts on voter turnout because all potential voters do not come to the polls, and campaigners presume that the increment that they turn out will be helpful to their winning margin.

The low levels of American voting turnout are rather well known to political observers. Between 60 and 65 percent of the eligible electorate normally turn out in presidential elections, although in two elections (1948 and 1972) the rate dipped to around 55 percent.[111] Presidential contests are the high point of electoral turnout; in all other types of elections the turnout rate is less. In off-year congressional and state elections, the turnout is normally between 45 and 50 percent of the electorate. Turnout in local elections varies greatly with the locality, but they range from 20 to 50 percent of the electorate. Primary elections normally bring out from 25 to 50 percent of the number of general election voters, except in one-party areas where a primary victory is tantamount to election. Figure 2.2 traces these variable turnout patterns in the city of Minneapolis over a decade. It is not unusual, however, for an electoral turnout to dip even below the range revealed in Minneapolis. In 1973 two Northern Illinois University students faced each other in a DeKalb contest for alderman in a campus ward with over 8,000 eligible voters. The vote tally was 81 to 71. In 1969, an Illinois, constitutional-convention-delegate primary election brought out 13 percent of the state's electorate. Many poverty program, community

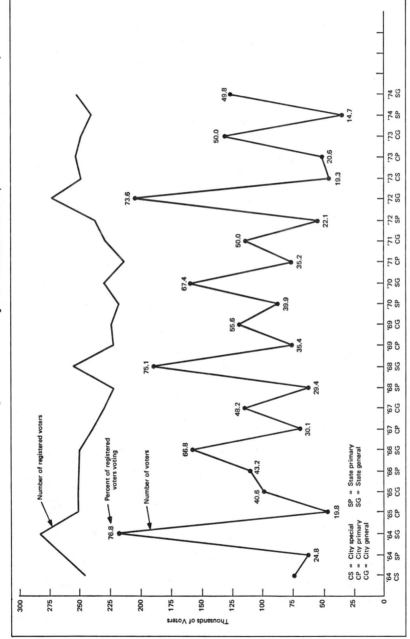

Figure 2.2 Minneapolis Election Turnout, 1964-1974

Source: Charles H. Backstrom, *Minnesota Political Almanac* (Minneapolis: Univ. of Minnesota, 1974), mimeographed.

council elections, designed to enhance "maximum feasible participation" by residents of poverty neighborhoods, have turnouts of less than 5 percent of the eligible voters.

Such rates, which compare unfavorably with other democratic nations, are relatively low because of the interrelation of a number of forces that tend to depress voter participation. These forces relate chiefly to the nature and frequency of individual elections and various obstacles to individual voting.

Americans are almost constantly faced with an approaching election and its preceeding campaign. There are presidential elections, state and Congressional elections, county elections, local city elections, school board elections, and primaries for most of these. In addition, there are special bond issue elections, a number of special district elections, and in some areas referendum elections. Of course, the long ballot system of electing many officials means that there are multiple contests in many of these elections. Some of these elections and contests obviously generate more interest than others, and voters do not react equally to them. Angus Campbell categorizes elections on the basis of the interest to the electorate. Some elections are *high stimulus*—the electorate sees the alternatives faced as implying important differences if one candidate or the other is elected. Under these conditions turnout is generally high. If such differences are deemed unimportant, it is a *low-stimulus* election and turnout will be correspondingly low.[112] While Campbell was referring to the differences between various presidential and off-year congressional elections, we can expect that interest will vary between any set of elections and differences in interest will vary from one election contest to another. It has been suggested that differences in the levels of interest between elections and between various contests are a result of—

- the differences in media coverage given the election,
- the significance attached by voters to the office,
- the importance of issues raised in the campaign, and
- the attractiveness of candidates.[113]

Variation of these factors leads to high-stimulus or low-stimulus elections.

The relationship between voter interest in various elections and their corresponding status as high- or low-stimulus elections helps explain the low turnout in many elections. Far more attention is given by the media to the contests for higher office, such as president, governor, and senator. Voters generally attach more significance to these offices, and they are more likely to identify issues related to these contests. It is hard to say whether the candidates for these offices are more attractive, but certainly they have more opportunities to make their attractiveness known. Local and county elections have lower turnouts than state and national elections because they are generally given less coverage in the media, voters follow these contests less, and voters place less importance on them.

There are exceptions. Voter turnout is generally high when local elections are given extensive coverage by the media, and when voters see the importance of issues and candidates in the campaign and thereby make the office contest more significant. Turnout once approached 98 percent of the registered voters in parts of Hastings, Minnesota in an off-year election because of the simultaneous effect of a closely contested race for governor and a hotly contested (over some important county zoning regulations) county board race between two attractive and well known candidates. The exceptions prove the rule.

In addition to variations in voter turnout due to the nature of the contest, there are also individual barriers to voting. That is, regardless of the interest surrounding any particular election, there are factors that prevent some individuals from voting. Converse has grouped these barriers to voting into three broad categories:

> Accidental factors, or odd events which intrude in the daily lives of individuals, such as personal or family illness, a sudden call out of town or last-minute failures in transportation, which can deter even the highly motivated person from voting. These randomly occuring barriers have one thing in common: they are not political, even though their consequences may be.

> Motivational barriers, or apathy or indifferences of one type or another to the citizen's obligation to vote. Two types of motivational barriers exist. First, motivation dependent on immediate external stimulation, for example, the excitement of a presidential campaign stimulates a larger vote than off-year elections. Secondly, internalized motivation or the stimulation to vote in any election on the basis of some educational or learning process. For example, a broad sense of the importance of participation in a democratic process even where the stakes are not high. Some persons do not vote because they are neither internally nor externally stimulated.

> Legal or institutional barriers, or the network of state and local rules defining who is to be allowed to vote. These barriers can disfranchise even the most highly motivated citizen, albeit temporarily.[114]

As Converse maintains, it is usually taken for granted that all non-voting is motivational, but any one of these three factors might be the cause.

The legal regulations for voting in the United States, particularly registration, foster low turnout, to a greater degree than most people assume. Barriers to prevent blacks from voting in the South, such as poll taxes, literacy tests, and grandfather clauses, have been eliminated. The major remaining legal hurdles relate to the length of residence and requirements for registration prior to the election. At one time some states required as much as a one-year residency in addition to a shorter period of residency in the county and a shorter residency in the precinct before a voter was eligible to register. The recent trend has been to shorten such periods of residence. However, the prospective voter must very often go to a central location, such as the city hall, during certain specified times to register. Election laws rarely allow in-precinct registration, and if they do, it is often only for a day or two. A universal, postcard registration bill has been before Congress in recent years, and at this writing is still pending. The registration period often closes long before the election. In Illinois, for example, registration generally closes about one month before the election.

Converse found that with Southern blacks excluded, almost half of the non-voters in the 1952 and 1956 elections did not vote because they could not meet the legal residency requirements.[115] In a more recent study, Kimball found that legal requirements remain a significant barrier that enmeshes voters in a web of prior restraints, and that they are more likely to affect the poor.[116] In a study of voter registration in 104 cities, Kelley and his associates concluded that, "local differences in turnout for elections are to a large extent related to local differences in rates of registration, and these in turn reflect to a considerable degree local differences in the rules governing, and arrangements for handling, the registration of voters."[117] Obviously, some areas make it easier to register, allowing shorter residence requirements and more convenient and lengthier registration periods, while others do not. These barriers to registration are presently being challenged in the courts, and the courts are generally deciding in favor of the relaxation of requirements, but rules for registration remain as voting barriers.

Lack of motivation to vote is due to unstimulating campaigns or some factor related to a citizen's life situation. An example of the former is that turnout can sometimes be associated with increased competition. As the race becomes more competitive, more people vote. As one might suspect this competitive turnout is likely to be a function of the interest generated by the campaign.[118]

Many different life situations affect voter motivation. Persons with higher voting records are more closely linked with the political system. Presumably their closeness stimulates interest which, in turn, leads to voting. In *The American Voter,* it was stated that the more intense the partisan preference, the higher the turnout rate.[119] It was also found that the turnout rate of persons with a high degree of interest in the campaign exceeded those with low interest by almost 30 percent.[120] Those who were more concerned over the outcome of the election were more likely to vote.[121] The greater the sense of political efficacy (the feeling on the part of voters that their vote, or their participation, has some meaningful effect on political decisions), the greater the turnout.[122] And the greater the sense of citizen duty (adherence to the norm that an individual has a civic duty to vote), the higher the rate of turnout.[123] Persons who are less partisan, less interested in the campaign, less concerned about the outcome of the election, less politically efficacious, and who have less of a sense of civic duty, are in many ways more personally remote from politics and elections and therefore do not readily link up with the political system by voting.

Social characteristics are associated with voting and non-voting as well as psychological factors. Many studies have indicated that voter turnout is associated with—

- age, both older and younger people tend to vote less.

- sex, men are slightly more likely to vote than women.

- education, college-educated persons are the most likely to vote. Those with grade school education are the least likely to vote.

- income, the higher the income level, the more likely one is to vote and the converse.

- occupation—the closer the occupation with political matters, the more likely one is to vote, such as businessmen, social workers, certain professions, and so on.[124]

Other factors, such as place of residence, religion, and ethnicity are sometimes related to voter turnout, but more slightly. The differences found in religious or ethnic groups are very often a result of other factors such as different levels of education or income among the group, or that the group is disproportionately young.

There are, of course, strata of habitual voters and habitual non-voters, with the bulk of the citizenry in between, who vote in some but not all elections. Flanigan claims that the social composition of voters and non-voters does not change significantly from one election to the next,[125] although the evidence rests on only presidential and off-year elections. In a study of non-voting in many different types of elections, Agranoff and Backstrom found that in each successive election, the "quality" of the electorate does not change markedly. In low-turnout, low-visibility elections, the proportion of well educated, high-status-occupation, high-income, male, middle-age voters does not increase.[126] Apparently, people from all strata of society make up the true habitual voters who vote in all elections, regardless of media or other attention.

On the other hand, there is a group of habitual non-voters who do not even vote in presidential elections. They amount to about 15 percent of the eligible electorate; almost half live in the South. More than two-thirds of this group are women; one-fourth are black. They are generally poor; more than 50 percent have incomes under $5000—twice the rate of low incomes as the rest of the population. Almost half of the non-voters are under thirty years old. One-third have a grade-school education or less, and over 60 percent live in working class households.[127]

TURNOUT
IMPLICATIONS IN THE CAMPAIGN

The campaigner must be as conscious of turnout patterns as voting patterns. The more astute campaigners do not seek to turnout voters indiscriminately, but try to focus their research and tactical efforts on those who are likely to support the candidate. Thus, knowledge about voting habits and turnout habits are usually combined by finding those likely to support the candidate and urging them to vote. Campaigners sometimes naively feel that it is their civic duty to urge all voters, regardless of predisposition or disposition, to vote. Congressman Frank Thompson resigned as head of the McGovern campaign committee because, among other reasons, the group around McGovern wanted him to expend efforts to register all voters, particularly new, young voters, regardless of party affiliation or candidate preference. Thompson, an intelligent politician, could read polls and they showed that McGovern's support was slipping among the young. In fact, it was almost evenly divided between McGovern and Nixon. It is usually the civic duty of such nonpartisan groups as the League of Women Voters and Boy Scouts to register and encourage all to vote. It is the civic duty of the campaigner to make the best competitive effort possible. This does not include mobilization of those who are least likely to support the candidate.

The campaigner must therefore capitalize on what is known about predispositions and commitments to the candidate by trying to mobilize such voters first. As will be demonstrated, it takes considerable effort to find out who votes, who does not vote in a particular election, and who is likely to support the candidate, but it is often worth the effort. Turning out those who are already committed is an important weapon in the strategic arsenal.

One might assume that the given turnout level in an election is constant. That other things being equal, about 60 percent will always turn out in presidential elections, 45–50 percent in off-year elections and one-third in local elections. The problem with that assumption is that other variables are never constant. Lack of interest in the election for president, dislike for the candidates, and the absence of key issues could combine to "depress" the electorate. This means the candidates for governor, attorney general, state legislature, or county board, at the same election, are facing a reduced electorate. If those who normally turn out are not distributed equally, it will also depress the chances for other candidates. This was the problem faced by many state Democrats in 1972. Pre-election polls indicated that three times as many Democrats as Republicans were not planning to vote because they did not like McGovern. To avoid serious losses in other races, extraordinary efforts had to be made to turn out Democrats who usually vote.

This suggests it is often likely that it takes a serious campaign effort just to get the turnout rate to a "normal" level. That is, perhaps the 60 percent rate in presidential elections occurs because parties and candidates are making the best possible effort to turn out voters, and that best effort is necessary to reach that figure. One often wonders, "if Candidate X had only turned out another 1 percent of his voters" could he have won? What we tend to forget is that Candidate X had to make an effort to get out the minimal proportion, and that might have been all that he could have done with what he had to work with. The low turnout rates we reach could very often represent the very best efforts of the campaigners involved.

In low-stimulus elections, there is a greater burden on the campaigner to create the interest that the media and voters help create in high stimulus elections. The media almost automatically report whatever a candidate for president or governor says. Reporters are even assigned full time to follow their campaigns. Because more information is available, voters more readily follow the campaigns of the candidates for these offices. This places an extra burden on candidates for other offices to create the interest that very often naturally flows in other elections. When these low stimulus contests occur at different times than general elections, the burden of creating attention and stimulating turnout is even greater.

A final set of turnout implications for the campaigner relates to dealing with individual barriers. Although accidental barriers may occur to many types of voters, if the campaigner has good records of supporters and a good get-out-the-vote operation, such nonvoting can be reduced by providing absentee ballots, baby sitters, transportation, and so on. Legal barriers can be dealt with by knowing the legal requirements and working within them by registering voters who are eligible within the alloted time. This sounds like trite advice but a surprising number of campaigners fail both to take account of the legal regulations and to work within them. The greatest challenge to the campaigner is to mobilize those eligible voters who do not vote because psychological and social barriers obstruct motivation. These nonvoters usually comprise the largest and the most difficult group to mobilize. Yet, it is from among this group that the "committed non-voters" must be shifted to "committed voters." Subsequent chapters will indicate that this is part of the hard work of campaigning.

Notes to Chapter 2

1. Robert Agranoff, *The New Style in Election Campaigns* (Boston, Mass.: Holbrook Press, 1972), p. 120.

2. For an overview of the early approaches see Peter H. Rossi, "Four Landmarks in Voting Research" in *American Voting Behavior*, Eugene Burdick and Arthur J. Brodbeck, eds. (Glencoe, Illinois, Free Press, 1959).

3. Bernard R. Berelson, Paul F. Lazarsfeld and William N. McPhee, *Voting* (Chicago: University of Chicago Press, 1954), pp. 306-10; Henry B. Mayo, *An Introduction to Democratic Theory* (New York: Oxford Univ. Press, 1960), pp. 41-49.

4. Angus Campbell et al., *The American Voter* (New York: John Wiley, 1960), p. 103.

5. Ibid., pp. 183-75.

6. Ibid., ch. 6.

7. Ibid., p. 121.

8. Ibid., p. 122-23.

9. These net figures do not reflect the possibility that considerable switching of party identification could occur within these aggregate distributions, see Douglas Dobson and Douglas St. Angelo, "Party Identification and the Floating Vote," *American Poltiical Science Review*, 69 (June 1975), pp. 484-86.

10. William H. Flanigan, *Political Behavior of the American Electorate* 2nd ed. (Boston: Allyn and Bacon, 1972), p. 121.

11. Campbell et al. *The American Voter*, pp. 244-45.

12. Ibid., p. 134.

13. Donald E. Stokes, "Party Loyalty and the Likelihood of Deviating Elections," in *Elections and the Political Order*, Angus Campbell et al., eds., (New York: John Wiley, 1966), p. 127.

14. Phillip E. Converse, "The Concept of a Normal Vote," in Campbell, *Elections and the Political Order*.

15. Stokes, "Party Loyalty and the Likelihood of Deviating Elections," in Campbell et al., eds., *Elections and the Political Order*, pp. 126-27.

16. Stanley R. Freeman, "The Salience of Party and Candidate in Congressional Elections: A Comparison of 1958 and 1970," *Public Opinion and Public Policy*, Norman R. Luttbeg, ed., (Homewood, Ill.: Dorsey, 1974), p. 130. The 1958 study is: Donald E. Stokes and Warren E. Miller, "Party Government and the Saliency of Congress," *Public Opinion Quarterly* 26 (1962): 531-46.

17. F. Gerald Kline, "Mass Media and the General Election Process: Evidence and Speculation," *Maxwell Review* 9 (1973): 50-52.

18. Campbell et al. *The American Voter*, pp. 143-44.

19. Ibid., p. 180.

20. Ibid., p. 97.

21. Ibid., ch. 7.

22. Donald R. Matthews and James W. Prothro, "The Concept of Party Image and Its Importance for the Southern Electorate," in *The Electoral Process*, M. Kent Jennings and L. Harmon Zeigler, eds., (Englewood Cliffs, N.J.: Prentice-Hall, 1966), pp. 159-62.

23. Donald R. Matthews and James W. Prothro, *Negroes and the New Southern Politics* (New York: Harcourt, Brace and World, 1966), pp. 396-401.

24. Ibid., p. 399.

25. Campbell et al., *The American Voter*, p. 143.

26. Flanigan, *Political Behavior of the American Electorate*, pp. 45-47.

27. V.O. Key, Jr., *The Responsible Electorate* (Cambridge, Mass.: Harvard Univ. Press, 1966), pp. 93-100.

28. David E. RePass, "Issue Salience and Party Choice," *American Political Science Review* 65 (1971): 398.

29. Matthews and Prothro, *Negroes and the New Southern Politics*, pp. 393-94.

30. James L. Sundquist, *Dynamics of the Party System* (Washington, D.C.: The Brookings Institution, 1973), p. 346.

31. Richard M. Merelman, "Electoral Instability and the American Party System," *Journal of Politics* 32 (1970): 122.

32. *Gallup Opinion Index*, no. 112 (October, 1974).

33. Campbell et al., *The American Voter*, pp. 162-63.

34. Sundquist, *Dynamics of the Party System*, p. 347.

35. Ibid.

36. Merelman, "Electoral Instability and the Party System," pp. 134-35.

37. Angus Campbell, Gerald Gurin, and Warren E. Miller, *The Voter Decides* (Evanston, Illinois: Row, Peterson, 1954), p. 109.

38. Ibid., p. 136.

39. Ibid., pp. 56-57.

40. Ibid., p. 60.

41. Ibid., p. 63.

42. Ibid., p. 140.

43. Phillip E. Converse et al., "Stability and Change in 1960: A Reinstating Election," *American Political Science Review* 55 (1961): 278.

44. Phillip E. Converse, Aage R. Clauson, and Warren E. Miller, "Electoral Myth and Reality: The 1964 Election," *American Political Science Review* 59 (1965): 331.

45. Ibid., p. 332.

46. Walter DeVries, "Taking the Voter's Pulse," in *The Political Image Merchants* Ray Hiebert et al., eds., (Washington, D.C.: Acropolis Books, 1971), pp. 76, 77, 79.

47. Ibid., p. 67.

48. Warren E. Miller, "Reflections on the 1972 Election," lecture at Northern Illinois University, December 18, 1972.

49. See, e.g., Denis G. Sullivan, "Psychological Balance and Reactions to the Presidential Nominations in 1960," in *The Electoral Process*, Jennings and Zeigler, eds.

50. Herbert F. Weisberg and Jerrold S. Rusk, "Dimensions of Candidate Evaluation," *American Political Science Review* 64 (1970): 1168.

51. For a detailed discussion see, Agranoff, *The New Style in Election Campaigns*, pp. 1-20.

52. Donald E. Stokes, "Some Dynamic Elements of Contests for the Presidency," *American Political Science Review* 60 (1966), p. 27.

53. Phillip E. Converse et al., "Continuity and Change in American Poltics: Parties and Issues in the 1968 Election," *American Political Science Review* 63 (1969): 1084.

54. Walter Dean Burnham, *Critical Elections and the Mainsprings of American Politics* (New York: W.W. Norton, 1970), p. 109.

55. Ibid., p. 120.

56. Walter DeVries and V. Lance Tarrance, *The Ticket Splitter* (Grand Rapids, Michigan: Eerdmans, 1972), p. 31.

57. Ibid., p. 34.

58. Ibid., pp. 49-54.

59. Ibid., ch. 3.

60. Ibid., ch. 4.

61. *Gallup Opinion Index*, no. 42, December 1968, p. 7.

62. Heinz Eulau, Betty H. Zisk and Kenneth Prewitt, "Latent Partisanship in Nonpartisan Elections: Effects of Political Milieu and Mobilization," in *The Electoral Process*, Jennings and Zeigler, eds., p. 219.

63. Campbell et al., *The American Voter*, pp. 128-39.

64. Ithiel de Sola Pool, Robert P. Abelson and Samuel Popkin, *Candidates, Issues and Strategies* (Cambridge, Mass.: M.I.T. Press, 1965), p. 88.

65. Private polls.

66. Warren E. Miller and Donald E. Stokes, "Constituency Influence in Congress," *American Political Science Review* 57 (1963); 56.

67. Berelson et al., *Voting*, pp. 268-69.

68. Campbell et al., *The American Voter*, pp. 130-31.

69. Ibid., pp. 173-74.

70. Ibid., p. 180.

71. Ibid., p. 183.

72. Key, *The Responsible Electorate*, pp. 7-8.

73. Ibid., pp. 27, 147-49.

74. Burnham, *Critical Elections*, p. 10; see also Walter Dean Burnham, "The Changing Shape of the American Political Universe," *American Political Science Review* 59 (1965), pp. 7-28.

75. RePass, "Issue Salience and Party Choice," p. 400.

76. Converse et al., "Continuity and Change in American Politics," p. 1097.

77. Ibid., p. 1098.

78. Ibid., p. 1099.

79. Gerald M. Pomper, "From Confusion to Clarity: Issues and American Voters, 1956-1968," *American Political Science Review* 66 (1972): 426.

80. Richard W. Boyd, "Popular Control of Public Policy: A Normal Vote Analysis of the 1968 Election," *American Political Science Reveiw* 66 (1972): 446.

81. John H. Kessel, "Comment: The Issues in Issue Voting," *American Political Science Review* 66 (1972): 462-63.

82. Ibid., p. 464.

83. Campbell et al., *The American Voter*, p. 170.

84. Ibid., p. 169.

85. Campbell et al., *The Voter Decides*, p. 169.

86. Ibid., p. 136.

87. Campbell et al., *The American Voter*, pp. 52-54.

88. Richard A. Brody and Benjamin I. Page, "Comment: The Assessment of Policy Voting," *American Political Science Review* 66 (1972): 456.

89. DeVries, "Taking the Voter's Pulse," p. 77.

90. Ibid., p. 80.

91. Weisberg and Rusk, "Dimensions of Candidate Evaluation," p. 1185.

92. Berelson, *Voting*, chs. 3-7; Paul F. Lazarsfeld, Bernard Berelson, and Hazel Gaudet, *The People's Choice* (New York: Duell, Sloan and Pearce, 1944), ch. 3.

93. Berelson et al., *Voting*, p. 147.

94. Lazarsfeld, *The People's Choice*, p. 26.

95. For a more complete explanation see, Campbell et al., *The American Voter*, pp. 24-29.

96. Henry W. Riecken, "Primary Groups and Political Party Choice," in *American Voting Behavior*, Burdick and Brodbeck, eds., p. 177.

97. Campbell et al., *The American Voter*, pp. 309-10.

98. William R. Keech, *The Impact of Negro Voting* (Chicago: Rand, McNally, 1968), pp. 29-36.

99. Matthews and Prothro, *Negroes and the New Southern Politics*, p. 224.

100. Raymond E. Wolfinger, "The Development and Persistence of Ethnic Voting," in *American Ethnic Politics*, Lawrence H. Fuchs, ed. (New York: Harper and Row, 1968), p. 192.

101. Ibid., p. 191.

102. Campbell, *The American Voter*, pp. 446-48.

103. Ibid., p. 453.

104. Ibid., p. 459.

105. Key, *The Responsible Electorate*, pp. 19-21.

106. Phillip E. Converse and Richard Niemi, "Non-Voting Among Young Adults in the United States," A Data Report to the American Heritage Foundation, published in *Political Parties and Political Behavior* 2nd ed., William J. Crotty, Donald M. Freeman and Douglas S. Gatlin, eds. (Boston: Allyn and Bacon, 1971).

107. U.S. Census, P-20, no. 192.

108. David Butler and Donald Stokes, *Political Change in Britan* (New York: St. Martins, 1969), pp. 283-92.

109. Campbell et al., *The American Voter*, p. 162.

110. Butler and Stokes, *Political Change in Britan*, p. 276.

111. Flanigan, *Political Behavior of the American Electorate*, pp. 16-17.

112. Angus Campbell, "Surge and Decline: A Study of Electoral Change," in *Elections and the Political Order*, Campbell et al., ed., pp. 41-42.

113. Flanigan, *Political Behavior of the American Electorate*, p. 14.

114. Converse and Niemi, "Non-Voting Among Young Adults in the United States," pp. 452-53.

115. Ibid.

116. Penn Kimball, *The Disconnected* (New York: Columbia University Press, 1972), p. 15.

117. Stanley Kelley, Jr., Richard Ayres, and William Bowen, "Registration and Voting: Putting First Things First," *American Political Science Reveiw* 61 (1967): 373-74.

118. Flanigan, *Political Behavior of the American Electorate*, pp. 12-13.

119. Campbell et al., *The American Voter*, p. 97.

120. Ibid., p. 102.

121. Ibid., p. 104.

122. Ibid., p. 105.

123. Ibid., pp. 105-06.

124. For a more complete explanation see, Lester W. Milbrath, *Political Participation* (Chicago: Rand, McNally, 1965), ch. 5.

125. Flanigan, *Political Behavior of the American Electorate*, p. 22.

126. "The Several Electorates," forthcoming.

127. Flanigan, *Political Behavior of the American Electorate*, p. 22.

For Further Reading and Research

Axelrod, Robert. "Where the Votes Come From: An Analysis of Electoral Electoral Coalitions, 1952-1968." *American Political Science Review* 66 (1972): 11-20.

Berelson, Bernard R.; Lazarsfeld, Paul F.; and McPhee, William N. *Voting*. Chicago: Univ. of Chicago Press, 1954.

Boyd. Richard W. "Popular Control of Public Policy: A Normal Vote Analysis of the 1968 Election." *American Political Science Review* 66 (1972): 415-28.

Campbell, Angus; Converse, Phillip E.; Miller, Warren E.; and Stokes, Donald E. *The American Voter*. New York: John Wiley, 1960.

_____ . *Elections and the Political Order*. New York: John Wiley, 1966.

Cantor, Robert D. *Voting Behavior and Presidential Elections*. Itasca, Illinois: F. E. Peacock, 1975.

Converse, Phillip E.; Campbell, Angus; Miller, Warren E.; Stokes, Donald E. "Stability and Change in 1960: A Reinstating Election." *American Political Science Review* 55 (1961): 269-80.

Converse, Phillip E.; Clausen, Aage R.; and Miller, Warren E. "Electoral Myth and Reality: The 1964 Election." *American Political Science Review* 59 (1965): 321-36.

Converse, Phillip E.; Miller, Warren E.; Rusk, Jerrold G.; and Wolfe, Arthur C. "Continuity and Change in American Politics: Parties and Issues in the 1968 Election." *American Political Science Review* 63 (1969): 1083-1105.

DeVries, Walter, and Tarrance, Jr. Lance. *The Ticket-Splitter*. Grand Rapids: Eerdmans, 1972.

Flanigan, William H. *Political Behavior of the American Electorate*. 2d ed. Boston: Allyn and Bacon, 1972.

Gallup Opinion Index: Political, Social and Economic Trends. Princeton, N.J.: Gallup International, Inc. Published monthly.

Inter-University Consortium for Political Research. Ann Arbor, Michigan: University of Michigan. Depository of survey research and other political data gathered and deposited by over 100 member academic institutions.

Jennings, M. Kent and Zeigler, L. Harmon, eds. *The Electoral Process*. Englewood Cliffs, N.J.: Prentice-Hall, 1966.

Kelley, Jr. Stanley and Mirer, Thad W. "The Simple Act of Voting." *American Political Science Review* 68 (1974): 572-91.

Lazarsfeld, Paul F.; Berelson, Bernard; and Gaudet, Hazel. *The People's Choice*. 3d ed. New York: Columbia Univ. Press, 1968.

Pomper, Gerald M. "From Confusion to Clarity: Issues and American Voters, 1956-1968." *American Political Science Review* 66 (1972): 415-28.

Roper Public Opinion Center. Williamstown, Mass.: William College, Depository of Roper, other commercial, newspaper, and academic survey data.

RePass, David E. "Issue Salience and Party Choice." *American Political Science Review* 65 (1971): 389-400.

Rossi, Peter H. "Four Landmarks in Voting Research." *In American Voting Behavior*, edited by Eugene Burdick and Arthur J. Brodbeck, pp. 5--54. Glencoe, Illinois: Free Press, 1959.

Campaign Processes

In the previous chapter we examined some factors that deal with the reasons why citizens turn out to vote in elections and why they vote as they do. Obviously, something happens between the time campaign appeals are made and the casting of ballots. This chapter deals with some important intermediate processes, particularly the participation of citizens in the campaign and the impact of communications on voters. These processes are introduced here as concepts for analysis and strategic thinking, leaving more applied research and specific applications to later chapters that deal with organization, media, and voter contact.

POLITICAL INVOLVEMENT

One very important way for the campaigner to view the citizenry is categorization by levels of political involvement. Table 1.1 (page 4) presented aggregate figures for a wide range of political involvement activities. The figures indicate that only a small proportion of the entire citizenry is involved in any form of political activity, and those activities that require the greatest commitment, or personal effort, involve the smallest number of people. Because involvement varies so considerably it becomes important for campaigners to understand its extent and quality.

Political participation, in general, and campaign involvement, in particular, is generally thought of as hierarchical in nature. Because political acts tend to involve fewer and fewer people as they require greater commitments, it is assumed that those who perform the more difficult political acts also perform all of the less difficult ones. Therefore, one assumes there are hierarchical levels of involvement (see Figure 3.1) with a steadily decreasing proportion of people involved, until only a handful are involved in extensive participatory (gladiatorial) activities. Using this type of conceptualization with data reported from a single time (usually in a single election campaign) Milbrath estimates that fewer than 1 percent of the adult population engage in the top two or three activities on the hierarchy; about 4 or 5 percent are active in a party or campaign or attend meetings; 10 percent contribute money; 13 percent contact officials; 15 percent display a button or sticker; 25 to 30 percent try to persuade another to vote a certain way; and, from 40 to 70 percent receive political messages and vote in any given election.[1]

Verba and Nie have offered a refinement that generally confirms that overall levels of political participation are low and roughly hierarchical, but suggests that levels of campaign participation are considerably higher than others would lead us to believe. Most of the measures of participation are taken from election surveys and are based on involvement in that particular campaign. When citizens are asked whether or not they have ever engaged in various political activities, or

Figure 3.1   A Hierarchy of Political Involvement

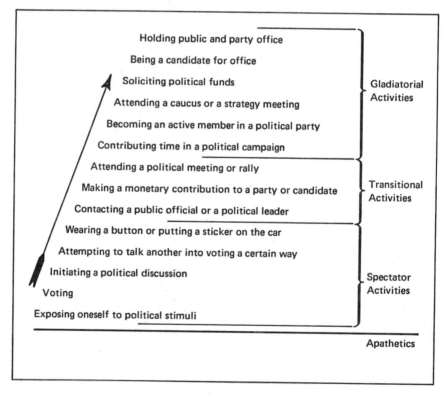

Source: Lester W. Milbrath, *Political Participation* (Chicago: Rand McNally, 1965), p. 18.

the survey examines a longer time period, the levels of involvement go up. Table 1.1 (page 4) indicates by this measure that 26 percent have worked for a party or candidate during an election, 19 percent have attended a meeting or rally in the last three years, and 13 percent have contributed money. Thus, measuring political activity over a longer time frame appears to raise aggregate levels of campaign involvement. As the authors suggest, "active political involvement is not sustained. . .a significant number of citizens move in and out of active political participation in the political process."[2] It could be that there are more than just activists and non-activists, but an occasional-activist category must be added.

The same study also revealed that the hypothetical hierarchy of political involvement is not, in fact, perfectly hierarchical. Some people participate in the "harder" activities but not in all of the "easier," as well as the reverse. Thus, the levels of political involvement appear to be not completely mutually exclusive— some people perform some campaign activities and not others. Verba and Nie find that 22 percent of the citizenry have been involved in campaigns at some time, 42 percent only vote, 4 percent have campaigned but do not vote, and 32 percent neither campaign nor vote.[3] Of the six hardest political activities (contacting state officials, contacting local officials, attending a rally, forming a group, giving money, being a member of a political organization) 53 percent of the citizenry report never having engaged in them, 24 percent have participated in one of these acts, 13 percent in two, 6 percent in three, 3 percent in four, 2 percent in five, and 1 percent in all six.[4] The fact that 6 percent of the citizens have engaged in four of the six most difficult political acts suggests that activism is more widely distributed than assumptions of full cumulation would lead one to believe.

Verba and Nie caution that their refinement should not be misinterpreted to assume that political activity is widespread. They conclude, with others, that it is low, it tends to be concentrated among certain citizens, and it is roughly hierarchical. That aggregate measures within limited time frames may have led researchers to overestimate the degree of structure in and amount of correlation among the different kinds of political participation is entirely possible.[5]

POLITICAL STRATIFICATION

Political scientists divide citizens into three categories of political activity: political activists, attentive publics, and general publics. The activists include those who *regularly* participate in politics, including key political leaders such as governmental officials, party leaders, key interest group leaders, candidates and their regular workers, and leading citizens whose positions allow them to make political decisions. Dahl, in a study of the city of New Haven, found that different people were involved in different decisions. Economic leaders were more interested and active in urban renewal. Social notables were concerned about education and the schools. The political party groups were more concerned about nominations for office. Each type of decision involved somewhat different activists. Elected officials were at the helm uniting the various political elements.[6] Dahl's work suggests that the political activists are variegated throughout the constituency and that they are neither confined to a few behind-the-scenes business leaders or a few political party "bosses."

In a study of a Congressional campaign in the state of Washington, Peabody and Gore identified two power centers of political activists generally bound together by similar ideological outlooks. One center was liberal; its leaders supported the Democrat. The other center was conservative; its leaders supported the Republican. Within each of these core power groups of several dozen leaders, complete cohesion of ideas, issue positions, or philosophies was nonexistent. However, there was general agreement over a common candidate, his policies, and his programs. The power of these influential political activists came from (1) the organizations, associations, or large industries they were able to speak for, and (2) their ability to produce the funds and skills required to construct a successful campaign. The power of these influentials, conclude Peabody and Gore, "stemmed not from the fact that they could direct these groups to take a particular stand, but from their willingness and skill in making themselves the instrument through which such groups mobilized their influence and gave it a common and hence forceful expression in the form of support for a specific policy or a particular candidate."[7]

The group between the activists and the general public is the attentive public, composed of interested and semi-active citizens who regularly follow politics in the news, magazines, and books, through organizational membership and participation and who try to influence others about political matters. The attentive public ordinarily shifts in size and shape depending on the particular issue—its makeup would be quite different regarding agricultural policy than it would be regarding civil rights on the national level, zoning, and day-activity centers for the retarded, on the local level. The attentive public rarely exceeds 10 to 15 percent of the population. V.O. Key, drawing from his research on public opinion in the United States, specualtes that practically every governmental policy area has a corresponding attentive public watching over it, some to protect their self interest, some with a more general interest in mind.[8] Among the various attentive publics are journalists, interest group activists and leaders, teachers, clergymen, veterans' organization leaders, feminist leaders, business, labor union officials, and farmers. Although attentive-public membership rises in direct proportion to higher social and economic status, there are some members from all levels of society. These attentive publics, explains Key, "as they monitor the actions of government and let their judgments be known, play a critical role in assuring a degree of responsiveness of government to non-governmental opinion."[9]

Although many prefer to believe that political messages are transmitted to the general public only through political activists, the attentive publics also play a key role. They too operate at critical points in peoples lives: they produce the news people receive; they "boil down" and transmit information to group members. As respected figures their views are valued, and very often, it is the attentive publics that shape the opinions of the general public. When messages conflict with the activists, the attentive publics very often prevail.[10] The authors of *Voting* found such "opinion leaders" to be very important points of linkage between the campaign messages of the activists and the general public. These campaign opinion leaders were both sought out by other voters in the community and they were more likely to seek advice. Their key role was attributed to a particular interest and competence in the sphere of discussion coupled with a capacity for greater interaction through more strategic social locations.[11]

For the campaigner the existence of the three publics means that one must add a corresponding third dimension to the campaign. It is clear that most candidates engage in mobilization of support of political activists, economic, social, and political group leaders. Even more obvious is the campaign to woo voters from the general publics. But attentive publics must also be included for special treatment in the campaign given their special role regarding opinion formation and transmission. Expanding the inside campaign to gain the support of attentive publics can be of utmost significance in aiding the outside campaign to win voter support.

When the inside or non-public aspect of the campaign is organized to include both activists and attentive publics, the "two-step flow" of influence will be facilitated in the campaign. The two-step flow is defined as the notion that ideas often seem to flow *from* the mass media *to* opinion leaders and *from them to* the less active sections of the population.[12] It was discovered, for example, that adoption of a newly marketed drug by most physicians was related to the influence of "opinion-leading" physicians who read the research materials and advertising on the drugs and then transmitted information about their usage of the drug to other physicians in their social relationships.[13] In *The People's Choice*, it was reported that people who made up their minds late in the campaign were more likely to mention personal influence as having figured in their decisions. They found that influence flowed from "opinion leaders" (people of special influence who were almost equally distributed at all levels of society). These "opinion leaders" exposed themselves to a greater number of the media for longer periods of time. Thus, it was hypothesized that information flowed in a two-step fashion—from media to "opinion leaders" (attentive publics) to the general public.[14]

Two other research findings shed further light on this notion. Those who most actively talked to people about the campaign and tried to persuade them to vote for someone were also those who had the greatest media exposure. Few of the people who were not exposed to media tried to persuade anyone to vote.[15] Stouffer also found community leaders, in this case, those persons we have defined as attentive publics, to be more likely to get their information about politics from the media, whereas the general public received its information in direct conversations.[16] Thus, the network of personal relations is probably important in the "trickle down" theory of communication. And as one might surmise, as information is transmitted, it is not neutral, but that people tend to "color, amplify, distort, limit, or otherwise change the information as it is passed along."[17]

The two-step flow can be used by the campaigner if one links up with the attentive publics, seeks their support, or reaffirms their support. Since they act as a buffer in communications, the campaigner can buttress his mass media messages in print, radio, or television by exposure to those who talk to and influence the general public. The attentive publics are in many ways at the front lines of a campaign. Voters listen to them because they are the personification of certain values (who one is); they are regarded as competent (what one knows); and, they are strategically located between the outside world of political matters and the inside world of the individual voter (whom one knows).[18] Even if the campaigner does not use the mass media extensively, mobilization of the attentive public is logical given the position, respect, and network of influence these people have. Perhaps this explains why candidates often spend so much time mobilizing key people in the community. Although they can cast only one vote each, they actually swing many votes.

THE IMPACT OF CAMPAIGNS ON VOTERS

Before reading this book, if any readers had the preconception that all voters are exposed to the campaign with a sort of "blank slate," and are thus potential supporters, or that every opposition supporter is a potential convert, our discussion of the relative impact of parties, issues, and candidates should be unsettling. The campaign does have an effect on practically every citizen, but its effect varies and is only partially a matter of conversion. A greater number of voters must be activated by the campaign because though not very political they will support a candidate if properly stimulated. For the greatest number of voters inclined to support a candidate, generally, only their predispositions need be reinforced. Such processes occur at various points in the campaign.

Reinforcement

In their study of the impact of campaign communications, Lazarsfeld, Berelson, and Gaudet found that the campaign propaganda produced no overt effect on the behavior of most voters, if by effect one assumes that it *changed* a vote. For many voters, they found that:

> . . . political communications served the important purpose of preserving prior decisions instead of initiating new decisions. It kept the partisans 'in-line' by reassuring them in their vote decision; it reduced defections from the ranks. It had the effect of reinforcing the original decision.[19]

The reinforcement process is predicated on the political communication assumption that most people want and need to be told that they are right and to know that other people agree with them. Very often campaign efforts result not so much in gaining new adherents, but in preventing the loss of voters already favorably inclined.[20]

Most, but not all, who are reinforced by the campaign are partisans. Others are partial to the candidate for diverse reasons. The predisposed voter makes available more of the campaign communication of those whom he is supporting by selective exposure to those messages that are congenial and support his position.[21] The process works something like this:

> The provision of new arguments and the reiteration of old arguments in behalf of his candidate reassure the partisan and strengthen his vote decision. Should he be tempted to vacillate, should he come to question the rightness of his decision, the reinforcing arguments are there to curb such tendencies toward defection. The partisan is assured that he is right; he is told why he is right; and he is reminded that other people agree with him, always a gratification and especially so during times of doubt. In short, political propaganda in the media of communication, by providing them with good partisan arguments, at the same time provides orientation, reassurance, integration for the already partisan. Such satisfactions tend to keep people 'in line' by reinforcing their initial decision.[22]

Thus, most of the predisposed are reinforced chiefly because people tend to protect themselves from the upsetting experiences associated with opposition arguments by ignoring them. The greatest number of voters in a campaign are generally reinforced; in the particular study illustrated, this group amounted to 53 percent of the electorate.[23]

Activation

Many voters hesitate to make a decision during the campaign and even may ponder the decision but, in the final analysis, they decide to vote consistent with their predispositions—particularly, but not exclusively, their partisan predispositions. What the campaign does, then, is to activate their predisposed views. In *The People's Choice*, for example, the authors identified a group of "crystallizers," who were undecided early in the campaign; two thirds of those predisposed toward the Republican party voted Republican; two-thirds predisposed toward the Democratic party voted Democratic.[24] The authors compare the activation effect to photography: the image is on an exposed negative, but it is not visible until the developer brings it out, faintly at first, but finally in sharp contrast. Campaign communication has a similar effect to that of the developer; it brings the voters' predispositions to the level of visibility and expression, it transforms the latent political tendency into a manifest vote.[25]

There are two types of activating forces of political communication,

messages delivered through the mass media—radio, television, newspapers, literature and direct mail; and direct personal influences—through opinion leaders,
attentive publics, campaign workers, family, friends, and associates. There are
four continuous steps in the normal process of activation:

1. *Propaganda Arouses Interest:* As the campaign gains momentum, people
   who have not been interested begin to pay attention. At this stage it is the
   rising volume of propaganda which initiates the changes.

2. *Increased Interest Brings Increased Exposure:* As people 'wake up' to the
   campaign, their aroused attention leads them to see and hear more out of
   the supply around them. The voter's initiative is more in evidence at this
   stage; but the relationship is circular. Increased attention brings increased
   exposure which further arouses interest and attention and adds to exposure
   and so on.

3. *Attention is Selective:* As interest increases and the voter begins to be aware
   of what it is all about, his predispositions come into play. Out of the wide
   array of available propaganda, he begins to select. He is more likely to tune
   in some programs than others; to go to some meetings rather than others;
   to understand one point in a speech than another. His selective attention
   thus reinforces the predispositions with which he comes to the campaign. At
   this stage the initiative is almost wholly with the prospective voter rather
   than with the propagandists. Whatever the publicity that is put out, it is the
   selective attention of the citizen which determines what is responded to.

4. *Votes Crystallize:* Finally enough latent lines of thought and feeling have
   been aroused and sufficient rationale has been appropriated from the campaign so that the decision is made. The latent has become manifest; the
   uncertainty disappears; the voter is ready to mark his ballot.[26]

Thus, the campaign serves to arouse political interest for many who in turn begin
to pay more attention to politics, but preconceived notions lead to selective
attention which channels the vote in the expected direction. As one might expect, the second greatest number, in terms of its impact, are activated to vote in
the direction of their predispositions, 14 percent in the study mentioned.[27]

Conversion

Some are indeed converted by campaign communication but they are fewer in
number than is generally assumed. The authors of *The People's Choice* found
that many barriers to conversion exist: half the people were decided before the
campaign began and clung to their decisions; others made up their minds when
they knew who the nominees were; most voted in relation to their deeply held
social, group, and political feeling; and most people who followed political
communication exposed themselves to information more supportive of their
position.[28] But, some people did break through the restrictions and voted

contrary to their predispositions. They were converted by campaign messages.

Most who are converted are "sold" by certain arguments in the campaign. For example, many Democrats who voted for Nixon in 1972 were convinced during the course of the campaign, through the campaign efforts of both Nixon and McGovern, that they should vote Republican on the basis of the "negative messages" against McGovern that broke through. The weaker the voter's preconceptions are, the more "convertible" the voter is. Others are doubters, persons with high levels of interest in the campaign who felt that there was something important to be said on each side and tried more or less conscientiously to resolve their doubts during the campaign, like the rational democratic stereotype voter.[29] In *The People's Choice* it was found that only 8 percent of the electorate was converted during the course of the campaign although some voters (3 percent) had switched but reconverted by election day.[30]

In the campaign in which these key processes were discovered, more than half of the citizens (53 percent) were reinforced by the campaign, 14 percent were stimulated to vote by the campaign in accordance with their initial predispositions, 8 percent were converted. 3 percent were reconverted, and the campaign had no effect on the remainder (22 percent). Because their estimates are based on relatively weak measures of predispositions, the authors believe that the estimates of the numbers of voters who were converted is somewhat high, and the figures representing those who were activated is probably low.[31] These figures were gathered at a time when party loyalties were more solid, and when mass campaign communication was not as prevalent and available as today.[32] Voters now hear more of the oppositions's messages, more people have access to a number of communications media, and party loyalties are not as steadfast as they once were. Thus, one would assume that a greater proportion could be activated or converted in contemporary campaigns. But undoubtedly the rank ordering is identical; most are reinforced, the next greatest number are activated, and the smallest number are converted.

Time of Voting Decisions

Research on the time of voting decision indicates that the forces that go into a decision occur, for many, before the campaign even begins. Decisions are made at many points during the campaign. Strong party ties are associated with early decisions.

Voting decisions are ordinarily made during the campaign by fewer than four in ten voters in any given presidential election. Table 3.1 indicates that from one-third to one-half of the electorate decides before the candidates are even nominated, and from about one-fifth to almost one-third decide during the nominating conventions. This means that as many as three-fourths of the electorate can decide before the campaign begins, as was the case in 1956, although normally about six in ten decide before the campaign begins. This leaves a margin of from 25 to 40 percent of the voters who decide during the campaign.

Table 3.1   Time of Voting Decision in Presidential Election,
1948–1972

	1948	1952	1956	1960	1964	1968	1972
Decided							
before conventions	37%	34%	57%	30%	40%	33%	44%
during conventions	28	31	18	30	25	22	18
during campaign	25	31	21	36	33	38	35
don't remember,NA	10	4	4	4	3	7	4
Total	100%	100%	100%	100%	100%	100%	100%
n =	424	1251	1285	1445	1126	1039	1551

Source: William Flanigan, *Political Behavior of the American Electorate* (Boston: Allyn and Bacon, 1972), p. 109. Data for 1972 compiled from Survey Research Center, University of Michigan. All data made available through Inter-University Consortium for Political Research.

Unfortunately, no research of this nature has been done on non-presidential elections, where the mixture of the stabilizing and unstabilizing factors is often different. But, there is no reason to believe that the number of voters who decide during the campaign is not within the wide 25- to 40-percent range.

As one would assume, those who make up their minds earliest are those who have the least difficulty in arriving at a decision. It has been found that the more cross-pressures one has (for example, the strong Protestant Democrat concerned about Kennedy's Catholicism in 1960), the later the decision. In *The People's Choice* it was found that the greater the number of such cross-pressures, the later the decision, although that voters actually experienced such conflicts could not be documented.[33] The strength of party loyalty is also related to the time of decision—the stronger the party ties, the earlier the decision. Independents and weaker partisans choose later in the campaign. Moreover, the more consistent the individual voter's attitudes are with the position of the party, the earlier the decision. Those who decide later in the campaign tend to be those whose attitudes are most inconsistent with the party's position.[34]

At one time it was believed that only those who were not much interested in the campaign decided during the campaign, and a great deal of campaign strategy was based on this assumption. It was also assumed that since the most informed and interested decided early, the simplest campaign appeals should be used on the remaining undecided, uninterested, and presumably uninformed voters. This evidence was gathered during the Roosevelt and Eisenhower periods when partisanship was more stable and when communication was less pervasive. It is likely that as more information about candidates and issues become available to people, and when this information is received with less solid party loyalty, that more and more late deciders are interested voters. The campaigner must meet this challenge by making information available to the interested and undecided.

Some political consultants blend notions of reinforcement, activation, and conversion, and the various times of decision into dividing the electorate into the committed, the undecided and the indifferent.[35] The undecided have to be converted and the indifferent have to be activated. The campaigner must also work to reinforce the committed. It is not accurate to say the campaign has no effect on those who decide before the campaign begins, but rather that it has no conversion or activation effect. As was stated in *The People's Choice*, parties who dispense with propaganda do so at considerable risk.[36] When party is not a factor in elections, one cannot write off the possibility that voters are committed on the basis of other factors, such as candidate image or known issue positions, and thus reinforcement is in order.

KEY COMMUNICATIONS
PROCESSES IN CAMPAIGNS

Enough variables affecting voting have become apparent to indicate that a campaign other than the type used to appeal to the classic democratic voter is needed. In fact, Stanley Kelley has established an ideal or debating model of campaign discussion in which: a great amount of candidate and issue information is offered to the public, differences between candidates are pointed out, and the sources of information on which the discussion is based become clear to the voter.[37] He is aware that it rarely, if ever, exists, and that there are restrictive barriers to the debating model. An examination of some key obstacles to the debating model reveals some important communication phenomena. Chiefly, our concern is with the conditions that make it difficult to change people's views, and the conditions that facilitate changes of opinion.

The Voter's Context

It is obvious that campaign communications find the voter in a context that includes primary groups, the personal influence of opinion leaders or attentive publics, organizational, ethnic, or other group loyalties, party loyalties, and previously formed opinions, attitudes, and beliefs about issues and candidates. This has some important implications. First voters are very likely to have preexisting views on the subject of the communciations. They may, for example, receive a message about policies within the context of their partisanship. These views are relatively stable. Second, the information received occurs within the web of interpersonal relationships, or within the social network of the individual. As Kelley suggests, these interpersonal relationships serve to anchor opinions and convictions, mediating the impact of any communication on them. The voter has to fit new ideas into a pattern which his associates have come to expect of him.[38] Third, it has been found that certain views are ego-involved attitudes (crucial to the self-images of people and central to clusters of related attidues) and are extremely difficult, if not impossible to change. Consider, for example, a white supremacist or a black power advocate. A candidate's positions on racial matters that are contrary to the voters views go against extensive personal attitudes of the individual.[39] Ego-involved attitudes are not exclusive to people at the extremes of the political spectrum. A steel manufacturer can be equally ego-involved in his views about antipollution enforcement, as can the citizen whose feelings about steel factory effluents are particularly cogent. When such feelings are so strong, they are next to impossible to change. Therefore, the context of media reception—the individual, his interpersonal relationships, and the political milieu in which he finds himself are factors that make it difficult for campaign communication to alter the views of voters.

Selectivity

In addition, the three processes of selection limit the effectivenss of campaign messages. The "defense mechanisms" most commonly used by voters are known as selective exposure, selective perception, and selective retention. Selective exposure refers to the tendency to expose oneself to mass communications in accord with one's existing interests and points of view, and to avoid unsympathetic material. In some voting studies it was found that most partisans follow only the information of the party with which they are affiliated.[40] Other findings from the study of both political and nonpolitical cummunications indicate that selective exposure is relatively widespread.[41]

Selective perception is the tendency to perceive in communications what one wants to perceive, what one has habitually perceived, or what one perceives in expectation of some form of social or physical reward. For example, when residents of Ann Arbor, Michigan were asked whether or not newspaper and magazine reports had convinced them that smoking was a cause of cancer, the relationship was accepted (perceived) by twice as many non-smokers as smokers.[42] Members of staunchly Republican social groups are likely to discuss a Democratic president's speech as "political" whereas a Democratic group can call it "statesmanlike." Not surprisingly, more Republicans thought Nixon won the first of the Kennedy-Nixon debates in 1960 whereas more Democrats thought Kennedy won.

Selective retention, which is closely related to selective perception, is evident when one relays communication to another but presents a distorted or incomplete report of its contents, sometimes because it is selectively perceived, or sometimes correctly perceived but not retained.[43] It was found that when persons were given pro- and anti-Soviet literature to read, and then asked to communicate it to others at different intervals, those who were pro-Soviet consistently gave the pro-Soviet side of the argument, selecting out anti-Soviet communications. The anti-Soviet group followed the opposite pattern of selectivity. Consider the strong, Republican, antiwelfare member of an attentive public who hears Senator Edward Kennedy say, "I believe that every qualified person who is unable to work because of physical disability, dependence, or is a head of household who must remain home to care for children is entitled to a minimum subsistence income guaranteed by the Federal government," and tells people with whom he discusses politics, "I heard Kennedy say that everyone who doesn't want to work should be given an income by the government." Selective exposure, selective perception, and selective retention are not used by all people for all campaign communications, but the available evidence indicates that these defense mechanisms function as a "protective net in the service of existing dispositions."[44]

These indicators from mass communications regarding reception and the process of selection suggest to the campaigner that communication is more likely to reinforce the existing opinions of voters than it is to change such opinions. Reinforcement seems to be related to the way in which influence is mediated by the factors, other than communication factors, related to the context of reception and the various selective processes.

Change and Conversion

Converson of views can occur, and it obviously does, in some situations. Minor changes in attitudes are possible, especially if they are not contrary to the individual's immediate context, or under conditions in which individual or group norms are not important.[45] This is perhaps why partisan voters who are unsure of their party's candidate are more likely to be undecided than automatically support the other candidate. Indecision is a halfway change. More important, when the information is new (when the context discussed above is nonexistent), campaign communication is likely to have a greater effect. As Klapper maintains, ". . .to the degree that the issue is really 'new' the communication is unlikely to run afoul of unsympathetic predispositions, unsympathetic group norms, or unsympathetic group leaders."[46] Therefore, if people are not previously inclined to one way or another, or if people in a situation are unlikely to have pre-existing opinions, the likelihood of formulating their opinions or "inoculating" people is greater.[47] Most research on the conversion effect thus indicates that it is most likely to occur when the forces of reinforcement are inoperative, or at least partially so. Klapper summarizes how inoperation can lead to conversion:

> Various extra-communication factors and conditions which ordinarily make for reinforcement appear to be less active, and occasionally to function in an atypical direction, in processes of conversion which involve mass communication.
>
> a. *The selective processes* (selective exposure, selective perception, and selective retention) which normally aid reinforcement are imperfect.

Further, when an individual is impelled ('predisposed') toward change by extra-communication conditions, the selective processes may sensitize him to communications suggesting change.

b. *Groups and group norms,* which often abet reinforcement, may well be less influential in regard to issues not salient to the group and among persons who do not greatly value their group membership. . . .

c. *Personal influence* appears to exercise a more crucial influence toward change than does mass communication when both such influences are present. However, personal influence does not appear to be a necessary factor in conversion, and its relative superiority over the media differs markedly from one topic of decision to another. . . .[48]

Converting people is thus limited in scope but possible. Consider the case of the Republican identifier whose basic campaign information is a television speech by a Democratic candidate; he is impressed by the Democrat's honesty and sincerity and does not discuss it with his Republican friends as he usually does. Consider further that his party loyalty has been weakening, and he has begun to surmise that there are good points and bad points in both parties. Consider further that his social network has slowly shifted from exclusively Republican to a mixed partisan group. Furthermore, this group frowns upon blind obedience to one's party, and advocates voting for candidates regardless of their party. In other words, the personal influence process is exerted, however subtly, toward a change in vote. These are ripe conditions for conversion, given the imperfection of the selection process, the absence of certain group norm barriers and the existence of facilitating group norms, and the personal influence directed toward conversion.[49]

IMPLICATIONS FOR CAMPAIGNS

The preceding discussion of opinion contexts and conditions for change obviously emphasizes the importance of reinforcement in campaigns. In Chapter 6 we will demonstrate how strategic thinking is based on the support that is either already existent, or is likely to be easily mobilized. Our examination of voter predispositions, early vote decisions, and communications coalesce into the conclusion that an important first step for the campaigner is discovering and appealing to those who are committed. It is primarily, but not exclusively, partisan commitment and it is ordinarily the important foundation upon which other processes are built upon.

The process of developing new information and motivating people on that basis is the next critical step which builds on the foundation of reinforcement. Candidate information is most important. Information about the qualities of the candidate are largely new sources of information for people, and thus are not as likely to be received with the usual barriers. The campaigner can fashion these candidate factors to be independent of party, organization, group, or other personal factors. What is said about candidates, particularly when the candidacy is new, are major factors in creating the candidate's image. As will be demonstrated, the campaigner has the greatest potential to control information about the candidate (as opposed to party and issue), and to the extent that it is new, it can be presented in a persuasive fashion. The implications, of course, suggest a less partisan strategy. To the extent that an issue is really new and people have no pre-existing context, the same process is at work. Campaigners try to capitalize on this by proposing solutions to problems or by making quick reaction statements to crises that arise during the campaign.

Although conversion is most difficult, the campaigner may not be able to avoid attempting it, particularly in constituencies that are predisposed to the opposition by reason of party, group, or other factors. Under ordinary circumstances it is easiest to convert people because of a candidate's image, less easy but possible because of issues. Party converson is the most difficult. It is easier to design messages to reformulate attitudes about an individual's personal qualities, issue stands, and likely performance in office, than it is to change ingrained views on welfare policy or an "inherited" party identification.

Conversion efforts must be combined with attempts to reinforce and activate the latent supporters. Many a losing campaign is one that has as its only real objective the goal of changing the partisanship of voter, or of changing the issue positions of voters. On the other hand, the campaigner must be aware that the contemporary trend toward weaker party loyalties combined with more extensive media messages is slowly increasing the small margin of opinion conversion. More information received outside of a party context also increases the likelihood that it will be received as new information, thus increasing the conversion component of the electorate. These changes undoubtedly lead to the increase in issue and candidate messages by candidates at all levels through person-to-person and mass media communications. But, it does not necessarily change priorities. Most voters remain partisans and are committed early, and the major effect of the campaign is reinforcement. Under normal campaign conditions all processes are working simultaneously; it is the relative emphasis among them that changes for different campaign situations.

Notes to Chapter 3

1. Lester W. Milbrath, *Political Participation* (Chicago: Rand McNally, 1965), p. 19.

2. Sidney Verba and Norman H. Nie, *Participation in America* (New York: Harper and Row, 1972), p. 32.

3. Ibid., p. 37.

4. Ibid.

5. Ibid., p. 40.

6. Robert A. Dahl, *Who Governs?* (New Haven: Yale Univ. Press, 1961), passim.

7. William J. Gore and Robert L. Peabody, "The Functions of the Political Campaign: A Case Study," *Western Political Quarterly* 11 (1958): 59.

8. V.O. Key, Jr., *Public Opinion and American Democracy* (New York: Alfred A. Knopf, 1961), pp. 544-45.

9. Ibid., p. 546.

10. Ibid., p. 201.

11. Bernard R. Berelson, Paul F. Lazarsfeld and William N. McPhee, *Voting* (Chicago: University of Chicago Press, 1954), p. 110.

12. Elihu Katz and Paul F. Lazarsfeld, *Personal Influence* (New York: The Free Press, 1955), p. 32.

13. Herbert Menzel and Elihu Katz, "Social Relations and Innovations in the Medical Profession," *Public Opinion Quarterly* 19 (1955): 337-52.

14. Paul F. Lazarsfeld, Bernard Berelson, and Hazel Gaudet, *The Peoples Choice* (New York: Duell, Sloan and Pearce, 1944), pp. 51, 151.

15. Key, *Public Opinion and American Democracy*, p. 361.

16. Samuel A. Stouffer, *Communism, Conformity and Civil Liberties* (New York: John Wiley, 1966), p. 227.

17. Melvin L. DeFleur and Otto N. Larsen, *The Flow of Information* (New York: Harper, 1958), p. 264.

18. Elihu Katz, "The Two Step Flow of Cumminication: An Up-to-Date Report on an Hypothesis," *Public Opinion Quarterly* 21 (1957): 73.

19. Lazarasfeld, *The People's Choice*, p. 87.

20. Ibid., p. 87-88.

21. Ibid., p. 89.

22. Ibid., p. 88.

23. Ibid., p. 103.

24. Ibid., p. 74.

25. Ibid., p. 75.

26. Ibid., pp. 75-76.

27. Ibid., p. 103.

28. Ibid., pp. 94-95.

29. Ibid., p. 99.

30. Ibid., p. 103.

31. Ibid., p. 104.

32. Robert Agranoff, *The New Style in Election Campaigns* (Boston: Holbrook Press, 1972), pp. 255-60.

33. Lazarsfeld, *The People's Choice*, p. 630, see also Berelson, *Voting*, p. 131.

34. Angus Campbell, Phillip E. Converse, Warren E. Miller, and Donald E. Stokes, *The American Voter* (New York: John Wiley, 1960), pp. 79, 82-83.

35. Stephen C. Shaddeg, *The New How to Win an Election* (New York: Taplinger, 1972), pp. 120-21.

36. Lazarsfeld, *The People's Choice*, p. 87.

37. Stanley Kelley, Jr., *Political Campaigning* (Washington, D.C.: The Brookings Institution, 1960), pp. 12-15.

38. Stanley Kelley, Jr., "Elections and the Mass Media," *Law and Contemporary Problems* 28 (1962): 310.

39. Joseph T. Klapper, *The Effects of Mass Communication* (Glencoe, Illinois: The Free Press, 1960), p. 45.

40. Lazarsfeld, *The People's Choice*, p. 89.

41. Klapper, *The Effects of Mass Communication*, p. 21.

42. Ibid., p. 23.

43. Ibid.

44. Ibid., p. 25.

45. Ibid., pp. 44-45.

46. Ibid., p. 61.

47. Ibid., pp. 60-61.

48. Ibid., pp. 94-95.

49. I am indebted to my neighbor, Richard Eike, whose discussions with me during the 1972 campaigns made it possible for me to conceptualize this process.

For Further Reading and Research

Best, James J. *Public Opinion.* Homewood, Illinois: Dorsey, 1973.

Devine, Donald J. *The Attentive Public.* Chicago: Rand, McNally, 1970.

Donahue, Thomas R. "Impact of Viewer Predispositions on Political TV Commercials." *Journal of Broadcasting* 18 (1973-74): 3-15.

Erickson, Robert S. and Luttbeg, Norman R. *American Public Opinion.* New York: Wiley, 1973.

Hawley, Willis D. and Wirt, Fredrick M., eds. *The Search for Community Power* 2d ed. Englewood Cliffs, N.J.: Prentice-Hall, 1974.

Katz, Elihu, and Lazarsfeld, Paul F. *Personal Influence: The Part Played by People in the Flow of Mass Communications.* New York: Free Press, 1964.

Key, Jr., V.O. *Public Opinion and American Democracy.* New York: Knopf, 1961.

Keynes, Edward and Ricci, David M., eds. *Political Power, Community and Democracy.* Chicago: Rand, McNally, 1970.

Kelley, Jr., Stanley. *Political Campaigning: Problems in Creating an Informed Electorate.* Washington: Brookings, 1960.

Klapper, Joseph T. *The Effects of Mass Communication.* Glencoe, Illinois: Free Press, 1960.

Lane, Robert E. *Political Life: Why People Get Involved in Politics.* New York: Free Press, 1959.

Meyer, Timothy and Donohue, Thomas R. "Perceptions and Misperceptions of Political Advertising." *Journal of Business Communication* 10 (1973): 29-40.

Milbrath, Lester W. *Political Participation.* Chicago: Rand, McNally, 1965.

Preston, Ivan L. "Logic and Illogic in the Advertising Process." *Journalism Quarterly* 44 (1967): 231-39.

Verba, Sidney and Nie, Norman H. *Participation in America.* New York: Harper & Row, 1972.

Warren, Roland L. *Studying Your Community.* New York: Free Press, 1965.

Strategic Assessment I — Raw Materials

The preceding overview of general campaign and voting processes forms a context of considerations from which strategic assessments can be made. They should help the campaigner formulate premises about the constituency, assess resources, calculate assets and liabilities, weigh advantages and disadvantages. This chapter, and the one that follows, will deal with how the campaigner gathers and uses the raw materials for strategic assessment, transforming knowledge and applied information into a field setting, using both "hard" and "soft" data.

Campaign research requires an equal blend of conceptual background and resourcefulness as well as the insight to apply it to a situation. Some would add expertise and money to purchase complex research services. To be sure, assessment can often be maximized by polls, computer analysis, and media research—ordinarily obtainable only by hiring consultants.[1] Their usage depends on their own situational factors: the size of the constituency, the amount of money available for research, the orientation of the strategists, and the political situation faced. Not all research is expensive and complex. Some involves the acquisition and interpretation of data already gathered by others. In other cases, campaigners will have to gather their own data. Some data will be simple enough to require only careful reflection, while others will require extensive background reading and or the advice of experts. Neither the level of complexity nor the expense of research entirely determines its importance in campaign planning. The true test is whether or not it will help transcend guesswork, avoid pitfalls, build vote potential, that is, whether or not it will be used.

There are many different kinds of materials which the campaigner can use to understand how previous research fits into a particular campaign. Many already exist in the community and are in ready-to-use form. Others are in the community, but must be investigated by the campaigner. Still others involve the community setting, but may require the assistance of others.

MAPS

Just as there are highway maps to guide the traveler, there are political and election unit subdivision maps to guide the campaigner. Political maps outline the boundaries of counties, Congressional districts, state legislative districts, judicial districts, school districts, special districts, cities, wards, and, that most basic of all political units, the precinct, or voting district. These printed maps are usually obtained from the office of the official who administers the election under consideration: state offices, multi-county constituencies, and Congressional from the Secretary of State; special districts, school districts, county divisions (if they are within a single county), from the county clerk; wards and precincts from the city clerk's office, or its equivalent. Occasionally, a special district is large enough in staff and facilities to have developed an extensive set of maps. If election maps are unavailable, the campaigner can obtain city street, county or township maps, study the districting bill which outlines constituency boundaries, and trace these boundaries on the appropriate map.

It is important that the maps used be accurate. The boundaries of election districts frequently change through reapportionment. State legislatures, county boards, and city councils are empowered to change district lines in accordance with population changes, and they often do so. Districts which appear on maps may have been changed, and, even with slight changes their makeup is different. Precinct boundaries are most susceptible to change, because a population change has a larger impact on these small units. But, they are the most difficult to detect. Precincts are generally organized for election administration, to achieve a balance of the number of voters who appear at each polling place. As the population moves about an election unit, some precincts can be divided and others consolidated, and thus, the numbers of precincts and the labels given them may and very often do appear to be the same when they are actually different. The campaigner can be sure that maps are accurate only by checking if there have been any bounary changes and then making the proper adjustments.

On occasion, a variety of maps that are developed for other purposes and are not divided by political subdivision may yield very useful information. The U.S. Census Bureau publishes maps to accompany its data sources and block-level maps in urban areas. Often, city or county planning offices draw economic development maps, zoning maps, land use maps, drainage maps, and conservation maps for their own purposes, but they may give the campaigner insights into the constituency, trigger possible problem areas, or even suggest an issue to use. These maps are often deposited at the map room of the city or county library.

Constituency maps have many uses throughout a campaign. They can be useful in planning, organizing, and implementing a whole series of area-divided

Figure 4.1 Election District Map of Geneva Township, Illinois

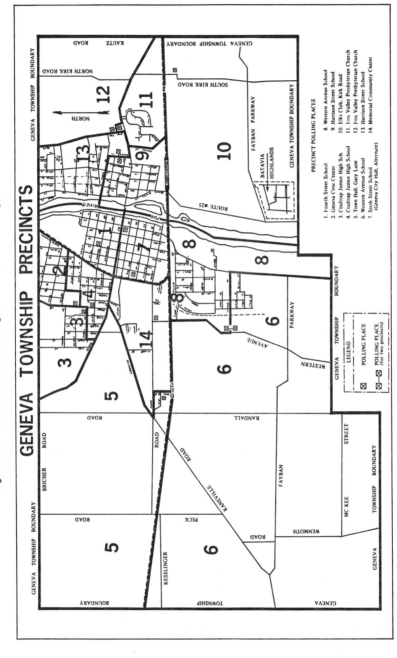

activities: voter identification, voter registration, voter turnout, house-to-house literature distribution, and other person-to-person activities. They can be merged with other data (particularly census with past voting) to increase information levels. They give campaigners an idea of the extensiveness of the task before them, and likewise, can help establish priorities. Constituency maps also may be needed to assist in interpreting other geographic data. For example, if a direct mailing is to be sorted by zip code, the campaigner should make sure that only the addresses within a constituency are included, since zip codes and election districts are rarely congruous. Thus, election maps give the campaigner the lay of the land and they are generally helpful at many points in the campaign.

HISTORICAL INFORMATION

The campaigner may wish to increase the depth of his or her knowledge of the constituency by reaching into the past for information which may help to understand and deal with the present. This may be particularly true in the case of large constituencies, such as in a statewide campaign when the campaigners want to know more about an area relatively unfamiliar to them, or in any constituency where the campaigners are new. College student campaigners, for example, often find themselves in strange territory. Historical area information is generally compiled and published in brief form by city and county historical societies, and usually are available at public libraries. On occasion, this information may be condensed into a city or county information booklet, available at courthouses or from local Chambers of Commerce. Neighborhood information is more difficult to obtain, although community surveys sometimes contain brief historical summaries for parts of cities.

Historical information can be used to help introduce the campaigner to the area in a similar fashion to meeting a political activist. In each case the campaigner wants to know something about past positions, possible influences, and likely behavior. Historical information offers a general idea of the distinguishing features of one unit as opposed to another. Also, the historical information gathered can be used to brief the candidate on the area when he or she makes an appearance in that area. The candidate may even wish to integrate bits of history into speeches given in that area, to demonstrate awareness of and interest in the area. Such information may shed light on why the local residents support a particular party. It may be a wealthy agricultural area and thus heavily Republican, or it may be a mining county heavily populated by Eastern European Catholics and, thus, overwhelmingly Democratic. Historical information could even generate an issue position. Take the example of a Minnesota candidate who discovers in a Stearns County Historical Society booklet that 20 percent of all American granite is extracted in Stearns County. He read a year earlier that the New England granite quarries were resisting the lowering of import quotas. The foreign competition situation can now be worked into a local issue. The use of such background information is well worth the minimal effort involved in acquiring and absorbing it.

CENSUS DATA

As is well known, each decade the Census Bureau enumerates and gathers characteristic information about the population of the United States. Other information is gathered in the time between the decennial census. Such information is gathered by many geographic divisions: state, county, minor civil division (city, township), congressional district, tract (an area of a larger city divided into units of about 8,000), enumeration district (about 400 population), and block face (the corner-to-corner "face" of a single square block). Many valuable characteristics are provided as well—race, nativity, level of education, type of occupation, income level, persons over 18 years of age, size of family, owner occupied or rented dwelling, ratio of welfare recipients, condition of housing, and so on.

In a negative vein, census data has increased in quality while the accessibility of the data has decreased. In addition, it does not relate well to voting units, except in the very largest or "over aggregated" units. A great deal of the previously available information, such as city tracts, remains in printed sources. But, as the amount of information has increased, the Census Bureau has availed

Figure 4.2 Census Tract Map for Geneva Township, Illinois

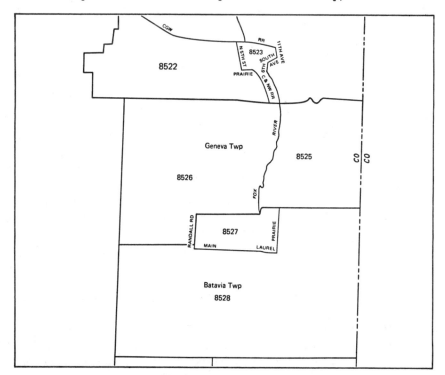

Source: U.S., Department of Commerce, Bureau of Census, *1970 Census of Population and Housing: Chicago Census Tracts.*

itself of modern technology and has stored the data on computer tape. There-fore, much of the relevant information must be obtained, specifying the tracts and characteristics, from those who have access to the computer tapes. The most important limitation is that small-unit data (or tracts and enumeration districts) do not correspond to the smallest voting unit—the precinct. Block face data can be turned into precincts, but concern for privacy has limited the information available. Block data only reports information regarding the numbers of people: in group quarters, who are Negroes, under 18 years, 62 years and over, lack plumbing facilities, in 1-unit structures, in structures over 10 units, in owner occupied dwellings, are renters, in one-person households, and in female-headed households. The typical campaign researcher is faced with dealing with small unit data, notwithstanding the problems, and with superimposing the small-unit social and economic data onto overlapping territories. Usually the campaigner can do little more than "eyeball" the census tract map and the precinct map and assign a precinct roughly to a tract.[2] All campaigners face problems of incon-gruity, incompleteness, and inaccessibility, unless they want to order a special reaggregation from the Census Bureau for a prohibitive price.

The campaigner must find some way to "link up" with the Census if he or she wishes to use area-based social and economic characteristics of the popula-tion. If there is to be no polling, much can be derived from the Census that is political. Published Census reports are availabe in U.S. government depository libraries, including most large city and university libraries. In addition to city tracts, enumeration districts, and block faces, much useful area-based informa-tion is still published for counties and minor civil divisions and in state reports. For congressional districts there is a *Congressional District Data Book*, although it rapidly becomes out of date due to population changes as the decade pro-gresses. Reapportionment requires supplemental publications, merely rearrang-ing the original information with no updating. The Census Bureau also publishes a continually revised *User's Guide* to familiarize the researcher with available data and how to obtain them. For the small-unit data on computer tape, un-fortunately, the researcher must have the knowledge and skill to acquire it, and must have access to it. Of course, one can seek the assistance of those who are capable of handling Census tapes. Short of these advantages, information access must be purchased. There are private, and, quasi-governmental national- and re-gional-service bureaus which will prepare specialized printouts of census mater-ials on order, usually for a fee. Several software systems, such as Control Data Corporation's CENSTAT package have been developed to extract Census data.

The actual use of census data for a campaign can range from a simple social and economic profile of the constituency to a detailed precinct-by-pre-cinct social area analysis.[3] Some candidates use the data merely to add hard and more current information to their historical background file. They consider the average level of education and income for the whole district, the numbers of welfare recipients, and the ratio of substandard housing for an entire city or legislative district. Such over-aggregation of data is generally useful only as speech and issue material; it will not assist the campaigner in determining how to

Table 4.1   Census Economic Data for Selected Maine Towns (partial)

Towns and Places	Mexico town	Millinocket Center (U)	Millinocket town	Milo town	New Gloucester town	Norway town	Oakland town	Old Orchard Beach Center (U)	Old Orchard Beach town	Old Town	Orono Center (U)
OCCUPATION											
Total employed 16 years old and over	1362	2469	2512	898	806	1531	1266	1947	1982	3629	3116
Professional, technical and kindred workers	114	441	445	82	93	126	149	210	210	610	1012
Health workers	18	62	62	15	19	32	34	23	23	107	83
Teachers, elementary and secondary schools	46	147	147	19	42	50	62	101	101	129	119
Managers and administrators	73	197	197	70	53	147	97	226	230	248	193
Salaried	53	149	149	62	42	100	57	163	167	199	184
Self-employed in retail trade	16	37	37	4	4	47	30	24	24	32	9
Sales workers	64	74	74	54	29	48	111	81	81	212	166
Retail trade	64	54	54	35	21	39	82	44	44	133	109
Clerical and kindred workers	173	265	265	101	106	148	124	276	285	522	499
Craftsmen, foremen, and kindred workers	228	414	414	223	119	209	237	268	283	517	192
Mechanics and repairmen	44	39	39	39	27	36	83	77	88	74	54
Construction craftsmen	71	87	87	57	48	53	39	93	93	174	88
Operatives, except transport	382	579	601	158	86	523	262	399	402	784	146
Manufacturing	359	550	572	122	59	500	233	377	380	706	70
Nonmanufacturing industries	23	29	29	36	27	23	29	22	22	78	76
Transport equipment operatives	40	110	110	62	67	58	24	102	102	115	40
Laborers, except farm	122	168	180	63	18	94	85	82	82	130	130
Farmers and farm managers	—	—	—	—	4	12	7	11	11	16	—
Farm laborers and farm foremen	—	—	—	—	27	20	12	10	10	—	86
Service workers	160	206	211	75	199	114	119	252	256	436	581
Cleaning and food service workers	94	115	115	26	88	90	57	145	145	244	432
Protective service workers	3	36	41	5	13	11	9	17	17	61	57
Personal and health service workers	63	41	41	44	89	13	45	73	77	100	86
Private household workers	6	15	15	10	5	32	39	30	30	39	71
Female employed, 16 years old and over	501	662	662	271	350	627	531	807	815	1495	1324
Professional, technical and kindred workers	54	207	207	30	73	81	103	106	106	246	378
Health workers	15	51	51	10	19	20	26	19	19	94	34
Teachers, elementary and secondary schools	26	120	120	5	39	27	56	53	53	82	83
Managers and administrators	6	41	41	—	—	6	24	54	58	28	40
Sales workers	36	43	43	26	16	32	22	35	35	86	46

Source: U.S., Department of Commerce, Census Bureau, *Characteristics of the Population,* vol. 1, pt. 21, Maine.

Table 4.2 Block Characteristics, New York City (partial)

| Blocks Within Census Tracts | Percent of total population | | | | | Year-round housing units | | | | Occupied housing units | | | | | | | | | | | | | | |
| | Total population | Negro | In group quarters | Under 18 years | 62 years and over | Units in— | | | | Owner | | | | | Renter | | | | | 1.01 or more persons per room | | One-person households | With female head of family | With roomers, boarders, or lodgers |
						Total	Lacking some or all plumbing facilities	One-unit structures	Structures of 10 or more units	Total	Lacking some or all plumbing facilities	Average number of rooms	Average value (dollars)	Percent Negro	Total	Lacking some or all plumbing facilities	Average number of rooms	Average contract rent (dollars)	Percent Negro	Total	With all plumbing facilities			
83																								
101	4309	9	—	29	14	1800	135	9	1591	14	2	4.7	…	—	1735	128	3.2	87	8	249	222	692	213	43
102	510	6	—	19	12	262	27	1	233	4	…	…	…	…	253	26	2.9	93	6	30	20	113	22	15
202	746	15	—	31	10	294	20	2	252	1	…	…	…	…	279	20	3.8	73	10	41	36	89	56	7
303	1062	4	—	15	15	603	81	4	512	8	1	4.4	…	—	567	76	2.4	103	5	82	71	305	40	19
304	1122	10	—	40	15	341	2	—	298	—	…	…	…	…	339	2	3.9	77	10	61	61	86	46	2
	869	10	—	38	17	300	5	2	296	1	…	…	…	…	297	4	3.8	75	9	35	34	99	49	—
84																								
102	300	10	—	6	17	235	53	3	147	—	—	—	—	—	229	53	1.5	178	10	32	29	179	5	13
103	24	17	—	—	17	22	—	2	4	—	—	—	—	—	22	—	1.8	134	18	—	—	20	—	1
201	66	18	—	—	35	63	42	1	59	—	—	—	—	—	63	42	1.0	113	18	3	3	60	1	—
202	31	7	—	3	13	24	—	—	6	—	—	—	—	—	20	—	2.5	120	5	2	2	13	—	1
203	13	8	—	—	39	12	1	—	1	—	—	—	—	—	10	1	1.6	130	10	2	1	7	1	—
	166	7	—	10	9	114	10	—	77	—	—	—	—	—	114	10	1.5	237	5	25	23	79	4	11
86																								
101	6377	9	22	7	29	3051	23	34	2728	943	3	4.7	60000	1	1864	18	3.1	248	—	70	69	1302	88	62
102	1361	40	99	2	52	8	—	5	3	—	—	—	—	—	8	—	5.1	…	13	—	—	8	—	—
103	1011	1	1	9	25	615	4	4	576	323	1	3.6	—	1	254	3	3.2	249	1	13	13	251	24	3
202	810	1	1	10	20	447	9	4	389	55	1	8.4	—	—	340	8	3.3	285	—	17	17	141	15	17
301	1342	1	1	8	26	856	6	14	742	96	—	6.5	…	—	718	5	3.0	223	1	18	18	469	20	22
302	576	1	—	7	14	340	1	1	302	42	—	5.0	…	—	277	—	3.3	266	—	4	4	127	10	13
303	519	—	2	6	25	446	2	4	400	149	—	3.6	…	—	252	—	2.6	244	—	16	15	245	13	5
	658	11	—	11	21	339	10	3	316	278	1	5.3	—	2	15	—	3.3	291	—	2	2	51	6	2

Source: U.S., Department of Commerce, Bureau of Census, 1970 Census Housing: Block Statistics, New York Metropolitan Area.

Table 4.3 Selected Tract Data for Waco, Texas (partial)

Census Tracts	McLennan County			Waco							
	Total	Waco	Balance	Tract 0001	Tract 0002	Tract 0003	Tract 0004	Tract 0005	Tract 0006	Tract 0007	Tract 0008
All housing units	52 529	34 408	18 121	916	299	209	2 390	1 998	490	924	1 083
Vacant--seasonal and migratory	24	8	16	—	—	—	—	—	—	—	—
All year-round housing units	52 505	34 400	18 105	916	299	209	2 390	1 998	490	924	1 083
TENURE, RACE, AND VACANCY STATUS											
Owner occupied	31 585	18 993	12 542	185	141	26	605	1 177	161	435	704
Cooperative and condominium	54	54	—	—	—	—	—	7	—	—	—
White	27 698	16 205	11 493	156	130	26	485	1 043	161	422	703
Negro	3 743	2 731	1 012	27	11	—	115	126	—	10	—
Renter occupied	16 534	12 511	4 023	612	120	183	1 558	661	258	389	300
White	13 311	9 705	3 606	481	83	179	1 365	591	253	372	299
Negro	3 118	2 731	387	129	37	1	181	62	3	16	—
Vacant year-round	4 436	2 896	1 540	119	38	—	227	160	71	100	79
For sale only	661	453	208	18	1	—	20	17	7	20	22
Vacant less than 6 months	419	304	115	11	…	—	10	7	4	14	14
Median price asked	$8 100	$8 500	$7 200	$6 900	…	—	$5000-	$5 500	$12 500	$6 900	$8 600
For rent	2 316	1 748	568	65	3	1	154	101	53	53	28
Vacant less than 2 months	1 021	776	245	27	…	—	63	35	25	30	13
Median rent asked	$61	$64	$50	$49	$34	—	$46	$43	$63	$54	$68
Other	1 459	695	764	36	34	—	53	42	11	27	29
LACKING SOME OR ALL PLUMBING FACILITIES											
All units	2 545	625	1 900	110	19	1	85	45	3	4	4
Owner occupied	1 137	182	955	9	5	—	17	13	1	1	1
Negro	566	92	474	3	—	—	6	3	—	—	—
Renter occupied	818	277	541	68	3	1	46	14	2	2	2
Negro	345	101	244	11	1	—	3	6	—	2	—
Vacant year-round	570	166	404	33	11	—	22	18	—	1	1
For sale only	37	13	24	6	…	—	—	—	—	—	—
For rent	209	94	115	16	—	—	19	3	—	—	—
COMPLETE KITCHEN FACILITIES AND ACCESS											
Lacking complete kitchen facilities	2 031	728	1 303	127	18	1	57	34	2	12	14
Access only through other living quarters	17	12	5	1	—	—	—	1	1	—	—
ROOMS											
1 room	474	361	113	123	—	2	64	4	7	8	3
2 rooms	1 370	1 058	312	131	4	4	147	50	45	42	11
3 rooms	5 187	3 915	1 272	251	42	53	794	208	103	151	70
4 rooms	11 961	7 676	4 285	169	113	110	576	695	88	142	168
5 rooms	17 426	11 050	6 376	117	79	14	487	661	101	229	416
6 rooms	10 514	6 737	3 777	65	46	6	192	286	60	172	281
7 rooms	3 516	2 217	1 299	17	15	9	73	65	33	78	93
8 rooms	1 252	816	436	20	—	8	30	22	24	52	27
9 rooms or more	805	570	235	23	—	—	27	7	29	50	14
Median	4.9	4.9	5.0	3.3	4.4	3.9	3.8	4.6	4.5	5.0	5.2

Source: U. S. Department of Commerce, Census Bureau, Census Tracts: Waco, Texas SMSA.

campaign in a particular locale. These district averages are net figures. For example, there are more well-educated people in some areas, poorly educated people in others, and moderately educated in others. These differences can affect the type of appeals made, and the extent of effort made in various areas. Only by "disaggregating" social and economic data to the lowest possible unit will the campaigner differentiate areas meaningfully. Even then there still will be some mix of people in each area.

Campaign researchers who deal with small unit data very often build indices by voting unit to expand their social and economic profiles. After dealing with the problem of merging the voting unit and census tract, they often average two or three social and economic indicators—income, number of laborers, and owner occupied dwellings—into an index of social and economic status. The higher the income levels of the precinct, the fewer the laborers, and, the higher the rate of owner-occupied homes, the higher the index. Republican strategists would then assign these high social and economic precincts a high priority, assuming from the voting literature that these areas are saturated with people predisposed to Republican candidates. Other indicies have been built on family makeup (e.g., number of young children, women in the labor force) and ethnicity (e.g., race, place of ancestors' birth, Spanish surnames). Acutally, there is no limit to the number and type of Census items used in forming such indices. Even single indicators can bear fruitful results. The researcher should bear in mind previous research on voting behavior. One should ask the question, "How can these data assist in telling me how the voters are likely to behave in the light of previous research on voting?"

PAST VOTING STATISTICS

An important part of the political history of the campaigner's constituency is contained in the records of votes cast in past elections. Here we are referring to what are commonly known as the voting results, election returns, voting statistics, or more precisely, aggregate electoral data. These figures contain the aggregated totals of all votes cast for various candidates, or measures for various constituencies and election units. There has been a great deal of discussion in the literature about use of these figures. It has been claimed that too many researchers made incorrect inferences about the behavior of individuals using these grouped data.[4] While this is probably true, aggregate election data can be used to study the behavior of electorates, and their shifts between parties and candidates. Moreover, since most campaigning is an attempt to mobilize aggregated electorates, that is, planned and executed on a group basis, usage of aggregating of votes by geographical unit seems especially helpful.[5]

Possible error in using aggregate election figures is reduced to a minimum when the campaign planner disaggregates the data to the lowest available unit, the precinct. People who live in close proximity tend to have similar lifestyles as well as similar political outlooks. Precinct election data corresponds closest to neighborhoods, and the various differences between people show up at this level. At the more aggregated levels—wards, counties, entire constituencies—the figures are the net results of all precincts. Thus, a 51- to 49-percent legislative race could easily be made up of many precincts that were two, three, or even four to one for one candidate or the other. The campaigner naturally wants to know where the one-sided and where the relatively even areas are. Results from wards or counties occasionally may be useful for planning the priorities in very large constituencies, but more often, they yield little more than a general picture of who won and who lost these areas.[6]

Election results are usually kept in the offices of the official who is responsible for administering the electon—usually city clerks, town clerks, county clerks, and secretaries of state. In some larger cities and counties, sometimes there are separate election boards or commissions who collect these figures. Ordinarily, any constituency that crosses county lines is administered by the secretary of state, or some other state official. In some states, returns from local races are deposited centrally, but in others, data (even on statewide races) is available only at county seats.[7] Once one has located the proper source one may have to persuade the official to release the figures. Despite the fact that these results are a part of the public record, researchers have reported many tales of the reluctance of election officials to make election figures available. The reasons range from fear of discovering something (perhaps incompetence more often than fraud) to disruption of office schedules. In some areas election officials are legally allowed to destroy the returns after a certain period of time, usually six months to one year, and they often do. The campaigner should be prepared for a less than warm reception.

Access is only the first problem with election returns. They are seldom in ready-to-use form. Rarely are precinct results published; they must be dug out of or photocopied from the official records. Data at the more aggregated levels are very often published, either in a small election-results booklet by the office of the official, or in some statewide publication. Most states publish a statewide "blue book," or canvassing-board report with some figures. They usually contain county and legislative results, although a few publish precinct results for some major races, perhaps only for the general election. County election figures on presidential and major state races are also published in the *America Votes* series, and the Inter-University Consortium for Political Research at the University of Michigan has accumulated vast bodies of past county figures, available on computer tapes to its college affiliates.

As researchers gain access to data, they will want to consider gathering a number of key items. First is data on registration and turnout. The total number of ballots cast and counted (some reports inaccurately substitute the highest contest on the ticket—all do not vote in this race) will yield the turnout figures. Registration figures for each election year may be listed on the returns, or they may have to be secured from another source, usually in the same election official's office. Second, the planner may wish to gather figures for the most visible or high stimulus races, president, governor, senator, mayor in order to compare them with the race under investigation. These are generally the contests that most people actually come out for, and comparisons with votes for these candidates are useful. Third, a measure of the levels of party support in each unit is generally desirable. Ordinarily, a race or set of races from the less visible candidates and races is used as a measure of benchmark party strength. In Illinois, the votes for University of Illinois Trustee or the Clerk of the Supreme Court are often used. Fourth, it is often useful to look at a race that did inordinately well compared to other party candidates, to get a measure of the areas of swing voting. Finally, if the past race for the office under investigation has not already been included, it obviously should be. The planner should keep these points in mind, examine the vote totals of the entire constituency to get a general picture, discuss them with colleagues, and have a clear idea of which races one is interested in before gathering the data from the precinct level.

VOTER LISTS

Another valuable campaign tool is the list of names and addresses of registered voters by precinct, ordinarily obtainable from the city or county clerk's office. These lists are the building blocks for many person-to-person voting-public contacts. Planners should be aware that the lists are constantly changing, due to residents moving, new registrants being added to the rolls and the deletion of names of citizens who lose their registration by not voting periodically. In some states, registration is by party affiliation and in others it is not. Still other states do not have party registration, but records are kept of which party's primary the voters participated in for each election. Fewer voters vote in primaries, and many who do, switch parties. Thus, primaries often represent a hard core of activists or a minimum party vote. Primaries with sharp factional battles often reveal differences by geographic areas that may be instructive for future campaigns.

There are many uses for voter lists, they will be detailed in Chapter 15. Briefly, they can be used for such activities as: checking against a city directory for nonregistrants and organizing a registration campaign; checking candidate preferences through telephone or door-to-door canvassing; conversion to precinct-worker and block-worker walking lists for canvassing and literature distribution; serving as a basic document for the get-out-the-vote campaign; and for direct mail appeals, if updated.

LEGAL SCHEDULE AND REGULATIONS

Every campaign operates within a legal context that regulates times and practices. When one is at the office of the election administrator, one should also check into all legal dates related to the election. Among the more important deadlines are: the filing deadline and last day to withdraw from a contest; the dates of the primary and general election; the opening and closing dates of registration, and, where applicable, differences in dates between courthouse, mobile, in-precinct, and door-to-door registration; the dates when any financial report statements might be required; dates for canvassing board meetings to certify results and notices of contest; and any other legally prescribed data that is peculiar to the state or constituency.

Other legal regulations also concern campaigning. Every state has a legal code, governing campaigns and elections, which amount to guidelines the campaigner must follow. In addition to the usual, corrupt practices codes of forbidden activities, there may be regulations covering campaigning at the polls, spending limits, reporting procedures, registration rules, and absentee ballot procedures. Minnesota law, for example, proscribes the giving of "anything of value" while campaigning for office, forbidding the often used matchbooks, pens, and litterbags, but allowing buttons, pennants, and stickers. Obviously, the campaigner must be aware of such regulations because they bear directly on the plans of the campaign. In some states, a printed book summarizing the relevant legal codes is available. If such materials are not available, as is true of other laws, it is the responsibility of the candidate and campaigners to know of such regulations and to operate within them.

PUBLISHED STUDIES

In many communities a number of published community surveys exist which can help the planner understand the constituency and identify potential issues and concerns. Included are economic surveys, business surveys, city, county or state planning surveys (land use, industrial growth, health care, educational needs, manpower needs, transportation patterns, population patterns, and so on). Sometimes they are broken down by state regions or city neighborhoods.

Two examples will illustrate how these surveys have been used for campaign purposes. A candidate for mayor of a medium size city was able to confirm from a state industrial planning agency report that industrial growth in his town had reached a plateau. His study of other reports, including local zoning regulations, transportaion patterns, land use, and the comparative tax base led him to conclude that industrial growth would increase only as a result of changes in these matters. His campaign included appeals on changes in taxation, transportation, zoning, and land use in order to accelerate industrial growth. In a second case, a candidate for the state legislature from an inner city district, with a large American Indian population pored over reports from the Model Cities program office and the state Indian Commission. He discovered that there were many things he could do nothing about, such as the high suicide rate of adolescent Indians, or the highest unemployment rates for urban Indians, but he understood these aspects of the situation better. There were other situations he could remedy. His reading of the report that urban Indians had the highest rate of communicable diseases led him to propose state supported store-front health clinics to complement the mobile clinics already in use for rural Indians. When he discovered that the average years of school for urban Indians was 9.2 years, he proposed an omnibus urban Indian education program, including special training for teachers, the teaching of Indian language and culture, and special vocational and technical training. These two cases illustrate how published surveys find their way into speeches, group appeals, issue appeals, and position papers.

Numerous sources generate such published works. Most of the government surveys come from the agencies that produce them, including city, county, and state planning departments; industrial development departments; health departments; tax departments; and so on. Chambers of Commerce or other business development firms may also publish some studies, and occasionally, a neighborhood or city development group may also have made their work available. Many university departments have conducted community surveys which are sometimes published, and in other cases are available as theses or dissertations, indexed in the university library. The campaigner has to scout the area to find out which materials might be available as well as useful.

Figure 4.3   Campaign Finance Reporting and Disclosure Law
(Partial), Iowa

1974 Session

Campaign Disclosure—Income Tax Checkoff

Senate File 1200

An Act Relating to the Campaign Disclosure-Income Tax Checkoff Law

Be it enacted by the General Assembly of the State of Iowa:

Section 1. *Acts of the Sixty-fifth General Assembly, 1973 Session, chapter one hundred thirty-eight (138), section six (6), subsection one (1), is amended by striking the subsection and inserting in lieu thereof the following:*

1. Every political committee which receives or expends any amount of money shall file a statement of organization within ten days from the date of its organization. For the purposes of this section, "political committee" means a person or committee, but not a candidate, including a statutory committee which accepts any contributions or makes any expenditures for the purpose of supporting or opposing a candidate for public office.

Sec. 2. *Acts of the Sixty-fifth General Assembly, 1973 Session, chapter one hundred thirty-eight (138), section six (6), subsection two (2), is amended by adding the following new paragraph:*

New Paragraph

A signed statement by the candidate or an officer of the political party which shall be in the following form:

"I am aware that I am required to file additional reports if I receive or expend more than one hundred dollars for the purpose of supporting or opposing any candidate for public office."

Sec. 3. *Acts of the Sixty-fifth General Assembly, 1973 Session, chapter one hundred thirty-eight (138), section six (6),* is amended by adding the following new subsection:

New Subsection

All affidavits of candidacy required by law shall contain a sworn statement by the candidate in substantially the following form:

"I am aware that I am required to file additional reports if I receive or expend more than one hundred dollars for the purpose of supporting or opposing any candidate for public office."

Sec. 4 *Acts of the Sixty-fifth General Assembly, 1973 Session, chapter one hundred thirty-eight (138), section seven (7), subsection one (1),* is amended to read as follows:

1. Each treasurer of a political committee shall file with the state commissioner or commissioner reports of contributions received and disbursed on forms prescribed by the state commission. The reports from all committees, except those committees for municpal and school elective offices, shall be filed on the twentieth day of January, May, July, and October of each year. The January and July reports shall be current to the end of the month preceding the filing. The May and October reports shall be current as of five days prior to the filing deadline. The January report shall be the annual report. Reports from political committees for municipal and school elective offices shall file reports five days prior to any election in which the name of the candidate which they support or oppose appears on the printed ballot and thirty days following the general or run-off election.

Sec. 5. *Acts of the Sixty-fifth General Assembly, 1973 Session, chapter one hundred thirty-eight (138), section seven (7), subsection two (2),* is amended to read as follows:

2. If any political committee, after having filed one or more statements of organization, dissolves or determines that it shall no longer receive contributions or make disbursements, the treasurer of the political committee shall notify the state commissioner or the commissioner within thirty days . . . .

Source: Iowa Legislative Service, *Acts and Resolutions 65th General Assembly*, St. Paul: West Publishing, 1974.

KEY POINTS AND PROJECTS

It is also useful, particularly in campaigns involving a large constituency, to list for each community, county, or city, the key industrial concerns, important industries and businesses, chief agricultural products, important government projects in the area, key governmental contracts awarded to local concerns, and all state and federal government projects in the area. This not only enhances the campaigner's knowledge of the constituency, but makes it easier to distinguish between various subunits of the constituency. When the candidate or any important campaigner who is unfamiliar with the territory arrives in the area, he or she should be apprised of all of these factors so that he or she has some familiarity with the local situation. Such area differences and distinguishing characteristics also can be the basis of the tailored appeals made on behalf of a candidate in a particular locality.

KEY POLITICAL OFFICIALS

Campaign planners often compile a list of all governmental units within the constituency, including special districts (school districts, conservation districts) and then fill in the names of current elected and appointed officers, as well as party officials of both parties at the county, ward, and precinct levels. Such lists must be compiled from a number of sources, including: city and county courthouses for their officials, state party headquarters for party officials, county party leaders for precinct chairmen, the secretary of state for state legislators and state officers, and other offices for their officials. Sometimes the League of Women Voters or other civic groups publish lists of officials for a given area. Such lists not only contain the most active political activists, but they give the campaigner an idea of who's who in area politics. In large constituencies, the candidate and those who campaign for him will want to know the "lineups" of local "players" when they campaign in the area.

ORGANIZATONS

Another useful list to compile early in the campaign is a list of the important organizations in the constituency, and the names and addresses of their leaders. It is through organizations that most of the meaningful political action takes place. Organizational leaders and activists make up the various attentive publics. Also, our survey of voting behavior indicated that organizational leaders can offer important voting cues to those who identify with the group and that many campaign messages are transmitted through group leaders. Obviously, not every group is predisposed to support a candidate, but some are, and others might, with some stimulation. The process of lining up group support is no doubt one of reinforcement, activation of latent support, and conversion, and it must begin with an inventory of groups.

Three types of groups, classified by interest to the campaigner are political, semi-political, and non-political. Among the political groups are: political party organizations; League of Women Voters; citizens reform movements, such as the Greater Philadelphia Movement and the Minneapolis-St. Paul Area Citizens League; ongoing local coalitions that work for local political causes, and local political parties not affiliated with the two major parties, such as the Good Government League of San Antonio, Texas.[8] Not all of these groups directly support candidates for office (see Chapter 5) but they are exclusively political groups and their leaders often occupy central points in the political process. Candidates are usually expected to make appearances before such groups, or, at least, issue positions are expected to be made known to them. In many areas, for example, the League of Women Voters have candidate forums where contestants are expected to appear. In some areas the League circulates issue questionnaires to candidates which are published as voter's guides in local newspapers. Because these groups contain the most politically interested and active citizens, they are difficult to bypass if a candidate were so minded.

A second category of groups are semi-political. Their mission and role is primarily non-political, but they do concern themselves with political matters. Labor organizations, business organizations, farm groups, professional associations, veterans organizations, public health associations, mental health associations, and many others are included in this category. These groups also contain key activists who may or may not be at the center of political affairs, but they are ordinarily important in their subject matter specialization. Candidates may be called upon to state their issue position on matters of interest to these groups. There also may be instances when it is to the candidate's advantage to make an issue position known to these groups. Moreover, their leaders are likely to be key opinion leaders, particularly on the political matters that relate to the organization, including candidacies. If a campaigner can get his message into the specialized communication of such groups he may penetrate a market of people not ordinarily responsive to straight political appeals.

The third category is the non-political groups, such as church congregations, fraternal groups, the YMCA, and many others. They generally avoid involvement in politics, but their associational nature makes them potential points of contact. Often they can be appealed to politically on the basis of some common identification, or by some issue of mutual interest. Candidates sometimes secure the schedule of public events of these groups and make appearances as a member of the crowd. Sometimes they acquire lists and send specialized mailings to these groups. One neophyte legislative candidate (with a not very Catholic sounding name) in a heavily Catholic area secured the lists for all the parishes in his county and in *that* mailing he stressed his membership in the Knights of Columbus, his graduation from Catholic schools and colleges, and his parish church.

In large constituencies, listing each group in these three categories will be difficult to accomplish, considering their large number and dispersion. The planner will simply have to make judgments as to which are most important. The relative status of groups as a campaign communication channel in large constituencies is less important because there is more reliance on mass media. The opposite is true for the small constituency. Yet, group membership may well overlap, particularly within the boundaries of a very small constituency. Ordinarily, group lists have to be compiled on a group-by-group basis, by asking others about such groups, and looking through the telephone directory under "Associations" and other various classifications. In some areas, "organization directories" that have been produced by city or county governments or by citizen groups are available.

COMMUNICATIONS MEDIA

As will be demonstrated in subsequent chapters, the mass media have become the most important campaign communicators. Thus, it is important to list the various communications media that cover a constituency. This list should be compiled very early in the campaign, so that campaigners know the number and type of media to be confronted. The printed media are listed in *Editor and Publishers International Yearbook;* radio and television are listed in the *Broadcasters' Yearbook.* Both list by state and county, and they are available in most libraries.

It will be readily discovered that the number and variety of media in a given area will force campaign planners to make some early decisions. In addition to daily newspapers, AM radio, and television, there are weekly newspapers, special group newspapers (ethnic, language and labor union, for example), small FM radio stations, and in some areas, cable television. The impact and reach of the media must be considered as well. Circulation by area, and audience by area and time slot must be investigated. The question of the cost of time and space also arises. These figures are usually supplied to the candidate, as a prospective user, by the individual medium. Most media markets are covered by data services, such as the Audit Bureau of Circulations, the Audience Research Bureau, and the Standard Rate and Data Service, which compile comparative figures for all media within a given market. These factors must, of course, be considered in conjunction with budgetary factors. The first step in this process is to list all media, assessing reach and cost factors so the campaigner can understand the boundaries of the media situation.

POLITICAL PARTY ORGANIZATION

Until now the suggested materials have been previously existing data or lists. The campaigner must also create some of his or her own data, or lists of factors, starting with an early assessment of the electioneering capability of the candidate's party organization. Some party organizations prove to be excellent debating societies, but may be poor at campaigning; some are good at both. Others are good campaigners, but there is little intellectual content to their meeting dialogue. Still others are mere "paper" organizations, the officers seeking or accepting the position for the prestige it may bestow upon them, or for some other reason. They neither debate nor campaign. Since the campaign planner is primarily concerned with the local organizations' electioneering prowess, one should seek ways to separate the party organizations into paper organizations, debaters, campaigners, or combinations that include campaigners.

There is no easy formula for determining the campaign strength of a party organization.[9] In Chapter 15, surveys of the activism of party organizations in performing various campaign activities will be revealed. Ordinarily, the campaigner will not have the opportunity to make an extensive survey of past party electioneering, rather, he must proceed informally by gingerly inquiring of other people and gathering various isolated indicators. One means is to ask previous candidates or their campaign managers what kind of help they received in the past, keeping in mind that there is a high rate of turnover in party organizations at all levels, and therefore, the situation could get better or worse. If handled diplomatically, it is even possible to ask party chairpeople, or their committees, a series of questions about how many workers they had in the last campaign, which campaign activities they performed, how much money they contributed to which candidates, and to which candidates they gave the greatest and least effort. Constituency party leaders could rate the activism of each precinct chairperson. The author once surveyed party organizations by asking these questions of all party officers individually in an area, and then pooling their (often) different responses into a single rating. After each unit is pooled, they were ranked. No matter how it is done, the campaigner must get a general picture of the electioneering capability of the relevant party organizations.

In addition to the regular party organization, campaigners should take into account any possible assistance that may be forthcoming from auxillary party groups, such as the Young Republicans, the Democratic Women's Organization, or other groups. Their members may be more enthusiastic about the candidate than the regular party, and an effort should be made to determine this.

The campaigner might also wish to investigate the strength of the opposition party's organizations in various areas, bearing in mind that less can be done about this situation. There may be a situation, however, in which the candidate's party is weak in a particular, high priority area, and the opposition party is strong. If discovered early enough, an extra effort to build a candidate organization in this area can be made, or perhaps another medium, such as direct mail or telephoning from headquarters can be substituted. What the opposition is doing should be a constant reminder to the candidate that the campaign amounts to more than the candidate's effort—another candidate, and perhaps another party, is also doing something.

CONSULTATION
WITH OTHER CANDIDATES

Our system of overlapping constituencies and periodic elections means it is likely that there will be other candidates with whom to consult, compare notes, and exchange campaign activities. The most logical candidates to consult with are, of course, those of the candidate's party running in other races, particularly in overlapping constituencies, or previous candidates from the same constituency, although there may be cases when other candidates are sought.

It might be very useful to seek out previous candidates from the constituency in order to benefit from their experience. Being former candidates often means they lost an election, but that does not render their advice useless. As in any other situation, the advice seeker must sift out the useful from the useless information. There are many questions one might ask. How did he approach his campaign? What factors did he emphasize? How was the campaign organized? How much money did he raise and spend? What were his sources of campaign contributions? From whom did he receive campaign assistance? From which organizations did he receive support? If the candidate had produced lists of supporters, both financial and otherwise, these might be available to the new candidate if the request is made diplomatically. Consultation with previous candidates may manifest certain bitter fellings, jealousy, or perhaps shame about previous actions, and prior candidates may be unwilling to cooperate. However, this type of advice and assistance can give the campaigner a head start.

Many advantages result from cooperating with other simultaneous candidate efforts in the constituency, although there are also pitfalls. The American long-ballot method of electing many officials at the same time makes this possible. Consider a candidate for the lower house of a state legislature. He could be running with a state senate candidate, a gubernatorial candidate, a congressional candidate, a U.S. senatorial candidate, a presidential candidate, three or four state constitutional officers, a special district officer or two, and several judges. An aldermanic candidate in a city election is likely to run with a mayoral candidate, candidates for city clerk and city treasurer, and perhaps a special district board or two. Not all of these candidates will be willing, or able, to assist another candidate's effort; they are concerned with their own races, their resources are scarce, and in many ways candidates from the same party "compete" for the same workers, dollars, and active supporters. If these problems can be overlooked and overcome, there are benefits to cooperation. The campaigner could seek the same type of information from other candidates running that was sought from previous candidates in the constituency. Likewise, the campaigner's information about the constituency could be pooled with other candidates to bolster their knowledge and offer them something in return. Division of labor is helpful on many fronts. Often in Minnesota congressional level candidates in the Twin Cities and the party organizations cooperate to handle voter registration, voter identification, and turnout from centralized telephone banks, while the legislative candidates and their volunteers have handled literature distribution and other door-to-door activities. In recent years, candidates for governor and U.S. senator have joined in these efforts. Minnesota Republican candidates at least pool their media buying to obtain the most advantageous rates. In other cases, candidates have had joint fundraisers and advertising. Candidates might also pool their lists of supporters, contributors, or the lists of raw materials we have referred to in this chapter. Sometimes factional differences among workers will prevent cooperation, or sometimes a candidate will not want to associate with the "head" of the ticket, such as the presidential candidate, if it appears he is going down the drain. This happened in the McGovern race in 1972. These cooperative efforts are not always easy to achieve. The American candidate-centered campaign almost dictates that it is every candidate for himself, but there can be advantages to such pooling of resources and information, and they should be explored in the planning stages of the campaign.

EXPLORING THE CONSTITUENCY

It is very often useful to have a general picture of the nature of the constituency from those who are outside of party and campaign politics. The electoral system naturally intersects other facets of political life, as well as the economic and social life of the constituency, and it is useful to tap these dimensions in some way. The campaigner will not have the resources to conduct a full-scale community survey, so he or she will have to proceed informally, bearing in mind that the investigation is a very informal one.

One way to proceed with such an inquiry is to discuss the nature of the constituency, its social, economic, and political problems with knowledgeable people in the community. Some people to talk with are the leaders of the three types of groups—political, semi-political and nonpolitical. In any case, it is important to touch as many bases as possible by going beyond politics to those who are in the economic and social spheres of the community. It is also advantageous to reach beyond the actual leaders by discussing community problems with attentive publics. If the candidate undertakes these efforts, he or she can also use these discussion sessions as an initial effort to sound out the likely support of these people and the groups they may represent. Thus, campaign planning and coalition building are combined.

Many new candidates and experienced candidates with larger or new portions of their constituencies follow this practice as the first formal step of their campaign. Two examples will illustrate the point. A new Congressional candidate, who is a politically active attorney in one of the nine counties of an Illinois district, made, as one of his first campaign efforts, a tour of the other eight counties to find out more about them and to test possible sources of support. He has lived most of his life in his home county and knows it well, through his law practice, his political, and associational life. In the other eight counties, he must now somehow create, in a few days, impressions similar to those he has spent a lifetime developing at home. In this particular case the candidate started with friendly attorneys in the other communities, and sought from them the names of other important persons with whom to talk. While talking to the persons named by the lawyers, the candidate sought out other names and later talked to them. Such snowballing techniques are frequently used to study communities.[10] In another case, a two-term state legislator, who is a smalltown hardware dealer and former county board chairman found a large portion of another county added to his district through reapportionment. He began to familiarize himself with his new territory long before the formal campaign started. Initially, he discussed the new territory with old friends (in the new county) from the County Board Association and fellow hardware dealers. He began to discuss legislative matters affecting that county with township officials, school board members, conservation district officers, and other lay people in the area. Since these people somewhat overlap in membership with area interest groups, he then found himself being asked to speak before Parent-Teacher Associations, the Farmers Union, the Chamber of Commerce, Izaak Walton, and other groups. After making a few acquaintances, he begins to understand the new constituency and can ask the right questions of the right people in the new territory, while getting a head start on campaigning. Of course, nonincumbents can follow similar procedures in unfamiliar territories.

If the candidate is a long standing member of the community, and the community and the constituency substantially overlap, he may have gathered all of this information over a period of time. But he may still wish to make such an early "tour," for however knowledgeable and well-known he may be, he has never faced political activists and attentive publics as a candidate before (unless they were sounded out before the candidate decided to run), and their reactions to the individual in the role of candidate should be explored.

This type of information about the nature of the constituency is difficult to gather in a precise fashion, and it naturally has a lesser degree of reliability than election statistics or Census data. There is no way to avoid using this type of "soft," judgmental, or unsystematically gathered information. A general picture of the constituency is needed so that there is some understanding of what campaigning in that particular territory entails; it adds an important qualitative dimension to premises about the constituency and campaign planning.

UNIT DATA BOOK

After all of the foregoing information has been compiled for purposes of campaign planning, important aspects of these data can be compiled into a *unit data book*, which has the potential of being an important campaign document. We will cite the case of a statewide campaign county data book as an example, although such a book could be compiled for any subunit of a constituency. Basically, the book organizes the information gathered on a county-by-county basis; some of which has been gathered that way, the rest of which should be broken down by county. Large metropolitan counties should be further broken down into appropriate units. In Illinois, Chicago wards and suburban townships seem to be the equivalent political subunits to downstate counties. The constituion of the Minnesota Democratic party breaks metropolitan party organizations into state senatorial districts. In California, the meaningful metropolitan unit for both parties appears to be the state assembly district. A suggested table of contents for each county unit will illustrate its nature.

1. Name of county: congressional and legislative districts, historical paragraph, population of county, county seat.
2. Chairman and members of county board and their political affiliations.
3. Name of city, population of city, mayor of city and key councilmen of cities in the county.
4. Names, addresses and phone numbers (business and home) of party officers, including precinct chairpeople.
5. Names, addresses and phone numbers (business and home) of the (statewide) candidates' chairpersons in the county.
6. Names, addresses and phone numbers (business and home) and duties of other persons with campaign responsibilities.
7. Composition of the state legislative delegation, addresses and phone numbers, and candidates for these offices.
8. Radio stations in the county and those outside with 50 percent or more coverage in the county.
9. Television stations in the county and those outside with ARB (Audience Research Bureau, size of station audience) of 50 percent in that county.
10. Daily and weekly newspapers, including metropolitan and Sunday papers outside of the county which have substantial circulation in the county. Note: media lists should include circulation figures, audience size, publishers, station owners, political editors, news directors, addresses and telephone numbers.
11. General statistics (population trends, voting trends, election indicies, vote ranking, swing rates, vote proportions).
12. Major plants (size of work force, shift times, number on each shift).
13. Names and offices of important organizations (approximate size and location of officers).
14. Location and date of county fairs or other civic celebrations.
15. Airports (length of runways, nature of surface, when lighted, radio facilities, fuel available, mechanical services, nearest all-weather field).[11]

The unit data book will have many uses throughout the campaign. In the planning stage, it will become part of the strategist's guide to setting priorities and becoming familiar with key persons throughout the state. As the campaign organization in each county unit is filled in, it becomes the basic directory for the inside or non-public campaign. It serves as a valuable reference book for any publicity efforts with a local cast or color; such as news releases or specialized direct mail efforts. When the candidate or important campaigners from outside the area make appearances in a county, they should be briefed from the materials in the county unit data book. Compiling this information in advance gives the campaigner ready access to information at a later time in the campaign when time is more precious.

Notes to Chapter 4

1. For an estimation of these costs see, Robert Agranoff, *The New Style in Election Campaigns* (Boston: Holbrook Press, 1972), p. 30.

2. For a more detailed discussion see, Charles H. Backstrom and Robert Agranoff, "Aggregate Election Data in the Campaign: Limitations, Pitfalls and Uses," in *The New Style in Election Campaigns,* p. 168.

3. See for example, Eshref Shevky and Wendell Bell, *Social Area Analysis* (Stanford, California: Stanford Univ. Press, 1955); Marvin S. Sussman, ed., *Community Structure and Analysis* (New York: Thomas Y. Crowell, 1959).

4. W.S. Robinson, "Ecological Correlations and the Behavior of Individuals," *American Sociological Review* 15 (1950); Herbert Menzel, "Comment on Robinson's 'Ecological Correlations and the Behavior of Individuals,' " *American Sociological Review* 15 (1950); Austin Ranney, "The Utility and Limitations of Aggregate Data in the Study of Electoral Behavior," *Essays on the Behavioral Study of Politics* Austin Ranney, ed., (Urbana: University of Illinois Press, 1962); W. Phillips Shively, "Ecological Inference: The Use of Aggregate Data to Study Individuals," *American Political Science Review* 63 (1969).

5. Backstrom and Agranoff, "Aggregate Election Data in the Campaign," *The New Style in Election Campaigns,* p. 165.

6. Ibid., pp. 173-75.

7. If the state does not require central collection of data then the data must be gathered in individual county or city collection places.

8. Penn Kimball, *The Disconnected* (New York: Columbia Univ. Press, 1972), pp. 210-20.

9. Among the party rating schemes are, William J. Crotty, "The Party Organization and It's Activities," *Approaches to the Study of Party Organization* William J. Crotty, ed., (Boston: Allyn and Bacon, 1968); Samual J. Eldersveld, *Political Parties: A Behavioral Analysis* (Chicago: Rand McNally, 1964), Ch. 13; Frank J. Sorauf, *Party and Representation* (New York: Atherton, 1963), Ch. 3, pp. 164-67.

10. See for example, Floyd Hunter, *Community Power Structure* (Garden City, N.Y.: Doubleday, 1963); James B. Kessler, "Running for State Political Office," *Practical Politics in the United States,* Cornelius P. Cotter ed., (Boston: Allyn and Bacon, 1969), pp. 122-34.

11. I am grateful to Michael A. Berman, former Administrative Assistant to Senator Walter Mondale, for calling the county data books to my attention.

For Further Reading and Research

Barone, Michael; Ujifusa, Grant; and Matthews, Douglas. *The Almanac of American Politics*. 2d. ed. Boston: Gambit, 1973. Profiles of U.S. Senators and Representatives, their records, states and districts.

Congressional Quarterly Almanac. Washington: Congressional Quarterly, Inc. Annual survey of national government and politics.

Congressional Quarterly. *Guide to U.S. Elections, 1789-1974*. Washington: Congressional Quarterly, Inc., 1976. Reference work on voting and demographic data, redistricting, electoral college, party convention ballots and platforms.

Congressional Quarterly. *Washington Information Directory*. Washington: Congressional Quarterly, Inc., 1975. Information on federal agencies, national associations, embassies, including who and where to call for various types of information. Annual series planned.

Congressional Quarterly Weekly Report. Washington: Congressional Quarterly, Inc. Summary of the week's major events in national politics and government, with some state political coverage.

Congressional Record. Daily, verbatim proceedings of each house of Congress. Bound edition is indexed by author, subject, and bills; and resolutions and bills are traced.

Congressional Reports, Hearings and Documents. Periodic reports on pending legislation.

Council on State Governments, *Book of the States*. Lexington, Kentucky: Council of State Governments. Annual comparisons and rankings of the states.

Editorial Research Reports. Washington: Congressional Quarterly, Inc. In-depth reports, with background information and proposed solutions, on various public affairs subjects, issued four times a month.

International City Managers Association. *The Municipal Year Book*. Washington, D.C.: ICMA. Resume of city level activities and statistics, published annually.

———— . *The Municipal Management Series*. Washington, D.C.: ICMA. Periodic publications on principles and techniques of administering cities.

Merritt, Richard L. and Pyszka, Gloria J. *The Student Political Scientist's Handbook*. Cambridge, Mass.: Schenkman, 1969.

National Journal Reports. Washington: Center for Political Research. Weekly reports on national government and politics, with some state political coverage.

Public Affairs Information Service Bulletin. New York: PAIS, Inc. Published weekly and cumulatively, containing listings of books, scholarly periodicals, pamphlets, and government reports on social, economic, and public affairs.

Peterson, Svend. *A Statistical History of American Presidential Elections.* New York: Fredrick Ungar, 1963.

Reader's Guide to Periodical Literature. New York: H.W. Wilson. An index to general and nontechnical articles.

Riker, William H. *The Study of Local Politics.* New York: Random House, 1959.

Scammon, Richard, ed. *America Votes.* Multi-volume work covering data on major office candidates since 1952.

Social Sciences and Humanities Index. New York: H.W. Wilson. Published quarterly, listing scholarly journal articles.

United States Code. Consolidation and codification of all U.S. laws in force.

United States, Department of Commerce, Bureau of the Census. *Congressional District Data Book.* Washington: U.S. Government Printing Office. Periodic.

———— . *Current Population Survey.* Large sampling to provide data between decennial census. Periodic.

———— . *County and City Data Book.* Periodic.

———— . *Directory of Federal Statistics for Local Areas.* Periodic.

———— . *Directory of Non-Federal Statistics for States and Local Areas.* Periodic.

———— . *Characteristics of the Population.* A periodic series, containing many specialized topics, including housing, income and employment, and voting and registration in elections.

United States, Library of Congress. *Monthly Checklist of State Publications.* Lists state publications deposited at the Library of Congress.

United States Statutes at Large. Includes statutes enacted during the calendar year of publication.

U.S., Superintendent of Documents. *Monthly Catalog of United States Government Publications.* Washington: Government Printing Office. A listing of documents issued by all three branches of the federal government plus information on access to them.

Strategic Assessment II — Modes of Analysis

This chapter deals with some of the methods by which the campaigner can transform the selected raw materials (discussed in Chapter 4) into analysis, which, in turn, can be used to plan campaign strategies. The process necessarily requires a combination of hard and soft information. The assessment techniques covered in this chapter include: social and economic profiles of the constituency; support assessments of political activists, party organizations and groups; voting habits research and polls; candidate assessment; opponent assessment; issues analysis; and comprehensive information systems. These techniques and systems are the most commonly used methods of understanding campaign situations. They are designed to assist the campaigner gather accurate campaign intelligence rather than mere impressions. Campaign research is ordinarily performed at the early, prestrategy formulation stages of the campaign.

SOCIAL PROFILES OF THE CONSTITUENCY

One of the important early steps in understanding constituencies is to combine the historical, census, business and economic, published study information and organizational listings into a social and economic profile of the constituency. This will give the campaigners a basic idea of the type of constituency and people they are dealing with, as well as pointing out many important campaign approaches. Gathering the relevant data into a profile will undoubtedly confirm some of the campaigners' hunches, challenge some preconceived notions, and yield new information that may be valuable for campaign planning. In large constituencies, it is useful to perform a similar analysis for various subunits of the constituency.

One method of building a profile is to combine various sources of hard data into a demographic profile of a district. The Republican State Central Committee of Washington has expended considerable effort and energy into building data profiles. Figure 5.1 is a portion of a demographic profile from a Spokane area district. By the mid-1970s the Washington Republicans had built 1970 Census data into their districting system so that they were able to profile districts with the following district-level median information: total population, racial composition, age distribution, years of school completed, place of birth, year moved to residence, source of income, occupation, family income, proportion below the poverty level, housing values, and monthly rentals. The same information can be broken down on a precinct-by-precinct basis.[1] Obviously, such data makes possible meaningful conclusions about key income, occupational, housing, educational, transportation and other patterns which in turn can be translated into social and economic premises, useful for planning a campaign strategy.

It also is useful to combine hard and soft data into socioeconomic profiles of the community. Here the researcher supplements the hard information with whatever relevant information is necessary to understand the constituency. Among the factors that might be included are: predominant religious or ethnic groupings, important area traditions, key community needs, and notable social patterns. The following case of a city ward in a medium size, pre-energy crisis mining town illustrates the hard and soft approach:

> Most of the residents of Ward 99 are moderate income workers, primarily coal miners. The median family income is $8916 and 760.98 persons per thousand are laborers, operatives and craftsmen. Three out of four families own the dwellings they live in, and the tax assessor's office report indicates the average market value of homes in this area at $19,291, a relatively modest level. The population is relatively stable, only one in ten has moved in the last year, one in thirty has moved from another county. Eight out of ten residents were born in this city. The ancestry of most of these people is eastern European. Although religious data is impossible to obtain, two Roman Catholic, one Serbian Orthodox and one Greek Orthodox church within the precinct strongly indicate the religious make-up. Reports from informed people in the area indicate that there is a heavy union membership in the neighborhood, that important social functions include church and union picnics, and Sunday lamb barbecues in the public parks. Also, while the homes are well kept the streets, curbs and gutters are deteriorating. The most severe local problem is the sharp rise in real estate taxes due to the cutback in mining operations, a net decrease in miners, stagnation in industrial growth and housing growth and, therefore, a greater tax burden on the remaining citizens.

This very brief social and economic profile of a single ward offers many cues to the aldermanic candidate as to how to campaign, where to campaign, and what appeals to stress. It will not be too surprising if a candidate from

Figure 5.1   Basic Demographic Profile of a Legislative District (partial)

	LEGISLATIVE DISTRICT No. 5-B	

Total Population   18,266

Race:	99.5% White	.5% Non-White
Origin:	82.8% Native	Foreign
		17.2% Foreign Stock

Net Gain or Loss of Population by Migration _____*

Top Five Nationalities:

1. Canada	4.4%	4. Sweden	1.5%
2. United Kingdom	3.8%	5. Norway	1.4%
3. Germany	2.4%		

Gender:
49.9% Male   50.1% Female

Age - 1960:
54.2% 21 and Over   4.2% 65 and Over   24.9% Median Age (Yrs.)

Age - 1964:
_____% 0 - 20   _____% 21-64   _____% 65 and Over

Number of Families   4,734

Family Income -
Median Income $6,634

0 -$3,000	7.6%
$3,000-$9,999	75.1%
$10,000-Over	17.3%

Employment:
Total Civilian Labor Force   6,896
       69% Male   31% Female
                       White Collar____%

Total Employed (Five major businesses by number employed):

1. Wholesale & Retail Trade	24.8%
2. Manufacturing	14.3%
3. Public Administration	7.6%
4. Construction	6.6%
5. Educational Services	4.5%

Location of Employment:

Remainder of Spokane Co.	18.1%	City of Spokane 76.8%
County	_____	
Other	_____	

Means of Transportation to Work:
       Car   83.7%   Bus   7.4%

Housing:

Owner Occupied:	86.4%		
White	99.7%	Non-White	.3%
Renter Occupied:	13.6%		
White	99.3%	Non-White	.7%

Residential Stability:
       _____% in residence in 19__ .

Education (25 years and older):
       Median 12.4 years
       High School completed   66.0%
       College completed   9.2%

*Blanks represent data compiled in other districts but not in District 5-B.

Source: Vote History and Demographic Analysis, Research Division, Republican National Committee, 1969, pp. 60-61.

this ward: seeks union support; discusses methods of property tax relief; promises to repair streets, curbs, and gutters; shakes hands at picnics and barbecures; and, if his background is like the average ward citizen, stresses these qualities in his campaign literature.

The social profile is an important step in translating social and economic familiarity with the constituency into political campaign considerations, for it requires the campaigner to assess the political implications of a social survey of the constituency.

MEASUREMENT OF POLITICAL
SUPPORT: Five Levels of Campaign Assistance

At some early point campaigners often tabulate the results of various support-seeking tours throughout the constituency, evaluations of party support, and preliminary discussions with group leaders into some weighted notions about how useful the contributions of these elements are likely to be. By the strategic planning phase, the campaign planner must have a fairly precise idea of what kinds of campaign activity the party organization is likely to engage in, and what it is likely not to do. The same is true for community leaders and interest groups in the community—some prove to be very helpful, whereas others ignore the candidacy. The campaigner must not only know whom to count on, but must know to what degree. Thus, a serious effort must be made at evaluating the degrees of political support from various forces, so that it can be blended into strategic thinking.

At least five different kinds of support that party organizations, groups and political leaders can offer in a campaign are noteworthy. First is active electioneering for the candidate either by many individuals or as a part of an official group effort. Some interest groups such as labor unions, farm groups, business associations, and professional associations engage in activities such as voter registration, voter turnout, and direct campaigning in various areas. Indeed, in some areas of the country, organized labor's campaign precinct activity has been known to overshadow that of either party.[2]

Second, a leader, party, or group can give a financial contribution to the candidate, but do little else. Many party organizations feel they have done their share after they send $250 to the Congressional candidate and $100 to legislative candidates, although many do not even do this. Unions and corporations are prohibited by statute from contributing to Federal offices, but they circumvent this by contributing to voter registration activities, or with contributions from voluntarily solicited funds, such as the AFL-CIO's Committee on Political Education (COPE). Moreover, in most states they are not prohibited from contributing to state and local candidates. On occasion, groups will assist candidates in large constituencies by giving employees temporary leaves of absence with pay to work in a campaign. Other groups, by tradition, shy away from even indirect financial contributions to candidates. The campaigner should investigate past contributory practices and traditions in the constituency and, of course, current laws.

Third, the group or party may formally endorse the candidate. Obviously, electioneering on behalf of and officially appropriating money connotes endorsement, but sometimes official sanction will be the extent of the organization's effort. A study of city council elections revealed that endorsements and paid advertisements in newspapers were the most prevalent form of group support.[3] Many state educational associations are beginning to endorse candidates for governor and legislature, but few have begun to work for them. In some situations it may be necessary for candidates to seek party endorsement. Two such cases are partisan endorsement of candidates running on a nonpartisan ballot (primarily in local elections) and preprimary endorsements.

A fourth and less official type of support is the willingness of party and group leaders to identify themselves publicly with a candidacy even though there is no organizational endorsement. In many local nonpartisan elections, party and group leaders subtly lend their support by offering their names for the campaign committee or the fund-raising committee letterhead, and they make appearances at official gatherings. In other elections, groups that traditionally shy away from being formally identified with campaign politics as organizations often make their sentiments known by their leaderships' overlapping participation in campaign committees or functions.[4] Campaigners can often persuade group leaders to make their identification known by allowing their names to be published in newspaper ads.

Another form of support, or more precisely non-support, is evident when an important person or group implicitly supports a candidacy by not opposing the candidate as was expected. On occasion, one candidate cannot seem to mobilize a certain group's support, but it appears that neither can the opponent. The leaders, by not acting for one candidate, do not effectively oppose the other. Many labor leaders and unions did not actively oppose McGovern by supporting Nixon in 1972, but neither did they work for the Democratic nominee as they ordinarily would. Some paid McGovern's candidacy lipservice only, and others did nothing at all. This type of campaign support by non-opposition occurs frequently.

The campaigner should keep these five types of support in mind while assessing party and political group leadership. Some of these commitments will, of course, come during the course of the campaign. Many organizations will want to know what the candidate's views are, or perhaps will want commitments on supporting actions before offering support. An analysis of the previous record, informal discussions, and preliminary assessments will, however, reveal some important early signals. It will give a picture of the relative importance of organizational support, where reliance can be placed, and where it cannot. Chapter 10 will investigate some of the techniques used in securing group support and campaign coalition building.

VOTING HABITS

The discussion of voting in Chapter 2 indicated that, while accounting for the social and economic forces behind voting is important, the political forces of parties, candidates, and issues are the primary motivators. The campaign planner thus needs some way to measure or approximate these political forces. Most campaigners use voting data because it is the most reliable and most readily available data concerning how people behaved in the past. The use of such data in campaigns is based on the assumption that voters within a given geographic area under investigation are likely to vote in the upcoming election in a somewhat similar fashion to preceding elections. Aggregate election figures are undoubtedly the most widely used sources of hard information—almost every campaigner at least peruses the results from the past election in the constituency. Such information can be indispensible in charting a path if the campaigner is aware of both its utility and limitations, and works within them. In this section a series of elementary aggregate-data calculations from a sample, four-precinct legislative district will be displayed with accompanying explanations. Obviously, most constituencies will contain a greater number of precincts, but the simplified district will make it easier for the beginner to follow.

Limitations

Since election figures constitute the sum of many individual actions, the campaign planner should beware of many misinterpretations, inferences, and pitfalls that may occur when using these data. In another place, Backstrom and Agranoff have discussed and illustrated these questions:

1. Aggregate election figures are "net" figures. Many different actions are aggregated when they are summed in a precinct, ward, or county. Thus, a ward may look dead even for two candidates but its precincts could have many one-sided totals.

2. Since it is more difficult to distinguish various areas from one another if they are large units, and since people who live together are more likely to be alike than those who live apart, it is preferable to use the smallest unit available for analysis, ordinarily the precinct.

3. One cannot make inferences about the behavior of individuals on the basis of correlations between the same variables based on groups of people as units; individuals do not necessarily exhibit both characteristics that show up together in the area they are in. Thus in a precinct that is 90 percent black, if the Republican candidate gets 10 percent of the vote we do not know if all whites are voting Republican or it is 10 percent of the black voters, or some combination of them.

4. If a high correlation is discovered between two variables, one can surmise but not necessarily *prove* that the association between them is related to a

particular factor. For example, when the correlation between Republican candidates for the U.S. Senate and Congress is very high, say .95, one would normally assume that it is their common partisanship, and that most voters cast their votes for the two because of their identification with the Republican party, but it could have been due to many different reasons, for example, position on the ballot, the ethnicity of the name, personal appeal, issue positions, or many other factors.

5. There are often changes in municipal boundaries, precinct boundaries, and constituencies which must be taken into account.

6. When measuring the same precinct over time, even with the same boundaries, one cannot be sure the same people are voting. Thus, if 67 percent of voters voted for a candidate in one election and only 55 percent in the next election, one cannot say that 12 percent changed their minds and voted against the candidate, because there is no proof that the same people were voting in both elections.[5]

These problems must be kept in mind when the campaign planner uses aggregate election data in order to avert overstepping the limitations of the information and thus reasoning fallaciously. Each requires an explanation more involved and complicated than space permits for inclusion here. The campaigner should consult reliable published sources or persons who are familiar with these problems.[6]

Registration

Registration figures are very difficult to deal with in advance of the campaign because they are constantly changing, owing to movement of voters, irregular voting, deaths, and registration of new voters during the campaign. This problem will become increasingly difficult, as the courts are beginning to strike down residency requirements of any length, which, in turn, has prompted legislatures to keep registration periods open longer and closer to election day. For many rural areas there is actually no preregistration, and the registration figures reported are actually the number of voters who show up on election day. Some areas even allow registration at the polls on election day. These factors make registration figures something other than fact. Nevertheless, the campaigner may want to investigate well the registration situation in the constituency before the campaign begins to determine if there are potential supporters who have not registered. This can be done by comparing the number of registered voters in a given area with the number of persons 18 years or older, as estimated by the census bureau. Then, the campaign planner may want to make a registration drive part of the strategy.[7] Depending on the size and nature of the constituency, the campaigner will find either extremely high or extremely low rates overall, or uneven areas of registration. However, the registration areas should be ranked by priority for the candidate under investigation—integrated with the other voting data. Registration plans that work from most likely to least likely areas of support for the candidate then can be made.

Party Support

A "base race" or indicator of party support should also be selected. Ordinarily, a low visibility office is used so that candidate and other factors associated with races for governor, senator and president are not involved. The easiest way to measure base partisanship is to calculate the two-party percentage for a given election for the base race office. On occasion, it may be useful to build an "index" of partisanship by combining two or more low visibility races, either from the same or from different elections. Since the number of votes cast down the ticket is different in each race, it is also useful to display the absolute vote for the office, which will give the planner an estimate of the minimum number of votes that can be expected in a precinct. Since it is generally agreed that for most races party is the single, most important factor in voting, one needs some indicator of it by geographic area. The base race will not reveal the proportions and numbers of party identifiers who are likely to vote for any partisan in an area, but often, it is the best estimate of party voting by area available.

Candidate Voting
and Ticket-Splitter (Swing) Voting

Since candidate voting has been on the rise over the years due to voters increasingly splitting their tickets, researchers have begun to measure the aggregate incidence of candidate voting. The aim here is to discover significant areas of deviation from normal party voting, ordinarily by comparing races or areas. Three measures are particularly useful, differences with high visibility races, comparisons with a representative race, and measures of split-ticket or swing voting.

Comparing the race under investigation and the base race with one or more of the higher visibility races is far more useful than for the sake of curious comparison. Since no two races are alike, the researcher should try to assess the similarities and differences between the high visibility contest under investigation and the race being planned. How much turnout difference will there be between a presidential election year (or any other election year) and the one under investigation? Will the turnout be differential by party? What is the differential in party-candidate voting likely to be due to the differences in the visibility of the races? Moreover, one must ask what vote total differentials between nonvoting in the race (falloff from turnout) under investigation and the high visibility race. These differences offer planning cues to the campaigner as to where one should concentrate certain activities.

An even more significant form of comparative analysis is designating a representative race, or a previous campaign which has as many situational

Table 5.1 Basic Aggregate Election Figures

1 DATA INPUT PRECINCT	2 RFG	3 VOTE	4.1 US SEN REP	4.2 DFL	5.1 USCON REP	5.2 DFL	6.1 GOV REP	6.2 DFL	7.1 M.SEN REP	7.2 DFL	8.1 M.REP REP1	8.2 DFL1
1CRYSTL 1	3503	2335	1102	1174	1370	832	1199	1117	1031	988	1353	699
2CRYSTL 2	3185	2288	1693	1125	1346	816	1194	1061	1026	1004	1315	751
A 3CRYSTL 3	3226	2119	819	1246	1034	958	883	1207	778	1105	1040	885
4CRYSTL 4	2947	1852	612	1190	830	892	666	1165	769	844	1107	551
5DIST TL	12861	8594	3626	4735	4580	3498	3942	4550	3604	3941	4815	2886
PRE REG		8594										

For ease of identification, each section of computer printout has been assigned a letter (A, B, C, etc.) and each column a number (1, 2, 4.1, 4.2, etc.). For example: A4.2 is the DFL vote for U.S. Senator; C4 is the DFL percentage of the two-party vote for governor.

A1 Precinct numbers for the legislative district; the name of the precinct; and the number of the precinct if it is within a city. Thus, there are four precincts in district 31A: Crystal 1, 2, 3, 4. The last number at the left (5 in this sample) is not actually a precinct, but merely indicates "district total."

A2 Number of registered voters in the precinct. If the precinct has no permanent registration, zeros appear in this column.

A3 Number of persons who actually voted.

A4 Precinct vote for U.S. Senate: 4.1 = vote for Robert Forsythe, the Republican candidate; 4.2 = vote for Walter Mondale, the DFL candidate.

A5 Precinct vote for U.S. Congress. In this example, 5.1 = vote for Clark MacGregor, Republican; and 5.2 = vote for Elva Walker, DFL.

A6 Precinct vote for Governor. 6.1 = vote for LeVander, Republican; 6.2 = vote for Rolvaag, DFL.

A7 Precinct vote for the State Senate. 7.1 = Republican vote (in this district, Welter); 7.2 = DFL vote (in this district, Parish).

A8 Precinct vote for the State House of Representatives. 8.1 = Republican vote (in this district, Forseth); 8.2 = DFL vote (in this district, Boyum).

Source: Minnesota Democratic-Farmer-Labor (Democratic) State Central Committee, "1966 Election Study: How to Interpret the Data." This report prepared by Robert Agranoff, Charles Backstrom, Henry Fisher and Betty Kane.

Table 5.2 Vote and Plurality Contributions

1	2	3	4	5	6	7	8	9	10	11	12	13
DISTRICT 311			PERCENT OF TOTAL VOTE					PLURALITY				
PRECINCT	REG	VOTE	USSEN	USCON	GOV	M.SEN	M.REP	USSEN	USCON	GOV	M.SEN	M.REP
1CRYSTL 1	27.24	27.17	24.79	23.79	24.55	25.07	24.22	72	-538	-82	-43	-654
2CRYSTL 2	24.76	26.62	23.76	23.33	23.32	25.48	26.02	32	-530	-133	-22	-564
3CRYSTL 3	25.08	24.66	26.31	27.39	26.53	28.04	30.67	427	-76	324	327	-155
4CRYSTL 4	22.91	21.55	25.13	25.50	25.60	21.42	19.09	578	62	499	75	-556
5DIST TL	100.00	100.00	100.00	100.00	100.00	100.00	100.00	1109	-1082	608	337	-1929
DFL PLURALITY								1109	62	823	402	0
REPUB PLURALITY								0	1144	215	65	1929

B2 Percentage of registered voters who live in each precinct of the district.

B3 Percentage of the total 1966 vote that was cast in each precinct of the district.

B4 Percentage of Mondale's total vote cast in each precinct of the district. In this example, 27.17 percent of the total 1966 vote was in Crystal 1 (B3) but Mondale received 24.79 percent of his vote in that precinct.

B5 Percentage of the DFL congressional candidate's vote cast in each precinct of the district.

B6 Percentage of Rolvaag's vote cast in each precinct of the district.

B7 Percentage of the state Senate candidate's vote cast in each precinct of the district.

B8 Percentage of the state House candidate's vote cast in each precinct of the district.

B9-B13 Plurality or loss which each of the DFL candidates received in each precinct of the district. For example, in Crystal 1, Mondale's plurality was 72 votes; Walker lost the precinct by 538 votes; and Boyum lost by 654. Three totals appear at the bottom of each of these columns. The first (Dist TL) line is the overall DFL candidate plurality. For example, the sum of Walker's plurality(B10), adding all plus and minus figures is: -1082 [(-538) + (-530) + (-76) + (62) = -1082]. The second total, labeled "DFL Plurality," represents only the DFL candidate's share of the plurality of only those precincts which he carried. Thus, in this district, Walker carried only one precinct, by 62 votes. If the DFL candidate carried no precincts (as in B13), the DFL plurality would be zero. The Republican plurality below is the total of all the precincts carried by the GOP candidate (recorded as minus figures). Thus, MacGregor's plurality in this case was 1144.

Source: Minnesota Democratic-Farmer-Labor (Democratic) State Central Committee, "1966 Election Study: How to Interpret the Data." This report

Table 5.3 Party Support Indicators and Comparisons

1	2	3	4	5	6	7	8	9	10	11	12	13	14	15	16	17
DIST 311	PERCENTAGE DFL OF TWO PARTY VOTE					DIFF. BETWEEN BOYUM AND M.REP					INDEX		INDEX COMPARISONS			
PRECINCT	USSEN	USCON	GOV	M.SEN	M.REP	USSEN	USCON	GOV	M.SEN	M.REP	INDEX	USSEN	USCON	GOV	M.SEN	M.REP
1CRYSTL1	51.6	37.8	48.2	48.9	34.1	-17.5	-3.7	-14.2	-14.9	0.0	45.9	5.7	-8.1	2.4	3.1	-11.8
2CRYSTL2	50.7	37.7	47.1	49.5	36.4	-14.4	-1.4	-10.7	-13.1	0.0	45.2	5.5	-7.4	1.9	4.3	-8.8
C 3CRYSTL3	60.3	48.1	57.8	58.7	46.0	-14.4	-2.1	-11.8	-12.7	0.0	55.4	4.9	-7.3	2.4	3.3	-9.4
4CRYSTL4	66.0	51.8	63.6	52.3	33.2	-32.8	-18.6	-30.4	-19.1	0.0	60.5	5.5	-8.7	3.1	-8.2	-27.3
5DIST TL	56.6	43.3	53.6	52.2	37.5	-19.2	-5.8	-16.1	-14.8	0.0	51.2	5.5	-7.9	2.4	1.1	-13.7

C1-
C6 Percentage of the two-party vote which each DFL candidate received in every precinct of the district. Thus, in Crystal 1 (C2), Mondale received 51.6 percent of the two-party vote and Boyum (C6) received 34.1 percent of the vote. In the bottom row are percentages for the entire district.

C7-
C11 Differences between the vote for the DFL house candidate and for each of the other candidates. For example, the figure -17.5 in C7 (Crystal 1) means that the House candidate ran 17.5 percent behind Mondale in that particular precinct. (This figure is arrived at by subtracting the data in C6 from C2. Zeros appear in C11 because the vote for the house candidate is being subtracted from itself.)

C12 DFL index for each precinct of the district. This index is a mean of only the partisan contests (U.S. Senate, Congress, Governor) in the precinct. In Crystal 1, the average of the three partisan percentages (51.6, 37.8, 48.2) = 45.9, and that figure respresents the DFL index of the precinct. The districtwide index appears at the bottom.

C13-
C17 Comparison between each of the five candidates and the DFL index. For example, Mondale (C13) ran 5.7 percent ahead of the index (51.6 - 45.9 = +5.7) while the House candidate (C17) ran 11.8 percent behind the index (45.9 - 34.1 = -11.8). The districtwide index comparisons appear at the bottom.

Source: Minnesota Democratic-Farmer-Labor (Democratic) State Central Committee, "1966 Election Study: How to Interpret the Data." This report prepared by Robert Agranoff, Charles Backstrom, Henry Fisher and Betty Kane.

Table 5.4   Falloff and Rates of Swing Voting

DIST 311	TOTAL RACE FALLOFF FROM TURNOUT						BOYUM FALLOFF FROM DFL VOTE FOR--			1966 GE VOTE FOR--		FALLOFF FROM REPUB VOTE FOR--				
1	2	3	4	5	6	7	8	9	10	11	12	13	14	15	16	17
PRECINCT	TURNOUT	USSEN	USCON	GOV	M.SEN	M.REP	USSEN	USCON	GOV	M.SEN	M.REP	USSEN	USCON	GOV	M.SEN	M.REP
1CRYSTL1	66.7	-2.5	-5.7	-.8	-13.5	-12.1	-40.5	-16.0	-37.4	-29.3	0.0	22.8	-1.2	12.8	31.2	0.0
2CRYSTL2	71.8	-3.1	-5.5	-1.4	-11.3	-9.7	-33.2	-8.0	-29.2	-25.2	0.0	20.3	-2.3	10.1	28.2	0.0
D 3CRYSTL3	65.7	-2.5	-6.0	-1.4	-11.1	-9.2	-29.0	-7.6	-26.7	-19.9	0.0	27.0	.6	17.8	33.7	0.0
4CRYSTL4	62.8	-2.7	-7.0	-1.1	-12.9	-10.5	-53.7	-38.2	-52.7	-34.7	0.0	80.9	33.4	66.2	44.0	0.0
5DIST TL	66.8	-2.7	-6.0	-1.2	-12.2	-10.4	-39.0	-17.5	-36.6	-26.8	0.0	32.8	5.1	22.1	33.6	0.0

D2   Percentage turnout of voters in each precinct. In Crystal 1, 66.7 percent of the registered voters turned out to vote. (In precincts with no permanent registration, D2 will contain zeros.)

D3-   Percentage of persons who went to the polls but failed to vote in certain races. In Crystal 1 (D3), 2.5 percent of the people who took ballots did not vote in the U.S. Senate race (regardless of party or candidate) and 13.5 percent did not vote for State Senate (D6).

*D8-   Falloff or swing vote for the DFL House candidate, as compared with each of the other DFL candidates. Thus, in Crystal 1 (D8), 40.5 percent of the people
D12   who voted for Mondale did not vote the the DFL House candidate. Although there are no plus figures in this sample district, there are many cases in which the House candidate received a higher vote than the other candidates. In such cases, a minus would not appear on the print. (D12 will always be zero because comparison is with the same vote.)

*D13-   Fall off for the Republican House candidate, as compared with each of the other GOP candidates. In Crystal 1 (D13) the GOP House candidate got 22.8 percent more people to vote for him than did the Republican U.S. Senate candidate. (D17 will always be zero because the comparison is with the same vote.)

*This is a measure of swing or split voting.

Source: Minnesota Democratic-Farmer-Labor (Democratic) State Central Committee, "1966 Election Study: How to Interpret the Data." This report prepared by Robert Agranoff, Charles Backstrom, Henry Fisher and Betty Kane.

Table 5.5 Rankings of Selected Indicators

DIST 311 RANKING OF PLURALITY

	1	2 BOYUM	3	4 1966 GE	5
	USSEN	USCON	GOV	M.SEN	M.REP
1	CRYSTL4 578.0	CRYSTL4 62.0	CRYSTL4 499.0	CRYSTL3 327.0	CRYSTL3 -155.0
G 2	CRYSTL3 427.0	CRYSTL3 -76.0	CRYSTL3 324.0	CRYSTL4 75.0	CRYSTL4 -556.0
3	CRYSTL1 72.0	CRYSTL2 -530.0	CRYSTL1 -82.0	CRYSTL2 -22.0	CRYSTL2 -564.0
4	CRYSTL2 32.0	CRYSTL1 -538.0	CRYSTL2 -133.0	CRYSTL1 -43.0	CRYSTL1 -654.0

G1- Rank-order of the precincts based on the plurality (see B9-B13) which each DFL candidate received in that precinct. In this
G5 district, the DFL State Senate candidate (G4) got his highest plurality in Crystal 3 (+327) and his lowest plurality in Crystal 1 (-43).

DIST 311 RANKING OF TWO-PARTY PERCENTAGE BOYUM

	1	2	3	4 1966 GE	5
	USSEN	USCON	GOV	M.SEN	M.REP
1	CRYSTL4 66.0	CRYSTL4 51.8	CRYSTL4 63.6	CRYSTL3 58.7	CRYSTL3 46.0
E 2	CRYSTL3 60.3	CRYSTL3 48.1	CRYSTL3 57.8	CRYSTL4 52.3	CRYSTL2 36.4
3	CRYSTL1 51.6	CRYSTL1 37.8	CRYSTL1 48.2	CRYSTL2 49.5	CRYSTL1 34.1
4	CRYSTL2 50.7	CRYSTL2 37.7	CRYSTL2 47.1	CRYSTL1 48.9	CRYSTL4 33.2

E1- Rank-order of the precincts based on the percentage of total two-party vote which each DFL candidate received (see C2-C6); rating
E5 is from highest to lowest. In this district, Mondale's best precinct was Crystl 4 (66.0) and his poorest was Crystal 2 (50.7).

DIST 311 RANKING OF PROPORTION OF VOTE BOYUM

	1	2	3	4 1966 GE	5
	USSEN	USCON	GOV	M.SEN	M.REP
1	CRYSTL3 26.3	CRYSTL3 27.4	CRYSTL3 26.5	CRYSTL3 28.0	CRYSTL3 30.7
F 2	CRYSTL4 25.1	CRYSTL4 25.5	CRYSTL4 25.6	CRYSTL2 25.5	CRYSTL2 26.0
3	CRYSTL1 24.8	CRYSTL1 23.8	CRYSTL1 24.5	CRYSTL1 25.1	CRYSTL1 24.2
4	CRYSTL2 23.8	CRYSTL2 23.3	CRYSTL2 23.3	CRYSTL4 21.4	CRYSTL4 19.1

F1- Rank-order of the precincts based on the percentage of his total vote (see B4-B8) which each DFL candidate received in that pre-
F5 cinct. For example, Rolvaag received the greatest proportion of his vote (26.5 percent) in Crystal 3 (F3) and the smallest proportion in Crystal 2 (23.2 percent).

Source: Minnesota Democratic-Farmer-Labor (Democratic) State Central Committee, "1966 Election Study: How to Interpret the Data." This report prepared by Robert Agranoff, Charles Backstrom, Henry Fisher and Betty Kane.

similarities to the race being planned as possible. The areas of the candidate's presumed strength can be tested against the areas of strength in the representative race which need not be for the same office, or even of the same party as the candidate. For example, a young, liberal, native son, city attorney in Illinois was running for county attorney. In the previous election, a young, liberal, native farmer who lived just outside of town and who had served on that town's school board had run for the state senate and narrowly lost the election but carried that county's portion of the senate district. The senate race should be an excellent indicator of potential areas of strength and weakness for the county attorney candidate. One consultant, in planning efforts for attracting Democratic votes in a Michigan Congressional race for a Republican candidate running against an incumbent in a heavily Democratic district, used the vote for the moderate Democrat in a primary contest between a moderate and a liberal. Of course the planner must keep in mind that no two races are exactly alike, and thus, the races will not be exactly comparable. Every election is somewhat unique; the candidates are different, they are making different appeals, the campaigns are different and the composition of the voters is different. Yet there is enough stability to voting, both party and candidate, to make useful comparisons between two races.

Campaigns that include partisan races may also want to develop a measure of swing or split-ticket voting, or extreme voter deviation from normal partisan voting. Split-ticket voting gives the campaigner an estimate of the areas which are best and worst prospects for candidate appeals. Those areas which display high rates of ticket-splitting reveal that significant numbers of voters are not locked into party voting.

Ticket-splitting can either be measured over time, that is, the examination of the rates of swing in precincts in a number of elections or the areas of high, moderate, and low swing in a single race can be examined. The computation of ticket-splitting is relatively simple. One means is to calculate the percentage difference between the base race and the representative race. Another means is the calculation of the percentage difference between the highest and lowest vote getters on a party ticket. In most cases two adjustments must be made to swing. Voter falloff must be accounted for; the number of votes needed in the race being planned might be higher and lower. Also, the variance in the number of votes cast per precinct or unit should be accounted for; some areas with lower rates of swing may be more significant than those with somewhat higher rates if they can contribute more absolute votes.[8] In some areas, records are kept on the number of straight and split ballots cast. This information is also helpful.

Rankings and Analysis

As the various races are selected as measures of party strength, swing, candidate equivalency, vote contribution, and others desired by the campaigner, they should be prepared in a form that can be readily calculated. If large numbers of precincts are involved, a computerized analysis might be in order. Simple rankings allow for demonstration of the relative position of each subunit of the constituency. As the computations in Tables 5.1 to 5.5 illustrate, most of the calculations necessary to plan a campaign are elementary mathematical procedures. A number of experienced data analysts have gone beyond the elemental computations and displays to more complex statistical analyses, such as simple and multiple correlations among vote percentages for different offices. Scattergram plots for two offices, which can reveal deviant cases that require further explanation, as well as the extent and areas of relationship between the races are used also.

This section is intended to be an overview of aggregate data in the campaign. Before actually undertaking a study, the planner should consult more extensive treatments of the subject and seek the help of knowledgeable resource people. The Backstrom and Agranoff work contains a case study of how aggregate election figures can be translated into a campaign strategy. If computer assistance is being considered, the planner should seek competent assistance. Simple programs do exist, or can be written to make these calculations. There are many questions, such as accessibility, time, cost, and format, which should be investigated in advance. Aggregate election data plans can be performed without a great deal of prior training, if the campaigner is willing to take the time to study the problem, work within the limitations, and to seek advice when necessary.

POLLS

Campaign polls have become increasingly popular in recent elections. Most estimates place the number of marketing and information firms undertaking candidate polls at somewhere over 200. Also, many polls are conducted by very small operators or *ad hoc* groups of researchers. Practically every large-scale campaign engages in some polling, and the practice of surveying voter attitudes for planning campaigns is beginning to permeate many small constituency campaigns. The advantage of polling over using only past voting figures is that it deals with the "here and now" of *individual* voters, that is, how specific types of voters are likely to behave in the coming election. For candidates running on modest budgets or without access to expertise, the greatest disadvantages of polling are high costs and the requirement of fairly sound technical knowledge.

The Uses of Campaign Polls

Campaign polls are based on those done for voting behavior and market research and are used to gather information for the planning of a campaign. Many assume that the most important function is to see how the candidate and his opponent "stack up," or the "horse race" contest between the two. Actually, this is a very minor aspect of campaign polling. While no candidate would ignore gathering such information while investing in a poll, conducting a poll only to determine how the election is likely to come out would be quite an expensive and involved undertaking. This would offer absolutely no planning information and campaign workers and the candidate would be either inflated or deflated about the results. More important to the campaign planner than who is ahead is information on what types of voters make up the likely vote total a candidate can get, and with what appeals. In other words, the candidate really wants to know how he or she can win on election day, not whether he or she would win "if the election were to be held today," as is usually asked. Why then is the "trial run" so often all the candidate will use out of an expensive poll? Because that is all potential financial supporters want to know before opening up their purses—whether the candidate has a chance, or is at least gaining on the opposition. However, a poll can provide unsurpassed opportunities for gaining useful strategic information.

Pollster Louis Harris, now retired from active candidate surveying, reports that candidates use polls to plan campaigns on the basis of three types of information. First, key group breakdowns indicate the political makeup of the constituency, including area differences, racial and religious patterns, nationality group differences, occupational patterns (unions, farmers) differences by size of place, and how the vote in prior years is now dividing. This vital group makeup enables the planner to figure out just where a majority can be put together, as well as possibly indicating where the candidate is not doing well for a member of his political party.

The second area of usefulness Harris refers to is tapping candidate images. Polls can give the campaign planner an indication of what the public thinks of both the candidate and the candidate's opponent as a public figure; how many are familiar with the names; what voters know of their records; and what are their favorable and unfavorable personal qualities. Accurate information, particularly when it is negative, is difficult to obtain. Moreover, candidates and political activists tend to inflate the extent of public knowledge of the candidates and their records, and polls can help bring them down to earth if the information is fed into the campaign-planning process.

The definition of key issues in the campaign is a third area of usefulness. Ordinarily, voters are allowed to express their own views on the problems of government, and they are asked to reply to specific questions. Issue positions are then analyzed by key groups, persons who are switching from their normal partisanship to the candidate, and by the undecided. As Harris maintains, the concept of switching is crucial. When the electorate is analyzed by the hard-core for each candidate, then the pollster can see which issues are firming up the solid base of a candidate, which are bringing voters over to him, and which are losing votes.[9]

In recent years polls are also coming to be used to tap media information levels and media habits of various voter types. Voters are handed a long list of media and asked as they make up their minds about voting which do they consider

Table 5.6 Voter Support Candidates by Selected Groups

Question: Now thinking in terms of the general election in November, who would you vote for in a race for governor between John Jones, the Republican and Sam Smith, the Democrat? Or, is it too early to say?

Group	Jones	Smith	Undecided
Total	34.9	38.2	24.6
Republicans	74.5	13.5	8.7
Democrats	13.8	58.6	23.4
Metropolis/City	23.2	42.9	28.3
Metropolis/Suburb	47.6	24.0	26.4
Rest of State	33.4	44.6	18.9
18–20 years old	36.4	21.2	36.4
21–24	20.6	54.4	23.5
25–34	35.4	34.8	25.5
35–44	29.5	41.7	28.8
45–59	31.7	42.6	22.8
60–64	32.4	37.8	21.6
65 and over	49.2	29.2	16.2
Professional-Technical	41.1	34.8	20.5
Manager-Proprietor	41.6	32.6	24.7
Clerical	30.3	33.3	33.3
Skilled-Foremen	28.7	39.5	29.3
Unskilled	20.8	46.9	27.7
Service Worker	31.2	39.0	29.9
Farmer	47.8	36.7	12.2

Source: Private campaign poll taken in 1972. The names have been changed but the data is actual. Jones was governor at the time of the poll.

to be the most important sources of information (see Chapter 10). This information is then crosstabulated with the other information in the poll, particularly candidate preference, decided-undecided, straight party voter, or ticketsplitter.[10] One consultant had polls taken to match the political and television viewing habits of constituents. The data indicated that persons who split their tickets tend to be more regular watchers of television—particularly talk shows—than straight ticket voters. The same consultant also determined what programs these voters tend to watch most often and bought time accordingly.[11]

While each of these tabulations is valuable in itself, mere summations of results do not by any means exhaust the power of a poll. What the planner really needs to know is more specific information about which kinds of people hold which views. Or, combinations of data, such as what kind of image is held by the people bothered by which issues? This is done by crosstabulating, that is,

Table 5.7   Candidate Identification and Candidate Image

1. *Identification*

   Question: "I would like to read you a few names. Would you please tell me if you have heard of the person before and, if you can, his present position?

Name	Not Heard of Him	Heard of Him But Not Occupation	Know Occupation
Robert Dugan (Mayor of Metropolis)	2.2	4.7	92.7
Carter Peterson (U.S. Senator)	1.4	16.6	81.7
John Jones (Governor)	1.2	11.0	87.5
Sam Smith (holds state constitutional office)	15.9	47.2	36.4
Adolph Samuelson (U.S. Senator)	3.6	32.6	63.5
David Weeks (Other democratic contender)	67.7	23.1	8.7

2. *Image*

   Questions: a) "What do you feel the present Governor (John Jones) has done particularly well? (PROBE)   b) what do you feel he has done poorly? (PROBE) . . . c) What—if anything—do you particularly like about John Jones?

Done Well		Done Poorly		Particularly Like	
Nothing	36.5	Everything	11.1	Nothing	31.0
Taxes/Fiscal Policy	11.5	Taxes/Fiscal Policy	32.9	His Policies	6.9
Transportation/ Highways	14.3	Education	8.2	Good Republican	0.4
Effective Executive/Good Politician	11.7	Not interested in Poor/ Elderly	5.6	Does Good Job	13.3
Law Enforcement/Keep Order	4.8	Too Political/ Corruption	9.3	Honest	16.4
Aid to Education/Parochial Schools	3.3	Pollution	1.3	Outspoken	7.5
Pollution	2.3	Aid to Metropolis City	3.6	For whole state	4.1
Welfare Crackdown	2.9	Housing	1.8	Doing best he can	9.0
Other	12.8	Other	6.2	Other	11.4

Source: See Table 5.6.

Table 5.8   Issue Identification

Question: First, what do you feel are the most pressing problems facing the state government in Capitol City? (If respondent answers more than one:) which do you feel is the single most important problem?

Issue	1st Issue Mentioned	2nd Issue Mentioned	3rd Issue* Mentioned	Single Most Important of those mentioned
Taxes	28.2	18.3	11.1	26.6
Education	15.8	15.6	16.7	16.7
Pollution/ environment	6.8	9.0	11.1	5.9
Transportation/ Highways	3.9	7.2	9.6	2.0
Crime/Unrest	6.8	10.8	12.1	8.5
Race	1.7	4.3	5.1	1.2
Housing	4.3	4.3	6.1	2.9
Welfare	11.5	11.7	11.1	11.2
Other	20.9	18.7	17.2	18.4

*602 of the 800 respondents did not mention third issue.

Source: See Table 5.6.

Table 5.9   Issue Positions by Groups

Question: "Children should not be bussed to schools outside the boundaries of their local schools" Agree Strongly _____ Agree _____ Disagree _____ Disagree Strongly _____

Subgroup	Agree Strongly	Agree	Disagree	Disagree Strongly
Republican	21.7	61.3	12.3	4.7
Democrat	21.5	42.4	33.7	2.3
Independent	17.2	50.0	25.0	7.8
Member Labor Union	20.9	47.9	27.4	3.7
Not Member Labor Union	19.7	52.2	22.5	5.6
Central City Residents	7.7	51.3	38.5	2.6
City Fringe	7.7	52.7	34.1	5.5
Suburban Ring	29.8	45.0	19.9	5.3
Exurban and Rural	20.9	56.0	19.8	3.3
Caucasian	21.7	51.0	23.2	4.1
Black	11.5	40.4	40.4	7.7

Source: Private Congressional Poll, taken by Decision Making Information, Inc., Santa Ana, Calif.

Table 5.10 Crosstabulation of What "Jones Has Done Poorly" Question
Intensity of Party Identification Question

	Refused Don't Know	Strong Repub.	Not so Strong Repub.	Independent Repub.	Independent	Independent Demo.	Not so Strong Demo.	Strong Demo.	Row Total
D.K., N.A., Nothing	2 / 1.0	30 / 14.4	38 / 18.3	15 / 7.2	24 / 11.5	14 / 6.7	42 / 20.2	43 / 20.7	208 / 39.0
Everything	1 / 2.7	5 / 13.5	2 / 5.4	2 / 5.4	2 / 5.4	4 / 10.8	10 / 27.0	11 / 29.7	37 / 6.9
Taxes, Fiscal Policy	3 / 2.7	8 / 7.2	11 / 9.9	11 / 9.9	13 / 11.7	10 / 9.0	30 / 27.0	25 / 22.5	111 / 20.8
Education	0 / 0.0	4 / 15.4	4 / 15.4	0 / 0.0	5 / 19.2	3 / 11.5	5 / 19.2	5 / 19.2	26 / 4.9
Not Interested in Poor, Old	0 / 0.0	1 / 6.3	3 / 18.8	0 / 0.0	1 / 6.3	1 / 6.3	3 / 18.8	7 / 43.8	16 / 3.0
Too Political, Corruption	0 / 0.0	4 / 12.9	7 / 22.6	1 / 3.2	7 / 22.6	3 / 9.7	6 / 19.4	3 / 9.7	31 / 5.8
Pollution	0 / 0.0	1 / 33.3	0 / 0.0	0 / 0.0	1 / 33.3	1 / 33.3	0 / 0.0	0 / 0.0	3 / 0.6
Aid to Metropolitan Area	0 / 0.0	0 / 0.0	3 / 25.0	0 / 0.0	5 / 41.7	3 / 25.0	0 / 0.0	3 / 25.0	12 / 2.2
Housing	0 / 0.0	0 / 0.0	0 / 0.0	0 / 0.0	2 / 40.0	0 / 0.0	1 / 20.0	2 / 40.0	5 / 0.9
Other	0 / 0.0	20 / 23.5	14 / 16.5	8 / 9.4	10 / 11.8	5 / 5.9	10 / 11.8	18 / 21.2	85 / 15.9
Column Total	6 / 1.1	73 / 13.7	80 / 15.0	37 / 6.9	70 / 13.1	44 / 8.2	1C7 / 20.0	117 / 21.9	534* / 100.0

*Based on estimated "likely" voters.

taking all the respondents of one position and breaking them down further. This is illustrated in Table 5.10.

The four areas of research obviously offer the campaigner very valuable information on individual voters. There is concrete planning information on a host of questions:

1. important issues to stress in the campaign, and to which groups.
2. likely vote switchers to the candidate.
3. how to campaign among various groups.
4. where geographically to place campaign emphasis.
5. how important party, candidate, and issue questions seem to be in the campaign.
6. candidate personality information, including what to stress in advertising.
7. important qualities of the office sought to stress.
8. how much candidate name familiarity needs to be pursued.
9. what is known and unknown about the candidate's record and therefore should be emphasized.
10. potential appeals to increase the number of switchers.
11. which voter types are undecided—their characteristics, their issue preferences.
12. the characteristics and issue preferences of ticketsplitters.
13. important sources of media-information for various voter types.
14. media habits of various voters.

The above fourteen items are not inclusive of all of the various types of information that can be used for campaign planning purposes. There are obviously many others. Indeed, each of these can lead to dozens of bits of information that can be used for planning purposes. Thus, the use of polls in campaigns goes far beyond the mere gathering of information on who is winning and who is losing.

The Cost and Services of Polling Firms

Despite their usefulness many candidates for office cannot poll because polls are an expensive item to buy, ranging from $10-30 per interview, with the number of interviews ordinarily ranging from 250-1,000, depending on the makeup of the constituency, the number of crosstabulations needed, and mostly on the error factor one is willing to tolerate. The size of the constituency is irrelevant in setting sample size. There are basically two types of errors. Sampling error is the mathematical difference between the estimate (based on the sample) and the parameter (the true population value). Generally, in campaign polls an error estimate of about 3 percent is tolerated, although in some cases pollsters have been known to reduce the size of their samples and accept a 4 or 5 percent error. The other type of error is called nonsampling error, which arises because of poor design of the interview schedules, interviewer error, poor coding, and analytical mistakes. Pollsters take several steps such as pretesting interviews, training interviewers, verifying interviews, and training coders to reduce this type of error. Candidates very often poll more than once in a campaign, which nearly doubles the price. The average congressional poll has about 400 respondents at $15 per interview, at a single poll cost of $6,000. A second poll would cost at least $4,000 unless it was taken as a telephone poll "tracking," using the same respondents as the first poll. Statewide candidate polls usually interview 600-1000 respondents two or three times during the campaign, making polling expenditures of $25-50,000 not unusual. The largest single cost item in polling is the labor charge for interviewing. But, the expense is also run up for supervision, sample design, questionnaire construction, coding of responses, data processing, report writing, and consultation.

Unless the candidate has access to proven expertise and experience in the field of marketing or survey research, polling services ordinarily must be purchased from polling or marketing research firms. Polling involves a combination of technical knowledge and experience, neither of which can be substituted by enthusiasm or economy. Sampling requires a knowledge of mathematical probabilities and tolerance of error. Questionnaire design requires a theoretical knowledge of voting and the psychology and mechanics of questioning. Supervision and interviewing requires prior training. Coding requires knowledgeable decision making and constant supervision. Data processing requires its own particular expertise. All of these facets are buttressed by the experience of previous surveying. There are literally hundreds of shortcuts, substitutes, and techniques that only the experienced can bring to bear on the campaign poll. This is not to say that a poll cannot be undertaken by an inexperienced person. There are some handbooks on polling such as Backstrom and Hursh's excellent *Survey Research*, written to guide beginners. But, the novice should still consult with and check each stage with one who is knowledgeable and experienced. Short of this type of access, if a poll is considered desirable, professional services should be purchased. There is enough precision required and the stakes of making a serious mistake can be costly.

If it is decided to use the services of a polling firm, campaign planners should take some elementary steps to investigate their reliability and methods. Polling firms range from large-scale national operations, conducting polls in many states, to small, even one-man operations that ordinarily operate within limited geographic areas.[12] There is a great deal of charlatanism or very deleterious shortcutting of methods for the dollar by some polling firms, large and small. The campaigner should ask prospective pollsters some very basic questions. The Democratic National Committe, relying on a widely circulated memo of Gerald Hursh, urges their candidates to get written proposals from at least three prospective pollsters. They suggest that the candidate look for the following:

Figure 5.2   Steps and Procedures in a Campaign Poll

The Elements of a Political Survey

```
┌──────────────────┐          ┌──────────────────────────┐
│    Research      │◄─────────│   Campaign Management     │
└──────────────────┘          └──────────────────────────┘
        │                                 │
        ▼                                 ▼
┌─────────────────────────────────────────────────────────┐
│                      Objectives                          │
└─────────────────────────────────────────────────────────┘
        │                                 │
        ▼                                 ▼
┌──────────────────┐          ┌──────────────────────────┐
│     Sample       │          │       Interview           │
└──────────────────┘          └──────────────────────────┘
        │                                 │
        ▼                                 ▼
            ┌──────────────────────┐
            │     Interviewer      │
            └──────────────────────┘
                       │
                       ▼
            ┌──────────────────────┐
            │     Respondent       │
            └──────────────────────┘
                       │
                       ▼
            ┌──────────────────────┐
            │        Coder         │
            └──────────────────────┘
                       │
                       ▼
            ┌──────────────────────┐
            │     Machine Data     │
            └──────────────────────┘
                       │
                       ▼
            ┌──────────────────────┐
            │      Computer        │
            └──────────────────────┘
        │                                 │
        ▼                                 ▼
┌──────────────────┐          ┌──────────────────────────┐
│   Tabulation     │          │  Statistical Analysis     │
└──────────────────┘          └──────────────────────────┘
        │                                 │
        ▼                                 ▼
            ┌──────────────────────┐
            │   Written Analysis   │
            └──────────────────────┘
                       │
                       ▼
┌─────────────────────────────────────────────────────────┐
│                      Evaluation                          │
└─────────────────────────────────────────────────────────┘
```

Source: Decision Making Information, Inc., Santa Ana, Ca.

The Overall Approach—The better pollsters usually develop a comprehensive plan of action rather than a one-shot affair. The poll is indicative only at the time it was taken; it is important to note the trends. This can be done only with a series of polls. Since there are many different approaches on this, it is wise to get a number of proposals.

The Sampling Methodology—Read this section of the proposal very carefully. If possible, get advice from a mathematician or statistician. Compare methodology carefully.

The Size of Sample—What are the reasons for selecting the number of respondents? What kind of groups will be analyzed? What size will that group be? Remember, cost and sample size are related. If you particularly like the approach of one firm but find the price too high, you might be able to cut back on the sample if you are willing to forego the analysis of certain subgroups.

The Type of Analysis—It is important to find out what you are going to get for your money. The best way to do this is to ask for an outdated report with the proposal. This is a reasonable request, and it helps you evaluate the quality of work.

The Data Runs—When the completed questionnaires are returned to the polling organization, they are coded and key-punched and the data are fed to the computer. The result: a printout with voluminous data that will be dissected by an analyst and from which a report will be prepared. But what happens to the printout? Usually it gathers dust in a back room.

A client with foresight will always ask for a copy of the printout. The pollster is then required to be certain that his data are clean and in good order. Next, if the pollster uses any special weighting formulas to make the sample more representative, he will be compelled to explain these variables clearly to the client. Most important, you are paying for the data and you are entitled to all the information. It can be extremely useful later in the campaign when you want to check something that was not included in the report. You should also think ahead to the next time around; it will be worthwhile to compare current data with past data.

The Costs—Candidates are prone to take the lowest bid of three proposals. This is often a grave mistake. Prices must be considered in context with what is being offered. Organizations of good reputation and wide experience are more expensive, and for a reason. They can draw upon a wealth of outside information to supplement the findings on a single poll. They have their fingers on the pulse of the nation, so to speak, and therefore view things in perspective rather than in isolation. They have a working familiarity with all advanced techniques.

The advantage of selecting a smaller, less-known organization is that you will pay less and receive more personalized service. Of course, it is often as much a learning process for the pollster as for the client—but if the candidate has a knowledgeable analyst on the staff, it can be a beneficial relationship for all concerned. . . .

Delivery Date and Presentation—One last and important thing is to be sure to get a hard delivery commitment which, if not met, will be costly to the pollster. Timing of polls is crucial to the client; their usefulness decreases over a period of time, and therefore the delivery should always be clearly specified.[13]

In addition, it is considered appropriate to ask pollsters for the names of past clients for purposes of securing references. These precautionary steps can give the campaigner a better picture of what he or she is getting and what he or she is paying for as well as avoiding problems or unnecessary expense.

In-House Polling Operations

There have been occasions when candidates have set up their own polling operations, usually with knowledgeable and experienced people at the helm. One method is to use volunteer but trained interviewers who will do nothing else in the campaign but door-to-door survey work. In 1968, the Democratic Party in Minnesota conducted polls for some of their legislative candidates by drawing a random sample from the voting lists of registered voters, after the registration period closed, and then used a team of campaign volunteers to conduct and code the interviews.[14] On some occasions, candidates have used student-organized surveys, who have conducted a candidate poll as a part of a class project. The student or students in charge generally participate in all phases of the survey— they draw the sample, construct the questionnaire in consultation with the campaign planners, recruit, train, and supervise the interviewers, recruit, train and supervise the coders, handle data processing and present a written report. Other candidates have simply turned over a polling operation to a willing candidate volunteer or set of volunteers. These persons range from the quite knowledgeable to those who are learning on the job.[15] Campaigners who decide to set up their own polling operations should take great pains to read as much information on the subject as possible, consult with a reliable person at each step, and above all, should attempt to make a clear assessment of exactly what they are getting for the price they are paying.

Mail or Telephone Polls

A frequently asked question in regard to surveying is whether or not the cost can be reduced by using mail questionnaires or telephoning? Mail surveys are by far the least expensive and least reliable—so unreliable that they are almost never used in campaign planning. The return rate of mail questionnaires is very low and is usually too unrepresentative to draw any conclusion from them. Even when a politically interested group is the target audience, the return rate rarely exceeds 50 percent. For a survey of all voters the return rate might be 15 to 20 percent.

Figure 5.3   A Basic Telephone Poll for a Legislative Candidate

Phone No.   Address   No Answer   Busy   Refused   Other

_____   _____   _____   _____   _____   _____

Hello, I am calling for the Mid-East Survey Organization. We are making a survey about the coming election. We have a few questions that will only take a few minutes and we are not selling anything. Your name will not be used and your answers will be kept confidential, O.K.?

1. Are you registered to vote? Yes _____ No _____ Don't know _____
   (IF THE PERSON IS TOO YOUNG OR IF THEY ARE NOT REGISTERED, TERMINATE THE INTERVIEW.)

2. As far as you are concerned, what are the most important problems for the governor and the state legislature to work on and do something about here in _(state)_ . _____

3. (IF TWO OR MORE PROBLEMS CITED) of these, which one would you say is the most important? _____

4. What do you feel the governor and state legislature should do for people like yourself? _____

5. One of the most important issues the governor and the legislature have to decide on next year is the question of state support for Metropolitan Regional Mass Transit. Are you in favor or against state support for establishing transportation systems in the metropolitan areas, utilizing existing public and private companies? (IN FAVOR) _____   (AGAINST) _____

6. How would you vote if the election were held tomorrow in these races? REVERSE THE ORDER—(DEM-REP)—FOR EVERY OTHER INTERVIEW. (CIRCLE CHOICE).

For U.S. Senator:	Carter Peterson, the Democrat or
	Adolph Samuelson, the Republican
For Governor:	John Jones, the Republican or
	David Weeks, the Democrat
For Congress:	Benjamin Blaska, the Democrat or
	Randolph Webster, the Republican
For the Legislature:	Tim Thorson, the Democrat or
	William Barrett, the Republican

7. Now, let's turn to a slightly different question. First what, if anything do you particularly *like* about Tim Thorson? _____

8. What, if anything, do you particularly *dislike* about Tim Thorson?

_____

9. What, if anything, do you particularly *like* about William Barrett?

_____

10. What, if anything, do you particularly *dislike* about William Barrett?

_____

11. During the last election campaign, from what sources did you become best acquainted with the candiates for the legislature—from newspaper or radio or television or magazines or talking to people or where?

Newspapers _____   Magazines _____

Radio _____   Talks with people _____

Television _____   Other _____

12. Finally, we would like to get some background information for our study. Sometimes people find it hard to vote in certain elections. . .because they can't get away from work or something like that. In your own case did you happen to vote in the last general (national) election, November 19—, or didn't you have a chance to vote? Yes _____ No _____

13. Can you tell me who you voted for in the race for Governor, John Jones, Republican, or Sam Smith, Democrat?

Jones _____   Smith _____   Other _____   Don't Remember _____

14. Generally speaking, in politics do you consider yourself to be a Republican, a Democrat, an Independent, or what?

Republican   *Democrat*   *Independent*   *Other*   *No Preference*

Would you say that you are   In general, do you consider yourself closer
a strong or not so strong   to the Republican or Democratic Party?
(Republican, Democrat)?

15. What type of work do you

does your husband   do _____?

does the head of household

16. What is highest grade of school or year of college you finished?

_____ (GRADE OF SCHOOL) _____(YEAR OF COLLEGE)

17. What is your present age?_____

18. In what city do you live? _____

Thank you very much!

Interviewer _____

Date of Interview _____

Telephone interviewing has become increasingly popular among pollsters and candidates who have commissioned their own polls. Their attractiveness is due to: 1) cost, the labor time can be reduced by one-half or less; 2) speed, as quick as 24 hours as opposed to four to six weeks? 3) a greater geographical dispersion of respondents in a sample; and 4) no personal security risks for interviewers on the street.

There are many disadvantages accompanying these very significant advantages. A telephone poll generally does not allow for the length, breadth, and depth of an interview that an in-the-field door-to-door survey allows. Most campaign planning polls require about 30 to 40 minutes of interviewing to obtain significant planning material; a telephone interview rarely exceeds ten minutes. Moreover, certain types of sensitive information is difficult to obtain. Race, which is usually recorded by observation, and income, which is reported by response to a display card are very sensitive issues. It is difficult to probe respondents on image or issue questions while speaking on the telephone. There is a tendency for more persons to call themselves independents, masking a true party affiliation on the telephone. Also, the rate of undecideds in the candidate-support ratings is almost always higher in telephone polls than they are in a field poll. Of course, any kind of questions that require a display such as scales, semantic differentials, or feeling thermometers are impossible to use on the telephone. There is also evidence that respondents tend to hide their true feelings, and give fewer negative responses than they do in the field. Some are reluctant to be negative when dealing with unseen strangers on the telephone.[16]

Sampling telephone numbers presents another set of problems. Telephone numbers or telephone books are generally used to draw numbers. If numbers are randomly drawn some will be business numbers and they must be bypassed. If books are used there is the problem of unlisted numbers; up to one-third of all telephones in some areas are unlisted. Then, there is the problem of households without telephones, estimated at 11 percent nationally, but as high as 33 1/3 percent in some areas. There is reason to believe that the absence of telephones or unlisted numbers is not random, but skewed toward certain populations and certain areas which can affect results.

Telephone polls are more frequently taken by public pollsters to get a quick reading of the public's response to a major event or issue which arises suddenly. Also, many candidates are beginning to engage in "tracking" their original sample in the field survey, that is, telephoning the same respondents to see if any changes have occurred, to see where the undecideds are going, to see if any significant switching is occurring and to test new issue positions. This can be done on the telephone since all the difficult to obtain demographic information has been retained. These *caveats* offered do not necessarily mean that telephoning should be bypassed. They are a good example of a cardinal rule of polling: every such shortcut reduces the cost *and* the quality and quantity of the results. Campaign planners should be apprised of what they are getting into by telephoning.

In sum, polling is a complex art and science which can yield very valuable information to the campaign planner if reasonable precautions are taken. Campaigners want to make sure they are not making decisions on faulty information. There are many steps along the way that can lead to faulty decisions. Consider the error factor of not accounting for unlisted telephone numbers built upon a foundation of a five percent error tolerance. Then if one adds in faulty questions or misinformation on party or candidate preferences the researcher is in serious trouble. There are many who would say polling is too difficult to be left up to the amateur or novice. This is not quite true, unless the careful steps of reading, understanding, and seeking advice are not taken.

INTEGRATED INFORMATION SYSTEMS

As campaign planners go beyond impressionistic campaign planning and actually undertake the gathering and analysis of many types of hard information, they often face a disorderly mountain of data. Somehow the yards of adding machine tape, computer ouptut, and sheets of figures do not jump out at the planners and tell them how to campaign or where. An important theme of this book is that neither the impressionistic nor the hard data alone best serve a well managed campaign, but, that it is the interface of one's experience and reasoned judgments with concrete information that best serve sound campaign management. Therefore, strategists have come to devise systems of information integration which combine political judgment and data, which basically establish priorities for subunits of the constituency. These system are then used for purposes of campaign planning, targeting subpopulations, organizing campaign work, identifying and making appeals, scheduling, fund raising, and for many other uses.

This concept will be illustrated by focusing on one of a number of integrated systems, the Precinct Index Priority System (PIPS) developed by the present Census Bureau Director Vincent Barabba, when he was a campaign consultant[17] PIPS is based on factors, considered significant by campaign planners, about which systematic information can be obtained. Thus, if a planner thinks that party registration or party support is important, and one can gain such information by precinct, that is included in a PIPS. Many factors can be used. Among the more common types are:

1. Social factors (e.g., number of school-age children, educational attainment, welfare recipients, condition of housing, etc.).
2. Economic factors (e.g., prevailing occupations, owner-occupied dwellings, women in the labor force).
3. Past voting behavior patterns.
4. Party preferences (e.g., party registration rates, party voting indices, summary of canvass information).

5. Survey information factors (e.g., how do people feel about the candidate, key issues, broken down by areas of the constituency).

6. Canvass information factors (candidate preferences, issues or any other items of interest that volunteers obtain).

7. Other items of information that the strategist may deem important (e.g., ethnic concentrations, rating of strength of party organizations).

After deciding upon and gathering the relevant data for each precinct, a further judgment, weighing each factor, must be made. PIPS does this simply by assigning each factor a weight on a scale of 1 to 6 based on the strategist's judgment. Thus, if it was deemed that party was the most important factor and occupation was only half as important, the former would be given a weight of 6 and the latter 3. The least important but relevant factors are given a 1. As each factor is recorded and scored (standard score) for a precinct, it is multiplied by the weight it is given.

PIPS is illustrated in Table 5.11, a plan for a Republican Congressional candidate running in a Democratic district. Table 5.12 explains the meaning of each heading used in this particular illustration. Precincts are listed in this example in PIPS order (rank order). Some strategists also like listings in precinct order for ready reference. The items listed here illustrate the wide range of items that can be used. Moreover, some types of information about which there is no available systematic data can be incorporated into the system by quantifying it, for example, the assessment of the candidate's party organization. Each precinct might be investigated and quantified into rankings, on a scale of 1 to 6, 1 to 100, or any scale can be assigned standard scores, and then weighted appropriately.

A priority system like PIPS can assist the campaigner in many ways. It is the basic system for "targeting" precincts. The highest scores become the high priority precincts for door-to-door campaign work, literature distribution, voter identification, neighbor-to-neighbor fund drives, scheduling of candidate door-knocking or other scheduling, areas of potential volunteers and other elements of strategy development. Also, if volunteers are scarce, they can be assigned on a priority basis. Barabba also explains how PIPS can be used to allocate scarce resources.

> Suppose a campaign strategist has decided that a special kind of letter should be mailed on a selective basis, depending on the needs, interests and importance of a precinct. Keeping in mind his total budget for the mailer, he simply lists: 1. Fixed printing costs for a minimum printing run, 2. Additional costs per thousand units, 3. Addressing and handling costs per thousand units, 4. Postage costs per thousand units. PIPS can now suggest the precincts to which the letter should be mailed, and at what costs, with a considerable saving of time and error.

> Further, suppose that a donor has just appeared with an extra $1000 which he will make available for this special mailing. But the strategist

Table 5.11   Precinct Index Priority System for "Center City"

CITY OR TWP	*PRE	GL	CT	REGOV P¹	REGOV SDS²	MODDEM P	MODDEM SDS	REPACN P	REPACN SDS	REMAY P	REMAY SDS	EDUCAT P	EDUCAT SDS	SCOUTS P	SCOUTS SDS	RECWEL P	RECWEL SDS	LOCIND P	LOCIND SDS	TRV	TVC	CUMTRV	CUMTVC	PIPS
CENTER CITY	82	H5	16	87	98	69	82	63	90	78	92	116	100	29	45	0	98	18	99	720.	610.	720.	610.	89
CENTER CITY	83	H6	37	88	99	83	99	65	94	79	92	226	76	44	70	0	98	33	76	544.	435.	1264.	1045.	89
CENTER CITY	80	H5	16	82	92	72	85	60	86	78	92	116	100	29	45	0	98	18	99	689.	547.	1953.	1592.	88
CENTER CITY	59	H5	38	77	86	70	82	53	77	75	88	199	82	45	72	1	96	30	81	436.	356.	2389.	1948.	83
SATURN TWP	9	G8	12	83	94	73	87	65	94	84	99	257	69	57	91	0	92	59	37	474.	453.	2863.	2401.	83
CENTER CITY	81	H5	16	76	84	59	69	50	72	69	80	116	100	29	45	0	98	18	99	923.	752.	3786.	3153.	81
CENTER CITY	58	H5	38	78	87	62	72	55	79	69	79	199	82	45	72	1	96	30	81	528.	464.	4314.	3617.	81
SATURN TWP	15	H8	12	82	91	75	89	63	92	75	87	257	69	57	91	0	92	59	37	386.	323.	4700.	3940.	81
CENTER CITY	84	H6	37	74	82	64	75	62	90	66	76	226	76	44	70	0	98	33	76	977.	783.	5677.	4723.	80
THOR CITY	2	A2	32	73	81	67	78	59	84	72	84	246	71	62	99	2	86	42	63	583.	448.	6260.	5171.	80
CENTER CITY	96	G7	41	73	87	69	81	55	75	74	86	298	49	49	78	0	95	40	66	903.	762.	7163.	5933.	79
CENTER CITY	56	H5	38	73	81	56	64	52	75	70	82	199	82	45	72	0	96	30	81	577.	481.	7740.	6414.	79
CENTER CITY	69	H6	37	72	80	64	74	53	76	70	81	226	76	44	70	0	98	33	76	727.	610.	8467.	7024.	78
SATURN TWP	8	G7	12	76	84	57	66	65	93	72	84	257	69	57	91	1	92	59	37	479.	441.	8946.	7465.	77
CENTER CITY	63	H6	35	80	90	63	74	61	89	80	94	273	65	23	36	1	92	47	55	945.	809.	9891.	8274.	77
THOR CITY	3	A2	32	69	76	62	72	56	81	67	78	246	71	62	99	2	86	42	63	745.	595.	10636.	8869.	77
TUONELA TWP	1	J2	6	76	85	68	80	58	84	72	83	271	66	50	80	1	93	60	35	556.	490.	11192.	9359.	76
VULCAN TWP	5	J5	15	71	79	75	89	58	84	73	84	292	61	31	49	5	64	25	88	722.	616.	11914.	9975.	76
ODIN CITY	4	J2	6	81	81	74	88	58	84	72	84	271	66	50	80	0	93	60	35	522.	409.	12436.	10384.	76
CENTER CITY	62	H6	22	70	78	58	66	50	72	66	76	224	76	38	60	0	98	28	84	712.	569.	13148.	10953.	76
CENTER CITY	55	J5	34	87	98	66	78	61	88	79	93	326	53	22	34	1	93	53	47	625.	520.	13773.	11473.	76
THOR CITY	4	B2	32	67	74	70	82	47	68	65	75	246	71	62	99	2	86	42	63	664.	524.	14437.	11997.	76
CENTER CITY	68	H6	37	68	75	63	74	46	66	64	73	226	76	44	70	0	98	33	76	652.	538.	15089.	12535.	75
CENTER CITY	57	H5	38	65	71	58	67	42	61	64	74	199	82	45	72	0	96	30	81	524.	425.	15613.	12960.	74
ODIN CITY	3	J2	6	69	76	69	82	55	80	72	84	271	66	50	80	1	93	60	35	724.	558.	16337.	13518.	74
CENTER CITY	70	H6	37	67	74	56	64	44	64	67	77	226	66	44	70	0	98	33	76	735.	611.	17072.	14129.	74
ODIN CITY	5	J2	6	70	77	65	76	57	82	70	81	271	66	50	80	1	93	60	35	544.	413.	17616.	14542.	73
SATURN TWP	10	G8	12	73	80	61	71	63	90	58	66	257	69	57	91	1	92	59	37	340.	307.	17956.	14849.	73
CENTER CITY	67	H6	37	64	70	59	68	41	59	66	75	226	76	44	70	0	98	33	76	675.	538.	18631.	15387.	73
PLUTO TWP	10	G5	8	81	90	79	95	69	99	62	71	377	42	39	62	1	93	64	29	435.	429.	19066.	15816.	73

Table 5.11   Precinct Index Priority System for "Center City" (Continued)

CITY OR TWP	*PRE	GL	CT	REGOV P¹	REGOV SDS²	MODDEM P	SDS	REPACN P	SDS	REMAY P	SDS	EDUCAT P	SDS	SCOUTS P	SDS	RECWEL P	SDS	LOCIND P	SDS	TRV	TVC	CUMTRV	CUMTVC	PIPS
SATURN TWP	12	G8	12	64	69	50	57	57	82	71	83	257	69	57	91	1	92	59	37	1400.	1158.	20466.	16974.	72
KRONUS TWP	5	F1	28	74	82	67	79	55	79	64	73	302	59	33	52	0	96	46	56	695.	557.	21161.	17531.	72
CENTER CITY	25	K6	10	67	73	71	84	43	62	68	78	291	61	43	68	1	92	48	54	598.	487.	21759.	18018.	71
CENTER CITY	48	H6	36	69	76	46	51	49	70	65	74	269	66	37	59	0	97	34	75	492.	416.	22251.	18434.	71
CENTER CITY	61	H6	22	64	70	60	70	42	61	56	63	224	76	38	60	0	98	28	84	565.	463.	22816.	18897.	71
ADONIS TWP	7	B2	33	67	73	32	33	54	78	72	84	212	79	27	42	0	99	37	70	582.	462.	23398.	19359.	71
THOR CITY	1	A2	32	57	61	64	75	43	62	65	74	246	71	62	99	2	86	42	63	524.	411.	23922.	19770.	71
ADONIS TWP	10	B1	31	67	74	46	50	61	88	67	78	287	62	41	65	0	96	49	52	613.	500.	24535.	20270.	71
CENTER CITY	49	H6	24	67	74	60	69	45	65	62	78	284	63	35	55	2	81	28	85	619.	516.	25154.	20786.	71
PHAETON TWP	3	G4	17	69	76	62	72	50	72	66	76	264	67	39	62	1	90	48	53	965.	804.	26119.	21590.	71
PHAETON TWP	5	G4	17	69	76	57	66	46	67	63	73	264	67	39	62	1	90	48	53	591.	514.	26710.	22104.	70
CENTER CITY	47	H6	36	65	71	60	70	41	60	64	73	269	66	37	59	0	97	34	75	643.	552.	27353.	22656.	70
CENTER CITY	74	H5	40	66	72	60	70	38	55	54	61	197	82	47	75	0	96	43	61	986.	755.	28339.	23411.	70
PHAETON TWP	4	G4	17	74	82	52	59	50	72	65	74	264	67	39	52	1	90	48	53	911.	725.	29250.	24136.	70
CENTER CITY	87	G6	39	64	70	63	74	40	58	62	70	247	71	34	54	1	93	40	66	446.	385.	29696.	24521.	69
CENTER CITY	94	G7	41	64	70	53	60	39	56	63	72	298	60	49	78	0	95	40	66	517.	407.	30213.	24928.	69
CENTER CITY	75	G5	40	66	72	61	71	38	55	52	58	197	82	47	75	0	96	43	61	458.	362.	30671.	25290.	69
SATURN TWP	14	H8	12	55	59	55	62	45	65	77	90	257	69	57	91	1	92	59	37	1251.	981.	31922.	26271.	69
CENTER CITY	72	H5	40	64	69	67	79	35	50	52	58	197	82	47	75	0	96	43	61	806.	649.	32728.	26920.	69
ADONIS TWP	8	B1	33	61	66	55	63	49	71	64	74	212	79	27	42	0	99	39	67	740.	562.	33468.	27482.	69

[1]percentage

[2]standard score: The highest precinct is given a score of 100 and the lowest a score of 0. Other precinct are given a score relative to 0 and 100. Standard score provides an indication of the relative differences in value.

* See Table 5.12 for Legend of Headers

Table 5.12 Center City P.I.P.S., Legend of Headers

Code	Weights	Description
City or Twp.		Name of city or township.
Pre		Precinct number
Gl		Grid location. (A grid drawn on the map of Center City enabled strategists to locate any precinct very quickly.)
Ct		Census tract. (In what census tract is the precinct located?)
Regov	6	Percent vote for the Republican governor in 1964. (The greater the percentage, the more important the precinct.)
Moddem	3	Percent vote for moderate Democrat candidate in the 1968 gubernatorial primary, which was between a liberal and a moderate candidate; the liberal, with union endorsement, won the primary election. (The greater the percentage for the moderate, the more important the precinct.)
Repcan	4	The results of a volunteer Republican canvass to determine the percentage of Republicans in each precinct. Voters do not register by party in this district. (The greater the percentage Republican, the more important the precinct.)
Remay	5	Percent vote for the Center City Republican mayoralty candidate in 1967. In the rest of this one-county district, the percentage voting for the Republican candidate for County Supervisor was substituted; both men won. (The greater the percentage, the more important the precinct.)
Educat	3	Educational ranking of census tract in which precinct is located; rank order based on number of people over 25 having an eighth-grade education or less. (It was the strategists' opinion that less educated voters would tend not to vote for the Republican candidate. Therefore, the more people with, or below an eigth grade education, the *less* important the precinct.)
Scouts	3	Number of girls registered in Brownies, Girl Scouts, or Senior Scouts in proportion to

Table 5.12 cont.

Scouts cont.		women between the ages of 14 and 44. (It was the strategists' opinion that familieis placing their daughters in such organizations would be more likely to have ambitions and hopes that would tend to make them vote Republican. Therefore, the greater the percentage, the more important the precinct. This factor is not a special device for finding Republican-thinking people but it does illustrate the range of political hunches that can be incorporated into P.I.P.S.)
Recwel	3	Number of welfare recipients in proportion to the number of heads of households. (It was the strategists' opinion that welfare recipients would tend not to vote Republican. Therefore, the greater the percentage, the less important the precinct.)
Locind	4	Percentage of laborers, operatives and craftsmen in proportion to the total working force. (It was the strategists' opinion that laborers, operatives and craftsmen would tend not to vote Republican. Therefore, the greater the percentage of these occupations, the less important the precinct.)
Trv		Total registered voters in the precinct.
Tve		Total votes cast in the precinct in 1966.
Cumtrv		This column keeps a running count of how many registered voters P.I.P.S. has described. (For example, the first precinct on the list contains 720 registered voters, and 720 appears in the CUMTRV column. The second precinct on the list contains 544 registered voters; then 544 is added to 720, and 1264 appears in the CUMTRV column.) The cumulative total enables the campaign planner to find the spot at which he has accounted for 50 percent of the total registered vote in his district, or 60 percent, etc.
Cumtvc (only on Chart V)		This column keeps a running count of how many of the total votes case in the district (in 1966) P.I.P.S. has described. (The CUMTVC column can be used in much the same way as the CUMTRV column described above.)
Pips		Precinct Index Priority System score. (When

Table 5.12 cont.

Pips cont.	all the information is combined, the P.I.P.S. score indicates the importance of each precinct in relation to all other precincts in the district. The Higher the P.I.P.S. score, the more important the precinct.)

---

heterogeneous than others and, therefore, likely to engender more and different kinds of issues. Some congressional districts encompass portions of a central city, some include all of a city, some are only suburban, some are rural. What if a district encompasses two or more of these components? Moreover, some areas may contain a higher proportion of interested, issue-oriented voters than others.

When settling on issues, it is important to keep three things in mind. First, the greater part of the electorate, generally, can identify only a small number of salient issues. Since their knowledge and interest is generally low, the information used for appeals need not be very detailed. CBS news once asked voters as they left the polls what was the most important factor in their vote decision for Congress. Eighty percent said issues. When asked to name one issue that was important, three-fourths of this group could not name a single issue. This does not necessarily mean, however, that detailed information on those subjects should not be gathered. Once the candidate speaks out on an issue, he will be called upon by community leaders, political leaders, news media representatives, and perhaps the opponent to answer questions, be specific, and generally exhibit knowledge on the issues. The campaigner must make the proper preparations. A one paragraph statement on the need for a property tax freeze for senior citizens may be enough for a throw-away handout, but the strategist had better prepare the candidate for such questions as: the actual property tax impact on senior citizens and others on fixed incomes; how many persons would this effect; how much actual dollar relief in the next year would they receive; how much revenue would be lost under the plan; and what proposals does the candidate have for making up the revenue loss. A few projection tables may even be in order.

That fairly careful and detailed research of a more specialized nature will have to be performed for issue appeals to political activists and attentive publics is a second and related consideration. They expect the type of issue sophistication illustrated above on the senior citizens' tax freeze. For example, if the candidate is to speak on community development to Kiwanis, Lions or the Chamber of Commerce, he must keep in mind that the development issue has been uppermost in *their* minds for a long time. This is not an occasion for slipshod programs or proposals. Many a candidate has "flunked" the question-and-answer section of the campaign appeal before a group of knowledgeable and interested citizens because the "homework" was not completed.

Third, the campaigner must consider even narrower issue appeals on subjects of interest to special publics, particularly if they are target groups. When speaking before a union council meeting, a senior citizens group, a gun club, or has only 48 hours for production, printing and mailing in order to have the letters reach their destinations with the greatest impact in terms of timing.

Again, P.I.P.S. can quickly suggest where the $1000 gift can best be utilized. It must be emphasized that P.I.P.S. does not dictate, but operates on instructions previously supplied.[18]

The individual items can also be used as indicators for appeals. For example, one's appeals on property taxes would be different in areas where the rate of owner-occupied dwellings is higher than in areas where it is very low. High pockets of welfare recipients suggest another set of appeals. Indeed, many direct mail appeals are differentiated by area on the basis of just such items.

There is no limit to the items included and the uses systems such as PIPS have except limits on the imagination and resourcefulness of the planner.[19] Use of the computer is not necessary, but it is helpful for speed, flexibility, and efficiency.

ISSUES RESEARCH

In the course of the processes discussed earlier in Chapters 4 and 5 (polls and historical, political, and social surveys) the planner should try to identify the issues that are likely to be important in the campaign. Some use, as a rule of thumb, that only polls can identify the two or three important issues which then are conveyed superficially to the electorate. Others, either unaware of or ignoring the findings of voting research, believe that the entire campaign should be based on the detailed, intricate, intellectual development of a large number of issues, including study groups, task forces, position papers, and detailed speeches and handouts. The key is obviously somewhere in between. Some issues *are* more important than others and not all voters are sophisticated issue watchers.

In planning issues research, the researcher must bear in mind that there is a mass electorate out there, but also that there are attentive publics; there is an opponent; there is the possibility of an opposing party administration; and, there is the likelihood that the candidate has a public record. Thus, issues research should focus on specific information about the important issues identified, the production of more detailed issue material to satisfy attentive publics, information about the candidate and the opposition.

Developing Specific Issues

After the issues have been identified it is time to think about research development. The advice on the number for a candidate to become expert in, and foster in speeches, literature, press releases, press conferences, and mailing ranges from none to infinity. There is no rule of thumb. Some constituencies are more a veterans club the candidate generally speaks on issues of interest to them which would not necessarily appeal to general publics or community leaders. If the membership is interested, they are likely to be knowledgeable, and the candidate will be expected to display a similar knowledge of the issues.

When gathering detailed information on specific issues, the planner will find a number of sources useful. The published studies referred to in Chapter 4, or other studies from study groups or interest groups (upon whom the campaigner is willing to rely), often make good sources. For example, the AFL-CIO and Chambers of Commerce at the national level and, in many of the states, periodically commission tax studies. The local library is a good source of published literature. A search through the *Readers Guide to Periodical Literature* and the *Public Affairs Information Service Index* will yield many sources of periodical literature. The *New York Times Index* references all the news and background materials that fit in that paper. For national races there are two important weekly news sources, the *Congressional Quarterly* and the *National Journal,* both of which contain detailed issue information, background information, roll-call votes, and current dispositions of pending bills. At the state level, many states have commercial legislative information services, which most libraries subscribe to. Of course, there is local newspaper coverage of issues, which are available upon subscription, at libraries, or newspaper morgues.

Many campaigns find it especially useful to have a special person or group of persons in the campaign clip newspapers for issue information. One can include news stories, feature articles, editorials, and columns concerning the candidate. Ordinarily, as items are clipped they are marked by topic, source, and date. The clippings are then filed by subject or by the candidate and his opponent. Commercial clipping services are also available in most states. Checking with the state newspaper association will reveal their whereabouts.

Some candidates designate task forces to conduct their issues research; some appoint a single issues research director, while others designate issue directors by topics. Volunteers are fairly easy to secure for issues research. There is the risk that task forces will take a longer period of time than the candidate is willing to tolerate, given their propensity to debate and come up with a "position." What the candidate ordinarily needs is as much background on the issue as possible, responsibly investigated, of a sophisticated nature, but not of the detail of a study commission. After the strategists and the candidate have had a chance to digest this information, and after it has been evaluated in the light of their political judgment, it can be blended into the strategy. Only the candidate and his strategists can make the final decision, since much more is involved than the information gathered.

Opponent Research

It is considered useful in many campaigns to compile as complete a record as possible on the candidate's opponent. Included in such an opponent file would be as much information as possible on that individual's party and personal positions, covering the entire scope of his political life. Generally, opponent's files contain all possible information on the individual's personal record, affiliations, special interests, and approach to public problems. It is also useful to collect quotations and issue statements and categorize them by subject.

The 1972 Watergate burglary and the allegations of campaign opponent's file containing potentially detrimental material held by the FBI, raises questions as to the propriety of opponent intelligence. What is being suggested here is merely the collection of items that are in the public domain; any "public" person is expected to be subjected to this type of scrutiny, and these activities should be considered normal, ethical and legitmate. What is considered unethical is interference with the free market of campaigning through illegal means, or use of government agencies to pry out harmful personal information.

A roll-call segment of the opponent's file is usually included when the opponent has a legislative record. Many state party headquarters collect roll-call information on opposition state legislators, and the two National Committees also collect congressional roll-call data. If such information is not made available by the parties, it will have to be extrapolated from the appropriate legislative journal. At the county, city, or other local level, roll-call positions ordinarily have to be taken from the official minutes of the meetings.

It is helpful to have the roll calls compiled and analyzed by a campaigner who is familiar with the legislative process and the constituency, so as to tailor the roll calls selected to the strategist's needs. The researcher should carefully analyze the issues and processes surrounding each roll call that is to be used publicly. The other strategists should attempt to ascertain why the opponent voted the way he did, as well as the direction of the vote. A careful study of the wording of the bill, proposed amendments, and the debate, may uncover the intent of the opponent. For example, if on nine of ten different roll calls for building new highways by appropriation a legislator voted against highway bills or amendments, but he voted for a highway extension program coupled with a highway bond funding provision, the candidate can charge that his opponent voted against new highway programs nine out of ten times. Then he can be prepared to debate his opponent over methods of funding highways. It is important to emphasize that each of these ten votes may have a different meaning, some procedural and some substantive. Great care should be taken to avoid inaccuracy in stating a public official's record, it may avert a charge of an unfair campaign practice, or the possibility of a libel or defamation of character suit. If the researcher wishes to go beyond counting to establish indices or scales, a techniques manual should be consulted, such as *Legislative Roll-Call Analysis*, by Anderson, Watts and Wilcox.[20]

Some campaign researchers like to go beyond basic issue material to investigate campaign promises, attendance, and missed roll calls. Absentee rates must match the attendance record of the opponent against the average of the entire body, since general rates of absenteeism can reach 25 percent. If the rate exceeds the average for the body, it can be used as campaign material. For missed roll calls, the researcher must be sure to count "pairs" and announced positions, for only yes and no votes are counted on the outcome of a roll call. Legislators who know in advance that they will not be present for a vote seek out a vote of a colleague who would vote the opposite way if he were present. Knowing their votes will cancel each other they "pair." Sometimes a legislator will go on the record without having his vote count by announcing for or against. On occasion, researchers have also compared legislators on their rate of missed controversial roll calls, sometimes called the "chicken factor." A number of predetermined controversial roll calls are selected out (25-100) and relative rates of nonvoting are compared. To investigate campaign promises, the voting trends results of the general issue roll-call analysis can be compared with the opponent's campaign statements of the past few campaigns, thus comparing what he said with what he did. Finally, to investigate performance, campaigners often assess the bill-passing record of an opponent by comparing it in absolute or relative terms to colleagues with similar periods of legislative service.

The researcher should also realize that the formal record contained in the roll call is not the complete record of a legislator. Much of the action of a legislative body goes on behind the scenes or in committee, without formal record. Much of the real legislative work is done in committee, some in sessions closed to the public. Roll calls give little indication of the progress of amendments, or of bills introduced. Also, many amendments and final bills are passed by voice or teller vote, with no formal record. Every effort should be made to gather as much information as possible. The researcher will find formal records and votes for committees to be irregular or nonexistent. The only way to gather such information is to think of it in advance and send "observers" to the legislative session to record behavior patterns and votes. Both Minnesota parties have enlisted, from time to time, volunteers to follow and observe target opposition legislators in committee and on the floor.

Opposing Administration

If the candidate is from the party other than that of the incumbent executive administration, or, simply is opposed to that administration, the incumbent's record is often appraised, even if it is a retiring administration. Such efforts do more than supply campaign fodder which reinforces the party faithful or candidate supporters. Since executive administration is such an important part of the governing function, it will offer a measure of expertise to the candidate as well as help place issues in a larger government program context.

Among the items the researcher can search for are: departmental actions, legislation signed or not signed, campaign promises not kept, and leadership not taken in dealing with problems for which the executive's constituency has a responsibility, such as welfare, environment, education, or consumer protection. One might investigate any act which can be argued as detrimental to the citizens of the constituency. In addition to the public sources mentioned in the Specific Issues section earlier, the public records of the administration should be examined to the extent that this is possible. Such an examination should include departmental policy statements, rules promulgated, administrative lobbying, public laws, and other "outputs" of the executive branch. Of course, if the candidate is seeking executive office, one would perform this research in minute detail, since it would constitute a major portion of the opponent's file.

The Candidate's Record

The public record of the candidate, particularly if he is a public official seeking re-election or another office, should also be a part of the issues research. Many of the same sources and methods previously mentioned apply here. If the candidate has a public record, how did he vote on key issues? Did he miss any key votes? Are there potentially embarrassing votes or actions which may be discovered by the opposition? If so, prior knowledge combined with prior preparation might prevent an embarrassing situation.

A search of the record may even reveal a pattern that was not previously evident, and which, perhaps, can be thematically emphasized. Take the example of a legislator running for Congress, whose researcher indicated, to his surprise, that over a period of years he had proposed and succeeded in securing passage of a notable number of the state's recent consumer protection bills. He had also followed the procedure through and made many enforcement recommendations to the attorney general. In a single year, each of these actions did not amount to much, perhaps a reason why they were not very evident, but cumulatively they are significant. Here is an emerging campaign issue theme which has significant transference from the office held to the office sought.

Although the candidate may be helpful, the campaigner should not count on him to provide all of the information about his votes or actions, particularly those which might be embarrassing. The candidate's memory may be imperfect, and an independent view of his record may uncover favorable and embarrassing aspects of his record.

NON-ISSUES OPPONENT EVALUATION

In addition to the issues research on the opposition, strategists should make an attempt at evaluating the opposition strengths and weaknesses, their likely moves, and resource allocations. This process can be conducted by reflecting on the strategic assessments suggested in this chapter.

A great deal of the research already conducted can be carried forth. The process of revealing areas of strength for the candidate should also reveal areas of strength for the opponent. In the process of identifying group support, undoubtedly some will be assigned to the camp of the opposition. Some political decision makers and attentive-public types will automatically go into the camp of the opposition. Areas of strength revealed in a voting analysis for the candidate will simultaneously point out strong areas for the opposition. If a poll is taken, the strong and weak points of the opponent's image, as well as key issues he may use, the important groups that are supporting him, his strengths and weaknesses among partisans and independents, and other types of information should be revealed.

Another dimension of opponent assessment is to try to anticipate what the opposition's strategy and tactics are likely to be. How much emphasis will be placed on candidate, issue, or party? What aspects of his personal record will be emphasized? Which issues will they stress? Will it be a party organization or candidate campaign? How much effort will be made door-to-door? Mass media? Telephoning? Direct mail? Will the candidate actively campaign, or will he remain in the background and leave it up to others? How much money are they likely to raise and spend? The answers to these questions will necessarily be speculative. As the campaign unfolds, some of the estimates will prove to be wide of the mark. But the attempt to account for them and estimate within a range will enhance strategic thinking. What one candidate is doing in relation to the other can at least be put into the context of campaign planning.

THE RELATIONSHIP
BETWEEN HARD AND SOFT DATA

The reader should have concluded that both "hard" and "soft" data have a place in strategic assessment. One should avoid impressionistic, "rule of thumb," "ballpark," "curbstone" political analysis, because it is so often inaccurate. One way to avoid this is to carefully take the steps suggested in this chapter and then use political judgments to supplement and help explain the research findings. The hard data should indicate that something is happening. The strategists then must interpret it and blend judgment into strategy formulation. The campaign strategist is analagous to manufacturing executives who plan production and sales campaigns. They would not ignore sales figures, market research, market locations, and market trends, when producing and planning products. Rather, their hard data, based on their knowledge, observation, and experience helps them make sound judgments. The campaign strategist must rely on similar guidelines.

Notes to Chapter 5

1. Justin P. King, "The Candidate Information Development System," (Olympia, Washington: Republican State Central Committee, 1972).

2. See, for example, Fay Calkins, *The CIO and the Democratic Party* (Chicago: University of Chicago Press, 1952); J. David Greenstone, *Labor in American Politics* (New York: Random House, 1969), chs. 6 and 7.

3. Heinz Eulau, Betty H. Zisk, and Kenneth Prewitt, "Latent Partisanship in Non-Partisan Elections: Effects of Political Milieu and Mobilization," *The Electoral Process*, eds. M. Kent Jennings and L. Harmon Zeigler (Englewood Cliffs, N.J.: Prentice-Hall, 1966), p. 230.

4. For a further elaboration of the group process see: L. Harmon Zeigler and G. Wayne Peak, *Interest Groups in American Society* (Englewood Cliffs, N.J.: Prentice-Hall, 1972), pp. 122-28; David B. Truman, *The Governmental Process* (New York: Alfred A. Knopf, 1951), ch. X.

5. Charles H. Backstrom and Robert Agranoff, "Aggregate Election Data in the Campaign: Limitations, Pitfalls and Uses" in *The New Style in Election Campaigns*, ed. Robert Agranoff (Boston: The Holbrook Press, 1972), pp. 165-68.

6. In addition to the preceding citation, both National parties have published materials on aggregate data; Democratic National Committee, *Campaign Manual 1972* (Washington, D.C.: Democratic National Committee, 1972), pp. 40-43; Research Division, Republican National Committee, *Vote History and Demographic Analysis* (Washington, D.C.: Republican National Committee, 1969).

7. Ronald N. Totaro has developed a system for estimating turnout differences between elections based on party registration, see Ronald N. Totaro, *How To Conduct a Political Campaign With the Systematic Analysis Study System* (New York: Vantage Press, 1971), pp. 18-19.

8. Republican National Committee, *Vote History and Demographic Analysis*, pp. 28-31.

9. Louis Harris, "Polls and Politics in the United States," *The New Style in Election Campaigns*, pp. 208-209; see also, Charles W. Roll, Jr. and Albert H. Cantril, *Polls: Their Use and Misuse in Politics* (New York: Basic Books, 1972), pp. 40-63.

10. Walter DeVries and V. Lance Tarrance, *The Ticket Splitter* (Grand Rapids, Mich.: Wm. B. Eerdmans, 1972), ch. V.

11. National Journal "Politicking on Television," *The New Style in Election Campaigns*, p. 290; see also, Leo Bogart, *Silent Poltiics: Polls and the Awareness of Public Opinion* (New York: John Wiley, 1972), pp. 30-32.

12. For more information see Agranoff, *The New Style in Election Campaigns*, p. 120.

13. Democratic National Committee, *Campaign Manual 1972*, pp. 46-47.

14. Robert Agranoff, "Managing Small Campaigns," in *The Political Image Merchants*, eds. Ray E. Hiebert et al. (Washington, D.C.: Acropolis Press, 1971), pp. 196-97.

15. For example see, Totaro, *How to Conduct a Political Campaign*, pp. 38-47.

16. Roll and Cantril, *Polls*, pp. 98-101.

17. Vincent P. Barabba, "Basic Information Systems-P.I.P.S." *The New Style in Election Campaigns*, pp. 192-205.

18. *Ibid.*, p. 203.

19. Other systems can be found in: Republican National Committee, *Vote History and Demographic Analysis*, pp. 34-62; Totaro, *How to Conduct a Political Campaign*, pp. 14-37.

20. Lee F. Anderson, Meredith W. Watts, Jr., and Allen R. Wilcox, *Legislative Roll-Call Analysis* (Evanston, Illinois: Northwestern University Press, 1966).

For Further Reading and Research

Anderson, Lee F.; Watts, Jr., Meridith W.; and Wilcox, Allen R. *Legislative Roll-Call Analysis*. Evanston: Northwestern Univ. Press, 1966.

Babbie, Earl R. *Survey Research Methods*. Belmont, California: Wadsworth, 1973.

Backstrom, Charles H. and Hursh, Gerald D. *Survey Research*. Evanston: Northwestern Univ. Press, 1963.

Bogart, Leo. *Silent Politics: Polls and the Awareness of Public Opinion*. New York: John Wiley, 1972.

Gallup, George. *The Sophisticated Poll Watcher's Guide*. Princeton: Princeton Opinion Press, 1973.

Greenstone, J. David. *Labor in American Politics*. New York: Random House, 1970.

Janda, Kenneth. *Data Processing: Applications to Political Research*. Evanston: Northwestern Univ. Press, 1965.

_____ . *Information Retrieval: Applications to Political Science*. Indianapolis: Bobbs-Merrill, 1968.

Kish, Leslie. *Survey Sampling*. New York: John Wiley, 1965.

Pool, Ithiel deSola; Abelson, Robert P.; and Popkin, Samuel. *Candidates, Issues and Strategies: A Computer Simulation of the 1960 and 1964 Elections*. Cambridge, Mass.: M.I.T. Press, 1965.

Republican National Committee. *Vote History and Demographic Analysis: A Manual for Utilizing Election Statistics*. Washington: Research Division, RNC, 1969.

Robinson, John P.; Rusk, Jerrold G.; and Head, Kendra B. (eds.). *Measures of Political Attitudes*. Ann Arbor: University of Michigan, Institute of Social Research, 1968.

Roll, Jr., Charles W. and Cantril, Albert H. *Polls: Their Use and Misuse in Politics*. New York: Basic Books, 1972.

Roper Public Opinion Research Center, *Current Opinion*. Williamstown, Mass.: Williams College. Monthly digests of public opinion from various poll sources.

Scoble, Harry M. *Ideology and Electoral Action.* San Francisco: Chandler, 1967.

Shaffer, William R. *Computer Simulations of Voting Behavior.* New York: Oxford, 1972.

Shively, W. Phillips. *The Craft of Political Research: A Primer.* Englewood Cliffs, N.J.: Prentice-Hall, 1974.

Stephan, Fredrick J. and McCarthy, Phillip. *Sampling Opinions.* New York: John Wiley, 1960.

Planning
Campaign Strategies
and Tactics

Discussions of campaign strategies very often fall into one of two camps. Either they posit rules, such as "fourteen steps to victory," or they vaguely say that strategy depends on the situation, failing to depict which situations are likely to lead to which strategems. That there are situational differences and from these, one might derive characteristic strategies might be an alternative position. Research on voting and campaigns has indicated that there are similar situations in which various campaigners find themselves. The research that individual campaigners perform is to discern their particular situation. Strategies can be formulated by examining the individual situation in the light of more general findings on voting and campaigns.

Strategy is one of the more awesome sounding words in our vocabulary. This is, perhaps, because it is so popularly used in the context of a notable winner: the coach who pulls a stunning upset, the general who pulls off a magnificent victory, the advertising executive who cleverly captures a huge share of the market, or the winning campaign manager. Since strategies involve employing organized strength to secure the objects of an election contest, including planning and directing operations in adjustment to the electoral arena, every campaign employs a strategy. Some are written, some are unwritten. Some are clever, some are not. Some reported accounts of strategies are really not planned events, but spontaneous reactions. Some moves which are reported as strategic undertakings are really unplanned. But somewhere along the line, whether researched or not, campaigners translate premises about the constituency, resources, assets, liabilities, advantages, and disadvantages, into charting a path or a plan. Strategy building, like other facets of campaigning, requires information, insight, and judgment applied to a particular situation. There is nothing awesome about campaign strategies if one understands these factors.

A very simplified case will illustrate the point. Assume that a Republican strategist has been poring over voting figures in his constituency for the past ten years, and has discovered that its very stable population has contributed an average of 65 percent of the vote to Republican candidates, with never more than a four percent deviation. One might surmise that party identification is an important factor in voting in this Republican district, and that a proper stratagem for the candidate is to identify with the party and somehow reinforce partisanship. Mobilizing and reinforcing partisans to register their pre-existing sentiments, by linking a party and candidate is a simple, straightforward means of maximizing conditions in the light of what research has told us is likely to happen. Now, consider his opponent. After studying some of the same information, in addition to weighing a different set of conditions, he will have to consider a different sort of strategy. Among other things, finding and activating latent supporters (non-voters) who might be supporters, candidate appeals, and conversion will be in order. This strategy will be much more complex, given the almost impossible task before this campaigner. Most strategies are somewhere between these two extremes of complexity. Charting a path based on accumulated "bits" of information such as this, based on considerations of voting behavior, campaign processes, and the investigations that strategists perform is what strategy formulation is about.

In this chapter we will try to illustrate how different situations lead to different strategies. Rather than offering specific formulas for plugging in strategies, various illustrations of how strategic thinking can lead to certain courses of action and campaign events will be offered. That is, after all, how strategies are formulated.

THE CRUCIAL SETTING OF THE CAMPAIGN

Many factors lead to the different situations in which candidates find themselves. The nation is large and diverse. There are rich areas and poor areas. Some areas are industrial whereas others are agricultural. In one part of the country, the people may be white old Americans while in another part of the country the people are multi-racial immigrants. In some towns the local officials are elected on a national, party-labeled ballot; in others they are elected without party labeling. Some areas are strongly Republican, some are strongly Democratic, and some are competitive. These and other factors contribute to the situational nature of campaigning, and each situation can be considered the setting of a particular campaign. Setting refers to the geographic-economic-social-political context within which each candidacy must operate.

Lewis Froman was one of the first political scientists to identify the importance of setting, in the context of a case study of a congressional campaign in Wisconsin. Froman conceived of setting to be primarily within the political factors of party, candidate or issues:

This discussion will begin from the basic premise that a candidate is severely constrained in his attempt to control the outcome of his campaign. That is, what is more important than the candidate's activities is the setting in which the campaign takes place. Many of the activities of candidates will be ineffective in increasing the probability of winning because of the structure of the setting itself.

Of all the factors involved in the setting which may impinge upon an election, by far the most important is the number of Democrats and Republicans in the electorate. . . .Other factors in the setting (the two most important being the appeal of the candidate himself as a person, and issues) may be treated as supporting or running counter to party preferences.[1]

Froman concludes that in the particular case he studied, most of the campaign resources were relatively equal, and there was a general absence of personality or issue factors. Thus, the Democrat won because there were more Democratic voters than Republican voters.[2]

The setting of the campaign involves much more than the relative partisan position of the two candidates. Charles Jones compared the campaigns of two incumbent congressmen running for re-election. The two districts are different in geographic setting as well as party registration, one being a rural district "safe" in party registration for the incumbent, the other being a portion of a city with a minority of registrants of the incumbent's party. The candidates did many of the same things: speaking in the district between elections, maintaining contact with voters while in Washington, both conducted active campaigns, and both had campaign organizations apart from the regular party organization. But, the two candidates conducted different campaigns which can be explained by differences in the political, social, and economic characteristics of the two districts, according to Jones. The districts he analyzed differed in the type of economy, geography, size, population density, occupational characteristics of the constituents, transportation and communication, racial and ethnic characteristics.[3]

Jones then contrasts the differing campaign styles of the two candidates, given their constituency differences:

Mr. Urban had an elaborate and well-financed organization. He had a campaign manager, a campaign chairman, a chairman of finance, a treasurer, and an executive committee of ninety-one prominent citizens. He had fifty different groups organized to support him—e.g., Doctors for Urban, Lawyers for Urban, Labor for Urban. He could rely on a large volunteer staff.

Mr. Rural traditionally had carried his organization around "in his hat." In 1960, he finally organized a Rural for Congress Committee, but continued to manage his own campaign. Because, in the candidate's words, 'I was never quite sure how to use it,' the Committee was principally used for fund-raising. Rural relied on regular party county chairmen to some extent, but only as advisors and friends.

The costs of the two campaigns differed enormously. Mr. Urban spent more on postage than Mr. Rural did on his whole campaign! Whereas the Congressional Campaign Committee's contribution to Mr. Rural comprised nearly half of his contributions, Mr. Urban (according to his campaign manager) didn't really need the contribution from the Campaign Committee—it was too small. A conservative estimate would be that Mr. Urban's campaign cost between ten and twenty times that of Mr. Rural.

As might be expected, on the basis of differences noted so far, the campaign plans of the two candidates differed markedly. Mr. Rural had no well-conceived plan; he operated mostly on intuition and personal relations. A rough pattern evolved as the campaign progressed, but comparatively little time was spent in precampaign strategy meetings.

Mr. Urban's campaign was planned in detail. Almost nothing was overlooked. An extensive campaign manual was prepared for all volunteers, outlining four phases of the campaign. In the first phase an attempt was made to get 5000 signatures on the candidate's petition (750 were needed). During the second phase, the preprimary phase, the organization made an effort to speak to all the voters of the candidate's party and urge them to vote in the primary. The third phase emphasized the registration of voters. The fourth and final phase was devoted almost entirely to visiting every member of the other party and independents to urge them to vote for the candidate.

The media of communication used by Mr. Rural were those designed to cover a large geographical area with low population density. Billboards, television, radio, newspaper advertisements, and direct mailing were all employed. Mr. Urban did not rely on television, radio, or metropolitan newspapers because these are not efficient campaign media for urban congressional candidates. These media give the urban candidate a much larger audience than he needs to have, which means that he has to pay for this large audience but has no guarantee that *his* audience—i.e., his constituents—will identify him as their Congressman. It is much more efficient to rely on personal contact media. Thus, Mr. Urban conducted a program of extensive telephoning, canvassing, and direct mailing. In addition, from three to five social gatherings every night were sponsored by constituents in the final phase of the campaign. The candidate would make a brief appearance at each of the gatherings.

Of course, both candidates relied to a considerable extent on personal handshaking and speaking tours of the constituency. Mr. Urban traveled by taxi, however, while Mr. Rural often spent as much time enroute—seeking out constituents—as he did in shaking hands. For example, on one typical day, Mr. Rural traveled 215 miles, spent seventeen hours, and met or talked to approximately 300 people. In the same time, Mr. Urban met or talked to from three to five times that many people and his travel distance was measured in city blocks.

The specific content of speeches and conversations for each candidate differed considerably. Both, however, spoke about local problems—what they had done for the constituency and what might be done. Mr. Urban spoke more about international and national issues; Mr. Rural concentrated on agriculture.[4]

The case of these two campaigns illustrates how each setting led to its own strategy.

In a very interesting case study of a 1966 Georgia congressional campaign, David Paletz suggests that campaigns operate within specific "contexts" and that strategy amounts to a candidate's attempted manipulation and modification of these contextual factors.[5] Paletz offers the following factors as constituting the context of the campaign he studied:

1. *The constituency.* Its geographic and political subunits, their population patterns and its growth, education levels, racial distributions, occupational patterns, the candidates views of the constituency and its voting habits.

2. *The candidates.* The incumbent—his appearance and personality, speaking skills, previous government service, previous issue positions as a moderate Southerner. The opponent—a 'new breed' Southern conservative, his appearance and personality.

3. *Other elections on the ballot which may have a bearing on the contest.* In this case they were the three-way Arnall-Maddox-Calloway race for governor, the neighboring Congressional District in which the incumbent Charles Weltner withdrew his candidacy because he could not keep a loyalty oath pledge and support Maddox, and Senator Richard Russell's unopposed race at the top of the ticket, allowing for differences in organizational efforts, turnout incentives and ticket splitting opportunities.

4. *The ballot.* The race under analysis was overshadowed by the gubernatorial contest and it was buried on the ballot. The contest was 88th on page three of a seven page ballot in the state's largest county. The voter had several choices: he could vote individually for the candidates for each office, write in a name, pull a straight party lever or vote straight-party and then select a candidate of the opposing party for one or more office.

5. *Party.* In this case party affiliations were highly changeable and while nominally there was a Democratic majority, Goldwater had carried the district in the previous election, suggesting there were two disparate meanings of the word Democratic.

6. *Incumbency.* The incumbent was better known and he benefited from the services of his Washington office as well as the federal benefits he brought to the district as a member of the President's party.

7. *Group support and opposition.* In this case given the previous record and identity of the two candidates the focus of group support was determined before the campaign began.

8. *Issues.* Candidates are somewhat confined in their choice of issues by their past deeds and pronouncements and by the electorate's concerns.[6]

Thus, Paletz suggests that the strategies of the two candidates operated within the context of these factors. The campaign organization, finances, the type of party appeals, the issues developed and the methods of campaigning were predicated on the context or setting of the race.[7] Paletz suggests that these considerations are the neglected context of analyzing campaign strategies.[8]

The Froman, Jones, and Paletz studies offer the campaigner the suggestion that strategies must be considered in the light of the context of the particular situation. These different settings led the strategists to formulate their strategies differently. In addition to the differences in setting illustrated by the campaigns investigated, the following considerations may become important:

1. Unique organizational problems created by districting. For example Congressional, legislative, judicial, school and park board districts often cut across the lines of other natural units (counties, wards), making relationships with party organizations, organizations, key leaders and zip codes more difficult.

2. The temper of the times. At this writing a great deal of national attention is focused on the "Watergate" and its attendant considerations, accompanied by a high degree of national cynicism about the political process and general distrust in politicians, as substantiated by the polls. A campaigner may have to account for such time bound forces, and deal with them.

3. The time of the election. This generally refers to conditions at the time an election is held. 1962 candidates were faced with the Cuban missile crisis, 1968 candidates were faced with the Indo-China war. It could also refer to the particular timing of a special election, i.e., the conditions accompanying the particular holding of such elections.

4. The particular office sought. A race for a city council seat or a city attorney's office may require different strategies. The visibility of the office sought varies—Presidential, senatorial, gubernatorial and some local races are highly visible. Races in the "middle of the ticket" generally compete against these for attention. A race for a judgeship may call for a restrained campaign.

5. The electoral system. The race could be partisan or non-partisan. The primary could be open to all voters or closed to registered voters of a single party. The timing between the primary and the general election could be important.

6. The potential pool of political resources. In the context of the particular contest how much in the way of manpower, skills and money can be mobilized.

7. The "electoral culture." In addition to voting habits, the constituency electorate's political norms, expectations, and the political styles and tactics they are likely to approve.[9]

While the exact potential effect of factors such as these are difficult to measure (although many of them are approximated by polling) strategists ordinarily consider factors of setting when formulating strategy. Campaign strategists use research and information to try to reduce the guesswork involved in assessing these factors as much as possible. Maximized information levels plus the campaigner's judgment on the particular situation contribute to establishing the context as the first crucial step in formulating campaign strategy.

ASSESSMENT OF THE CONSTITUENCY:
Resources, Advantages,
Disadvantages, Assets, Liabilities

Establishing the context of the campaign represents a crucial first step in identifying the broad outlines of a campaign strategy. Ordinarily, more detail is required to bridge the gap between what is suggested by the situation and which specific activities or tactics should be undertaken. One method is to translate the raw materials (Chapter 4) and strategic analysis (Chapter 5) into a specific strategic assessment in the light of voting behavior (Chapter 2) and campaign processes (Chapter 3). We are suggesting that strategists formulate a sort of balance sheet of resources, advantages, disadvantages, assets, and liabilities. The actual ledger need not be written, but it should be as complete as possible, and a written check list and written records can aid in avoiding incompleteness. Naturally, this step should be taken when all the research (including social and political surveys, assessment of groups and leaders, voting studies, polls, media listings) has been gathered, analyzed, synthesized, and reported in a form usable for planning purposes. These reports then can be combined with the collective judgments of strategists, as they proceed to discuss, assess and weigh various factors. Such a suggested checklist follows:

A Checklist for Strategic Assessment

I–Partisanship and Party Support

A. Rates of party voting: base races for party candidates over time, votes of key partisans on the ticket, votes for fellow partisans running for similar offices (to measure fall off), precinct or area priorities by party support.

B. Poll results: support for candidate (and opponent) by partisan identifiers, strength of partisanship; comparisons with other partisans running; images of candidates by partisans; key issues or other factors, characteristics of partisans leaning or supporting opposition; polarity image (left, right, center) partisans have of candidate; support and disposition of independents.

C. Evaluation of party organization: degree of support-endorsement of subunits of constituency party, estimate of willingness to electioneer for candidate, specific activities in specific areas that subunits of the party can handle for campaign.

D. Support of party organization leaders and the extensiveness of their commitment.

E. Party canvass or party registration: existence or absence of them; specific areas of the constituency where party canvass exists, areas where canvass in progress, known commitments of other candidates to voter identification.

F. Other candidates running and their likely impact.

II–Group Support

A. Social and political surveys combined: how various demographic groups are likely to line up in this race, occupational groups, religious groups, ethnic groups, income level areas, race.

B. Poll results: demographic differences in rates of partisanship, support for the candidates, issues, image of the candidates, media habits.

C. Organized group support: a listing of political, semi-political and non-political groups by the degree of their potential or already determined support.
    1. Groups that will electioneer, extent of.
    2. Groups that will contribute, extent of.
    3. Groups that will endorse only.
    4. Groups from which leaders will lend their names to this cause.
    5. Groups from which non-opposition is the most likely outcome.
    6. Groups which will oppose the candidacy and not support opponent.
    7. Opposition support levels.

III–Candidate and Personal Factors

A. Personal attributes of the candidate and opponent likely to be assets or liabilities: ethnicity, group support, party support or nonsupport, known or unknown in community, name recognition, personal qualities, personality, net personal minus or plus for each candidate.

B. Personal advantages or disadvantages: incumbency or non-incumbency, previous office holding, particular experience or expertise in subject matters, relative wealth of candidates, length of residence in constituency, amount of non-occupational time available for candidate campaigning.

C. Candidate voting: areas of personal strength (as against party strength) and weakness for candidate and opponent if a voting record exists, swing areas of the constituency, comparison of representative race for areas of strength.

D. Poll results: composite images of the candidates, images by demographic groupings, groups, partisans, candidate supporters, undecideds, issue images. ability to do the job, personal ratings and feelings of the candidates. Expectations of the office sought.

IV—Early Voter Support and Weaknesses

Known indicators of strength at this early point of the campaign, to indicate possible areas of extension.

A. Types of groups indicating favorable and unfavorable responses to candidacy: unions, civic groups, farm groups, mental health association, professional groups, business organizations, nursing home association, bankers, etc.

B. Key occupational categories indicating favor or disfavor: lawyers, optometrists, teachers, physicians, plumbers, electricians, occupational therapists, etc.

C. Poll results: geographic, occupational, ethnic, religious or demographic areas of support or weakness. In comparison with similar support for other party candidates.

D. Areas of potential support suggested by analysis of past voting, census, historical information and other community survey information.

E. Support of key political decision makers, political leaders and governmental officials.

F. Given the candidate's party, occupation, age, political standing and philosophy, what are other expected sources of support and opposition?

V—Latent Sources of Support

A. Unregistered voters: in areas of high priority or potential strength, new groups of voters in the constituency, new age-eligible voters in the district.

B. Low turnout voters: areas of high concentrations of low turnout in various types of elections, areas with high number of people with social characteristics associated with low turnout, registered but occasional voters as a target group from existing canvass, accidental factors, absentees.

C. Areas of high rates of nonvoting among voters in particular races (falloff).

D. Poll results: latent supporters, undecideds, characteristics of voters leaning to candidate or weak supporters, independents, ticket splitters or any other indicators of potential voter types.

E. Legal rules, barriers, deadlines as facilitators or hinderances to voter registration, straight-or split-ticket voting.

F. Any latent areas of support suggested by analysis of social and political surveys, census, community studies, historical information, etc.

VI—Issues

A. All possible issues suggested by published studies, historical studies, census analysis, community surveys, etc.

B. Issues suggested by discussion with key people in the constituency, research on issues, group visitations and discussions with attentive publics.

C. Poll results: key issues by subgroups, candidate supporters, partisans, strength of partisanship, independents, decideds, undecideds as well as the most important constituency-wide issues.

D. Filter out key constituency-wide issues to use in general advertising appeals, filter out key issues for segments of the constituency.

E. Important issues for the "issue-electorate," special issue publics.

F. Existing, well-known issue positions of the candidate which can be extended.

G. Less well-known issue positions which can be crystallized.

H. Issues the opposition is likely to use, issues on which the opposition can be challenged, issues that can be used against opposition administration.

VII–Attentive Public Support

A. All key groups, group leaders or organizations in the constituency.

B. Separation of likely opposition and support.

C. Ranking of groups, leaders, organizations in order of likelihood of support.

D. Availability of mailing lists or other sources of contacting organization leaders and activists of high priority.

VIII–Material Resources

A. Money: amount available at present; realistic projection of money that can be raised, within a range, a total unbudgeted, working figure.

B. Skills, available and acquirable: fund raisers; persons who can get the support of influentials, groups; researchers, issue and voting, computer skills; press relations and writing; advertising and media; organization.

C. Personnel: volunteers in addition to party volunteers or workers, a realistic assessment at this time of the potential to draw volunteer workers given the candidate, the office sought, the election, etc.

D. Organization: existing or *de novo*, potential for building or re-establishing a candidate organization, given the candidate, office sought, the election, etc.

E. Any known commitments of other candidates in the constituency that are reliable to cooperate or perform campaign tasks.

IX–Media

A. Listing of radio, newspapers, television, print media, direct mail estimates in the constituency: costs per unit for each one, potential reach for each one, cost per voter contact for each one.

B. Potential vehicles of uncontrolled media: radio stations, television, newspapers and other vehicles of news coverage, editorials, interview formats, talk shows, question and answer formats.

C. Media as a potential source of support/non-opposition or opposition: likely editorial support, areas of favorable and unfavorable coverage, potential media hostility, support for the opposition.

D. Media ratings: ranking of important circulation and audience rates, type of audiences for special papers and smaller radio stations, key media patterns suggested by polling, demographics of audiences.

This check list is representative of the various premises of the constituency, resources, assets, liabilities, advantages and disadvantages that campaigners must typically evaluate when formulating a strategy. The list does not, of course, mean that every item should be assessed, or that information must be gathered for each factor. Different situations will call for different combinations of these, and judgment should be used as to which fit the candidacy and which do not. In nonpartisan races, for example, when party is likely to be less relevant, candidate factors will weigh much heavier than partisan factors. In some cases, such as in a very small constituency campaign, party may also be irrelevant. Assessment of each of these factors should at least be considered, and if it is not included, there should be substantive reasons for exclusion. The familiar response, "We don't need voting analysis because our candidate knows his district and the people in it," should not be an excuse for not undertaking voting studies or polls. Inevitably, the evidence will show the candidate merely thinks he knows what he does not know. How could one person possibly know the partisan support indices, swing rates, registration ratios, vote contribution rates for literally dozens of precincts, as well as how various groups of voters are likely to line up in the next election, their media habits, or what they think of the candidate? Polling or voting analysis, or any other item for that matter, may be excluded because of lack of time, insufficient expertise, or insufficient resources, but, no item of information should be excluded because the strategists think they know it all in advance.

A checklist is, of course, a skeletal accounting of the range of considerations that strategists can and do apply. In each situation the principals involved will have to add "flesh" by selecting the items, conducting the investigations, and using their judgment to interpret the findings.

MUTABILITY AND STRENGTH AS STRATEGIC ASSESSMENT FACTORS

While proposing that candidates have little control over the outcome of the election because of the importance of setting in election campaigns, Froman suggests that this proposition becomes less true under two conditions: "(1) the more competitive the district, the more impact the campaign can have on the outcome; and (2) the greater the inequality of resources of the candidates, the greater the control over the outcome by the candidate with the greater resources."[10] These qualifying conditions are additive, says Froman; that is, as the district becomes more competitive, inequality of resources becomes more important.[11] Paletz argues that while the impact of contextual factors on the outcome of elections cannot be denied, the impact of the campaign might well be judged on the extent to which it maximizes the candidate's impact within these contextual constraints.[12] These two writers are suggesting that, *given the context of a particular campaign setting, the campaigner can have an impact on the outcome if he works with those factors which he can do something about, proceeding from those factors over which he can have the greatest control to those of lesser importance.* In a word, the candidate should deal with mutable factors from strength.

It is the setting which determines whether a resource or other strategic factors can be mobilized in a campaign, but the strategist makes that judgment and takes the steps to mobilize them. Judgments must be made as to how mutable a particular resource, asset, or advantage is, and how to mobilize it. Kingdon, for example, found that candidates tended to assign factors such as their own hard work, their reputation, their campaign plans and their publicity efforts as within their control, and such factors as the party makeup of the district, national and state trends, their opponent's familiar name, and superior monetary resources as beyond their control.[13]

A case in point is the single disadvantage of a minority-party candidate running in a legislative district. Political scientists, following the importance of party identification and party voting, use party competition in a variety of typological settings because competiveness of the district is presumed to effect the behavior of candidates as well as public officials in a variety of ways. Because party identification is stable and lasting, the minority candidate is faced with a majority electorate predisposed against him. Moreover, candidate and issue very often run in the same direction as party. Does the minority-party candidate give up because of the competitive situation? No, but he probably does not exploit partisanship much, or engage in partisan conversion. Obviously, the key is to exploit what one can, such as candidate and issue positions that run counter to party support, and to do other things which are possible such as turning out latent supporters and exploiting superior resources. Some factors that can contribute to victory are within the ability of the campaigner to grasp and deal with. Some are not. Strategists, then, ordinarily concern themselves with those strategic factors which are mutable and immutable; each strategic factor must, in a sense be lived with if it is immutable and possibly dealt with if mutable.

Among the more obvious factors which cannot be changed in the context of a campaign are: the incumbency of an opponent, the relative youth (or age) of an opponent; a small number of union members in a district for a Democratic candidate; a two-to-one opposition-party support level; an opponent's vast advantage of previous governmental experience; the campaign laws, regulations and prohibitions; and certain longstanding individual and group affinity for the opponent or opposition party. These factors must be dealt with by emphasizing something else; trying to shift the ground of the campaign to more mutable factors.

Many other factors can be changed in the course of the campaign, and they can be integrated into the strategy. They range from those which require considerable effort to change to those which can be changed more easily, although with considerable effort. Examples of those which can be changed only incrementally are: if the opponent is personally wealthy or has the wherewithall to raise large sums of money, the candidate group will have to live with only a portion of the opponent's financial treasury but may try to make "buying the election" an issue; the opponent's personal organization is longstanding and extensive, but the campaigners can build one *de novo;* and, though many group leaders are predisposed to the incumbent, early visits may neutralize their opposition.

Still other factors can be changed markedly with a campaign effort: a low name-recognition factor can be raised; large numbers of latent supporters (party or candidate) can be registered and turned out; weaker partisans can be motivated to split their tickets; candidate appeals can reinforce, activate, or convert voters; key constituency issues can be stressed; a weak party organization can be circumvented by a strong candidate organization; and neutral groups, leaders, and attentive publics can be mobilized.

Crosscutting considerations of changeability are considerations of strength. Simply stated, one maximizes the impact on the setting by working from those in which the greatest impact on the outcome can be obtained. That is to say, the strategist must work from a position in which he uses those factors which are most likely to maximize votes, employing those processes and factors which offer the greatest yield. It is sort of a cost-benefit procedure in which one tries to maximize the greatest benefit balanced by the least possible cost. This is not to say that there will be no cost at all, but that a given commitment will yield the greatest return on the investment. As an example consider the fact that: 1) in legislative and congressional campaigns partisanship is the single most important factor in voting; 2) combined with the fact that most partisans have not heard of either candidate; 3) but, they are more likely to vote for a candidate if they have heard something about him, particularly if he is of the same party. In districts leaning toward or safe for one party, one might deduce that important stratagems might include: partisan appeals, primarily through identifying strong party areas or individuals, designed to reinforce voters partisanship; messages that link the candidate with the party; and voter registration and mobilization drives in strong party areas. That is dealing from strength.

Using a continuum of only the three factors of party support, group support, and personal popularity, Kindon has demonstrated that candidates vary in their security of positon. A candidate at one end of the continuum is quite secure because he has achieved at least one, or a combination of the following: the party identification of a majority of voters is identical to his; he has built a coalition of groups in the district sufficient to elect him; he has established a remarkable degree of personal popularity. At the other end of the continuum the candidate is relatively helpless—he is of the minority party, without significant group support, and unknown.[14] Kingdon's data indicated that those candidates relatively near the "secure" end "concentrate on bolstering the support they already enjoy: they appeal to the groups in their coalitions, they campaign in their strong areas and neglect their weak areas."[15] They deal from strength.

TRANSLATING CORE FACTORS
INTO A STRATEGY: *Strategic Thinking*

As a bit of useful redundancy we emphasize that it is situational differences that determine which core factors are deemed important by strategists in formulating a strategy, within the crosscutting considerations of mutability and strength. In this section we will examine how such factors can be translated into a working plan.

While earlier sections of this chapter revealed that many different considerations can be taken into account, we will only use a few in order to simplify strategic thinking. Along the dimension of strength we will consider party, candidate, issue, and group support. Along the crosscutting dimension of mutability we will consider money, organization, incumbency, and attentive publics.

To further simplify strategic thinking in terms of the strength dimension, we will arbitrarily divide each dimension in a hypothetical electorate. Figure 6.1 contains representations of the divisions by the various strategic factors. Since the electorate is hypothetical and the divisions arbitrary we have assigned the party component of the electorate equally in the district. Notice that the candidate dimension is not assigned equally. One-fourth of the electorate is assigned to each of the four support categories, in this case giving the candidate an advantage. The issue dimension assigns equal amounts of the public to each candidate, and gives each candidate the possibility of succeeding waves of "issue possibles," close to the candidate's views and close to the candidate's existing supporters. Likewise, group support is hypothetically divided between the most friendly to the most hostile.

At this point, it should become clear how strategic thinking proceeds from strength. Along the party dimension one would expect partisans to be the most likely voters from strong to weak, in that ordering. One would least expect the strong partisans of the opposition to be voters. Thus, a strategy which included a partisan dimension would move from strong party supporters to weaker party supporters, to independents (or those without a party affiliation), to weak supporters of the opposition candidate's party. The stronger supporters of the opponent's party would ordinarily be ignored, since that would be dealing from weakness.

Candidate, issue, and group dimensions are predicated along similar lines. Strategic thinking ordinarily proceeds from mobilizing definite supporters to

Figure 6.1 Some Strategic Divisions of a Hypothetical Electorate

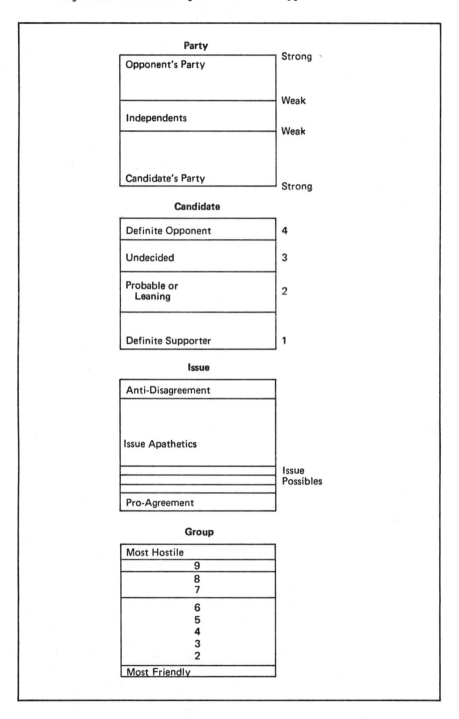

probable supporters, to undecided voters, ordinarily ignoring opposition supporters. Issue voters are usually smaller in number, but strategic thinking would
proceed from mobilizing those who are definitely pro on issues to each succeeding (and perhaps smaller) wave of likelies, ignoring the improbable issue apathetics and improbables. Group coalitions are formed in a similar fashion, working
from those closest to the candidate, his supporters, and their values, to the next
closest group, to succeeding groups. Similar strategic configurations, including
such dimensions as key political leaders, attentive publics, ethnic or religious
groups, can be formulated depending on the situation, similarly proceeding from
strength to weakness. Naturally, these groups are not mutually exclusive, and
the degree of overlap will have to be considered in actual strategic thinking.

The mutability or relative degree of change can be represented similarly by
a hypothetical example. For ease of explanation we will again depict only four:
incumbency, money, organization, and attentive publics. Figure 6.2 contains
these representations for a hypothetical challenger. In the case illustrated,
the challenger can do nothing about his non-incumbent disadvantate. An extensive fund-raising effort can have the modest effect of reducing the fund

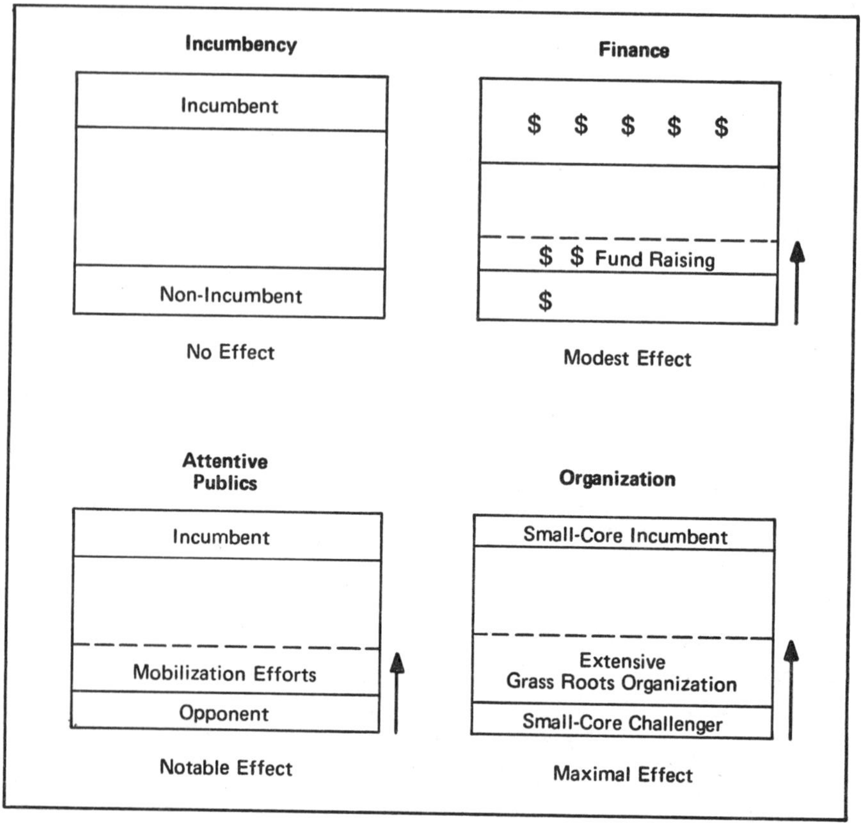

Figure 6.2 Some Considerations of Mutability in Campaign Settings

deficit from 5-1 to 5-2. The attempt to work the attentive publics can notably mobilize as many of them as the opponent. Building a grass-roots organization can have the maximal effect of placing the opponent at a disadvantage. Just as factors of strength in strategic thinking proceed from the most probable to the least likely, these factors of setting ordinarily proceed from those in which there is likely to be a maximal effect to those with lesser effects, to those with no effect.

While these and other considerations of strength and mutability are treated separately, at some point they have to be combined into meaningful strategic considerations. Parties, candidates, issues, and groups are not independent of organization, attentive publics, and monetary considerations. Organizations have to be built in areas of party or candidate strength. Friendly groups may have to be wooed into the grass-roots organization. Attentive publics have to be appealed to on the basis of issues. This is one factor contributing to the complexity of strategic thinking. Not only do many things have to be considered at once, but they must be considered in terms of their many dimensions.

The end product of this stage of strategic thinking is ordinarily a rough ranking of the relative importance of each of the factors weighed. Carrying forth the examples already used; what is the relative importance to be in the campaign of party and partisanship, candidate appeals, issues, and what issues? How many and which groups are to be encouraged to join the coalition? How important and how much money might be needed? Which attentive publics might be targets? What type of organization is necessary? At this stage the strategists should have a fairly accurate estimate of where they are going and what it will take to get there.

How to get there is also an important element of strategic thinking. Here, the reference is to the specific campaign processes—reinforcement, activation of latency, and conversion—and their linkage to voting and other campaign elements. Unfortunately, there is no neat formula for relating processes with voting, another reason why strategic thinking is difficult. A necessary part of strategic thinking is trying to associate processes with the strategic factors already decided upon.

Some examples and generalizations will substitute for formulas. Party appeals are generally reinforcers, although some latent party supporters are activated by party. The campaign generally has the effect of reinforcing those who are already committed. Candidate appeals are usually designed to reinforce some committed voters, to activate latent support of the undecided and the weak partisans, and to convert to the candidate. Candidate activation is often used on the undecided or the weak supporters as new information. Issue appeals are designed to reinforce partisans and committed voters; but they are also designed to activate the latent support of issue voters, undecided but interested voters, and to convert a few voters. Key attentive publics and secondary groups may be from the same source in a campaign, although one could conceivably mobilize a group's leaders but not its followers. In other words, each of these processes can be designed to accomplish different things at different times, depending on various strategic aims. No single process has a single effect.

Combining these campaign processes with considerations of strength and mutability would yield practical examples such as the following. A well known minority party candidate in a normally 2 to 1 district would not seriously consider partisan converson of the opposition, but may well consider intermediate activities such as identifying and activating latent supporters, making issue appeals to undecided but interested persons in conjunction with his primary activity of reinforcing, activating, and even converting a few on the basis of his personal appeal. Of course his opponent, would have a somewhat different set of factors, although he too will undoubtedly be using the mutable and dealing from strength. Few candidates would seriously undertake a strategy that dealt only with issues, trying to convert voters on that basis, appealing only to indifferent voters, stressing issues related to difficult-to-change attitudes. In American political jargon, such a candidacy is known as a "kamikaze race."

Using strategic factors that signify strength does not necessarily mean that other factors are rendered inoperable, but only that the emphasis is weighted toward elements of strength, yet another element in the difficulty of strategic thinking. One common problem is that campaigners must adopt stratagems and tactics to please supporters or financial contributors, however unsound the tactics may be. For example, the McGovern forces in 1972 would have preferred avoiding issues such as abortion, marijuana, homosexual rights, and guaranteed incomes, but coalition supporters forced these issues on the campaign. Campaign spending is often for nonstrategic purposes, such as the purchase of inordinate amounts of display advertising because a large contributor has business interests in outdoor advertising, or expenditures on buttons, skimmer hats, and other gimmicks to please insistent volunteers. One should also realistically consider strategic efforts that make the most of deficient resources, disadvantages, and liabilities. Minority-party candidates ordinarily identify, reinforce, and mobilize what available partisans there are in a constituency, particularly if they are in pockets of strength. Finding potential nonvoters or new voters as partisans is another stratagem. If the organization is deficient, or few volunteers are available, the available ones can be assigned to priority projects or priority areas. Monetary disadvantages mean that every dollar must be budgeted more effectively and that no waste is allowed. Non-incumbency may mean the campaign has to begin earlier than the incumbent's campaign. A lack of name recognition may mean a considerably greater media expenditure. Thus, the strategist tries to discern stratagems which minimize deficiencies, disadvantages, and liabilities.

In sum, there are four reasons why strategic thinking is a complex enterprise in a campaign. First, variations in setting lead to variations in the strength and mutability of various strategic factors in each campaign. Second, the multi-dimensionality involved in cross-cuting considerations of strength and mutability makes it difficult in a particular campaign to piece strategic elements together. Third, there is no perfect match between strategic elements and campaign processes; a single undertaking can reinforce, activate, or convert, or combine these effects. Fourth, charting a strategic path, including strength and major effects, does not necessarily mean that is all a campaigner undertakes; non-strategic activities must also be undertaken. These reasons help explain why there are no easy formulas for broadly applicable campaign strategies. Until such formulas are developed, campaign strategists will have to combine the best information possible with the best reasoned insights possible; they must think strategically.

TRANSLATING
STRATEGIC FACTORS INTO TACTICS

Campaign tactics refer to those activities designed to accomplish strategic ends. Thus, a direct-mail appeal to known partisans linking the candidate to the accomplishments of the party is tactically designed to support the strategic principle of reinforcement of partisans. As one campaign strategist has said, "There are different fish and they can't all be caught with the same bait."[16] The activities in which one engages on the basis of candidate and issues differ from those of party tactics. Reinforcement may require one set of activities, activation of latent voters other tactics, and conversion, still others. In some cases it is possible that a single campaign tactic can serve a combination of campaign processes.

Tactics are ordinarily designed to support the important strategic factors that are to be emphasized in the campaign. For example, in an aldermanic challenge race: 1) it is decided that party support and the reinforcement of it is not very important; 2) that the major strategic factors are to be activating the latent support of ward residents toward the popularity and previous public service of the candidate; and 3) candidate conversion of some partisans of the other party, because the incumbent has recently voted for an unpopular tax proposal. A minimal amount of party campaigning is in order. The candidate should make speeches about the unimportance of party in deciding most city council matters. Literature, radio, display advertising, and newspaper appeals should not mention the candidate's party, but should stress instead his important personal qualities and public service. The candidate's differences in the tax matter should be underscored, perhaps as the "theme" of a mailing to identified opposition-party supporters. If voter identification is to be undertaken for purposes of registration and get-out-the-vote, it should be done on the basis of identified candidate support rather than party support. These activities are designed to buttress the strategic principles of activating the latent support of a candidate as well as converting members of the opposing party to support a single candidate.

Since there is no exact tactical derivation of a particular strategic factor, strategists must engage in tactical thinking or use tactical applications similar to the strategic-thinking process. Indeed, some tactics can serve many strategic factors. Literature can be designed to reinforce party, activate latent candidate

support, help convert on the basis of issues, appeal to the interested but the undecided; however, it probably cannot be used effectively to activate or convert
indifferent undecided voters or convert partisans. Activation of indifferent
voters will ordinarily require a heavy tactical investment in identification of
them, perhaps registering them, getting them out to vote, including the use of
telephoning, transportation, and perhaps providing babysitters. Display materials can be used to link the candidate with the party and, of course, serve as an
all important device for name recognition and candidate appeal. Direct mailings,
if properly targeted to the voter audience, can reinforce partisanship, or activate
latent support; offer partisan, candidate, or issue support; and can serve as a
converting force. Newspaper, television, and radio advertising are considered to
be the best means of developing candidate image appeals and candidate-issue
appeals, and to a lesser extent issue appeals, particularly longer spots or larger
ads. Shorter formats are used to reinforce candidate support and activate latent
candidate support. Uncontrolled mass media, or free media coverage stimulated by the campaigner, such as news releases, news panels, talk shows, interviews, and press conferences are used primarily to develop candidate-issue
appeals and issue appeals.

The effectiveness of appearances by the candidate at gatherings or meetings depends on the audience: a speech at a party meeting or a gathering of
campaign workers ordinarily reinforces the audience's support, as would a talk
to a group committed to support a candidate; a talk to a more neutral group will
reinforce only those already committed, but more importantly it may have the
effect of activating the latent support of some members of the audience, gaining
some, or further, recognition, and perhaps converting a few from the attentive
public. A speech to a hostile group will do little except, perhaps, to neutralize a
few and reinforce the commitment of the majority against. Such appearances may
be a waste of time, unless it is politically unwise to pass up such a gathering.
Person-to-person campaigning is used by the party organization to reinforce
partisanship, whereas, when the candidate organization undertakes this task it is
generally to develop and stimulate candidate identification and to a lesser extent
candidate appeal, given the brief nature of its message. In many low-stimulus
elections, person-to-person appeals by the candidate can be an important means
of conversion, in as much as few alternative cues exist in the election. In other
words, in some campaigns door-to-door or other personal campaigning can fill
an information vacumn and have a conversion effect. Of course, person-to-
person campaigning gains its importance in conjunction with other activities.
Another form of personal campaigning is the candidate's personal public-relations activities, such as lining up the support of key leaders, political activists,
attentive publics, contacts with the media, and appearances at important gatherings. Depending on the situation, these important activities can reinforce the
committed, activate the undecided, and convert the neutral and a few who are
hostile.

Therefore, the campaigner should envisage some tactics in a campaign
that support a number of strategic principles, depending on the nature of the

appeal and the format of it. Of course, just as all strategies are a mixture of candidate, party, issue, reinforcement, activation of latency and conversion, so too are the tactics which support these stratagems. The list below is a suggested, though not comprehensive, list of tactics, organized by whether they primarily reinforce, activate or convert, designed to indicate which kinds of campaign activities support which strategic principles in a campaign.

A Selected List of Campaign Tactics, By Strategic Principles

A. *Reinforcement*—Primarily Partisans and Committed

1. Determine partisan or committed supporters, candidate supporters through voter identification techniques; door-to-door survey or telephone canvass. Implement a get-out-the-vote campaign.

2. Door-to-door campaigning by the candidate in areas of strong support, linking candidacy with party or previous candidate support.

3. Speaking to groups of known supporters; the party organization, friendly groups or associations.

4. Utilization of electioneering activities (voter registration, get-out-the-vote appeals, etc.) of groups willing to campaign among their memebers (unions, business groups, other associations).

5. Use of the party organization for party campaigning in strong party areas in which they are effective.

6. Special literature (designed for distribution among partisans or heavy party areas) stressing the party's accomplishments, linking the candidate with a fellow partisan mayor, governor, senator or president.

7. Appointing party officials, elected party officials to the campaign committee.

8. Speaking to party or campaign workers or campaigning among them.

9. Using display advertising, yard signs or media advertising which identifies the party of the candidate.

10. Buttons, gadgets, party fund raisers, candidate fund raisers.

11. Testimonials (used in advertising) by fellow partisans for the candidate.

B. *Activation of Latent Support*—Primarily Weaker Partisans, the Less-interested, Weakly Committed Supporters

1. Voter registration campaigns in areas of support which have low voter-participation rates. Voter turnout efforts in the same areas.

2. Voter registration and voter turnout efforts, transportation, provide baby-sitters, among identified individuals who are not registered or who have a low voting turnout record who could be supporters (independents, undecideds).

3. Reminders (telephone, direct mail, or others) to vote for your candidate if the race is down the ticket from the high visibility races.

4. Use of a candidate-centered organization to campaign in more marginal areas or areas of opposition-party strength.

5. Use of citizens committees to demonstrate broad, nonparty, community-wide support.

6. Personal door-to-door campaigning by the candidate stressing candidate and issue appeals.

7. Candidate image development and candidate-issue appeals in newspaper, radio, and television advertising.

8. Use of uncontrolled media—press releases, interview shows, talk shows—to develop candidate-issue appeals.

9. Use of bumper stickers, billboards and other displays without party to develop name recognition.

10. Testimonials by leading citizen types stressing candidate and issue qualities.

11. Development of issue appeals that may generate interest.

12. Appearances before semipolitical and nonpolitical groups.

C. *Conversion*—Primarily Weaker Partisans of the Opposition Party, Weaker Opposition Candidate Supporters, Uninterested but Latent Opposition Supporters.

1. Use of issue appeals on the opponent concerning issues about which his weak supporters disagree with him.

2. Stress the positive aspects of the candidate's record and experience, particularly when they compare unfavorably to the opposition.

3. Exploit unpopular stands, unpopular public commitments, or unpopular votes on the part of the opposition.

4. Linkage of the opponent with an unpopular administration of the opposition party.

5. Use of targeted advertising, such as direct mail or special literature, to specific types of opposition-party or candidate supporters containing messages based on 1, 2, 3, and 4 above.

6. Establish a bi-partisan citizens committee.

7. Personal door-to-door campaigning in low stimulus elections.

It should be obvious that each of the strategic factors decided upon should have a set of tactics related to them. In other words, at this point, the strategists should have a clear notion of what they want to do and what activities are designed to support them. The campaign planners should have a long list of activities they plan to undertake, but every single one of them should be justifiable on the basis of some strategic principle. Too often, candidates undertake activities because they always have been done, because supporters urge them on strategists, or because the opponent is doing them. These are neither necessary nor are they sufficient reasons for undertaking campaign activities. As an example, the way it has always been done is not always effective, (even if it is a winning campaign) plus the opponent, in all likelihood, has a different strategy. Spending a lot of time attending party meetings may be all right for an incumbent from a safe district, but his challenger may well wish to steer clear of his party, both in terms of organizational association and in appeals, not to speak of his possible disadvantage in name recognition or familiarity among voters, which would mean party meetings could be a waste of time.

After the strategists have compiled all of the tactics which they plan to employ, each of them supporting a strategic factor or set of factors, the final step in strategy building—ordering into priorities—can be undertaken.

SETTING AND ORDERING PRIORITIES

By this time, the strategists have undertaken a serious analysis of strategic possibilities, including: 1) the best analytical sources and techniques available; 2) a realistic and suitable-to-the-setting set of strategic principles; 3) a proper mix of reinforcement of partisans and the candidate-committed, activation of latent candidate supporters, weak partisans, issue and candidate conversion, and so on; and 4) have arrived at a set of campaign tactics necessary to support them. The process of establishing and ordering strategic priorities, then, is relatively easy (although following them may not be). The essence of establishing priorities in campaign strategy is to maintain the same mix in implementation that was established in strategy building.

A simple explanation is in order. Suppose it is decided by a Democratic candidate in a 2-to-1 Republican district that party reinforcement will be least important in a strategy in which candidate reinforcement, issue conversion, and activation of latent support on the basis of candidate, and a little issue are the most important, in roughly that order. This means that when forming a committee and making issue appeals, tactically, the candidate will steer clear of his party organization, and avoid much close identification with his party in advertising. If he appeals to his partisans or union members it will be either through direct mail or party, or union contacts with known partisans or union members. But these activities should be a minor part of the campaign. The major efforts should be aimed at developing *candidate* identification and linkage of the candidate with key issues likely to activate or convert persons predisposed to support the other party (if they have had no other campaign cues). All the advertising, the committee setup, the groups appealed to, and themes in the campaign should support a candidate orientation. Identified and known candidate supporters should be reinforced as supporters of the candidate and not necessarily as partisans, since roughly more than one-third of the electorate cannot be of the candidate's party in order to win. The latter set of strategic principles have other consequences for the campaign: Since it is not party oriented, a candidate organization must be built up; building an identity means advertising with its attendant requirements of cost and expertise; much of the campaigning, including door-to-door, will have to be undertaken by the candidate; many more group appearances have to be made than merely attending ward clubs; and many others.

There are three major principles which relate to setting and ordering priorities to be derived from this example. First, despite the fact that one has set a number of priorities in the campaign, lesser-priority strategic principles still have to be performed. In this case, the partisans must be held, or reinforced, and some campaign efforts have to be expended toward that end. This is what makes campaign strategies so difficult to establish and to implement. One cannot ignore party, candidate or issue, reinforcement, activation of latent support or conversion; they must be put in their proper place.

Second, at the same time that many or most of these strategic principles and corresponding tactics are being implemented, the campaigner must take the greatest of care that lesser priority tactics do not overshadow the more important activities. In the example cited, the party must maintain a low profile: the candidate cannot spend a great deal of time addressing the party faithful. He must resist efforts on the part of loyalists to identify the party and its accomplishments on displays, in literature, and in advertising. Most money must be channeled into the high-priority projects; workers must be sent to high priority areas. Candidate workers must resist the requests to peddle all of the party's literature when they are going door-to-door. Voter identification must be candidate and not party identification; the citizens' committee should not be overloaded with prominent, strongly identified, party members. And all other attempts by the party to get the candidate's organization to do its work must be resisted. If this is not accomplished, the strategy will have been altered. If this is done at the expense of other activity, the likely consequence could be a "super-reinforced" one-third of the electorate. There must not only be a mix of strategic factors, but they must be carried out in rough approximation of the strategic priorities. There can be no exact formula for this and even a rigid ratio of 2:1, 3:4, or 4:2 may be difficult to accept. But somehow, the campaigner must make sure that first things really do come first.

Third, the fact that many things must be done simultaneously, yet by priority in terms of effort, will inevitably lead to some major consequences for the structuring of the campaign. In each situation it will be somewhat different. The major consequences of the nonparty-centered campaign exemplified above include: building a separate organization, a heavy commitment to personal campaigning by the candidate, raising a large amount of funds to promote candidate image and advertising, and greater use of the mass media. In a setting where the candidate is of the majority party, and that advantage is relatively large, one can run a more party-centered campaign, particularly if the party organization is active. Thus, the major theme of implementation must be structured to serve a set of simultaneous and priority-ordered set of strategic principles.

In this final stage of setting and ordering priorities, the strategists should strive to *maintain* the proper mix established when the strategic factors were set. If this is accomplished and relevant tactics are established to support each principle, then a set of activities in the campaign will have been decided upon, and an approximate ordering of their importance will have been established.

In conclusion, this chapter has attempted to convey the notion that strategy building requires the application of strategic assessment factors to the setting of the campaign by engaging in strategic thinking. From these considerations, strategists can establish a strategy based on an approximate mix of voting forces and campaign process with appropriate tactics or specific campaign activities suitable to each particular setting. Placing priorities on strategic factors, and then ordering them, complete the process of establishing campaign strategies.

Notes to Chaper 6

1. Lewis A. Froman, Jr., *Congressmen and Their Constituencies* (Chicago: Rand McNally, 1963), pp. 51-52.

2. Ibid., 57-58.

3. Chalres O. Jones, "The Role of the Campaign in Congressional Politics," *The Electoral Process,* ed. M. Kent Jennings and L. Harmon Zeigler (Englewood Cliffs, N.J.: Prentice-Hall, 1966), pp. 29-30.

4. Ibid., pp. 30-31.

5. David Paletz, "The Neglected Context of Congressional Campaigns," Polity II (1971): 197.

6. Ibid., pp. 197-205.

7. Ibid., pp. 205-210.

8. Ibid., pp. 212-217.

9. Alexander Heard, *The Costs of Democracy* (Garden City, New York: Doubleday and Company, 1962), pp. 27-30; Conrad Joyner, "Running a Congressional Campaign," in *Practical Politics in the United States,* ed. Cornelius P. Cotter (Boston: Allyn and Bacon, 1969), p. 162; Frank J. Sorauf, *Party Politics in America,* 2nd ed. (Boston: Little, Brown, 1972), p. 245.

10. Froman, *Congressmen and Their Constituencies,* p. 53.

11. Ibid.

12. Paletz, "The Neglected Context of Congressional Campaigns," p. 212.

13. John W. Kingdon, *Candidates for Office: Beliefs and Strategies* (New York: Random House, 1968), p. 29.

14. Ibid., p. 133.

15. Ibid., p. 133.

16. Joyner, "Running a Congressional Campaign," p. 162.

For Further Reading and Research

Barkan, Joel D. and Bruno, James E. "Operations Research in Planning Political Campaign Strategies." *Operations Research* 20 (1972): 925–41.

Campaign Insight. Wichita, Kansas: Campaign Associates, Inc. Twice-monthly newsletter of campaign techniques.

Campaign Practices Reports. Washington: Plus Publications, Inc. Twice-monthly newsletter on campaign finance and other campaign legislation, national and state.

Election News. Washington: Heldref Publications. Monthly newsletter for election officials.

Federal Election Commission Record. Washington: Federal Election Commission. A monthly survey of FEC procedures, advisory opinions, and court decisions affecting campaign regulations.

Fishel, Jeff. *Party and Opoosition: Congressional Challengers in American Politics*. New York: McKay, 1973.

Ripon Society and Brown, Clifford W. *Jaws of Victory*. Boston: Little, Brown, 1974.

Weil, Gordon L. *The Long Shot: Geoge McGovern Runs for President*. New York: Norton, 1973.

White, Theodore, H. *The Making of the President, 1960*. New York: Athenum, 1961.

_____ . *The Making of the President, 1964*. New York: Athenum, 1965.

_____ . *The Making of the President, 1968*. New York: Athenum, 1969.

_____ . *The Making of the President, 1972*. New York: Athenum, 1973.

Wilcox, William H. and O'Brien, James. "How to Win Campaigns: Critical Path Method." *National Civic Review* 66 (1967):265–69.

Campaign Organization

In each campaign, regardless of the size of the constituency or visibility of the office sought, campaigners must undertake some effort to put things together, and, therefore, some form of organization exists. Just as the strategy is based on the setting of the campaign, the organization is based on the setting and strategy. Campaigns for high visibility offices, covering large, diverse constituencies and undertaking many tactics, are generally more elaborately organized than those for low visibility offices in small, homogenous constituencies, undertaking a narrower range of activities. Setting and strategy notwithstanding, campaigns range considerably from the well-organized to the very poorly organized. The organizational function of the campaign is multi-faceted: to divide the labor, to conduct strategy and tactics, to connect the operations, to demonstrate support, to schedule and advance, to raise funds, to conduct direct voter-contact activities, to conduct research and issue development, to appeal to special interests, and generally to be part of the campaign resource base.[1]

Studies of campaign organization are quite scant in the literature, and few detail the campaign effectiveness of one type of campaigning over another.[2] In Burdett Loomis' interesting study of 102 marginal congressional districts, it was discovered that less centralized decision-making campaign structures and more professionally run media campaigns tend to achieve better results than previous campaigns of fellow partisans.[3] Most works on campaign organization, however, do not go beyond an account of the campaign structure and campaign roles. Yet, they do indicate that campaign organizations vary considerably in the extent and the manner in which they are organized.

THE RANGE OF ORGANIZATIONS

Campaign organizations range from one-man operations literally run under the candidate's hat, to multi-divisional, multi-million-dollar operations run by vast numbers of personnel. The Nixon campaign for re-election in 1972 (The Committee for the Re-election of the President) was perhaps the most extensive campaign organization in history. It's budget, which exceeded 50 million dollars, organized 337 paid staff members and thousands of volunteers into: a separate finance division; its own advertising agency, The November Group; a polling organization; 11 direct-mail and 250 telephone centers throughout the country; an advance division; a field organization division; a vote security division; a number of special interest group divisions and subdivisions; as well as the now famous but ill-fated security division,[4] whose operatives were apprehended while burglarizing the Democratic headquarters in the Watergate building in Washington, D.C. At the other end of the scale, many successful campaigns are organized on a much less extensive basis, having only a small number of persons performing the various functions. The typical congressional campaign has five or fewer paid employees and as many as 300 to 350 volunteer workers.[5] Legislative and aldermanic contests generally operate with many fewer volunteers and without the benefit of paid workers. In these smaller constituency campaigns, the functions that are divided among many specialists in large campaigns, if performed at all, are performed by a few generalists.

The setting and strategy play a large part in both the style and extent of campaign organization. In a given election, the office sought, the nature of the constituency, and the candidate will be important determinants of the type and extent of organization. A gubernatorial candidate running against an incumbent of the majority party in a state may need a large-scale, multi-divisional, multi-media, citizens' organization effort. On the other hand, a legislative incumbent seeking re-election in a safe district may be able to rely primarily on himself and perhaps a few key party people around the district to erect a few signs and sell tickets to fund-raising events. Candidates running for parks and recreation boards need not gear up for extensive volunteer and media effort, but presidential candidates must. Strategic decisions may mean different organizational forms: working through the party organization, creating a new citizen organization, or a candidate organization consisting of a hybrid of the two. A dearth of funds and a relatively large number of workers may call for an extensive person-to-person volunteer structure, whereas the reverse may require more mass media and a different organization. Strategies that primarily reinforce partisanship can be structured through the party more easily. Strategies that primarily try to activate latent candidate sentiment need separate organizations, employing face-to-face contact on behalf of the candidate, having a candidate-centered finance base, and creating and using mass-media candidate messages in addition to any efforts to reinforce that candidate's partisan supporters.

The size of the office does not always dictate the extent of the organization. Many incumbent congressmen, particularly those from very safe districts, have casual organizations. Their organizations very often have been tested over time, and "campaigning" is a continuous activity, particularly the public relations aspect. Moreover, the organization is being constantly developed, added to, refined, and extended. Its outward appearance may be casual, with few functional divisions, little division of labor or "divisions," but they are suited to the incumbent's style.

There are, then, no proven formulas for imposing an organization on a campaign, since each organization is dependent on setting and strategy. It would be convenient but inappropriate to proffer an ideal campaign organization, as many manuals do. Huckshorn and Spencer report that the novice campaigner is often tempted to rely on the advice of others, formulas suggested by manuals, or, they may revert to the campaign style appropriate to previous election contests.[6] Such temptations should be resisted at all costs in favor of the more difficult but appropriate task of suiting the campaign organization to the exigencies of setting and strategy.

MODES OF ORGANIZATION

There are many forms of organization in campaigns, all established to meet various campaigners' conceptions of connecting the operations for creating and managing a strategy within a setting. Sometimes the campaign is organized functionally by having a single person or committee head a group of activities throughout the entire campaign. In some campaigns, the constituency is divided by area into subunits, and one person takes charge of all activities concerning that unit. In other campaigns, a few generalists perform some or most of the campaign activities. In nearly all large scale campaigns there are specialists at the higher or constituencywide levels, but many of the activities performed in the counties, towns, and precincts are undertaken by a multi-purpose group. We will elaborate on these four modes of organization for purposes of illustration.

Functional-Specialist Organization

One of the more common forms of organization is the functional or specialist mode in which various activities are divided throughout the campaign. It is the one most often recommended in campaign manuals, party pamphlets, and how-to-do-it books. For example, campaign consultant Hank Parkinson recommends that most campaigns should be run by a campaign chairman and four other executive committee chairmen who head the five major committees: fund raising, youth activities, women's activities, publicity, and direct voter contact. Statewide campaigns should be expanded to include research and advertising committees.[7] Extending Parkinson's suggestion, each large subunit or area should also be organized on a functional basis, with a different person in each subunit of the campaign responsible for finance, publicity, youth, women's activities and direct voter contact. Naturally, the existence of each of these functions at the campaignwide or subunit level, depends on the setting and strategy. Other functional divisons might include such clientele interests as labor, students, senior citizens, and business and professional people.

This form of organization has the advantage of allowing for neat expansion and contraction of activity as strategy dictates. It also allows for a total campaign perspective on each of the important activities, for example, all direct voter-contact activities in all areas report and consult through a single person, making responsibility clear cut and easily accountable. The system makes use of specialization; some workers are better at or prefer fund raising, others prefer setting up and carrying out door-to-door activities, others, coffee parties. In many campaigns it is common to put young volunteers in charge of organizing youth or students, women direct women's activities, and union members conduct labor activities. A final advantage is that as each function is broken down by relatively large subunits there is the flexibility to assign workers to priorities within the subunit.

The chief drawback to this system appears to be that in many campaigns even this simple division may be too rigidly specialized. Youth, women's and voter-contact activities may overlap in some campaigns to such an extent that divisioning may be difficult. Moreover, there inevitably will be activities that do not neatly fit into the established categories, meaning that committee chairmen may try to include them for purposes of expansion, or repel them to avoid

Figure 7.1   A Functional-Specialist Organization

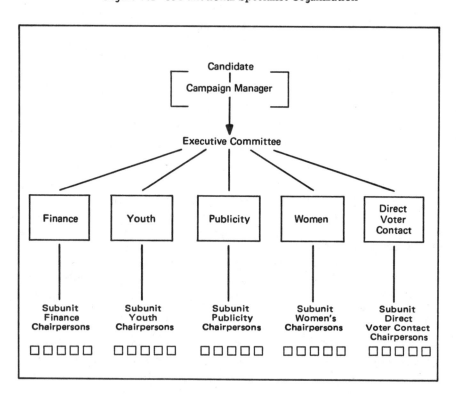

more of a burden. Finally, this system may operate rather well with a few persons at the top, but it may be difficult to find five capable and willing specialists for each subunit of the campaign.

Generalist Organization

The generalist form of organization is one that is often used to deal with the problems of a small number of workers and rigid specialization. It is best characterized as an organizational form in which the workers perform whatever tasks are necessary, in any part of the constituency to carry out the strategy. It's counterpart in athletics is much closer to a hockey team than a professional football team. Whether the task at hand is literature distribution, raising money, or putting up display advertising, all available workers pitch in to get the job done. No known campaign manual ever suggests this form of organization, but it is probably the most prevalent. In its purest form, generalists should, of course, work anywhere in the constituency deemed important by the campaign group. This form of organization does not mean that there is absolutely no division of labor; one person may write the press release and another take charge of the treasury. It is assumed that with the exception of a few such tasks all

Figure 7.2   A Generalist Organization

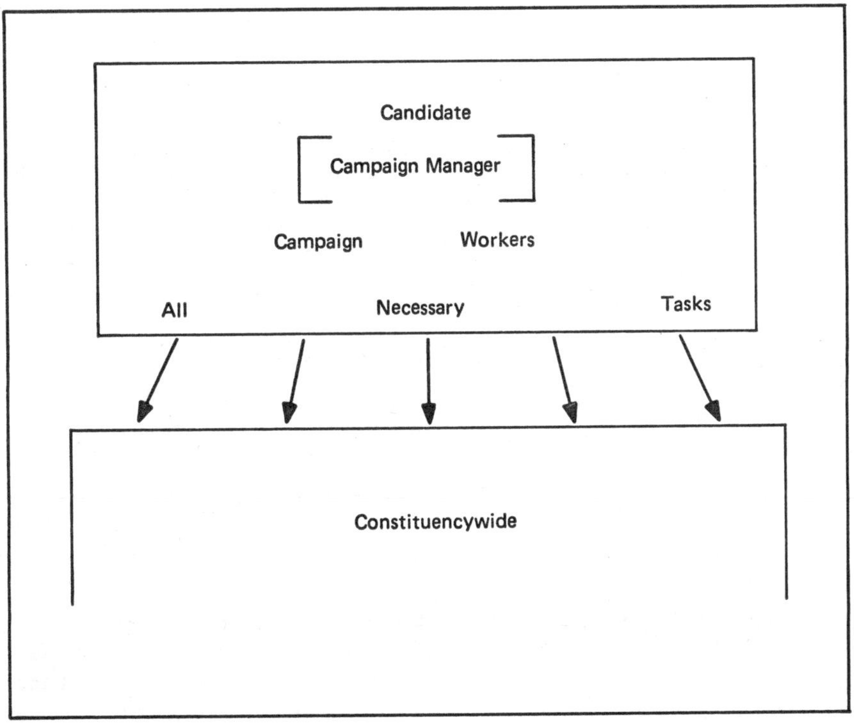

workers are generalists.

A variant of the generalist form of organization is frequently used by experienced campaigners for high visibility offices: a small group of decision makers collectively plan the strategy and labor is divided loosely. Bibby and Davidson characterize Senator Abraham Ribicoff of Connecticut as following such a relaxed or informal manner:

> As in all of Ribicoff's campaigns, there was little formal organization. Decisions on strategy and tactics were in the hands of an informal directorate of four men. The candidate himself made all of the final decisions, especially when differences of opinion arose among his advisors. Newman (his Washington administrative assistant) as campaign director was in charge of coordination and certain day-to-day operations, such as issuing press releases. He was stationed in Hartford and rarely accompanied Ribicoff on his campaign swings. Herman Wolf (a long time friend and close political advisor, a public relations executive) contributed indispensible advice and expertise, especially in over-all strategy and the preparation of media materials. Finally, Wilbur Randall headed the advertising agency hired by the state party and its major candidates. Randall's office served as agent for the state party and for candidates Ribicoff and Dempsey in contracting radio and TV time, preparing advertisements, planning layouts, and handling the technical work relating to campaign literature and the mass media.[8]

The campaign under discussion took place after a twenty-four-year career in Connecticut politics, including the state house, Congress, two terms as Governor and as a member of the Cabinet. Ribicoff obviously was established in state politics, was well known both inside the party structure and to the public, and had experienced many campaigns. Apparently, he continued a pattern of organization based on previous successful efforts. Thus, a rather extensive media-oriented campaign for a high visibility office in a statewide constituency can operate without an extensive or complex organizational structure.

This form of organization naturally maximizes the efforts of workers in campaigns that have very few workers, very often, but not exclusively, for low visibility offices in small constituencies. The candidate has so few volunteers that he needs workers willing to do a little bit of everything. Frequently in such campaigns, the strategy is not complex and the corresponding tactics and tasks to be performed are not so diverse, thus, a generalist orientation may be the most logical as well as the most practical. The candidate, who very often is the campaign manager in such situations, or the manager has a clear sense of what to do and has very little problem deciding who is to do it. The carrying out of priorities is somewhat simpler under a generalist system because the "team" can be moved easily from task to task without a great deal of concern for specialities or organizational "turf." Incidentally, students who campaign for course credit very often find that they learn the most about campaigning as one of a few generalists, experiencing a little bit of many activities, rather than as a small cog in large machine, such as serving in a specialized role as dormitory voter-registration chairman for a presidential campaign.

The generalist organizational form, however, does not make use of special training or talents that persons might bring to a campaign, or, it may exclude people who by temperment will only raise funds or distribute literature. Furthermore, because one does not specialize, it often happens that generalists do what they like to do best, leaving some necessary activities partially completed or undone. It is not impossible in a generalist organization for a candidate to end up with six speech writers and no fund raisers, press-agents, or workers to distribute literature.

Areal Organization

Two other common forms of campaign organization are actually hybrids of the specialist and generalist models, presumably established to maximize the advantages and minimize the disadvantages of the two. Many campaigns are organized with a loose division of labor at the top and by area in the subunits of the constituency. The area units generally are called upon to perform a number of tasks for the management. Subunit chairpersons report to or deal with any or all of the unit or division leaders. Subunit or divisional leaders are called upon to organize the entire campaign in the area for which they are responsible. They are the chief fund raisers, direct-voter-contact organizers, publicity directors, and special projects organizers for their area. They work under the supervision of all of the campaign directors, depending on the activity to be performed. The system is very often found in large constituency campaigns, but generally organized on a smaller scale. It has the advantage of a more collegial form of organization, yet also takes advantage of specialization at the planning and organizing stage. (See the section in this chapter: Volunteer Activities: A Case Study.) At the subunit level, the areal form recognizes that manpower shortages may require more of a generalist orientation, and that it is better to have a few workers performing many tasks than running the risk of having a lot of workers doing little.

A very common organizational problem inherent in this system is the rivalries between directors for the loyalties and task performance of area chairpersons, contests which on occasion seem to overshadow the contest to be fought at the polls. Area chairpersons do not always know what to do first or to whom they should listen, particularly when they receive conflicting advice. If these problems can be overcome, the areal form makes for efficient use of specialization where it is needed most and for organizational ability and, hopefully, enthusiasm at the unit level, which may well be the prime requisites for generalist type activities at this level.

Large Scale Organization

The other modified form is often found in the largest campaigns, in which strategies are complex, tactics are diverse, and the constituency is very large.

Often it is necessary to organize the campaign to handle a large number of specialties and to organize a number of activities, yet, only a portion of them need be carried out at the lower levels. Thus, a large scale mode of organization combines specialist divisions with subunit generalists who perform only a limited number of campaign tasks. Most modern presidential campaigns, and a great number of gubernatorial and U.S. Senate campaigns are organized along these lines. Under this system, ordinarily one person, often called a field director, is directly responsible for supervising the activities of the subunit campaigners and other directorial personnel deal through the field director if they wish to contact subunit chairpersons.

Ordinarily, the various specialty divisions coordinate with each other at the campaign management level. Some divisions naturally work closer with each other than others. Polling results and other voter information is attuned to advertising, publicity, and direct mail. Issue research is responsive to special groups and publicity. Finance is typically a more separate operation, since it is not linked to other forms of activity. Indeed, in many such campaigns, the finance structure is an operation independent of the campaign organization.[9] In this form of organization, almost all media, publicity, finance, and special

Figure 7.3   An Areal Organization

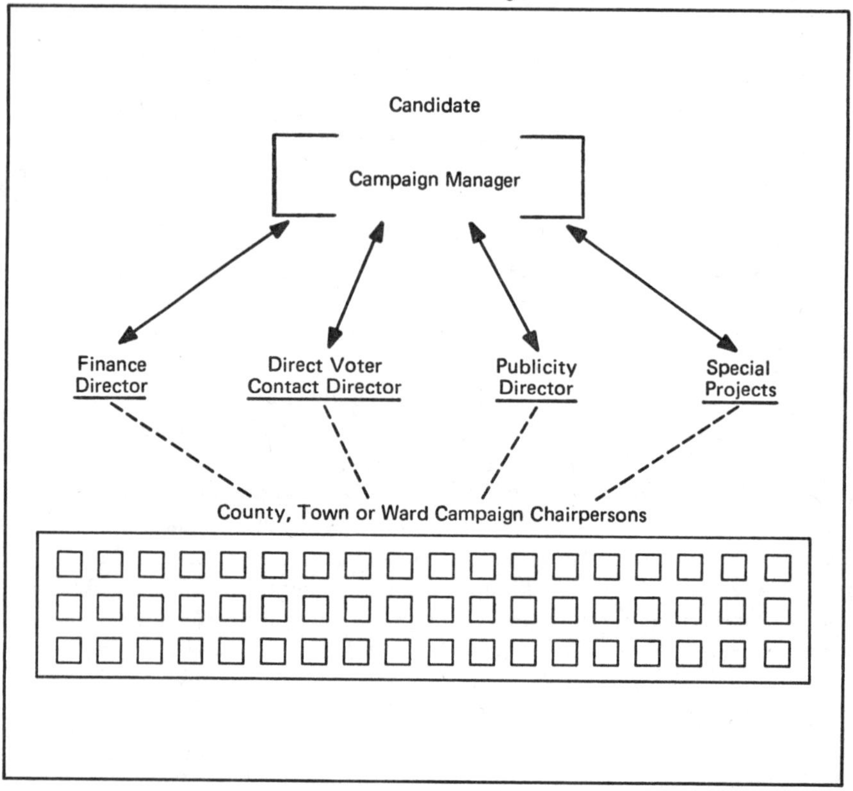

Figure 7.4 A Large Scale Organization

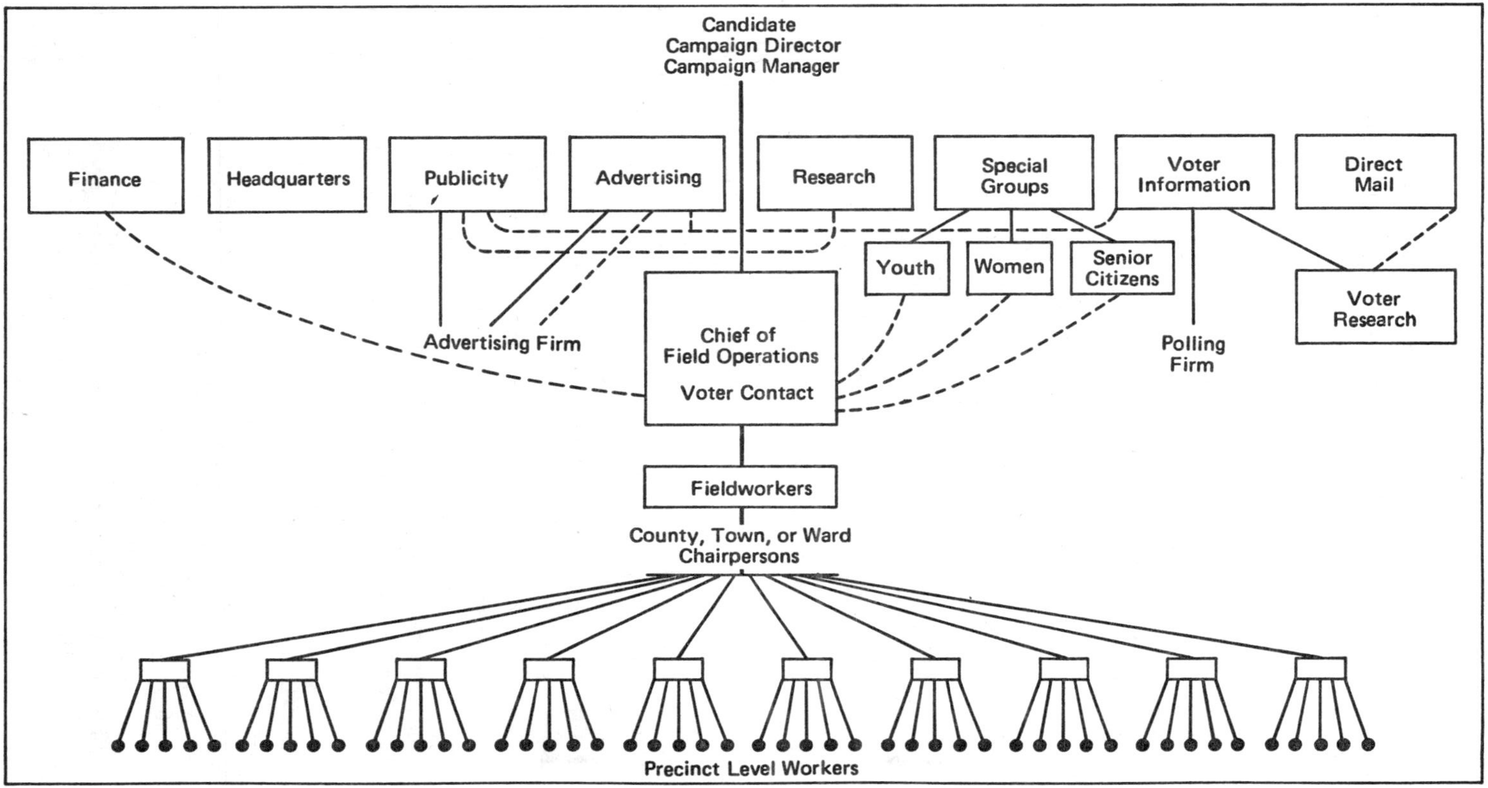

group activities are conducted at the campaign level. Generally, voter contact activities such as voter identification, voter registration, literature distribution, and get-out-the-vote activities are supervised by a field director and very often by a series of field persons who recruit, train, and supervise a series of county, ward, or town chairpersons who, in turn, are responsible for organizing activities at the precinct level. Since the scale of the campaign is large and dependent on a number of specialists and even specialty firms, many of the activities are carried out on a constituencywide basis. By having a relatively large number of workers available, if the direct-mail division needs envelope stuffers on a given day, volunteers from headquarters can fill the supply. Other divisions rarely, if ever, need large numbers of volunteers. The bulk of the volunteers are reserved for the activities which require the most manpower—direct voter contact. The large scale organization mode has developed in response to the changing campaign: media oriented, specialty-based, and constituencywide, yet retaining the earlier forms of face-to-face contact in the precincts.

William Brock's campaign when he unseated Tennessee Senator Albert Gore was typical of this form of large scale campaign organization. Brock, who was then a congressman, set up an organization that included the regular Republican party organization, auxillary groups, his own candidate-centered group, and outside political consultants. (See Figure 7.5.) Undoubtedly, Brock's organization was based on the problem of extending his campaign from a single, safer congressional district to a statewide and more competitive situation, and, of course, running for a more visible office against a well-known challenger.

The four forms of campaign organization are only approximations of the types of organizations found in campaigns. In the actual setting, campaigners will probably find some form of these with a great deal of additional hybridization. No manual can neatly depict the organization that is ideal for so many different situations. Clever campaigners are always making adjustments to fit the available resources to the strategy, tactics, and corresponding organization. As cooperative endeavors intended to accomplish goals mutually, organizations should be designed to serve individuals rather than having individuals serve them. Campaigners therefore would be wise to avoid the pitfall of being slaves to an organizational chart or ideal model.

CAMPAIGN AUTHORITY STRUCTURE

In Chapter 1 reference was made to Lamb and Smith's identification of Goldwater's campaign organization as hierarchical and based on centralized decision-making. After weighing the consequences rationally, decisions were to be made at the top; the appropriate plans were to be carried forth without serious questioning, room for contingencies, new developments, or new information.[10] By contrast, the campaign organization of his opponent, Lyndon Johnson, was incremental in nature. It emphasized adjustments, contingencies, new developments within a framework of systematic design, and rational choice. With this

Figure 7.5 Brock Campaign Structure

Candidate		Policy Committee (11) Pat Brock, Chairman
		Advisory Committee Lewis Donelson, Chairman All Committee Chairmen
Campaign Chairman Nat Winston		
Campaign Coordinator Ken Rietz		Vice Chairman Womens Division Susan H. Boone

Finance Chairman David K. Wilson	Co-Chairman	District Chairmen (8)
Finance Director Lewis Dale		

Research Director	Ballot Security	
Issues Research	State Executive Committee	
Opponent Research	Legislators	Speakers' Bureau (6)
Polling Research	Young Republicans	Truth Squad

Publicity (3)	Advertising Director Harry Treleaven	District Coordinators (13)
	Advertising Comm. (5)	District and County Chairmen
		City and Precinct Chairmen

Field Staff (9)	Staff Assistants	Citizens Chairman
General Counsel	Canvass	Democrats Independents Doctors Lawyers Barbers Cooks Real Estate Insurance Kiwanis Rotary Mayors Farmers Educators Walking Horse People
Treasurer	Brockettes	
	Advance	
Support Staff (15)	Driver and Aide	
	Young Volunteers for Brock	
	YVB Fieldmen (3)	

Source: *National Journal,* September 26, 1970, p. 2082.

approach, the Johnson organization established a loose organizational structure, using primarily the means and techniques that were used in the past, allowing them to: 1) take up only the most pressing problems, delegating and ignoring the others; and, 2) make collective decisions coordinated through bargaining and mutual adjustment in a decentralized and flexible organizational structure.[11]

Each of the models in their ideal form has its appeal as well as its deficiencies. The more hierarchical model used by Goldwater, though generally unpopular among politicians, has the appeal of allowing for greater management (in a business sense) in that rational decisions based on information, weighing of alternatives, coordination, and the carrying out of a plan is attractive. But the model is not without its problems: it is difficult to reach permanent agreement on goals—information is never complete. There are likely to be contingencies, the organizational costs of this type of decision making may exceed the benefits, and different "actors" in the campaign have their own criteria for effectiveness.[12] On the other hand, the more incremental model used by Johnson is appealing to many because it is more "realistic," "practical" and "like we have done before,"[13] and is similar to the realities of party politics. It allows for more, shared decision making with the lower ranks, the ability to meet new situations, and to deal with larger problems. This form too has its problems: the structure is neither firm or sharply delineated, offering a considerable range of choice in which to fit decisions. It may be too crude to offer effective decisional guidelines. The focus on the familiar, the precedented, and the practical can promote bias against new opportunities. Orientation to pressing problems and remedial solutions directs attention away from larger problems that emerge slowly from a long line of incremental decisions. And, where conflicts over goals and values are irreconcilable, coordination is frustrated.[14] Thus, one model of decision making, in its ideal form, appears too rigid and inflexible and the other appears too loose and flexible.

To what extent do campaign organizations fit into the idealized models derived from these two cases of campaign decision making? In a study of 102 congressional campaign organizations, it was found that most campaign organizations can be characterized as centralized in decision making and "flat" in structure. In four of the five campaign-policy areas studied, Loomis found at least 75 percent of all campaign decisions were made either by the candidate or the campaign manager. Republican campaigns tended to be slightly more decentralized, in that they tended to hand more authority over to paid consultants than the Democrats. In terms of decision making concerning overall strategy, Democrats remain firmly in control of their strategies, whereas the Republicans tend to be more decentralized, as indicated in Table 7.1. Loomis does point out that the image of campaign organizations being highly centralized is tempered by findings that: 1) many separate activities, such as mailings or research tended to be more decentralized; and, 2) the campaigns tended to be geographically decentralized. Most specific tasks are executed by individuals or groups other than the candidate or campaign manager, and the campaigns studied averaged more than 15 separate auxillary organizations or offices, spread through their respective districts. This study also pointed out the basically "flat" nature of the campaign structures, that is, that there are few hierarchical levels between the decision-making core of the candidate, campaign manager and the workers who perform campaign tasks. Perhaps, this is due to the relatively small number of workers available in most campaigns.[15] Thus, most campaign decision making is highly centralized and non-hierarchical in nature.

Campaign organizations rarely resemble other, more permanent organizations. This is due to many factors: their impermanence, the need to rely on volunteers, the need to perform so many activities, the general inexperience of the operatives, and the lack of a technology. For example, businessmen who believe their methods are superior and universally applicable often become frustrated with the lack of business techniques in the campaign. The late Robert Humphreys, longtime public relations man for the Republican National Committee, thought businessmen could often bring important skills to the campaign: their ability to organize, their ability to keep records, their tendency toward more rational decisions, their greater tendency to follow through on decisions, and their willingness to invest in training.[16] On the other hand, Humphreys' experience with businessmen also led him to observe some very serious drawbacks to including them in campaigns: businessmen's inordinate suspicion and low opinion of politicians and political activists, their belief that money will solve all problems, the fallacious belief that politics needs business methods, when unlike business, one can rarely weigh, measure, test, gauge, and calculate, the impatience of business people with political protocol, and most important,

Table 7.1 Centralization of Authority in Planning Overall
Congressional Campaign Strategy

Person(s) Responsible for Making Final Decision	Party	
	Democrats(46)	Republicans(53)
Candidate	71%	42%
Manager	19	28
Paid Consultant	2	8
Single Individual (Volunteer)	8	2
Committee	2	8
Staff as a whole	4	13
	100	101[*]

[*]Rounded—figures represent percent of all the parties' campaigns which allocate authority. No multiple answers permitted.

Source: Burdett A. Loomis, "Campaign Organizations in 'Competitive' 1972 House Races," Unpublished Doctoral Dissertation, University of Wisconsin, 1974.

their inability to grasp the chain of authority—the chain exists in politics but seldom the authority.[17]

The American form of campaign organizational authority appears to be unique—strong strategic authority and decision making at the top, with decisions often carried out by semi-independent task operatives in the middle, built on top of a voluntary base, with very little distance between top and bottom. Frequently position is not based on outside prestige, but on the needed political skills one can offer and the time one is willing to commit. In other cases, position is based on proximity to the candidate. Within this framework, however, one must often gain the acquiescence in decisions of many volunteers, active attentive publics, group and party leaders. Those who have had a say in past political affairs will expect to be heard in the present campaign. On the other hand, those who are new and constitute the candidate's differential base of support will also expect to be heard. All of these characteristics and many others give the campaign its own structure.

One can thus conclude by returning to the two models of campaign decision making: the structured, hierarchical comprehensive and the contingency based adjustment incremental pattern. Few campaigns are very comprehensive. However, more rational decisions based on information can be built on the more incremental structure with which most campaigners find themselves. Somehow the organizational structure must allow for information, weighting of alternatives, shared decision making with information from those below, coordination between units, and planning. Yet, the ability to change, meet new situations, innovate, and deal with the larger problems must be retained. Those designing organizations to be like the comprehensive model should consider becoming more incremental. Those who find themselves incremental should consider moving toward the comprehensive.

MANAGEMENT AND ORGANIZATIONAL ROLES

The vast range in campaign organization size, staffing, and resources makes it difficult to state precisely what a given campaign should have in terms of a particular person or set of persons performing designated management tasks to fulfill organizational requirements of the division of labor. Moreover, one might assume (correctly) that the other aspects—setting and strategy—help determine the proper division of labor. Therefore, it appears more appropriate to speak in terms of management and organizational roles, some of which will be performed by individuals, some will be performed collectively, and some will be performed by the candidate alone. Of course, considerations of setting and strategy will determine the roles.

Campaign Manager

The campaign manager or campaign coordinator is the person who puts it all together. Theoretically, the manager is responsible for coordinating the entire effort, including supervision of staff and committee chairman and all operations, to ensure that the strategy is implemented. In many campaigns the manager takes on other responsibilities including: scheduling of the candidate; liason with the party, other campaigns and elected officials; approving of organizational, media, and print expenditures; sometimes setting up and running the head-quarters; establishing a subunit organization; and, fending off impractical but well-meaning "cinch" ideas for winning the election from loyalists. In other words, the managerial function is to establish and maintain the organization, guiding it toward its stated goal of electing a candidate. When the manager and the candidate are separate individuals, it frees the candidate to concentrate on personal campaigning. In the words of two experienced politicians, "The candidate meets and speaks; the manager schedules and stimulates."[18]

The advice on the important characteristics a manager must have is legion. Stephen Shaddeg, for example, suggests that the manager should know the constituency, be acquainted with the media, interested in politics, able to work with people, able to say no (even to the candidate), coldblooded and hard-nosed about spending funds, able to resist the unreasonable demands for the candidate's time by party leaders, and understand how the voter is motivated.[19] There are many such lists.

Campaign managers are both professional and amateur, recruited from various sources. In congressional campaigns the sources of managers are: (1) the candidate serves as his own manager, relies on his wife, family members, or close relatives; (2) the candidate relies on trusted and available friends or business associates; (3) the political party provides a full or part-time campaign manager; (4) the candidate hires the services of a professional manager; (5) incumbent officials frequently use one of their staff members as manager, ordinarily by temporary removal from government payroll to the campaign payroll; and, (6) professional campaign management firms take over the operation of the campaign.[20] The Huckshorn and Spencer study of losing congressional candidates found that 60 percent selected friends or business associates, 22 percent managed their own campaigns or relied on close relatives, 14 percent used party officials; only 4 percent used professional managers. Thus, over eighty percent of the campaigns they studied had nonprofessional or amateur campaign managers.[21] Leuthold's study of 19 California congressional campaigns indicated that three of them retained the services of professional management firms, whereas most Congressmen used a staff member as manager, and the remainder of the candidates hired managers who were knowledgeable in campaigning, but most were running a congressional campaign for the first time.[22] No systematic information on campaign managers exists at other levels, but it can be expected that as one moves to the higher visibility races for governor, sentaor, and president, managers are almost always experienced and professional. Conversely, the lower visibility races are more likely to have the candidate either serving as his or her own manager or relying on a close relative or friend.

Most experienced politicians suggest that the candidate should never serve as his own campaign manager. One adage is, " 'He who defends himself in a court of law has a fool for a client,' in the same way a candidate who campaigns under his own management invites disaster before he begins."[23] Consultant Shaddeg says, "In baseball the same man cannot be both pitcher and catcher. In politics the candidate cannot successfully manage his own campaign—a truism which was painfully demonstrated when I attempted to manage my own campaign for the Republican nomination for the United States Senate in 1962."[24] These observations are made from the vantage point of high visibility campaigns. In general, it is much easier to leave the organizational details to a manager, and, almost all campaigns waged in large constituencies have managers, yet the scant but revealing evidence presented earlier regarding congressional candidates suggests that in the smaller constituencies and for the lower visibility offices this may cause problems. Smaller amounts of money and a dearth of skilled personnel or other workers may make it impossible for anybody but the candidate to serve as manager. If the candidate is lucky, he may find a loyal and willing person whose availability in terms of time is the only requisite for selection as manager. Many a campaign is run under such conditions. Thus, a better rule of thumb may have to be, "It is better to have the candidate or some other available person manage the campaign than to not manage it at all."

It is becoming increasingly popular for some candidates to retain the services of a professional campaign management firm. The extent of their services ranges from occasional consulting, or auditing a campaign plan, to management of the entire campaign. The specific tasks performed by these firms include information, planning, management of the day-to-day operations of the campaign, handling of the candidate, media, and advertising.[25] These firms are able to relieve many of the management problems that often confront candidates, particularly when they are new and inexperienced. Many pitfalls can be avoided by employing them.[26] On the other hand, their retention fees make their services prohibitive to all but the affluent candidate. A congressional candidate is likely to pay such a firm a $10,000 to 25,000 management fee plus expenses, and, in some cases the 15 percent commission for placing advertisements is also collected by the management firm. Even short consulting or auditing sessions are expensive, ranging from $350 to $1000 per day plus expenses.

On occasion a campaign director is selected in addition to a campaign manager. This individual is ordinarily well-respected and has many political connections with party officials, elected officials, and fund-raising sources. Some activities the "director" ordinarily assumes are: generating the support of political activists, key attentive publics, and interest groups; generating support for the candidate among party officials and elected officials, including securing their participation at campaign functions; and, participating in special fund-raising activities including negotiating for support from other candidates, tapping special sources as well as established party sources of funds. After the 1972 Democratic Convention the McGovern forces selected out-going National Chairman Lawrence O'Brien to perform the campaign director's role, in an effort to link the McGovern forces with older party activists, organized labor, and traditional fund-raising sources.

Public Relations and Media Director

It is becoming increasingly important for the candidate to make use of mass media and public relations techniques, as constituencies are becoming larger and more diversified, the number and types of media formats are expanding, and voting is less party-oriented. Evidence on campaign spending indicates that the largest proportion of increases comes in purchases of media time and space.[27] Even when access to media is by unpaid means, it requires considerable campaign-staff-development time, commitment, and often expense. In addition, most candidates are constantly engaged in the public relations activities of meeting groups, dealing with newspeople, and preparation of advertising materials. Whether the format is paid or unpaid, or the activity is public relations or advertising, considerable skill is required to arrange and supervise such activities. That is why candidates often feel the need to select a public relations and media director.

The duties of the media director, of course, vary considerably with the setting and strategy. Among the activities this person might become involved in are: developing relationships with newsgatherers, including newspaper, radio, and television; arranging meetings or interviews for the candidate with editors and reporters; writing and distributing news releases; preparing media lists; arranging for the candidate to appear on interview shows, talk shows, news shows, in news conferences and possibly in debates; writing speeches; preparation, editing, and placement of advertisements or making last minute changes, and checks if an agency is involved; working with photographers; ensuring news coverage at campaign events; developing written materials by-lined by the candidate, including articles, published questionnaires, or letters to the editor; arranging for public appearances of the candidate before groups or other large audiences; and, arranging for contacts with attentive publics.

As the preceding assignment sheet indicates, the job ideally calls for someone who is knowledgeable and skilled, particularly in working with the news media. Many candidates find it useful to hire a skilled newsperson; some hire public relations consultants; and, some simply use persons who have the ability to get news coverage and have the time to devote to the campaign. Incumbent officials who have press secretaries or another staff person in charge of stimulating and working with the news almost always use this staff person as campaign media director. One study of non-incumbent congressional candidates indicated that only about one-fourth had separate media directors and another one-fourth assigned public relations and media to the campaign manager. Nearly one-half had advertising and public relations firms to assist in all or part of their campaigns.[28] Advertising and public relations firms can lend skill and knowledge of the media to a campaign, particularly if they operate in similar media markets as the constituency. If they handle news work they disadvantage the candidate in that they are not available for the everyday, late breaking, or emergency news work.[29] Candidates often need releases sent from late night meetings, coverage of a notable who attends a dinner or rally, or reaction to a last-minute development. Many firms are likely to adhere to a nine-to-five schedule.

The Campaign Legal Advisor

Every campaign is conducted within a web of state or national legal regulations on campaigning and campaign finance. Campaigns using the broadcast media are also subject to a set of national communications campaign regulations. Where and when one can campaign, the requirements of reporting and deadlines for filing them, what one can and cannot do to get elected, from whom one can and cannot collect money, and how much can be spent are but a few of the proscriptions in the legal code of campaigning. The 1972 presidential campaign and the Watergate hearings focused national attention on campaign violations and campaign spending excesses. These incidents, coupled with the already more stringent Election Reform Acts of 1971 and 1974,[30] have created a climate of reform which will lead to even greater legal control over campaigns and campaign spending.[31] A number of states tightened the campaign portion of their election codes considerably in the years following that election, and many other states and the U.S. Congress are on the verge of doing so. This means that the campaigner increasingly will be forced to operate within a more involved and stringent legal code, and that enforcement (and penalties) will no longer be token. The campaign enterprise is likely to face a legal context similar to that involved in public utilities, transportation, housing, or many other such enterprises. Therefore, every campaign can benefit from legal advice, either by retaining a counsel or by securing the services of a volunteer lawyer.

The legal advisor has many important campaign tasks. First, after becoming familiar with the legal code of campaigns and elections, legal advisors often provide explanations and summaries of applicable laws to the campaign staff and volunteers, particularly in regard to direct voter-contact activities. Second, the counsel can monitor all legally prescribed requirements, such as filing deadlines, nominating petitions, and financial statements both for time and legality. Third, the legal advisor can consult with the finance chairmen to assure that donations or other fund-raising techniques are within state and federal law. Fourth, the legal counsel can review legal contracts for goods and services, particularly when they involve extensive campaign commitments. Fifth, the legal advisor may be called upon to interpret the Federal Communications Act on behalf of the candidate when a radio or television station is not properly interpreting the law. Sixth, he may be called upon to review the literature of the candidate or the opposition for any violation of the libel laws, or for any other monitoring of the opposition for questionable practices or possible violations of the law.

On occasion, the legal advisor may have to handle a legal challenge on behalf of the candidate. For example, in Jay Cooper's successful 1971 bid to become the first black mayor of Pritchard, Alabama, his legal counsel sought legal remedies for the public issuance of ward voting lists with no addresses on them. This situation posed quite a serious problem to a black candidate in a small Southern town; it had the effect of voiding voter challenges, even though such challenges are provided by Alabama law. Since the voter list had not been purged of ineligible voters, and since black voter registrants had been regularly discouraged and misinformed, it was to the Cooper campaign's advantage to gain some meaningful role in the supervision of the election. Thus, their legal counsel formally requested the Justice Department to send in federal observers under the Voting Rights Act of 1965.[32]

In many cases the legalities of campaigning are not as involved as this Alabama case, and operating within the law is a relatively routine matter. For this reason most candidates are able to secure the services of an attorney on a volunteer basis. Many lawyers are active in politics and very often are willing to perform this very minor (in the context of all the legal work they do) legal service for a friendly candidate. Indeed, in even the largest campaigns, the legal work is very often done on a contributory basis, if a lawyer is not already part of the campaign group. Some campaigns expand their legal staffs on election day to have a network of volunteer lawyers, available by telephone at their law offices, to deal with legal challenges at the polls. Poll watchers in various areas are provided with the telephone number of the lawyer covering their area, in the event a voter is to be challenged or an illegal activity is occurring at the polls. Because legal advice is a short-term voluntary service, it should not be regarded as unimportant. Many a petition has been denied, an injunction has been ordered, or even a winning candidate unseated for failure to follow regulations.

Research Director

In some campaigns it is often necessary to have a separate research operation, or at least a research director responsible for coordinating issue type research and voting research. Some campaigns, particularly the larger ones, choose to separate the two areas of research. Among the areas of responsibility of a research director are: voting records, background material, and personal information about the candidate and his opponent; researching and developing campaign issues (including tabulation of the opposition's stand on the issues), the candidate's stands on the issues, and preparing "backgrounds" and position papers; collecting newspaper information and developing clipping files; gathering and analyzing political history and voting habits of a constituency, and; working with strategists on targeting key precincts. Most of these activities are covered in Chapters 4 and 5. In many campaigns, the staff is fortunate to have the volunteer services of one or a number of persons skilled and knowledgeable in these areas. Somehow, issues or voting research draws a commitment from volunteers that other activities do not. If no separate director's title is given to someone, some of these activities will have to be performed by campaign workers.

Finance Director

Campaign finance is generally organized through a finance director or treasurer, a finance chairmen or a finance committee. Of all of the campaign roles, the finance role is the one most likely to involve the work of many people, since sources of funds and contacts are quite diversified. Thus, candidates very often find it necessary to make this a multiheaded function.

Financial allocation as well as the better known fund-raising are the two major activities of the finance director. Very often the fund-raising aspect (including planning dinners, soliciting donors, planning direct mail campaigns, seeking group contributions and projecting financial needs) is the province of the committee, if there is one. The finance chairman, treasurer, or finance director is generally responsible for spending, signing the checks, serving as campaign accountant by keeping the books, reporting finances when legally required, and overseeing purchases ranging from printing to headquarters insurance. Often, the finance structure is separate from the campaign. Chapter 8 deals with campaign financing in detail.

Coordinator of Volunteers

In campaigns that enjoy the benefits of a very large number of volunteer workers, one person is often placed in charge of handling volunteer efforts. Volunteers can be a valuable campaign resource but they must be dealt with in a systematic and professional manner. Among the tasks a volunteer chairperson might have are: recruitment of personnel, transportation, training, scheduling, assignment to priority projects and areas, keeping volunteer records, and coordination with other branches of the campaign in order to supply them with manpower needs and priorities, as dictated by the campaign plan. Since it is the volunteers who are being supervised, the coordinator should possess the necessary personality characteristics that we commonly label "ability to deal with people."

Field Organization Personnel

As the various organization plans depicted earlier indicate, certain activities of the campaign that are neither constituencywide nor face-to-face in nature are organized on a subarea basis, often by congressional district, county, town, or some other political subdivision. Also, political parties, one of the prime sources of support for campaign assistance, are organized on this basis. Campaigners, therefore, very often find it useful to designate a person or persons to organize and oversee these activities in the various subunits by which the campaign is organized.

Field organizers or field workers generally travel throughout their assigned areas, working with campaign workers and party leaders. Their duties include recruitment of area chairpersons; instructing them; being present at important subunit campaign meetings; checking on campaign registration, voter identification, and get-out-the-vote drives; serving as liason with local party leaders; distributing campaign materials; dealing with complaints at the local level; and reporting happenings in the field to the campaign leadership.

Experienced campaign field personnel are difficult to recruit and expensive to retain. Expenses to maintain fieldworkers can often double salaries. The work is short term, and pay generally low, and the hours and miles are long. Those persons who last beyond one campaign generally move up to more prestigious and less demanding positons. Incumbents, of course, have the advantage of using staff persons. But the typical fieldworker is a willing but only a semi-experienced campaigner. Thus, use of paid field personnel is an expensive proposition, despite their usefulness.

Many campaigns use volunteer area coordinators to perform some of the functions of fieldworkers. Congressman William Steiger of Wisconsin used a series of county coordinators in his 1970 campaign. Their duties were to supervise all Steiger campaign activities in the county, to arrange speaking engagements, meetings, and caravans, and then arrange for literature distribution. Steiger and his campaign manager carefully coordinated the activities of these county campaign leaders with the county party chairmen.[33] Use of volunteer subunit coordinators can be a valuable substitute for a paid field staff or a supplement to one, but work with such part-time personnel requires a great deal of instruction, attention, and supervision. The campaigner should be prepared for a great deal of unevenness in activity among these coordinators. That is, some will accept the title and do nothing; other will perform only token tasks, and others will put in a great deal of time and effort, performing well.

Special Group Coordinators

In many campaigns, the leadership makes a special effort directed at certain groups which cut across the geographic lines along which the campaign is ordinarily organized. Among the more common special group efforts in contemporary campaigns are women, students, youth, labor, nationality groups, occupational or professional groups, and senior citizens. In addition, some candidates find it necessary to form some sort of auxiliary nonparty organization or citizens' committee to provide an avenue for persons who wish to participate but want to steer clear of any partisan implication. Such groups are becoming less important as candidate-centered campaigns become more visible. The purpose of citizens' committees is to mobilize and convey support for the candidate among the particular group.

The activities of these groups in various campaigns range from nominal paper organizations to full-blown mini-campaigns. Very often the candidate's news operation publicly announces the formation of the committee listing the names of the group, particularly group "achievers" from a variety of fields and geographic areas, including the prestigious, honorary chairpersons and working chairpersons. The group may receive a separate area and an individual telephone listing at headquarters, its own stationary, with perhaps the same design motif carried over to other display or advertising. Very often, the next step is the formation of similar groups in subunits of the constituency, for example, county, women's, or student coordinators. Among the activities these groups might engage in are: special voter registration, literature distributions, get-out-the-vote and absentee voter drives; fund-raising activities; organization of callers to talk-show broadcasts or letter-writing campaigns; and liaison with any organized groups of a similar category.[34] Depending on the strategy and the setting, the formation and use of such groups can be valuable auxiliary forces, ensuring the right people in attentive and voting publics are mobilized.

Campaign Aide

It is often useful to employ an aide who can travel with the candidate and who handle many of the details of the campaign confronting the candidate as he meets with various groups and individuals throughout the constituency. This is particularly true in very large constituencies where the distances to be traveled are great, and there are many new people to meet. The aide very often serves as a driver, particularly in those campaigns that are wholly dependent on the automobile for travel. The aide maintains the itinerary, and upon arriving at the destination, checks to see that arrangements are as agreed, handles any distribution of campaign materials, and records any problems, questions, and or requests. In sum, the aide relieves the candidate of everything but personal campaigning while on tour. This may appear on the surface to be a superfluous, ego-satisfying or fringe position in a campaign, but aides prove valuable when hundreds of miles must be traveled, thousands of people must be met, and details must be managed. Indeed, it is not uncommon for a small campaign operation in a large constituency to have no other campaign staff but an aide. Many candidates for state offices, such as treasurer, secretary of state, attorney general, or state board offices, have only an aide on their campaign staff.

VOLUNTEER WORKERS

The managerial roles thusfar depicted can be performed by either amateur or professional campaign workers, paid or unpaid personnel. In the larger campaigns, these management tasks tend to be performed by the professional and paid workers, in the smaller campaigns, workers tend to be unpaid amateurs.

Congressional campaigns are intermediate between the large and small campaigns, and their staffing patterns reflect this. Table 7.2 reflects the extent and quality of personnel in 102 marginal-district House campaign organizations with between eight and nine full-time people working in the congressional campaign, and about five of them paid. The average of thirty two experienced workers, means that these congressional candidates could not rely on many persons with campaign experience. As the very low ratio of full-time staff to total, organizational-size figures indicates, campaigns are not highly professional, even in competitive congressional districts.

Most campaigns rely on volunteer labor—from a few members of the candidate's immediate family and close friends in some, to thousands who have never met the candidate but are supporters, in others. Volunteers perform many of the non-managerial tasks, carrying out the strategy on an everyday basis. They perform many necessary chores, such as ringing doorbells and stuffing envelopes, doing what is dictated by need and dependent on their previous experience.[35] In addition to the free labor performed for the campaign, volunteer activity ordinarily reinforces the supporters' commitments to the candidate. Strongly committed workers can also be "missionaries." Each highly motivated volunteer can represent several votes, if that person stimulates the votes of their immediate family and close friends. In large campaigns, volunteers can reach thousands, and in presidential campaigns, the number is in the hundreds of thousands.

The Experienced Volunteer

Campaign workers, in transition between the more professional managerial roles and the unpaid amateur roles are the experienced volunteers who contribute their services to the campaign. Many such individuals who have participated in numerous campaigns, generally donating a particular skill, exist in various locales. Most of these persons are party loyalists who have participated in campaigns over the years and have become experts in various aspects of campaigning, or they have occupational skills which are useful in the campaign. The skills these persons contribute include fund raising, setting up a campaign headquarters operation, media counseling, ordering materials, securing printing, and

Table 7.2   Average Size, Experience and Professionalism of
House Campaign Organizations

	All Campaigns	Republican	Democratic
Size (total personnel)	216	239	192
Full-time workers	8.8	8.1	9.6
Salaried workers	4.8	4.5	5.1
Experienced workers (total working in previous campaigns for candidate)	32	39	24
Ratio of full-time staff to total staff size	.21	.19	.25

Source: Burdett A. Loomis "Campaign Organizations in 'Competitive' 1972 House Races," Unpublished Doctoral. Dissertation, University of Wisconsin, 1974.

setting up various phases of a voter-contact operation. On the Illinois Demo-cratic scene, Angelo Geocaris, a Chicago attorney and businessman, has con-tributed his time and skills to various campaign fund-raising efforts, extending back to the Paul Douglas Senate campaign of 1948. Ronald Stinett, a former Humphrey staff member and later a political consultant, was a perennial volun-teer precinct work organizer and coordinator in Minneapolis mayoral and state-wide campaigns while he was a full-time graduate student at the University of Minnesota. Advertising executive Miles Spicer, who once ran for the Minnesota Senate himself, has been a regular, unpaid advisor to Democratic candidates, par-ticularly those running in small constituencies who could not otherwise afford his services. Such skilled personnel can be a valuable addition to the campaign, and while their services are gratuitous, their experience hardly makes them amateurs.

The Typical Volunteer

Most campaign volunteers have little experience, and they tend to perform the necessary but more menial tasks. Their involvement in the campaign is almost always part-time, ranging from an hour-or-two to a near full-time number of hours on a regularly scheduled basis. Studies indicate that about 3 to 5 percent of the voting-age population engage in volunteer campaign work in presidential or midterm election years. About 12 to 20 percent, depending on the survey, claim to have worked in at least one campaign sometime. Survey evidence reveals that the potential pool of volunteers is considerably larger, with about three in ten American voters claiming that they would be willing to work in a cam-paign.[36] Campaign volunteers tend to be better educated than the general public, have higher income levels, and hold higher level occupations.[37] For ex-ample, Leuthold's study of California congressional campaigns indicated that about 50 percent of the volunteers were college graduates compared to 12 per-cent of the population. Nearly 25 percent of the volunteers had family incomes over $15,000 per year, whereas the figure for the general population was 7 per-cent.[38]

The number of workers in a campaign appears to vary with the candidate's party and the competitive situation. Unfortunately, no comparative studies exist on the differences between various levels of office, or even comparisons between races at the same level but of different visibility. Illustrative data do exist on the congressional level from two studies that can cast some light on the subject. The Huckshorn and Spencer study of a large number of non-incumbents indicated (see Table 7.3) that the average number of volunteers ranged from 49 to 301. Candidates running in marginal districts (45% to 55%) had a greater success in garnering volunteers than those running in losing districts. Those marginal candidates who ultimately won averaged three times more helpers than those who lost. Republicans tend to get more volunteers regardless of category. Leuthold's study of 19 campaigns seems to point in the same direction. He found the range in actual numbers to be from less than 20 to over 1000, varying with the amount of activity and available precinct workers. The average number of workers was: 330 for all campaigns; 450 for Republicans and 220 for Democrats; 240 for sure winners; 600 for contests in competitive districts; and 175 for those who were classified as sure losers. Incumbents had only a slight advantage in the average number of volunteer workers.[39] These figures appear to be within the same range as those reported in Table 7.2, which represent an average for all marginal districts. While these data are limited in scope, one can surmise that a proportionately greater number of workers will be available in gubernatorial and senatorial campaigns by party and competitive situation, and a somewhat smaller number in lower visibility, small constituency campaigns.

The data on sources of workers in congressional campaigns are also suggestive as to where volunteers are likely to come from in other campaigns. Table 7.4, also from Leuthold's study, indicates that more than half of all campaign workers are from political clubs, which are the party organization in California. The next largest number of workers were from a previous campaign in which a candidate has been involved, and fewer than one-fifth were friends of the candidate before the campaign. Incumbents have an advantage in recruiting previous campaign workers, presumably a greater number of them from prior congressional races. Competitive district candidates are also advantaged, particularly in recruiting party workers. Leuthold concludes that in a campaign of the scale of a congressional campaign, the number of workers who are not friends of the candidate underscores the need for candidates to secure help from large numbers of people that they meet on the campaign trail, in addition to an initial base of friends.[40] The number of campaign workers available from the party organization varies from area to area with the activism of the organization. In higher visibility races, one would probably have to add an additional category of

Table 7.3   Average Number of Volunteer Workers Per Candidate
by Party

Class of Candidates	Republicans	Democrats	Both Parties
All Losing Candidates	99 (N* = 108)	49 (N = 85)	77 (N = 193)
All Marginal Candidates	135 (N = 26)	113 (N = 27)	119 (N = 53)
Marginal Winners	301 (N = 5)	132 (N = 10)	189 (N = 15)
Marginal Losers	96 (N = 21)	86 (N = 17)	91 (N = 38)

*Number of Campaigns

Source: Robert J. Huckshorn and Robert C. Spencer, *The Politics of Defeat: Campaigning for Congress* (Amherst: University of Massachusetts Press, 1971), p. 114.

candidate supporters who are neither party activists nor friends of the candidate, and have not worked for the candidate previously. In other races, there appears no reason to assume that the same pattern of friends, party workers and previous volunteers does not exist, although the relative proportions from each source may be different.

Why They Volunteer

There are many reasons that motivate people to volunteer to work in a campaign; some occur in combination. Volunteers work because they have ideological or issue preferences and regard assisting a candidate as a vehicle for pursuing their concerns. Others work simply out of loyalty to the party with which they are affiliated. Others work because they are friends or neighbors of the candidate and wish to advance his or her cause. Others may work because they are politically ambitious themselves, and see activity on behalf of others as an inroad to politics. Still others work because they see it as part of their civic responsibility, or they envision it as a vehicle to economic rewards, or, perhaps they find campaign work socially fulfilling.[41]

A study of campaign workers in Los Angeles state assembly districts indicated that party loyalty, issue concerns, and candidate orientation (in that order) were the most important reasons given as to why volunteers became active in politics. Party loyalty appeared to be more important to Republicans, whereas Democrats were more likely to stress issue concerns.[42] In a comparison between campaign workers and a sample of the general public, Leuthold found

Table 7.4   Source of Campaign Workers

Categories of Candidates	Friends of Candidate	Political Club Members	Workers for Candidate in Previous Campaign for any Office
Democrats (9)	100	280	100
Republicans (10)	30	90	60
Incumbents (8)	70	170	160
Non-Incumbents (11)	55	175	25
Sure Winners (6)	60	120	120
Competitive (6)	70	300	110
Sure Losers (7)	40	110	10
All candidates	65	175	80

Source: David A. Leuthold, *Electioneering in a Democracy: Campaigns for Congress* (New York: John Wiley and Sons, 1968), p. 93.

workers to be oriented more toward issues (by almost a 3 to 1 margin) and less oriented toward candidates and parties, when judged by the reasons given for vote decision.[43] But party loyalty was also important to these volunteers, 72 percent considered themselves to be strong partisans, compared to 35 percent of a national sample for the same year.[44] Leuthold concludes that it is really the interaction of the appeal of an attractive candidate, the party to which a worker is loyal, and the issues the worker believes in:

> . . . among the 3 to 5 percent of the adult population participating in a particular year are a fair number of regular party workers who volunteer to work for the candidate whose personality and issue orientation most appeal to them that year. Similarly, in the reservoir of 5 to 10 percent more who participate now and then, are a fair number who are loyal to their party or are quite concerned with issues but work only if they find an attractive candidate who takes positions that they can enthusiastically support.[45]

Recruitment of Volunteers

Workers are recruited by a variety of techniques. Some are asked directly by the candidate. Some come from the card files of the state, county, or local party. Others are recruited from party clubs or auxiliary party units, such as the young Republicans or the Democratic Women's club. Others come from lists of volunteers from the candidate's previous campaigns, or perhaps another candidate's campaign in the area, or a previous candidate's campaign. Enlistment is often through direct mail appeals to voters, or in fund-raising appeals to more specialized groups. Volunteers can be recruited from unions, businesses, civic clubs, or other organized bodies of activists. Finally, volunteer cards are often handed out at party gatherings, coffee parties, and at other appearances by the candidate. Of course some volunteers do not have to be recruited, they drop into the headquarters or telephone in their services.

The listed sources of volunteers are obviously those most likely to say yes to a request to participate in politics. As one moves from likely political activists to less motivated types, the success rate of recruitment diminishes. Attempts have been made to solicit workers by telephoning from a list of registered party voters, but the return rate is very low, ranging anywhere from one worker per hour of calls, to a low of two or three per day. Sometimes voters are asked if they would be willing to work during a telephone canvass, an economy of scale, but the process does not ordinarily yield any more workers. Door-to-door soliciting would yield about the same low rate of volunteers, although if it were combined with candidate appeals, it again would yield economies to scale. The reason why such "shot gun" techniques do not work, of course, reflects the small number who do actually volunteer, and their greater motivation regarding issues, stronger partisanship, plus a very strong attraction to the candidate, setting them apart from most members of the general public. Their special status as a minority political activist group makes such recruitment techniques more appropriate.

Volunteer Activities—
A Case Study

The list of tasks for which volunteers can be used can be as long as the activities in the campaign. Large scale campaigns generally employ volunteers to perform a host of menial tasks: addressing and stuffing envelopes, assembling duplicated material, stenographic and clerical work, telephoning, running errands and providing a messenger service, research and fund-raising assistance, clipping newspapers, monitoring radio and television coverage, voter contact work, baby-sitting, transportation, and literature distribution. In smaller campaigns, volunteers perform many of these chores plus take on one or a number of the management roles depicted earlier.

Figure 7.6   A Volunteer Card

Yes, I'll help BILL McCONKEY —to help I will

☐ Donate $ _____   ☐ Address Envelopes in my home

☐ Hold a Coffee or Party   ☐ Work with Local Campaign Groups

☐ Work at the Headquarters   ☐ Take 10 McConkey voters to Polls

☐ Work in my Block   ☐ You may use my NAME

☐ Display a Yard Sign

☐ Sign up 10 more volunteers
                               _____
                                          NAME
☐ Distribute Literature in my _____
  neighborhood and/or at work   STREET
                               _____
                                   CITY & ILLINOIS ZIP
☐ Help during Election Week   _____
                                  PHONE

Source: Citizens for McConkey, Aurora, Illinois, 1974.

Volunteers can also take on activities that range between menial tasks and managerial responsibilities. An illustrative case is former Minnesota Congressman Clark MacGregor's reliance upon volunteer area chairmen, who operated in their respective areas with a great deal of autonomy:

> . . .The MacGregor Volunteer Committee included precinct and ward workers and was headed by a chairman and chairwoman for each village, town, and legislative district. The organization was directed by an advisory committee composed of a chairman, a chairwoman, and five close aides of the Congressman. These seven worked with MacGregor in planning campaign activities and provided a liaison between the entire volunteer organization and MacGregor's offices in Washington and Minneapolis. . . .
>
> The MacGregor volunteers were officially sent into action on September 12, when the Congressman opened the campaign headquarters in Robbinsdale—his first major appearance after the primary. Actually the volunteers had been at work weeks before, distributing MacGregor window stickers, automobile aerial pennants, and lawn signs. Now they were busy mailing the campaign postcard (a photograph of the congressman and his family) to every Third-District voter. Volunteers also handled special mailings throughout the campaign: the legislative questionnaire results, the congressman's voting record, and some of his House speeches.
>
> Volunteer organizations in each locale enjoyed a high degree of autonomy. The chairman and chairwoman in each village or town were expected to recruit precinct volunteers. A form letter to be sent to potential workers was supplied by the Washington office. District organizations operated on their own budgets and planned their own activities. Volunteers could request MacGregor's appearance at particular events by means of a form submitted to the Washington and Minneapolis offices, which were in daily telephone contact. The Congressman's activities were coordinated by Bob McCann, his Minneapolis staff man, and Stan Langland, his administrative assistant in Washington. In addition, volunteers were encouraged to make informal personal contacts with voters and occasionally to write letters to newspaper editors.[46]

The MacGregor case demonstrates how volunteer efforts can be used to perform many of the middle-management or subunit level campaign organizing tasks, with a great deal of independence. Other such tasks at a campaign headquarters might include: distribution of campaign materials, buttons and gadgets; help organize rallies, fund-raising work, and maintaining campaign records. Whether in the field or at the headquarters these activities, which generally require less supervision, depend on a cadre of reliable volunteers.

The Quality of Volunteers

Whether the tasks performed are managerial, menial, or somewhere in between, experience has indicated that volunteers not only differ widely in skill levels, but they also vary in terms of their reliability. Many campaign volunteers prove to be unsatisfactory: they do not have the skill to do the job assigned, they do not like what they have been assigned, they are called from campaign duties by regular occupations or family obligations, they tire of campaign work, they do not show up at assigned times, or they agree to perform tasks which they simply do not perform. Therefore, it becomes necessary to secure replacements during the course of the campaign. As in so many other aspects of campaigning, incumbents have the advantage of being able to rely on those volunteers who have performed adequately before. For the most part, they must replace only a few turnover personnel and perhaps a few who proved to be unsatisfactory in the last campaign. Volunteers never seem to be "stable" for the duration of the campaign. Rather, supervisory personnel must constantly "field test" their work force and make appropriate replacements due to the unevenness in the quality of volunteers.

THE CAMPAIGN ORGANIZATION AND THE PARTY ORGANIZATION

At many points in this book the organizational implication has been made that except in rare circumstances, the campaigner must not rely on the party organization but put together a candidate-centered group. Only at the presidential level, can a campaign effort rely, with any assurance, on the party grouping because the *raison d'etre* of the national party committees is to do the bidding of the candidate. And even in this single case, the trend has been toward movement away from the party organization to the candidate organization. Political parties have many functions: leadership recruitment, informing the public about political matters, simplifying complex and numerous political choices, representing peoples' interests, self-maintenance, attempting to run the government, and mobilizing the voting public behind party candidates for office. Only the last is the function of candidate groups.

The type of party cooperation in the actual organization and operation of the campaign ranges from comprehensive packages of management advice, research and technical assistance[47] to virtual party ignorance of the party candidate's effort. Only in rare cases does the party organization undertake the entire campaign operation, and it should not be expected by candidates or campaigners unfamiliar with party operation. Local parties show considerable diversity in their campaign performance, ranging from those which contribute most of the money and do most of the electioneering for a candidate, to the paper organization which does not do much campaigning.[48]

Most typical of the party role is assistance or coordination. Very often at the statewide level an informal campaign coordination group evolves to exchange information and candidate schedules and to arrange joint appearances. Rarely are strategies discussed or arranged in depth. If any joint campaigning is undertaken, such as billboards, transit display, or other advertising, it is often arranged by the party organization. Sometimes candidates pool certain efforts, such as buying media time or printing, but they are coordinated by the candidate groups as often as the parties. The most likely campaign activities to be organized, financed, and operated by the party organization are a series direct voter-contact activities including voter registration, voter identification, get-out-of-the-vote drives, poll watching, and the like. Again, the extent to which these activities are performed by the party varies, and candidate organizations themselves are increasingly involved in direct voter-contact activities.

Liaison with the party is often maintained with a campaign advisory group of party, party-related, and non-party people. In this way important liaison is maintained with both party and community. Such an advisory group typically reviews campaign strategies, tactics, and other campaign plans. Presumably, such groups should be composed of those who know something about campaigning and they very often include former candidates, experienced but retired campaign managers, important party and interest group officials, as well as community leaders. If these groups are formed as serious advisory groups, special attention is paid to balancing of skills to include, for example, the media, public relations, fund raising, voter contact, and other facets of campaigning as well as their previous campaign experience and loyalty to the candidate. Many manuals suggest such a group. But, like other facets of campaigning, there is no hard and fast rule that an advisory committee should be formed. Because there are no rules, the advice of others, including party organization, should be sought whether in committee form or not. As one astute observer has noted, the advisory committee is more important for the means it provides to involve important community and political people in the campaign than for the advice it gives.[49] Thus, one can conclude that the important advisory function can be undertaken either through informal consultation or with the dual purpose of public involvement in the campaign organization.

Notes to Chapter 7

1. Xandra Kayden, "The Political Campaign as an Organization," *Public Policy* 21 (1973): 270–86.

2. Works on campaign organizations include, Robert J. Huckshorn and Robert C. Spencer. *The Politics of Defeat* (Amherst: Univ. of Massachusetts Press, 1971), ch. 4; John H. Kessell, *The Goldwater Coalition* (Indianapolis: Bobbs-Merrill, 1968); Karl A. Lamb and Paul A. Smith, *Campaign Decision-Making* (Belmont, California: Wadsworth, 1968), ch. 2; David A. Leuthold, *Electioneering in a Democracy* (New York: John Wiley, 1968), ch. 7.

3. Burdett A. Loomis, "Campaign Organizations in 'Competitive' 1972 House Races," Ph.D. dissertation, Univ. of Wisconsin, Madison, 1974), p. 3.

4. *The New York Times*, 10 September, 1972, p. 25.

5. Huckshorn and Spencer, *The Politics of Defeat*, pp. 104, 114-15; Leuthold, *Electioneering in a Democracy*, p. 91; Loomis, "Campaign Organizations in 'Competitive' 1972 House Races."

6. Huckshorn and Spencer, *The Politics of Defeat*, pp. 100-01.

7. Hank Parkinson, *Winning Your Campaign* (Englewood Cliffs, N.J.: Prentice-Hall, 1970), pp. 46-47.

8. John Bibby and Roger Davidson, *On Capitol Hill* 1st. ed. (New York: Holt, Rinehart and Winston, 1967), p. 43.

9. See Finance Organization in chapter eight.

10. Lamb and Smith, *Campaign Decision-Making*, p. 21.

11. Ibid., pp. 30-32.

12. Ibid., pp. 26-28.

13. Ibid., p. 23.

14. Ibid., pp. 34-35.

15. Loomis, "Campaign Organizations in 'Competitive' 1972 House Races."

16. Robert Humphreys, "Material for Off-Record Speech to Businessmen," Republican National Committee, memorandum to Leonard Hall, July 7, 1959. Reported in Harold Lavine, *Smoke-Filled Rooms* (Englewood Cliffs, N.J.: Prentice-Hall, 1970), p. 153.

17. Ibid., pp. 150-52.

18. Marshall Loch and William Safire, *Plunging Into Politics* (New York: David McKay, 1964), p. 3.

19. Stephen C. Shaddeg, *The New How to Win an Election* (New York: Taplinger, 1972), pp. 33-34.

20. Huckshorn and Spencer, *The Politics of Defeat*, p. 94; Conrad F. Joyner, "Running a Congressional Campaign," in *Practical Politics in the United States* ed. Cornelius P. Cotter (Boston: Allyn and Bacon, 1969), pp. 146-47; Leuthold, *Electioneering in a Democracy*, pp. 87-88.

21. Huckshorn and Spencer, *The Politics of Defeat*, p. 95.

22. Leuthold, *Electioneering in a Democracy*, pp. 88-89.

23. D. Swing Meyer, *The Winning Candidate* (New York: James H. Heineman, 1966), p. 29.

24. Shaddeg, *The New How to Win an Election*, p. 32.

25. For an explanation of each of these management functions see Robert Agranoff, *The New Style in Election Campaigns* (Boston: Holbrook Press, 1972), pp. 54-57.

26. On professional campaign management see, Agranoff, *The New Style in*

Election Campaigns, pp. 52-116; Robert J. Pitchell, "The Influence of Professional Campaign Management Firms in Partisan Elections in California," *Western Political Quarterly* 11 (1958); Stanley Kelley, Jr., *Professional Public Relations and Political Power* (Baltimore: Johns Hopkins Press, 1956); David Lee Rosenbloom, *The Election Men: Professional Campaign Managers and American Democracy* (New York: Quadrangle Books, 1973).

27. Cf., David Adamany, *Financing Politics* (Madison: Univ. of Wisconsin Press, 1969), pp. 127-29.

28. Huckshorn and Spencer, *The Politics of Defeat*, p. 106.

29. For one account of a public relations firm in operation see, Harry N.D. Fisher, "How the 'I Dare You' Candidate Won," in *The New Style in Election Campaigns*.

30. "Campaign Spending Controls Under the Federal Election Campaign Act of 1971" *Columbia Journal of Law and Social Problems* vol. 8 (1972); Roscoe L. Barrow, "Regulation of Campaign Funding and Spending for Federal Office," *Journal of Law Reform* vol. 5 (1972).

31. Herbert E. Alexander, "Impact of New Federal Election Laws in the United States," paper presented before International Political Science Association Congress, Montreal, Canada; August, 1973.

32. John Dean, *The Making of a Black Mayor* (Washington, D.C.: Joint Center for Political Studies, 1973), pp. 20-21.

33. John F. Bibby and Roger H. Davidson, *On Capitol Hill* 2d ed. (Hinsdale, Illinois: The Dryden Press, 1972), p. 59.

34. For further information see, Democratic National Committee, *Campaign Manual 1972* (Washington, D.C.: Democratic National Committee, 1972), pp. 13-21; Huckshorn and Spencer, *The Politics of Defeat*, pp. 108-12.

35. For a discussion of the role of campaign volunteers see, Dwaine Marvick, "The Middlemen of Politics," *Approaches to the Study of Party Organization* ed. William J. Crotty (Boston: Allyn and Bacon, 1968).

36. Angus Campbell, Phillip E. Converse, Warren E. Miller and Donald E. Stokes, *The American Voter* (New York: John Wiley, 1960), p. 91; Samuel J. Eldersveld, *Political Parties: A Behavioral Analysis* (Chicago: Rand McNally, 1964), p. 19; *Gallup Opinion Index*, no. 15, (August, 1966): 11; Robert E. Lane, *Political Life: Why People Get Involved in Politics* (Glencoe, Illinois: Free Press, 1959), pp. 53-54; Julian A. Woodward and Elmo Roper, "Political Activity of American Citizens," *American Political Science Review* 44 (1950): 872.

37. Quoted in Leuthold, *Electioneering in a Democracy*, p. 92.

38. Ibid.

39. Ibid., p. 93.

40. Ibid., p. 92.

41. Robert R. Alfrod and Harry M. Scoble, "Sources of Local Political

Involvement," *American Political Science Review* 62 (1968); Eldersveld, *Political Parties*, p. 132; Lane, *Political Life*, chs. 8 and 9; Lester W. Milbrath, *Political Participation* (Chicago: Rand McNally, 1965), chs. 2-5; Sidney Verba and Norman H. Nie, *Participation in America* (New York: Harper and Row, 1972), ch. 8.

42.   Dwaine Marvick and Charles Nixon, "Recruitment Contrasts in Rival Campaign Groups," *Political Decision-Makers* ed. Dwaine Marvick (Glencoe, Illinois: Free Press, 1961), p. 208.

43.   Leuthold, *Electioneering in a Democracy*, p. 94.

44.   Ibid., p. 95.

45.   Ibid., p. 96.

46.   Bibby and Davidson, *On Capitol Hill*, pp. 80-81.

47.   Robert Agranoff, "The Role of Political Parties in the New Campaigning," *The New Style in Election Campaigns*.

48.   Frank J. Sorauf, *Party and Representation* (New York: Atherton Press, 1963), pp. 46-47.

49.   Joyner, "Running a Congressional Campaign," *Practical Politics*, p. 157.

For Further Reading and Research

Archibald, Samuel J. (ed.). *The Pollution of Politics: A Research/Reporting Team Investigates Campaign Ethics.* Washington: Public Affairs Press, 1971.

Brown, Jr., Sam W. *Storefront Organizing.* New York: Pyramid, 1972.

Center for American Women in Politics. *Women State Legislators.* New Brunswick, N.J.: Rutgers Univ. Press, 1973.

Chartrand, Robert L. *Computers and Political Campaigns.* New York: Spartan, 1973.

Costikyan, Edward N. *Behind Closed Doors.* New York: Harcourt, Brace and World, 1966.

Dean, John. *The Making of a Black Mayor: A Study of Campaign Organization, Strategies and Techniques in Pritchard, Alabama.* Washington: Joint Center for Political Studies, 1973.

Democratic National Committee. *Campaign Manual.* Washington: Democratic National Committee. Issued every two years.

Felknor, Bruce L. *Dirty Politics.* New York: Norton, 1966.

Kayden, Xandra. "The Political Campaign as an Organization." *Public Policy* 21 (1973): 270-86.

Kenrick, Frank; Fleming, Theodore; Eisenstein, James; and Burkhart, James.

Strategies for Political Participation. 2d ed. Cambridge, Mass: Winthrop, 1974.

Lamb, Karl A. and Smith, Paul A. *Campaign Decision-Making.* Belmont, California: Wadsworth, 1968.

May, Ernest R. and Fraser, Janet. *Campaign '72: The Managers Speak.* Cambridge, Mass.: Harvard Univ. Press, 1973.

Murphy, Jr., William T. and Schneier, Edward. *Vote Power.* Garden City, New York: Doubleday, 1974.

Republican National Committee. *Campaign Manual.* Washington: Republican National Committee. Issued every two years, with periodic separates on special topics.

Walzer, Michael. *Political Action: A Practical Guide to Movement Politics.* Chicago: Quadrangle, 1971.

Campaign Financing

A great deal of public attention has been focused on campaign funding in recent years, particularly on the amount of money spent by candidates, the sources of funds, and spending patterns. Campaign finance practices and possible abuses of them were crystallized in the public mind by the Watergate break-in at the Democratic headquarters, "black advance," and other so-called dirty campaign tricks. Many felt that with its $60.2-million-dollar campaign treasury, the Committee to Re-elect the President had a surplus of funds, permitting it to engage in such antics. This benchmark in campaign affluence was the culmination of a decade of high cost campaigns in which "disadvantaged" presidential candidates spent $10 million in 1968 and $42 million in 1972, and, statewide candidates in the larger states were spending anywhere from one to six million dollars in their campaigns. During this period, several members of the "millionaires club" sought office, spending personal or family funds, capped by the six-million-dollar effort of the Rockefeller family to re-elect Nelson Governor of New York. By 1972, the Government Accounting Office estimated that presidential-election spending after April 7, 1972, when a new federal disclosure act came into effect, was $110 million. The total campaign spending for all races in that year reached $425 million, an increase of 42 percent from the previous presidential election year.[1]

Contrary to what many people commonly assume, money is not everything in a political campaign, but, because it is a very valuable general political resource, it is among the more important campaign resources. David Adamany has explained the importance of money as a campaign resource in terms of its convertibility and transferability. *Convertibility* refers to the extent to which a resource can be exchanged for other resources, and money is the most easily convertible in as much as it can purchase most of the other resources, or their functional equivalents. Adamany explains that it is much more difficult to convert manpower into an effective mass media campaign or to convert access to mass media into manpower, than it is to convert money into either media exposure or campaign workers.[2] Money is not perfectly convertible to other campaign resources; it cannot be converted into incumbency or a partisan advantage, but money can be used to offset these advantages through creation of a favorable candidate image in paid media and news coverage. As will be demonstrated, however, conversion is a good deal more complex, since money and other campaign resources tend to run together.

Less complex a notion is the transferability of resources, with money again being the most easily transferable. As Adamany suggests, "Money is more easily allocated to the locale where most politicians want it than are most resources."[3] Volunteers may be plentiful in one area, but it may be difficult to transfer them to other areas, whereas money "moves easily,"[4] buying campaign organization in one subunit of the constituency as well as in others. As Adamany concludes, since resources are the basic ingredient of political combat, money must be considered among the most commonly used and most useful because of its convertibility and transferability.[5] In other words, money makes it easier to plan and implement a strategy; one can do much more with adequate levels of funding.

Current discussions of the importance of money in campaigns, total spending costs, and the large sums expended in large constituency campaigns tend to mask two important facts about campaign finance. First, though absolute levels of campaign spending are high, the relative increases are not great. One report revealed that the median per-vote expenditure for all spending in five state political systems and the total American system from 1964 to 1968 was $3.99, with a mean of $3.66. The 1968 total election spending bill of $300 million represented only .03 percent of the GNP, a proportional decline from the 1964 spending level of $200 million which was .05 percent of the GNP. Adamany claims that personal income is a more relevant comparison since the bulk of campaign contributions in the United States are from private contributors. By this measure, the amount spent is minimal. In the six American political systems he studied, less than .50 percent of personal income is spent on campaigns, with half of the spending closer to .25 percent. Nationally, only .043 percent of personal income went for campaigns.[6] A cross-national study of campaign finance published in 1963, which compared expenditures per vote as a ratio of average hourly wages of manufacturing workers, indicated that expenditures in the United States (1.12), ranked above Australia (.27) and Great Britain (.67), but below Germany (1.40), Japan (1.40), Italy (4.50), the Phillipines (18.90), and Israel (21.10).[7]

That thousands of campaigns, particularly those in small constituencies or those for low visibility offices, are conducted with relatively modest sums of money is a second, less well known fact about campaign finance. Some of them are financed adequate to the setting and strategy, and some of them are underfinanced. At the same time that Rockefeller was spending $6 million for his 1966 re-election, his opponent, Frank O'Connor, spent $500,000. More typically, candidates in the smaller constituencies spend much less. Congressional campaigns very often spend more than $100,000. The average reported expenditure for competitive district races in 1972 was $71,500.[8] Many candidates, particularly minority candidates in sure districts for the other party, can raise only a few thousand dollars. The available evidence regarding state legislative office spending indicates an average ranging from $359 for the lower house in Kentucky to $27,464 for California senate seats. The range is from no expenditures in Oregon and Wisconsin to $122,294 for a single California state senate seat.[9] These considerably wide ranges suggest that in spite of the vast sums associated with more visible campaigns, spending for the bulk of offices is at a more modest level, and, for many offices securing sufficient funds to support a strategy is problematical.

This chapter will focus on some important research findings and implications for operating a campaign, with particular attention to spending levels, sources of funds, and finance organization. The following chapter will cover the more practical aspects of campaign finance. There is an emerging and extensive literature on the subject of political finance,[10] and inferences from it can assist the campaigner.

CAMPAIGN SPENDING

In spite of the considerable range of campaign spending for various office levels and settings, it is clear that the absolute costs of campaigning are rising in all jurisdictions. These increases are in part a product of the increases of prices and income levels. For example, between 1964 and 1968 the consumer price index rose 12.1 percent and national income rose 36 percent whereas campaign costs increased 78 percent.[11] Other factors, obviously are working with price increases to raise the costs of seeking office.

Before examining the reasons behind the increasing costs of campaigning, we must investigate representative campaign spending and cost increases. Table 8.1 reveals costs for individual races in large constituences and average expenditures for smaller constituencies for eight jurisdictions. These figures, of course, reflect earlier spending levels. They are meant to illustrate the relative costs and increases in various areas, and the statewide average figures mean that some campaigns cost much more than others. The figures demonstrate rapid spending increases. They appear to be just as rapid in the small constituencies as the larger ones. The average cost of a Connecticut House seat (Republican) has increased 91 percent per election year, with the layout being $2,329, compared to a mere $150 fourteen years earlier. By contrast, in spite of very high absolute dollar increases, presidential spending has increased at a more modest pace.

The stricter campaign reporting regulations of the 1971 Federal Elections

Table 8.1   Levels and Increases of Campaign Spending for Selected Areas

Jurisdiction	Office, Party[a], Year, Election[b]	Amount	Office, Party[a], Year, Election[b]	Amount	Average Increase Per Year (%)
United States	President R-1952-G	$7.4 million	President R-1968-G	$24 million	15
United States	President D-1952-G	4.8 million	President D-1968-G	11 million	14
Connecticut	U.S. Senator D-1952-G	106,100[c]	U.S. Senator D-1968-G	592,600	29
Connecticut	Governor D-1954-G	69,000	Governor D-1966-G	242,000	21
Wisconsin	U.S. Senator D-1950-PG[d]	35,900	U.S. Senator D-1968-G	470,000	68
Wisconsin	Governor D-1950-PG[d]	26,300	Governor D-1968-PG	220,000	41
California	Governor D-1958-G	790,000	Governor D-1966-G	2.1 million	21
California	Governor R-1956-G	916,000	Governor R-1966-G	2.7 million	27
New York	Statewide[e] 1952-56-G	1 million	Governor R-1966-G	5 million	29
Oregon	Statewide[e] 1952-56-G	150,000	U.S. Senator R-1968-G	391,000	10
Tennessee	U.S. Senator D-1948-P	75,000	U.S. Senator D-1960-P	325,000	28
Virginia	Statewide[e] D-1952-56-P	80,000	U.S. Senator D-1966-P	228,600	13
Connecticut	U.S. House of Rep. D-1952-G	7,800[f]	U.S. House of Rep. D-1968-G	53,300[f]	36

Jurisdiction	Office, Party[a], Year, Election[b]	Amount	Office, Party[a], Year, Election[b]	Amount	Average Increase Per Year (%)
Connecticut	U.S. House of Rep. R-1952-G	8,100[f]	U.S. House of Rep. R-1968-G	53,600[f]	35
Wisconsin	U.S. House of Rep. D-1950-PG	3,900[f]	U.S. House of Rep. D-1966-PG	17,900[f]	22
Wisconsin	U.S. House of Rep. R-1950-PG	6,100[f]	U.S. House of Rep. R-1966-PG	29,600[f]	24
Connecticut	State Senate D-1952-G	400[f]	State Senate D-1968-G	2,827[f]	39
Connecticut	State Senate R-1952-G	400[f]	State Senate R-1968-G	2,486[f]	33
Wisconsin	State Senate D-1950-PG	512[f]	State Senate D-1966-PG	3,368[f]	35
Wisconsin	State Senate R-1950-PG	1,453[f]	State Senate R-1966-PG	4,649[f]	14
Connecticut	House of Rep. D-1952-G	150[f]	House of Rep. D-1968-G	2,285[f]	89
Connecticut	House of Rep. R-1952-G	150[f]	House of Rep. R-1968-G	2,329[f]	91
Wisconsin	Assembly D-1950-PG	164[f]	Assembly D-1966-PG	1,304[f]	43
Wisconsin	Assembly R-1950-PG	364[f]	Assembly R-1954-PG	1,614[f]	21

a) D = Democratic; R = Republican.

b) P = primary election; G = general election

c) Average of expenditures in two U.S. Senate campaigns waged by the Democrats in 1952. One campaign was for a full term, the other was to fill a vacancy caused by the death of the incumbent.

d) In 1950, both the gubernatorial and senatorial nominations were heatedly contested; in 1968, neither was. The rate of increase, therefore, tends to be understated because the earlier expenditure figures represent two full-scale campaigns while the later ones portray the cost of only one serious electoral effort.

e) Based on figures reported by Heard, *The Costs of Democracy* (cited in the notes for Chapter 1), p. 425.

f) Average of the expenditures in all districts in the state.

Source: David W. Adamany, *Campaign Finance in America* (North Scituate, Mass.: Duxbury Press, 1972), p. 44-45.

Act allow for precise figures for the first time on 1972 Congressional spending. House and senate general election candidates spent a total of $66.4 million. The amount spent for house races depended on a number of situational factors:

	Total Spending
Democrats	$ 47,479
Republicans	49,564
Democrats in races with no incumbent	90,074
Republicans in races with no incumbent	90,030
Races wherein incumbents were defeated by nonincumbents	
Incumbent	86,075
Winning challenger	125,521

Similar factors were present in 1972 Senate patterns:

No Incumbent	Total Spending
Democrats	$481,156
Republicans	458,484

With an Incumbent	
All Incumbents	495,424
All Challengers	244,126
Democratic Incumbents	381,080
Republican Challengers	312,403
Republican Incumbents	559,742
Democratic Challengers	205,720[12]

These figures represent spending from April 1972 to the end of the campaign. It is clear that levels of spending depend on a number of situational factors. The average house candidate spent almost $50,000. When there was no incumbent that figure was $40,000 higher. Those challengers who defeated incumbents spent considerably more. Senate spending patterns demonstrate the advantage of incumbency (although four Republican races skew these figures), and the absence of it as an equalizing factor. Of the 66 senate campaigns in 1972, 18 exceeded $500,000 in expenditures, 25 exceeded $400,000, and 3 races exceeded $1 million.[13]

Systematic information on spending for aldermanic, mayoral, and county office is unobtainable. There is, however, some comparative evidence of legislative district spending, which is illustrative of the range of spending for small constituencies. Table 8.2 depicts average spending levels in four states plus the range of spending. It illustrates that expenditures for the same offices differ considerably, and that some candidates still spend very little, while for others spending can readily exceed $10,000 for a single race. California legislative spending is even higher, given the generally large size of their districts. The average 1970 cost for an assembly seat was $12,258 and a sentate seat averaged $27,464. These costs were, by comparison, $3,253 and $5,077 in 1958.[14] Thus, there are great differences in spending in small as well as large constituencies.

Many diverse factors contribute to the broad range of expenditures and increases revealed above. Among the more generally recognized variables are:

1. *Price Level Increases* Even if candidates for office were doing the same thing year after year the costs of the goods and services needed to do these things would go up. As candidates turn away from personal campaigning to a greater reliance on paid (and more skilled) staff plus the increased use of the media, costs increase because the costs of these items generally exceed general price level increases.

2. *The Importance of the Office* The higher the prestige of the office, the greater the expenditures. The importance of contests in national, state, and local elections usually goes along with the powers and prestige associated with the office, its location at or near the top of the ballot, the amount of

Table 8.2 Legislative Campaign Spending in Four States

State	Year	House and Election[a]	Number	Democrats Average	Range	Number	Republicans Average	Range
Upper Houses								
Connecticut	1968	S/G	35[c]	$2,827	$ 50-15,045	33[c]	$2,486	$118- 8,045
Kentucky	1967	S/P	29[b]	1,156	47- 5,697	26[b]	716	15- 3,164
Kentucky	1967	S/G	21[c]	1,157	216- 6,651	20[c]	1,247	512- 3,242
Oregon	1968	S/G	12[c]	1,914	0- 4,342	14[c]	2,648	0- 9,971
Wisconsin	1966	S/P-G	15[c]	3,368	50-15,015	15[c]	4,649	369-10,514
Wisconsin	1964	S/P-G	14[c]	1,190	200- 6,449	15[c]	4,107	377-10,888
Lower Houses								
Connecticut	1968	L/G	140[c]	2,285	25- 4,088	138[c]	2,329	15- 3,579
Kentucky	1967	L/P	135[b]	631	20- 3,269	71[b]	359	15- 1,925
Kentucky	1967	L/G	79[c]	894	19- 2,452	94[c]	947	12- 3,835
Oregon	1968	L/G	47[c]	1,243	25- 6,861	55[c]	1,883	00-16,404
Wisconsin	1966	L/P-G	56[c]	1,304	24- 4,177	56[c]	1,614	32- 4,336
Wisconsin	1964	L/P-G	80[c]	962	6- 2,726	70[c]	978	00- 2,901

a) S = State senate or upper House of the legislature; L = lower House of the legislature; G = General election; P = primary election.
b) This is the number of candidates rather than the number of contests. The 29 Democratic senate candidates campaigned for 12 nominations, the 26 Republican senate candidates for nine nominations, the 135 Democratic House candidates for 54 ballot places, and the 71 Republican lower House aspirants for 30 places.
c) This is the number of candidates who faced opponents in their districts; unopposed candidates and their (usually) nominal spending were excluded from these calculations.

Source: David W. Adamany, *Campaign Finance in America* (North Scituate, Mass.: Duxbury Press, 1972), p. 42.

media attention given to the contest and to the incumbent in that office. Another factor which can often contribute to the importance of a contest is the possible use of the office as a stepping stone to other, more important offices.

3. *The Size of the Electorate* As the number of voters in a constituency increases, the costs will increase, even if the campaign tactics are the same as in previous, smaller sized constituency campaigns. Of course, some costs rise faster than others. In mass mailings, postage increases at a fixed rate with more voters, whereas printing, stuffing, or volunteer distribution do not necessarily increase proportionately. Moreover, as the population of an area increases certain costs also increase, even though the increased number of voters may be small, such as in the case of media costs, which rise by the number of viewers, listeners, or readers.

4. *The Geographic Size and the Population Density of the Constituency* The more dispersed the population, the greater the cost. In the larger districts travel costs, headquarters costs, and organizational maintenance are the major cost factors. Contrast for example, the differeing geographic cost problem in a U.S. Senate campaign in California and Rhode Island. Adamany found expenditures in Connecticut to be directly related to the size of the constituency, with the per vote cost decreasing as the size of the constituency diminished, until a "threshold" was reached in the smaller constituencies, where personal campaigning and other techniques change spending patterns.[15]

5. *The State of Political Organizations* The party organization, the candidate organization, other political groups active in electioneering, or some combination of the three affect spending levels. The stronger and more active these groups are in performing the important voter-contact activities, the less campaigns will cost. Where party organization is strong, and voters are regularly canvassed and mobilized behind the party ticket, the cost to the individual candidate is less, although we have cited evidence that party is less effective organizationally and in holding voters' loyalties than it once was. Moreover, old-style party organizations very often expect "subventions" of $100 to $200 per precinct from candidates, to turn out the vote. In large cities having from 2,000 to 5,000 precincts, this can become an expensive practice.

6. *The Nature and Use of Campaign Technology* The techniques a campaigner decides to use depend on many factors, but some methods are more expensive than others. Media advertising, particularly television, is more expensive than other forms of voter contact. The use of computers for research, record keeping, and mailing are used by many, and the cost of campaigning is thereby increased. When polls are used, the cost of campaigning is also higher. Of course, the use of the new techniques of campaigning varies greatly from place to place; one ordinarily does not use television for small constituency offices or when it is impracticable in larger constituencies. Running for a New Jersey statewide office would require using the New York and Philadelphia television markets, with considerable waste. Interestingly, it appears that technological advances also increase costs

because new expenses do not displace expenditures for pre-existing activities; campaigners appear to avail themselves of new techniques as well as old ones.[16]

7. *The Available Pool of Resources Which Are Convertible to Money* In a study of Wisconsin finance, Adamany reports the important resources that are potentially convertible are party ideology, candidate and party program, incumbency, candidate charisma, and the degree of electoral competitiveness.[17] Each of these factors has the potential to attract contributions. For example, a candidate's program could yield contributions from unions, or certain trade and business interests. Candidates who look like sure winners very often draw upon broad sources of support.

8. *The Skill of the Campaign Fund Raisers* This is particularly variable since spending generally follows available funds. Adamany contends that a homogeneous, well defined constituency generally permits centralized fund raising to a well-defined group, whereas it is more difficult among broader-based coalitions.[18] Certainly the more homogeneous Goldwater and McGovern constituencies of 1964 and 1972 yielded large numbers of contributors, although it appears to have come at considerable electoral cost. Nevertheless, it is safe to say that skilled fund raisers can be a considerable contributing factor to the amount of money available for spending.

9. *The Nominating Process Facing the Candidate* A stiff primary contest or a contested convention may cost thousands more than a "free ride" to the nomination. Presidential candidates today, of course, face both primary costs, state convention costs, and national convention as well as preconvention activity costs. In many situations the costs of seeking the nomination exceed general election costs.[19] A total of $32.3 million was spent by Democratic candidates in 1971-1972 seeking their party's presidential nomination, close to the $29.8 million spent by McGovern in the general election campaign. In a primary contest, the cost of the campaign is extended over a longer period of time, with similar organizational, media, and travel costs. Of course, many of the same factors which affect general election costs also affect primaries.[20]

10. *The Degree of Electoral Competition* Studies of party competition at the legislative and congressional level suggest that spending is higher in the more competitive contests.[21] The Common Cause Campaign Finance Monitoring Project revealed considerable differences in 1972 House-of-Representatives expenditure patterns by level of competition:

Winning Percentage (range)	N	Winners Expenditure (averages)	Losers Expenditure
70% to 90%	97	$ 38,729	$ 7,479
65% to 70%	66	42,212	16,060
60% to 65%	91	55,065	30,483
55% to 60%	60	73,616	54,600
up to 55%	66	107,378	101,166[22]

Obviously, as the race became more competitive, the total spending levels increased. Presumably, as contests become closer, politicians and contributors perceive this, a greater effort is expended in raising money, more money is received, and more is spent. Heidenheimer suggests that costs increase with competition because there is a greater potential for persuading voters to change their political choice. Whatever the reason, more competitive contests generate higher expenditures.[23]

These ten factors clearly relate to how the setting and strategy of a campaign affect the amount of money spent. In a sense, they define the parameters of the finance setting of the campaign, determining the relative cost a campaigner is likely to face. Strategic considerations, the nature of the office sought, the availability of organizations, the competitive situation, and other factors have an important effect on spending.

MONEY–ONE AMONG MANY RESOURCES

Just as there are many factors that contribute to the cost of campaigns, we have argued that campaigns entail many concerns and resources, and that no single factor or resource is likely to determine or condition the outcome of a campaign. This should be obvious to any campaigner who engages in many activities in the course of the campaign. Yet, too often, money is selected as the resource that assures victory. It is not an uncommon notion that the campaign with the most money has the greatest chance of winning, or, the even more widespread saying that those who spend the most money win. Certainly money is a key campaign resource, and a paucity of funds can be critical disadvantage, especially when one's opponent has an abundance. But, money is only one among many resources (and assets, advantages, etc.) in a campaign, and contrary to folk wisdom, "No neat correlation is found between campaign expenditures and campaign results."[24]

Since this book is devoted in part to the discovery and mobilization of resources, there is no need to discuss in detail the resources which can join with money. In his study of the political influence process of New Haven, Connecticut, Robert Dahl bases the key political resources on his common sense observation of the scene, including: an individual's own time; access to money, credit, and wealth; control over jobs; control over information; esteem or social standing; the possession of charisma, popularity, legitimacy, legality; and the rights pertaining to public office. In addition, he included *solidarity* as a resource, defining it as the capacity of a member of one segment of society to evoke support from others who identify him as like themselves because of similarities in occupation, social standing, religion, ethnic origin, or racial stock.[25] In this book we have also focused on party support and key issue positions as resources. The interplay of these resources in a campaign makes it difficult to accept that money alone can determine the outcome of a campaign.

The belief that money determines victory probably came about during the first three decades of this century when campaign fund information became availble, and it was revealed that the winning candidates (chiefly Republican in that era) always spent more of the funds. After 1932, however, the Democrats captured five consecutive victories (though outspent on each occasion), spending only 35 percent and 39 percent of the campaign monies in 1940 and 1948.[26] This aroused the suspicion of campaign finance students who felt that money as as a resource is difficult to isolate from other resources, and that money does not equal victory. The number of very wealthy candidates who have won electoral victories is almost equal to the number of unsuccessful wealthy candidates. In spite of Republican financial advantages in California in state and national offices from 1950 to 1970, it was, for the most part, a period of Democratic dominance. The greatest disparity was in the Democrat's best year, 1964, when Republicans spent seven out of every ten California campaign dollars.[27] People like to cite the Rockefeller victories in New York, West Virginia, and Arkansas, but each of these Rockefellers has also lost an election in which they made use of family money. In many districts, an incumbent from the majority party will be outspent by his opponent by 10, 20, or 30 to 1, and will still win, obviously relying on party and incumbency as resources.

This is not to say that under some circumstances a financial advantage is not decisive, for it certainly can be. Some argue that if Humphrey had had money earlier in 1968 or had had more money, he would have won. There are also the cases in which no amount of money spent could have changed the outcome. Our knowledge of voting behavior and campaigns is unfortunately imprecise. The relative impact of money over other factors has not been determined yet. One can surmise that many of these resources operate together, and that they are somewhat cumulative, and therefore, money often flows with other resources.

THE INTERDEPENDENCE
OF MONEY AND OTHER RESOURCES

Rather than assuming that money is independent of other campaign resources, it should be regarded as a part of a total flow of campaign resources which are interdependent. Thus, candidates who are well known and popularly established in their constituencies will have an easier time raising funds than will a rank unknown. Similarly, persons who are thought of as winners, because of some measure of their electoral support such as a public poll, often draw sources of money. The converse happened to Humphrey in 1968. Since he was so far behind Nixon in the polls, contributions dried up. As he began to close the gap, his aides used private and public polls to show potential contributors his increased public support. Money can even follow issue positions. In both the Goldwater campaign of 1964 and the McGovern campaign of 1972, large numbers of small contributions were collected from attentive supporters who were more to the political right and left respectively. Thus, the flow of money into a campaign often follows those candidates who have favorable balances of other resources: electoral support, key issue positions, popularity, and other favorable personal qualities.

Incumbency is an advantage that in many ways symbolizes electoral support and visibility. Not surprisingly, it is interdependent with fund raising. In 1972, for example, the average contribution to U.S. Senate incumbents running for re-election was $525,809 as compared to $243,070 for their challengers. A similar pattern existed for the House of Representatives. The average contributions to Democratic incumbents was $56,364, and $32,090 went to their Republican challengers. The average contributions to Republican incumbents was $60,842, and $29,656 went to their Democratic challengers. When the incumbent is not running, average contribution levels tended to equalize: $89,430 for House Democrats and $88,375 for House Republicans, $496,297 for Senate Democrats and $465,264 for Senate Republicans.[28] Using 1972 as a case, congressional incumbents were able to use their positions to raise almost twice the amount of money as non-incumbents, thus demonstrating the interrelationship between holding office and fund-raising ability.

In a study of money as a campaign resource in Tennessee primaries, it was found that a certain minimum campaign fund, essential and available to most leading candidates, and those who had a reasonable balance of other resources, such as visibility, personal style, incumbency, could combine their resources with funds to attain victory or at least make a good showing. Some candidates had ample finances but had few other resources, and thus could not convert them to personal qualities and visibility (the important resources in Tennessee primaries). Money alone could not do it for them because they had fewer workers, or a less experienced organization, compared with what the more successful candidates had.[29] One interesting bit of evidence demonstrating the interdependence of resources is the relationship found between two resources, money and volunteer work. Table 8.3 clearly indicates that many of those who worked at least one day in the campaign also made a financial contribution. This relationship suggests that others may exist: those who contribute may be spokesmen for the candidate to voting publics; since workers are avid supporters, the number of supporters helps determine the amount of money raised; and, the perceived or demonstrated support is reflected in money and volunteers.

Although this evidence is merely suggestive, the dynamics of the campaign process lead one to conclude that, under normal circumstances, money flows from the maximization of other, related political resources. Its convertibility, as discussed earlier, also suggests that money, in turn, can lead to the maximization of some other resources. Money is an interdependent campaign resource.

USING OTHER RESOURCES
TO SUPPLEMENT FINANCIAL DISADVANTAGES

Since a number of resources must be accumulated in a campaign, it is also possible to use advantages in other resources to compensate for financial disadvantages. In the Tennessee study, the authors concluded that money could not be easily converted to certain other resources, such as appeal to likeminded persons on national issues, but, that candidates who were known and had well developed issue positions could use these to overcome financial disadvantages.[30] Likewise, Truman used appeals to loyal Democrats on New Deal–Fair Deal issues to bring them back into the fold, in spite of a financial disadvantage in 1948.[31] Some candidates who find themselves financially disadvantaged are blessed with a relative abundance of workers due to their visibility on issue positions, their popularity, or, perhaps, to previous service in the community. The most obvious resource to counteract financial deficiencies is pre-existing electoral support, whether on a party, candidate, or issue basis.

For the financially disadvantaged candidate, then, it is reasonable to try to maximize those resources which can compensate for financial handicaps. If a large number of volunteers are available, they can be used to distribute literature that cannot be mailed due to lack of funds for printing and postage. Volunteer workers can be used to engage in a host of face-to-face voter-contact activities to compensate for inability to purchase media. If one is from the majority party, but financially on the minority side, an appeal to partisanship and use of the party organizations can make up for it. In many small constituencies, the personal door-to-door campaigning of the candidate can make up

Table 8.3   Interdependence of Campaign Resources,
The Case of Time and Money

Days Spent Campaigning	Size of Gift				
	$10	$100	$250	$500 up	Total
Senatorial Campaigns					
1 to 9	14%	18%	4%	1% =	37%
10 to 19	5	11	6	4 =	26
20 or more	3	12	9	14 =	38
Total	22%	41%	19%	19% =	100% = 548
Gubernatorial Campaigns					
1 to 9	11%	12%	3%	5% =	31%
10 to 19	3	9	6	11 =	29
20 or more	3	7	10	20 =	40
Total	17%	28%	19%	36% =	100% = 470

Source: William Buchanan and Agnes Bird, *Money as a Campaign Resource: Tennessee Democratic Senatorial Primaries, 1948–1964* (Princeton, N.J.: Citizens Research Foundation, 1966), p. 83.

for serious financial disadvantages. Even when a candidate is doubly disadvantaged—lacking two crucial resources—other resources can be maximized. When Lawton Chiles was a little-known impoverished candidate for the U.S. Senate from Florida, he stimulated almost daily news coverage by walking the length of the state. Other candidates, including Senator Richard Miller of Iowa and Governor Daniel Walker of Illinois, have since followed suit, attempting to develop visibility and an image without purchasing media time.

Some campaign factors are, therefore, not as convertible as money, but they can supplant funds. For example, an organization, which has been through the process of campaigning, whose leadership is aware of the many pitfalls involved, and whose leaders know the constituency and its key players, is difficult to purchase. Financially deficient campaigns must make extra effort to convert factors, such as an experienced organization, into an advantage.

WHO CONTRIBUTES
TO POLITICAL CAMPAIGNS?

Almost all of the information that has been gathered regarding the number of contributors, the characteristics of contributors, and the sources of funds has been obtained from presidential or other high visibility campaigns. Nevertheless, our evidence of political participation suggests that, with few exceptions, activists are generally active at many levels, whereas non-activists are inactive at all levels. Therefore, the inferences drawn from this material should be suggestive of candidate efforts at all levels.

Two of this country's leading survey organizations have been surveying the percentage of the national voting age population which contributed to campaigns since 1952. As Table 8.4 indicates, since 1956 nearly one-tenth of the population ordinarily contributes something to political campaigns in a presidential-election year. The available data on solicitation indicates that nearly half of those asked did contribute. The highest number of persons actually solicited is about one-fifth of the adult population (much less than the number of voters). It is interesting to note that the ratio of those solicited to those giving is relatively high, just under 40 percent in 1968. Since so few are actually contacted, this figure suggests that there is a reservoir of potential contributors. Indeed, Gallup polls of the 1960s consistently indicated that between 40 and 50 percent of the unsolicited citizens would contribute five dollars if asked.[32] If these figures are even partially accurate, candidates have an untapped source of small contributors who could solve many financial problems.

As suggested in Chapter 3, those who do contribute tend to fall into the level of political activity between those who only vote and those who actively participate. Of course, contributors are more likely to be active in politics than non-contributors, but, there is a group of contributors who, beyond giving money, do not actively participate. Political giving is one component of a general dimension of political involvement: about half also work in a campaign, attend meetings, or belong to a political group.[33]

Studies depicting the social and economic characteristics of contributors like to point out the large number of wealthy and corporate donors. These funds do make a significant impact at the national level. In 1968, 13,000 individual contributions of $500 or more totaling $17.5 million were reported. Of these, the Republicans accounted for 72 percent of the number of contributions and 73 percent of the dollars; the Democrats received 19 percent of the contributions and 17 percent of the dollars.[34] There is no way of prorating this to local campaigns, but, significantly, Leuthold found that wealthy contributors who regularly gave to the party's national level committees also gave to San Francisco Bay Area Congressional candidates.[35] The list was acquired by examining the public record of all those who contributed $500 or more to a congressional campaign.

It comes as no surprise that party identifiers are more likely than independents to contribute to campaigns. In 1968, twice as many contributors had a party identification. According to Survey Research Center estimates, 13.6 percent of Republican identifiers made a contribution (compared with 19 percent in 1960 and 1964) and 6 percent of the Democratic identifiers (compared with 7 percent in 1960 and 1964). It appears, then, that Republicans are two- to three-times more likely to contribute than are Democrats.[36] Table 8.5, depicting SRC survey data on contributors, further indicates that political giving is skewed in the direction of higher income persons and professional,

Table 8.4 Percentage of National Adult Population Solicited
and Making Contributions

Year	Organization	Solicited by			Contributed to		
		Rep.	Dem.	Total	Rep.	Dem.	Total
1952	SRC				3	1	4
1956	Gallup	8	11	19	3	6	9
1956	SRC				5	5	10
1960	Gallup	9	8	15	4	4	9
1960	Gallup						12
1960	SRC				7	4	11
1964	Gallup				6	4	12
1964	SRC	8	4	15	6	4	11
1968	SRC	8	6	20	3	3	8
1972	SRC				4	4	8

Source: Herbert E. Alexander, *Financing the 1968 Election* (Lexington, Mass.: D.C. Heath, 1971), p. 143; Survey Research Center, Inter-University Consortium for Political Research.

managerial, and business persons. Lower income persons contribute least. Rates of giving also seem to increase among the middle-aged, more politically active age groups, although there is very little difference except at the youngest and oldest age groups.

Information on the sources of funds contributed indicates that campaigns normally rely on the combination of personal contributions, individual contributions, party organization contributions, group contributions, and funds

Table 8.5   Campaign Contribution Rates by Income Level,
Age, and Occupation, 1952–1972

	Election Year					
	1952	1956	1960	1964	1968	1972
Annual Family Income						
less than $3,000	2%	2%	3%	2%	3%	2%
$3,000–$4,999*	3	6	8	6	3	3
$5,000–$7,499*	7	12	9	7	7	6
$7,500–$9,999*	14	17	20	15	8	6
$10,000 and over	17	31	30	21	12	14
Age						
18–20	—	—	—	—	—	3%
21–24	4	6	7	5	4	9
25–34	3	7	12	10	7	8
35–44	5	13	11	14	8	13
45–54	4	12	13	9	7	9
55–64	6	11	14	10	10	9
65 and over	4	6	9	7	8	5
Occupational Group						
professional	18%	19%	22%	25%	11%	20%
business & managerial	14	18	15	20	7	15
white collar	6	7	8	12	7	8
skilled	3	8	13	6	10	6
unskilled	1	7	10	5	8	5
farm operator	1	6	2	9	11	2
retired	3	6	12	6	8	5
housewife	2	6	16	8	7	7

*For 1968 and 1972 these two categories are respectively: $5,000–$7,999 and $8,000–$9,999.

Source: Survey Research Center, University of Michigan. Made available through the Inter-University Consortium for Political Research.

raised at events. Of the $62.3 million contributed to congressional candidates in 1972: 35 percent ($21.7 million) was from 41,600 persons who gave $100 or more, over half of whom gave $500 or more; 26 percent ($16.5 million) came from contributions of more than $100 from political and special interest committees; 32 percent ($19.6 million) came from contributions of $100 or less, presumably from individual donors and 7 percent ($4.4 million) reflects net loans of more than $100.[37] Table 8.6, which depicts the source of funds for

Table 8.6   Source of Connecticut Republican and Democratic Campaign Funds

		Republican		Democrat	
	State Campaign[a]	U.S. House of Representatives	State Senate	State Central Committee	Senator
Individual Contributions	45.9%	43.7%	61.1%	92.7%	89.5%
$ 0- 99	11.5	20.1	32.6	6.7	6.6
100-499	18.3	16.6	19.8	75.3	19.5
500 plus	16.1	7.0	8.7	10.7	63.4
Party Organizations	6.8	48.4	15.2	1.1	3.9
town committees	3.1	15.2	12.8	.2	.1
state central committee		11.4	.2		
other party units	.7	3.6	2.2	.9	d
national party units	3.0	18.2			3.8
Labor		.1	1.0	4.6	5.8
Political Events	1.2	5.6	4.2		
Candidate Contributions	6.1	.7	12.6		
Associations		1.6	1.9		.2
Other	40.0[b]		4.0	1.7	.6
Totals	100.0	100.1	100.0	100.1	100.0
Amount[c]	$733,223	$220,236	$88,966	$118,779	$553,926[e]

a) State central committee and gubernatorial campaign receipts combined because of centralized financing.
b) Reported debts and loans of $289,000 (39.4 percent) and a cash operating balance at the beginning of the reporting period of $4,571 (.6 percent).
c) ...Disparities between receipt and expenditure totals occurred in the filed reports.
d) Less than .1 percent.
e) ...Disparity between receipt and expenditure totals occurred in the filed reports.

Source: David W. Adamany, *Campaign Finance in America* (North Scituate, Mass.: Duxbury Press, 1972), pp. 127-28.

both parties and candidates in a single state, is illustrative of the proportions from each. The largest single share of funds comes from individual contributions, the larger individual contributions concentrated at the large constituency level. Organizations, and notably labor, contribute a relatively small proportion of the total, with the single exception of Congress, which is a focal point of labor electoral activity. An even smaller amount is contributed by the party organizations, although its impact is greater at the congressional and legislative level. One should also note that the individual candidate's contribution becomes more significant in the smaller constituencies. Finally, political fund-raising events, which are often regarded as important sources of funds, actually contribute a small portion of the total.

Studies of congressional and small constituency campaigns indicate that the candidate's personal contribution, contributions of family and friends, and contributions of active partisans make up the largest share of funds. Leuthold found very large personal contributions on the part of four Democratic candidates—between $25,000 to $100,000 or more. He also estimated that each congressional candidate contributed an unreported $2,000 to $4,000 in hidden living expenses, including meals, travel, clothing, telephone, and tickets to fund-raising events. [38] Another study reported similar findings: among congressional sure losers and marginal candidates of both parties, the personal contributions of the candidate and help from friends and supporters was far more important than party financial support from national level congressional committees or other party sources.[39] A study of state senate campaigns in Oregon similarly indicated that financing was generated primarily by the candidate personally, then in the immediate business and professional circles of the candidate, with some support from groups such as labor.[40]

The Oregon study, like so many others, found the financial base to be narrow, with the number of contributions ranging from ten to sixty in an individual campaign. Leuthold's study indicated that personal and family contributions amounted to one-third of all funds in the twenty campaigns he studied.[41] A study of Wisconsin campaign finance between 1950 and 1964 indicated that the statewide base of contributors ranged from 635 in 1950 to 24,085 in 1962 for the Democrats and from 2,003 in 1954 to 18,055 in 1964 for the Republicans—in a state with over one million voters.[42] On the national level, Herbert Alexander has projected the number of individual contributors to be: 3 million in 1952, 8 million in 1956, 10 million in 1960, 12 million in 1964, 8.7 million in 1968, and about 8.5 million in 1972.[43]

On the basis of the brief evidence presented on fund sources and contributors, one can conclude that the campaigner is faced with having to raise most funds from individual contributions within a relatively narrow base of contributors that include family, friends, and associates of the candidate, plus other committed supporters, particularly partisans. On the other hand, there is a hint that the potential exists to broaden the financial base. The evidence also suggests that campaigners should not be deluded into expecting generous party and group financial support.

FINANCE ORGANIZATION

The fund-raising operation is most frequently a separate or independent facet of campaigns. The chief fund raiser and his committee, if any, are generally prestigious persons who have wide community contact, particularly regarding money sources. Somehow or other their prestige and fund-tapping contact make them the sort of persons who do little else in the campaign but raise money. Given the critical importance of money and its almost universal perceived scarcity, this is considered to be a necessary and proper division of labor. Also, the campaign-reporting laws governing contributions and spending were sufficiently loose enough before the 1970s to encourage clandestine activities, so that a separate, less public, lower profile campaign finance activity was considered desirable. New legislation at the state and national levels, requiring very detailed expenditure reports and disclosure of amounts contributed, and from whom, will inevitably make campaign finance operations more public, but the nature of the fund-raising process and the fund raisers is likely to continue the separatism.

The chief sources of funds—individual contributions and, to a lesser extent, groups and political events—all require that they be solicited from their source by some means of contributor contact. Since a large share of American campaigns at all levels are financed by large contributions, this further implies that the contact must very often be a personal one. This is why the chief fund raisers in the campaign are most often important civic leaders who have contacts that cut across many sources. Ordinarily, they are persons who are socially able to ask prestigious persons to contribute. Outstanding finance chairmen and fund raisers are considered very difficult to find, and more difficult to enlist. The political campaign may be competing with the unified community fund, the Heart Fund, the Leukemia Fund, the March of Dimes, or some other charity. Political consultants Baus and Ross reveal the situation of the campaign finance chairman:

> Of course, he is a volunteer, and asking for money is not a sport men enjoy. For one thing, everybody he asks for important money will later be ringing *his* doorbell for some other 'good cause.' Reciprocation is a primary rule in the fund-raising fraternity.
>
> Nobody loves a finance chairman and a deaf man can hear him tiptoe at a distance of 20,000 yards. But there will be a good man who will take the job if someone is persistent enough to dig in and find him.
>
> The important (and always the lucky) thing is to get for finance chairman a good political geologist who knows by instinct and experience where the gold is, and has the punch to go in and get it.[44]

Those who are involved in raising the funds are more often generalists in community affairs than are the other campaign workers, and thus, use their contacts within the campaign to become specialists at fund raising.

Normally a fund-raising committee is established with broad geographical and special interests in mind. Formal divisions are more critical in large campaigns. Functional division—business, labor, professional—is necessary in many campaigns to use prestigious fund raisers within the community. The constituency is simply too large to use a few fund raisers throughout the campaign. Very often, active partisans with a proven record in fund raising for the party or some previous candidates are chosen to head fund-raising in subunits of the constituency. In the very large campaigns, separate committeees were establihsed to appeal to special interests (and previously to circumvent spending limits): Physicians for Smith, Educators for Senator Jones, Professionals for Congressman Doe, and so on. Smaller campaigns, of course, employ a more generalist system, with one or a few community notables performing most of the chores regardless of functional and geographical lines. The key is to use some system which uses willing and able people who have access to different segments of the community.

In many campaigns, the campaign treasurer serves as the chairman of the fund-raising committee. This individual is often very close to the candidate, and is the person legally responsible for fund-raising efforts. In the 1972 presidential campaigns, Maurice Stans and Henry Kimmelman held these posts for Nixon and McGovern respectively. Larger campaigns also employ full-time, paid, fund-raising directors who work with the volunteer committees, handle much of the paper work, organize mass fund raising, and perform some of the direct solicitation.[45] In the larger campaigns, special fund-raising events such as dinners often have full-time, paid, temporary staff that handles organization, arrangements, paperwork, and solicitation.

It is important for campaigners to realize that the two major parties have somewhat different modes of finance organization. We have portrayed American campaigns as candidate-centered, and as one might suspect, the finance operation follows this pattern. Herbert Alexander has depicted American political finance as double-diffused: *vertically,* in which various layers of party—national, state, county, ward, and precinct—raise, control, and disburse funds at their own level; and, *horizontally,* in which candidates, nonparty committees, labor committees, and business committees raise, control, and disburse funds for their own purposes.[46] Under this sytem the parties and candidates are free to raise their own money. Party organizations often do not work in conjucntion with or contribute much directly to the candidates who similarly have their own operation. Thus, each party level and candidate effort taps its own (but very often overlapping) sources of support, and spending is normally limited to efforts on behalf of the group that raises the funds. This system, as Alexander and others have observed, most typically fits Democratic party finance at all levels.[47]

In many areas, the Republican party practice is to form separate "united finance committees" which conduct cooperative fund drives, combining party organization and candidate efforts. At the national level and in many states, independent finance committees supply funds to the state committees and to various campaign committees. Very often, quota and allocations are made by which the political organizations raising the funds retain some of the funds, with the rest going into a finance pool, chiefly for candidates. The extensiveness of this united effort varies considerably from state to state, and the extent to which it reaches into the local level or the extent to which funds are contributed to minor-office candidates or local office candidates varies. Very often these efforts are limited to statewide efforts for gubernatorial and senatorial candidates. On the other hand, these united efforts can be extensive. Adamany describes the Connecticut Republican organization:

> The main organ of fund rasing is the Republican state finance committee. Each town is asked to name a finance chairman to work with the state central committee; and Republican leaders report that most towns do provide local leadership but late appointments and high turnover are common. Notwithstanding these weaknesses, the state finance committee cooperates with each town and each candidate to develop a budget. Most money raised by town finance committees is deposited directly in the state committee's account; towns may then draw on these funds up to the agreed upon budget or the amount raised in the town, whichever is lower. Budgets are also prepared for statewide candidates, and their campaigns are supported, as funds become available, to the extent of the agreed budget. In 1966 and in most previous years the state central committee actually administered the state campaign, so that party and candidate support budgets were merged in an overall effort.[48]

Centralized Republican efforts do not always have the impact and reach of the Connecticut effort. Campaigners should become familiar with particular, party financing patterns in their constituencies.

Whether the finance organizaton is centralized through the party or whether it is candidate-centered, the candidate will inevitably play a large role in fund raising. Some argue that the candidate should never be bothered with the time consuming, obligation-rendering task of soliciting money. There is no rule of thumb. In many small campaigns, the most effective fund-raising individual may be the candidate, and money may take precedence over time as a scarce resource. In both large and small campaigns, many potential contributors will only talk to the senator, representative, governor, mayor, alderman, or board member, or the future senator, representative, and so on. Moreover, the candidate should know from whom the funds come, and he or she may want to approve or disapprove of certain sources. Since the candidate's time is so valuable during the later stages of the campaign, it is deemed desirable for the inevitable involvement of the candidate to come at the early planning and support-gathering stages of the campaign.

The candidate's fund-raising and early support-gathering efforts often can be combined or at least initiated early—during the inside campaign to political leaders, community notables, and key members of the attentive public. One of the most popular sayings in campaign fundraising is, "If you can get someone to contribute something, he will be an avid supporter." Positive evidence has already been presented. This can also be reversed: those who are supporters are the most likely contributors. As the candidate is mobilizing key, individual support, he is also making an initial contact for fund raising. If it is considered inappropriate to solicit funds at the time, support is requested and these contacts should be followed up. The important people in a community are used to being asked for their support—for candidacies, civic projects, and public policies—and they are very often asked to contribute money. Some of these individuals are, possibly, the large contributors to the campaign. Thus, the inside campaign is often an important base of financial support.

Next to the inside campaign, those who volunteer for the campaign and volunteer for the candidate's party are important bases of support. Some argue that one cannot ask a volunteer for time and for money. But those who volunteer are committed, and there is evidence that people ordinarily demonstrate their commitment on more than one level. In addition to party and campaign workers, loyal supporters who do not work are another base of support. Lists of those who will put up lawn signs or those who have indicated in a telephone survey that they support the candidate, regularly support the candidate's party, or persons who are registered with the candidate's party all make better-than-random prospects for fund raising. Some fund-raising efforts are combined with voter contact activities by asking voters if they would be willing to make a financial contribution after they have given some indication of support. Of course, the positive response rate is low, but it is another economy of scale plus a measure of commitment. Like the process of garnering supporters, fund-raising efforts often radiate outward from the inside campaign to direct, voter solicitation.

Notes to Chapter 8

1. Herbert E. Alexander, *Financing the 1972 Election* (Lexington, Mass.: D.C. Heath, 1976), in preparation; *Chicago Tribune*, 24 March 1974, p. 10.

2. David Adamany, *Financing Politics* (Madison: Univ. of Wisconsin Press, 1969), pp. 8-9.

3. David W. Adamany, *Campaign Finance in America* (North Scituate, Mass.: Duxbury Press, 1972), p. 3.

4. Ibid.

5. Ibid., pp. 3-4.

6. Ibid., pp. 30-32.

7. Arnold J. Heidenheimer, "Comparative Party Finance: Notes on Practices and Toward a Theory," *Journal of Politics* 25 (1963): 798. Recalculated by Adamany, *Financing Politics*, pp. 52-55, 274.

8. Burdett A. Loomis, "Campaign Organization in 'Competitive' 1972 House Races," (Ph.D. Dissertation, University of Wisconsin, Madison, 1974).

9. Adamany, *Campaign Finance in America*, p. 42; John R. Owens, *Trends in Campaign Spending in California, 1958-1970: Test of Factors Influencing Costs* (Princeton, N.J.: Citizens Research Foundation, 1973), p. 60.

10. See notes to this and the next chapter.

11. Herbert E. Alexander, *Money in Politics* (Washington, D.C.: Public Affairs Press, 1972), p. 36.

12. Campaign Finance Monitoring Project, Common Cause, August 1973.

13. Ibid.

14. Owens, *Trends in Campaign Spending California, 1958-1970*, p. 62.

15. Adamany, *Campaign Finance in America*, pp. 54-55.

16. Ibid., pp. 62-63.

17. Adamany, *Financing Politics*, p. 72.

18. Ibid., p. 74.

19. Alexander, *Money In Politics*, p. 16.

20. Alexander Heard, *The Costs of Democracy* (Garden City, New York: Anchor Books, 1962), pp. 335-43.

21. Adamnay, *Financing Politics*, pp. 74-86; Adamany, *Campaign Finance in America*, p. 65; David A. Leuthold, *Electioneering in a Democray* (New York: John Wiley, 1968), p. 80.

22. Campaign Finance Monitoring Project, Common Cause, September, 1973.

23. This entire section on factors which relate to spending levels is based on the works of Adamany, *Financing Politics*, pp. 66-86; Adamany, *Campaign Finance in America*, pp. 51-72; Heard, *The Costs of Democracy*, ch. 14; Heidenheimer, "Comparative Party Finance"; Leuthold, *Electioneering in a Democracy*, pp. 77-83, 104.

24. Heard, *The Costs of Democracy*, p. 17.

25. Robert A. Dahl, *Who Governs* (New Haven: Yale Univ. Press. 1961), p. 226.

26. Heard, *The Costs of Democracy*, pp. 18-19.

27. Owens, *Trends in Campaign Spending in California, 1958-1970*, pp. 51-52.

28. Campaign Finance Monitoring Project, Common Cause, September, 1973.

29. William Buchanan and Agnes Bird, *Money as a Campaign Resource: Tennessee Democratic Senatorial Primaries, 1948-1964* (Princeton, N.M.: Citizens Research Foundation, 1966), p. 87-89.

30. Ibid., pp. 87-88.

31. Bernard R. Berelson, Paul F. Lazarsfeld and William N. McPhee, *Voting* (Chicago: Univ. of Chicago Press, 1954), ch. 12.

32. *Gallup Opinion Index*, 15 (August 1966): 11; Gallup Opinion Index, 36 (June 1968): 10.

33. Heard, *The Costs of Democracy*, pp. 40-41.

34. Herbert E. Alexander, *Financing the 1968 Election* (Lexington, Mass.: D.C. Heath, 1971), p. 162.

35. Leuthold, *Electioneering in a Democracy*, p. 82

36. Alexander, *Financing the 1968 Election*, p. 144.

37. Campaign Finance Monitoring Project, Common Cause, September, 1973.

38. Leuthold, *Electioneering in a Democracy*, pp. 79-81.

39. Robert J. Huckshorn and Robert C. Spencer, *The Politics of Defeat* (Amherst, Mass.: Univ. of Massachusetts Press, 1971), pp. 127-28.

40. Donald G. Balmer, *Financing State Senate Campaigns: Multnomah County Oregon, 1964* (Princeton, N.J.: Citizens Research Foundation, 1966), pp. 37-38.

41. Leuthold, *Electioneering in a Democracy*, p. 80.

42. Adamany, *Financing Politics*, pp. 191-92.

43. Alexander, *Financing the 1968 Election*, p. 144.

44. Herbert M. Baus and William B. Ross, *Politics Battle Plan* (New York: Macmillan, 1968), p. 87.

45. Michael A. Berman, *Organizational Suggestions for a Statewide Campaign in Minnesota*, Minneapolis, Minnesota, pp. 77-78.

46. Herbert E. Alexander, *Responsibility in Party Finance* (Princeton, N.J.: Citizens Research Foundation, 1963), pp. 31-35.

47. Ibid., pp. 34-37; Heard, *The Costs of Democracy*, pp. 267-71; Cornelius P. Cotter and Bernard C. Hennessy, *Politics Without Power: The National Party Committees*, (New York: Atherton Press, 1964), pp. 176-79.

48. Adamany, *Campaign Finance in America*, pp. 133-34.

For Further Reading and Research

Adamany, David W. *Campaign Finance in America*. North Scituate, Mass.: Duxbury, 1972.

_____. *Financing Politics: Recent Wisconsin Elections*. Madison: Univ. of Wisconsin Press, 1969.

Adamany, David W. and Agree, George. *Political Money: A Strategy for Campaign Financing in America*. Baltimore: Johns Hopkins, 1975.

Alexander, Herbert E. *Financing the 1968 Election*. Lexington, Mass.: D.C. Heath, 1971.

_____ . *Money in Politics.* Washington, Public Affairs Press, 1972.

_____ . *Political Financing.* Minneapolis: Burgess, 1972.

_____ . *Responsibility in Party Finance.* Princeton, N.J.: Citizens Research Foundation, 1963.

Buchanan, William and Bird, Agnes. *Money as a Campaign Resource: Tennessee Democratic Senatorial Primaries, 1948-1964.* Princeton, N.J.: Citizens Research Foundation, 1966.

Common Cause. *Campaign Finance Monitoring Project.* Washington: Common Cause, 1972. Periodic reports.

Dunn, Delmer D. *Financing Presidential Campaigns.* Washington: Brookings, 1972.

Heard, Alexander. *The Costs of Democracy.* Garden City, N.Y.: Doubleday, 1962.

Heidenheimer, Arnold J., (ed.) *Comparative Political Finance: The Financing of Party Organizations and Election Campaigns.* Lexington, Mass.: D.C. Heath, 1970.

McCarthy, Max. *Elections for Sale.* Boston: Houghton Mifflin, 1972.

Nichols, David. *Financing Elections: The Politics of an American Ruling Class.* New York: New Viewpoints, 1974.

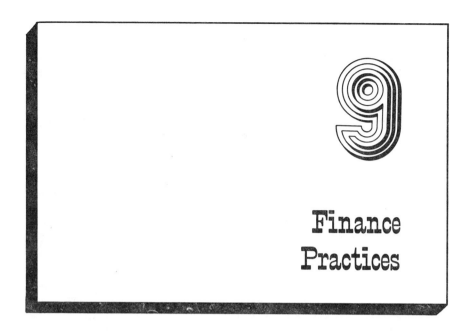

Finance
Practices

The most important problems in campaign financing for candidates are fund raising and management of those funds to support the strategy. Spending levels are related to a number of the systemic factors listed in the previous chapter. In addition, costs probably relate to strategists' expectations about spending in previous campaigns, meeting the spending expectations of their key supporters, and the opponent's spending level. Sometimes spending levels are set at the high water mark of a previous successful campaign. (Before meaningful disclosure, they were obscure and often inflated by outside observers.) Alexander also points out that as new techniques are accepted and, to some extent, replace older ones, few candidates are willing to use the unconventional methods alone.[1] Rather than relating spending levels to setting and strategy, campaigners frequently select a total figure first, after which a budget and spending pattern is determined. Sometimes this becomes a magical figure. "It will take at least $100,000 to beat X in this district," without any regard to what one plans to do or how it is to be done, is a familiar refrain. In the meantime, as these various factors increase costs, the campaigner faces the problem of raising funds from a narrow and competitive political finance base. As costs increase, it is not clear that the number of contributors has increased proportionately or that the necessary dollar amounts from the contributor groups will be forthcoming in every situation.

The dual problems of costs and available funds, therefore, make it imperative that campaigners relate finance practices to setting and strategy, avoiding any idiosyncratic spending or fund-raising factors. Fund-raising techniques should be appropriate to the level of the office and the organizational abilities of the campaign. Spending levels should follow a set of established tactics, which, in turn, should follow strategic assessment. Costs then relate to such factors as personal campaigning and number of volunteers, both of which tend to lower costs for printing, postage, media time, and consultants, all of which tend to raise costs. Relating costs to strategy will not necessarily lower costs, but it may avoid some unnecessary spending or overspending, and it may avoid some fund-raising pitfalls. This chapter will cover some of the practical aspects of fund raising, spending, budgeting, and financial management, as well as recent legal concerns, and how these practices might be related to strategy.

FUND RAISING: A CATALOGUE OF IDEAS

Raising money can be one of the most time-consuming aspects of a campaign. Some candidates, trapped by unrealistic dollar objectives with little prospect of reaching them, react by spending most of their time fund raising almost to the exclusion of all other campaign activities. Most campaign accounts indicate that the acquisition of money as a resource is one of the more problematical aspects of the campaign. Fund-raising efforts are often undertaken unrealistically, too late, with little planning, and they consume other valuable campaign resources. This section deals with identification of various fund-raising techniques and their implications as a part of the campaign process, including some suggestions of how to raise funds.

Direct Personal Solicitation

Data has already been presented which indicate that: (1) raising money from direct contacts is the largest, single source by far; and (2) an even greater potential exists because many unsolicited persons appear willing to contribute if and when asked. That personal contributions to candidates "radiate out" from the candidate's family and personal friends, to business and professional associates, to strong supporters and to fellow strong partisans, and then to milder partisans and supporters has also been demonstrated.

The apparent key to personal solicitation, as with so many other fund-raising techniques, is to work from the most likely prospects to lesser prospects. This ordinarily means securing and compiling lists, and keeping records on priority prospects, solicitors, and special-event contributors. Lists of likely prospects include: party contributors, previous campaign donors, lists shared with other candidates, lists of contributors to previous political events, lists of contributors to other causes, published state and national reports of large campaign contributions in the constituency, and lists of potential contributors compiled by the finance committee. If the finance committee is broadly representative of various community, party, business, and labor interests, acquisition and compilation of lists will be greatly facilitated. One of the most sought after Democratic lists is the McGovern contributor list for 1972, which can be easily broken down by various constituencies. An unprecedented total of 600,000 contributors are named on that list.

Personal solicitation can be either person-to-person or by telephone. Some experienced solicitors claim that very large contributions are more successful in person-to-person contacts than by telephone. Because fund raisers are often very busy, face-to-face solicitation may be impossible, and the method used depends somewhat on how well the solicitor knows the prospective contributor. The greatest problem in personal solicitation of large contributions is the combination of fear and underestimation. Campaigners are reluctant both to ask busy people to solicit funds and also to ask persons to give. Furthermore, there is a tendency to ask for less money than actually can be raised. Most prospective large contributors are used to being asked for money. Parting with $100 or $1000 is much less painful to them than parting with smaller amounts is to the more moderate-income person. The greatest problem in personal solicitation of smaller contributions is usually organizational; parties and campaigns are not normally prepared to make extensive appeals. This is the reason why more candidate efforts have turned to direct mail or to combine fund raising with voter-contact activities.

Direct solicitation techniques, of course, depend on the availability of campaign workers to solicit such contributions. Resources may be too scarce to allow volunteers to raise funds, particularly if they appear to be unsuited and unwilling to perform such chores.

Political Events

Campaign fund-raising events ordinarily accomplish the dual function of bringing the faithful together, reinforcing and encouraging them to work for the campaign as well as to bring in money. Fund raisers can be very simple and easy to do—garage sales, bake sales, voluntary-donation coffee parties, cocktail parties, movie nights, and bridge sales. They can be moderately complicated—progressive dinners, barbecues, pool parties, pancake breakfasts, pot-luck suppers, bean feeds, tours, ice cream socials, boat cruises, square dances and hay rides. They can also be very elaborate or complex: dinners, dinner dances, all day picnics with games and prizes, auctions, or a refreshment stand at a fair. Fund raisers raise less money than is commonly believed, particularly in small campaigns where it is ordinarily difficult to bring in masses of people and there are fewer "natural" contributors who might have an interest in government contact. Their role in congressional, gubernatorial and senatorial campaign fund raising is much more important, but less than half of all funds raised in those campaigns are generally raised through such events.

Two very important costs make fund-raising events a painful way to garner funds for all but a few campaigns. First, there is ordinarily a cost of the goods sold. A dinner with a $10 to $25 ticket price will cost between $5 and $7 per plate, not including other overhead costs. Boat rides, movies, hayrides, and ice cream also cost money. Even if the goods are donated, there may well be overhead expenses. A second and perhaps more important cost, is the organizational inertia and number of scarce campaign-worker resources expended on these events. The involvement required to plan, staff, organize, and promote these events often drains off workers into projects which then exclude them from other, more important campaign work. Too often in small campaigns volunteers spend so much time and energy on dinners or sales that they lose their taste for the more necessary work. If the monetary returns are low for the effort made, these two costs are indeed a high price to pay for funds. By contrast, the harvest from direct solicitation is nearly free, with the exception of the time of solicitors who often would do little else in the campaign anyway. When fund-raising events involve hundreds of hours over a period of weeks for a relatively miniscule return, they function more as reinforcing and cohesive forces than as money-raising devices.

The case of the campaign dinner is representative of the considerable work involved in fund-raising events. A coordinator and a planning committee must be selected and they in turn must set the ticket price, select the date and place. An honorary dinner committee and chairperson may have to be selected. Lists of those to be invited must be secured and or compiled. If a speaker is to be used, a confirmation will be needed very early. Invitations, mailing envelopes, return envelopes, and reservation cards must be designed and ordered from the printer. Records must be kept on the returns, to be followed up by a telephone call to those who do not reply. A week or so before the dinner, the tickets will have to be mailed out. Many last minute details are involved: the head table must be set up; press arrangements must be made; parking facilities must be checked; ticket sales at the door will have to be arranged; the public-address system will have to be tested; the program must be arranged; publicity for the dinner and the speaker will have to be planned; plus a hundred or so details involving the caterer, florists, flags for the head table, elevation of the head table, lighting and bar arrangements, and so on. These and other details indicate that careful planning and skilled management are required to make fund-raising events, such as dinners, a success.

Fund-raising events must be carefully weighed in advance to estimate whether the organizational and financial costs will yield the benefits that might be had from direct solicitation or other, less costly methods.

Direct-Mail Solicitation

Raising funds by mail ordinarily means relatively large numbers of small contributions. The success of using the mails obviously depends upon the selectivity of the list used and the common appeal to which the people in that category might be most responsive. Occasionally campaigners attempt mass direct-mail appeals, such as a mailing to all those on the voter registration list, property tax rolls, automobile registrations, city directories, or voters and canvass lists, but, the costs of such efforts are high and the return relatively low. Data indicate that even when solicited, only about one in five are willing to contribute.

The key to direct-mail solicitation is to somehow reduce the odds and the

Figure 9.1   Campaign Pledge and Contribution Forms

Lawyers' Committee for **DOUGLAS M. HEAD for GOVERNOR**

☐ You may use my name in connection with a list of lawyers who support DOUGLAS M. HEAD for GOVERNOR.

☐ Enclosed is my check in the amount of $ _____
(Make checks payable to: Lawyers for Head Volunteer Committee)

(Please Print)

_____   _____
(Last Name) (First Name)   (M/I)   (Signature)

_____   _____
(Street)   (City)   (County)   (Zip)

_____   ☐ Please contact me if I can
(Office Phone)   (Home Phone)   be of further help.

PRECINCT NO

MARRIED ☐   SINGLE ☐   A |1|2|3|4|5|

OCCUPATION _____   FIELD   POSITION

SOLICITOR _____

DATE SOLICITED MO ___ YR ___

AMOUNT PLEDGED ___ DOLLARS ONLY

PAID NOW ___ DOLLARS ONLY

BALANCE DUE   SEMI ☐   QUAT ☐

LAST NAME _____
FIRST NAME _____   MIDDLE INITIAL ___
TITLE ___   JR ☐   SR ☐   II ☐   III ☐   IV ☐
STREET NUMBER _____   IF ½ ☐
STREET DIRECTION ___   STREET NAME _____
STREET TYPE ___   APT - BOX NO ___
ZIP CODE _____   COUNTY CODE ___

CAPITAL '70 CLUB   PAYMENT BEGINS MO ___ YR ___   TELEPHONE NUMBER _____

DEMOCRATIC DATA SERVICE   1712 SHERMAN STREET   DENVER, COLORADO 80203 costs of mailing to non-contributors by selecting those most likely to contribute and to stress some issue or group principle that will motivate them to give. The best lists are obviously those of previous contributors to a related or similar campaign. Other lists might include: active party members or those who have contributed to the party, lists of persons who have attended precinct caucuses to elect delegates to political conventions, or lists of persons who have contributed to other political causes that can be construed as related to the candidacy. Examples of the latter would include contributors to civil rights causes, to citizens lobby groups, consumer groups, and neighborhood action groups, if such lists for a given constituency are available. Other often used lists include interest groups or organizations—labor unions, service clubs, business groups, church lists, veterans groups, and other special interest associatons—whose primary mission may not be political, but membership in the group indicates a sufficient degree of attentiveness and community activism suggesting that their prospects for a contribution are greater than that of the general publics. Appeals based on something the members of the list share in common are then made in the letter: their trade union status, their opposition to open-housing legislation, their commitment to the civil rights movement, their practice of supporting Republican candiates, their concern for gun-control legislation or their role as property owners.

Those experienced in direct-mail fund raising suggest that the letter should be as personalized as possible, straightforward in style, on a single page, giving the reader a reason why he or she would benefit from making a contribution, and, a specific amount should be suggested. Since the appeal necessarily will be short, a campaign brochure, or some other specially prepared insert, is included. Return envelopes, color coded to identify the list, should be included, providing space for names, addresses, amount of the contributions, or any other pertinent information. Letters are, of course, modified for each list, and some campaigners make the effort to eliminate duplicates, but the effort may be greater than its worth if the lists are long. Some fund raisers feel that the return envelopes must have return postage, others do not. Return postage raises the cost, and thus, diminishes the potential dollar yield.

Unfortuantely, there is no reliable evidence as to the amount a direct-mail campaign will yield, and lists vary greatly as to their fund-raising potential. Each list must be estimated individually. Sometimes it is possible to determine the effectiveness of lists from other campaigns, when the same lists are used. Many fund raisers and direct-mail experts recommend the testing of lists, by sending letters to a portion of people listed (about 10 percent), to examine its yield. In the case of very large lists, several letters are often tested. Various lists and letters may be tested simultaneously. Senator Walter Mondale's 1972 re-election campaign staff also tested the printed letter against the more personalized computer-generated letter on established campaign-donor lists and found little difference between the two. In testing the mailing, records can be kept on the ratio of responses to pieces sent, average and total contributions, the cost of the mailer, and funds raised or lost, as in Table 9.1. If the returns from a particular list (combined with any volunteer effort involved) exceed the costs of the mailing to a degree that, in the judgment of the fund raisers, justifies the effort, it is worthwile to proceed with the mailing. If costs exceed funds, the list may be useful for campaign appeals, but it should be disregarded for fund-raising purposes.

Direct-mail fund raising requires some organizational effort, particularly if the work of preparing mailing will be undertaken by volunteers. Since the fund-raising steps should come relatively early in the campaign, volunteers need not diminish any voter-contact activities if they are planned in advance. Advance planning, sufficient lead time, and estimation of the organizational and financial costs are all important facets of using direct mailings.

Table 9.1   Direct-Mail-Fund-Raising Test Data

Identity	No. Sent	No. Response	Percent Response	Average Contri- bution	Total Contri- bution	Cost	Profit/ Loss
List A Letter 1	1000	100	10%	$7	$700	$100	$600
List A Letter 2	1000	50	5%	$10	$500	$100	$400
List B Letter 1	1000	200	20%	$4	$800	$100	$700
List B Letter 2	1000	75	7.5%	$1	$75	$100	-$25

Source: Michael Berman, *Organizational Suggestions for a Statewide Campaign in Minnesota,* private campaign memo, 1969, p. 83.

Group Appeals for Contributions

Chapter 5 indicated that groups vary in the degree to which they support candidates, and that contributions from the group or one of its political committees is one demonstration of support. The amount of money raised from groups is generally less than is often assumed, and the total amounts of group monies is also overestimated. In 1972, contributions from registered interest groups amounted to only 14 percent of the total monies contributed to congressional candidates, although they accounted for 26 percent of all contributions over $100. Nevertheless, group financial support can help the treasury as well as demonstrate support.

Among the better-known groups that make contributions to candidates are:

1. labor auxiliary groups, such as the AFL-CIO's COPE and the Teamsters' DRIVE, which are based on the voluntary contributions of members, (primarily for president, senate and congress) because direct union (or corporation) contributions to candidates seeking national office are illegal. Individual unions also contribute funds nationally through their voluntary political action committees, and AFL-CIO central body affiliates and union locals contribute at the state and local level. Political union groups not belonging to the AFL-CIO, such as the railroad brotherhoods and the longshoremen, also contribute.[2]

2. campaign "arms" of business associations, such as the Bankers Congressional Committee, Shoe Manufacturers Committee, and others which are either interested in specific economic issues or a wider range of public policies.

3. domestic policy oriented committees of a conservative persuasion such as Americans for Constitutional Action (ACA), American Medical Political Action Committee (AMPAC), and Business and Industry Political Action Committee (BIPAC); or liberal groups such as Americans for Democratic Action (ADA) and National Committee for an Effective Congress (NCEC).

4. other organizations and businesses at the state and local level which habitually contribute money to candidates (in states where direct organizational contributions are legal). The practice of organizational contributions to candidates is too varied to generalize. The most reliable means of finding out is to check the public record of reported contributions from a previous campaign, and to seek such information from local groups.

The amount of money contributed to candidates by these groups is very often overestimated. It has already been demonstrated in Table 8.6 (page 000) that the proportion of funds from such groups is small, rarely exceeding 20 percent in large campaigns and much less in the smaller campaigns. As an example, Adamany reports that the total dollar amount of such group contributions in Connecticut in 1968 to candidates and party committees was—

- labor organizations: $109,605 to the Democrats and $1,755 to the Republicans.
- business and professional organizations: $86,233 to the Republicans only.[3]

Often, the gross amount of business or group contributions reported in a campaign year distorts the amount received by the individual candidates. For example, two milk-marketing cooperatives (including the Associated Milkproducers of San Antonio, Texas) contributed $38,800 to Illinois candidates in 1972. They included: $11,000 to Daniel Walker, candidate for governor and $5,200 to Richard Ogilvie, his opponent; $2,500 to Roman Puchinski, Democratic senatorial candidate and $5,000 to Charles Percy, his opponent. With the exception of one $8,100 contribution and one for $2,000, the rest of the congressional contributions ranged from $500 to $1,500.[4] Likewise, organized labor committees contributed a total of $1,106,494 to 1972 senate candidates. The money went to thirty-nine candidates, with a mean contribution of $33,000 to thirty Democrats and $11,000 to nine Republicans.[5] Union money raised by voluntary contribution to auxiliary committees at the national level averages about five or six cents per union member and, thus, it takes many gifts to aggregate large sums contributed to candidates, or to match a large individual contribution ranging from one to five thousand dollars.[6] Labor contributions to candidates are probably the most overestimated. Table 9.2 depicts the allocations by labor to candidates for the 1964 elections, according to some important aspects of the campaign setting. The average labor contribution to congressional Democratic candidates in 1972 was closer to $5000, which amounted to less than 10 percent of funds raised.[7] These figures suggest that only a few thousand dollars can be expected by Democrats in campaigns that easily run from $50,000 to $100,000. Even "safe" and marginal incumbents, or challengers with even chances to win can only expect a relatively small portion of the funds. Though not unimportant, group contributions (such as labor giving) should be realistically assessed so that campaigners will not expect much financial support.

Table 9.2   Mean Labor Allocations to House Democrats by
Type of Constituency

Candidate Category	Urban	Rural
Safe Incumbents	$2,704 (86)[*]	$1,877 (37)
Marginal Incumbents	$3,842 (10)	$3,617 (21)
Marginal Challengers	$3,182 (23)	$2,402 (41)
Marginal Candidates for Open Seats:		
FD	$3,357 (7)	$1,650 (4)
FR	$4,369 (7)	$2,267 (6)
Hopeless Challengers	$1,092 (31)	$1,610 (28)
Hopeless Candidates for Open Seats (FR)	$2,450 (1)	$2,750 (1)
Safe Candidates for Open Seats (FD)	$1,123 (7)	$1,588 (4)

[*]Figures in parentheses indicate the number of candidates in that category who received labor contributions.

Source: Kevin L. McKeough, *Financing Campaigns for Congress: Contributions of National Level Party and Non-Party Committees, 1964* (Princeton, N.J.: Citizens Research Foundation, 1970), p. 75.

Most groups that do contribute to candidates follow established procedures for lending support. For example, labor political action committees, such as COPE, ordinarily announce public meetings in which prospective endorsees are screened. After all the candidates who have sought out endorsement are screened, the committee meets to endorse and allocate funds. The candidate must seek out and obtain the endorsement prior to receiving funds. Screening announcements appear in the labor and sometimes the local newspapers. If in doubt, a telephone call to the union hall or union officer at a very early stage in the campaign is in order. Other groups have somewhat different procedures, depending on the level of the candidacy, geographic area, and the procedures established by the particular group. Campaigners who plan to seek funds from groups should become aware of the procedures and schedules of the various groups.

Professional Firms

A very recent trend in campaigns has been to employ the services of professional fund-raising firms, applying some of their contacts and expertise in other areas to politics. Such firms ordinarily raise money for hospitals, universities, charities, retirement homes, and other enterprises which depend upon voluntary contributions. They ordinarily work for a certain proportion of the funds raised plus expenses. Since they have channels of access to regular donors to many different causes, candidates have been known to take a chance that the money raised (after the firm has been paid) will be greater than the sums they themselves can raise. The use of professional fund-raising firms has been slower to catch on than the use of other types of campaign firms, because political sources of money are often passed on through party channels, and political donors are not always identical in characteristics to those who give to non-political causes. The cost of retaining such a firm would ordinarily be prohibitive to small constituency campaigns. The most profitable use of such firms appears to be for the large constituency campaign in which the candidate is relatively new and unfamiliar with normal party sources of funds.

Direct-mail firms can handle the entire direct-mail fund-raising portion of a campaign, or they may sell lists of possible contributors. The lists range from the nearly useless, such as all persons with children under 5 years of age (very useful for photo processors), to the highly useful, such as Richard Viguere's extensive list of contributors to conservative political causes. Potential buyers should be careful when purchasing any lists of non-political givers: their transferability is often questionable. These firms develop their lists to sell to advertisers and promoters, and the more times the same list is sold the greater the profit margin to the seller. Firms that specialize in political mailings such as Viguere of Washington, D.C. (Republican), and Valentine, Sherman of Bloomington, Minnesota (Democratic) can often supply more reliable, special lists, such as lists of union members, teachers, small business owners, and retired military officers. They also sell their computerized direct-mail capabilities. The cost of the lists are not expensive. Production and handling costs are quite expensive, with personalized, computer-generated letters often running between fifteen to twenty cents per letter.

THE COSTS OF FUND RAISING

One should conclude from this very brief account of various fund-raising techniques that raising money for a campaign costs more than money. Fund raising for charities, organizations, and other enterprises has more enduring structures, personnel, and procedures. Campaign enterprises are less permanent, and the fund-raising drive comes at the same time the organization gets established, personnel selected, plans initiated, and other resources surveyed and acquired. Except for incumbents, campaign-funding drives are less likely to be repeats of previous drives. Because the process if often initiated with and simultaneous to many other incipient activities, efforts to raise money have to be considered in the light of total campaign efforts. The cost of a specific fund-raising technique may well be the loss, dilution, or exhaustion of valuable personnel resources needed elsewhere or later. The use of a talented fund raiser to sell five-dollar tickets to a dinner, or to peddle literature, may cost the campaign much wasted money and effort. Using the candidate to raise needed funds in the last month of the campaign weakens the voter-contact activity effort. When raising funds, timing, techniques, efforts, and personnel must be considered in relation to the entire campaign effort.

BUDGETING

The campaign budget should be an important document, formally signifying that campaigners have translated setting and strategy into tactics, and, therefore, financial plans reflect these activities. Too often the budget, if there is one, is a reflection of the practices of doing what has been done before, or it is an effort to please supporters without regard to the strategic principles to which it should apply. Campaigns following this procedure often begin and remain underfinanced because they undertake activities which are beyond their means. More typical in small campaigns is a non-budgeting process in which campaigners do not plan but simply begin campaigning and raising and spending money (not necessarily in that order) with little concern for where they are going, how much it will cost, and how to get there.

The advice from campaign specialists on how to budget is legion. Ordinarily, the candidate is told to spend half for media and public relations, to be sure to rent a headquarters, that fund-raising events should bring in half, or "If you cannot afford paid staff in all areas, hire at least a public relations person/writer. Such advice very often comes from those who have worked in large campaigns and is less useful to those handling small campaign or a portion of a large campaign in a particular area. It is more important that budgets must reflect the strategy based on the setting. Half of one's budget for media and public relations probably does not follow if one is running in a very small, geographically concentrated constituency of a large city, particularly if it is a majority party setting where party volunteers do campaign. Much of the effort and expenditures of this party-reinforcement campaign setting will be devoted to raising money from partisan activists and spending it to support their activities. By the same token, if one is a town or campus organizer for a presidential candidate, much of the media and public relations for that campaign is undertaken elsewhere, and the funds raised will probably be devoted to special printing for voter registration, get-out-the-vote, or other such activities. If the campaigner tries to link the budget process to the strategic assessment and formulation process, then the campaigner has reasonably integrated finance, setting, and strategy. For this reason, it will be suggested that campaigners consider both program and line-item budgets.

Timing

Conventional advice always admonishes the candidate to raise money early for purposes of planning expenditures, particularly those which require considerable preparation such as media production and time, and for purposes of freeing the candidate and campaigners for later activities. Although difficult to contradict, the campaigner should bear in mind that some money will inevitably come in late because it flows with other campaign processes. Since politics is not uppermost in the minds of many people, they may not be contacted or they simply may not be enthusiastic until the candidate makes an impact, and, therefore, will not contribute until the later stages of the campaign. The money resource follows (or at least is interlocked with) other resources. In the 1968 presidential campaign, Hubert Humphrey began to overcome his financial disadvantages while he was closing the voter support gap. Also, as more campaign activities are undertaken, such as direct voter contact activities, more solicitors are reaching more potential contributors. The public enthusiasm the candidate generates will always generate some late money.

On the other hand, evidence regarding who contribute suggests that the bulk of important individual contributions comes from persons socially and politically close to the candidate—family, friends, associates, and fellow partisans. They are persons to whom the enthusiasm of the candidacy ordinarily comes earlier, permitting funds to be raised earlier. Since most money actually comes from these sources, "early" money as a base which allows for planning and integration is more possible than most expect. Incumbents have a particular advantage in this regard, because they widen their political and community circles during their tenure, have been through the process before, have already established a more public following, and can stage fund-raising events, such as "appreciation dinners," well in advance of formal campaigning. Whether the campaign is for an incumbent or a non-incumbent, the financial base of the campaign does make it possible to depend on some funds raised in the early stages.

Therefore, the ideal budget should begin with a large proportion of the funds raised in advance of much formal campaigning, yet make allowance for money raised later.

Spending, Setting, and Strategy

Since it has been argued that budgetary considerations should reflect what a campaign is trying to accomplish strategically within a given setting, it is difficult to posit rules of spending that tell campaigners how much money to spend on a given activity or what proportion of their money should go for each. It truly depends on the stituation. In some campaigns 80 percent of the funds spent for personnel and headquarters expenses will be consistent with the strategy. In others, 80 percent for media will be equally consistent.

The campaigner, as budgeter, should establish the financial needs required to support the strategy as opposed to day-to-day expenses. How much are the organizational, public relations, media, and direct-voter contact activities likely to cost in terms of dollars? Are the projected and actual funds adequate to support such activities? If there are gaps, then reassessments will have to be made as to additional fund-raising efforts, reduced expenditures, increased contributions, or similar adjustments. These activities lead inevitably to the establishment of program budgeting.

The Program Budget

A seldom used managerial campaign technique is the program budget—a form of financial accounting that stresses the activities undertaken and their programmatic thrust, rather than detailed line items. Program budgets are used in public finance to ensure that spending programs reflect the policy goals and objectives of the policy makers. Applied to the campaign, a program budget should reflect the allocation of finances in relation to strategic principles. If the strategy is based on creating public recognition and independent identity for the candidate, the program budget will reflect heavy expenditures for media production and purchases of time, with less for organizational activities. More partisan strategies will reflect less media expenditures and more support of and reliance upon party organization, including the possibility of financial support to the party.

The following is an excerpt from a hypothetical campaign program budget, for a legislative campaign for a minority party challenger in a rural, small town district. The strategy is based on capitalization of the candidate's well-known name in part of the district, candidate appeal, opposition to the incumbent's stand on aid to private schools and his stand for gun-control legislation, with minor emphasis on the candidate's own party support. Of the projected $4000 raised from the various activities deemed strategically necessary—

A. Door-to-door work by (the candidate) will constitute a major effort in direct-voter contact. Since he will begin in friendly territory and work out to less known territories, travel expenses will be light, most of which the candidate has agreed to pay—$300.

B. Media appeals, including newspaper advertising and radio spots will be designed to create visibility for the candidate as a person and will emphasize his previous experience and qualifications—$1100.

C. Issue appeals on gun control and aid to schools will be targeted to church groups and sportsmen's clubs, unions, and veteran's clubs by direct mail—$500.

D. Party support activities are less important, since the campaign is independent of the party, yet certain activities should be supported such as joint telephone bank activities, participation in literature distribution in high, party support areas plus attendance at functions—$250.

E. Most campaign support activities will be based on volunteers and donated activities. The headquarters will be donated. Nevertheless, preparation of press kits, media materials, postage, telephone, stationary will require about one-eighth of the budget—$500.

This portion of a program budget allocating $2,650 of a $4,000 campaign indicates how strategic principles are translated into the weighting of a program budget. Notice how issue and candidate appeals were supported by expenditures of $1,100, whereas party related expenditures were weighted significantly smaller. Support activities or administrative expenses are also put into their proper perspective by the ability to contrast them with other activities. Formulating such a program budget gives the campaign planners an opportunity to determine if their all-important spending activities are consistent with what is to be accomplished in the campaign.

Line-Item Budget

After a program budget is established, translating the large expenditure allocations into the necessary detailed items is an easier task. Again, the itemized budget should contain activities that are consistent with the strategy of the campaign, as presented in the campaign plan and the program budget. If an item is inconsistent with the strategy as formulated, it is an obvious choice for immediate cost reduction.

When formulating the line-item budget, the very important step of obtaining cost estimates is crucial. All suppliers, those offering professional services, and other vendors should be required to submit minutely detailed cost estimates. Too often this activity is left to guesswork and the costs are either budgeted too high or too low. If the campaign is organized on a large scale or functional basis, these estimates (along with the total itemized budget for that phase of the campaign) should be obtained by the appropriate division heads. Upon receiving all estimates and quotations, items can then be detailed, shifted, and totaled.

No attempt will be made to itemize an ideal budget for an ideal campaign, since it has been maintained that the "fit" would be very difficult. Figure 9.1 depicts an outline for a line-item campaign budget, most likely to fit a congressional campaign. Some items listed are not as relevant to smaller campaigns, particularly television, payroll, and certain headquarters expenses. This budget depicts the range of items which might be necessary to a campaign, and they can be expanded and contracted according to campaign plans. Notice that this particular budget form is scaled over a six-and-one-half-month period, allowing for ready comparison of revenue with those expenses required at any given point. Item budgets should unfold throughout the campaign if revenue and expenditures are integrated in this way. In a given month and throughout the campaign, a combination of the reserve fund (those funds already raised) and incoming expenditures should match those funds needed for activities, if not in reality at least as an objective.

Constraints on Spending

Until now, the discussion of budgeting has been predicated on strictly managerial concerns. We have been encouraging a sort of "management by objectives" based on setting, strategy, and program budgeting, while urging that expenditures be based on these concerns to the exclusion of extraneous, nonstrategic items, The aim is to condition campaigners, in their own budgeting, to think along the same lines as governmental and business executives.

In reality we know that budget makers operate within a political context, and thus, a set of restraints impinge on the ideal, objectives-based budget. Since campaigning is a political process, managerial activities in politics, like government budgeting, are likely to face their own contextual limitations. These limitations make the ideal set of expenditures sometimes impossible to achieve. David Adamany has developed a set of restraints on campaign spending, any one or a combination of which the campaigner, as budgeter, might encounter.

1. The practicability of certain stragegies and tactics; for example the use of television or major metropolitan dailies for legislative candidates, despite the fact these media are the most important means of reaching voters. Their extensive reach and circulation make them expensive and, thus, not cost-effective.

2. The unavailability of certain types of competence and skill; if large numbers of campaign workers are not available through patronage or

Figure 9.2   A Basic Time-Scaled Campaign Budget

	PROPOSED BASIC CAMPAIGN BUDGET MONTHS BEFORE THE ELECTION						15 Days	Total Budget
	6	5	4	3	2	1		
ADMINISTRATION								
Payroll (Hqs.)								
Payroll Taxes, etc.								
Office Rental (Hqs.)								
Equip. Rental (Hqs.)								
Stationery, Supplies, Postage								
Telephone & Telegraph (Hqs.)								
Travel (Hqs.)								
District-wide Meetings								
Miscellaneous								
Contingencies								
TOTAL ADMINISTRATION								
PUBLIC RELATIONS								
Publicity								
Travel								
Telephone & Telegraph								
Mats								
Release Sheets								
Envelopes								
Photography								
Postage								
Stencils								
Press Relations								
Contingencies								
TOTAL PUBLIC RELATIONS								
RESEARCH TOTAL								
ADVERTISING								
Newspaper								
Space — Dailies								
Space — Weeklies								
Space — Trade & Professional								
Magazines & Journals								
Production								
TOTAL NEWSPAPER								
Television								
Time								
Production								
TOTAL TELEVISION								
Radio								
Time								
Production								
TOTAL RADIO								
Outdoor								
Space								
Production								
TOTAL OUTDOOR								

Figure 9.2   A Basic Time-Scale Campaign Budget (Continued)

Continued	PROPOSED BASIC CAMPAIGN BUDGET MONTHS BEFORE THE ELECTION						15 days	Total Budget
	6	5	4	3	2	1		
Direct Mail								
Production								
Cost of mailing								
permit, stamps								
Distribution								
TOTAL DIRECT MAIL								
Other Promotion								
Signs								
Bumper strips								
Literature								
Stickers								
Miscellaneous								
TOTAL OTHER PROMOTION								
CAMPAIGN								
Travel								
Telephone & Telegraph								
Poll Workers								
Miscellaneous								
TOTAL CAMPAIGN								
FINANCE								
Supplies & Postage								
for Treasurer								
Bank Service Charge								
Donations required of								
Candidate								
TOTAL FINANCE								
RESERVE FUND TOTAL								
GRAND TOTAL ADMINISTRATION								
GRAND TOTAL PUBLIC RELATIONS								
GRAND TOTAL RESEARCH								
GRAND TOTAL ADVERTISING								
GRAND TOTAL CAMPAIGN								
GRAND TOTAL FINANCE								
GRAND TOTAL RESERVE								
TOTAL CAMPAIGN COSTS								

Source: Democratic National Committee, *Campaign Manual, 1972* (Washington, D.C., 1972), pp. 23–25.

by other means, or if skilled campaigners are not available, spending and strategies will not have to include such resources and expertise.

3. The candidate's personal qualities, such as speaking ability, physical appearance, or personality may make him more amenable to one format over another, thus limiting spending patterns. If the candidate is not good at unstructured give-and-take formats, more money may have to be put into controlled, well produced formats.

4. A candidate's supporters and allies may impose constraints on the way funds are spent, often in the form of demands that a portion of funds be channeled in their direction. For example, in some areas monetary contributions or "subventions" to local party workers (to recognize and encourage their support) is an expected practice, even when party campaigning is not an important part of the strategy.

5. Inadequate information, such as campaigners being unaware of certain campaign techniques or appeals, is a common restraint. Sometimes campaigners do not undertake certain projects, such as computerized individual appeals to specialized groups, in part because their costs are prohibitive, but many candidates lack knowledge of such techniques.

6. Perceived public lack of acceptance of certain techniques. If politicians believe voters will react negatively to certain styles or messages, they will not engage in them.

7. Other techniques may not only be deemed publicly unacceptable but the campaigner's own values may preclude some activities as unethical or improper, even though they may be legal.

8. Spending patterns of campaigners may be limited by legal regulations. National and state campaign regulations have established a framework of rules which depict limits on spending, set media limits and proscribe certain types of campaign activities. The latter range from vote buying which is illegal in all states, to giving constituents anything of value such as pencils, matches or litterbags. Campaigners ordinarily will not spend money for purposes which are understood as violations of the law.[8]

Just as the government or corporation budgetary processes operate within their respective political contexts, the campaign process operates within such constraints on campaign expenditures.

LEGAL, BOOKKEEPING, AND AUDITING CONCERNS

Since campaign finance is regulated by law as well as by tradition, the financial aspect of the campaign is the one where regular documentation and record keeping is most important. The Watergate incident and attendant campaign spending excesses created a climate of reform during which the states and the nation have made the laws governing campaign finance more enforceable and more stringent. Regulation has increased the importance of the accounting and auditing function of the campaign. Under national and many state codes, campaigners are required to submit very detailed records of contributions and expenditures, often with carefully proscribed limits.

Traditionally, campaign spending laws at the state and national levels have come in five basic formats:

1. *Ceiling on expenditures* to meet the rising costs and disparities in funds available to various candidates. The federal government and 23 states limit the amount that candidates can spend on campaigns.

2. *Prohibitions on contributions from certain interests,* to spare candidates from obligations from special interests. Corporations, national banks and labor unions are prohibited from making contributions, but officers, leaders or political action affiliates can make such contributions.

3. *Public reporting requirements* to disclose possible monetary influences upon elected officials and to help curb excesses and abuses by increasing risks for engaging in such practices. The federal government and 44 states have some form of reporting requirements.

4. *Laws to protect civil service employees* from "spoils system" like pressured solicitation practices.

5. *Federal law requires broadcasters to yield rival candidates equal free time on the air,* equal access to paid time to prevent partisan domination of the airwaves. (In 1975, the FCC excepted news conferences and debates.) Use of the mails by incumbents has also been restricted.[9]

The Watergate scandal and other, well exposed violations of these finance rules triggered a wave of state and national reforms. At the state level a great deal of experimentation with new legislation was adopted in the mid 1970s. All but three states now have some form of campaign finance disclosure requirements, and the trend has been for the legislatures to tighten up requirements, lower the amount of funds required for disclosure, and require filings more frequently and more timely. Many states have established enforcement commissions with power to subpoena records and prosecute violators. Nearly half of the states now have some limits on campaign spending, some using fixed ceilings while others scale the limits to population figures or past voter turnout. A few states limit media expenditures, while California limits incumbents' expenditures to 90 percent of that allotted to challengers. Some states limit the size of individual or group contributions, although they have been generally high, affecting only the wealthy. Some states are experimenting also with public financing and tax incentives: five have adopted the one-dollar check off in effect at the national level; two have approved one and two dollar tax surcharges; twelve have approved tax credits or deductions. States are getting into public financing with public fund matching at a much slower pace. Among the states that have enacted public financing, Maryland (in 1978) and New Jersey (in 1977) will provide public funds to candidates after candidates raise an initial amount in small contributions. As the states have experimented with cleansing and improving elections, they are undoubtedly creating different election systems and finance contexts that campaigners must understand and within which they must operate.[10]

Similarly, campaign finance reform at the national level has changed the system confronting campaigners. In 1971 the Revenue Act was adopted allowing a one-dollar income-tax check off to finance presidential elections beginning in 1976. Taxpayers have the option of indicating on their returns whether or not they wish to allocate one dollar to the Presidential Election Campaign Fund. After a slow start, about $30 million was collected by the end of 1974. The General Accounting Office is anticipating a sum of $72 million by 1976. In the same year, the first, new, federal campaign-finance legislation in fifty years was adopted. It basically represented more of the same—reporting, disclosure, limits on spending, including the media, and contributions. The Federal Election Campaign Act of 1974 makes the 1971 act more effective. It mandates spending limits of $10 million in nomination races and $20 million in general elections for presidential candidates. Senate candidates are limited to eight cents times the voting age population ($100,000) in primaries and twelve cents times the voting age population ($150,000) in general elections, in each case, whichever is greater. Parties can spend additional funds to support their candidates. Individual contributions in federal contests are limited to $1,000 in each nomination and election contest, and annual gifts are limited to $25,000. A candidate's contributions to his or her own campaign are limited to $50,000 for president, $35,000 for senator, and $25,000 for representative. Political committee gifts are limited to $5,000 to each candidate for federal office in each nomination and election contest. Candidates and political committees are now required to make full disclosures, including total contributions, expenditures, loans, and other financial transactions. Reports are required quarterly and annually before and after each election. Moreover, all names, addresses, and occupations of contributors of more than $100 must be reported. Money must be channeled through a candidate's principal campaign committee to make information more easily available, and funds similarly have to be handled through a single depository bank account to simplify auditing. A Federal Election Commission has been established to supervise the federal campaign law and to investigate alleged violations.[11]

However, the 1974 act is most innovative regarding public financing of campaigns. In general elections, major party presidential candidates have the option of receiving the full spending limit of $20 million in public funds or to accept private contributions. Major party candidates seeking the presidential nomination may receive matching grants for each individual contribution up to $250, after meeting the basic qualification of raising $5,000 of these small contributions in each of 20 states. Matching grants are limited to $5 million, half the statutory spending limit. Major parties may draw as much as $2 million to finance their national nominating conventions. Minor parties are eligible for proportional public funding based on the vote received in the past election. These public subsidies are financed by the income tax checkoffs.[12] There was considerable effort to add public funding of congressional campaigns to the bill but it failed, leaving presidential campaigns the only ones publicly financed at the national level. It will be closely watched in the 1976 and subsequent elections as a means to overcome the inequities of political money and to encourage broader participation in financing campaigns.

In a climate of increased regulation and concern for campaign finance, more stringent reporting and accounting procedures, and the initiation of public funding, the candidate and the campaign treasurer should become familiar with the relevant election codes. All financial regulations and reporting requirements should be discusssed with the legal counsel of the campaign. The stringent reporting requirements of the elections acts of 1971 and 1974 have made it necessary in the case of large scale campaigns to obtain the services of an accounting firm to keep their records in order and within the law. Reporting requirements may well make accountants the newest breed of political consultants.

The campaign treasurer ordinarily accounts for all contributions to and expenditures from the campaign fund and preparation of the appropriate forms for reporting purposes. The American Institute of Certified Public Accountants Committee on State Legislation recommends the following in regard to contributions:

- that they be made with appropriate deposit slips and copies filed with the report to the secretary of state,
- that state laws on prohibited contributions should be researched and the list be made known to all solicitors,
- that any contribution sources deemed inappropriate by the candidate or treasurer or limits on amounts contributed should be made known in advance of any fund raising.[13]

In regard to campaign expenditures, the Institute of Certified Public Accountants recommends that prior to the formal announcement of a candidacy no money should be spent on behalf of the candidacy, including radio, television, display and newspaper advertising, printing of literature, or rental of facilities. Some states prohibit these acts by law. However, reservation of media time or commitments to take office space are not included. Moreover, the accountants' group recommends that campaigners adopt internal rules governing campaign expenditures prior to the formal opening of the campaign. Among the rules that they suggest are—

- that no payments be made for the privilege of speaking before a group, either by the candidate or by a person speaking on behalf of the candidate,

Figure 9.3   Campaign Treasurer's Pre-Election Report to the Secretary of State

Name of Candidate: _____

Address: _____

Candidate for: _____

Expenditures previously reported	$_____
Expenditures this report	$_____
Total expenditures to date of this report	$_____

List of all expenditures authorized, incurred or made to date of this report.

Date	Name and address of party to whom expenditure is made	Purpose of Expenditure	Amount

Contributions previously reported	$_____
Contributions this report	$_____
Total contributions to date of this report	$_____

List of contributions (with names and addresses of contributors)

Date	Name	Address	Amount
	* *Schedule attached*		

I hereby certify that the above and foregoing statement is true and correct: Dated at _____ this _____ day of_____19___ .
(City and State)

By:_____
Campaign Treasurer

For:_____
Candidate

*Attach photostat of Campaign Deposit Slip

Source: American Institute of Certified Public Accountants, *Campaign Treasurer's Handbook* (New York: AICPA, 1974), p. 16.

Figure 9.4 Selected Campaign Treasurer's Forms

CONTRIBUTIONS AND EXPENDITURES

_____ BANK
(Campaign Depository)

Date	Payee	Vo. No.	Receipts and Contributions (Cash Only)	Expenditures	Bank Balance	Explanation

Note: The above information is taken directly from the Campaign Deposit Slip and Order for Payment (check) forms. If the expenditures are numerous, you may wish to distribute them by category. This can be easily done by adding more columns to the above form and extending the expenditure to its proper column.

MONTHLY CAMPAIGN TREASURER'S REPORT
Month — February, 1972

	Actual	Budget	Variance
Contributions	$	$	$
Expenditures:			
Radio Advertising			
Company Literature			
Newspaper Advertising			
Bumper Stickers and Posters			
Travel Expenses			
	$	$	$

Source: American Institute of Certified Public Accountants, *Campaign Treasurer's Handbook,* (New York: AICPA, 1974), pp. 18–19.

- that the payment of money or anything else of value to an elector in exchange for his or her vote be prohibited (by law in some states),
- that a schedule of payable items be established
- that written authorization, signed by the campaign treasurer, be required for each expenditure, to be accompanied by a certificate from the person claiming the payment which states the purpose of the claim and that no other person is interested directly or indirectly in the payment of the claim.[14]

It is also important for the campaign treasurer to keep very detailed and accurate records of individual contributions and expenditures. In many states the candidate and or the treasurer is required to submit a sworn statement of contributions made and expenditures incurred prior to the time of qualifying and since the last preceding election. In most states and on the national level, the treasurer must thereafter file periodic reports of contributions and expenditures. The treasurer should be prepared to make periodic reports to the candidate and other members of the campaign staff. Some campaigns. particularly the very large ones, also commission an audit of the treasurer's accounts by a certified public accountant who is independent of the campaign. The keeping of sound accounts and records may appear to be overly bureaucratic in many a campaign, but such diligent documentation is becoming increasingly important for compliance with the law, and observance of the regulations can avoid the pitfalls of legal penalties, fines, or even the removal of a winning candidate from office.

The 1972 presidential campaign and campaign spending legislation adopted in 1971 and 1974 generated a great deal of attention to the reporting and non-reporting of contributions and expenditures. The new agency of federal campaign finance found that some contributions and expenditures on behalf of candidates of both parties were hidden and obscured. Many were quick to conclude that "everybody does it, they just got caught." Not everybody does. While there is little substantial evidence, the vast bulk of the hundreds of thousands of campaign treasurers probably do not willfully evade the law by obscuring contributions and expenditures. Given their underfinancing and narrow financial base, plus the limitations of their own values, they probably have little to gain by hiding anything. Most citizen campaign treasurers keep their campaign books in the same fashion they would for the church brotherhood, the civic club, or the businessman's association. The 1972 violations, applying to campaigns in which millions of dollars from millions of contributors were at stake, came at a time when the law was in transition. Most small campaigns for which the financial records are kept by a close associate involve hundreds of dollars from dozens of contributors. The stakes, in either case, are simply not worth violating the law.

Notes to Chapter 9

1. Herbert E. Alexander, *Money in Politics* (Washington, D.C.: Public Affairs Press, 1972), p. 22.

2. For a detailed discussion see Kevin L. McKeough, *Financing Campaigns for Congress: Contribution Patterns of National Level Party and Non-Party Committees, 1964* (Princeton, N.J.: Citizens Research Foundation, 1970), pp. 58-79.

3. David W. Adamany, *Campaign Finance in America* (North Scituate, Mass.: Duxbury Press, 1972), pp. 141, 148.

4. *Chicago Daily News*, 25 October 1973, p. 10.

5. Campaign Finance Monitoring Project, Common Cause, October, 1973.

6. Herbert E. Alexander, *Financing the 1968 Election* (Lexington, Mass.: D.C. Heath, 1971), p. 194.

7. Campaign Finance Monitoring Project, estimated from various data.

8. David Adamany, *Financing Politics* (Madison: Univ. of Wisconsin Press, 1969), pp. 110-14.

9. Alexander, *Money in Politics*, pp. 183-84. See also, Herbert E. Alexander, "Communications and Politics: The Media and the Message," *Law and Contemporary Problems* 34 (1969); Roscoe L. Barrow, "Regulation of Campaign Funding and Spending for Federal Office," *Journal of Law Reform* 5 (1972); Jeffrey M. Berry and Jerry Goldman, "Congress and Public Policy: A Study of the Federal Campaign Act of 1971," *Harvard Journal of Legislation* 10 (1973); Carleton W. Sterling, "Control of Campaign Spending," *American Bar Association Journal* 59 (1973).

10. For a discussion of state finance reform see Herbert E. Alexander, "Campaign Finance Reform: What is Happening—Particularly in the Individual States?" in Robert Agranoff, ed., *The New Style in Electon Campaigns* 2d ed. (Boston: Holbrook Press, 1976).

11. "Congress Clears Campaign Financing Reform," *Congressional Quarterly Weekly Report*, 32 (October 12, 1974), pp. 2865-70.

12. For a discussion of the 1974 act see David W. Adamany, "Financing National Politics," in Agranoff, *The New Style in Election Campaigns*, 2d ed.

13. Committee on State Legislation, American Institute of Certified Public Accountants, *Campaign Treasurers Handbook* (New York: AICPA, 1972), pp. 7-8.

14. Ibid., pp. 8-9.

For Further Reading and Research

Adamany, David W. "Financing National Elections," *The New Style in Election Campaigns*. 2d. ed. Edited by Robert Agranoff. Boston: Holbrook Press, 1976.

Alexander, Herbert E. "Campaign Finance Reform: What is Happening-

Particularly in the States." in *The New Style in Election Campaigns* 2d. ed. Edited by Robert Agranoff. Boston: Holbrook Press, 1976.

——— . "Communications and Politics: The Media and the Message." *Law and Contemporary Problems* 34 (1969): 255–77.

——— . and McKeough, Kevin L. *Financing Campaigns for Governor: New Jersey, 1965.* Princeton, N.J.: Citizens Research Foundation, 1969.

American Institute of Certified Public Accountants. *Campaign Treasurer's Handbook.* 2d. ed. New York: AICPA, 1974.

Barrow, Roscoe L. "Regulation of Campaign Funding and Spending for Federal Office." *Journal of Law Reform* 5 (1972): 159–92.

Berry, Jeffrey M. and Goldman, Jerry. "Congress and Public Policy: A Study of the Federal Election Campaign Act of 1971." *Harvard Journal of Legislation* 19 (1973): 331–65.

Congressional Quarterly, "Liberal Fund Raisers: A Tighter Squeeze in 1974." (June 15, 1974): 1151–55.

Fay, James S. "State Campaign Finance Laws: The Issue of Enforcement." *National Civic Review* 62 (1973): 603–07.

Ferman, Irving. "Congressional Regulation of Campaign Spending: An Expansion or Contraction of the First Amendment?" *American University Law Review* 22 (1972): 1–38.

McKeough, Kevin L. *Financing Campaigns for Congress: Contribution Patterns of National-Level Party and Non-Party Committees, 1964.* Princeton, N.J.: Citizens Research Foundation, 1970.

National Municipal League. *Model State Campaign Contributions and Expenditures Reporting Law.* New York: National Municipal League, 1973.

Smolka, Richard. *The Cost of Administering Elections.* New York: National Municipal League, 1973.

Sterling, Carleton, W. "Control of Campaign Spending: The Reformers' Pardox" *American Bar Association Journal* 59 (1973) 1145–53.

Thayer, George. *Who Shakes the Money Tree? American Campaign Finance Practices From 1789 to the Present.* New York: Simon and Schuster, 1973.

Winter, Jr., Ralph K. *Watergate and the Law.* Washington: American Enterprise Institute for Public Policy Research, 1974.

Campaign Public Relations: Mobilizing Attentive Publics and Groups

A neglected topic in most treatises on campaigning is also the most frequently engaged in set of activities by candidates and campaigners; the public relations tactics of lining up the support of political decision makers, community notables, attentive publics, opinion leaders, groups, and political activists. To many a candidacy in small constituencies, neither the party organization effort nor the mass media campaign is nearly as important as the public relations campaign. The large campaign, the party campaign, the mass media campaign, or some combination of these usually contain public relations efforts as a part of the strategy. The influence and communication processes in campaigns reviewed in Chapter 3 definitely indicates that certain individuals play key roles in the transfer of political information, the offering of cues to those who may identify with the cue giver, and in convincing people to support and vote for someone. This chapter will discuss the techniques and approaches of public relations campaigning and will illustrate some techniques used by candidates in their public relations efforts.

CAMPAIGN PUBLIC RELATIONS

Among the many definitions of public relations the most straightforward is that of long time public relations consultant Edward Bernays: "Public relations is the attempt, by information, persuasion, and adjustment, to engineer public support for an activity, cause, movement or institution."[1] Adjustment refers to the process of coming to some mutual accommodation among various people, groups, and organizations, including the attempt to gain understanding by overcoming any possible ignorance, prejudice, apathy, or distortions. Information and persuasion are necessary tools in adjusting conditions. In its most advanced form, information includes use of the findings and techniques of communication, including research in mass operation, the psychology of communication, social aspects of communication, and media research. Persuasion, a constitutionally protected right, refers to the attempt to convince people by structuring information since few people make up their minds by evaluating all facts objectively.[2]

One need not be a public relations specialist to see the importance of public realtions to the campaigner. Much of the effort made on behalf of the candidate involves the use of information, persuasion, and adjustment to mobilize support for the candidacy. Campaigning is, in a sense, another special case of public relations, in which the most important findings and techniques refer to information about parties, candidates, issues, political groups, political decision makers, community leaders, opinion leaders, attentive publics, and groups and their members. A special kind of persuasion is the task at hand: to get others to support, work for, contribute to, and vote for a candidate. As supporters and the candidate are informing and persuading, they are doing so in the face of a public with less commitment, less understanding and somewhat different goals and values, and they are making adjustments.

HOW PUBLIC RELATIONS HAVE BEEN USED IN ELECTION CAMPAIGNS

In his landmark study of political public relations, Stanley Kelley, Jr., points out that the earliest efforts of public relations men in politics were extensions of business P.R. efforts to enhance their image, to gain favorable public support for their philosophy and aims, and to influence government.[3] Kelley claimed that the political public relations man works in a variety of ways: helping clients adopt policies designed to earn public confidence and insure against governmental interference; staging information campaigns so that political decision makers will find it easier, or more difficult, to make particular decisions; managing campaigns for pressure groups desirious of putting initiative and referendum measures into law; attempting to give political parties an advantageous publicity position; and, working to build men into public figures and to put them into the offices of government.[4] The methods used for such political activities are similar to those used in business to gain public support for their aims, and thus, most public relations specialists are involved in both business and political activity.

The use of public relations in campaigns ranges, of course, across many of the functions which have been discussed in this book. Research, lining up support, messages, media preparation, and media channels are all a part of information, persuasion, and adjustment. As one public relations expert who has also had considerable experience with campaigns sums up, the public relations approach to political campaigning involves—

- turning an otherwise dead possession into a function.
- carrying this function into the arena of public opinion.
- breaking down public opinion into specific target audiences.
- researching the past voting behavior and current opinions of each target audience.
- selecting the most powerful ammunition to present to these targets.
- priming the media or delivery systems with the most appropriate communication tools.[5]

Public relations is an integral function; media priming, delivery systems chosen, certain key individuals and groups, are based on researched and developed information which is focused on the various subgroups of the electorate. Public relations in campaigning is a functionally separate but related communications process in which the voting behavior and interests of the various types of individuals and groups who make up the electorate are investigated, appropriate messages are developed; and channels of delivery are selected.

One example of how this public relations approach has been utilized is the campaign approach used by Whitaker and Baxter, considered to be the original campaign P.R. firm. After accepting a campaign, Whitaker and Baxter liked to research the key factors (setting) in the campaign, blueprint a campaign plan, establish a time sequence of action, select the issues, place them into a theme, which in turn were integrated into speeches, news stories, and printed literature. Then media and approaches were selected, including paid and unpaid media, public speeches, relations with media, news releases, securing the endorsements of editors, key people, and the support of groups.[6] Whitaker and Baxter ordinarily had complete control over the campaign, including its finances, but they considered the integration of these functions to be the *sine qua non* of bringing public relations to the campaign.[7]

How The Public
Relations Firm Handles Campaigns

Given the nature and functions of public relations firms it was only natural that they began to handle political campaigns regularly. A study of the emergence of California firms in campaigns, by Robert Pitchell, revealed that it was a combination of increased mass interest in politics, the weakness of party organizations in campaigning, and the expansion of mass media that accounted for their ascendence.[8] Pitchell identified three main types of people involved in the political campaign, public relations industry: the campaign management firms, which specialize in the complete management of campaigns; advertising and public relations agencies whose primary campaign activity is to serve as publicity arms for candidates' campaigns, serving as public relations experts rather than as management experts; and, various professions, such as newspapermen, academic people, lawyers, labor unionists, civil servants, and political assistants, whose common characteristic is some specialized or technical knowledge of public opinion formation or mass media use. The latter group, though skilled, do not practice commercial public relations or advertising work between campaigns.[9] These three groups are still operative on the contemporary campaign scene.

The business of campaign public relations grew considerably in the 1960s. David Rosenbloom's study of the campaign management industry in the late 1960s revealed that about 60 public relations firms claimed to do most of their work in political campaigns, about 100 firms offered complete campaign management services (as opposed to 41 in 1957) and an additional 200 firms around the country offered professional campaign management services as a part of their business.[10] The study revealed that the firms increasingly are involved in campaigns at all levels, with an 842-percent increase in the number of races served in 1964-69 over 1952-57 in congressional races, and a 626-percent increase for statewide races, and a 298 percent increase for local races, comparing the same time period.[11] Based on the 2,292 campaigns studied from 1964 to 1969, it was estimated that the number of campaigns served by professional firms in the 1970 election was 900, including 150 House-of-Representatives races and 300 state-legislature races.[12]

The involvement of firms has not only grown rapidly in number but the range and sophistication of services has also broadened. Full-time campaign management was offered by firms eight times more frequently for congressional races in the 1960s than in the 1950s.[13] Among the other services offered by campaign public relations firms are: information, planning, handling of the candidate, fund raising, lining up group support, media preparation, media placement, and other appeals.[14] One of the most comprehensive firms in the United States is Spencer-Roberts of Los Angeles, California which works for Republican candidates. Spencer-Roberts offers all of the services mentioned earlier, and they will handle such activities as: recruiting and coordination of volunteers, raising funds, distribution of printed brochures, arranging coffee parties, arranging news conferences and lining up group and individual support. They handled the announcement of actor Ronald Reagan's candidacy for governor of California in 1966 by putting together a series of planned events: a massive news conference, a reception for 6,000 supporters, a dinner with community leaders, and a statewide television special. This wide range of services offered has led one political analyst to label the Spencer-Roberts operation, "California rent-a-party."

Perhaps more typical is the part-time involvement of the public relations firm in campaigning, and on a less complete basis. A case in point was that of Stemler, Barton, Fisher and Payne. More particularly, public relations director, Harry Fisher, who handled John Danforth's successful 1968 race for attorney general of Missouri. Danforth, a moderate Republican from an old (Ralston-Purina) St. Louis family, used the firm to: do media research; formulate his campaign theme, "I dare you" (based on a book written by his grandfather); wove the theme into speeches, advertising copy, and brochures; selected and developed a color scheme for billboards, brochures, bumper stickers and television commercials; handled relations with media representatives; production and placement of advertising; production and distribution of news releases; sought editorial support; and, created "events" to be covered by the media, such as his tour of prisons. The entire campaign was coordinated by a campaign manager and included an issues research director, a person to handle speaking and travel arrangements and other logistical matters, a chief of volunteers, a Kansas City press representative, a driver and necessary office and clerical helpers.[15] This pattern, in which only the public relations and media facets of the campaign are handled by the firm and the rest of the operation is handled by the candidate-centered group, is more representative of the degree of involvement and type of services of P.R. firms working in campaigns.

Use of Public Relations
By Candidates and Campaigners

Whether a professional firm is retained or not, all candidates or campaigners must use some of the very basic public relations techniques. Even if the setting of the campaign and the strategy do not dictate a great need for mass media coverage, other P.R. techniques will be required. Examples of the various public relations techniques employed in campaigns include: advancing and arranging candidate tours; utilizing speakers on behalf of the candidate; appearances at public gatherings and group meetings by the candidate or by the candidate's supporters; establishing rapport with the media, including meetings, advancing for the press, press conferences and news releases; development and distribution of issue information to interested segments of the public; production and distribution of information on the candidate; seeking the support of important segments of the voting public at the leadership, opinion leader, and mass level; relations with the party organization; and, all personal campaigning by the candidate.

PERSONAL CAMPAIGNING

Whether it is the personal campaigning of the candidate or some type of personalized campaigning by the campaigner's organization on the candidate's behalf, this activity is to be considered public relations. When conducting this type of personalized campaigning, the campaigner should face this "inside" and "inside-outside" aspect of the campaign with similar strategic and setting principles in mind by which one is guided when selecting important groups of voters. Seeking out the support of leaders and groups requires a similar targeting, based on the type of support coalition a candidate running for a particular office in a particular setting is likely to expect. This is why one finds Democrats more often shaking hands at plant gates and seeking union endorsements and Republicans more often talking to the businessmen on main street and seeking the support of BIPAC. One's strategy and campaign plan should indicate very clearly not only the types but the very key political and community leaders, groups, opinion leaders, and attentive publics one seeks out for support.

Public relations often goes beyond these targeted groups to include direct voter contact by the candidate. This is particularly true in smaller constituency campaigns in which the candidate can make a greater personal impact because greater numbers of voters can be contacted. In many areas it is traditional that the candidate go door to door, personally appealing to voters, a technique that can offer voters an important candidate stimulus, and one that is considered most likely to break through voter disinterest or difficulty in receiving messages about small-constituency candidates. Personal campaigning is not, however, limited to the small constituency. Senator William Proxmire of Wisconsin, in his many campaigns for statewide office, has made it a practice of personally campaigning at shopping centers, factory gates, parades, sports events, and other places likely to draw a crowd, and has estimated that by the time he approached his 1970 campaign he had met more than 1.5 million of the state's 2.2 million voters.

Personal campaigning is not always confined to the formal campaign period. Indeed, we have argued that much "inside" support-gathering activity should ordinarily precede the opening of the campaign. Candidates, and particularly incumbents who ordinarily have an earlier and more concrete idea of where they are going and how they are going to get there, often engage in informal campaigning. Bibby and Davidson depict how former Minnesota Congressman Clark MacGregor combined mass media coverage and personal campaigning into precampaign public relations:

> Each week during the congressional session, for example, MacGregor prepares a one-minute television tape consisting of commentary on a current national issue. The tape is sent to the four stations in the Minneapolis area, and they use it as their schedules permit. At the same time, he makes a weekly five-minute radio tape that is distributed to a number of stations. Two or three of them broadcast the entire tape as part of their regular schedule, while others insert excerpts in newscasts. A transcript of the radio tape is distributed to all Minneapolis newspapers, and several of the suburban papers publish it as a weekly column entitled "Congressman MacGregor Reports."

> In June of 1964 MacGregor's office sent to every Third-District resident listed in the telephone directory the 'MacGregor Legislative Questionnaire,' which requested opinions on ten major proposals before the Eighty-eighth Congress. Responses were tabulated in his Minneapolis office, and each respondent later received a reply from Washington. A summary of the questionnaire results was inserted in the *Congressional Record* and was reprinted and mailed to Third-District residents. A device used by many members of Congress, the questionnaire enhances a congressman's image while satisfying perfectly the norms of representative government.

It is through frequent personal visits to his district that a representative can most effectively keep his name before the electorate, while gauging the climate of opinion among his constituents. Thoughout the session preceding the election MacGregor tried to return to the district at least one weekend a month, and by July he was traveling home nearly every weekend.

MacGregor sometimes holds public meetings to inform constituents on legislative issues and to solicit their views. These meetings are usually planned around a specific issue, with his district office issuing invitations to constituents presumed to be particularly concerned. During the 1964 session MacGregor called a meeting of ministers, school superintendents, and schoolboard members to discuss the Supreme Court's school-prayer decisions and the so-called Becker amendment. Meetings were held on mass transportation and medical care for the aged during the previous session. The typical format of a MacGregor meeting consists of a fifteen-minute speech in which he summarizes the issues and proposals, then answers questions from the audience. Though the press is excluded from the sessions, a stenographer prepares a summary of the discussion.

About four times a year, MacGregor regularly holds a public luncheon in downtown Minneapolis. Invitations are sent to all persons on the district mailing list, and admission is by tickets issued upon request by the district office. Attended mostly by business and professional men who work downtown, these affairs are largely social, although MacGregor sometimes talks briefly on legislative issues.[16]

As the authors explain, such informal campaigning made the formal contest in large part an intensification of activities taking place during the intercampaign period, and allowed for a gradual build-up of campaign activity.

These support-gathering activities should be consistent with the previously decided posture and appeal structure of the campaign, based upon setting and strategy. That is, the candidate should be presented to possible sources of support in a manner consistent with the way the image of the candidate is to be developed, the issue positions taken, the interests to be represented, and the type of public official the candidate is to be. A study of a congressional campaign in the state of Washington revealed that in one of Rep. Thomas Pelly's early campaigns he tried to present himself as a moderate, "can do," elected official who was a fair-minded person capable of protecting and furthering the interests of all of the people in his Seattle area district. These themes were integrated into appeals by the candidate to individuals, organizational presentation plus mass media.[17] Of course, this does not mean one cannot be selective within these broad boundaries, speaking to individuals and groups about what interests them and how they expect to be represented. Pelly discussed the Puget Sound Naval Shipyard question with over 50 different business, labor, and civic groups, but he also talked peace, atomic power, and farm subsidies to others. These various discussions were consistent with his previously decided posture and appeal structure.

POWERFUL SUPPORT

In Chapter 3, the existence of power structures in communities and specifically how they formulated in the context of Congressman Pelly and his opponent's campaign were mentioned. We have also listed many possible sources of community leadership. Power structures are sometimes conceptualized as generalized—one set of powerful leaders are important in many areas, or more specialized, (different) leaders are important in different areas of public policy. There is a considerable controversy as to how one discovers the power structure of a given area. Some rely on the reputational ascription rating of experts;[18] some believe the holders of key institutional positions are the powerful;[19] others believing that one must look at who makes the decisions;[20] and still others who believe one must investigate who controls the agenda-setting process, and that non-decisions are as important as decisions.[21]

Questions of how general or specialized are power structures or appropriate methodologies of discovery are beyond the immediate task of the campaigner. Indeed, only the rarest of campaigns will be able to undertake an extensive community power study. It has been suggested earlier, therefore, that campaigners proceed with the assumption that the powerful exist and that determinations be made based on the best judgment and astute observation of campaign strategists. This may include combinations of reputational assessments, those who are important by viture of their positions, those who are likely to be important in decisions and non-decisions, plus any other informal observational data that may be helpful.

The importance of the informal judgment should not be underestimated. One campaign anecdote, from the campaign of James Kessler for the Indiana state senate is illustrative:

> On the way back to Bloomington, I noticed something about the names on the country mailboxes. I saw Hudson, Hudson, Hendrix, Hendrix, Hudson, Abrams, Hendrix, Abrams, Hudson all the way down the road to Ellettsville, which is just over the line in Monroe County. This gave me some insight into one aspect of Greene County politics. Families are large and interrelated. Maybe there were a few key people to see in each family. I soon found out that this is the case. Two days later I came back down the road looking for the heads of families. I was looking in particular for Wayne Abrams at Hendrixville, I found Wayne in back of his house. He and several other farmers were in the process of moving a privy. When I walked up they were too busy to bother with introductions. Instead, they yelled for me to give them a hand, which I did. After we set the privy in place, they asked me who I was. I told them my name and that I was a Republican candidate for the State Senate. They grinned and said, 'Well, we'll give you a few votes around here. Give us some posters and cards.'[22]

This particular campaign experience illustrates how the process of discovering who are influential depends on the resourcefulness and insight of the campaigner.

Kessler's account of his personal campaigning for the state senate also indicated how he used his personal knowledge and experience as a party activist and participant in community and state affairs as the initial basis for knowing whom to contact in terms of seeking out leadership support.[23] After receiving positive indicators from these familiar sources, he began to broaden his support by seeking indications of support from various factions in his county party organization, and from key office holders in that county. Next, he sought out other important civic and political people in his county. After he had developed a party (parties are relatively important in Indiana) and community base of support in his own county, he began to develop similar support in the other two counties in the district, based on leads offered him by his own county supporters and state political leaders sympathetic to his cause. Candidates and campaigners very often follow similar procedures in lining up support from key people.

GROUP SUPPORT

Earlier portions of this book developed some of the dynamics of groups and campaigning, including the differing degrees of political interest and activity of groups, the various levels of support groups offer in campaigns and certain considerations of group financing of campaigns. The techniques used to gain support and the particular groups selected to coalesce with the candidate are a part of the strategy as defined in each situation. Not surprisingly, the setting of the campaign makes a difference in the particular group coalition built by the candidate.

In his study of Congressional campaigns, Leuthold reported five principal techniques for securing group support:

1. Presenting a suitable record on public issues. Some groups compile voting records, thus appearing to endorse those congressmen who voted for the groups' objectives most frequently.

2. Requesting endorsements or help from representatives of the group or from prominent individuals in the group.

3. Requesting official endorsements, which are given most regularly by the political action committees of labor unions.

4. Making appeals to the group membership by means of speeches, letters or advertisements. Some times such appeals are made by the formation of a "Veterans for Jones" type group, the usual purpose to legitimize some mailings or press releases.

5. Purchasing endorsements, such as purchasing advertisements (and thereby endorsements) in ethnic newspapers or payment of membership fees in groups.[24]

As Leuthold reports, only the first category does not involve any active solicitation by candidates. Consequently, an important component of the solicitation of group support was the candidate's willingness to ask for this support.

Three very important considerations of setting are the candidate's position on issues, the candidate's vote-getting ability, and the candidate's personal situation. If the candidate's ideology is generally acceptable to the group, he or she is more likely to be supported by the group. Leuthold found that incumbents referred to their records on bills before Congress, explaining the arguments for and against the bill and justifying their stand. Non-incumbents were more often expected to give specific and acceptable answers about issues not yet before Congress. [25] The more likely the candidate looks like a sure winner, the more likely the group will endorse that candidate. This is in part to avoid alienating him, particularly if the group feels they may agree with him occasionally. There is some evidence that groups sometimes support sure winners, even though the group may not agree with them, to make their slate of greater appeal to a broad audience.[26] Indeed, Scoble found that labor unions give more support to sure winners than competitive candidates.[27] Also, candidates who are members of a group or who have personal friendships with leaders of a group have somewhat of an advantage, since garnering group support frequently requires personal contacts, and meetings with personal friends are more likely to be profitable than with strangers. Leuthold reports the turning of a personal contact into a group endorsement to be a frequent occurence in the San Francisco Bay area. For this reason, active candidates worked hard to make personal contacts, using such techniques as writing letters to newly elected group officers or appointing group officials to patronage or campaign positions.[28]

The particular type of coalition of groups a candidate builds depends upon various factors in the setting. One very important factor is party. When Kingdon asked Wisconsin legislative, congressional, and statewide candidates to rate the principal support coalitions in the campaign they had just conducted, he found dramatic party differences in coalitions. Kingdon identified three basic types: business oriented, including professional and several other non-labor groups; labor and several other non-business groups; and, coalitions that straddle the business labor dichotomy. A few candidates claimed they had no group support or refused to recognize these categories. As Table 10.1 indicates, Democratic candidates were essentially labor oriented and Republican candidates tended to be business oriented in their coalition building. Not a single Democrat listed a coalition that included business and professional groups but not labor, and not a single Republican mentioned a labor-oriented coalition. Kingdon considers these results to be the most striking findings of his study of candidates' perceptions, in that they show extreme party differences in terms of supporting groups, at least as seen by the candidates.[29]

The type of constituency was also important in coalition formation. Kingdon found rural candidates of both parties more likely to build a mixed labor-business coalition than urban candidates. Among Democrats, rural candidates were less likely to have a labor base and Republicans in the urban areas were more likely to have a business base. Thus, the labor-business dichotomy was more in evidence in the more urban parts of the state than rural or small-town areas.[30]

In local elections with a nonpartisan ballot election a somewhat different constellation of groups seems to emerge. Eulau, Zisk, and Prewitt studied 123 councilmen in 23 cities in the San Francisco Bay area. They were interested in the particular milieu of the city, whether it was predominantly Republican, Democratic, or competitive, since they were examining the degree of latent partisanship in these cities. As Table 10.2 indicates, group support was most likely to be forthcoming in Democratic milieux, with almost the same level in competitive areas with less support in Republican areas. The type of group giving support varied with the area, with union support of importance in Democratic and competitive areas, neighborhood or service clubs following similar patterns, and business of little importance in any areas. Political clubs were not reported to be active in any but competitive areas, and then only of moderate significance. Of most significance were the local good government or reform groups (sometimes ad hoc) organized for the purposes of council campaigns, even though a smaller proportion of councilmen in competitive settings mentioned such groups. This constellation of group perceptions led the authors to conclude that "organizational support in council campaigns is of a highly informal nature: it comes to only a very limited extent from traditional interest groups but, rather, from voluntary, spontaneous groups rarely of permanent character."[31]

Table 10.1   Parties Supporting Coalitions

Type of Coalition	Party	
	Democrats	Republicans
Labor-oriented	72%	0%
Business-oriented	0	43
Neither: both labor and business, farm, noneconomic	22	30
Refused to discuss groups, no group support	6	27
	100%	100%
n	32	30

Source: John W. Kingdon, *Candidates for Office: Beliefs and Strategies* (New York: Random House, 1968), p. 48.

The process of establishing group support is a part of the coalition building process requisite in campaigning. John Kessel has described this process, the joining together of a set of groups, with a:

set of attitudes lying within the intersection of the sets of attitudes of the member groups, and its set of behaviors is comprised of those activities which form an interdependent system. . . .A group requires interaction; a coalition only interdependent activity. . . .The attitudes of the member groups lead to certain conclusions about the likelihood of coalition formation, and the problems of coalition leadership.[32]

Kessel suggests that formulation of groups into a coalition begins at a very early stage in the campaign, in presidential elections in the prenomination process. Ordinarily it moves from a core group around the candidate, to the candidate's home state or regional supporters. Then the candidate's most natural allies are included, the groups whose defining attitudes have the greatest extent of overlap with the candidate's own attitudes. After the core group is expanded to include those persons of shared attitudes, the coalition is expanded to include less likely but, nevertheless, persons of somewhat similar or at least interlocking attitudes. Appeals to this wave of groups may be on the basis of the support already gathered rather than on ideas, since the candidate coalition is now dealing from

Table 10.2 City Councilmen's Reports of Group Support

Reports of Group Support	Democratic Milieu (N = 26)	Competitive Milieu (N = 54)	Republican Milieu (N = 29)
Was Group Support Forthcoming?*			
yes	62%	56%	41%
no	38	44	59
total	100%	100%	100%
Type of Groups**			
reform/good government	75%	40%	67%
labor unions	25	37	0
neighborhood/service	25	27	8
political clubs	0	20	0
business	0	7	8
other	12	33	8

*The question: "In your last campaign for the council, were there any community groups or organizations which supported you? What kind of things did they do?
**Percentages may total more or less than 100 because respondents could name more than one group or, as was the case in the Republican milieu, none.

Source: Heinz Eulau, Betty H. Zisk and Kenneth Prewitt, "Latent Partisanship in Nonpartisan Elections," in M. Kent Jennings & L. Harmon Zeigler (eds.), The Electoral Process (Englewood Cliffs, N.J.: Prentice-Hall, 1966), p. 229.

strength. Kessel thus concludes that the recruitment of groups ordinarily proceeds from the most natural to the least natural allies, and the less natural allies can be wooed because of the increased leverage which stems from the already committed.[33]

ATTENTIVE PUBLICS: A CASE STUDY

Interested citizens who follow and discuss politics and are likely to convince voters to take a position on a candidate are important links in the flow of communication in the campaign. Yet, identification of attentive publics is often difficult since they are less visible in the community than a prestigious community leader or an organized group.

A number of different means have been used in campaigns to identify attentive publics. Since campaign workers and campaign finance appears to radiate from a core of the candidate's family, friends, and immediate associates, lists of attentive publics have been built, "snowballing" from these persons as a base, and then asking persons on the list to add their own friends and associates. Another means is the time honored form of recruiting "citizens committees" such as "Lawyers for Doe," "Senior Citizens for Doe," and "Educators for Doe." Key persons from each category who are active and known supporters, and ordinarily among the more politically active or at least attentive of the group, recruit like-minded attentive members of their professional, occupational, or whatever group. Campaigners have also identified attentive publics by gathering or compiling lists of attendees at important civic meetings such as: the city council, the school board or county board meetings; meetings to discuss civic projects, such as school bond, referenda discussions, hospital building program meetings, or civic improvement meetings; civic or politically interested groups, such as Rotary, Kiwanis, unions, farm groups, or the Chamber of Commerce; and, other meetings that bring people together, such as church fellowships or the Boy Scouts. The assumption here is that attending a meeting is an indication of a commitment to civic, political, or organizational life and such persons are likely to be politically attentive. Still another indicator of commitment and possible attentiveness that has been used is to compile lists of officers of organizations in the community and to use them as a basis of identifying attentive publics.

The most elaborate method of identifying and utilizing attentive publics in a campaign is the "social precinct" technique developed by political consultant Stephen Shadegg. In the many campaigns he has managed in Arizona and elsewhere, Shaddeg identifies enthusiastic, knowledgeable, candidate supporters who would not be labeled or identified as members of any special (candidate- or party-related) organization, and who could enlist other supporters, disseminate information, keep the campaign staff informed of opposition tactics and infiltrate centers of support unnoticed by the opposition.[34]

The typical member of a social precinct has a somewhat different network of friends and associates than the more political person, and he intersects with the community differently than the political campaigner.

> John Smith is a certified public accountant, forty-three years old, married, the father of three children. His home address is 74 Elm Street. He works in an office downtown, approximately seven miles from his residence. He is a member of the Kiwanis Club, the Old Pueblo Luncheon Club, Quail Run Golf Club, the State Society of Accountants and CPA's, the Methodist Church, and because one of his children was born with a birth deformity, he is extremely active in the Society for Crippled Children.

> John Smith sleeps in a bedroom of his house on Elm Street, and eats most of his meals at home. But most of his life is spent outside of Jefferson Precinct. He is active in seven social precincts. He has a great many friends in the Kiwanis Club. He frequently meets his clients, lawyers and other CPA's in the Old Pueblo Club for lunch. He has a different group of friends at Quail Run Golf Club. He is regarded with respect by the members of the CPA society, he has friends and contacts in the Methodist Church whom he rarely sees except on Sunday, and because of the contribution of energy and money to the crippled children's effort, he is highly regarded by the members of this particular special-interest group.

> John Smith has never canvassed Jefferson Precinct in his life. If he did, he would present himself to the people in his neighborhood as just the man who lives down the street. But in these social precincts he has far greater influence. When the members of John's Kiwanis Club hear him praising a particular candidate they listen respectfully. At lunch he can influence the opinion of his clients. There are fifteen or twenty members of Quail Run Golf Club he can influence because they know him and like him.

> John Smith would be like a fish out of water canvassing the people who live near the bedroom where he sleeps. He can be an effective and skillful politician in his Social Precincts.

> The foundation of a successful Social Precinct organization requires a wide acquaintance with the individuals in the constituency. It isn't at all necessary that the individuals selected be close friends of the candidate.[35]

The plan Shadegg employs involves entering into the inner circle of the social-precinct worker and gaining access to and using information not available to the general public. Lists of "workers" are built from the candidate and campaign worker's close personal friends, close political associates, and individuals who are known, but not close friends or associates. His candidates have culled their correspondence files, persons they had contact with on the basis of mutual interest, selected business associates, service club or church contacts, or party members who would otherwise qualify. Shadegg's researchers have then tried to obtain as much additional information on these individuals as possible, including their financial situation, banking connection, relationship with the hometown newspaper, church or lodge identification, occupation and family connections throughout the constituency. Lists are kept separate and coded by occupation, economic status, and geographical location, particularly in the larger campaigns.

The initial contact made with selected individuals is by an individualized, personal letter, ordinarily from the candidate but sometimes from the supplier of the name. Shadegg uses a personal approach in the letter, and addresses the appeal to some issue of mutual interest, but does not initially seek campaign support. The purpose is to cement the relationship between the recipient of the letter and the candidate, and to develop this interest to the degree the recipient will identify with the candidate's fortunes. He uses the example of a letter used on a prospect who was a bank stockholder or bank board member discussing a bill to give protection to depositors. The letter was concluded with a request for advice on the bill. The request provides the writer with a logical and legitimate reason for writing the letter, and it requires the recipient to react by answering the letter or by responding in some other way. If a return letter is received, a social-precinct worker has been recruited.

The second response is also by personalized letter and its tone assumes a continuing relationship. In the case of very prestigious individuals, the personal approach is continued for some time, but ordinarily the contacts are shifted to bulk mail. Shadegg has used various vehicles for these mailings: editorials from an out-of-state newspaper, reprints from the *Congressonal Record,* a copy of a letter the candidate has sent to someone setting forth his position on an issue, an advance copy of a speech, and advance information on the candidate's travel or other plans.

Some individuals respond by asking what they can do to help, others are asked to help after they have been recruited. They are asked to do a number of things. First, they are used to provide an index of public sentiment toward the candidate, either by telephoning or some other means of registering support. Second, they can keep the campaign staff advised on activities and tactics of the opposition. For example, Shadegg has used them to record and report media usage in various areas of the state of Arizona. Third, he has used social-precinct workers to counteract opposition statements, such as answering a last minute charge by the opponent or to help quell a rumor. Fourth, he has used them to "prepare a climate of disbelief by suggesting in their everyday conversations that 'your opponent will probably follow a certain course of action or make certain declarations.' "[36] Prediction of this future action of the opposition makes it possible to turn what might be a liability into an asset. Finally, and most important, social-precinct workers are used to mention the name of the candidate favorably to persons they meet. Since the social-precinct worker is not publicly identified with the candidate or party organization, their views are more readily accepted, particularly in their social circles, including contact with persons who do not have strong political convictions. Shadegg points out the importance for the campaigner to keep the social-precinct workers supplied with valid reasons for injecting the candidate's name into every conversation—inside information which will, in turn, become natural points of departure for discussing the candidacy favorably.[37]

Shadegg's plan for mobilizing the social precincts is among the more elaborate, involved, and expensive. The personal letters used in recruitment are time consuming. If the number of workers is large, mailing expenses can make these efforts costly. But the system illustrates recognition of the key role of attentive publics and how they can be put to use in a campaign. Other candidates have similarly recognized the importance of attentive persons or likely opinion leaders and have adopted less elaborate techniques. One California city councilman told Heinz Eulau and his associates that, "I would select an influential person on every street, go and have a cup of coffee with them and talk. I found out that they really liked that."[38]

THE PERSONAL ORGANIZATION

The candidate centered organization can become an important branch of the public relations aspect of the campaign through the many means that organizations campaign for the candidate: circulating the candidate's nominating papers, appearing on behalf of the candidate at public meetings, campaigning at shopping centers, holding coffee parties, or putting on a public rally for members. Many of these activities not only entail adjustment, information, and persuasion of others, but, serve to reinforce the commitment of those already in the fold. Circulation of nomination papers, for example, has been used very frequently to test the willingness to work of the circulators, to build up a basic list of possible workers or contributors, to get the word out that the candidate is running and that a campaign is about to begin.

Campaigning at shopping centers and coffee parties gives the impression that the candidate is reaching down to the neighborhood level, particularly in the early stages of the campaign before door-to-door activities are operational. They can be conducted with or without the candidate, and if the candidate is involved they can be scheduled between public appearances. Coffees ordinarily involve the committed, undecided, and sometimes those opposed, and this opportunity should be capitalized by ascertaining the degree of commitment and willingness to work. Shopping centers are busiest when other activities are in slack periods. Many campaigners like to call attention to the effort with a car, van, or trailer decorated with campaign material or some other attention getter. If the candidate is alone, he will ordinarily greet people as he walks through the center. If the organization is working on his behalf they ordinarily distribute literature and very briefly state their purpose. Experienced, shopping-center campaigners claim that a single blitz through the center is enough unless it is extremely large. In that way, as many as six or seven centers can be covered in a single day.

The public relations function of the personal campaign organization can be illustrated by expanding on the case of a campaign rally in which the candidate makes an important policy speech. The organization must, incidentally,

handle many managerial details: checking the site selection, obtaining cost estimates and accommodations; arranging seating and floor arrangements; ordering
sound equipment; decorating the hall; publicizing the rally, including making
sure a crowd is present by expediting it through the party and campaign organization, and other channels; and cleaning. The media aspects of the rally
include: preparation and distribution of the news release announcing the rally;
placement of any advertising for the rally; following up with reporters, column-
ists, and news directors of radio and television stations to ensure adequate coverage; preparation, and duplication of the candidate's speech, arranging for
photography, and furnishing newspapers and TV with photos and copy. The
program can serve many campaign public relations functions. Among the more
important are: as a reinforcer and as a morale booster, volunteers can meet
the candidate and like-minded people, and feel good about the relationship and
hopefully feel enthusiastic enough to work harder and spread the word; media
coverage can extend the reach of the rally to readers and listeners, and if the
rally is enthusiastic and well attended, it will spread the impression of a "moving" campaign; since other party and political people are either in attendance or
will hear about the rally, it can serve to impress, re-establish, and reinforce
favorable contact with influential politicians; and, rallies can serve as a vehicle
for portraying the candidate dramatically and, it is hoped, forcefully.[39]

DOOR-TO-DOOR
CAMPAIGNING BY THE CANDIDATE

One of the most vital, continuous, inexpensive, and potentially effective public-
relations techniques is door-to-door campaigning by the candidate. Its potential
impact is greatest in the smaller constituency, because a greater portion of
voters can be contacted and because it is an indispensible means of breaking
through the greater candidate visibility given to candidates for large constituency office.

The importance of door-to-door campaigning rests on two related sets
of findings. First, few voters know very much about candidates for less visible
offices, and thus, rely on party as a cue. But, if they do happen to know something about the candidate, they are more likely to vote for that candidate, regardless of the candidate's party. Second, few of the voters are ever reached by
many of the other personal modes of citizen contact. A recent Harris poll of
elected officials and citizens revealed that 88 percent of all local and state
officials regularly make speeches and appear at public functions, but only about
50 percent of the public has ever attended such a speech or function. Similarly,
70 percent of these officials held regular office hours, but only 14 percent of
the public has ever visited a state or local official at his office. Fifty-six percent
of the public officials regularly attend social functions, such as weddings, wakes,
and christenings, but only 19 percent of those surveyed have ever seen a public

official at such events.[40] Contacting voters in their homes, offering candidate or other cues, is a means of bridging the gap between the electors and those who hope to be elected, particularly where mass media is not a decisive campaign factor.

Door-to-door work requires little advance knowledge or preparation, and it can be handled in a very personal, individualized manner. The candidate has virtually complete freedom to act naturally, and it allows the voter to personally experience the candidate. Despite this ease and importance, there is evidence that of three forms of personal campaigning: door-to-door, asking others to campaign, and speaking to small, informal groups, local office candidates are most reluctant to engage in door-to-door work.[41] This reluctance could be due to reticence, to the pressure of the candidate's other business, or to local tradition. If one can somehow overcome these obstacles, door-to-door candidate work can help considerably in reducing or neutralizing a significant party or personal visibility disadvantage.

The techniques are very simple, but carrying them out requires a considerable personal commitment. Candidates who attempt to cover their entire constituency often begin as early as five to six months before the election. State Representative Helen Somers of Washington personally knocked on doors in 102 of the 156 precincts in her district between July and the September primary, avoiding only those areas with locked security apartments and those which were too geographically dispersed.[42] Some candidates are so well organized and knock on doors so regularly that they cover the entire constituency before the election, returning to areas which were not personally covered or revisiting areas of strength. The best time to find people at home is between 5:00 to 8:00 PM on weekdays and beginning at 10:30 AM on Saturdays and 1:00 PM on Sundays. In cities, one should be able to cover nearly forty homes or seventy-five apartments per hour, farm-to-farm work takes considerably longer, depending on the location of farms and road conditions. It is advisable to develop a block-by-block work plan in advance, mapping out the priorities and areas to be covered each week of the campaign. Since one should always work from areas of strength to weaker areas, candidates ordinarily cover their top priority precincts first (based on party strength, where the candidate is likely to be known, areas of the opponent's weakness, etc.), marking off on a block map the areas which have been covered. Weeks of self-hypnotizing activity will make it impossible to remember where one has been, even in familiar territory.

The object of the voter contact is to be personable, succinct, and relevant. What one says in these informal contacts should be suited to one's taste. One example would be: "Hello! My name is John Doe, and I'm a candidate for the School Board. I just wanted to meet you, to say 'hello,' and give you some of my literature. I'd like your support. Thank you. Goodbye." After a smile and a handshake, one moves off to the next house. Experienced door-to-door campaigners say, "keep moving and do not get involved in long conversations and discussions."

Some campaigners who feel the task is overwhelming will have someone go with them and cover one side of the street, using a slightly different message and pointing out the candidate across the street. Of particular significance is the use the candidate's spouse or other members of the family, showing commitment. Former State Representative E.W. Quirin of Rochester, Minnesota is the father of nine children, and he always had his children help him do door-to-door work, working in teams of two or three covering the opposite side of the block that he worked.

For doors with no one home candidates either carry duplicated messages or handwrite a message, personally signed with a brochure. The message could say, "Sorry you weren't at home when I called. I'd appreciate it if you would read my pamphlet. Sincerely, John Doe." Other persons going door-to-door can leave the same message. Some active candidates follow up personal contacts with direct mail. Minnesota State Senator Clarence Purfeerst has a volunteer secretary write one of three appropriate letters after a door-to-door or farm-to-farm tour: a sorry-I-missed-you letter; a new supporter letter; or, a noncommittal letter. State Representative Somers used the reverse directory to prepare a special mailing to the security apartment dwellers she could not reach, explaining that she had tried to meet them personally ". . .I've doorbelled your neighborhood. . .I wanted to meet you personally. . .but I respect your privacy and understand the regrettable need for security."[43] A by-product of door-to-door campaigning can be the identification of some who might do volunteer work, make a contribution, or display a lawn sign. Candidates ordinarily carry a few volunteer cards for these purposes.[44]

All of this appears to set a strenuous course for the candidate, but the rewards, particularly in a constituency where media cannot penetrate, or it is wasteful, or prohibitively expensive, are gratifying, both personally and from a vote mobilization standpoint. Indiana candidate James Kessler was working a small village in his district. He entered a store looking for Lavon Yoho who was a storekeeper and township trustee:

> When I got inside, there was a little old-fashioned pot-bellied stove. Four or five farmers sat on an ancient wooden bench. A cracker barrel and a pickle barrel stood nearby. When I walked in, these farmers, dressed in their bib overalls, looked up, sort of grunted, and went on talking. This was a picture from Norman Rockwell's drawing board. I introduced myself, passed out candidate cards, and announced that I was a candidate for the State Senate. They asked me what party—I told them Republican. They said, 'Right party.' Comments like that always made me feel good.

> Lavon wasn't there, but his father, Dwight was. I introduced myself to Dwight. Lavon came in a few minutes later, offered me a Nehi pop and we talked politics. At the end of the conversation, he said, Well, you'uns is the first to ask. Give us one of your posters. Evidently, we struck it off all right. In the primary I received fifty-two votes in Lavon's precinct, to two for my opponent, Star Brown. When I thanked Lavon for his support, he

Figure 10.1 Door-to-Door Follow-up Letters

William J. Stangler
R.R. #4
St. Peter, Minn.

Dear Bill,

Thanks much for your time when I
visited with you, and nice meeting
you again.

Your thoughts and opinions were most
interesting. I would appreciate
your support this fall, and the vote
of the entire Stangler household.
Anything you may be able to do would
certainly help in my campaign to give
us the type of representation that
I feel we all deserve in the Minnesota
State Senate.

Anytime you have any questions or
suggestions, please get in contact
with me.

Sincerely,

Clarence M. Purfeerst
Clarence M. Purfeerst

Eugene McAllister
R.R. #4
St. Peter, Minn.

Dear Eugene,

I am sorry that I missed you when I
stopped at your home on Monday.

I was seeking your thoughts and
opinions regarding my candidacy for
state senator this fall. Any thing
that you may be able to do would
certainly help in my campaign to give
us the representation that I feel we
all deserve in the Minnesota State
Senate.

At any time you have any questions or
suggestions, please get in contact
with me.

Sincerely,

Clarence M. Purfeerst
Clarence M. Purfeerst

Robert Kaveney
R.R. #4
St. Peter, Minn.

Dear Bob,

Thanks much for your time when I met
you at Demers. May I again wish you
the best of luck at the National Plow-
ing Contest in Denmark this September.

Your thoughts and opinions were most
interesting. I appreciated your offer
of support, and hope for the vote of
the entire Kaveney household. Any
thing you may be able to do would certainly help in my campaign to give
us the type of representation that I
feel we all deserve in the Minnesota
State Senate.

Anytime you have any questions or
suggestions, please feel free to
get in contact with me.

Sincerely,

Clarence M. Purfeerst
Clarence M. Purfeerst

said, 'Well, that was a pretty good vote, but we're still wonderin' who them two was.'[45]

The personal campaigning of the candidate can also be an important campaign weapon in campaigns for higher office or in large constituency campaigns. Connecticut Senator Abraham Ribicoff's method of personal campaigning is not uncommon in large campaigns:

> Ribicoff's usual campaign technique was the 'walking tour,' interspersed with a few scheduled engagements. Accompanied only by his driver, Ribicoff would go to a town and begin walking up the main street, in and out of shops and stores, shaking hands and talking briefly with businessmen and customers. He also liked to tour factories and greet the workers. If the town was a large one, a whole day would be devoted to the tour; otherwise, several towns might be covered during a day. The driver carried with him a large black notebook filled with information concerning the local political scene—town Democratic leaders, city officials, and past voting records of the area. This information would then be relayed 'on the run' to the candidate. At campaign headquarters, a volunteer worker plotted out the precise routes that were to be followed by the driver the next day.
>
> The pattern was illustrated on July 26 when Ribicoff opened his campaign, as he traditionally does, in the northwest Connecticut town of Canaan. At 10 AM he began making the rounds, starting with a drug store at the town's main intersection. 'I'm superstitious.' Then he moved down the street, stopping at an assortment of stores. 'Hellow, I'm Abe Ribicoff,' he would say as he greeted people and shook hands. There were no large gatherings, though the candidate ended his tour with a brief speech. On the stroll Ribicoff was accompanied by Joseph Foley, Canaan Democratic town chairman. This routine was repeated more than a hundred times before the campaign ended.[46]

While not always as systematically organized as depicted in this case, most candidates for large and small offices try to develop the candidate dimension by personally campaigning at some point in the campaign.

MEDIA AND PUBLIC RELATIONS

Media has become so significant in modern campaigning that it receives the attention of the four following chapters. The focus of this chapter is on the more personal campaign techniques of candidates and campaigners as public-relations techniques. Though treated separately here, in the campaign, personal and media campaigning are connected public-relations processes. In this section, the linkage of candidate campaigning, activities on behalf of the candidate, news coverage, and advertising will be discussed as examples of public relations integration.

A few practical examples centering around a candidacy announcement will aid in understanding how linkages can be established. When the candidate makes a formal announcement of his or her candidacy, news releases ordinarily go out to the appropriate media, with accompanying pictures and background materials, making sure the announcement is timed for publishers of weeklies. Before the announcement is made public, many candidates write all party officers, including precinct committeemen (and sometimes vice-committeemen), and other key people in the community also announcing the candidacy and seeking help. Writing social-precinct, attentive-public campaigners who have been identified at this point, with advance word would help elicit support from this group. The immediate pre-announcement period is also a good time for the candidate to make a public-relations tour visiting editors, political writers, and news directors. Sometimes campaigners stage campaign events around announcements, such as receptions, dinners, or the opening of a series of store-front headquarters. Historic dates or places are also selected to maximize the impact. Democratic presidential hopefuls like to announce from the Senate Caucus Room, where President Kennedy announced. Many Republicans choose Lincoln's birthday as a time. All of these activities make the announcement more than just a media event but a campaign organization activity as well.

Press advance and press relations efforts in general can be seen as the integration of public relations with media. In the very large scale campaigns, one person knowledgeable of the workings with the press is responsible for press arrangements, including travel, accommodations, and ensuring that reporters and correspondents are at the right place at the right time. Victor Gold, who was later to be press secretary for former Vice President Agnew, had these responsibilities in the 1964 Goldwater campaign, and was referred to as a "combination mascot, mother-hen, and pressure valve to newsmen—some of whom feel the best part of a campaign day is watching Gold bring his bus in on time with the heroic derring-do of the U.S. Cavalry."[47] Even in smaller campaigns the two can be linked. A speech to a business group on a plan for economic development can be publicized by a special meeting with or a release to the business page editor. If the candidate is male, the wife's campaign activities can be linked with the women's page by contacts with the appropriate editor or writers. John Lindsay's staff always made it a point of informing the media where he would be "street campaigning" and which store front headquarters he would be working out of, in his campaigns for Mayor of New York City. He received considerable news coverage of his personal campaigning.

A final example of media linkage is the campaign TV party. Inexpensive television time is selected in daytime, non-prime hours, taking care not to pre-empt any favorites. Certain persons are selected by telephone to, in turn, recruit enough available persons to fill up a modest size television studio. Questions are fielded by the candidate from the audience. A telephone in the studio is placed beside the candidate. Meanwhile, other persons who are supporters, have TV parties in their homes, asking friends and neighbors to come over and watch the show. During the show the candidate calls the parties and allows those in attendance to ask questions, always identifying the address of the call and the person asking the question, keeping answers brief so as to maximize the number of questions. At the parties, campaign literature, display materials, and a donation box can be placed in a prominent location. TV parties not only reach voters through mass media, but allow less committed people to become more exposed to the candidate by being part of a semicaptive audience in a friend's or neighbor's home, and they facilitate and display the enthusiasm of the more committed as sponsors or by attendance in the studio.

TV parties, press relations, and key supporter contacts in conjunction with the announcement of a candidacy are but a few examples of merging the more personal contact activities with mass media. One facilitates the other, since they both are different ways of dealing with publics.

THE CANDIDATE'S POSTURE

Although we know very little about this subject in a systematic fashion, the *posture*, or the sum of the characteristics, or assumed bearing the candidate takes is a vital part of the public relations aspect of the campaign. The uncertainty over its definition reflects the difficulty in including only relevant postural dimensions without saying it is everything in the candidate's image. Perhaps the following quote about President Calvin Coolidge will illustrate the flavor of one's posture as a candidate:

> I remember two photographs of Calvin Coolidge taken while in office. One showed him, a look of outraged obedience on his face, wearing a full Indian warbonnet. The second showed him, in his high stiff collar, coat off, staring distrustfully at a fishing rod. Both publicity shots were catastrophies, and I have always suspected that his refusal to run for re-election was based on the conviction that he had lost forever the Indian, cowboy and fisherman votes.[48]

This public relations man obviously believed that this very "stiff," taciturn man, should never have taken on the type of publicity stunts that were either inconsistent with his personality or the office which he held.

When former Michigan Governor and Housing Secretary George Romney was seeking the 1968 Republican presidential nomination (in the pre-primary period) he took on actions which were inconsistent with his posture as a candidate. Perhaps in order to appear Kennedyesque or perhaps simply to appear more youthful, vigorous, and athletic, Romney skied in New Hampshire and shot baskets in a Milwaukee gymnasium. Both ended in disaster, and they were covered by national media. On the ski slopes he fell, blasting into a group of young people, and in the gym he missed something over twenty consecutive shots on the basket, then gave up. These seemingly minor events occurred at a time when Romney's campaign was coming apart at the seams; he was being trapped on issue positions, funds were scarce, and he was making no impact in the polls against Richard Nixon. The national networks depicted these two events as symbolic of a floundering effort. Romney's posture was, unfortunately, too consistent with the way his campaign was going, but not necessarily consistent with a serious looking, gray-haired, near 60-year-old business executive turned governor, seeking the presidency.

Among the dimensions of candidate posture which can serve to illustrate this facet of public relations campaigning are: becoming known, establishment of an identity, relating posture to strategy, consistency of the individual with candidate image, consistency with campaign themes, issue familiarity, speech making and personal demeanor—interpersonal relations and cosmetic considerations as a campaigner. Since there are no established principles in regard to this facet of the campaign—and there may never be because of the individuality involved—case material regarding some of these dimensions will be presented.

Establishing an Identity

One important dimension of the candidate as an individual is the process of becoming known for something, or being an individual recognized for something in the community. Many a citizen has carried civic or charitable work into a candidacy. Others have become known for their work in regard to urban renewal, union affairs, farm organizations, or economic development. That the visibility created for this previous work should be exploited as a candidate is natural. It is an area of knowledge, expertise, and interest with an already created, public identification, and thus, enhances the credibility and legitimacy of the candidacy.

Congressman James Schuer of the Bronx became known in New York for his work in housing and civil rights. Three things became important in his pre-election establishment of an identity. First, Schuer became a known leader in these two issue areas before they became important issues. He had even won the Urban League man of the year award for his work on legislation. Second, he became an active participant on public boards and commissions identified with the two key issues; state housing for the aged, an urban redevelopment group, and a slum clearance committee. Third, when party and other political leaders avoided an issue, the citizen formed his own committee on an issue of public concern. In this particular case it was state aid to higher education. Schuer formed a committee which made a detailed study and released a report.[49]

Obviously, this strategy for establishing an identity on an issue involves more than an eleventh hour commitment to become involved in public affairs. It takes months or years of advance commitment. However, many a candidate or potential candidate is at some midpoint in this process. It would take only some public speaking and news stimulation to turn a campaign asset into an advantage.

Becoming Known beyond the Community

Many constituencies extend beyond the immediate geographic or issue community of the candidate or potential candidate, and it becomes necessary to become widely known. Certain techniques used by candidates to broaden contacts have been illustrated in Chapter 3 in connection with lining up the support of key people in the community. Of equal and sometimes more critical importance is broadening support to include party or key people involved in being nominated.

An interesting case in broadening support is U.S. Senator Birch Bayh's attempt to gain his first senatorial nomination. He was a four-term member of the Indiana legislature, including service as Speaker of the House. Yet, he felt he needed to broaden support and visibility beyond his immediate political circle. The following are excerpts from a pre-nomination master plan by the Bayh campaign:

1. Arrange for systematic contacts between our supporters and those of Governor Welsh's organization.
2. Set up a hospitality suite for the Jackson-Jefferson Day Dinner.
3. Contact county chairmen, vice-chairmen and mayors throughout the state. Select a personal representative in each county. Follow up each Bayh visit with a personal letter.
4. Form four teams of two men each to systematically call on all delegates to the last convention.
5. Commence an active speaking tour with both political- and civic-type speeches.
6. Have committee representatives contact all Democratic organization people within one or two weeks after Bayh visit.
7. Trip to Washington for conversation with Hartke and congressmen. Have pictures taken with national figures. Check possibility of meeting with Bob Kennedy. Meeting should perhaps be at the time of National Unemployment Conference called by the AFL–CIO.
8. Initiate systematic mail campaign to full mailing list. This to be sponsored by the Sixth District committee (Bayh's home district) and stress the need for a strong candidate.
9. Arrange weekly meetings, skull sessions with experts at Indiana University to keep the group abreast of advanced thinking on current national and international affairs.[50]

Because parties are relatively strong in Indiana, and because senatorial candidates are chosen at state party conventions, Bayh's particular plan for broadening his support was party-oriented.

Relating Posture to Strategy

As a candidate becomes known for some particular subject or area of specialization, these particular subjects usually find their way into a central part of the strategy, especially in terms of the issue themes. If one is known for civil rights, economic development, or crime control, specific issue appeals are formulated to capitalize on already developed visibility, for usage before attentive groups and the media. In the 1972 campaign for the Democratic presidential nomination, Edmund Muskie tried hard to capitalize on his years of work on pollution and environmental problems as a Maine legislator and governor and then seantor, by stressing ecology issues in speeches, news releases, and commercials. Candidates who have some special expertise in foreign policy or defense policy, try to weave these themes into strategy, since foreign policy competence is an important expectation of the presidential office. Thus, in addition to all of the other important strategic principles and requisites of office, campaign strategists often try to play the "strong suit" of the candidate into strategy by posturing the candidate as a specialist.

A case illustration is from Abraham Ribicoff's first try for the Senate, after he had resigned as Secretary of Health, Education, and Welfare. Ribicoff and his advisors had identified twenty-two campaign issues, but the major themes were based on his experience as HEW secretary. Education and medicare, along with commuter problems, civil rights, air and water pollution were his most important speech topics. A study of Ribicoff's major speeches and press releases showed a predominance of education and medicare themes. The candidate also delivered from three to ten informal speeches daily, in which he touched on educational problems in every speech, with medicare running second.[51] Ribicoff was a well known political figure in Connecticut, but he had developed expertise in a new area since he had last run for office, and he thus tried to exploit expertise in education and welfare issues as a part of his posture by weaving it into his strategy.

Consistency with Image

Another important dimension of the posture of the candidate is the attempt to gain some consistency with the image being portrayed. Indeed, the posture the candidate takes is contributing to that image. Analysis of candidate images in Chapter 2 indicated that there were three important dimensions of candidate image which may influence voter evaluation of candidates: personality and personal characteristics, candidate-issue dimensions, and the ability to do the job.

Previous sections have already illustrated the importance of issues. Strategists also attempt to formulate individual appeals with knowledge of important personal qualities or requisite qualities for the office sought in mind.

Richard Nixon's 1968 strategists certainly must have been concerned with creating a posture for him consistent with his image, or at least their perception of his image. The following excerpts from private campaign documents are illustrative:

> It is my belief that the most effective posture for Mr. Nixon is that of *challenger*—which means, of course, that we always regard Mr. Humphrey

as a key member of the incumbent administration, sharing responsibility for past and present policies and committed to their continuation for the years ahead.[52]

In developing actual advertisements and commercials, we should observe two general guidelines.

First, the style of advertising must be *appropriate*—to the man, to his background, to the office he is seeking. We are representing in our advertising a former vice president of the United States, a man with specific and well known personality traits, a candidate for the most important office in the world.

Second, we must not, in our zeal (or in our preoccupation with the loser image), forget that *our candidate is* the favorite.[53]

Generally, it has been agreed that all advertising for Mr. Nixon must communicate his *acceptability* to the masses. This 'acceptability factor' is considered a very important element in persuading voters that he is the man qualified by far. Furthermore, it is agreed that Mr. Nixon's acceptability is currently an open question. It is an open and unanswered question because he is not always loved, he is not particularly glamorous, and he has been depicted as cold, objective, and, even ruthless.[54]

These particular documents were written by Nixon's media strategists. They were introductory notions which were later woven into plans. They suggest how the image to be portrayed is part of the posture of the candidate.

Consistency with Theme

Political campaigns, like other public relations efforts, very often contain a theme. In public relations a theme is the equivalent to the story line in a work of fiction. A theme embodies the major idea to be conveyed. Themes are generally expressed repeatedly, in varied form. They condition all that is verbally or visually presented through the various media of communication.[55] Since campaigns ordinarily contain a series of events and activities based on multiple approaches of party, candidate, and issue appeals with reinforcement, activation of latency, and conversion effects, they are very often tied together with a campaign theme. "Tippecanoe and Tyler too," and "I like Ike," "Nixon's the One," and "All the Way with LBJ," referred primarily to candidate appeals whereas "Forty Acres and a Cow," "Fifty-four Forty or Fight," "Communism, Corruption and Korea," and "Let's Get America Moving Again," refer to issue appeals.

Themes can be woven through the entire campaign. Milton Shapp's first primary election for Governor of Pennsylvania was based on his opposition to the party slate-making process. "The Man Against the Machine" was his theme and it permeated his campaign, including the content of his media, where he spoke, and the people who staffed his campaign. He used outside consultants and non-party people to put his campaign together. He rarely sought party support or spoke before a party group. All of his radio and television time and a very extensive direct mail campaign to registered Democrats was based on his opposition to party bossism. His consultants produced a half-hour film documentary entitled *The Man Against the Machine*.[56]

Former Minnesota Governor Karl Rolvaag used a similar theme, when he was denied party pre-primary re-endorsement in 1966 as an incumbent. After twenty bitter ballots, the state party convention endorsed Lt. Governor A.M. Keith. Rolvaag opposed Keith in the primary election, and his strategists chose "Let the People Decide" as the theme to represent the evil actions of party bosses. While Keith attacked Rolvaag's lack of leadership as governor, the Governor and his strategists stuck to a simple theme:

> Rolvaag did not reply to Keith's attacks. He was busy campaigning, hitting as many towns as possible. He did not talk about his opponent, and wherever he appeared he limited himself to the same simple message, one which had always struck a responsive chord with the people of Minnesota: the party bosses were trying to run the show, and he was out to stop them. He was the lonely defender of 'the democratic process of allowing the people to pick the candidate.' The people's great hope lay there, in the primary, a final check against 'boss-ruled conventions.' Occasionally this theme got out of hand, as at the Blue Earth County Fair in Garden City, where he suggested similarities between his role and 'the American boys who are fighting today in Vietnam to preserve the principle of free elections,' but always Rolvaag's message won applause. His slogan, 'Let the People Decide,' was an echo from the days of the old Nonpartisan League, and so was his solution: 'Vote the Twenty-first Ballot.'[57]

Rolvaag's speeches, which were well covered by the press, were buttressed by an extensive billboard campaign with "Let the People Decide". . .Karl F. Rolvaag in gold letters with a maroon background (University of Minnesota colors) plus an extensive last week newspaper ad campaign with the same theme. Rolvaag thus connected his entire (successful) primary campaign around his stated theme of taking the candidate selection process away from the party and to the people. His posture as the man beaten by the organization who could be saved by the voters was integrated with the theme.

Issue Familiarity and Presentation

The question of issues has been dealt with at many different points in this book. Generally, it has been stated that issues are not as important in voters minds as most assume, yet the outside or public campaign requires the development of a small number of constituencywide issues. A large number of issues targeted to special interests and special audiences as a part of the inside-outside campaign are required. It has also been suggested that the candidate will inevitably have to go beyond the few issue areas and develop some familiarity with the problems of the groups he speaks before and whose support he seeks. The candidate's posture is obviously enhanced by demonstration of a wide-ranging knowledge and understanding of issues, the proposal of solutions to problems, particularly if they are sympathetic to the views of the group or persons being addressed.

This is not to suggest that the candidate or campaigners calculate the issue positions of groups and adopt their stands. Ordinarily, the process of coalition formation is one in which the candidate builds from groups with similar values. The decision to run may, in part, be based on the desire to represent certain groups or interests. Thus, selection of issues is natural in these cases. New groups or interests will arise which also may deserve attention and support in the course of campaigning, and there may be a desire to personally support such issues. There is no reason why a candidate must support any issue in which he does not believe. Indeed, some argue that the stronger the convictions, the more effective the appeal; or at least it is difficult to sell something one does not believe in. Whatever the particular package of issue appeals, those which are most visible contribute to making up the posture of the candidate, what he will be known to be for, or conversely, what he will be known to be against.

A publicly identified candidate is very often called upon to take stands on many issues. A candidate for the state legislature, for example, receives mail and personal appeals from dozens of organized interest groups asking him or her to take stands on issues of interest to the group. These groups can include: conservation groups, divorce reform associations, those supporting and opposing abortion, mental health and mental retardation groups, civil rights and civil liberties groups, women's rights groups, veteran's associations, labor associations, education groups, farm groups, good government associations, taxpayers' groups and many others. These requests are routinely sent to candidates listed on the filing rolls. Experienced campaigners ordinarily handle these requests with considerable discretion. Depending on the issue or interest of the candidate, some are carefully filled out, some are worked through the group's representatives in the constituency, and some are ignored.

The active candidate often gives from two to ten speeches in a single day. There is no way to completely separate a single appeal for each group. Candidates very often overlap their issue appeals by beginning their talks with the more general or theme related appeals, and then, moving to the specific issues related to the group. Another approach is similar to Senator Ribicoff's, who used what he knew best—education and medicare—for secondary themes in nearly every talk he gave. Indeed, repetition can be turned into an asset, by linking themes with issue appeals. In 1960, John F. Kennedy tried to use his theme of "let's get the country moving again" by leading into speeches with appeals such as, "We've been doing all right, but we can do better," and then, launching into a talk about defense, foreign policy, economic growth, or civil rights, depending on the audience. When these appeals are put together, they are part of the candidate's posture.

The advice given to campaign speakers is abundant and often contradictory. Some argue that one should be witty; others would rather not be witty, and still others say do not be witty unless the speaker is known to be funny. Some say always be controversial, others say do not be controversial, still others say do not be too controversial. Some say refer to dramatic historical events; others say deal with the here and now—real events. Some political speech advisors say that different audiences should be approached differently: present one side of the issue to friendly audiences, both sides to hostile audiences. If the audience is thoroughly familiar with the issue and unbiased, the candidate should be candid and neutral. More educated audiences should be approached rationally and logically, avoiding emotion; less educated audiences should get more emotion and more graphic approaches.[58] Others feel audiences should be treated equally. The evidence to support one side of the issue or the other is not conclusive enough to mention.

The important variable from all of this advice is the speech-giving ability of the candidate. Some are very able and articulate public speakers, and others are not. Some may have excellent speaking abilities, but they may be lacking in organizing speech material, or may know more about one subject than another. What candidates very often need is the speech development support of other campaigners. The following is a succinct version of advice given to city office candidates on how to carry foreward research and issue development into speech assistance, and then to link it with the rest of the public relations effort:

> The 'guts' of the job lies in having quick, accurate access to facts. These facts you should have—from the 'Situational Analysis,' 'Political Analysis,' lists and so forth you obtained from your City Chairman in the beginning. You also have at hand the Party Platform or 'Action Program,' in which the theme and major issues of your campaign are stated. You also have other factual information from local publications, libraries, etc.

> The idea is to marshal facts behind *one* key point, develop this into an interesting, logical, challenging declaration—in conversational form—and keep it all within the situation at which it'll be given. In other words, direct it to the 'audience'—if the audience is to be a Rotary Club, peg it to a set of professional ears; if the audience is to be a labor union, peg it to 'pocketbook' ears. Tailor it to fit the time allowed—10, 15, or 20 minutes.

> Polish the text after consulting with the actual speaker, so that he can use *his words* where necessary to express the ideas you're suggesting.

> Make him either learn it, or rehearse it (several times). Give him a set of 5 × 7 cards, with the speech text either summarized or typed out in full (if so, triple space, capital letters, with cards boldly numbered).

> KEEP IN MIND: 'KISS.' This means: 'Keep It Short, Stupid!' In practice, that means stick to the point, don't ramble, be interesting.

> Write your press releases from these speeches, pegging them to actual speaking engagements. In one put the 'lead' on one point; in another,

on another 'point,' and keep these moving in sequence so that you build a 'snowball' effect—both to listeners and to others who get the message through the press.[59]

This simple advice can assist in translating issue familiarity into presentations which can enhance the candidate's posture.

ADVANCE AS A PUBLIC RELATIONS FUNCTION

An increasingly important function in the public relations component of the campaign is advancing—or preparing and arranging campaign events in advance. As campaigning has expanded beyond party work to include media, electioneering by non-party groups, and increased public involvement, the need has arisen to coordinate the various elements as they work together on such events as dinners, rallies, parades, speeches, or tours by the candidate.

The advance function ranges from the extremely simple early checking of plans and schedules, to elaborate teams of advance men, charged not only with arrangements but building up huge crowds to greet the candidate. In its basic form the person advancing a candidate (or some other person campaigning on the candidate's behalf) travels to the site of the appearance a few days before the actual visit. All physical arrangements, including space, sound equipment, which persons are to be contacted, where the candidate will eat and sleep are checked. The advance person tries to get local supporters to carry out all details and ensures that there are no failures in plans. At the same time the advance person can collect local information for the candidate regarding local problems and personal ties which can prove helpful to the candidate as he visits the area.

In larger campaigns, where visible candidates make appearances in many different locales, often making more than a single appearance in the area, the advance person must make a number of different kinds of arrangements. The most famous of all advancemen, Jerry Bruno, relates the major tasks he has undertaken in the many presidential and senatorial campaigns he has been in:

> It's my job in a campaign to decide where a rally should be held, how a candidate can best use his time getting from an airport to that rally, who should sit next to him and chat with him quietly in his hotel room before or after a political speech, and who should be kept as far away from him as possible.

> It's also my job to make sure that a public appearance goes well—a big crowd, an enthusiastic crowd, with bands and signs, a motorcade that is mobbed by enthusiastic supporters, a day in which a candidate sees and is seen by as many people as possible—and at the same time have it all properly recorded by the press and their cameras.

I'm almost never there when a speech is being made, because I'm figuring out how to get the candidate from the hall to his next appearance as effectively as possible. Or I'm calling to another city to find out why the high-school band isn't already waiting at the airport, or why the automobile dealer has decided not to lend us twelve cars for our triumphant motorcade into town. Or maybe I'm trying to convince the press that those twenty thousand people who met us in downtown Cleveland were really fifty thousand, or that the empty streets in front of the hotel were empty because we urged people not to show up there—not because nobody cared about the candidate.[60]

The advance work performed in larger campaigns is predicated on the notion that the particular event planned goes beyond those immediately attending or participating in the event; that the crowds and enthusiasm generated there will be reverberated to other voters through direct media coverage of the event and reporters' accounts of public events. Somehow, crowded streets and shopping centers, filled halls and screaming audiences are to be regarded as demonstrations of widespread support.

Thus, the central part of any advance person's role is the building of a crowd. The success of the campaign stop depends on how many people turn out to cheer, and how this is reported through the media. Therefore, advance persons do not leave this up to chance. Advanceman Jerry Bruno explains his techniques for filling a field house with 7,500 people in a town of 250,000:

> If you leave it to a handful of political leaders, they might put an ad in the paper or rely on a mailing to turn out a crowd. Then you'd find a candidate facing a lot of empty seats.
>
> But if you break it down, if you have a wide variety of interest groups trying to get out small numbers of people they know well, you're likely to have a much more successful turnout. My list would run something like this:
>
> *Labor:* Personally contact 200 shop stewards and union officials, and instruct each of them to bring 5 workers 1200
>
> *Business:* Ask 100 friendly businessmen and professonal people to bring 5 friends and colleagues 600
>
> *Bands:* Get two 30-piece bands, and 'allow' each member to invite his parents and 5 friends 480
>
> *Schools:* Approach principals, school superintendents, and members of the Board of Education, and persuade them to dismiss school for this historic occasion. If possible give personal invitations to each student for himself plus 3 friends or members of his family 2400
>
> *Political Workers:* Invite ward chairmen and chairmen

of surrounding villages and towns, and get a promise
from each of them that they'll bring 30 party workers
and citizens   2480

Patronage Holders: In a town with a Democratic
mayor who's more or less friendly, get 50 jobholders
of some influence to bring 15 friends and workers
(who can be encouraged to come by circulars,
letters, and conversation)   800

Senior Citizens: Provide, say, three buses from
homes to and from the hall, and you can get about
150 out   150

Hostesses: Give 50 housewives the title of 'hostess,'
and give them the job of inviting 10 people, with calls
to be made from their homes (saves money)   550

This means that more than 500 people are actively working to turn out a crowd, and that more than 8,500 people have been personally invited by friends or colleagues *before* you invite the general public (which is always done). In this way, people have a stake in turning out a crowd; it means that if a lot of people never do any work (which always happens) you still have a very good chance to get an overflow crowd.[61]

Bruno then enhances the event by having a number of local committees to: handle press arrangements, invite as many bands as possible, arrange for local entertainment, secure cars for the motorcade, make hotel arrangements, create homemade signs, distribute leaflets advertising the speech, organize a telephone committee to call all registered Democrats, and have candidate girls dress alike to perform cheerleader functions.[62]

There was extensive use of advance work on the local level in Jay Cooper's campaign for Mayor of Pritchard, Alabama in 1972. A good part of his public relations campaign included walking and shopping center tours, a motorcade through the city, and a park rally. The tours were advanced by physically checking key populated areas, determining which stores or neighborhoods were to be visited, seeking permission from the store management as to the degree of campaigning permitted, checking times and distances to and from the site by car and on foot, checking the route to be taken at the site, printing and distribution of handbills, creating media messages, engaging in leadership contacts, securing and setting up loud speaker systems for crowd gathering, and preparing a minute-by-minute schedule incorporating all of these steps. Advancing the motorcade and rally included the following techniques of preplanning and checking: finding a stage and having it delivered, getting sound equipment and testing it, determining the location and condition of exterior electrical outlets, finding entertainers and briefing them on their part of the program, arranging for security and its deployment, generating a crowd, determining the positions of the cars, arranging for car and site decoration, determining and timing the route to be taken, seating plans for the stage, appropriate media publicity for the event, arranging literature distribution, making arrangements with park authorities, and developing the agenda.[63]

Presidential campaigns very often are staffed with large numbers of advance men, whereas in smaller campaigns usually one or two will suffice. In 1968, Hubert Humphrey's campaign used 125 advance men which appears to be a record high. Advance men often work prior to major candidate appearances for one week to ten days. Advance men come from many walks of life—lawyers, salesmen, public relations men, executives—and most have campaign experience. They rarely are paid a salary, usually working for expenses, but the expenses of an advance man can easily reach $1000 per week. Often the expenses are paid by the local committee sponsoring the campaign event.

All of the advanced events are designed to create the impression that the appearance of the candidate triggered an outpouring of enthusiasm and support for the candidate. One cynic has thus labeled the work of advance men as planned spontaneity.

Notes to Chapter 10

1. Edward L. Bernays, *The Engineering of Consent* (Norman: Univ. of Oklahoma Press, 1955), pp. 4-5.

2. Ibid., pp. 7-8.

3. Stanley Kelley, Jr., *Professional Public Relations and Political Power* (Baltimore: Johns Hopkins, 1956), pp. 9-17.

4. Ibid., pp. 37-38.

5. D. Swing Meyer, *The Winning Candidate* (New York: James H. Heineman, 1966), p. 12.

6. Kelley, *Professional Public Relations and Political Power*, pp. 46-60.

7. This firm's approaches are discussed in, Robert J. Pitchell, "The Influence of Professional Campaign Management Firms in Partisan Elections in California," *Western Political Quarterly* 11 (1958), pp. 286-94.

8. Ibid., pp. 278-79.

9. Ibid., pp. 280-81.

10. David Lee Rosenbloom, *The Election Men: Professional Campaign Managers and American Democracy* (New York: Quadrangle Books, 1973), p. 50.

11. Ibid., p. 51.

12. Ibid., p. 53.

13. Ibid., p. 52.

14. Robert Agranoff, *The New Style in Election Campaigns* (Boston: Holbrook Press, 1972), pp. 54-57.

15. Harry N.D. Fisher, "How the 'I Dare You' Candidate Won" in *The New Style in Election Campaigns.*

16. John Bibby and Roger Davidson, *On Capitol Hill* 1st ed. (New York: Holt, Rinehart and Winston, 1967), pp. 58-59.

17. William J. Gore and Robert L. Peabody, "The Functions of the Political Campaign: A Case Study," *Western Political Quarterly* 11 (1958): 66.

18. Floyd Hunter, *Community Power Structure* (Garden City, N.Y.: Doubleday, 1963), ch. I.

19. C. Wright Mills, *The Power Elite* (New York: Oxford Univ. Press, 1956).

20. Robert A. Dahl, *Who Governs* (New Haven: Yale Univ. Press, 1961).

21. Peter Bachrach and Morton S. Baratz, "Two Faces of Power," *American Political Science Review* 56 (1962); Peter Bachrach and Morton S. Baratz, "Decisions and Nondecisions: An Analytical Framework," *American Political Science Review* 57 (1963).

22. James B. Kessler, "Running For State Political Office," *Practical Politics in the United States* ed. Cornelius P. Cotter (Boston: Allyn and Bacon, 1969), p. 129.

23. Ibid., pp. 122-34. Kessler presents an excellent account of personal campaigning.

24. David A. Leuthold, *Electioneering in a Democracy* (New York: John Wiley, 1968), p. 65.

25. Ibid., p. 66.

26. Ibid., p. 67.

27. Harry Scoble, "Organized Labor in Electoral Politics: Some Questions for the Discipline," *Western Political Quarterly* 16 (1963): 683.

28. Leuthold, *Electioneering in a Democracy*, p. 68.

29. John W. Kingdon, *Candidates for Office: Beliefs and Strategies* (New York: Random House, 1968), pp. 48-49.

30. Ibid., p. 49.

31. Heinz Eulau, Betty H. Zisk and Kenneth Prewitt, "Latent Partisanship in Nonpartisan Elections," in *The Electoral Process* eds. M. Kent Jennings and L. Harmon Zeigler (Englewood Cliffs, N.J.: Prentice-Hall, 1966), pp. 231-32.

32. John H. Kessel, *The Goldwater Coalition* (Indianapolis: Bobbs-Merrill, 1968), pp. 14-15.

33. Ibid., pp. 29-31.

34. Stephen C. Shaddeg, *The New How To Win an Election* (New York: Taplinger, 1972), p. 104.

35. Ibid., pp. 105-06.

36. Ibid., p. 118.

37. Ibid., pp. 107-18.

38. Eulau, "Latent Partisanship in Nonpartisan Election," p. 228.

39. Meyer, *The Winning Candidate*, pp. 51-53.

40. Cited in *Campaign Insight*, 1 May 1974, p. 2.

41. Eulau, "Latent Partisanship in Nonpartisan Elections," p. 227.

42. *Campaign Insight*, 1 January 1974, p. 5.

43. Ibid.

44. Lois Mizuno developed portions of this section in her work on the *1968 DFL Legislator's Campaign Manual.*

45. Kessler, "Running for State Political Office," pp. 128-29.

46. Bibby and Davidson, *On Capital Hill*, pp. 44-45.

47. Quoted in Meyer, *The Winning Candidate*, p. 115.

48. David Baldwin, "A Political Campaign, Its Public Relations," in *Campaign Technique Manual* ed. Robert D. Buehler (Washington, D.C.: National Association of Manufacturers, undated), p. 111.

49. From Meyer, *The Winning Candidate*, pp. 15-16.

50. Quoted in Michael J. Kirwan, *How To Succeed in Politics* (New York: MacFadden, 1964), p. 76.

51. Bibby and Davidson, *On Capitol Hill*, pp. 45-46.

52. Harry Treleaven, "Notes re NFP Advertising—Phase One," publ. in Joe McGinniss, *The Selling of the President, 1968* (New York: Trident, 1969), p. 233.

53. Ibid., p. 175.

54. Ibid., p. 218.

55. Bernays, *The Engineering of Consent*, p. 16.

56. Richard B. Stolley, " 'Hopeless' Case of Milton Shapp," *Life Magazine*, May 27, 1966; James M. Perry, *The New Politics* (New York: Clarkson N. Potter, 1968), ch. 3.

57. David Lebedoff, *The 21st Ballot* (Minneapolis: University of Minnesota Press, 1969), pp. 167-68.

58. Meyer, *The Winning Candidate*, p. 64.

59. Indiana Democratic State Central Committee, *A Handbook on Publicity, Public Relations, and Advertising for a Democratic City Election in Indiana*

in 1967 (Indianapolis: Democratic State Central Committee, 1967), pp. 19–20.

60. Jerry Bruno and Jeff Greenfield, *The Advance Man* (New York: Bantam, 1972), pp. 28–29.

61. Ibid., pp. 48–49.

62. Ibid., pp. 49–51.

63. John Dean, *The Making of a Black Mayor* (Washington, D.C.: Joint Center for Political Studies, 1973), pp. 16–17.

For Further Reading and Research

Bernays, Edward L. *The Engineering of Consent.* Norman: Univ. of Oklahoma Press, 1955.

Boyarsky, Nancy. "The Image Makers: Behind the Mystique of the Powerful but Unseen Manipulators of the California Political Process." *California Journal* 5 (1974) 149–55.

Bruno, Jerry and Greenfield, Jeff. *The Advance Man.* New York: Bantam, 1972.

Coffman, Tom. *Catch a Wave: A Case Study in Hawaii's New Politics.* Honolulu: Univ. of Hawaii Press, 1973.

Dunn, Richard E. and Glista, Martin D. "Illinois Legislative Races: Separating Winners from the Losers," *Public Affairs Bulletin* Southern Illinois Univ. 6 (1973): 1–5.

Evry, Hal. *The Selling of a Candidate.* Los Angeles: Western Opinion Research Center, 1971.

Gore, William J. and Peabody, Robert L. "The Functions of the Political Campaign: A Case Study." *Western Political Quarterly* 11 (1958); 55–70.

Kelley, Jr., Stanley. *Professional Public Relations and Political Power.* Baltimore: Johns Hopkins, 1966.

Meyer, D. Swing. *The Winning Candidate.* New York: James Heineman, 1966.

Perry, James M. *The New Politics: The Expanding Technology of Political Manipulation.* New York: Clarkson N. Potter, 1968.

Pitchell, Robert J. "The Influence of Professional Campaign Mangement Firms in Partisan Elections in California." *Western Political Quarterly* 11 (1958) 278–300.

Rosenbloom, David Lee. *The Election Men: Professional Campaign Mangers and American Democracy.* New York: Quadrangle, 1973.

Shadegg, Stephen C. *The New How to Win an Election.* New York: Taplinger, 1972.

Media in Campaigns: Structure and Dynamics

The ubiquity of mass media is obvious, including their marked impact on many societal patterns and practices. This includes, of course, the conduct of campaigns. Auditory perception specialist Tony Schwartz claims, for example, that it is resonance not content which is the apparent principle creating modern communication, because so much material that is stored in the heads of the audience is also stored in the brain of a communicator, by viture of a shared media audience. In communicating at electronic speed, Schwartz claims we no longer direct information into an audience, but try to evoke stored information out of them, in a patterned way.[1] Schwartz represents but one of a number of hypotheses about the structure and impact of a communications system which is electronically oriented, rapid, and pervasive.

The newer media have combined with the old to make campaigning multi-channeled. In addition to reliance on intermediate structures—key political leaders, group leaders, activists, and the party organization—there is direct contact with voters, that is, direct candidate communication with the voter, either by a person, an organization, or through mass media (newspapers, radio, television, direct mail, display) reaching large proportions of the electorate. These direct media contacts are made through two basic forms, news coverage and advertising. The availability of the then-new media appeared to have come at a propitious time for campaigners: parties were declining in activism, constituencies were increasing in size, and voters were more amenable to voting contrary to their party line. These factors combined with media availability to make them all-important in campaigns. And it is not only in the large constituency, inactive-party swing-voter situation that media are important. Practically every candidate has to go beyond the intermediate structures and engage in some form of direct contact. That can be accomplished only through face-to-face contact and through the mass media.

Advertising and news coverage are a sort of information mass production counterpart to the machine in manufacturing. They have an accelerating force, reaching many people rapidly at low cost. Just as product advertising can increase sales and turn prospects into customers in large numbers and at high speed, campaign media appeals can speed up reinforcement of the committed, activate large numbers of latent supporters, and convert some of the undecided.[2]

The use of advertising and communications media is one of the very important reasons why campaigns have become more candidate-centered. Access to the media requires either money or skills, or both, and political parties have failed to monopolize these. Candidates have been better able to raise sufficient money to buy time and space, gaining access to those skilled in the creation and production of media messages. Since the candidate began to employ those who produced the communication, the messages were tailored to the candidate, who began to speak to the electorate as an individual rather than as a part of a party grouping.[3]

An interesting analogy to this process is the need for product advertising as a result of the changes in the methods of merchandise distribution. A century ago when products were delivered in bulk to retail stores, the shopkeeper performed many of the services now embedded in the product at the point of manufacture: measuring, packaging, and informing. Shopkeepers had to rely on the integrity of the wholesalers with whom they dealt. The buyer put his or her trust in the retailer and knew little about the manufacturer of the goods. The retailer knew most customers, their wants, and their tastes. Contemporary methods of distribution are different. An increasing number of stores allow self-service. The buyer confronts an array of competing varieties; perhaps the only encounter with an employee is with the cashier. The shopper must know a great deal more about the goods before setting foot in the store. Among the shopper's sources of information are the brand labels and instructions on the goods, as well as media advertising.[4] With the advent of increased use of mass media and advertising in campaigns, a similar process has occurred. Media have been substituted for the shopkeeper and the party precinct worker. Candidates have formulated messages to sell themselves, building up a personal franchise with the public, relying less on wholesalers, such as interest groups, and shopkeepers, such as party organizatons. The result is a reduction of the personal element of campaigning. The candidate and his or her appeal is clearly the equivalent to the brand name, wishing to distinguish themselves from the product—another member of the party ticket.

Candidate orientation to media obviously compounds the importance of media understanding, skill, and usage to all campaigners, and accounts for the extensive treatment given here. In this chapter, some important structural properties and dynamics of media for the campaigner will be revealed. The three chapters that follow will cover media planning, news coverage, and advertising.

THE REACH OF MEDIA

Campaigners have turned to mass media because of their impressive reach. In Richard Nixon's exhaustive personal-contact tour of all 50 states in the 1960 presidential campaign, it was estimated that 10 million people saw him. A single national political broadcast can reach 20 to 25 million voters, and the Kennedy-Nixon debates in 1960 averaged 71 million viewers. On a more local level, a single radio ad for a candidate can reach anywhere from 500 to 500,000 listeners, and, while many of them are doing something else. At the same time that 1,000 or 100,000 newspaper readers are seeking information about a wide range of subjects, or comparison shopping, they may run across information about or advertising for a candidate. A single news item read by a TV newscaster or a spot ad placed by a candidate has the potential of reaching from 5,000 to 150,000 viewers in small listening areas and from 50,000 to 1.5 million viewers in large media markets.

Though political party or candidate organizations are not always extensively organized and capable of distributing information over a wide range of areas, the media are. There are over 1,700 daily newspapers in the United States, with a total circulation of 63 million. In addition to these suburban, metropolitan, and city papers, the small towns and rural areas are serviced by over 8,600 weekly newspapers with a total circulation of 29 million. There are over 5,000 radio stations in the United States. Almost all of them are distinctively local—they are not network oriented, and they reach for only a share of the total audience. The number of television stations in the United States is close to 900, almost all of them network oriented and reaching out to a more general audience. On the receiving end, 98 percent of all households with electricity have one or more television sets; they are used for an average of over five hours per day. There are about 1.5 radios in use in the United States for every inhabitant, with about 350 million presently in existence. In the spring of 1972, it was estimated that 85.4 percent of all Americans 18 and over listen to an average of 4 hours and 10 minutes of broadcasting each weekday.[5] A single, computer generated letter can be composed, interspersing paragraphs with different information, and addressed from a tape file, to one million households in a single working day. Over a period of a month or two, a billboard can be noticed by 100 percent of the persons passing a particular place—hundred of thousands in some well traveled locations.

Less important but noteworthy mass media for campaigners are magazines, films, and books. The big, general interest, weekly and monthly magazines have given way to those that cater to special interests: 750 consumer magazines, 60 hunting and fishing magazines, 87 for boaters and yachtsmen. Although theater attendance is at record low, 75 percent of all filmgoers are under 30 years old, making movies a special audience. American book publishers now issue more than 35,000 titles per year, including trade and text books, again appealing to different readers with different interests.[6] Rarely are books, films, and national magazines of interest to any but the presidential campaign, where campaign biographies, books, and articles on newsworthy subjects, written by or about the candidate, can be significant. Theatre advertising, magazine articles, and specialized magazine advertising are of more importance to some campaigners, especially when coverage can be broken down into units similar to the constituency.

The extensive reach of media has its impact on political campaigns. Since 1952 the Survey Research Center has measured the extent of media exposure to political campaigns, a time period which spans the television era (Table 11.1). Campaigns have been followed in the newspapers by about three-fourths of the electorate over the years. In contrast, radio listening appears to have dropped off since 1956, but just under half of the voting-age population continues to follow the campaign by that medium. About 4 in 10 persons of voting age are exposed to some information about the campaign from magazines. The greatest share of individuals obtain their campaign information by watching television programs, rising from half of all citizens in television's first campaign year, until it became established in 1964 as a source of campaign information for nine out of ten persons of voting age.

Such figures not only indicate the importance of the mass media for campaign information, but illustrate the wide range of sources of campaign information. Some persons obviously obtain campaign information from more than one source, yet, a single medium is often the important source for some. Table 11.2 (page 313) summarizes the most important source of media in presidential campaign years. Television has clearly become the single most important media source—the prime source—for about six in ten by the 1960s and 1970s. This dominance of television has probably come at the expense of radio, whose audience appears to have shrunk steadily since the advent of TV. Almost one in four people claim that newspapers are the most important source of their campaign information, a proportion that has held constant despite television. Magazines, as a prime source, hold the allegiance of a very small proportion of the information-seeking audience. Clearly, newspapers and television are the dominant media during presidential campaigns.

The mass media appear to be equally important sources of information in state and local campaigns. the data in Table 11.3, (page 314) from a national sample of the voting-age population, include interpersonal conversations as a source of information. In state and local campaigns, the relative influence of newspapers and radio is greater. Television is also the number one source of information in state campaigns, although newspapers are nearly as important. Only about one in ten persons listed interpersonal conversations or radio as a source of information. For local offices, a more diverse set of campaign information sources appears. Newspapers are clearly the number one source of information about local candidates, although television is also an important source. Radio is about the same as at the state level, being mentioned by one in ten. As might be expected, the role of personal conversations about candidates is nearly twice

Table 11.1 Campaign Media Exposure in Presidential Election Years

Media	1952	1956	1960	1964	1968	1972
Read newspaper articles about the election						
Minimum to Regularly	79.0%	68.6%	79.5%	78.4%	75.4%	57.4%
None	21.0%	31.4%	20.5%	21.6%	24.6%	42.6%
	N=1,707	N=1,760	N=1,780	N=1,437	N=1,348	N=1,115
Listened to speeches or discussions on Radio						
Minimum to Regularly	69.7%	45.4%	41.9%	47.9%	40.8%	42.9%
None	30.3%	54.6%	58.1%	52.1%	59.2%	57.1%
	N=1,703	N=1,758	N=1,814	N=1,441	N=1,335	N=1,116
Read about the campaign in Magazines						
Minimum to Regularly	40.2%	31.1%	40.8%	39.0%	35.7%	32.9%
None	59.8%	68.9%	59.2%	61.0%	64.3%	67.1%
	N=1,703	N=1,751	N=1,808	N=1,438	N=1,342	N=1,117
Watched programs about the campaign on Television						
Minimum to Regularly	51.3%	73.8%	86.6%	89.1%	89.2%	89.3%
None	48.7%	26.2%	13.4%	10.9%	10.8%	11.7%
	N=1,634	N=1,758	N=1,818	N=1,446	N=1,341	N=1,116

Source: Survey Research Center, University of Michigan. Made available by the Inter-University Consortium for Political Research. 1952–1964 data compiled by Dan Nimmo, *The Political Persuaders* (Englewood Cliffs, N.J.: Prentice-Hall, 1970), p. 116.

as important as for state campaigns. In another survey of sources of information in suburban local elections, it was found that newspapers proved to be the major source of information about campaigns; few respondents recalled receiving any information about the local electons from radio and television (even though it was available).[7] The picture of sources of campaign information that emerges is that as one moves from national to state to local campaigns, media become more diversified, specialized, and tend to be more personal.

CAMPAIGN INFORMATION FLOW

Thus, it becomes clear that there are many sources of media in a campaign, and that people place a greater or lesser reliance on various sources. Actually, these studies of media sources do not include all of the possible modes of communication in a campaign. While it would be quite difficult to measure their relative weight, a complete study of the sources of communication would have to include all conversations, literature, billboards, buttons, bumper stickers, and other modes, in addition to the media sources usually studied. Despite these gaps in studying the overall impact, it has been demonstrated that the amount of information flow in a campaign varies with individuals, and this has further consequences for the campaign.

In the very earliest voting study, *The Peoples Choice*, it was discovered that during the last twelve days of the campaign, 54 percent of the respondents had heard of at least one of five major political talks broadcast on the radio, 51 percent had read at least one campaign story which appeared on the front page of their favorite newspaper the day before the interview, and 26 percent had read at least one campaign article in current, popular magazines. The authors point out the striking fact that at the peak of the campaign, about half ignored stories regarding the campaign or talks by the candidate, and three-fourths did not read about them in magazines.[8] In a later study by the same group, it was found that there was a difference between how much attention people claimed to pay to the campaign and how much attention they actually payed. Only 38 percent claimed to be paying a great deal of attention to the news about the election, but when measured in terms of more objective measures, such as following the conventions, recall of newspaper items, or campaign speeches, the number substantially increased. Seventy-four percent recalled a reasonably specific item from one of three media, 67 percent remembered reading about a current news item in the newspaper, and 77 percent read or listened to something from one of the three media.[9]

It was also discovered by the authors of these early studies that contrary to their expectations, political materials tended to pile up and concentrate on certain groups of people. Those who were exposed to a lot of campaign propaganda through one medium of communication were also exposed to a lot in other media; those exposed to a little in one were also exposed to a little in

Table 11.2   The Most Important Media Source of Information

Source	1952	1956	1960	1964	1968
Newspapers	22.9%	24.3%	22.3%	24.5%	19.1%
Radio	28.1%	10.6%	5.3%	3.7%	2.9%
Television	31.9%	49.4%	60.9%	57.8%	52.6%
Magazines	5.2%	4.6%	4.3%	6.9%	5.0%
Newspapers & Radio	2.2%	.6%	.1%	.2%	.2%
Newspapers & TV	1.0%	1.2%	1.7%	1.8%	1.1%
Radio & TV	1.2%	.2%	.2%	.4%	.2%
Magazines & one other	.9%	.2%	.5%	1.1%	.4%
Any other combination	.2%	.5%	.2%	.4%	.4%
Did not follow campaign	6.4%	8.4%	4.5%	3.2%	18.1%
	N=1,561	N=1,595	N=1,729	N=1,397	N=1,328

Source: Survey Research Center, University of Michigan. Made available by the Inter-University Consortium for Political Research. 1952-1964 data compiled by Dan Nimmo, *The Political Persuaders* (Englewood Cliffs, N.J.: Prentice-Hall, 1970), p. 116. Not available for 1972.

others.[10] They also found that persons who read more campaign material in the newspapers also read more in magazines and listened to the radio; persons who paid more attention to campaign matters in June were also paying more attention in October; persons who followed the Republican convention more closely followed the Democratic convention. Thus, there was an overlap of channel, time, and events.[11]

These early findings concerning different levels of information have been repeatedly replicated, and it is now standard procedure to stratify the electorate in terms of media audience.[12] For example, V.O. Key explains that the audience for political communication can be stratified according to interest and involvement in politics. The greater the sense of political involvement, the greater exposure to political communications tends to be. Moreover, Key explains that the highly and continuously attentive stratum contains relatively large numbers of readers of magazines, books, and quality newspapers. This group listens to more radio and TV programs with a high, public affairs content. This group (estimated, by Key, to be about 10 percent of the public) undoubtedly includes most of the political activists. At the opposite end of the pole are those who pay little

Table 11.3   Source of Campaign Information for State
and Local Offices

	11/64 %	1/67 %	11/68 %	1/71 %	11/72 %
Local Offices:					
Newspapers	42	44	40	37	43
Television	27	32	26	32	28
Radio	10	10	6	6	7
People	18	16	23	20	22
Magazines	1	1	1	1	1
Other	7	6	4	5	5
Total mentions	105	109	100	101	106
State Offices:					
Newspapers	41	41	37	30	42
Television	43	50	42	50	43
Radio	10	9	6	6	7
People	8	9	9	9	10
Magazines	1	1	1	1	1
Other	4	4	4	4	4
Total mentions	107	114	99	100	107

Source: Burns W. Roper, *What People Think of Television and Other Mass Media 1959-1972* (New York: Television Information Office, 1973), pp. 6-7.

or no attention to political communication, with the size of the stratum depending on which measure is used. Nearly 10 percent do not follow national campaigns at all. To almost one-fourth of the voting-age public, the day-to-day attention to politics is light, their followership is limited to the easier media—radio, TV, and tabloid type media. Between these two strata is a large intermediate group that is moderately involved, votes, and gathers information from newspapers and TV, but are less attentive and less involved than the informed, multi-media, high exposure group.[13]

The information available to illustrate these stratification groups is sparse, yet very instructive. One means of measurement is to see which type of media are attended by the more knowledgeable people. Table 11.4, from the Key study, is a simple comparison of the media habits with issue familiarity. Although small in number, citizens who rely on magazines rank higher in willingness to express opinions on issues and in their disposition to appraise governmental performance on issues than other media followers. Next most important were those who relied on a combination of media, usually magazines, newspapers, radio, and TV. The relationship is clear throughout. The more informed citizens attend the harder to follow media—magazines, newspapers, or combined media; and, the less informed citizens follow the easier media—radio and TV.[14] Of course, those who do not follow the campaign at all tend to rank lowest in issue familiarity. It appears that the issue-familiar audience gets its information from different channels than the less informed voters.

Table 11.4 Most Important Source of Campaign Information
in Relation to Issue Familiarity[a]

Issue Familiarty	Most Important Source					
	Maga-zines	Combina-tions of media	News-papers	TV	Radio	Didn't follow campaign
High 4	54%	42%	35%	32%	24%	11%
3	25	32	28	25	23	12
2	14	11	21	20	15	14
Low 1	7	15	16	23	38	63
	100%	100%	100%	100%	100%	100%
N	80	47	423	862	185	147

[a]The question was: "Of all these ways of following the campaign, which one would you say you got the most information from—newspapers, radio, television or magazines?"

Data Source: *Survey Research Center, University of Michigan, 1956.*

Source: V.O. Key, Jr., *Public Opinion and American Democracy,* (New York: Alfred A. Knopf, 1961), p. 347.

As one would expect, those who follow media more closely in campaigns have different political characteristics than persons with less media exposure. The higher the level of media exposure (as measured by the number of media the respondent reported exposure to during the campaign), the more likely one is to talk to others to persuade them to vote for one of the parties or candidates. Almost half of those who attended all four media measured tried to convince someone, whereas only 18 percent of those who followed one medium claimed to have done so, and less than one in ten of those who did not follow the campaign in the media talked to someone.[15] Stouffer's study of the relationship of community leaders and nonleaders revealed that the leaders were more likely to obtain their public affairs information from the media than in "conversations" with people, suggesting that community leaders are more likely to attend the media.[16] It has also been found that those high in campaign media exposure (measured by recall of campaign media items and recognition of sample items) belong to more community organizations.[17] In the same study it was also found that the higher the person's level of general mass media exposure, the greater the level of political media exposure.[18]

These various studies of the campaign communication audiences appear to identify three types of campaign followers: (1) heavy followership of a few who closely follow the campaign through a number of media; (2) the vast group of persons who moderately expose themselves to the campaign, through one or two of the easier media, and, (3) those who do not follow the campaign. These groups vary in levels of political information, involvement, and personal characteristics—those who attend more than one media being more informed and more involved.

With these characteristics in mind, political scientists have begun to study the dynamics of the relationship between the flow of information and the vote. In a well-known study, "Information Flow and the Stability of Partisan Attitudes," Converse confirmed the contention that interelection vote changes (persons who change either their turnout or vote-direction intentions between elections) tend to be those having the lowest levels of political information. Interelection changes in the vote are most likely among those who are least exposed to political communication. Table 11.5, a compilation from a number of studies, provides support for the proposition that the least informed or least exposed voters are also the most apt to change from one election to the next. Converse explains this phenomenon on the basis of the fact that more informed and attentive voters are more likely to be in a party context, and the information they receive is channeled into what they already know and think, whereas the less attentive are more subject to the short-term forces of the particular campaign. (The most changeable voters were those minimally exposed to mass media.) But, since these voters are less attentive, something of a paradox is presented:

On the one hand, such voters show a high susceptibility to short-term change in partisan attitudes *provided that any new information reaches them at all.* On the other hand, when the flow of information through society is weak, these are the individuals who are *most* likely to experience no new information intake, and hence are individuals *least likely to show changes in patterns of behavior,* if indeed they are constrained to behave at all.[19]

Converse thus assumed that in any single election, the early intentions of those who experience no new information intake should remain stable and correlate with existing party loyalties. Those who are less involved should be pure partisan voters.[20] Since the most and least involved are expected to be the most stable in their vote intentions for different reasons, Converse predicted and found the most changeable groups within an election were the groups between those with the very highest and very lowest exposure to communication.

Edward Dreyer tested the Converse assumptions over a period of four elections, using the same tests and procedures. Dreyer found that with each succeeding election from 1952 to 1968 Converse's assumptions began to break down. Over the years, there came to be very little difference in the changeability of the vote between those of low and high exposure. More importantly, Dreyer found that in each succeeding election the relationship between party identification and the party vote declines at virtually every level of media exposure. Dreyer concludes that Converse's 1952 findings may be the exception rather than the rule.[21]

Table 11.5   Vote Stability and Change in Relation to
Political Communication

	Proportion Supporting Same Party by Exposure to Political Communication				
	Lowest				Highest
Converse's panel, 1956-60[a]	44%		61%		81%
Butler and Stokes' British panel, 1960-64[b]	57	71	75	80	83
SRC American recalled at[c]					
1960-64	47	58	67	67	71
1964-68	50	64	68	66	75

[a]Recomputed from data presented in "Information Flow and the Stability of Partisan Attitudes," Table 8-1, p. 139.

[b]*Political Change in Britain,* Table 10.4, p. 221.

[c]Inter-University Consortium for Political Research, 1964 and 1968 Presidential Election Studies.

Source: Edward C. Dreyer, "Media Use and Electoral Choices," *Public Opinion Quarterly,* XXXV (Winter, 1971-72), p. 547.

Dobson and St. Angelo have attempted to clarify both Dreyer and Converse by examining the relationship between changes in party identification, vote switching, and media use in a panel study (re-examination of the same respondents over time). They discovered three related findings. First, there are clear patterns of variation in party attachments over time. Second, voters with low media involvement did not seem to be disproportionately represented among vote switchers. Almost half of those voters who were unstable between the two presidential elections studied attended the media at a high rate, whereas the low media attenders accounted for less than 20 percent of the vote switchers. Third, those who ranked high in media involvement and changed their vote and party identification tended to change in a linear fashion—to the next or to a close degree of party attachment, whereas low-media-involvement voters who switch tend to do so in a more random fashion.[22] By examination of the actual movement of individual voters over time (the other studies examined different groups of individuals representing the same electorate at different points in time) the authors demonstrated that there, indeed, is more fluctuation in voting among high media attenders.

THE CHARACTER OF MEDIA AUDIENCES

There are not only different levels of media attendance in terms of numbers, but, as one would expect, there are notable behavioral and demographic differences among the audiences of the various media. Different political stratification groups pay different levels of attention to the campaign, attend different kinds of media, put their faith in different media, receive different levels of information, and select certain portions of the media.

Overall media exposure is high in the United States, particularly in the case radio, television, and newspapers, when compared with other countries, developed and less developed. While there are some differences according to levels of education and income, American media attendance is quite high for all population groups, even in comparison with similar countries, particularly in the low effort electronic media, where the cost of obtaining equipment is not a prohibitive factor.[23]

Within this broad spectrum of exposure there are different characteristics of American media audiences. Newspapers and magazines are considered "high-effort" media, and they are read by the more educated, those with more professional and managerial occupations, high-income persons, those with a high socioeconomic index, and those who consider themselves to be middle class. By contrast, the greater proportion of non-readers are semi-skilled and skilled workers, farmers, those with less than an eighth-grade education, those with incomes under $5,000, those with a low socioeconomic index, and those who consider themselves to be working class.[24] A study of the news-following effort of ghetto residents indicated that they depend almost entirely on the evening television newscast for news outside the neighborhood. They did not supplement that news with additional information from other media.[25] It has also been demonstrated that use of the "high effort" media—newspapers, magazines, and books—is not only positively correlated with high education, but also with the skills one has and the role created by education. The job an educated person has blends with more opportunity to follow printed media, as compared to the less educated or those with occupations which do not afford as many reading opportunities. Moreover, the time demands of the more educated reduce the amount of time available to spend attending media, and when the educated select media other than television, the time that would otherwise be spent viewing is pre-empted. The less educated person has fewer role demands on his time and is able to view at a greater level of satisfaction.[26]

The media also vary in terms of the credibility placed on them. A number of studies have indicated that people are more inclined to believe reports of news on television than in newspapers. About half of all citizens tend to believe TV, about one-third believe newspapers, and about one in ten say they are most inclined to believe radio or magazines.[27] Television apparently is given high marks because the person can "see what is happening" more readily, and newspapers are also given a higher bias rating. Those that believed newspapers more tended to express confidence in the completeness of the account and the greater amount of time available to digest the accuracy of the account.[28] Younger people tend to put considerably more confidence in television than persons over fifty.[29] One study revealed no relationship between party identification and media credibility, or even among independents who leaned toward one party. Independents who do not lean to either party are the only group most likely to rate newspapers more truthful and accurate. This study also revealed that those who are active in three or more organizations, or are organization leaders, place greater faith in newspapers than in television.[30] Nevertheless, most persons of various occupational, income, and socioeconomic groups rated TV as more believable.[31] Television's greater believability was attributed by one journalist to the fact that "In terms of the receiver the more sense modalities involved the greater the realism. In terms of the message, the more dimensions or channels involved, the greater the realism. . .television news, presented with sound, pictures in motion and even color, outclasses other media in stimulating reality for the receiver."[32]

Television is not only the most believed medium, but it is the most available and, thus, the best attended. The high-effort media require one to not only select the medium, but, attend it for the most part, to the exclusion of other activities. McLuhan refers to print media as "hot media" because one cannot read and do other things, and, because reading requires more total concentration. Electronic media are "cooler" because attendance requires less attention, and it is possible, and very often probable, that one is doing something else simultaneously.[33] Moreover, the overall audience for TV is highest, those who attend the high-effort media also attend the lower-effort media, such as radio and TV. Indeed, Converse found that media attendance for political information very closely follows Guttman scalar patterns from the highest to the lowest effort media:

That is, people who report having drawn political information from magazines are very likely to report having monitored newspapers and a spoken medium as well. People who report the monitoring of newspapers do not in large measure read magazines, but are very likely to have monitored radio or television. Among people who have monitored one of the spoken media, there are a disproportionate number who have monitored nothing else.[34]

Converse's findings preceded the dominance of television. Today, television is undoubtedly the most universal source of political information.

Television not only reaches the largest audience, but it has a greater chance of reaching a broader spectrum of voters in a campaign. Television makes it possible to see the candidates personally, despite tendencies of people to seek favorable information. (See Chapter 3.) It seems difficult to avoid candidate television appearances. A study of candidate exposure by the Cunningham and Walsh advertising agency revealed that only 14 percent saw neither candidate, and about one in ten saw only one of the candidates. More importantly, as Figure 11.1 indicates, about two-thirds of the electorate saw both candidates—Rockefeller voters saw Harriman and Harriman voters saw Rockefeller. Few voters were selective in viewing candidates in this New York gubernatorial campaign. Television apparently made it difficult for voters to select out the opposition candidate.

When television formats are shorter and the candidate does not necessarily appear, the rate of attendance and nonselectivity appears to hold up. A study of the amount of viewing of Colorado campaign spots on television revealed that between 70 and 80 percent of viewers, regardless of the amount of TV viewing they did, viewed spots for both candidates. The more interested the viewer was in the campaign, the more likely the person was to view both candidates. Supporters of the Republican candidate Love and the Democratic candidate Hogan showed only a slight tendency to select out spots favorable to the candidate they preferred, most followed both. Those who were undecided showed a slightly greater tendency to follow both. The data are presented in Table 11.6. The authors of this study concluded that voters tended to view a greater number of ads for the candidate who was advertising most heavily, and the pervasiveness of TV spot advertising apparently overcame selective exposure tendencies.[35] In a similar vein, a study of Nixon and McGovern commercials revealed that recall of commercials for both candidates increases with the amount of viewing time, the level of political interest, among split-ticket voters, and among independents. Overall viewer awareness also increased with the frequency of advertising by the candidates.[36]

Merely attending a medium does not necessarily mean one follows it closely, the attention given to a medium varies considerably. The study of TV spots in Wisconsin and Colorado revealed that only 28 percent of the exposed voters payed close attention to the ads, 42 percent paid some attention, and 29 percent paid little attention. A similar process of selectivity occurs with

Figure 11.1 Television Exposure of Voters to Candidates

	TOTAL VOTERS	ROCKEFELLER VOTERS	HARRIMAN VOTERS
Saw Neither	14% (100%)	15% (100%)	13% (100%)
Saw Mr. Harriman Only	9%	8%	9%
Saw Mr. Rockefeller Only	11%	12%	9%
Saw Both Candidates	66%	65%	69%
Saw Either or Both	86%	85%	87%
Saw Mr. Rockefeller	77%	77%	78%
Saw Mr. Harriman	75%	73%	78%

Source: Cunningham and Walsh, Television and the Political Candidate (New York: Cunningham & Walsh, Inc., 1959), p. 16.

newspapers. A newspaper in Ohio once plastered the front page with an editorial endorsement of a presidential candidate, and during the campaign followed it up with front page editorials. Yet a few months later, in the heat of the campaign, 59 percent of the sample did not know which candidate the paper was supporting.[37] A survey of newspaper readers in Albany, New York once revealed that 47 percent read only the headlines and skimmed the paper for national and international news whereas less than 10 percent read the paper very carefully and another 19 percent read the paper carefully but skipped some things.[38] Exposure does not guarantee attentiveness.

Table 11.6   Campaign Television Advertising Recognition in the 1970 Colorado Gubernatorial Campaign

Ads Noticed	Amount of TV Viewing:		
	Light Viewers	Moderate Viewers	Heavy Viewers
	N=46	N=102	N=102
Both candidates	74%	81%	85%
One candidate only	26	19	15
	Interest in Campaign:		
	Low Interest	Moderate Interest	High Interest
	N=22[*]	N=85	N=97
Both candidates	77%	82%	85%
One candidate only	23	18	15
	Candidate Preference:		
	Favor Love	Favor Hogan	Won't Say, Undecided
	N=100[*]	N=51	N=53
Both candidates	82%	80%	89%
One candidate only: Love	11	4	2
One candidate only: Hogan	7	16	9

[*]Excludes respondents viewing less than one hour of television per day, to help control the effect of the opportunity factor.

Source: Lawrence Bowen, Charles Atkin, Kenneth Scheinkopf and Oguz Nayman, "How Voters React to Electronic Political Advertising: An Investigation of the 1970 Election Campaigns in Wisconsin and Colorado," Paper presented to the 26th Annual Conference of the American Association for Public Opinion Research, 1971.

This brief reveiw of media audiences reveals that there is considerable differentiation on the basis of the number and types of media attended, the interest and involvement in politics, attentiveness to the campaign, demographic characteristics, credibility, amount of exposure, and selectivity of exposure. The mass media audience is not necessarily an undifferentiated audience. As the authors of a well known communications text claim, mass communication does not mean communication for everyone, but a selection of *classes*—groups or special publics, which might be large numerically—within the *masses*. The media and the audiences come together through a process of mutual selection. Although these may be overlapping, the audience may be quite different from one medium to another. Even within a single medium, the audience may differ in composition between units. The various media and their audience come together by the content that is presented.[39] This is why voters, audiences, readerships, information bits, time slots, and positions are so often based on segmentation.

TYPES OF CAMPAIGN MEDIA MESSAGES

It is now common practice to divide campaign media into two categories, controlled and uncontrolled. The former refers to those communications which the campaigner can create, produce, purchase, and place—advertisements, brochures, telephone messages, billboards, and campaign-worker appeals. The latter refers to communication activities over which the campaigner does not have direct and complete control--news coverage, press conferences, debates, newspaper and magazine stories, editorials, interviews and talk shows.[40] A very popular book (*The Selling of the President*) about how Nixon's 1968 campaign media team controlled his media presentation, and made Mr. Nixon into something that he was not, actually covered only the controlled media portion of the campaign. As political consultant Joseph Napolitan claims, it is not unusual to find a candidate who appears very slick and smooth in his paid material, and not so slick and smooth in his uncontrolled media. Some handle both well, and consultants increasingly recognize the importance of both, and spend considerable effort in coaching candidates to handle both.[41]

The reason why both types of media are important in a campaign is because information flows from both. Voters do not get party, candidate, and issue information exclusively from spots, billboards, and brochures, but also from news stories, talk shows and educational programs. Walter DeVries' study of ticket splitting and undecided voters attempted to get voters to rate the importance of various controlled and uncontrolled media in terms of their voting decision. A 1970 sample of Michigan voters was asked to examine a list of 35 possible media sources. Each medium was rated on an eleven point (0 to 10) scale in terms of how important an impact the medium might have on the way they make up their minds on political matters. DeVries categorized those rankings 5.0, or higher, as very important; 3.0 to 4.9 as important, and media rated

2.9, or lower, as not important. Using this rating, those ranked highest included contacts with candidates, talks with friends, newscasts, news stories, editorials, documentaries, and educational programs. In the intermediate category were talks with party workers, political mailings, advertisements, brochures, and party appeals. In the least important category were billboards, telephone messages, magazine advertisements, and entertainment formats. As DeVries points out, except for contacts with candidates, the more important media were the uncontrolled media—television news and documentaries, newspaper stories and editorials, television educational programs, television editorials, and talk shows (in that order). Many controlled media commonly used in campaigns ranked very low: newspaper ads (22nd), brochures (23rd), television ads (24th), mail (27th), billboards (31st) and telephone messages (32nd).[42]

DeVries' analysis is centered on the conversion effect. He unfortunately does not indicate whether or not controlled media has a relatively greater effect on the large group of decided voters, that is, do advertisements have the effect of reinforcing those who are committed. Similarly, controlled media might be instrumental in activating latent feelings, particularly of straight-ticket voters and those who decide during the campaign. Also, certain low-ranked, controlled media may have other effects besides influencing a voting decision—telephone messages may stimulate citizens to turnout at the polls and vote. Moreover, there are those who would argue, given the complex processes involved in a voting decision, that it is difficult for a voter to really know which media are indeed the more important, not to speak of the fact that voters may claim that certain uncontrolled media are important to sound more informed, when in fact it was something else. No self-respecting poll respondent would admit to being influenced by a billboard. Nevertheless, the data presented earlier indicates that there is a news and educational format—information seeking strata of the voting population and DeVries and Tarrance perform the important service of indicating the importance of *both* controlled and uncontrolled media; particularly in reaching the important and increasing group of voters who split their tickets and decide during the campaign.

Patterson and McClure studied the relative influence of campaign television viewing in the 1972 campaign with particular attention to spots. The thrust of their findings indicates a much more significant role for controlled media and a less significant role for uncontrolled media. First, they found that exposure to television news had only a minimal impact on voters awareness of candidates' issue positions. Second, when impact due to television news exposure existed, it was limited to a few issues and to voters who had low exposure to newspapers, whereas newspapers had a substantial impact on almost all issues. Third, exposure to television political spots had a significant impact on voters' issue awareness. They found the commercials to have significant issue content and the exposure to them contributed significantly to attitude change, to movement of voters, and to vote switching (most likely in the direction of basic predispositions), and that commercials can penetrate voter defense mechanisms about as frequently as other information sources. Fourth, the

Table 11.7 Rating of Controlled and Uncontrolled Media
Factors in Influencing Voting Decisions,
Gubernatorial Undecideds and Ticket-Splitters*
(May, 1970; N = 809)

Media	Guber-natorial undecided	Ticket-splitters
Inter-personal		
Talks with family	5.5	5.6
Contact with candidates	5.0	5.2
Talks with friends	4.8	5.0
Talks with political party workers	4.3	4.2
Talks with work associates	4.3	4.3
Talks with neighbors	3.8	3.9
Audio-visual		
Television newscasts	6.7	6.8
Television documentaries and specials	6.5	6.6
Television editorials	5.7	5.6
Television talk shows	5.6	5.6
Television educational programs	5.6	5.9
Television advertisements	3.6	3.6
Television entertainers	2.6	2.5
Movies	1.8	1.8
Stage plays	1.4	1.4
Audio		
Radio educational programs	5.3	5.5
Radio newcasts	5.3	5.5
Radio talk shows	4.5	4.9
Radio editorials	4.2	4.5
Telephone campaign messages	2.3	2.0
Phonograph records	1.3	1.1
Print		
Newspaper editorials	5.8	5.9
Newspaper stories	5.8	6.0
Magazine editorials	4.3	4.2
Political brochures	3.8	3.6
Magazine stories	3.8	4.0
Newspaper advertisements	3.8	3.7
Books	3.6	3.6
Political mailings	3.4	3.3
Magazine advertisements	2.9	2.6
Billboards	2.4	2.1
Organizational		
The Democratic Party	5.3	4.5
The Republican Party	3.6	4.1
Membership in religious organizations	3.4	3.1
Membership in professional or business organizations	3.2	3.4

*Market Opinion Research.

Source: Walter DeVries and V. Lance Tarrance, Jr., *The Ticket-Splitter* (Grand Rapids, Michigan: Eerdmans, 1972), pp. 75–76.

effects of political advertising were most obvious among voters with low exposure to news sources. The authors conclude that television news had minimal effects because it simply did not provide voters with much information about candidates' issue positions, preferring action film of campaign activity and pseudo-events, whereas television advertising contained more issue content (twice as much in the last two months). They explain that the format for TV news is an obstacle to presenting issue information. The brevity of its stories often precludes explicit linkages of events with candidates' issue positions.[43]

The Patterson and McClure studies must be understood in their context. In addition to significant methdological and technique differences as compared with DeVries, their studies are based primarily on issue information. Next to party, candidate factors seem to be the most important (and most ascendent) in voting. A great deal of candidate information can be conveyed and sought through television news. Indeed, there is some evidence that voters place more emphasis on television for candidate information and newspapers for issue information.[44] Also, television and other news exposure may serve to call attention to a candidacy and campaign, thus cueing voters to attend to paid advertising. The reverse is probable too. Another question raised is whether or not political advertising contributes equally according to political information levels, or does it contribute disproportionately to low-effort media attenders? Some will contend that neither television newscasts nor commercials constitute the totality of coverage; there are longer news formats, talk shows, telethons, and paid program time. Other questions will undoubtedly be raised about the Patterson and McClure studies. However, they do serve to indicate that political spots (the element of controlled media that are commonly labeled as easy to tune out and ineffective and have been attacked for being issueless) are not only effective but deliver issue content.

CAMPAIGN MESSAGE STRATEGIES

Presently there appears to be two schools of thought concerning use of media in campaigns to reinforce, activate, and convert. One interpretation, represented by Dan Nimmo, following much of the research on communication audiences and voting behavior in the past two decades, breaks down campaign media audiences into two groups. The first group is composed of users and believers of print media. They are also likely to be multi-media users, members of interest groups, concerned and interested in political affairs, and possessing moderate to strong loyalties to one of the two dominant parties. These voters are the likely early deciders in a campaign. All of these factors lend to appeals designed to reinforce their existing commitments, not to convert them. In the second, and growing, group are those who rely on electronic media, primarily television, and are persons who isolate themselves from other media. While containing voters from all socioeconomic strata, within it are large numbers of persons with: low to moderate incomes, with high-school educations, little interest in politics, and more experience in evaluating television, film and recording personalities than in deciding ambiguous public issues. This voter, says Nimmo, is a member of the vast audience built primarily by commercial television and radio for purposes of marketing products, and does not care much about politics. It is the group which occupies the attention of professional media men.[45] Appeals presumably are designed to activate latent support and convert voters in this group.

The other, somewhat different interpretation is based on the notion that persons who are exposed to a greater number and quality of campaign information are more likely to stray from their professed party identification and become ticket splitters. Their arguments are based on findings similar to the Dreyer study, that indicates a steadily declining influence of party identification on the vote, at all levels of media exposure, even among those who follow many media.[46] A national survey by Market Opinion Research reported by DeVries indicated that ticket splitters are among the heavier media users: they are highest in readership of newspaper campaign stories, they ranked between regular Republican voters and regular Democratic voters in magazine reading, and they were the largest group of viewers of political talks or shows.[47] DeVries and others reveal that ticket splitters tend to come from all socio-demographic groupings, although they tend to be the moderate income, professional and technical person, who is more interested in politics.[48] From findings like these, media people are beginning to formulate appeals aimed at the ticket splitter, with heavy doses of uncontrolled media, and controlled media which has the appearance of a news announcement or story; aimed at activating and converting more regular and more interested followers of the campaign.[49]

While these two formulations represent different approaches to media strategy, the dynamics of the voting process are such that most campaign communicators must engage in reinforcement, activation and conversion, and that some attention is aimed at the committed and some to the switchable. Media strategies, like general campaign strategies really are aimed at all of these processes.

One can then link what has been illustrated about voting, strategies and media communications by the following summary:

1. Campaign settings make a difference in the type of media campaign one would have. One would design vastly different messages and use different media for an incumbent from the majority party running for re-election to the U.S. Senate than a minority party challenger running for the county board.

2. Recent studies of voting behavior and the increased number of split outcomes indicate that fewer persons are locked into a party affiliation when voting. Media appeals and formats can be designed to reach the increasing proportion of ticket splitters.

3. Whether partisan or ticket-splitter, reinforcement or conversion, these themes usually represent the *emphasis* of a media campaign, rather than the

totality. Ticket-splitter oriented campaigns ordinarily have the task of holding the party faithful in line, and some media and messages are designed accordingly. Likewise, media campaigns designed at reinforcement of those already committed involve some attempts to convert. Indeed, the electronic media have not proven to be very good instruments of partisan reinforcement, so that the campaign predicated on this stratagem ordinarily makes other appeals via radio and television.

A final point in regard to media in campaigns refers to the difficulty of determining the precise impact of a particular message. Communications research is not at the point where one can determine the conditions under which certain messages can be linked with categories of voters who are reinforced, activated, or converted. Moreover, it is highly possible that a single message through a single medium can have multiple and even unintended effects. The communication process through media in campaigns may have many consequences, only a limited number of which have beeen explained.

In fact, the findings exceed the explanations. Communications research has indicated that personal sources, such as the personal integrity of the presenter, count for more than the method of presentation. When the communicator's name is known to the audience, and is considered to be believable, the image of the medium is enhanced, particularly on television.[50] A study of the impact of television in campaigns indicated that voters were considerably more likely to recall the occasion of a television appearance than to recall the content.[51] These isolated findings reveal the complexity of the communication process, and the many implications of them.

Media campaigns based on such inferences should be considered as part of an integrated package. Spots and billboards may not contain sophisticated issue information about the candidate, but they may call attention to the fact that a candidate is running so that voters will then read or view the information on a news program or article. A television newsclip showing the candidate campaigning at plant gates may cue a voter to read an editorial about the candidate or to peruse a piece of literature left on the door step. Many things happen between the multiple stimuli of campaign communication and the response of a vote. As John Maloney explains, the work of translating (advertising) research into mass persuasion is predicated on the most basic elements that are common to almost all communication and behaviorial science theory:

1. We are always dealing with STIMULUS, INTEGRATION and RESPONSE.

2. The audience takes in or attends to those stimuli which stand out most against background noise or competing stimuli, favoring those most compatible with pre-existing memories, interests or curiosities.

3. These stimuli are integrated with memories from prior learning or experience and the effects of such integration are stored in the

memory structure. They remain there until they are themselves buried (that is, 'forgotten') or alerted by later inputs, or until they are reactivated to form a decision, a response or a pattern of response.

4. Meanwhile the imbalance, or unfinished business within the audience's memory structure, provides the interests or feedbacks which partially control attention to subsequent inputs.[52]

Campaign communication, then, requires the use of many media and messages to break through competition, ensure compatibility, stimulate curiosity, link with prior experience, and retrieve from memory storage, ranging from personal conversation to television.

Notes to Chapter 11

1. Tony Schwartz, *The Responsive Chord* (Garden City, New York: Doubleday, 1973), p. 25.

2. With apologies to Fredrick R. Gamble's definition of advertising, quoted in William C. Rivers, Theodore Peterson, and Jay W. Jensen, *The Mass Media and Modern Society* 2nd ed. (San Francisco: Rinehart Press, 1971), p. 236.

3. Robert Agranoff, *The New Style in Election Campaigns* (Boston: Holbrook Press, 1972), pp. 15-20.

4. Lester G. Telser, "Advertising and the Consumer," in *Advertising and Society,* ed. Yale Brozen, (New York: New York Univ. Press, 1974), pp. 26-27.

5. Rivers, The Mass Media and Modern Society, pp. 18-19.

6. Ibid., pp. 18-20.

7. M. Margaret Conway, "Voter Information Sources in a Nonpartisan Local Election," *Western Political Quarterly* 21 (1968): 71-72.

8. Paul F. Lazarsfeld, Bernard R. Berelson, and Hazel Gaudet, *The People's Choice* (New York: Duell, Sloan and Pearce, 1944), p. 121.

9. Bernard R. Berelson, Paul F. Lazarsfeld and William N. McPhee, *Voting* (Chicago: Univ. of Chicago Press, 1954), p. 240.

10. Lazarsfeld, *The People's Choice*, pp. 121-122.

11. Berelson et al., *Voting*, p. 241.

12. Phillip E. Converse, "Information Flow and the Stability of Partisan Attitudes," in Angus Campbell, Phillip E. Converse, Warren E. Miller and Donald E. Stokes, *Elections and the Political Order* (New York: John Wiley, 1966); Edward C. Dreyer, "Media Use and Electoral Choices: Some Political Consequences of Information Exposure," *Public Opinion Quarterly* 35 (1971-1972);

V.O. Key, Jr., *Public Opinion and American Democracy* (New York: Alfred A. Knopf, 1961), pp. 357-69.

13. Key, *Public Opinion and American Democracy,* pp. 348, 357.

14. Converse, "Information Flow and the Stability of Partisan Attitudes," pp. 152-53.

15. Key, *Public Opinion and American Democracy,* p. 361.

16. Samuel A. Stouffer, *Communism, Conformity and Civil Liberties* (New York: John Wiley, 1966), p. 227.

17. Berelson, *Voting,* p. 243.

18. Ibid., p. 244.

19. Converse, "Information Flow and the Stability of Partisan Attitudes," p. 144.

20. Ibid., p. 143.

21. Dreyer, "Media Use and Electoral Choices," pp. 552-53.

22. Douglas Dobson and Douglas St. Angelo, "Party Identification and the Floating Vote: Some Dynamics," *American Political Science Review* 69 (1975): 487-88.

23. Bradley S. Greenberg and Hideya Kumata, "National Sample Predictors of Mass Media Use," *Journalism Quarterly* 45 (1968): 644-66.

24. Bruce H. Westley and Werner J. Severin, "A Profile of the Daily Newspaper Non-Reader," *Journalism Quarterly* 41 (1964): 46; see also, Key, *Public Opinion and American Democracy,* p. 349 and Berelson, *Voting,* pp. 241-43.

25. Thomas H. Allen, "Mass Media Use Patterns in a Negro Ghetto," *Journalism Quarterly* 45 (1968): 525-27.

26. Merrill Samuelson, Richard F. Carter and Lee Ruggels, "Education, Available Time, and Use of Mass Media," *Journalism Quarterly* 40 (1963): 492-96.

27. Richard F. Carter and Bradley S. Greenberg, "Newspapers or Television: Which Do You Believe?" *Journalism Quarterly* 42 (1965): 31-32; Harvey K. Jacobson, "Mass Media Believability: A Study of Receiver Judgments," *Journalism Quarterly* 46 (1969): 23; Burns W. Roper, *What People Think of Television and Other Mass Media,* 1959-1972 (New York: Television Information Office, 1973); Bruce H. Westley and Werner J. Severin, "Some Correlates of Media Credibility," *Journalism Quarterly* 41 (1964): 326.

28. Carter and Greenberg, "Newspapers or Television: Which Do You Believe?" p. 33.

29. Ibid.

30. Westley and Severin, "Some Correlates of Media Credibility," p. 331.

31. Ibid., p. 328.

32. Jacobson, "Mass Media Believability," p. 27.

33. Marshall McLuhan, *Understanding Media* (New York: McGraw-Hill, 1964), ch. 1.

34. Converse, "Information Flow and the Stability of Partisan Attitudes," p. 152-53.

35. Lawrence Bowen, Charles K. Atkin, Kenneth G. Scheinkopf and Oguz B. Nayman, "How Voters React to Electronic Political Advertising: An Investigation of the 1970 Election Campaigns in Wisconsin and Colorado," Paper presented to the 26th Annual Conference of the American Association for Public Opinion Research, 1971.

36. Thomas E. Patterson and Robert D. McClure, "Political Advertising on Television: Spot Commercials in the 1972 Presidential Election," *Maxwell Review* 9 (1973): 59-62.

37. Elmo C. Wilson, "The Press and Public Opinion in Erie County, Ohio," *Journalism Quarterly* 18 (1941): 14-17.

38. Key, *Public Opinion and American Democracy*, p. 352.

39. Rivers, *The Mass Media and Modern Society*, pp. 278-79.

40. Joseph Napolitan, *The Election Game* (Garden City, New York, 1972), p. 67.

41. Ibid.

42. Walter DeVries and V. Lance Tarrance, *The Ticket-Splitter* (Grand Rapids, Michigan: William Eerdmans, 1972), pp. 77-78.

43. Thomas E. Patterson and Robert D. McClure, *Political Advertising: Voter Reaction to Televised Political Commercials* (Princeton, N.J.: Citizens Research Foundation, 1973), pp. 10-35; Thomas E. Patterson and Robert D. McClure, "Television News and Televised Political Advertising: Their Impact on the Voter," paper delivered at the National Conference on Money and Politics, sponsored by the Citizens Research Foundation, February, 1974.

44. F. Gerald Kline, "Mass Media and the General Election Process: Evidence and Speculation," *Maxwell Review* 9 (1973): 43-44.

45. Dan Nimmo, *The Political Persuaders* (Englewood Cliffs, N.J.: Prentice-Hall, 1970), pp. 117-18.

46. Dreyer, "Media Use and Electoral Choice," p. 552.

47. Republicans were nearly as high as ticket splitters in most cases, suggesting that socioeconomic correlates of high media use may have greater explanatory power, DeVries, *The Ticket-Splitter*, pp. 78-85.

48. Ibid., ch. 3.

49. Hank Parkinson, *Winning Campaigns With Publicity* (Wichita, Kansas: Campaign Associates Press, 1973), p. 15.

50. Leslie W. Sargent, "Communicator Image and News Reception," *Journalism Quarterly* 42 (1965): 41-42.

51. *Television and the Political Candidate* (New York: Cunningham and Walsh, 1959), pp. 21-22.

52. John C. Maloney, "Advertising Research and an Emerging Science of Mass Persuasion," *Journalism Quarterly* 41 (1964): 525-26.

For Further Reading and Research

Conway, M. Margaret. "Voter Information Sources in a Nonpartisan Local Election." *Western Political Quarterly* 21 (1968): 69-77.

Dobson, Douglas and St. Angelo, Douglas. "Party Identification and the Floating Vote: Some Dynamics." *American Political Science Review* 69 (1975): 481-90.

Dreyer, Edward C. "Media Use and Electoral Choice." *Public Opinion Quarterly* 35 (1971-72): 544-53.

Greenberg, Bradley S. and Kumata, Hideya. "National Sample Predictors of Mass Media Use" *Journalism Quarterly* 40 (1968): 644-66.

Kelley, Jr., Stanley "Elections and the Mass Media." *Law and Contemporary Problems* 28 (1962): 307-26.

Patterson, Thomas E. and McClure, Robert D. "Political Advertising on Television: Spot Commercials in the 1972 Presidential Election." *Maxwell Review* 9 (1973): 57-69.

——— . *Political Advertising: Voter Reaction to Televised Political Commercials.* Princeton, N.J.: Citizens Research Foundation, 1973.

Lang, Kurt and Lang, Gladys. *Politics and Television.* Chicago: Quadrangle, 1968.

Mickelson, Sig. *The Electric Mirror: Politics in an Age of Television.* New York: Dodd, Mead, 1972.

Schwartz, Tony. *The Responsive Chord.* Garden City, N.Y.: Doubleday, 1973.

Rivers, William L.; Peterson, Theodore; and Jensen, Jay W. *The Mass Media in Modern Society,* 2d ed. San Francisco: Rinehart, 1971.

Roper, Burns W. *What People Think of Television and Other Mass Media, 1959-1972.* New York: Television Information Office, 1973.

Rubin, Bernard. *Political Television.* Belmont, California: Wadsworth, 1967.

Media
Planning

The use of media in campaigns, just as its counterparts in nonpolitical areas, is based on a complex of findings, propositions, hypotheses, and conventional wisdoms. As for so many other endeavors that involve the application of techniques based on the study of human behavior, much of it is limited in scope and explanation, conjectural, contradictory. Media techniques are, therefore, a combination of art and science, but resemble art more. Some is unsophisticated and successful, some is sophisticated and unsuccessfull, and the converse. The media planning process, similar to so many other facets of the campaign, is ordinarily based on translating the best scientific information available into reasonable judgments about the voting processes one wants to achieve, defining the messages which will ahieve those results, selecting the vehicles for communication, and implementing the plans.[1]

The approach of advertising and media people who work in political campaigns reflects this scientific uncertainty in their art. Sound specialist Tony Schwartz, a follower of Marshall McLuhan, believes in a "nonlinear" approach to "getting inside people." To do this Schwartz uses multiple sound tracks, reflecting his conviction that the younger generation, freed by television from the linear, print-oriented world of their elders, can absorb two or three different levels of meaning simultaneously. For example, Schwartz used ink blot associations on the screen to link mothers, Medicare, and Hubert Humphrey.[2] In contrast, Roger Ailes believes that voters want neither dramatic presentations of the candidate and his family nor short spots. Consequently, he produces longer issue-oriented presentations, with the candidate talking.[3]

THE PLANNING PROCESS

The television viewer who observes that well-produced campaign ads are interspersed with his or her favorite programming ordinarily does not think about how the ad came about. Perhaps he or she feels that the timing is coincidental. Experienced campaigners know that some very careful analysis and plans produced the finished products. Those spots were probably planned by a combination of: the various account, creative, and art people of some ad agency; a production team; and the results of researchers, based on the demographics of audiences—the size of audiences, rates, polls, voting patterns and other population data. These are the basic inputs of the media-planning function. Obviously, many of the campaign assessment activities suggested in Chapters 4 and 5 can also be valuable tools in planning the media portion of the campaign. As will be demonstrated, media plans need not be very elaborate, but some planning based on the assessment of information judged in the context of the setting and strategy of the campaign is extremely helpful.

In larger campaigns, when media planners are used, the process is fairly standard. The first step is ordinarily a political briefing of the consultant, including political information on the district, the opponent, and, of course, the personal and political background of the candidate. Then the media specialist is given access to the information assessment in the campaign, including media, voting, census and polling (some consultants, such as Napolitan, insist on performing their own research). Where polls are used, they are ordinarily planned in consultation with the media person. At this stage media consultants and strategists decide on the need for an advertising agency, a decision which is based on a combination of whether the campaigners want to select their own creative team or accept the agency's, the amount of further media research an agency can provide, whether any agencies have the requisite political experience, and whether the planners wish to have an agency purchase their time and space.[4] In smaller scale campaigns, where the use of polls and media consultants is rare, candidates get their media-planning advice from friendly volunteers who are knowledgeable of media and advertising.

Among the more important types of media research information which are often used in campaign planning are:

1. Demographic characteristics of station coverage areas, program audiences, newspaper circulation areas and special publication readerships.
2. Station ratings, program ratings, and circulation rates, including station or paper dominance of a market.
3. An estimate of the amount of public service uncontrolled media time available in the various media.
4. Time and length of programming time available, space availability, particularly prime times and locations.
5. Station and newspaper policies regarding disclamers and length of material (e.g., some stations will not accept spots).
6. The availability and penetration of cable television and public broadcasting, and their audiences. How do color. UHF and VHF mix in the area.

7. Past histories of political broadcasting, including consultation with former candidates or other candidates who have run before.

8. Estimates of the amount of political advertising for other candidates and opposition ticket candidates that can be expected during this period.

9. Time and space purchased by opponent (advertising agencies should be able to get this information from the stations and from papers).

10. Amount of correspondence between markets for various media and identifiable voting groups.

11. Are there any peculiarities of time buying near election day, e.g., a special program or a football game.[5]

With such questions in mind, the media planner investigates all media outlets that cover the constituency.

In addition to these mass media investigations, the media planner may have to explore other advertising forms. Commercial printing firms are ordinarily checked for rates, capabilities to print different kinds of materials, copy and art requirements, production periods and deadlines, and payment arrangements. Local billboard or poster companies (listed in telephone book yellow pages) should be checked for available locations, copy services, required production time, prices for board space, paper costs, and contract terms. Mail service firms should be investigated for their scope of services, the lists they have available, time factors in production, and prices. Finally, catalogues should be obtained from novelty companies for buttons, stickers, and gadgets, plus any necessary information on ordering, delivery, and billing.

The section on polling in Chapter 5 should suggest valuable data that can be plugged into media planning: image information on the two candidates, issue identification and perceptions of issue differences among the population, size and demographic makeup of supporters, the undecided and ticket splitters, media habits by voter types, visibility and identification of the candidates, and, if the opponent is an incumbent, what is his or her job performance rating. Short of poll data, voting patterns and census information may help pinpoint the location of various voting blocs, such as regular partisans or ticket splitters, or population groups, such as high-income homeowners or pockets of high unemployment, which then can be matched with certain audience or circulation patterns. The political situation, such as any local party disputes, or conditions which relate to other candidates running for office or other contributors to the setting should be taken into account when making media plans.

Experienced media planners also like to consider the candidate's media ability as an ingredient in media plans. Which of the media will be most suitable to projecting the candidate favorably? Will the candidate appear better on radio and TV with some coaching? If the candidate does not go over well in relaxed, uncontrolled formats, then more controlled situations have to be built into the plan. These decisions are judgmental, of course, but media planning like so many other facets of campaigning, involves a combination of hard and soft data.

MEDIA SELECTION

There are many factors which go into the selection of media or the mix of media in the campaign. The initial context of considerations in the planning stage are the characteristics of the various media and their operant principles in the campaign. These characteristics and principles can be derived by blending considerations of voting, campaign and media structure, and processes with media practices. Four of the most prevalent campaign media modes—display, radio, television, and print—illustrate some important considerations for media campaigners:

1. *Display:* Used for name recognition, a quick impression, or reminders linked to other media and messages, with very short messages. A reference point for possible future action. Calls the voter's attention to candidates by using a slogan or jingle which will stick in one's mind and can connect with other media messages. Also used to reinforce the committed, through buttons, rally signs, lawn signs, etc. Requires considerable lead time and the cost per unit of contact can be expensive.

2. *Print:* For a more informed, more selective audience but more flexible in terms of targeting audiences, particularly direct mail. Can also be used to promote name recognition and reinforce campaign themes which are being projected through other media. Newspaper articles allow for more detail about candidates and issues, "fleshing out" the images of visual and auditory media, at least to the more interested and informed readership. Newspaper editorials are not as powerful as some believe, but can be influential, particularly in nonpartisan elections. Newspaper ads offer great flexibility in timing and creativity. The space can be readily broken down into a size suitable to an advertiser's budget and needs. They are less selective in terms of target audience, but have a high noticeability rate. Magazines can be used to target very specific audiences, and they reach many readers per dollar invested, but the combination of narrow audience plus cost often make them prohibitive. Literature is important for supporters to "have something," but it also can carry more detailed information, blend with themes used in the other media, and can be highly selective if different printings are targeted to different groups. Print requires less lead time and is realtively inexpensive.

3. *Radio:* A great deal of overlap between this audience and other media audiences, but can be used to reach an audience missed by the other "low effort" medium—television, particularly commuters, older people conditioned in the radio era, busy housewives, or the younger generation. Radio can be very selective, since many stations ordinarily divide up a small share of the market, appealing to different audience groupings. Radio ads are very often repetitious, serving as reminders of the candidate's name or very short messages linked to other facets of the campaign. AM radio advertising is ubiquitous and mobile; each individual listener can move and be always surrounded by its sound. Uncontrolled radio formats, such as interviews and talk shows, can be used to build up the image of a candidate. Radio can be particularly important in small constituency campaigns or where television is

not feasible. It can also be used to gain attention in campaigns where television coverage is monopolized by high visibility campaigns. Radio is the fastest or most current medium. It requires relatively little lead time and is inexpensive.

4. *Television:*   Used to reach a large audience which is relatively uninterested and uninformed about political matters, and which largely ignores print media.[6] Of all media it comes closest to the intensity of interpersonal confrontation and it permits the candidate to encounter the voter in a relaxed frame of mind, ready for whatever entertainment the medium will bring. The approach is generally less selective, although, controlled and uncontrolled media can be designed to reach various segments through spots adjacent to programs, special documentaries and news releases. News coverage can be used to convey a positive impression of the candidate, combining sight and sound. Very useful at activating latent candidate support and candidate conversion. Television has proved to be the best way for an unknown candidate to become known quickly to a large number of voters. Requires a great deal of lead time and is very expensive.[7]

In evaluating a medium one must think in terms of what one will get out of timing, scheduling, size of the audience, character of the audience and cost.

In addition to the capabilities of the media in the abstract, there are important considerations in the number of media selected. The larger the scale of the campaign the more likely campaign planners are to think in terms of a combination of media to accomplish strategic aims. The small or low budget campaign may have complex media needs but money may limit access to a single medium or limited coverage in a few media. If possible, campaigners use a number of media to get their messages across, which is known as a "media mix." A media mix is considered to offer a number of advantages over concentration in a single medium: it extends coverage and the chances of getting attention beyond what one would normally achieve with a single medium, with the advantage of diverting part of it to new sectors of the audience; it permits the communicator to segment the audience by delivering different forms of the message with different themes or appeals through different media; it permits the same individuals to be contacted within different psychological contexts, presenting the possibility of attracting attention in one environment which might not be noticed in another; and some assert that the use of multiple channels of persuasion working together improves the odds of breaking through audience defenses.[8]

Crosscutting these most basic media considerations are setting and strategy factors—the characteristics of the constituency, the nature of the office, the situation of the candidate, how the strategists have charted a path, and what they plan to do to get there. Among the most important concerns are considerations of allocation of a campaign budget in terms of the boundaries of the office sought and the boundaries of the media. The particular media chosen have "boundaries" in that they reach out into certain areas or have limited areas of coverage. A newspaper has a circulation area, a radio or television station has a particular reach, and display is primarily seen by people who live within a defined geographic area. Somehow the media planner tries for the best fit by selecting the medium which will maximize the coverage within a constituency. In a district that is made up of a portion of a city, it will ordinarily mean that electronic media will be ruled out, and campaigners will have to use direct contact or direct mail, whereas in a geographically dispersed area, newspapers, radio, and television may be the only means of maximizing reach. The office sought also helps determine media allocations. The more visible offices draw more attention-making news coverage. Also, the nature of the office sought "expects" the use of certain media. A candidate for governor or senator cannot very well remain hidden from radio, television, and newspapers; but, a candidate for state treasurer or alderman can readily run a non-media campaign. The amount of funds raised, which is somewhat determined by the size of the constituency as well as the office, also sets media allocation constraints. A campaign media planner may have to select less expensive media due to lack of funds. These three factors ordinarily work in conjunction, and they set important limitations on media selection.

One must also consider any peculiarities of the media or the voting research which may dictate the selection of certain media. For example, if a large bloc of undecided voters happen to be avid sports fans, some television adjacencies may be purchased. If, on the other hand, a particular ethnic group which traditionally supports the candidate's party appears to be slipping away, some partisan reinforcement ads in ethnic or neighborhood papers may be in order. Of course, the intent of the message is as important a consideration as the medium selected. The practicalities of these issues will be considered with a great deal more detail in this and the next two chapters. They form the initial context of media selection.

INTEGRATING MEDIA, STRATEGY, AND THEMES

While not every media tactic in a campaign needs to be part of a central theme or relate to each other exactly, campaigners ordinarily attempt to relate their basic planning themes based on their strategy to controlled and uncontrolled media plans. In a word, they try to *integrate* theme and media with strategy. The commercials that are written, where they are placed, the subject matter of news conferences, press releases and background papers, the content of radio and television programs, and other forms of advertising are designed to demonstrate some predetermined strategic principles, and they operate in some relationship to each other. In product advertising, this effort is sometimes referred to as blending messages and image creation into a "state of mind" about a product rather than attention to particular technical points. Automobile advertising, for example, very often pays less attention to information about the technical features of the machine, for messages about what the car will do for the individual, whether it be status, economy, or appeal to the opposite sex. Similar states of mind are stimulated in political campaigns by a process of integration of themes.

One interesting case study of theme integration is former Maryland Senator Joseph Tydings 1970 re-election campaign. Tydings' strategists worked out themes with a Baltimore advertising firm:

> Salter and his associated sat down with key Tydings aides sometime in the spring to talk about the campaign. Drawing upon findings from its panel interviews, the agency staff drew three ideas that they wanted to stress in advertising materials: Tydings' personal concern about individuals, his ability to 'get things done,' and his toughness of mind. These themes, it was believed, would build on the candidate's strengths—experience and independence—while dispelling suspicions about his 'aloofness.' The themes were accepted and embodied in media advertising, but they by no means constituted the overarching structure of the campaign. A campaign strategy, whether well conceived or not, may not actually be carried into daily decisions that shape speeches, press releases, and the like. Furthermore, events during the campaign may demand shifts in strategy.

> Five sixty-second 'spot' announcements were prepared for television, and they were crucial to the tone of the campaign. One, called the 'needs' spot, features a series of film clips illustrating Tydings' contributions to the state: a stoplight at a dangerous intersection, treatment for the elderly and chronically ill, and the preservation of Assateague Island for recreation. Then, as the camera showed Tydings listening intently to an out-of-focus figure in the foreground, the scene froze, and the announcer concluded: 'Joe Tydings cares. And he listens to people. Then he does something. Constructive and positive.'

> Another sixty-second spot, generally conceded to be among the most effective, featured film footage of Tydings talking to voters in various campaign settings. Meanwhile the Senator's wife was heard to say:

>> That's my husgand. . .Joe Tydings. [Noise from campaign scene heard under Mrs. Tydings' voice]. . .and this is another campaign. And that means early breakfasts. And late dinners. Eighteen hours a day. Hundreds and hundreds of people to meet. But he seems to thrive on it. He loves the chance to get out of the office and meet people. And hear about what they're thinking. He loves the chance to be able to respond to people. Firsthand.

>> [Location noise swells, then goes under as Mrs. Tydings continues] We've talked about it. And I now he's in a tough fight this year. But that's all right. It's times like these when he's strongest. He's taking his record to the people. Because he believes in the truth of what he's accomplished in the past six years. For all the people of Maryland. I think I'd admire a man like that. Even if he weren't my husband. Besides, he's my Senator. Too.

A third spot featured a crowd of children singing the state song, 'Mary-land, My Maryland.' Between stanzas the sound track went silent as the camera cut to scenes of Tydings around the state, talking to a police-man, greeting a crowd of people, sailing on an oyster boat. All three spots were designed to illustrate Tydings' personableness, forthrightness, and ability to 'get things done.'[9]

These main themes were supported by their uncontrolled media efforts, plus they tried to react to any late breaking events. A steady offering of press confer-ences, statements, news stories based on speeches, challenges to the opponent, and backgrounders were used, primarily to add flexibility to the more rigidly controlled media campaign.[10] Thus, the Tydings effort allowed for planning, integration, and flexibility by using the more controlled formats to build up the 'state of mind,' with support from the uncontrolled campaign.

In a similar fashion, the 1970 Milliken re-election campaign for Governor of Michigan was predicated on enhancing the image of the incumbent, through both controlled and uncontrolled formats. A poll indicated that an overwhelm-ing portion of the undecided voters liked Milliken for candidate factors, par-ticularly his ability to handle the job. In the final stage of the campaign, the im-portant issues in the campaign shifted to economics, and Milliken was able to capitalize on that shift through building issue appeals on top of his earlier image work, especially through print media, such as personalized direct mail and 3 million Sunday paper supplements. As a result, DeVries' research indicates Milli-ken carried the later deciders (last 5 to 7 days) by a margin of two to one. DeVries credits this shift to the campaign's ability to integrate tax issues with the earlier themes of competence in office.[11]

Blending Controlled and Uncontrolled Media

The two types of media messages are usually mixed in a campaign and some-times combined. One means is to use paid spots in a news format. Candidates reserve time very early in the campaign, and, when an important news event hap-pens, a spot is rapidly developed (usually within 24 hours) with the candidate appearing on radio and television commeting on the event. It could be after an important disclosure, a raise in rapid transit fares, a natural disaster, or any other important news. Consultant Napolitan once noticed a flaw in a statement made by an opposition Alaska candidate for governor before a hearing. He immedi-ately dictated a 60 second spot, telephoned it to an announcer who read it, re-corded it, and then fed it to a radio wire to all stations in the state, all in a matter of a few hours.[12] Consultant F. Clifton White believes that candidates should take advantage of events because of the instantaneous nature of tele-vision. A candidate appearance at an emotional event, such as the site of a natural disaster, a community confrontation, or a demonstration, identifies concern in the voter's mind, and is likely to be covered by the news media.[13]

In recent years there has been increasing effort to link controlled media with the news. A frequently used technique is the "beeper" system, sending short news release messages by telephone to radio stations. This has now been extended to television through "telenews," making sure candidates get on news programs by providing stations video tape of what the candidate says and does. A number of 1972 presidential candidates hired television production trucks to follow the candidates, tape their activities and feed it to television stations. The McGovern staff, for example, hired a TV crew to cover the Senator's California appearances. The crew video taped his talks, edited portions out, and delivered video clips to 35 stations throughout the state, mostly in small markets with limited news gathering facilities.[14] Other techniques frequently used to link the two include: building commercials that use news formats, such as those that sound and look like news; producing sound-on-film documentaries that are oriented toward news and current events, appearing as news documentaries; placing spots adjacent to newscasts, specials, and documentaries; attempting to schedule the candidate on talk and interview shows, with confrontation and conflict situations being particularly interesting; and using portions of newspaper editorials in advertisements.[15]

DeVries built a great portion of Michigan Governor William Milliken's 1970 re-election strategy around the concept of reaching the ticket-splitting and undecided voters through the uncontrolled media. The campaign was planned on the premise that the campaign must be newsworthy. The candidate must say and do important things for the reporters covering the campaign and for voters watching it. News releases were designed for audio and visual coverage, they provided tapes and clips for radio coverage. Major policy statements were handled through structured press conferences rather than large audiences. They aided those covering them by providing visuals, such as slides, tables, and charts. In addition, they used the standard techniques: telenews, employing news formats, adjacencies to newsprograms and specials, and appearances on talk and educational programs. These uncontrolled media techniques, says DeVries, means that one views the campaign as a series of news events; one thinks as a newsman.[16]

It becomes readily clear that not all uncontrolled media are completely uncontrollable, when one stimulates or attempts to structure media. Some would say these are semi-controlled media messages. However, all uncontrolled media messages are qualitatively different from messages produced and placed by the candidate, not only because what is said is not controlled, but also because the format through which it is delivered is considered to be more neutral and authoritative, and is regarded by the audience as information rather than propaganda. For these reasons contemporary campaigners make use of both controlled and uncontrolled media, the latter with various degrees of structuring by the strategists.

CREATING MESSAGES

The foregoing should suggest that messages are created to do something in a campaign; the creators have a motivational objective or strategic principle in mind. Ad man David Ogilvy believes that the advertisers "who dedicate their advertising to building the most favorable image, the most sharply defined personality for their brands are the ones who will get the largest share of these markets at the highest profit." To Ogilvy, "Every advertisement must be considered as a contribution to the complex symbol which is the brand image."[17] Of course, not all messages, product advertising or political, are predicated on building up images, but professional message creators ordinarily link messages to motivational objectives similar to Ogilvy's desire to build images.

In terms of political campaigns, we are suggesting that message creators do not forget what has already been examined in this book, in particular voting behavior, campaign communication processes, and strategic principles. Thus, campaign messages are created—

- to build up attention to the candidate to enhance candidate visibility.
- to contribute to candidate image creation; to build a state of mind about the candidate.
- to link the candidate with issues which are important to the constituency, or segments of it.
- to create new issue visibility, or activate latent feeling on an issue, then, link the candidate to this important issue.
- to identify or associate the candidate with a party grouping or other important groups in the constituency.
- to reinforce existing supporters, whether on a partisan, candidate, or issue basis.
- to activate citizens' participation in the political process, hopefully in the candidate' direction.

Therefore, campaign messages should be a product of the process of examining what the campaigners are trying to do. Some messages will reinforce partisanship, while other will be part of an image creation effort, still others will have different effects. What is important is that the message-creating mixture reflects the strategy.

This can be illustrated with the example of candidate image creation, or building up a state of mind about the candidate. In Chapter 2, it was suggested that there are at least three dimensions to image: candidate personality, ability to do the job, and candidate-issue domains. Assuming that the candidate is relatively unknown, long and short messages are created, to cover all three dimensions. Display and short spots can call attention to the name and connection with one theme linking the candidate to job competence and personal qualities. Longer spots and films, and uncontrolled programs, can be used to develop all three dimensions in depth, particularly issue concerns. Stimulation of news coverage can be designed to stress issues and job competence, at the same time they enhance visibility. Literature can be designed to do all three, depending on the design. Therefore, messages can be written to do more than one thing, but they should follow some motivational purpose, either establishing candidate personality, demonstrating job competence, or linking with issues.

There are occasions when all three are not paramount. Incumbent officials or well-known figures are usually established along the personality dimension. What they need to do is to link their established visibility with job competency and key issues. For example, Nelson Rockefeller's campaign for re-election in 1966 found him faced with a high visibility factor and extremely low ratings in the polls. The Governor's tenure in office was being associated with many public problems uppermost in the minds of voters. Rockefeller's strategists and his ad agency decided to deemphasize the candidate's personality in favor of a series of issue spots which were linked to "Governor" Rockefeller at the end. In the first wave, problems in the state of New York were portrayed as being on the way to solution, including: drug abuse, higher education, highways, pollution, and juvenile delinquency. In the second wave new messages on the same subjects were concluded with some linkage to the incumbent governor, usually through a voice over, but neither the candidate nor pictures of him were shown. Only in the final days of the campaign did Rockefeller personally appear on the screen, tying in with the issue dimensions and job competency portrayals in the earlier two waves.[18] In this particular campaign, the candidate and his personality was well known. Indeed, polls indicated almost too well known. Messages were created on issues and job competence, linking Governor Rockefeller to solutions of the problems, identified by citizens.

Some media messages are designed for and are more successful at reinforcement, some at activation, and some at conversion. Examples from campaigns can illustrate this point. In 1960, Senator John F. Kennedy had the problem of holding the majority Democrats in the fold, particularly Protestant Democratic identifiers who might cross over because of Kennedy's Catholicism. In his prepared speeches Kennedy said:

> Mr. Nixon, as you know, ordinarily runs as a rather ambiguous figure who is not really attached to any party because parties have no significance these days. But the other day. . .Senator Barry Goldwater got him in a room in Arizona and said, 'Dick, you are a Republican and you have to admit it.' So Nixon came out of the room rather shame-facedly and said, 'Yes, I am a Republican and I endorse every Republican candidate from top to bottom with great pride.' *I* have been saying that I am a Democrat for the past fourteen years because I believe the Democratic party is associated with progress. . .and I do not need Barry Goldwater or anyone else to remind me that parties are important.[19]

> I stand tonight where Woodrow Wilson stood, and Franklin Roosevelt, and Harry Truman stood. Dick Nixon stands where McKinley and Taft—listen

to those candidates—Harding and Coolidge, Landon, Dewey. Where do they get those candidates?[20]

These messages, obviously, were intended to reinforce the partisanship of Democrats.

By contrast, recent Republican campaigns for the Presidency have been predicated on persuading a certain number of Democrats to cross over and vote for the candidate. Even slogans such as, "I like Ike," and, "Nixon's the One," are predicated on conversion. Nixon repeatedly has stressed such themes.

> [Don't]. . .make that choice on the basis of the party labels they wear [candidates], but make it on where they stand on the great issues, and if they stand closer to you—regardless of the party label—vote the man who agrees with you more than the other man. This is the way to make the choice.[21]

> . . .across this country a big team has been assembled, all working together, not just for a party, but for a victory that will be bigger than a party, a victory that will bring to our ranks, Democrats, Independents. . .

> . . .A new voice is being heard across America. . .they cover all spectrums, they are laborers and they are managers, and they are white people and they are black people. . .who cry out. . .that's enough, let's get some new leadership.[22]

Still other messages are designed to activate latent feelings of support. In the turmoil of the 1968 presidential campaign, with many liberal, dovish Democrats uncertain about Hubert Humphrey, the strategists tried to capitalize on positive feelings toward vice-presidential candidate Muskie and negative feeling toward his counterpart Spiro Agnew. A television spot showed a bobbing line and the "bleeping" of an oscillograph, recording a heartbeat, followed by the message, "Muskie. Agnew. Who is your choice to be a heartbeat away from the Presidency?"[23] In the 1970 senatorial campaign in Illinois, Republican Ralph Tyler Smith's strategists attempted to convert Democrats away from Stevenson, on the "social issue." Their strategy was based on associating the liberal Stevenson with recent social unrest. The video portion of one commercial showed a series of still shots: a bus load of school children, student mobs at a university, Chicago policemen, and a photo of Stevenson. Moving slowly in on Stevenson, and superimposing red on the screen, the voice over said:

> "Why doesn't Adlai Stevenson speak out against bussing?
>
> Why doesn't he denounce those students who force our universities to close?
>
> What has Adlai got against the FBI and Chicago police?
>
> Why doesn't he admit he's a liberal and put an end to all pretense?
>
> Why doesn't he?
>
> Ask any Democratic Precinct Committeeman."[24]

Strangely, this particular commercial ended with a "Vote Republican" sign, which probably was confusing. Ordinarily activation of latency attempts try to link up with candidate vote appeal.

PRODUCING MESSAGES

The job of producing media messages is one that requires very specialized talent. Yet, only a few of the more experienced campaigners appear willing to accept this fact and make the financial as well as the other commitments to secure professional help. The campaigners around the candidate are likely to be knowledgeable about the strategic principles, issues, themes, and so on, but they may not be the best suited to translate such ideas into a format which can be understood by the public, and which can motivate. Advertising often requires simplification of complicated subjects, and writers must stretch precise words to cover large areas. When the appeal is visual as well as verbal, the advertising art must catch the attention of the viewer in such a way that he is favorably inclined toward the message.[25] Somehow or other, the message producer must translate a forty-page position paper on balancing employment with pollution control into a 60-second message that is moving, attracts attention, and links up with a strategic principle. Even a three-column ad buried inside the weekly newspaper has to break down themes, attract attention, and motivate. These tasks are not easy for the inexperienced hand, even those who are well versed in the details of politics and campaigns. That is why the media production enterprise is hired out or why consultation is sought.

One of the many ways a professional advertising agency translates ideas into messages is by working from a "campaign theme" or set of themes. The primary responsibility is often with the creative group. The group is presented with factual information on the problem, thinks about it, and a second meeting produces one or more possible themes. Ads are then prepared in rough form, and the group meets a third time to look over the advertising that the suggested themes have inspired. As the rough ads are mulled over and picked apart, the group usually comes up with a single direction toward which they want to proceed. After the creative group has decided on a direction, they will try to sell the account executive, and of course, the campaign strategists. Some agencies include the account people at the earlier stage; others rely more on their research departments.[26] For television, the creative and production work is somewhat different, with less emphasis on the word orientation and more on "dramatic timing."[27] Again, there are differences among producers, but most agree television must move, show something relevant, be interesting and hold the viewers' attention.[28] The creative television people ordinarily produce a complete shooting script, plus a set of plans (television-screen-size rough drawings) to guide the film or television director. The actual production of television material is ordinarily subcontracted to a film or television production company.

The contemporary political message is produced as a simplification of more complicated information centered on dramatic, visual presentation of a singular theme. Candidate and issue themes are developed into scripts written around them, usually with one issue per theme. They ordinarily are focused on the two or three important issues or candidate themes identified by voters in the campaign, somehow linking the candidate to a solution to the problem. Our analysis of voting has revealed the low degree of political interest and information among most voters, and the fact that only a few issues are important, in addition to the increased importance of candidate voting. The people responsible for the media production of campaign messages have a feeling for this voting data too, and that is why candidate-issue messages are created as they are.

In large campaigns, not one but many creative teams may be called upon to produce campaign messages. For example, in 1968 Joseph Napolitan coordinated the Humphrey media team of free lance operators and entrepreneurs. They included Shelby Storck: a 30-minute documentary and some spots; Robert Squier: uncontrolled television, coaching, production of studio programs, arranging for Humphrey to be on "Meet the Press," "Johnny Carson," the regular network programs, and producing the pre-election-night Humphrey telethon; William Wilson: (from the Lennen and Newell advertising agency), served as an independent producer and produced two films; Tony Schwartz: radio and some television spots; Harry Muheim: writing radio spots; Sid Aronson: a 30-minute documentary on the Democratic Party and two programs on Senator Muskie; Hal Tulchin: produced Schwartz's television ideas; and, Charles Guggenheim: documentaries and programs.[29] So large a team is not always used in big campaigns, but the team approach recognizes that some producers are better at some phases of production (or some media) than others. These determinations are ordinarily made by campaign managers or professional consultants on the basis of their reputation for work in other campaigns or from some of their commercial work. Most moderate size campaigns that engage agencies for creative and production work use the same "home town" agency that is working on placement.

The cost of production can be considerable, therefore, it is an important ingredient in the financial aspect of media planning. One rule of thumb that is often used when planning advertising costs is—television is 20 to 30 percent of time costs, radio is 15 percent of time costs and newspaper 25 percent of space costs. Of course, a single program, if elaborately produced, can cost as much or more than the time. Production costs is an area where many an inexperienced campaigner feels that corners can be cut, assuming that anything that is put on television or radio will motivate voters. Not all media messages gain votes. Some do nothing, and some lose votes. Thus, attention and cost commitment to the production of messages is considered to be a necessary expense. Even uncontrolled media can involve high production costs, when news coverage is telecommunicated or when consultants are employed. Some of the media outlets—newspapers, radio, and TV stations—offer production assistance to their advertisers, and they should be checked out at an early point for both extent and quality.

PLACEMENT OF POLITICAL ADVERTISING

Media scheduling is considered to be predicated on balancing three objectives: reach, frequency, and the size of the message within an available budget. *Reach* refers to the extent of coverage or the percentage of people brought within exposure range of the advertising over a stated period of time. A single candidate ad in a large circulation daily can reach hundreds of thousands. Dozens of weekly ads on the same day will fall very short of this, sometimes reaching only a few thousand readers. *Frequency* refers to the number of times the exposure takes place. The candidate ad can be run one or any number of times, depending on how important it is to catch the attention of the audience. Not even the largest product advertisers can get the maximum of both reach and frequency. One must always be sacrificed for the other. Media scheduling is then planned in relation to two characteristics of what is being advertised: the breadth of the audience and the intensity of the audience's involvement or interest. If the potential audience is small but quite interested in political matters, a focused or concentrated placement pattern is in order. Conversly, if the audience is large and mildly interested, broader mass media placements are needed. Leo Bogart adds a third dimension to frequency and reach—the *size of the message*. Within any given budget, the smaller the unit, the greater the number of different vehicles that can be used in the schedule, and the more often each can be used. A large ad is more likely to attract attention; it can carry more information and it can use more elaborate devices to capture audience interest. But, if the message can fit well in a smaller unit, it can be run more times for a given sum of money. Contrast, for example, a five-minute trailer on economic policy with the slogan: "Nixon's the One." The latter is well suited to numerous forms of advertising, whereas the issue program may not fit anywhere else. Within a given campaign advertising budget, reach, frequency and size of the message unit interact. While some advertisers try to balance these considerations, they ordinarily try to emphasize one at the expense of the other two.[30]

The purchase of time and space of controlled media is determined by the many technicalities and operating procedures of the display, newspaper, radio, and television business. It is, therefore, often left to the expertise of the advertising agency or an independent time buyer. Purchase of time and space not only requires a knowledge of the key voting concerns and location of voter types, but the purchaser must also look at the range of possible media in which advertisements could appear, and then decide on some important questions. For example, should the approach include the entire electorate once in a while, or a small segment of the population over and over again? Should the advertising be applied in small amounts over the entire course of the campaign, or should it be concentrated in the last few days? Crosscutting these are concerns of the operational procedures of the media: the availability of non-network time, broadcast time-period ratings, and attendant rates, quantity discounts, frequency discounts, and special plans and legal regulations. Each medium has to be analyzed in terms of its political impact; media placement involves a blend of political judgment, media acumen, and technical skill.

Buyers of time and space, first of all, know the market well. Their experience in following the thousands of newspapers, radio, and TV stations allows them to add a lot of flavor or interpretation to the cold figures in the media-rate cards, published ratings, and audience counts. They may know, for example, that an area's steel mill shifts begin at 6:00 and 7:00 A.M. in a certain area and therefore radio drive time is between 5:30 and 7:30 rather than the usual 7:00 to 9:00 A.M. They know if a particular newspaper runs its grocery ads on Tuesdays rather than the usual Wednesdays. Suppose a particular program in the afternoon has a 4 percent rating, but, the time buyer knows from the content of the program and from placing ads for geriatric, patent medicines and retirement land in the Southwest that it appeals to viewers over sixty; it may be the perfect fit for the senior-citizen spot. Second, the time buyer must interpret media demographics and relate them to the strategic principles of the campaign; time and space must be purchased in slots when the voters they were produced to appeal to will attend to them. For example, if a large number of undecided voters are heavy television talk show followers, a number of spots will have to be purchased adjacent to such shows. Similarly, special appeals to farmers, women, and the young must be placed either adjacent to their favorite programs, on radio stations they listen to, or in the parts of the newspaper they are most likely to read. Third, when electronic media are involved, time buyers must understand the Federal Communications Commission regulations and the broadcast campaign spending limits. An experienced time buyer can exert leverage on a station to sell certain types of time, or to release purchase information by the opposition or to make time and space available to the buyer when they would resist the candidate as advertiser. Perhaps the best known time buyer is Ruth Jones of New York, an independent, whose knowledge of media and politics makes her the most sought after by candidates of both parties. Jones is one of the few who view, listen and read all political advertising before making purchases, to get a feel for what is being said and to whom.

Various plans are used in putting together a series of media buys, to support different strategies. *The Flat Buy*, amounts to purchases at a constant rate throughout the campaign. This plan is often used when the candidate is well known or is known to be leading in the polls, and basically is a reinforcement strategy. Nixon's 1968 and 1972 campaigns followed this pattern. The *Accelerated Finish* is a buying pattern which begins two weeks to ten days before the election and increases in frequency to a highly saturated finish. This plan is used when spot packages alone are used or when candidates do not have the money for an extended period. It capitalizes on the increased attention to the campaign and focuses on activating latent supporters and converting last-minute deciders. The *Spurt Schedule* is a series of early, saturated spurts of advertising, staying on for a week or two and then disappearing. The spurt schedule often is instituted over a six- to nine-month period. This technique has been used by candidates with low visibility or those who do not have a clearly established image in the minds of voters. Incumbent officials have also used this plan to overcome image problems, such as Nelson Rockefeller's three-wave plan. Also, the late Governor John Burns of Hawaii used the spurt schedule in three waves in his 1970 primary battle. The first was devoted to Burns' record in office, the second in which the Governor was shown but did not speak was devoted, in part to Burns accomplishments, and the third wave was devoted to Burns, the man. The spurt technique is often followed by a flat buy or an accelerated finish at the end of the campaign. A fourth plan, the *Event Schedule,* is a spurt schedule tied to an event, such as an announcement of candidacy, a press conference or a rally. A spurt of electronic media purchases accompanies the event, having the effect of being a "multiplier" on the event. California Governor Ronald Reagan's consultants, Spencer-Roberts, purchased media in this fashion around his original announcement in 1966, to maximize the impact of linking this famous name with the office being sought. Each of these plans, or variations of them, are usually designed to support strategic principles and to facilitate campaign processes.[31]

Almost all advertising agencies (except the very smallest) maintain a media-purchase department to handle their volume work, such as buying space for a single ad in 300 to 400 newspapers or a commercial for 500 radio stations. In campaign work, the scale is smaller but the skill and technical knowledge required is equally important. In some larger campaigns, the practice has been to employ independent time buyers, such as Ruth Jones, on a negotiated-fee basis rather than the standard agency commission of 15 percent, to save a considerable amount of money. In recent years, several independent time-buying agencies have emerged, which offer their services at lower fees than full service agencies, and their role in campaigns will undoubtedly become increasingly important. Some media may offer time and space assistance themselves, but it may not extend beyond the issuance of audience ratings and rate sheets. Time and space purchases are made by inexperienced campaigners who sit and pore over rate charts, audience ratings, time and space classifications, federal and state regulations, and operating policies of the individual media. The work should be checked with someone who understands the media.

TIMING OF MEDIA—NEWS STIMULATION

Unlike the purchase of access to controlled media, the timing flow of uncontrolled media is somewhat easier to grasp. Since the final determination of whether or not the particular message is carried is up to the news producer in uncontrolled media, the campaigner must do something to ensure it's coverage, primarily gearing the message flow to the schedule of operations of the various media. The essence of message timing in uncontrolled media is a part of the campaigner's relations with the press, that is, learning important working schedules, peak and slack times, deadlines, and operating within them. What follows are some conventions of timing which appear to fit in most situations, but one always should check schedules and deadlines with media in their constituencies for the best fit in their situation.

Filing for office can be timed for maximum news media coverage. One of the old "conventions" of politics is to play it cagey and hold off until the very last minute; keep everyone in suspense and then file. The problem is that filings usually close on Tuesdays or Fridays, both relatively heavy news days. Moreover, usually one story is written after filings close to cover the filing of all candidates, including those covered earlier. To avoid having their candidate's filing buried in a list of candidates for many offices, experienced campaigners often time filings toward the middle of the filing period, often late on a Friday afternoon to get evening radio and TV coverage and Saturday morning newspaper coverage.

As the preceding paragraph suggests, the days of the week often make a difference in the likelihood of coverage, particularly with newspapers. Monday is a very important news day and one's message may have to compete with other news events, but if weekly papers are important in the campaign, then Monday may be the most important news day. A release, or an important press conference, or some other coverage that reaches the weeklies on Monday will give their editors time to get the story in for the Tuesday press run and Thursday distribution. Tuesday material is too late for weeklies and faces the thinnest daily newspaper of the week. Fewer advertisers use Tuesday, thus, there is less space available, given a normal amount of news activity. The same reasons tend to make Wednesday and Thursday outstanding prospects, because papers are expanded to accommodate department store and grocery advertising. There is a need for more copy to fill around the ads. Friday is less reasonable, but some messages will be held and covered in weekend editions, since there is less news then. Saturdays and Sundays are not good for anything that requires the presence of news-gathering staff, since most are off work, but these days are excellent for release materials because something is needed to fill Monday's editions.[32] On late Sunday afternoon, many an experienced campaigner has delivered coverage of a Sunday afternoon appearance, or an advance release on something the candidate is going to say the next day, in order to make the morning papers. The same is true for television, since sports events, traffic fatalities, or the occasional catastrophe are the major Sunday news. Candidates find this a good day to release film clips of the candidate campaigning, or some other message. Since the time has already been sold to sponsors, the news broadcasters need news copy on weekends to fill that time.

Timing within a day is usually a matter of finding the right balance point between differing news deadlines. Radio is the most flexible, since news can be put on the air almost immediately. If an important announcement is to be made, it is often geared to the drive time (7 to 9 A.M. and 4 to 6 P.M.) news or the noon news. If a number of stations are involved and some sort of recording is fed to the stations, a two hour lead time may be necessary to cover all the stations. Television news, and, in particular, the two evening slots are the most important sources of news. Generally, messages must be timed anywhere from two to four hours before afternoon air time, depending on the extensiveness of the station's operation. A good rule of thumb is no later than 2:00 P.M. to make the 5:00 P.M. news. Morning newspapers generally want material by no later than 2:00 P.M. on the day before the item is to be carried. Afternoon papers require items by 8:00 A.M. and no later than 10:00 A.M. on the day the story is to be carried, although a day in advance would be more helpful. While weeklies have a copy deadline that runs from noon Monday to noon Wednesday, many experienced campaigners mail releases on Saturdays, paticularly those designed as "exclusives for weeklies," to reach the editor at the time he is concerned about news. Advertising is the main concern of these small newspapers, late in the week, and only after the advertising has been sold can editors concern themselves with copy to fit around the ads. This usually happens near Mondays. Another timing device used by experienced media campaigners is to call the wire services (United Press International and Associated Press) at the same time releases are mailed to give them a "half day lead " By calling the bureaus at the normal, early evening mail release time, they in turn will feed the media that are their subscribers in time to make the 10:00 or 11:00 P.M. TV news, nightly radio news and the morning paper. A release is then double covered, in that it comes in over the wires as well as through the mail.[33]

A balance between all of these media and their schedules must necessarily be struck. Generally, the campaigner has to consider the most important medium given the strategy and setting. If television is the most important medium in terms of coverage, then timing has to be geared for the afternoon, which will also catch the morning papers. In most large cities, this is ideal because morning papers generally have a larger circulation than afternoon papers. If there are no morning papers or if TV coverage is not a likely prospect, then time schedules have to be shifted earlier to reach afternoon papers. The smaller town dailies are usually afternoon papers, and their deadlines vary, but if they are the major news source for the campaign, an afternoon mailing for the next day or an early morning, hand delivery would be optimum timing.

There are also controversies over whether releases should be labeled to be held for a certain date or always be labeled FOR IMMEDIATE RELEASE. Some ask the media to hold releases so that they can ensure perfect timing. Some try to maximize coverage by mailing releases on Saturdays to weeklies and dailies and asking it to be held until Wednesday, in order to accommodate the weeklies. Daily editors often resent being lumped with their smaller brothers, and weeklies feel they will be scooped by their big brothers. This has brought on the "exclusive for weeklies." Those who do not believe in labeling releases for hold say newspapermen do not file materials very well and are likely to throw them away.[34] Obviously, these and other questions related to timing have to be worked out during the course of the campaigners developing relations with the press.

MEDIA AND CONSTITUENCIES

In most constituencies, the electorate is made up of several crosscutting interests—racial, ethnic, occupational, social, and economic—which can be reached by channeling messages through the media outlets followed by various groups. Persons who make up these groups share enough in common, and they are sizable enough to warrant some special mass communication focus, whether it be a special program slot, special time or space, or some exclusive form of communication. On the national level, if one wanted to reach the opinion-making segment of the attentive public, utilizing The *New York Times* and *The Washington Post* plus some of the small circulation magazines, such as the *New Yorker, The New York Review of Books, Harpers,* and *Saturday Review,* would be more efficient than many larger circulation publications. These publications have a high readership among this group. Locally, farmers can be reached on rural country-western radio stations and the noon news on rural stations, house-wives can be reached best in spots adjacent to soap operas. In addition, there are ethnic and racial newspapers and radio stations and, of course, weekly and suburban papers.

The most frequent form of this type of specialization are general media which have specialized audiences. These include weekly newspapers, suburban papers, and radio stations with highly specialized audiences.

Weeklies rarely try to compete with the dailies for state, national, and international news. Indeed, they may cover very little political news, covering instead civic, social, and gossip type news within the county borders. For this reason, weeklies appeal to a very special group, a more apolitical audience which is oriented to the local community.[35] These papers normally contain a plethora of local names tied to civic, social, and gossip events. Campaigners therefore gear releases to this audience by naming the locals on various committees, or naming those who attended a statewide or regional dinner from the local area or by placing an ad with the name of, or testimonials from, local notables. Issue releases are also geared to special mention or special problems of the local area, although they have less chance of being published. Weekly newspapers cannot compete with dailies in either speed or extensiveness of coverage, so they gear themselves to people who live in the readership area and campaigners try to adjust to this format.

Suburban papers are somewhat different in that they are more political even though their readership is tied to geographic area (a single city or a few). The suburbs are populated by a generally younger more attentive population which is uprooted from the central city, and their community identity is not solid. Also, these communities are growing, they face the problems of expanding schools, building streets, establishing services, zoning, and rising taxes. The grow-ing suburban press tries to face this by covering local news on these issue sub-jects and by carrying news of governmental processes within the circulation area, with some emphasis on civic news. There is somewhat less emphasis on the social and gossip. Both controlled and uncontrolled messages are therefore geared with this orientation in mind: issue and candidate material with problems of a par-ticular local community and some attention to local personages.

Many radio stations have very specialized audiences. In a given consti-tuency area there could be: a "rock" station, which appeals primarily to the young; a "soul" station, which has primarily black audiences; a "country" station, which once had a primarily rural audience, but which is becoming more general; a "contact radio" or a call-in station, which appeals primarily to older citizens, persons who are frequently home, and persons interested in controversial political issues; a "classical" FM station appealing to a more educated and politically attentive group; and a Spanish station. These stations not only vary in audience but also in news or public affairs broadcasting content, ranging from almost none on "rock" stations to extensive coverage on the classical stations. In addition, the emphasis in coverage of news is often different from station to station, depending on the interest of the audience. Experienced campaigners meet this diversity by differentiation in both controlled and uncontrolled media. Classical, rock, and soul stations are likely to have small audiences for coverage of farm problems, but country stations are likely to have large audiences for such coverage. Messages regarding job opportunity, public housing, and health care are targeted to soul and Spanish stations. A register-and-vote appeal would be most suitable for the rock stations and least suitable for the classical stations. Messages can be channeled through advertising, news, or public affairs programming to the specialized audiences which listen to certain radio stations.

Some media are channeled to specialized groups exclusively, such as black newspapers, the ethnic press, and other specialized magazines and newspapers. The distinguishing feature is some perceived commonality or shared sense of identity. Their readerships are composed exclusively of the group. Actually, one can reach far more members of the group through the more general mass media, but using these channels can serve to build an identity among the group as a candidate favorable to the group's concerns. There are about 175 black newspapers and about 50 black magazines and periodicals circulated in black communities. Each nationality has its own generally circulated newspaper or newsletter, usually containing a mixture of social and political news. Additionally, there are publications for veterans, religious publications, social and civic publications, and occupational publications. These may be much larger in scope than the constituency, but they may be an important means of reaching that group's attentive publics, if the group is important to the strategy. In larger campaigns, advertising in and stimulation of these specialized group publications may be the most efficient and economical way of reaching these voters. Thus candidates often advertise in the various religious, ethnic, occupational, and special interest bulletins.

To reach these media, candidates normally prepare small, general ads suitable for adjustment to the situation. Language newspaper ads are normally translated to appear consistent with the rest of the paper. Uncontrolled media can be tailored to the audience through coverage of an event showing the candidate with group members, special issue appeals, or special candidate appeals. Religious publications like to print material on the candidate's family life, veterans' groups publish stories on the candidate's service record, and service clubs will publish stories on the candidate's good civic deeds. Some examples of more frequently used issue appeals are: support for Israel in Jewish publications; support of bilingual programs in the schools in Spanish language outlets; social services, jobs, and housing in black publications; and anti-Communist appeals to Eastern European ethnic groups.

It is also important to recognize that the general appeal media have within them more specialized outlets. Any time a program has a very special or predominant audience, or a newspaper section has a special readership there is potential to reach a targeted group. Programs which reach farmers, women, senior citizens, and the young have already been mentioned. There are also special language programs on radio and television stations, some newspapers publish a Spanish language page, and there are often special newspaper inserts on seasonal sports, the home, or community development. Each of these special formats has a primary appeal to a certain group. Campaigners very often find out about their appearance in advance and tailor relevant appeals to such audiences, either through stimulating coverage around these special slots or purchasing advertising in adjacent time and space.

THE MEDIA PLAN

The media plan need not be elaborate or very detailed. The only requirement is that they are based on what the campaigners are trying to communicate and through which media it is to be done. An excellent case in point is the media plan which Joseph Napolitan used to guide Hubert Humphrey's 1968 presidential campaign. After Humphrey was nominated, Napolitan found the following situation: the candidate was behind in the polls from 12 to 15 points; there were no media plans, nor was any meaningful advertising being produced; campaign polls were planned but not yet implemented, so that source of information was not available; and there was no money in the campaign treasury at that time.[36] Napolitan drafted a media plan during Labor Day weekend of the campaign which was based on: the Democratic Party identification lead they had to work with, Humphrey's identification with various groups which make up the Democratic coalition, Humphrey the person, Napolitan's perception of key issues, and their money problems. The media plan was in the form of a memo to campaign manager Lawrence O'Brien:

MEMORANDUM

To: Larry O'Brien

From: Joe Napolitan

1. Here is a brief report on media at this time:
   a. There are three people I consider indispensable to the success of the media campaign—Charles Guggenheim, Shelby Storck and Tony Schwartz.
   b. I have spoken with all three. Storck and Schwartz are aboard, with terms to be arranged.

   c. Guggenheim said he was at the point of exhaustion after putting the Kennedy memorial film together. (This film later won Guggenheim an Academy Award for the best documentary of the year.) I am to call him Tuesday. I think we can work this out; Charlie always needs to be wooed a little—but he is the best in the business.

2. Here is what I propose to do with these people and with Doyle Dane Bernbach:

   a. *With DDB:*   meet with Bill Bernbach this week, tell him to proceed with the spots we found acceptable and to come up with any creative ideas they could for new spots. I also will inform them that we have other people working on TV and radio spots, and that we will select those we want to use from all that are produced. DDB will place all material. I will work with them on time-buy and placement schedules. I also want the agency to begin quickly preparing some print pieces for utilization by Democratic organizations through the DNC. There are a few good Humphrey pieces around; we need a greater variety and more emphasis on specific areas (farms, minorities, etc.). Also need a superb general-purpose picture piece. I'll worry about these with the agency.

   b. *Guggenheim and Storck:*   I want them to work on these projects, either together or independently as they wish:

     1. A 30-minute *emotion-packed* documentary.

     2. Some 5-minute and 15-minute programs (including one of each length about Mrs. Humphrey) for off-prime TV time—particularly at times when women watch. I also would envision a 5-minute and 15-minute program about Muskie.

     3. A spot package on Humphrey the Man. These will be current and emphasize the candidate's positive qualities. The package will include 60's, 30's, 20's and 10's.

     4. If it appears feasible—a 30-minute film on the Democratic Platform. This has never been done before, there is an awesome amount of good emotional material in the platform (if it is properly visualized) and Humphrey and Muskie and other Democrats—Franklin Roosevelt, Harry Truman, John Kennedy, Lyndon Johnson—can be woven through it. I think this kind of film would be a new departure from conventional political rhetoric, and could be extremely effective. There also is a logistical reason: this film consists largely of *editing*, with a strong narration, and could be started at once.

   c. *Schwartz:*   This guy is a true genius in his field. I want him to work on *issues-oriented* spots, both radio and television. He is best by giving him a problem—Vietnam, crime, law and order, racial tension—and let him work out a solution. I would guess we would get five or six television and maybe six or eight radio spots from Schwartz. The best way to work with him is give him the problem and let him go.

3. I am going to make a determined effort to get everything but the Humphrey documentary ready as quickly as possible, and work out a system for various state committees to get copies of prints, tapes or

discs and get them on the air in their states—at their expense—as soon and as often as possible. This would supplement, not interfere with, our regular media program. So far as I know, no one has ever made maximum use of this procedure, although several candidates have made stabs at it.

4. At the moment I am contemplating only two kinds of newspaper ads for placement out of our budget: fundraising ads and film promotion. In addition, I think we should go into production at once on some ads for mats and reproduction proofs, and get these in the hands of state and local committees for placement. (Incidentally, advertising agencies resist such techniques because they do not receive the commission, but I really believe that the economic wealth of the agency is secondary to winning the campaign.)

5. If the Vice-President is going to be in Waverly for a few days, I would like to get a film crew up to shoot some stuff of him at home. We'll never get a better opportunity.

6. With any luck, I should have this program in motion by the end of the week.[37]

The entire controlled media portion of the campaign unfolded from this very brief, working document. Napolitan largely used this plan, with adjustments for contingencies, to contribute to the very successful campaign effort of nearly closing that 12 to 15 point gap.

As in other aspects of campaign planning, media planning entails a consideration—that the particular medium selected and the messages to be created, as well as the target audiences should be designed with those voting and campaign processes in mind which are related to strategy. Will the chosen media and the planned appeals support a related amount of candidate, party, and issue appeals? Is it designed to reinforce, activate, or convert in consistent proportions with what has been planned? Can the time slots and message themes be traced back to earlier plans? Are the hundreds of dollars designed for print and display justified in terms of something the campaign is trying to do? A great deal of campaign research and planning will be wasted unless the media and advertising effort is based on the plans formulated earlier. Many a campaign wrongly bases its media portion on what has been done before, something clever which others have done, or what appears to be current, rather than basing it on the path that strategists have charted.

Notes to Chapter 12

1. Joseph Napolitan, *The Election Game* (Garden City, N.Y.: Doubleday and Company, 1972), p. 2.

2. Thomas J. Fleming, "The Product Named Hubert Humphrey," *New York Times Magazine*, October 13, 1968, pp. 45-46.

3. Morton Knodracke, "Television and the Elections—A Double Image," *Chicago Sun-Times,* November 8, 1970, sec. 2, p. 4.

4. Napolitan, *The Election Game,* pp. 8-11.

5. Democratic National Committee, *Democratic Campaign Manual, 1972* (Washington, D.C.: Democratic National Committee, 1972), pp. 62-63.

6. John F. Becker and Eugene E. Heaton, "The Election of Senator Edward W. Brooke," *Public Opinion Quarterly* 31 (1967); Ray E. Hiebert, et al., *The Political Image Merchants* (Washington, D.C.: Acropolis Books, 1971), pp. 117-36.

7. For a more complete discussion of these principles see, Leo Bogart, *Strategy in Advertising* (New York: Harcourt, Brace & World, 1967), pp. 98-104; Martin Mayer, *Madison Avenue, U.S.A.* (New York: Harper & Brothers, 1958), pp. 205-08; Maurice McCaffrey, *Advertising Wins Elections* (Minneapolis, Minnesota: Gilbert Publishing, 1962), passim; Napolitan, The Election Game, ch. 3; Dan Nimmo, *The Political Persuaders* (Englewood Cliffs, N.J.: Prentice-Hall, 1970), pp. 118-40.

8. Bogart, *Strategy in Advertising,* pp. 112-14.

9. John F. Bibby and Roger Davidson, *On Capitol Hill* 2d ed. (Hinsdale, Illinois: Dryden Press, 1972), pp. 35-36.

10. Ibid., p. 37.

11. Walter DeVries, "Taking The Voter's Pulse," in Hiebert, *The Political Image Merchants,* pp. 76-80.

12. Joseph Napolitan, "Zeroing in on the Voter," in Hiebert, *The Political Image Merchants,* pp. 48-49.

13. F. Clifton White, "Balancing the Campaign," in Hiebert, *The Political Image Merchants,* p. 60.

14. Hank Parkinson, *Winning Political Campaigns With Publicity* (Wichita, Kansas: Campaign Associates Press, 1973), p. 123.

15. DeVries, "Taking the Voter's Pulse," pp. 73-74.

16. Ibid., pp. 70-71.

17. Quoted in Mayer, *Madison Avenue, U.S.A.,* p. 36.

18. Richard Donnelly, "How TV Turned A Race Around," *Television Magazine* 23 (1966).

19. Theodore H. White, *The Making of the President 1960* (New York: Atheneum, 1961), p. 327.

20. Ibid., p. 329.

21. Ibid., p. 270.

22. Theodore H. White, *The Making of the President 1968* (New York: Pocket Books, 1970), pp. 403-04.

23. Napolitan, *The Election Game*, p. 49.

24. Published in "Politicking on Television," *National Journal* 2 (1970): 2144.

25. Mayer, *Madison Avenue, U.S.A.*, p. 316.

26. Ibid., pp. 120-21.

27. Ibid., p. 132.

28. Tony Schwartz, "The Inside of the Outside," *Politeia* 1 (1972): 3-9.

29. Napolitan, *The Election Game*, p. 43.

30. Bogart, *Strategy in Advertising*, pp. 143-46.

31. *Democratic Campaign Manual 1972*, p. 64; Napolitan, "Zeroing in on the Voter," in *The Political Image Merchants*, p. 49.

32. Parkinson, *Winning Campaigns with Publicity*, p. 35.

33. Ibid., pp. 37-38.

34. For further discussion see, Chester G. Atkins, *Getting Elected* (Boston: Houghton Mifflin, 1973), p. 159; Parkinson, *Winning Campaigns With Publicity*, p. 54.

35. Robert K. Merton, *Social Theory and Social Structure* rev. ed. (New York: Free Press of Glencoe, 1957), pp. 406-13.

36. Napolitan, *The Election Game*, p. 34.

37. Ibid., pp. 35-37.

For Further Reading and Research

Braodcasting. Weekly coverage of the broadcasting industry, including political campaigns.

Broadcasting Yearbook. Basic marketing information for radio and television.

Congressional Quarterly. "Campaign Consultants: Pushing Sincerity in 1974." (May 4, 1974): 1105-08.

Devlin, L. Patrick. "Contrasts in Presidential Campaign Commercials of 1972." *Journal of Broadcasting* 18 (1973-74): 17-25.

Donnelly, Richard. "How TV Turned a Race Around," *Television Magazine* 23 (1966): 38-45.

Hiebert, Ray; Jones, Robert; Lorenz, John; and Lotito, Ernest. *The Political Image Merchants: Strategies in the New Politics.* Washington: Acropolis, 1971.

McGinnis, Joe. *The Selling of the President, 1968.* New York: Trident, 1966.

Mendelsohn, Harold and Crespi, Irving. *Polls, Television, and the New Politics.* Scranton, Pa.: Chandler, 1970.

Napolitan, Joseph. *The Election Game.* Garden City, New York: Doubleday, 1972.

Nimmo, Dan D. *Popular Images of Politics.* Englewood Cliffs, N.J.: Prentice-Hall, 1974.

Schwartz, Tony. "The Inside of the Outside." *Politeia* 1 (1972): 3-9.

Uncontrolled Media: Stimulating News Coverage

Coverage of news about candidates, issues, and parties makes the news portion of the media important determinants of campaign agendas. When stories are covered, they focus attention on certain issues, build up images of political figures, present objects, and suggest what people should consider, of what they should be aware and about what they should have feelings.[1] Bernard Cohen once pointed out that press coverage, . . . "may not be successful much of the time in telling people what to think, but it is stunningly successful in telling its readers what to think *about.*"[2] Regardless of any possible effect of the direction or intensity of attitudes, the agenda-setting function of the media is based on the notion that news coverage makes the issue or the candidate a topic for consideration. Issues and candidates not placed on the agenda by the news media may be doomed to exclusion from the deliberational process.[3]

    In a very important study of the kinds of images which presidential candidates and their running mates projected in the 1968 campaign, Doris Graber found that the images presented by the press depended heavily on direct reporting of the candidate's words. Figure 13.1 dramatically demonstrates that more than half (54.5%) of the eleven newspaper story sources studied could be attributed to the candidates for president or vice president. Her analysis of 3160 stories in a sample of twenty newspapers further revealed that even information from other sources, such as from columnists, editorial writers, or letters to the editor, took their cue largely from what the candidates were saying. As Graber concluded, "This shows the tremendous impact which the candidate-created images have on the campaign, for good or ill. What the candidate says receives the lion's share of publicity."[4] And research on the 1972 presidential campaign revealed that the candidate who made the most news—who worked at or otherwise made an effort to create news—received the most news coverage.[5] Ironically, in presidential campaigns a large contingency of newspersons, photographers, televisions crews, and accompanying electronic equipment travel with the candidate's party, yet the greatest portion of reportage comes from the candidate. Thus, uncontrolled media appears to be a very real challenge.

The normal campaign is not, however, a clearing house for news gathering. Newspeople gather a great deal of their political news in such places as the city hall, the county courthouse, the legislature, the court house, government office buildings, and from presidential campaigns. Campaigns are rarely on the list of "places" where newspeople can obtain volumes of copy in a short time. Candidates and campaigners, perhaps impressed by the stories filed by newsmen concerning presidential candidates, or by the importance of their running for office, or both, often expect reporters to flock to them, favoring them with interviews and coverage. A number of factors make this a rare occurrence: the relative lack of interest on the part of most citizens in following campaigns, the large number of campaigns, the pressures of continuous news gathering in non-campaign areas, and the fact that newspeople like copy that is convenient for them. The campaign's publicity function normally has to work to bring the news to the news gatherers.

THE CHARACTER OF NEWS STIMULATION IN CAMPAIGNS

Uncontrolled media often attract campaigners because they are easy to develop and the time and space is free. Candidates often turn to uncontrolled media because, with tight budgets, they feel the mass exposure will come through the news anyway, so money that might go for advertising can be channeled elsewhere.

However, some *caveats* are in order. First, by its nature, uncontrolled media can be more difficult to manage. One cannot produce it, control it, or present the candidate in exactly the fashion desired by the strategists. If the candidate is not a good media personage, it can be harmful. George Romney was devastated in 1968 on the interview panel circuit. Edmund Muskie started to fall apart in some of the news coverage of the 1972 presidential campaign. Many candidates simply do not make a good appearance in such formats. Thus, not all mass exposure is automatically good exposure. Second, uncontrolled media requires a considerable effort. Candidates very often will work days on a prepared speech intended for a few hundred committed supporters, and then make an off-the-cuff remark to a TV camera which reaches several hundred thousand viewers. Those with media experience in campaigns consider relations with the newspeople, preparation of news material, and preparations for appearances before the media to be as important as advertising. Third, serious efforts at uncontrolled media are not without their costs; experience, preparation, materials, and equipment all go into effective news stimulation. Fourth, uncontrolled

Figure 13.1 Source of News Stories in the 1968 Presidential Campaign

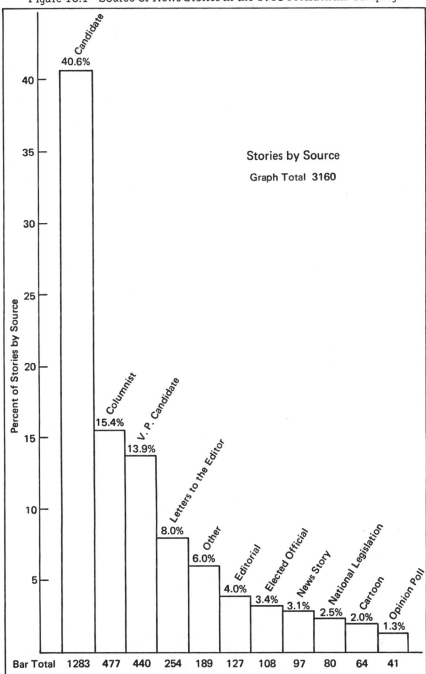

Source: Doris A. Graber, "Presidential Images in the 1968 Campaign," a paper presented at the 1970 Midwest Political Science Association Meeting.

media is not always a substitute for controlled media. Some voters, or potential voters, cannot be reached through news stories, newscasts, interview panels, or talk shows because they ignore them. They have to be reached either by advertising spots adjacent to their entertainment programs or through some direct, controlled format such as literature, direct mail, or advertising on the comics page of the newspaper. If reaching this segment is part of the overall strategy, then use of news formats solely will not be appropriate.

The reader will notice that in this introductory section we have successfully resisted the use of "press" except where the reference is to newspapers, and we have attempted to de-emphasize media. Use of the term "press," as in "press release" and "press conference," is apprently considered to be anachronistic by electronic journalists, who rightly claim that there are no presses in their news production operations. To journalists, media is apparently considered to be layman's term, journalists do not think of themselves as members of the media. Media has a closer connotation to advertising. It is a term in the advertising man's sales pitch to advertisers about the cost-effectiveness of their advertising dollar. Media is a quantitative term to measure the relative effectiveness in cost per thousand of potential audience to those thousands by newspapers, magazines, radio, television, direct mail or billboards.[6] Thus, the approach will be to treat news stimulation generically.

NEWS RELATIONS

Since one of the objectives of uncontrolled-media campaigning is to facilitate coverage, news relations is a particular type of public relations aimed at those who gather, report, and produce the news. The ultimate goal of news relations is to make it as easy as possible for newspeople to cover campaign news. This includes such means as proper timing, complete information, and reducing logistical problems—in other words, to break down as many barriers to campaign news coverage as possible. News relations has become one of the cornerstones of the modern campaign.

In the largest campaigns, the campaign news relations operatives expend much effort to accommodate the large news corps which travels with the candidate. In 1972, each of the major candidates for the presidential nomination had an entourage of reporters and correspondents following them and filing stories. By the fall campaign between McGovern and Nixon, the traveling news corps, including national political reporters, campaign reporters from large prestige papers, reporters from smaller dailies, radio and television network correspondents, and wire service people, was large enough to fill three buses and a charter jet. In addition to constant information, traveling newspeople are faced with making travel arrangements, accommodations, room service, arranging for telephones and typewriters at campaign stops, as well as meeting other reportage problems. These details are usually handled for the news corps by persons on the campaign news-relations staff. All of this is necessary in such mammoth operations which hop from media market to media market because the reporter "endures many hardships, compounded by the fact that he is at the mercy of whims and schedules commanded by others. He must absorb cataracts of words, distilling them into compact pieces of sparkling copy. . . .But when he is relieved of the dirty details of housekeeping by far-sighted campaign pros, he is freed to do his work uncluttered."[7]

In most campaigns, the candidate, or the appropriate person in the campaign, must establish some working rapport with the newspeople, learning some of the relevant working procedures and working within the guidelines. This involves some very basic (to grasp but not necessarily to implement) and important steps. If it is physically possible, the candidate should visit newspaper editors, news directors of radio and TV stations, and in the case of larger operations, the political reporters. The purpose of the visit is to exchange information with the important newspeople of a particular medium. Very early in the campaign, explanations should be given to newspeople concerning the candidate's background, who is to handle news in the campaign, and a brief outline as to how the campaign intends to use a particular medium for both news and advertising purposes. Many questions should be asked, including: What are their news and editorial policies? What kind of news and publicity releases are they likely to cover? What style and format should be followed? How are pictures, graphics, transparencies, films, tapes, or other visuals handled? What are their deadlines? And, for radio and TV, are there any special needs, such as more limited time available for news and public service broadcasts? The editor or news director should be asked if there are any other persons at the paper or station that are important to contact.

The discussion format then shifts to include advertising details. Inquiries should be made as to advertising rates, copy deadlines, policies concerning time slots or positions, rules concerning political disclaimers, size or time limitations for political ads, or any other special rules concerning political ads at that particular media outlet. Some papers and stations offer assistance in design and layout of ads, so, inquiries should be made. Terms of payment and billing procedures should be established. (Very often payment in advance is required for political work.) Sometimes questions are raised about suggesting advertising schedules. In larger operations, these questions are directed to the advertising manager; in smaller stations and weekly papers, there is usually no such role specification.

Many experienced campaigners also try to use this meeting to sound out the editor or news manager about the politics of the area. Questions could be asked about important problems in the community, likely important campaign issues in the community, important people to talk to in the community, any community squabbles of which the candidate should be aware, and the newsperson's perceptions of any particular segments of the community where the candidate is likely to be strong or weak. Inquiries on these subjects will not only yield campaign information, but will aid in establishing rapport by dealing with the newsperson as an expert on community affairs.

There are, of course, many other practices that news-relations people have worked out through their campaign experience.[8] Important diplomatic hints, such as writing a letter or telephoning in advance of the visit for an appointment, or arriving at a slack news time, and avoiding trying to get the news executive to change working policies during the campaign, are but a few of the dozens of bits of advice which are important in building a good rapport. Since many of these issues are situational, novices have to learn such details through the experience of adjusting to situations. But, visits to the media by the candidate, or, if that is physically impossible, by an important campaign news officer, can build significant bridges. They are considered to be the most important steps in news relations.

Beyond the initial session, relations are continued (by building on the rapport established) on a face-to-face basis. These can be boiled down to some conventions of news relations. First, a close working relationship should be developed between some person in the campaign and the working newspeople. Newspeople should come to believe that there is some person who is responsible for news and campaign information. This relationship should become as close and personal as is professionally appropriate. The campaign representative should be available to reporters at all times. Second, the more the campaigner thinks and acts like a newsperson, the better the relationship. This includes having a sense of what is news for the information and events behind the news item, the working procedures of the news media, and differences between various media. Third, an awareness of the mountain of information that passes over a news desk helps. Most of it is barely scanned and then discarded, so that presentation of newsworthy information which can get past the critical eyes that sort this material is crucial. The copy should be sound, with relevant information. Fourth, candor and equal treatment is said to pay off in the long run. Hidden information or favored treatment usually backfires. If reporters have a feeling that they are getting all of the information possible to give, they feel better about covering the campaign. Fifth, technical efficiency also helps get material past the jaundiced news eye. This includes presentation according to mechanical specifications, correct format, appropriate supporting materials, and meeting deadlines. The greater the amount of a busy newsperson's work that is done, the greater the possibility of coverage. These conventions are based on the experiences of persons who have dealt with the press in campaigns at all levels.[9]

NEWS ADVANCE—THE NEWS KIT

An emerging speciality in larger campaigns is the media advance person. As candidates in the large constituencies now communicate with the voting public more through the media, they require diplomatic work and arrangements similar to those needed for personal campaigning. The media advance person learns the media territory and trys to work within it before the candidate makes an appearance, and then he or she works out a local schedule of uncontrolled media appearances. Among other activities, media advance involves: becoming aware of local media schedules and requirements, arranging for meetings and interviews with newspeople, providing background information to the newspeople before appearances, making sure the candidate meets schedules for interviews or programs, working the candidate into interview or public service braodcasts, and providing anything newspeople may need. The media advance function is designed to maximize the coverage and appearances for the candidate in the local newspapers and on radio and TV. A separate, media advance staff is sometimes created because the knowledge and skills required to advance media and personal appearances are somewhat different than advancing meetings and rallies.

In smaller campaigns, most of the media advance work, or its equivalent, is performed by the candidate or a designated media person. Indeed, much of the earlier-mentioned news relations amounts to the bulk of the important advance work performed by most candidates.

Another frequently used technique of advancing the news in campaigns is to put important news material together into a news kit; a packet of background information and immediately usable material which is then given to every person on the news list. News kits are used both as background material on the candidate and for campaign events. They provide those who produce the news with any needed information not contained in news releases, interviews, or press conferences, which may be useful in the preparation of feature stories, editorials, or news stories. News kits are ordinarily pocket folders (prominently labeled on the outside) containing: biographical information about the candidate; some detailed information about the important issue positions of the candidate, either through position papers or a specially prepared fact sheet; a piece of campaign literature; a list of key campaign committee persons and staff persons, highlighting the appropriate news contact; 5 X 7 glossy photos for newspapers, normally a head-and-shoulders shot and optionally one or two action or family shots; and, for television, two or three 35-mm, horizontal, color slides showing different candidate poses, one or two 16-mm, color film clips of the candidate.[10] These kits are rather inexpensive to compile, since most of the written material can be duplicated, and the visual materials can be produced through loan of the equipment and expertise of skilled persons. They are distributed very early in the public portion of the campaign, as a service to the news. News kits or portions of them have also been used for other purposes such as to provide background information to potential donors, volunteers, or attentive publics. The news kit is a relatively important means of maintaining good relations with the newspeople, particularly in small campaigns. The material in such kits often finds its way into print or on the air.

NEWS RELEASES

The most important, continuing news contact with voters during the campaign is maintained by supplying news releases—a story for newspeople, but prepared so that it can be used verbatim. It is designed to convey information to news gatherers for story preparation. Very often, however, they find their way into the news in the fashion supplied by the campaigner, particularly in small news operations.

Most campaigns involve so many activities by the time they go public that it becomes impossible to deal with the news media on a one-to-one basis, even if there are only a handful of relevant outlets. Campaigners ordinarily meet this problem by building on previously developed personal relations with newspeople, releasing stories to them. Moreover, the reach of a personal appearance, the reaction to a late event, or a proposal to solve a public problem, can be extended through the news. Since most voters follow the campaign through mass communication rather than by personal contact, campaigners attempt to meet the demand for campaign information by increasing the supply to the communicators. Thus, a mainstay of information flow is the news release, a rapidly produced and distributed single-subject missive which brings *news* of the campaign to the public.

Since newspeople ordinarily receive anywhere from one to several cubic yards of release material daily, the key to receiving coverage is obviously in presentin ໑something that really is news. In fact, a growing number of news editors refuse to cover any releases not pegged to some event, such as a special appearance before a group or a campaign tour with a high level office holder. Journalism has produced many, many volumes on what constitutes news.[11] Political consultant Hank Parkinson suggests that without consciously creating these categories, news editors consider a release to be news if at least one of eleven things happen: if it is out of the ordinary, timely, significant, has local appeal, is emotional, has general interest, if there is an element of conflict, if it will jolt the reader or listener, if it happened locally, if it mentions other names, and or if it is what other people are talking about. These are the screening devices editors use when receiving news releases, he claims.[12] Within these guidelines, Parkinson says that he has had success in getting campaign news releases published if they are related to one of sixteen "politically newsworthy happenings": contemplating the race; announcing a candidacy; filing for office; committee appointments; personal appearances by the candidate; releasing the candidate's schedule (listing a series of appearances in the future); announcing a stand on issues; releasing poll results; publicizing fund-raising events; announcing testimonials and group endorsements; appealing to specific economic, age, racial, religious or regional interests; attacking the opponent; denying an accusation; a "sidebar," or feature which runs parallel to a release, offering background on the main release; releasing white papers, special studies, books, or unusual research; and postelection thank-you messages.[13] Campaigners ordinarily follow the procedure of weaving a news story around one of these campaign events.

The format for presentation has been relatively standardized, in order to work within the requirements of most news operations. Releases are ordinarily typed double-spaced with wide margins on 8½"-by-11" white paper. The name of the news contact, the campaign name or campaign committee name, the telephone number and the address is placed in the upper left corner. The release date and time is placed in the upper right corner. The story starts down the page, about one-third, to leave room for an editorial lead, head, and comments. Each paragraph is indented five spaces. If the story runs longer than one page, type "more" at the bottom of the page. Indicate the end of the story by the notation "--30--" or @ UF25.[14]

Beyond the requirements of format, there are some journalism conventions that go along with release preparation. They should be short (up to 150 to 300 words; no paragraph longer than six or seven lines), cover only one subject, be stated in direct and simple language, and flow easily from paragraph to paragraph. The first, or lead, paragraph is supposed to contain the five *W*'s of journalism: *Who? Where? What? When? Why?* For example, "Senator Joe Doe, 1976 Democratic presidential hopeful accused the Ford administration of being more concerned with protecting the profits of energy producers than in ensuring adequate supplies at reasonable prices to consumers, yesterday, before the AFL–CIO Executive Council meeting in Bal Harbor, Florida." This is the most important part of the release; editors often stop reading here. What follows the lead paragraph should be of decreasing importance so that if an editor shortens the release, it can stand by itself, each succeeding paragraph elaborating on the lead.[15]

The intervals and volume for news release flow is difficult to discuss in the abstract. They vary in campaigns from a few, pegged to very significant campaign events, to one per day during the late stages of the campaign. Some campaign news coordinators peg releases to practically every appearance by the candidate or every campaign event, filling in any gaps that may occur with the names of committee persons or some local color. Releases are normally sent to everyone on the media list, either addressed personally to the newsperson, city editor, political editor, or news director. The constant flow of releases should, of course, be designed to accomplish what is planned in the strategy-formulation stage.

Some adjustments to the normal procedure have to be made with radio and television. Print media ordinarily require only a mailed, mimeographed release. Although some stations will read material supplied on paper, they prefer a format more suited to their delivery system. Radio releases are often sent by having the candidate record highlights of the release on tape, and then someone feeds the messages to the stations by telephone. Television stations like to receive either film clips or tapes of the candidate actually campaigning (actualities). The latest, relatively inexpensive technique is to film the candidate and send or deliver the undeveloped film immediately to the station for development

Figure 13.2   A Sample News Release

SMITH FOR MAYOR COMMITTEE
451 Hemlock
Brushtown, Georgia 21504

(412) 564-5112

Contact: James W. Smith   April 1, 1975

FOR IMMEDIATE RELEASE

                    (leave five to eight spaces)

        Anne X. Smith, Action Slate candidate for Mayor, today
appointed William Crittenden as her campaign manager.

        Ms. Smith announced the appointment of Mr. Crittenden
at the Tuesday weekly luncheon meeting of the Action Slate
supporters, before some 100 persons at the Chestnut Tree
restaurant here.

        "Mr. Crittenden is an outstanding citizen of Brushtown,"
said Ms. Smith, adding: "he has long been active in community
affairs, knows the problems and needs of our city, and
possesses the organizing and leadership abilities to bring
active and progressive government to our city."

        Mr. Crittenden, 53, of 220 Laurel Lane, is operations
manager for the Zenia Manufacturing Company here. He is a
graduate of Georgia Tech.

        Other campaign officers will be announced later.

                            --30--

Figure 13.3   An Issue News Release*

CONLEY FOR HOUSE
Headquarters: 222 Elm
               Elmtown, Idaho
(812) 444-4512

Contact: Joe Conley   October 15, 1976

FOR IMMEDIATE RELEASE

                (leave five to eight spaces)

     Joe Conley, Democratic candidate for the State House in
the 12th District, today pledged to support a strong code of
ethics for legislators if he is elected and he called on his
opponent to make a similar pledge.

     "There is no place in our Legislature for persons who use
their positions of public responsibility for private gain,"
Conley said. "Recent news accounts of conflicts of interest
in the Idaho Legislature are shocking and intolerable. It's
time to take some firm, tough action to see that these conflicts
are eliminated once and for all.

     "People have a right to expect that their elected officials
will give 100 percent of their time and energy to their constituents, and not to their own private interests. And yet a
number of lawyer-legislators are in reality 'inside lobbyists'
who go so far as to sponsor bills for individuals or groups who
are their private clients.

     "This is an inexcusable practice, but it is only one example
of the way in which some legislators fail to make any distinction
between their public and private responsibilities. This is why
I plan to vigorously support a legislative code of ethics that
will contain at least three basic points:

     "1) Lawyer-legislators be prohibited from practicing before
          state agencies.

     "2) Attorneys and other professional persons serving as
          legislators should not be retained professionally by
          anyone having business before the legislature.

     "3) Each lawmaker should make a full disclosure of any
          personal interest he may have in pending legislation.

     "In addition, I plan to support a strong lobbyist
disclosure law, so the public can see how much money is
being spent, and how it is being spent. by different groups
to affect legislation.

     "This is the kind of issue that everyone in public life
ought to agree on, and therefore I hope my opponent, who has
been silent on this issue, will join me in supporting these
measures."

          --30--

Source: *Adapted from a news release written by Richard Moe.

(they have the facilities a candidate would not have) and use. Video tapes are also fed into stations in a similar fashion.[16] Of course, whether the release is by mimeographed words, magnetic audio tape, magnetic video tape, or audio tape, the news source should already have some visuals on hand, namely, the photos, slides, or film clips supplied in the news kit.

Since the news release is such a basic component of public campaigns, many written works have covered these techniques in detail.[17] Campaigners planning to use this tactic would do well to consult other written sources, as well as to seek out the advice of the experienced.

NEWS APPEARANCES

The availability and importance of appearances for news conferences and interview, talk, and panel shows in a campaign depends on a combination of the visibility and importance of the office sought, the number of available channels of uncontrolled media formats, the importance of uncontrolled media in the campaign strategy, and the strategist's judgment as to how effective the candidate might be in informal media appearances.

In general, those who seek higher level offices have more of these opportunities, because these are the more news oriented offices. In fact, many unannounced candidates for president, governor, and senator use such vehicles as an important public forum, for one does not have to assume the posture of a candidate. Stations welcome the appearances of prospective candidates because it brings important newsmakers before their cameras, microphones, or readers, plus their formal non-candidate status means they do not have to adhere to FFC, equal time regulations. Candidates for lower visibility or small constituency offices will ordinarily be excluded from such coverage in the national news forums and the twenty or so major media markets in the U.S., but the opportunities to stimulate coverage through appearances in the many medium sized and small media markets are much better.

If campaigners scan their constituency media lists, compile the results of their news-relations tour, account for the programmed public service time available on electronic media, and analyze local newspapers for public affairs coverage, a reasonable idea of available coverage can be determined. If it is deemed important to reach voters through such means, then steps can be made to integrate media appearances with other appearances (although they will necessarily be infrequent) by simply contacting the persons in charge at stations and newspapers and making it known that the candidate is available. Of course, such strategic decisions should be based on a positive assessment of the candidate's likely impact through these appearances. To sum up, the availability and importance of using news appearances operates within their own context or setting.

The news conference is one such example. Newspeople are more likely to attend news conferences of candidates for higher office. Incumbents have an even greater advantage, since their position is a natural forum for much important information. Moreover, there are newsgatherers assigned to follow their offices. The President of the United States or the Mayor of New York can call almost daily news conferences and get attendance and coverage. Other candidates or officials ordinarily use them more infrequently, reserving them for a very important announcement or the release of important information. For example, one state senator with gubernatorial ambitions had his campaign researchers check the property tax relief available, through a recent act of the legislature, given to the largest businesses in the state, compared with the average homeowner relief under the same bill. His data was broken down by county, with the names and the amounts of relief to the ten largest businesses in each county. About twenty newspeople attended the event, including all four local television stations. The news conference was extensively covered, including articles on the front page of the metropolitan dailies and televised news coverage. The data alongside the names of familiar companies made for interesting news copy. Similarly, most candidates will need to have extraordinary news with some hard information, such as a plan for economic development, a government reorganization plan, or a three-step program to end pollution. Campaigners will sometimes select a more dramatic setting to highlight their news conference, such as in front of a steel mill for pollution, a slum neighborhood for urban renewal programs, or in front of the police station to protest police brutality. News conferences are normally arranged, however, in a place accessible to the equipment for electronic media, with written notice to the media list a few days in advance, and with written copy to be made available at the conference.

Interview shows, talk shows, and panels are subject to similar considerations of setting. If the candidate does well in informal situations, talk shows an be an important means of developing candidate images and enhancing issue position development. Although the audiences for these shows are small, there is an important qualitative factor; they tend to be well informed, often undecided during the campaign, and likely ticket splitters. The same type of audience is likely to follow a public affairs broadcast over cable television. CATV outlets may even give time to the candidate that can be structured or semi-structured, since their outlets rarely have any news-gathering staff. Panel interview shows are another available outlet and means of exposure. If the right questions are asked, a candidate has an excellent opportunity to develop issue positions and demonstrate an aura of job competence before important issue publics. However, reporters or other questioners who appear on these shows tend to ask warmed over questions from national issues which either not apply to the local situation, or the answers require longer than the short time allowed for an answer. Another appearance format is the question-and-answer format, where a panel of carefully selected citizens ask candidates the questions. These are really controlled formats, where the candidate ordinarily purchases the time and tapes two or three times the time available, editing the best portions.

The standard news formats are not the only means of stimulating coverage of candidate appearances. In some cases, the news media will cover an important speech or appearance before a group. An emerging practice in high visibility campaigns is the creation of "media events," or coverage of the candidate engaged in ordinary campaigning. Senator Eugene McCarthy tried this in his 1968 presidential-nomination campaign, using a walk along the beach, a visit to the elderly, a plant gate appearance, or anything else that was visually interesting. Former Mayor John Lindsay of New York City turned his neighborhood visits into "media events." While geared primarily to television news, they often receive radio and newspaper coverage. Such appearances are normally accompanied by mobs of people on the scene who may or may not be supporters, all brought within the range of the camera through the planned spontaneity of the advance person.[18]

OTHER MEDIA EFFORTS

Among the other interesting means of getting uncontrolled media attention in campaigns, are through feature stories, call-ins, or letters to the editor, often appearing to be spontaneous but actually planned. Except in the most visible of campaigns, feature stories are not written by a reporter assigned to seek out background information on the candidate. Campaigners must either write them or cooperate with newspeople in their production. The latter is achieved by discussing possible subjects with editors and news directors. Feature stories ordinarily deal with the candidate's background, family life, hobbies, or any other special interest. They can be either print, print and photo, audio or audio-visual. Feature stories are an exception to the hard news dicta mentioned in relation to news releases. They have an audience appeal to those interested in lifestyle information, including many who do not follow political news very carefully. They depict the human side of the candidate's image through media, a significant dimension to convey.

Supporters are often encouraged to participate in the news campaign by writing letters to the editor or being a part of call-in shows. Somehow the words and name of a local reader on the editorial page have a considerable attraction and believability. Campaigners therefore stimulate publication of letters among supporters, ordinarily by providing them with subject information only, so that the letters appear genuine. In the 1972 presidential campaign, McGovern and Schriver had an official letters-to-the-editor section, complete with a published manual and organizers in the states.[19] Call-in shows are increasing in number, both the continuing, open-to-any-subject variety and special shows devoted to candidate appearances. In both cases, campaigners attempt to stimulate favorable media coverage by encouraging supporters to call-in with favorable or flattering comments or to ask favorable or leading questions. This places more candidate controlling into a basically uncontrolled situation by structuring, plus crowding hostile questions and comments off. Call-in show appearances give the candidate an appearance before audiences that do not necessarily follow campaigns in harder to follow newspaper, magazine, and public affairs program broadcasting.

Notes to Chapter 13

1. Kurt Lang and Gladys Engel Lang, "The Mass Media and Voting," *American Voting Behavior* eds. Eugene Burdick and Arthur J. Brodbeck (Glencoe, Illinois: The Free Press, 1959), p. 468.

2. Bernard C. Cohen, *The Press and Foreign Policy*, (Princeton, N.J.: Princeton Univ. Press, 1963), p. 13.

3. Maxwell E. McCombs and Donald L. Shaw, "The Agenda-Setting Function of Mass Media," *Public Opinion Quarterly* 36 (1972): 176-87.

4. Doris A. Graber, "Presidential Images in the 1968 Campaign," paper presented at the 1970 Midwest Political Science Association Annual Meeting, p. 3.

5. Robert G. Meadow, "Cross-Media Comparison of Coverage of the 1972 Presidential Campaign," *Journalism Quarterly* 50 (1973): 485.

6. With thanks to Theodore H. White for calling this distinction to my attention in his *The Making of the President 1972* (New York: Bantam Books, 1973), p. 332n.

7. Herbert M. Baus and William B. Ross, *Politics Battle Plan* (New York: Macmillan, 1968), pp. 307-08.

8. Indiana Democratic State Central Committee, *A Handbook on Publicity, Public Relations and Advertising for a Democratic City Election in Indiana in 1967* (Indianapolis: Democratic State Central Committee, 1967), p. 7; Charles A. Mosher, " 'Getting Along' With Local Newspapers," in Robert D. Buehler, *Campaign Technique Manual* (Washington, D.C.: National Association of Manufacturers, undated), pp. 114-15.

9. Chester G. Atkins, *Getting Elected* (Boston: Houghton Mifflin 1973), pp. 151-55; Sam W. Brown, Jr., *Storefront Organizing* (New York: Pyramid Books, 1972), pp. 64-76; D. Swing Meyer, *The Winning Candidate* (New York: James H. Heineman, 1966), ch. 13.

10. Film clips are especially appreciated by small, understaffed television news operations.

11. For example, Ben H. Bagdidian, *The Information Machines* (New York: Harper & Row, 1971); Douglas Cater, *The Fourth Branch of Government* (Boston: Houghton, Mifflin, 1959); William L. Rivers, *The Adversaries: Politics and the Press* (Boston: Beacon Press, 1970).

12. Hank Parkinson, *Winning Political Campaigns With Publicity* (Wichita, Kansas: Campaign Associates Press, 1973), pp. 31-32. These points are discussed on pp. 18-28.

13. Ibid., pp. 31-32. These points are discussed on pp. 32-49.

14. The common notation -30- apparently dates back to the early linotype operators. Upon completion of setting a story, the convention began of reaching up to the top line of the keyboard and hitting the first three keys, "-30," instead of the lengthier, "The End." Someone apparently made it symmetrical by adding another dash. Advancing technology is putting an end to -30-. As the typesetting function is increasingly being taken over by electronic optical scanners which "read" copy, and high-speed, tape-operated photocomposition machines that put "cold" type on film, these more literal machines have to use another symbol to signify the end of a story: @UF25 (-30- would simply transcribe as the number 30).

15. For further information on how to write news releases see *Democratic National Committee, Democratic Campaign Manual 1972* (Washington, D.C.: Democratic National Committee, 1972), pp. 67-69.

16. Parkinson, *Winning Campaigns with Publicity*, p. 23.

17. Brown, *Storefront Organizing*, pp. 76-82; *Democratic Campaign Manual 1972*, pp. 66-74; Meyer, *The Winning Candidate*, ch. 12; Hank Parkinson, *Winning Your Campaign* (Englewood Cliffs, N.J.: Prentice-Hall, 1970), pp. 89-110; Parkinson, *Winning Campaigns With Publicity*, pp. 51-68; Republican National Committee, *How To Get Publicity* (Washington, D.C.: Republican National Committee, 1965), pp. 3-8.

18. Joseph Napolitan, *The Election Game* (Garden City, New York: Doubleday, 1972), pp. 97-98.

19. Mary Meehan, *Letters-to-the-Editor for McGovern-Schriver* (St. Louis, Mo.: New Democratic Coalition, 1972).

For Further Reading and Research

Bagdikian, Ben H. *The Information Machines.* New York: Harper and Row, 1971.

Biegel, Len and Lubin, Aileen. *Mediability: A Guide for Non-Profits.* Washington, D.C.: Taft Products, Inc., 1975.

Crouse, Timothy. *The Boys on the Bus: Riding with the Campaign Press Corps.* New York: Random House, 1973.

Ferguson, James R. and Plattner, Marc F. *Report on Network News' Treatment of the 1972 Democratic Candidates.* Bloomington, Ind.: Alternative Educational Foundation, 1972.

Frank, Robert S. *Message Dimensions of Television News.* Lexington, Mass.: D.C. Heath, 1973.

Graber, Doris A. "Personal Qualities in Presidential Images: The Contribution of the Press." *Midwest Journal of Political Science* 16 (1972): 46-76.

——— . "The Press as Opinion Resource During the 1968 Presidential Campaign." *Public Opinion Quarterly* 35 (1971): 168-82.

Klein, Theodore and Danzig, Fred. *How to be Heard: Making the Media Work for You.* New York: MacMillan, 1974.

Lowry, Dennis T. "Measures of Network News Bias in the 1972 Presidential Campaign." *Journal of Broadcasting* 18 (1974): 387-402.

Meadow, Robert G. "Cross-Media Comparison of Coverage of the 1972 Presidential Campaign." *Journalism Quarterly* 50 (1973): 482-88.

Minnow, Newton; Martin, John Bartlow; and Mitchell, Lee. *Presidential Television.* New York: Basic Books, 1973.

Parkinson, Hank. *Winning Political Campaigns with Publicity.* Wichita, Kansas: Campaign Associates Press, 1973.

Pollock, Art. "Public Broadcasting and Politics: Florida's 'Politithon '70'." *Journal of Broadcasting* 18 (1973-74): 39-47.

Perry, James M. *Us and Them: How the Press Covered the 1972 Election.* New York: Clarkson N. Potter, 1973.

RePass, David E. and Chaffee, Steven H. "Administrative vs. Campaign Coverage of Two Presidents in Eight Partisan Dailies." *Journalism Quarterly* 45 (1968): 528-31.

Controlled Media
and Advertising Practices

Controlled media electioneering is required in virtually every campaign. Included in the controllable media are personal campaigning by the candidate and campaigner, party organization efforts, and all advertising efforts, whether they be through mass media or delivered on a smaller scale. Because of high costs, because the setting is not amenable, or perhaps because their personal values avoid use of the mass media, many candidates rely on the more personal and more exclusively political means of delivering controlled messages. Others assess their situations and find the purchase of time and space to be the most effective means of carrying out strategy.

The level of office appears to be the most significant factor in use of advertising as a means of controlled messages. Using braodcast time purchases as a measure of campaign advertising, the FCC reports that $58.9 million was spent for all offices in 1968. In 1970, with no presidential contest, the spending was nearly $50 million, due in large part to many, large state gubernatorial elections. The only election year with limits on broadcast spending at the national level was 1972. Yet, total broadcast spending was $59.6 million, a slight overall increase. Total presidential broadcast spending was $14.3 million, and total congressional spending was $13.8 million. Candidates for governor and lieutenant governor spent $9.7 million, and broadcast spending for all other state and local contests totaled $21.7 million in 1972. State and local elections are not subject to national spending limits.[1] The limited evidence available on broadcasting at other levels reveals that purchases are modest at best. One study of Michigan legislative candidates revealed that the "average" legislative candidate spent less than $300 on broadcast time; the range extended from zero to nearly $6,000. Less than one-third of the candidates spent over 50 percent of their budgets on radio and or television. Well over half of those who did use broadcasting used only one station. Those who used broadcasting extensively tended to be candidates from rural districts, those with larger and more complex campaign organizations, and those who spent more money overall.[2] A study of Illinois legislative campaigns revealed a similar pattern—paid political advertising and billboards ranked very low in usage. The most utilized techniques were, in order of importance: door-to-door, printed pamphlets, speaking to large groups, speaking to small groups, and newspaper advertisements.[3] The most important barriers to utilizing broadcast media in both studies were limitations of cost and setting; most candidates thought it was important and effective, but the nature of their district in relation to the station's reach, combined with the rates for purchasing time, precluded access.[4] Thus, they had to rely on other means of controlled media and advertising.

There are definite settings and strategies that call for use of controlled media. In general, the larger the constituency, both in terms of size and number of voters, the more important it is to use controlled media, particularly mass media. Wherever traditional party loyalties are not likely to be important in voting, or where the party organization is not particularly extensive or active in campaigns, controlled messages often must be used. The media are sometimes found to be necessary as supplements to or substitutes for small or inactive campaign organizations. When candidates lack public recognition or a firm identity, controlled media is ordinarily used to create it in the relatively short span of a campaign. When campaigners feel the need for more time and space than uncontrolled media are ordinarily used to create it in the relatively short span of a often developed and purchased. When uncontrolled media coverage is considered to be insufficient, unfavorable, or both, campaigners often select controlled media. Many other situations—whenever there is a need to reach large numbers of voters at relatively low cost, with the intention of motivating them by messages created by the campaigner—also dictate the use of controlled media.

This chapter examines the conventions and practicalities of campaign advertising. In the planning of a campaign, once campaigners decide to undertake controlled media and have decided which to employ (Chapter 12), they still must be familiar with the various approaches and techniques. After considering the nature of the campaign advertising function and the role of agencies in media, each major campaign medium—television, radio, newspaper, direct mail, literature, display and materials—is examined. They are treated individually because they are different in campaign advertising; an understanding of differential applications is critical. For each medium the approach is to examine its character as an advertising vehicle, special considerations for political campaigns, conventions of advertising techniques in campaigns, and relative costs.

ADVERTISING

Most controlled media messages can be considered advertising. Early in Chapter 11 it was explained how product advertising is used to rapidly expand markets by acceleration of information. Just as product advertising is designed to build up favorable brand images, campaign advertising is predicated on building a positive identity for the candidate.[5] The means used are varied: slogans, short messages, frequent messages, capsule descriptions, lengthy programs, positive image themes, hard-worker themes, young-vigorous themes, problem-solver themes, and so on. The vehicles are varied: newspapers, direct mail, display, printed literature, radio, and television. The object is also similar: instead of motivating a consumer to purchase a particular brand, one is motivating a voter to vote, and in a certain direction.

The advertising business actually has three integral components: clients, agencies, and the media. Clients are ordinarily the companies that produce the branded products and pay to advertise them. The media are, of course, those entities that carry messages to the public, each newspaper, broadcasting station, or billboard being an individual medium. Agencies prepare and place advertisements. In campaign advertising, the clients are normally candidate organizations, the media are similar, and agencies or persons in the campaign organization similarly have a role in the development and placement of ads.

WHAT AD AGENCIES DO IN CAMPAIGNS

Agency involvement in campaigning reaches farther back in history than the age of television. Broadcast expert Sig Mickelson traces their involvement back to Charles Evans Hughes' retention of the George H. Batten agency for his 1916 presidential campaign. Agencies were commonly used in the 1930s for the placement of newspaper and radio advertisements and for buying time for speeches to be broadcast over the radio.[6] But it was the advent of electronic media campaigning, particularly television, that brought ad agencies to a central role in the creation, production, and placement of political advertisements. Today the advertising agency is undoubtedly the single most frequent entrepreneurial participant in campaigns.[7] One study indicated that advertising services were the most frequently mentioned services offered in general election campaigns by all of the various types of consulting firms involved in campaigns.[8]

An unfortunate aspect of the role of ad agencies in political campaigns is that much more has been written about the proper ethics of advertising in politics, than about important operational questions. Questions such as how agencies work in politics, how effective their techniques are, how their methods differ from those of other political actors, or the impact of their techniques on the political system, have been virtually ignored. Many stereotypes and misconceptions have arisen about advertising personnel in politics. Among the more popular are—

- that advertising is used to create false impressions of candidates,
- that advertising is used to distort issues and candidate-issue preferences,

- that it is morally wrong to sell candidates like soap or cereal,

- that there is no way that the most commonly used short formats in advertising can offer serious discussion of candidates and issues.

The advertising people have established a common line of defense. They do not approve of distortion and false impressions. Most voters will not follow long programs. They do not create something that is not there; they convey what is there.[9] Supporters of both sides have proposed many reforms portrayed as quick and easy solutions. These discussions have been largely emotional rather than informational. It appears that only when we begin to understand what advertising does and what its impact is can we discuss reforms meaningfully.

The activities of advertising agencies in campaigns range from a rare case of managing the entire campaign, to such limited controlled media activities as placement of media. A few large agencies handle the publicity and public relations functions for campaigns, but ordinarily that is a separate function. (See Chapter 10.) Persons who are unfamiliar with communications often incorrectly regard advertising and public relations as identical. Typically, the advertising agency performs a more limited role: the preparation of advertisements, selection and placement of media, and measurement of the impact of the messages.

From our discussion of media time buying in Chapter 12, one rightfully would suspect that it is the complexities of controlled media which cause candidates to turn to ad agencies. The steps which precede placement are equally involved and require a blend of knowledge and experience. They may involve research into the constituency, surveys of population strata, or in-depth panel interviews with various voter types. Messages have to be designed, written, "story boarded," and finalized. Agencies can quickly produce designs for the entire complement of printed matter—stationery, posters, bumper stickers, brochures, and signs—that dot campaigns. They generally can produce or arrange for production in print, photo, sound, film, or video tape in a rapid and efficient manner, since they regularly deal with photographers and various audio-visual studios. Media are quickly selected on the basis of the buyer's familiarity with station personnel, audience reach and impact, pricing policies, and legal regulations. Agencies are also experienced purchasers of buttons, posters, car top cards, transit displays, and billboards. In some cases the agencies can even pretest advertisements to get a picture of the results before the ads are built into the campaign. Since the advertising portion of the campaign requires such a wide range of talent and experience, candidates often turn to agencies for assistance.

Campaigners often report difficulties in working with advertising agencies because advertising people feel that their experience in media also qualifies them as experts in politics and political campaigns. They claim that it becomes very difficult for the campaigner to make any meaningful political input when ad people have convinced themselves that they know all the answers.[10] Some advertising people are much more humble, admitting that their expertise is limited to a knowledge of media product advertising, and they seek the input of the campaigner. Still others fall somewhere in between these two extremes. Wherever a particular agency's people happen to be on this score, campaigners ordinarily insist that their ideas be put into action, and that someone in the campain be designated (often the uncontrolled media person—advertising agencies are usually not set up to perform day-to-day news chores) to act as liason with the agency. Many business advertisers operate on this principle. Their own advertising departments do the research and present the ideas to the agency for production and placement, with their own representatives working as liason. Candidate-advertisers ordinarily insist on similar arrangements.

When campaigners assess whether or not they are going to use an agency, and which agency to choose, they ordinarily try to discern something about the character, experience, range and depth of services, and cost of an agency. Nicholas Coleman, Majority Leader of the Minnesota Senate, from a dual vantage point as head of his own advertising agency and as an experienced campaigner, once promulgated a set of questions that a campaigner could ask an agency:

1. How would you characterize your basic interest in serving as the advertising agency for _____ candidate?

2. Will you be handling any other political campaigns at any level in _____ (year)?

3. What political advertising and public relations experience has your agency had?

4. If you were to handle this campaign, who would compose the account team? Who would handle the day-to-day account responsibility, and what other accounts does this individual have? (How much of his time would he be able to devote to _____ campaign?)

5. Specifically, what public relations staffing does your agency have and in what manner might this help be available for the campaign?

6. In general, how would you propose to handle a political campaign of this nature? Please detail how you would propose and develop campaign ideas.

7. On what basis would you be willing to make a presentation?

8. Would your agency have any interest in handling only the mechanical production and details in media selection and buying only? If so, how would you charge?

9. Would your agency be interested in handling the details on the mechanical and the media *plus* public relations only? If so, how would you charge for this?[11]

Colemen has worked for large and small agencies, and in addition to his own state senate campaigns, he has had experience in gubernatorial and U.S. Senate campaigns and he directed President Johnson's campaign in Minnesota in 1964. His questions may be important for other campaigners to ask.

As the preceeding paragraphs suggest, the services offered by agencies are useful, but not always essential. In larger campaigns, agencies are sometimes circumvented by campaign media coordinators putting together their own team of specialists, or by forming their own in-house agencies. The latter approach was used by the 1972 Nixon re-election campaign; the advertising agency known as The November Group was formed by bringing together a varied set of specialists on loan from established agencies. In smaller campaigns campaigners do without them.

Are Agencies Necessary?

Despite the fact that advertising agencies are the most numerous of entrepreneurial firms involved in campaigns, thousands of campaigns advertise without them. They are not employed for a host of reasons: there is not enough advertising through mass media; the cost is too high in relation to the perceived benefits; the campaigner does not see any benefits in using an agency; or, it simply does not occur to candidates to use an agency.

The crucial deciding factor appears to be the extensiveness of mass-media advertising used. One can almost hypothesize that the greater the number of media messages to be employed, the greater the amount of time and space; and, the greater the number of individual media outlets, the more likely an advertising firm is to be used. Some campaigns involve little more advertising than a card or brochure, and perhaps a newspaper ad or two. By contrast, other campaigns involve literally dozens of different messages using print, display, newspaper, radio, television, and direct mail channeled through hundreds of individual locations, local papers, stations, and individual mailings. Under these circumstances, campaigners face the question of whether or not they can internally design, create, produce, and place all of these dozens and hundreds, and still create and maintain the organization, raise funds, carry out the public relations, implement direct voter-contact activities, and all of the other things necessary to the campaign. If completion of these other as well as advertising activities are deemed unfeasible, then often the work is given to specialists.

Where the media-advertising effort is not extensive, particularly in small constituency campaigns, the advertising is created, produced (or hired out directly by the campaigner) and placed internally. Thousands of candidates follow this practice, many of them win, sometimes over opponents who use advertising agencies. They do this by either handling their own comparatively miniscule advertising or by selecting a public relations and media director who either knows or can learn enough basic advertising to do the job. Another frequent pattern is to utilize the volunteer skills of media and advertising persons in addition to, or in lieu of, a campaign contribution. In some areas there are persons who may be willing to lend their political-advertising skills from other campaigns to the present one. Persons in related media areas, such as public relations and advertising employees for businesses and organizations or university journalism people will often lend a hand. If the more extensive involvement of specialists is not available, perhaps their services can be employed to review advertising plans and creative work. A few campaign consulting firms are now reviewing advertising plans established by campaigners, with variable fee structures. In some cases the media themselves provide some advertising assistance.

Still another information resource is the advertising salespeople who peddle campaign wares, such as billboard space, printing, buttons and gadgets, broadcast time, and newspaper space. While these persons are necessarily biased in favor of selling their services, much valuable information can be gleaned from them, particularly if one seeks and sifts out the comparative advice of a number of salespersons. Therefore, one can consider also the availability of occasional consultation as a factor to be considered along with the extensiveness of media.

The cost of an agency's services also has to be considered. Agencies normally charge a standard 15 percent of all time and space billings plus creative costs and expenses. The media ordinarily allow a 15 percent discount on advertising placed through agencies, and the agencies then charge the amount the client would have paid, keeping the discount money as its fee. Larger campaigns with huge amounts of media placement are able to negotiate this fee downward. For the average campaign with modest advertising budgets (up to $500,000) this fee structure is rarely negotitated. These costs have to be blended in with other factors.

TELEVISION ADVERTISING

The dynamics of citizens' political attentiveness and entertainment habits have coalesced to make television advertising a central portion of many political campaigns. It has already been revealed that most people receive their campaign information from TV; indeed, a great body of voters are exclusively TV watchers. We also know that interest in political affairs, in general, or the seeking out of political braodcasts is not high on most citizens' lists of viewing preferences. Therefore, television campaigners try to place political messages before viewers by a combination of advertising in slots adjacent to the programs people usually watch, and by making the political productions interesting and exciting enough to keep this low-interest audience. The large audience of modern campaigns tends to be the less political people at home, not those who attend political meetings and rallies. The essence of television campaigning is to adjust to the medium and to adjust to the audience.

Characteristics and Problems of Television Advertising

The major difference between television and other media is that it combines the audio and visual components of them into a live or moving scenerio. According to media consultant Jay Weitzner, it therefore has the potential to develop involvement:

> Television has an inherent mobility. It moves. It captures time and makes a record of it. I can repeat for an infinite number of times an event that was recorded for television. A still photograph or a printed word is static, it does not move forward or backward. Furthermore, it takes a much more willful effort to ignore that which stimulates two of our senses than that which strikes only one. In other words, that which I see and hear involves me more than that which I just see. Once I am involved, I become a participant and add something of myself to what I see and hear. I add my own impressions and attitudes. I have become part of a circle of communication. I see a politician and add something of what I believe a politician should be. Gestalt psychology says that if we see an incomplete circle, we tend to complete it. Applying this to political communications, we can say that we try to complete as much as possible a circle of communication between politician and electorate by filling in the circle with attitudes learned about the voter and then letting him complete the figure.[12]

There are almost as many different techniques to successfully motivate voters on television as there are television people. But, practically all agree that one must capitalize on involving sight and sound.

To a certain extent the candidate has to become a rival performer to the television personalities that fill the air waves, both in news and entertainment formats. Indeed, one television consultant believes that the essence of gaining involvement is to portray political candidates in a similar fashion as the heroes that viewers see on westerns, crime, and other dramatic shows.[13] Short of such heroic portrayals, it is an advantage of controlled media to portray the candidate in the best light possible. An adjudged poor TV performer is rarely put in front of a live camera. If the candidate does not appear well in motion, then sound on video or scenery or places are used. Candidates who do project well are filmed or taped in their most natural settings. The television consultant tries to make the candidate look as good as his or her fellow performers, and short of that, to the best of his or her capabilities.

Then, of course, the average television candidate has other political performer rivals; the candidates for high visibility office. Most candidates cannot compete in attention, money, time, or expertise with the stars of political television. Candidates for president, governor, and senator appear more frequently in more professionally produced segments that draw larger audiences than other candidates. This consideration of setting is important to other candidates, and adjustments must be made. For example, long documentary programs over commercial television are probably not worth the money and effort for most candidates, even if one could afford them, given the size of the audiences they would likely attract.

While setting is important in the determination of a television advertising strategy, it need not preclude utilizing the advantages of television as a medium. Here the reference is to the common practice (in hundreds of medium size and small television markets) of presenting as political advertising the usual visual "radio" programs, speeches beside the flag, stand-up lectures, and scenes of the family (with dog) sitting on the living room sofa. Too often, campaigners fail to capitalize on the potential for moving involvement. The price that one pays is undoubtedly loss of audience, loss of attention, loss of motivation, and the risk of invidious comparison with the smoothly produced work of the high visibility candidates.

Conventions of Advertising Content

Political television is a long way from the stage where rules to capture moving involvement exist, but some conventions of reaching this objective may be useful. It has been suggested already that political television advertising is adjusted to the habits of the audience and to the capabilities of the performer. Beyond this, the conventions relate to content:

1. The image of the candidate and a few overriding issues are ordinarily stressed.
2. The visual portion is considered to be a representation of the message in support of the audio portion. This is sometimes done through a trial presentation of the story without the audio portion to see if it holds up. Depending on the image or issue to be conveyed they could be traffic jams on the freeway, cars driving up to closed gas stations, combines and tractors in action, ships and planes on the move, the candidate canoeing in a polluted stream or the candidate playing ball with a ghetto boys club. The audio is either the candidate or an announcer identifying and discussing the visual presentation.
3. The background for the visual is considered to be important. The sounds of farm machinery, boys yelling or the noise of the crowd add authenticity and drama. In large crowds the camera often pans the crowd to pick up reactions—signs of empathy depicting a wide range of supporters.
4. Candidates are portrayed as knowledgeable but not geniuslike, appearing competent to handle the office. Scripts are often written to magnify the candidate's virtues (without him or her personally dwelling on them) and by indirection, the opponents liabilities are made known.
5. Longer program formats need a great deal of planning, imagination, and production. They must quickly grab and hold audiences with such techniques as filmclips, newsreel segments, audience shots, and other illustrations. If the candidate speaks, it should be for shorter periods of time within the action shots.
6. Shorter spots require similar imagination, planning and production but ordinarily are limited to a single idea, issue or theme. They also require a less subtle approach to selling, ordinarily by directly asking the voter to vote for the candidate and naming him, or telling the voter to vote for the candidate

and naming him, implying that everyone else is voting for the candidate and naming him, or by having the candidate ask the voter for his vote and naming him.[14]

Within these very broad conventions of television advertising, there are no specific formulas that will create an impression in the minds of voters. The multiple answers are to be found in the minds of the voters. Naturally, the expectations, preconceptions, and predispositions of voters, through voting research, offer the most direct clues for developing themes and techniques.[15]

Matching Time Slots with Audience

That campaigners seek the maximum audience possible is another important principle of television advertising. Because of the low interest in politics, one must often locate and reach captive audiences. Carroll Newton once claimed that the audiences for political programs are determined by: (1) the size of the audience looking at the program immediately ahead, (2) the audience which tunes in for entertainment for the time for which a purchase is made, (3) the attraction values of the programs on other stations, and (4) the ability of a program to hold its audience varies in inverse proportion to its length.[16] Newton's rule of thumb is that 30-minute, set political speeches average ratings one-third below the programs they replace, 15-minute slots average between 5 to 10 percent. Sixty-second commercials show no loss.[17] Consequently, the trend has been to "buy television at times when the largest number of viewers habitually use their receivers and smaller units of time will reach more voters for your dollar."[18] Thus, much of television advertising has turned to short spots and five-minute trailers which are more effective because voters "have to listen before they can get up and switch them off."[19] It is within this context that the discussion of spots, programs, documentaries, and other formats should be understood.

Therefore, campaigners have turned to spots as the backbone of their advertising efforts because of the impressive advantages they offer. First, if the constituency is large enough and the geographic fit between the constituency and station audience is close, they offer the lowest cost per thousand in terms of reaching voters. Second, they not only reach audiences, but they are more likely to hold people, as compared to long paid programs. Third, they reach voters of all persuasions—Republicans, Democrats, Independents, committed, undecided, indifferent. Fourth, poll or research information can be quickly translated into production, conveying bits of information about images or issues. Fifth, they are relatively quick to produce compared to long television programs. In a few days time, poll results and ideas can be transformed into a tape or film. Sixth, they can be easily concentrated by priority, either by placement in certain markets, or by adjacencies to programs reaching certain audiences.

Television spots are of 10, 20, 30, and 60 seconds in length. Ordinarily they occur on the hour and the half-hour of programming. There are also 60-

second slots during programs, but on most stations, the networks sell them to national advertisers, and thus, they are prohibitive to all but presidential candidates. Occasionally they are available to local advertisers, particularly during non-prime time. Non-network stations, which specialize in sports and re-runs, ordinarily have program time slots available. Since all political advertising must contain a disclaimer (a statement that the ad is a political advertisement sponsored by the candidate's committee), and in some states the name of a responsible person is also required, the length of material must be reduced from 6 to 8 seconds. Unless the disclaimer is cleverly (and legally) woven into the text, spots are really about 52, 22, or 12 seconds long, making 10-second spots for campaigns all but impossible to run.

In sum, the structural advantages to using spot advertising for campaigns have much in common with their non-political advertising counterparts. According to Mickelson, "There's a single theme; a single copy approach; an opportunity for colorful and terse writing, and for attention-compelling graphic arts."[20] Themes can be presented in uncomplicated ways, making them understandable to virtually all viewers. Ordinarily, they serve to match a message to basic attitudes already existing in the viewer's mind, or to call attention to a candidate name or personality, or to some issue position.

In order to develop the candidate image or issue positions in a more detailed fashion, campaigners must turn to longer, controlled formats. What is lost in audience is gained in offering broader dimensions to those viewers who remain in attendance. Hopefully, not all who stay with the paid political program are supporters; the contemporary approach is to build in some of the drama, excitement, and action of the program it is replacing. Ordinarily, they are produced in a newsreel style, a combination of the candidate speaking and sound-on-action film.

The half-hour film or campaign documentary is becoming increasingly important in many large campaigns. They are generally used to either build up the image of the lesser known candidate or to document certain unknown accomplishments or ideas of a visible incumbent or an otherwise known candidate. Most presidential candidates who have been thrust on the national political scene quickly have used documentaries to introduce themselves to the electorate. Among them are Stevenson, Eisenhower, Kennedy, and McGovern. Those who were already known, such as Nixon, Humphrey, and Johnson, had the task of demonstrating to voters what they had accomplished in government over the years. In 1968, Humphrey used the documentary route to try to portray his earlier struggles for peace, civil rights, and economic security to newer voters; the young, the poor, and to blacks. Political consultant Napolitan suggests that the half-hour political documentary must:

1. Have an engaging opening; it must grip people in the first minute, or they'll switch off.
2. Be entertaining as well as informative, because it is competing against the best that commercial television has to offer.

3. Be properly promoted, unlike the accidentially viewed spots, one must get voters to tune in for it.[21]

Since about 1966, the half-hour documentary program has taken on these characteristics, generally replacing the half-hour television speech.

A compromise between the half-hour format and the spot is the five-minute program. Many stations will sell the first or last five minutes of certain programming segments. The times available vary from station to station; some will only sell them during the day, some will sell segments just before and post-prime-time hours, and some will sell them during prime-time programming. Of course, one should pay careful attention to the size and character of the audiences in each segment purchased. Five minutes gives the candidate an opportunity to discuss more elaborately one or two issues or to detail one or two important facets of a candidate's leadership potential or performance. The same attention to catching and holding the audience applies, but promotion is not as necessary, since the aim is to catch the audience of the program it has shortened.

Television time costs vary at a given station with the length of time of the format and the size of the audience or the importance of the time. Stations in larger markets charge more than stations in smaller markets. Rate structures for prime-time 30-second spots can cost as much as $3,000 for a single spot whereas non-prime time (after midnight) can be as low as $50 on the same station. Smaller stations ordinarily charge less, ranging from $50 to $150 per 30-second spot. A single network spot announcement for a presidential candidate can easily cost over $25,000. Program time ranges from about $1,500 to $2,000 for a half-hour show on a smaller station to over $80,000 for a half-hour of network prime time. Broadcasters are now required to make time available to political advertisers at the same rate as non-political advertisers, and they must make time available for purchase to all candidates if they sell time to one.

Cable Television

Cable television (CATV) offers an opportunity for controlled television as well. There are over 2,000 CATV systems in the United States, offering free time and selectivity. Since cable relies on subscription rather than on the sale of time, and because of the availability of extra channels, cable television offers notable advantages. The capabilities of CATV studios vary: some have "live" capabilities; others "cablecast" through video tapes, 16-mm films, slides, or audio tapes; and some stations have all of these. Programs are often repeated in several time periods, including prime time. This allows the candidate to reach a wider audience at no cost. While the audiences are smaller than commercial television, CATV also offers selectivity, in that it offers access to specific identifiable communities, both in a geographic and demographic sense. Many cable-television studios will accept candidates for office in controlled formats.

RADIO ADVERTISING

Radio has become so much a part of our surroundings that it is hard to recognize its importance and existence. The surveys reported in Chapter 11, depicting television as replacing radio as the most important source of campaign information and indicating the low ratings given radio, masks the fact that radio still has an important role. The hundreds of millions of radio receivers in existence and the hours spent listening to them while one is driving, doing household chores, working, studying, or relaxing with a game or magazine make it difficult to see the importance of radio; one almost always is doing something else with radio in the background. Also, it was suggested that radio is a much more segmented medium than television. Audiences can be broken down by station and program listeners. There are stations which appeal to the young, blacks, Spanish-speaking citizens, the middle-aged and older, the well-educated, and the higher-income. There are programs which appeal to ethnic groups, women, senior citizens, and farmers as well. There are time slots within stations which appeal to the same groups. Unlike television stations, radio stations are more likely to gain the loyalty of listeners; viewers select television programs regardless of the channel, whereas listeners tend to select stations based on knowledge of previous programming.

In addition to being more selective, there are other important differences between radio and television. First, radio advertising is much lower in cost. For example, one can purchase about four radio spots for the cost of one TV spot. Except in the very largest of stations, the cost of program time is well within the reach of any campaigner. In addition to its low cost, radio offers the advantage of relative speed and ease in production and acquisition. Since the only absolutely necessary production equipment is a tape recorder, ideas can be quickly turned into scripts which can be recorded for immediate replay. Radio can thus capitalize on instant information, making it possible to respond to an event, offer a solution to a late-breaking crisis, or answer a charge from the opposition. These same characteristics also make it possible to produce a greater number of appeals, at relatively little proportional increase in one's media-production budget. It is much easier and cheaper to cut a senior-citizen spot, Spanish-language spot, youth get-out-and-vote spot, etc., for radio than to do the same for television. Also, radio's low cost, speed, and flexibility combine to make it easier to saturate a given market with coverage. While there is no exact formula for saturation, one adman's conservative estimate would be a minimum of twenty-four spots per week per station or alternatively 120 per week, in a five station market.[22] Such extensive coverage is closer to the reach of the average candidate than any television saturation formula.

Campaign radio advertising formats are similar to TV formats—spots, programs, and special programming; and, they are of similar lengths.

Radio Spots

Radio spots are to be approached with much the same general objectives in mind as television spots. They are probably most frequently used in establishing and reinforcing candidate identification, thereby calling attention to or cueing the voter to other controlled and uncontrolled media. Because the listener is ordinarily doing something else while listening to the spot, special effort is often placed on gaining attention or moving the listener's ear momentarily from the background to the foreground. Light distinctive effects are sometimes used, such as an alarm clock, a train whistle, a police whistle, or other sound effects, to cue the listener to the spot. Often these effects are repeated with different copy as a link to candidate identification. To make the body of the spot interesting, multiple voices are often used through such means as an announcer introducing or questioning the candidate, having some citizen type ask the candidate a question, using multiple testimonials, or a short interview. Repetition and identification are sometimes conveniently combined. The 1968 Illinois gubernatorial candidate, Richard Ogilvie, led into and trailed out of his spots with an announcer shouting, "OGILVIE! OGILVIE! OGILVIE!. . .OGILVIE! OGILVIE! OGILVIE!" Needless to say, the 20- and 30-second spots had time for little else.

Spot campaigns can be planned with a reasonable amount of self-preparation, although they may require some consultation. Spots must be aired repeatedly, and they must be timed within braodcast hours in order to reach the intended audience. In order to accomplish this, one must decide what segment of the voting public one wishes to reach with what messages, and then consult the audience breakouts, program schedules, and station advertising manager. Settings and strategies vary so greatly that it is difficult to state how many spots one should purchase and for how long. It is not at all unusual to begin a schedule two months in advance of the election, working up to an accelerated-finish schedule in the last week or two of the campaign. Stations often offer discounts for quantity purchases, the actual number varying from around one hundred at small stations to many more in the larger stations. Sometimes quantity discounts really are not bargains in as much as the station may insist on running them at low audience times or at times when the intended audience is not listening. The largest audiences are morning and evening drive times, and particularly the evening slots just before the national television news and prime-time viewing start. Before and after the local news in the morning, at noon, and in the evenings are particularly good times too. Special times for special audiences should be checked carefully.

The rate structures for radio spots are figured in a similar fashion to television, i.e., they vary according to the size and reach of the audience for any given program time. The highest prices are normally around the drive and news times. The cost range is vast, from about $100 per one-minute spot in the very largest audience stations, to as low as one or two dollars per ten-second spot (in large quantities with no time specification) in small rural stations. As examples of what a total campaign spot schedule would cost, congressional candidates have been known to put together: a 425-spot, three per day, three week 11-station rural schedule for $2,143; and in an urban district, a 543-spot, four per day, three week, 10-station schedule for $6,008.[23] Legislative district cost structures are considerably lower, since there are rarely more than three or four stations. A fairly extensive three-week package can be built for $500 to $1,000.

Programs and Longer Formats

Radio programs ordinarily come in more flexible time slots than television. Since few stations have much in the way of programming anymore, programs are generally available in 5-, 10-, 15- and 30-minute portions. Given the audience habits of listeners, most campaigners steer clear of longer programs.

In order to hold an audience with a political program that brackets the news or that pre-empts a favorite program or music segment, one must be as imaginative or creative as in television. Various techniques and effects have been used to avoid the radio speech, such as: the interview format; a panel of experts and citizens questioning the candidate; on-the-spot interviews at the candidate's office, store, or farm; talks before live audiences; or varied formats around a short speech. Again, effects, such as the sound of the farm in the background, the crowd applauding, background conversation, a lead-in with a sports event or news-like commentator, are used to catch and hold the audience. In general, any device to keep the normal audience from moving the dial to an entertainment format should be used. To hedge their bets, radio program scripts often are subtly interspersed with spot-like candidate identification and requests for a vote.

The cost and benefits of radio programs very often make them worthwhile. The cost of purchasing blocs of radio time may sometimes be less than an equal number of sponsor spot minutes. Thirty minutes of mid-range time (evening or daytime) on a major city station ordinarily sells from $200 to $300. Smaller city stations and small stations sell program time for much lower rates, sometimes under $50. Five-minute programs vary similarly, with prime-time programs selling for around $100 each in the very largest of stations, others for much less. Statewide candidates have been known to set up very inexpensive statewide radio networks; one in Oregon bought thirty evening minutes on twenty-five stations in 1972 for $732.[24] While these audiences are not huge, they are considerably larger than audiences reached by personal appearances. Moreoever, radio programs often have other effects. Often, the news department will lift out portions for coverage in the day following the broadcast. A printed copy to the newspapers will also elicit coverage. Using programs along with spots reaches the information-seeking, multimedia voter. Additionally, if spots and programs are used, it allows the candidate to say that he has invested money in trying to inform voters, against any who might assail a spot campaign.

Audience size, audience quality, news coverage, cost, and other factors have combined to work the radio address back into campaign popularity. Among others, President Nixon turned to this vehicle in 1968, and to an even greater extent in 1972. In addition to the advantages of low cost, reaching the informed voter, and relatively good news coverage his radio speeches received, the

President and his media advisors found other advantages to the radio setting. First, they found it easier for him to prepare for them, one advance read-through as opposed to studios, make up, lights, concern about expressions, beard, and so on. Second, they simply felt his style and voice were better on radio than TV. Third, radio is less demanding of audience attention, and it can reach audiences that TV might miss. Fourth, the President and his advisors wished to capitalize on the fact that radio is more conducive to discussion of issues. Fifth, they felt that there was less risk of overexposure, or wearing out one's welcome on radio. Television being a dominating medium can get the public "up" too often. And sixth, the size of the audience is not insignificant. His media advisors estimated the audiences to be as high as 10 million. Nixon's radio addresses were considered not so much an alternative to TV but to giving speeches at rallies or dinners where the audiences were a thousand or two at most.[25]

Although radio advertising does not have nearly the impact of television, radio's potential in terms of low cost, production accessability, coverage, and ability to reach special groups should not be underestimated. Its potential for fitting into the setting and strategy of the average candidate is considerable.

NEWSPAPER ADVERTISING

Campaign advertising in local newspapers has many attractive advantages. The newspaper is a regular part of its readers' daily experience, with a habitual place and time of reading. This gives it an intimacy and sense of identification on the readers' part. Formats, in terms of the size and the location of the ads in the paper, can be suited exactly to advertisers' specifications. The cost of obtaining space is relatively inexpensive in comparison to the potential number of voters to be reached. Both creation and production, in terms of accessability, skill, and cost, are the easiest for the amateur to master. Newspaper advertising is also speedy; when billboards are booked up and when radio and television time is sold out, newspapers can always make room for that late advertising money. While they ordinarily have a twenty-four-hour dealine, newspapers have been known to take ads in a few hours; the normal process of layout, finished art, photos, copy, typesetting, paste-up and engraving is regularly performed on a highly accelerated schedule.[26] Since the newspaper is the most complete or the only source (for some campaigns) of news about local politics, campaigners can meet seekers of such political information by advertising in their medium. It may also be an important source of establishing campaign credibility, particularly in campaigns where the other media offer no coverage, and advertising in electronic media is not possible.[27] Finally, newspaper advertising can do many of the things that other forms of advertising can; it can create candidate identity and image, convey issue information, and identify party, among others.

Advertising in newspapers should not be undertaken, however, without an understanding of its limitations in comparison with advertising in the other media. First, as was demonstrated in Chapter 11, the audiences are neither as large nor as loyal as the electronic-media audiences, both in terms of sheer size and as a source of campaign information. Second, the exact audiences that newspapers reach are difficult to define. A circulation of 50,000 does not mean that 50,000 people will read the paper or even see an ad, given the erratic habits of newspaper readers. Since newspapers do not identify which homes their papers reach, the difficulty of targeting audiences is compounded further. By comparison, direct mail and literature can be placed in the exact hands or homes one wishes. Third, newspaper ads are less flexible than other print advertising; they are rarely cut out, and they rarely sit around for a few days before being read. And fourth, an ad in the paper cannot be as flexibly designed as other print advertising. An ad only appears once, whereas letters or literature can be used at many events, distributed in a number of places at differeent points throughout the campaign.[28]

Types of Campaign Newspaper Advertising

Newspaper ads can be broken down into four basic types: those that identify, those that endorse, those that promote, and those that narrate. All ads, to a certain extent, convey identification, but some are small billboards with little more than a slogan and the candidate's name in large type. Since most candidates from the congressional level on down the ticket suffer a serious lack of candidate identity, this is not an unimportant function of advertising. The second type comes in three different forms: an endorsement from a prominent public official; a testimonial or set of testimonials, with a citizen or citizens explaining why they support the candidate; and ads which list columns of names of people who are supporting the candidate. Advertising people seem to be split evenly on the effectiveness of this type of promotion. Endorsements probably have more of a party reinforcement effect, since it is almost always a fellow partisan. Testimonials usually portray ordinary citizens, telling a short, interesting, seemingly impartial story, rather than the usual politician's patter. Lists of supporters printed in the paper (usually paid for by the small contributions of those who appear) convey a sense of broad support and have considerable appeal as local citizens like to peruse the list for familiar names. Some ads are designed to promote attendance at campaign rallies or party meetings, to build up an audience for radio or television shows, to encourage volunteer supporters, or to raise funds. These ads are normally small in size and include candidate identification. Volunteer and fund-raising ads must contain both a coupon and a return address and telephone number. The fourth type of ad is the long format wherein a background story on the candidate is told, issue positions are spelled out in reasonable detail, or the candidate writes a column. These ads are often made to look like news columns, but the disclaimer will identify it as an advertisement. There is no reason why these longer-copy ads cannot contain bold type identifying the candidate, art work, or photos; many of them do.[29] These longer formats, in combination with other types of controlled and uncontrolled media, may be the most important means of getting information to the interested, issue voter. In the campaign for which electronic media is unreasonable, they may be the functional equivalent to purchased programs.

Attention may have to be given to placement of the ads, securing positions that will reach the intended public. Examples are women's appeals on the society or women's page, men's on the sports or business page, longer issue or development ads on an inside news page; testimonials on the local news page. Program promotion ads are almost always placed on the page containing program listings. The top right-hand corner of each page is the most read portion of the page. All these positions usually have to be reserved in advance, and they are priced according to readership.

Composition and Cost

Preparation for newspaper ads should take into consideration the variations in composition. Regular size newspapers vary from 18 to 22 inches in depth, and tabloids from 14 to 16 inches. Column widths vary from 11 picas to 2½ inches; most newspapers have eight columns with 310 lines per column, but, more are using six, wider columns (e.g., six 13.5-pica columns with 303 lines per column) and a smaller overall size. Mats (paper reproductions from engravings) are often used for multiple reproductions of the ad. Large ads may present a problem for some small town newspapers, since their mat casting boxes take a minimum ad of 5 columns by 10 inches. Larger ads must have more than one mat, and the ad must have natural separations. Papers that are printed by offset presses require reproduction proofs rather than mats. The campaign advertiser has to check the specifications and special requirements for each paper. When ads are submitted, it is advisable to include special instructions for increasing or decreasing the size of the ad so the newspaper can tailor it to its specifications.[30]

The cost of newspaper advertising varies enormously with the circulation of the paper, the size of the ad, and the position in the newspaper. A full-page ad in the prestigious "Week in Review" section of *The Sunday New York Times* costs around $9,000. Small town dailies charge from $300 to $500 per page, and weeklies are much lower, sometimes as low as $75 to $100 per page. Few campaigners purchase many full-page ads, and rates are scaled down accordingly. Space is usually sold at a certain rate-per-column line, ranging from around $1.00 in small weeklies to $3.30 in metropolitan dailies. Basic rates are for run-of-paper, i.e., anywhere in the paper, any page, any position, at the top or bottom of a column or wherever it happens to be placed. Specific pages or positions are at an extra charge.[31] Rates are quoted both as open (for smaller single purchases) and by volume discount.

Although the fundamentals of newspaper advertising are relatively simple to grasp, it would be wise to check one's plans and work with knowledgeable people. Like every other medium, newspapers reach certain persons and can do certain things, but they have limitations. The decision to use them should not be based on easy accessability or low cost alone, but rather on strategic principles.

DIRECT-MAIL ADVERTISING

Using the mails to appeal to voters is a mass medium only in the sense of the number of voters contacted by a single effort. Most campaigners who use direct mail differentiate the electorate in some way, usually by selecting out a group of people on a list who share some characteristic in common, and then tailoring a message to them. Political consultants like to depict direct mail as the rifleshot approach, whereas they term the other forms of advertising the shotgun approach. If used to tailor specific appeals to individual voters, direct mail is the most individual of the mass media.

It is this "individuality" which makes direct mail so attractive to many campaigners. It is the only mass medium which assures the campaigner that *specified individual voters* (as opposed to groups of individuals) receive the messages sent. Categories of specified individuals can be expanded or contracted, and portions of categories can be singled out, depending on strategy, cost, and other decisional factors. Virtually any stratification group—Republicans, undecided, farmers, residents of Elm township, St. Joseph's parishoners, auto licensees, or infinite portions or combinations of them can be included or excluded. The messages can be changed to appeal to the various groups. In the more sophisticated data-processing systems, for example, one could write about the accomplishments of the Republican party for farmers in paragraph one, the candidate's support for parochial schools in paragraph two, and the need for no-fault insurance in paragraph three, and then ask the recipients of the letter and their neighbors to support the candidate. Many variations and alternatives of this letter can be generated, e.g., for a Democratic, supporter, salesman, resident of Spruce City, St. Luke's Luthern parishoner, who owns no automobile. Direct mail also can be the central vehicle of mass communication in constituencies where electronic media or newspapers are difficult to use. In districts that are small portions of large cities or in very remote areas, mail can substitute for media, or can at least extend the reach in areas where coverage is not adequate.

Along with advantages, direct mail also suffers from its own set of reservations. One can be certain that the messages are sent to individual voters, but one cannot be certain that they are read very carefully, or even read at all, by the recipient. Political mailings, of course, range from those which appear identical to the individually typed business letter, to those which appear identical to junk mail. Regardless, unless the political mailing technique happens to be new to the area, voters appear to be able to sense "mass mailing." While the exact rate of readership is unknown, it obviously is not 100 percent. The return rate on direct-mail sales is two to four per hundred; the voter motivation rate is yet to be determined. A second and related problem is more like a dilemma. Direct mail letter writing has tended to be dull, pious, black and white sheets of copy which do not "grab" the reader. On the other hand, movement toward slick production, art work, color varied print, and involved layout also gives the letter away as an advertising piece. It may attract attention, but it also moves the letter far from the personalized appeal. The contemporary practice is to use succinct, individualized business letters, and, if desired, a piece of campaign literature is added. Two other reservations will become clearer later. Direct mail can be logistically difficult to deal with, requiring considerable managerial time and skill, and it can be costly.

Computer-Generated Letters

The advent of computers has added enormous flexibility to making selective appeals. A simple example will illustrate. Suppose a data bank with names and addresses of persons in households also contained the following information:

Republican identifier	Supporter of candidate	Laborer-union
Democratic identifier	Leans toward candidate	Business-sales
Independent	Undecided	Farmer
	Opposition supporter	

This information could be gathered in a voter canvass, allowing flexible letters to be written on the basis of location, political leanings, candidate support, and issues. Suppose the candidate is a Democrat running in a district with five counties. A basic letter could be formulated in which: in the first paragraph, the partisan accomplishments could be heralded or a bipartisan appeal made, depending on the recipient's party identification; the second paragraph could either reinforce the support of the voter, try to activate latent support, or try to convert; the third paragraph could contain an appeal to one of three specific issues based on the occupation of the head of household; the fourth paragraph could stress some issue or project of appeal and interest to the voters of the particular county; and the closing paragraph could ask the voters in the household, by name, to join with their fellow (Democrats) (Neighbors of the County) (Republicans) (union members) in supporting the candidate. Many different variations on this can be created, by either expanding or collapsing the information. This package could be written with fifteen basic letters (with location and party as the basis), but could easily be expanded to include 180 different letters.

Some computers can easily put out over 1,000 letters per hour. The computer and its auxiliary equipment can also add other personal touches, such as putting the recipient's name in two or three places throughout the letter, sign an authentic looking signature (with smearable ink), stuff the envelope and, of course, address it.

Lists and Appeals

Less elaborate direct-mail schemes can easily be developed without a computer. Campaigners often merely select lists of people and robotype (automatic typewriter), print, duplicate, or manually type the same letter to every person on a list, with different letters being composed for each list. Sometimes very simple variations are created for the same list. The letters are always addressed to a particular interest or situation one assumes the voter to have, based on the way they are categorized. Thus, property taxes are discussed with homeowners, schools are discussed to the parents of young children, flood control to the residents of a flood plain, labor issues to union members, streets to residents of pot-holed streets, and crop insurance to farmers.

Campaigners working for Wes Uhlmann's successful capture of the Seattle mayor's office in 1969 used tremendous ingenuity in direct-mail appeals. They went to the assessor's office for lists of applicants for special senior-citizen tax exemptions. They were sent a mailing that said Uhlmann believed property tax relief for the retired should be greater. Voters whose homes were in the path of a proposed freeway received a special mailing, as did school teachers, retired school teachers, policemen, retired policemen, and employees of the Seattle electric company. Mailings also went to ethnic groups, alumni of denominational schools and universities, and members of religious groups. Heads of households in selected neighborhoods got personalized letters reading "People in _____ community have long been overlooked. . . ." In all, 75,861 letters were sent before the primary and 156,000 before the general election.[32]

There are many different types of lists and sources of lists. In some states registered voters are separated by party registration as well as residence. In others, lists of voters are available and the partisanship or candidate disposition must be canvassed. Another candidate from an overlapping constituency or a previous candidate may also be willing to donate lists. Many other lists are available, either from donation by a friendly source or by purchase. Sometimes professional associations, church groups, labor unions, politically oriented groups which are also friendly to a candidacy (e.g., peace groups, AMA, ACA, Farmers Union) or other community groups will make their lists available. Direct-mail firms have commercial lists available which can be used for political purposes: physicians, lawyers, clergymen, small businessmen, college students, working women, and parents of parochial school children; lists of people by the value of their homes, their income levels, and the ownership of certain goods, such as boats or airplanes. Ordinarily these lists cover wide geographic areas, but they can be sorted to suit the constituency.

Letters are not the only means of direct-mail advertising. Special ads, flyers, or literature are also delivered through the mails. A commonly used direct-mail technique in many campaigns is the personalized post card. Volunteers ordinarily hand write personalized messages to persons they know. In small campaigns the candidate and his or her family often write them personally. A variant of this is to print the candidate's name, picture, and a few words across the top of the post card, leaving room for a personalized, handwritten message.

Mechanics and Cost Considerations

Beyond the strategic decisions to select individuals from various groups and the appeals to them, there are many intricacies involved in direct-mail work. The many steps include: selecting lists; writing copy; securing paper, envelopes, or other inserts; arranging for stuffing; and understanding and meeting the postal requirements (proper addressing and sorting procedures). A few examples will illustrate how complex mailings can be. Three sheets of sixteen-pound paper, a 3 by 5 return card, and a number nine envelope weigh slightly less than one ounce. The same card and three sheets of twenty-pound paper and a number ten envelope weigh slightly more than one ounce, increasing the postage bill. Bulk mail, if it exceeds one ounce, is cheaper than first class under current rates, but its use requires a different set of procedures and regulations. There is a charge for a bulk rate permit application and an annual license fee, which means that the volume of mailing should be sufficient to offset the initial costs. Also, bulk mail must be handled precisely according to postal regulations, one of which is counting, sorting and tieing by zip code. Metered mail of all classes must be sorted and tied. Another intricacy is the type of addressing machinery one might have to employ. There are at least five types: hand-addressed, hand-typed (gummed labels or on the envelope), address plates, Cheshire (a computer-printed label that is cut and affixed by a special machine which takes computer paper) and pressure-sensitive. These are but a few of the many details involved in mailing. Obviously, plans for a mailing, including the exact system, calculating costs, and estimating the labor involved, must be determined in advance. Persons who take on the responsibility should become familiar with various procedures and costs, visit the post office for an explanation of their requirements and procedures, and seek the advice of experienced direct mailers.

The cost of direct mailing is not insignificant. A printed mailing to 1,000 households, with donated labor, will cost between $150 to $200, or fifteen to twenty cents each when printing, paper, envelope, and postage are considered. If lists are purchased, that cost must be added; ordinarily between $25 and $50 per thousand names. Computer-generated letters are more, currently between twenty-five and thirty cents each. Direct-mail houses offer a wide range of services for a fee, of course. If a campaign has a large number of volunteers, much of the handling, stuffing, and addressing can be done at headquarters. But one cannot escape the basic costs of printing, duplicating, materials, and postage. Volunteers cannot deliver letters to mail boxes. There are private postal services in some metropolitan areas which claim they can deliver mail for 40 to 60 percent less than the U.S. Postal Service.

Direct mail can be an important means of reaching specifically identified voters with controlled messages, but plans, cost estimates, details, and advice are required before serious commitments are made.

LITERATURE

Printed literature seems to be that aspect of the advertising campaign which is most universal. In almost every campaign someone goes to the local print shop and orders a basic piece, ranging from the 2-by-3 inch black and white calling card to the four-fold, four color 2-by-3 foot foldouts. Perhaps they are so universal because so many other candidates have used them and others follow suit. Even in the small campaign, printed literature is some sort of benchmark of authenticity. Literature does have its function in the controlled media section of the campaign; and a better understanding of what those functions are and their applications to a particular setting should help determine its usage.

Literature can be used strategically to appeal to different segments of the constituency. For this reason many campaigners do not have a single piece of literature, but several, each designed to an important segment of the constituency. For example, if one had a large farm and labor population to appeal to, a brochure designed for each of these groups would be appropriate. Large campaigns often have as many as a dozen different pieces of literature. In fact, one of the biggest failings in campaign literature is the practice of designing it without the intended audience in mind.

Literature also seems to be necessary to convince the candidate, active campaigners, and supporters that there is movement to the campaign, that something is happening because literature is available for distribution. More importantly, candidates and campaign workers usually do need something to hand out as they campaign door-to-door or meet people at plant gates, shopping centers, church entrances, and fairs. Literature serves to ease the personal contact between the political and less political person, somehow conveying to them that here is something we worked on and paid for, therefore, we are authentic.

Printed matter should always be designed with strategic principles in mind. What is the card or brochure trying to do, and to whom? Literature can be designed to serve one of several purposes: to create and establish candidate identity; to develop issue positions; to reinforce support, particularly partisan; to urge voters to participate in election-centered events, such as attending an event, contributing to the campaign, registering to vote, or turning out to vote; and to call attention to the fact that an election is going on.[33] Sometimes more than one stratagem is contained in a brochure. It appears easier to mix some of these strategic purposes than it does to combine targeted groups, but care should be taken to avoid doing too much.

Production of Literature

Like other forms of advertising, the strategic principles should be translated into production with considerable care. The experts usually recommend that the writing style should be succinct or crisp, and yet informative. The design should be graphically appealing, containing some design, color, and action photographs. The important consideration to keep in mind is that this piece is going to be delivered to many who are not very political, and that they get most of their campaign information watching television. They know little about the candidates except for those running for a few offices. Thus, brochures are ordinarily attractively designed with a picture, slogan, or theme, and above all, the name of the candidate in large print on each face of the piece (like a billboard), making it possible for the recipient to at least have the picture or graphics call attention to the name of the candidate in the event that the copy is not read. Candidates often believe that because they have put a lot of thought, work, and money into a brochure, voters will somehow know this and read every word of it. The brochures dropped in a 100-foot radius of central distribution points, such as parking lots and fair grounds, make that a tenuous assumption. Thus, care in design is as relevant as care in creating the message.

The technicalities of brochure production are not difficult to grasp, but nevertheless, they should be investigated and established in advance. There are many size variations, the most basic are 8½-by-11-inch variations with a single fold or the 5½-by-8½ half size. Some suggest a smaller pocket or postcard size (3½ by 5½ or 3 by 5) to avoid the quick drop problem. The number required also varies with need and scale, and it is usually less than most people order. In a small constituency campaign 2,000 or 3,000 should suffice, and between 10,000 and 20,000 in larger campaigns are generally all that are used. Many campaigners will have to consider the necessity of a union label ("bug") on their printed matter, particularly if there is a large union membership in the constituency or the campaign has a union relationship.

Lead time is very important. It not only ensures that the printing will be ready at the time of distribution, but time is necessary to check and recheck material in order to avoid costly mistakes. Also, printers are not usually enthusiastic about interrupting jobs they have from regular customers for a small, political job.

The steps involved in preparation are relatively simple: define the purpose; prepare the copy, assemble photographs, and art work; prepare a rough sketch of the piece; secure approval for the copy; get bids from printers; the printer prepares a mechanical; proof reading for typographical errors or imperfections; final approval; and printing.[34] As in the case of other forms of advertising, checking plans and designs with experienced persons and asking questions of printers while seeking price estimates is ordinarily done, even by the experienced. Some printing firms do offer design and layout services, and most will have display samples on hand.

The cost of print advertising varies with the type of package to be put together. The most important variables are the printing process used, the paper quality, the size of the piece, the number of colors used, the engraving required, and the quantity to be printed. The normal range is broad; between one and ten cents per piece. The only way to establish cost is to check well in advance, carefully specifying every possible detail.

Print literature, whether a single sheet pamphlet or a brochure, can be an important facet of conveying controlled campaign messages. It has greater lasting power than other media, in that it can remain in the voters' possession for a long period of time. It also can have the advantage of longevity—being used throughout the entire course of the campaign. On the other hand, the readability rate of literature, notwithstanding effectiveness levels as motivators, is yet to be established. Campaigners should use literature if it is decided that its use is consistent with setting and strategy, and the design should follow these guidelines.

DISPLAY ADVERTISING

Campaign display—billboards, transit cards, lawn signs, posters, and window signs—has very limited uses in the controlled media portion of the campaign. Since the audience almost always passes by the message very fast (up to sixty miles per hour) and rarely has a chance to study it, display must be restricted to a very few words. Display media distracts viewers from what they are doing, for a fleeting glimpse or series of glimpses. Some feel that these quick views should leave an impression on the subconscious, and people are unaware that an impression is being made. Repetition of the impression should make it indelible for the time required.[35] Display advertising, therefore, is ordinarily restricted to a single message.

In most campaign displays that single message is either to simply identify the candidate or to link up the name of the candidate with a very simple theme, the election, or the candidate's party. Thus, display ordinarily contains—the name of the candidate and the office sought; the name, office, and party; the name, office, party, and election date; the name, office, and a slogan, such as "A New Leader"; the name and office blended into a slogan, such as "A Congressman of Action"; or some variation of these. The single most important function of display is name identification. They are a signal to people that the candidate is running. Display calls attention to the campaign; to the fact that an election is going on; that the person who appears on the sign is in that election; and, as a cue to people, that other media will contain additional information. Display often appears first in the campaign, before radio, TV and newspapers "kick in;" it gives the campaign that initial boost that voters and activists often need. Candiates who lack identity need display early in the campaign to let people know they are running. Established candidates need it less for identity purposes, but they too use it as an early warning signal that they are running again.

Location and Format

Since people view display in passing, location is the most important technical consideration. Simply put, one tries to put display in the busiest locations without a great deal of concern for segmentation of the electorate. The only quantitatively established locations are those of billboard sites. Outdoor display companies have established and ranked locations by the number of people who pass a given location. These "showings" are projections of the proportion of that number of people in a given area who will see a billboard message at least once during a week. In some areas a showing ranked 100 will require hundreds of boards, whereas in small towns the same rate can be achieved with 5 or 10 boards. Rates are set by whether a board has a 50, 75, or 100 showing rank. Transit rates are set by similar means. Securing locations for billboards and transit requires the most lead time of any controlled media. Choice locations are reserved from one year to eighteen months in advance. Many candidates reserve space as soon as they decide to run and cancel or subcontract the space later, if they decide not to use it. Billboards and transit are contracted on a monthly basis, and they are run for 30 or 60 days in a campaign. The only way that locations for other types of display can be established is on the basis of the judgment of someone who knows the area. This is why one often finds local supporters placing their own display signs in a campaign.

The format for most display is simple to grasp, in principle, but may require the assistance of someone with experience. The message rarely contains more than from 5 to 10 words. Pictures are ordinarily not used unless some action can be blended in, such as the candidate at the steps of the city hall or state capitol. The design must make the name stand out. Often the name is made larger then the rest of the words, to avoid running it together with the less important words.[36] Within these very broad outlines of display format, there are many nuances of design, color, ink, and timing for which experienced advice should be sought before any commitments are made.

Posters, window cards, and lawn signs follow similar format considerations. Posters must be made of stock and ink durable enough to withstand the elements. They also face ecological considerations; should one deface the environment and risk some sort of adverse reaction by tacking signs everywhere. Lawn signs and window cards not only display, but they are a sign of the displayer's commitment. Many veteran campaigners keep lists of sign locations from year to year, and ask residents and store owners if they wish to continue the practice. Window cards and posters can go up very early in the campaign, but lawn signs suffer the ravages of wind, rain, and vandals, and therefore, they are not erected until the last few weeks of the campaign. If a longer display period is desired, then a ratio of 2.5 signs to every location is normally planned, to allow for replacements. There are poster distribution services which will distribute and tack up posters, but ordinarily campaigners will have to plan, staff, seek locations, and implement their own display campaigns.

The cost of display varies considerably with size, location, and cost of printing and painting. A 24-sheet poster (standard billboard), which is 8' 8" by 19' 6" will vary in cost from $40 per month in a rural area (with inexpensive printing), to $500 to $600 in an urban area. Larger, (12' by 50') painted poster boards in high traffic areas can cost as much as $1,000 per month. Paper posters can be printed for 25 to 35 cents each. Signs vary in cost with the weight of the board and the cost of printing. The two most standard sizes are 10 ply and .050 board, with two colors; the cost will be from 40 to 50 cents per sign. For lawn signs, one must add about 12 cents each for posts. Like questions of format, display costs should also be estimated in advance.

BUTTONS, STICKERS, GADGETS, AND HANDOUTS

Campaign materials are the most enduring of all types of political advertising, dating back to the earliest campaigns. In an era of mass-media campaigns, paraphernalia, are, to many, an anachronistic hangover from an earlier era, an expensive symbolic luxury of campaigns gone by. Like other forms of campaign advertising, little is known about their actual campaign effectiveness. They could be more important motivators than most critics assume; but the logic of the situation indicates otherwise. There is a relatively high cost per unit and low-yield reach for hats, banners, ribbons, buttons, pens, matchbooks, litter bags, tie pins, earrings, emery boards, rainhats, kitchen utensils, calendars, football schedules, *et cetera*. In comparison to any of the mass media, they could not possibly be very effective. One must really look to other functions to justify their use in campaigns.

Materials relate more to the inside campaign than they do to the outside communications. Their messages usually contain candidate identification but they have a low circulation beyond an inner corps of supporters. They are usually handed out or sold at headquarters, meetings, rallies, dinners, or other places attended by only the firmest supporters. No one knows how many different times the average supporter will continue to display a button or other material, but the number is miniscule compared to a 100-showing billboard. Most of the gadgets are tucked away for the exclusive use of the recipients. Materials really serve to link campaign workers with the "inside" of the campaign; they are receiving things that others are not. A button or sticker is also a ready means of identification for workers as they campaign for the candidate. For the non-worker supporters, recipients are marginally linked with the active campaign; it is the lowest degree of involvement with the campaign next to merely voting for the candidate.

Composition of Campaign Materials

The requisites for makeup of these materials are similar to display. Only a brief, single message is possible since the passing glance is all one can expect from those who view or handle them. Bumper stickers are very small in size compared to the total field of vision of their viewers, thus little more than the name is printed ordinarily. The convention in bumper stickers is to select stock that will easily come off and ink that will not fade. These materials are so common that difficult as it may be, a search for something unique may magnify their impact. They are ubiquitous because everyone seems to want them, because they have always been around campaigning in the area, a loyal supporter insists on them at a campaign meeting, and the other candidates already have them. They have a great sameness about them.

The High Cost of Small Items

The cost of these materials is considerable. President Nixon's 1968 campaign items included 20.5 million buttons, 9 million bumper strips, 560,000 balloons, 28,000 straw skimmers, and 12,000 paper dresses and jewelry items, at a cost of over one million dollars. The overall dollar impact may be even greater in a small scale campaign.

Many items are made by some sort of pattern, casting, or die, where there are great economies to scale. Buttons, for example, can cost only a few cents each if a million are ordered, but several hundred cost closer to 25 cents each. Bumper stickers can be purchased for around 1 to 2 cents each in lots of 100,000 or more, but small lots of a few hundred to 1,000 range from 10 to 15 cents each. Very small (1¼ to 1½ inch) one color (plus another background color) celluloid buttons cost from $75 to $100 per thousand. Metal lithographed buttons are cheaper, but ordinarily larger lots (10,000 to 50,000) offer the real economy, at about $35 to $50 per thousand. One can begin to see that in a very minimal, low budget campaign, $125 worth of bumper stickers, $100 worth of buttons, and $100 for some other item could eat away a good portion of the advertising budget.

This $325 can easily be compared with an equal expenditure for some radio, television, or newspaper ads, a few billboards, or some combination of them in terms of the number of people reached. After arriving at an estimate of the mass media expenditure for sheer exposure to voters, the qualitative dimension should be considered. Where are the latent supporters who need to be activated, the undecided, and the convertible most likely to be reached? In large scale campaigns, materials may be necessary to placate and identify hundreds or thousands of volunteer workers. But expenditures for such materials are now a very low proportion of campaign budgets; about 1 percent in presidential campaigns. Campaigners should carefully consider the impact and reach of such items, materials, or paraphernalia before they commit one-fourth to one-third of their budgets to what may be a passing fancy.

ADVERTISING AND THE CAMPAIGN

There is a very popular adage in campaign advertising: "Fifty percent of all advertising money is wasted in campaigns. The only problem is, no one knows which 50 percent it is." We do know very little about the specific effects of various campaign appeals and about the relative effectiveness of various media in carrying these messages. Now that political scientists and communication specialists have discovered the relative importance of media and advertising in campaigns, they are beginning to study their effects. What is presently known about the structure and impact of media in campaigns appears to be a more sufficient basis for planning media and advertising than doing it because it has been done before. Like other facets of campaign management, reflection and judgment based on the available information filtered and bent within the setting and strategy is the most likely means of avoiding the 50 percent level of waste.

An increasing number of campaigns have turned to mass media and away from the volunteer worker to directly contact voters. Nevertheless, a large number of campaigns in the smaller constituencies are forced by circumstances to continue to rely on workers who engage in face-to-face contact. The immediate future is likely to see an important blend, where both the use of media is increased, and campaigners will also contact voters face-to-face. In this mixed appeal system, the relationship between the two should be kept in mind. One study of party leaders and campaign workers indicated that political advertising not only has an effect on inactive voters but effects activists as well. Political advertising boosted the morale of workers, and the confidence that the candidate was going to win the election. The ads also served as a source of information in the campaign, providing ideas and arguments to use in persuading voters.[37] Mass media and face-to-face contact obviously are not unrelated. Ideas, issues, themes, and candidate virtues are either carried via media through a two-step flow of information, or they are designed to be carried to voters through face-to-face media. And thus, our attention turns to direct-voter contact.

Notes to Chapter 14

1. U.S., Federal Communications Commission, *Survey of Political Broadcasting,* 1968, 1970, 1972.

2. Robert H. Prisuta, "Broadcast Advertising by Candidates for the Michigan Legislature: 1970," *Journal of Broadcasting* 16 (1972): 455-56.

3. Richard Dunn and Martin Glista, "Winners and Losers: Illinois Legislative Campaigns," *Campaign Insight,* 15 October 1973, p. 5.

4. Ibid.; Prisuta, "Broadcast Advertising by Candidates for the Michigan Legislature," p. 455.

5. Maurice McCaffrey, *Advertising Wins Elections* (Minneapolis: Gilbert Publishing, 1962), p. 4.

6. Sig Mickelson, *The Electric Mirror: Politics in the Age of Television* (New York: Dodd, Mead, 1972), p. 108.

7. Despite the obvious prevalence of agencies in campaigns, there is little written work on these firms and no published research studies. Most writings on firms in campaigns deal with public relations or campaign consulting firms, see, Peter Hamill, "When the Client is a Candidate," *New York Times Magazine,* 25 October 1964; Walter Troy Spencer, "The Agency Knack of Political Packaging," *The New Style in Election Campaigns,* ed. Robert Agranoff (Boston: Holbrook Press, 1972); Martin Mayer, *Madison Avenue, U.S.A.* (New York: Harper & Brothers, 1958), ch. 18.

8. David Lee Rosenbloom, "Managers in Politics," (doctoral dissertation, Massachusetts Institute of Technology, 1970), pp. 172-73.

9. See Agranoff, *The New Style in Election Campaigns*, pp. 40-43; Stanley Kelley, Jr., "Afterthoughts on Madison Avenue Politics," *Antioch Review* 17 (1957); "Do Agencies Belong in Politics?" *Printers Ink* 270 (1960); John E. O'Toole, "And If Elected, Here's What I'd Do About Political TV Spots," An address to the San Francisco Ad Club, November 17, 1971. Available from Foote, Cone & Belding Communciations, New York.

10. For a discussion see, Joseph Napolitan, *The Election Game* (Garden City, New York: Doubleday, 1972), pp. 7-10.

11. Nicholas Coleman to Warren Spannaus and Harry MacLaughlin, "Mondale Advertising and Public Relations Staff," 1966, St. Paul, Minnesota.

12. Jay Weitzner, "Handling the Candidate on Television," in *The Political Image Merchants*, Ray E. Hiebert et al. (Washington, D.C.: Acropolis Books, 1971), p. 105.

13. Gene Wyckoff, *The Image Candidates* (New York: Macmillan, 1968), pp. 216-17.

14. McCaffrey, *Advertising Wins Elections*, pp. 81-96; Dan Nimmo, *The Political Persuaders* (Englewood Cliffs, N.J.: Prentice-Hall, 1970), pp. 147-55; Stephen C. Shaddeg, *The New How to Win an Election* (New York: Taplinger, 1972), pp. 156-63; Weitzner, "Handling the Candidate on Television," pp. 100-05.

15. Weitzner, "Handling the Candidate on Television," p. 106.

16. Stanley Kelley, Jr., "Campaign Debates: Some Facts and Issues," *Public Opinion Quarterly* 26 (1962): 357.

17. Mickelson, *The Electric Mirror*, p. 62.

18. Kelley, "Campaign Debates," p. 357.

19. Ibid.

20. Mickelson, *The Electric Mirror*, p. 61.

21. Napolitan, *The Election Game*, p. 81.

22. Mayer, *Madison Avenue, U.S.A.*, p. 167.

23. McCaffrey, *Advertising Wins Elections*, pp. 77-78.

24. Hank Parkinson, *Winning Political Campaigns With Publicity* (Wichita, Kansas: Campaign Associates Press, 1973), p. 111.

25. Jules Witcover, "More Nixon Radio," *Washington Post*, 12 February 1973, sec. A. p. 16.

26. McCaffrey, *Advertising Wins Elections*, p. 123.

27. Chester G. Atkins, *Getting Elected* (Boston: Houghton Mifflin, 1973), pp. 146-47

28. Ibid., p. 146.

29. McCaffrey, *Advertising Wins Elections*, pp. 97-120.

30. Ibid., p. 124.

31. Mayer, *Madison Avenue, U.S.A.*, p. 153.

32. Betty Kroll, "Building Blocks, Direct Mail, Targeted TV Do The Trick," *Campaign Insight*, April, 1973, p. 7.

33. Atkins, *Getting Elected*, pp. 135-36.

34. D. Swing Meyer, *The Winning Candidate* (New York: James S. Heineman, 1966), p. 161.

35. McCaffrey, *Advertising Wins Elections*, p. 52.

36. Ibid., p. 59.

37. Kenneth G. Schienkopf, Charles K. Atkin, and Lawrence Bowen, "Political Advertising and Campaign Workers: Prompting the Political Persuaders," paper presented to the Association for Education in Journalism, Columbia, South Carolina, August, 1971.

For Further Reading and Research

American Association of Advertising Agencies. *Political Campaign Advertising and Advertising Agencies*. New York: AAAA, 1972.

American Newspaper Publishers Association. *Winning Ideas for Political Advertisers*. New York: ANPA, 1969. Other publications available.

Advertising Age. Weekly coverage of advertising and advertising agencies, including some political campaign reporting.

Bogart, Leo. *Strategy in Advertising*. New York: Harcourt, Brace, and World, 1967.

Devlin, L. Patrick. "Contrasts in Presidential Campaign Commercials of 1972." *Journal of Broadcasting* 18 (1973-74): 17-26.

Direct Mail Advertising Association. *How To Win Your Election With Direct Mail*. New York: DMAA, undated.

Farney, Dennis. "You're Hearing It: New Machines in the New Politics." *Smithsonian* 5 (1974): 62-68.

Fochs, Arnold. *Advertising That Won Elections*. Duluth, Minn.: A.J. Publishing, 1974.

Kleppner, Otto. *Advertising Procedure* 6th ed. Englewood Cliffs, N.J.: Prentice-Hall, 1974.

Kraus, Sidney ed. *The Great Debates*. Bloomington, Ind.: Univ. of Indiana Press, 1962.

McCaffrey, Maurice. *Advertising Wins Elections.* Minneapolis: Gilbert, 1962.

MacNeil, Robert. *The People Machine: The Influence of Television on American Politics.* New York: Harper and Row, 1968.

National Association of Broadcasters. *Political Broadcast Catechism.* 7th ed. Washington: NAB, 1972.

O'Keefe, M. Timothy and Sheinkopf, Kenneth G. "The Voter Decides: Candidate Image or Campaign Issue?" *Journal of Broadcasting* 18 (1974): 403–412.

U.S., Federal Communications Commission. *Survey of Political Broadcasting.* Annual reports on paid broadcast media usage.

Wanat, John. "Political Broadcast Advertising and Primary Election Voting." *Journal of Broadcasting* 18 (1974): 413-422.

Wyckoff, Gene. *The Image Candidates.* New York: Macmillan, 1968.

Person-to-Person
Contact

Direct or person-to-person voter-contact activities are a central part of every campaign because all citizens, as voters, do not fulfill the expectations of the classical democratic theorists. Enrollment of voters on the voting lists is required in most areas, but not all voters bother to register and vote. It has been estimated that nearly one-third of the voting age population is unregistered. Not all of those who are registered vote in any given election. Nationally nearly 60 percent of the eligible voters vote in presidential elections, about 50 percent vote in off-year elections, from 25 to 50 percent vote in local and primary elections and some community elections, referenda draw less than 10 percent. Not all of those voters who go to the polls vote for every office on the ballot. The fall-off rate, or level of non-voting in a contest ranges from 1 or 2 percent in the high visibility, top-of-the-ticket races, to one-third in the less visible, bottom-of-the-ticket contests. The rate can climb to one-half in nonpartisan ballot races. Even when these three conditions are met, the campaigner cannot be sure of a vote, since votes are also cast in a direction, and voters are not always clear as to the proper relationship between the candidates, issues, and parties in each and every contest. Campaign voter-contact activities are at the same time democratically virtuous and candidate self-serving; they are designed to help voters perform their civic duties of registering, voting, and being informed.

In the days before extensive mass media campaigning, direct contact by campaign workers, primarily by partisan operatives, was the most important means of voter contact. Historical accounts reveal that most persons were part of a party grouping; their loyalty to a party was an article of faith similar to a religious, ethnic, or occupational group following.[1] Because the mass media were less relevant (the low-effort media had not been developed), the important means of contacting the large group of non-activists was by party person-to-person contacts. Home visits primarily stimulated the predisposed to vote.

That the era of strong parties has given way to stronger candidates has been demonstrated throughout. The development and usage of low-effort media, declining party loyalties, declining party organization strength and activism, the newer techniques of campaigning, and social attitudes have all contributed to this reversal. In a mass media era, those who are less interested are more likely to be stimulated by campaigners' appeals; party is a less important cue. Yet, the mass media alone do not always "break through" and stimulate every marginal voter to vote, nor do they reinforce, activate, or convert all voters. All campaigners' mass media efforts do not reach all voters because all campaigners do not always use the media voters are most likely to follow. Radio and television are inaccessible, letters are not read, newspaper stories are ignored, and signs are not linked to the other media. Nor can appearances before large and small groups reach many voters, since so few voters ever attend them. It is to this unreachable group of voters (in some campaigns it may be the major voter-contact effort) that direct-voter-contact activities are directed. Faced either with declining party activism in these areas or simply the need to make individualistic appeals, candidate electioneering efforts increasingly focus on such activities.

The specific person-to-person contact activities referred to here include: voter identification, voter registration, absentee ballot campaigns, get-out-the-vote efforts, poll watching and poll judging, and other support efforts, such as providing transportation or babysitting. Each of these can be organized and conducted on a party, candidate, or coalition of candidates basis. Except in the few remaining areas where patronage workers are available, they are not ordinarily performed by party exclusively; they are performed by campaign volunteers, interest groups, and partisans. Sometimes they are conducted by telephone, sometimes by personal contact at the doors of voters.

The purpose of this chapter is to examine the role of person-to-person contact in the campaign process and to highlight the important administrative and practical concerns in organizing for direct voter contact. As in other subject areas, a review of the literature is presented to suggest its utility and limitations—situational factors, campaign processes, activity levels, and vote increments. The critical aspects of planning all person-to-person activities are considered, the interrelated concerns of operations, priorities, and personnel. Then, each of the major activities are examined in terms of relevant legal, election administration and political factors; planning and task analysis unique to the activity; internal management and information handling; and implementation, that is, practical applications and techniques. Campaigners who understand the function of direct contact, and plan in the context of setting and strategy, can add vote increments.

THE PLACE OF VOTER-CONTACT ACTIVITIES IN THE CAMPAIGN

Like other campaign efforts, face-to-face activity can have three important effects:

- increasing the turnout;
- encouraging a vote in a race that otherwise would be ignored; and
- influencing the direction of the vote by reinforcing, activating, or converting.

Many studies have revealed that, although not always overwhelming, significant margins can be gained by campaigners who engage in such activities.

The Impact of Direct Contact

A number of studies exist which illuminate the role of direct voter contact. They employ a variety of methodologies, varying greatly in the character and representativeness of their samples, and occurring in a variety of political settings. Moreover, most of them examine the role of political party organization activity exclusively, or mistakenly lump party and candidate efforts together rather than undertake a comparison of individual candidate efforts. Nevertheless, an overview of these experimental studies suggests important parameters of the direct-voter-contact effort. In addition, previous research on the subject can help to answer recurring questions campaigners have about the utility of various techniques and different delivery systems, placing voter contact in its proper campaign context.

A study in Ann Arbor, Michigan of apathetics—persons who vote in national and state elections but not in local elections—found that a 25-percent increment of those personally canvassed turned out to vote, whereas only 10 percent of those stimulated by mail efforts bothered to vote. While the actual proportion of apathetics turned out by the efforts seems small, the authors point out that a similar study conducted in a presidential-election year yielded substantially high turnout increments of those who had never voted. Very little difference in city election turnout was found between those canvassed by telephone (24%), party workers (29%), and by students (25%).[2] Also, it was found that a personal contact stimulus was considerably more likely to be remembered than a mail contact (50% compared to 18%).[3] In a study of a low visability, nonpartisan election in a suburban Maryland community, Margaret Conway found that electoral turnout increased with candidate contacts. Seventy-five percent of those contacted four or more times (by the candidate, workers, campaign flyers, mailed statements, and telephone calls) voted; about 6 in 10 of those contacted one to three times voted, and only 4 in 10 of those not contacted voted. Personal contact proved to be a very important means of stimulating voters in this campaign, inasmuch as there was very little mass media coverage, and even less voter recognition of the coverage that existed.[4] The results of these studies suggest that there is a group of non-voters who are resistent to various stimulation efforts, but, campaign efforts, and in particular the personalized approach, can make notable inroads into this non-voting group.

A study by Janowitz and Marvick utilizing a national sample found that among those who were not canvassed, 27.9 percent were non-voters; among canvassed persons only 12.7 percent did not vote. For the latter voters the authors concluded that the party had an activating effect. The authors also found that a considerable number of persons highly disposed to vote anyway (based on such factors as their political activity, interest and high SES) were canvassed, thus making the canvassing effort inefficient.[5] In a study covering a national sample in four presidential-election years (1952–64) Kramer tested both turnout and preference effects. The author found significant levels of turnout stimulation by those who were contacted by a campaign worker for president or congress, but found few significant effects on voter preferences when contacted by a worker. There were some small but notable preference effects in local contests. The most notable preference effects for high visibility office were in the 1964 presidential race, when both parties engaged in an extraordinary effort.[6] The author concludes that the obvious strategic implication is, "To be effective, a canvass should concentrate on turning out the vote among voters and in neighborhoods likely to support the party; and it must avoid contacting opposition voters."[7]

Cutright and Rossi found that in very close primary elections, where relative party strength is obviously not a factor, the campaign effort of the official party organization can swing a decisive vote in favor of a local candidate, even when that party's favored candidate is less well known.[8] The same authors found that in Gary, Indiana general elections, after one controlled for the normal, estimated vote and allowed for a slight "breakage effect" (the slight increment the majority party in an area often receives), there remains a marginal increment as a result of campaign workers talking to people. In fact, the more persons the party worker talked to, the higher the vote total for the worker's party; a gain of 1.8 percent for high Democratic activity and of 2.5 percent for high Republican activity.[9] The greatest gain came in the marginal districts, with a Republican or Democratic effort difference of about 6 percent.[10] Since the two parties are often working at cross purposes, the authors also investigated precincts where both worked, as well as where only one worked. They found that in Gary, a Democratic city, the majority party gained most when its partisans were active, and the oppositon was inactive. Where both were active, the minority Republicans had a slight edge.[11] Using another election, Cutright followed this up by comparing Gary with a nonpartisan city. When controlling for the normal party vote, the author found a 3 percent effect of party work in the nonpartisan city, and a 4 percent effect in Gary.[12]

In a similar study in Detroit, Katz and Eldersveld tested the effects of party workers in a number of electoral activities, enabling them to test the impact of strong and weak leadership at the local level as a contribution to the vote in national elections. They found notable differences if one party had a strong local leader and the other party did not. For example, in the precincts with strong Democratic and weak Republican organizations, the Democratic presidential candidate received 5 percent more votes than the expected vote from the precinct. Where there was a strong Republican leader but a weak Democratic leader, the candidate's vote fell 5.5 percent below the expected total.[13] Overall, there was a total of about a 10-percent effect of the efforts of campaigners on their candidate's votes. Since the authors found few precinct leaders consistently carrying out the necessary tasks for mobilizing the vote, they suggest that organizational activity at the precinct level has great potential.[14]

Raymond Wolfinger examined the potential impact of precinct work by a well-organized party in a low stimulus election, a local charter effort in New Haven, Connecticut. As a test of party effort, he examined their relative effect in the absentee ballot portion of the campaign. He found a significant difference between the absentee ballots and the voting machine totals; 34 percent of the variance could be explained by the party effort. The author concludes that in local elections such as the one he studied, when the outcome is related to important rewards, such as jobs, favors, or contracts, or, when party identification and the appeal of well-known candidates is absent, the impact of local campaign effort is substantially greater.[15]

The results of a study of priority-precinct canvassing in Tennessee make it clear that one should be cautious in speaking of a general "canvass effect." Price and Lupfer found that the turnout effects of selected priority-precinct canvassing ranged from 0.6 to 3.9 percentage points. The magnitude of effects appeared to be contingent on environmental factors. Canvassing appeared most likely to increase voter turnout in areas where: (1) a large majority of the voters are sympathetic to the candidate's position; but, (2) turnout tends to be low. The authors note that work in these precincts increased the total vote received by the majority candidate, but the increase in his percentage of the vote may be negligible, particularly if it is already approaching 100 percent.[16]

William Crotty argues that any test of the impact on the vote must be gauged against a broader party performance effort. He tested the impact of party activity variables (campaign activities, time spent in party effort, money spent in campaigns, the number of precincts organized, etc.) in North Carolina counties, controlling for demographic variables and party competition, and found that party activity variables raise the variance accounted for from 28 to 60 percentage points. In terms of the impact on a race, this meant party effort could increase the vote from between 4 and 20 percentage points, with the greatest impact in local races (sheriff, legislature) and a lesser impact in races for president and governor. When Crotty isolated the highly competitive counties for analysis, he found the margin of party effort increased to the 17- to 23-percent range.[17] Thus, the inclusion of party structural variables appears to indicate a marked effect for such activities, particularly in competitive areas. It suggests that candidates running with active party organizations will benefit by added increments, particularly in competitive constituencies.

John Blydenburgh conducted a controlled experiment study designed to measure the effects of door-to-door canvassing and telephone solicitation at the precinct level. Specifically, he measured the impact of the two types of campaigning on voter preference in a race for the Monroe County, New York Legislature (county board), in which he got the two parties and candidates to cooperate by performing all door-to-door canvassing, all telephone solicitation, or no contact in four experimental districts. When Blydenburgh compared tele-phone solicitation with personal canvassing, he found no (statistically) signifi-cant effect of telephone solicitation on the outcome of the election (the sign was in the positive direction), but door-to-door canvassing produced a 4.5-percent higher vote than would be normally expected.[18] Then he measured preference effect—the differences in the direction of the vote where all canvassing oc-curred—and found that each party campaign significantly altered the normal out-come to their advantage by about 3.2 percent.[19] The latter result, in particular, differs from the results of those who found small preference effects, primarily using high visibility races as data bases. Blydenburgh points out the crucial difference:

> When a voter is deluged with free and conflicting information from the mass media and elsewhere, personal contact becomes just another bit of information to evaluate. Most voters, by the time they are exposed to personal contact campaigning, have made their decision, thus additional exposure to campaigning would only serve to remind them of their obli-gations to vote. Thus we get a turnout effect for personal contact in elections where the voter gets exposed to a great deal of information. . . .
>
> For voters in the election for Monroe County Legislature, an office largely ignored by the mass media and by both parties' campaign use of mass media, personal contact was the only bit of information on which voters could base their decision. . . .[20]

In the Tennessee study of priority precincts, preference effects were found to be greatest in areas where the pull of trends was in the opposite direction. In this case, canvassing had the greatest impact, helping Democrats remain firm and vote for the Democratic senatorial candidate, Albert Gore. The authors suggest, that by having its most significant effect when voters are experiencing pressures to shift to the opposition, canvassing's preference effect was more to prevent than to produce conversions.[21] The authors offer the following strategic advice based on this finding, ". . .areas more evenly balanced between the parties and especially those displaying marked transitions in electoral behavior might offer relatively large returns for canvassing, even when their levels of political interest and voter turnout are already high.[22]

The preceeding evidence reflects a wide variety of party and candidate settings, with differing methodologies. It seems to suggest that within certain boundaries, however broad they may be, the person-to-person contact activities in a campaign can make a noteworthy but not necessarily overwhelming con-tribution. Obviously, the campaigner should understand and plan within these limits. In fact, following the evidence of such early researchers as Katz, El-dersveld, Cutright, and Rossi, many experienced campaigners think in terms of a 5-percent rule. That is, if a substantial effort is put forth, other things being equal, it will bring the campaign an increment of up to a 5-percent vote margin; in the absence of an effort, one could lose 5 percent. In the absence of any opposition efforts, it may be slightly higher.

Direct Contact
and Selected Campaign Processes

Much less is known about the specific voting and campaign processes operating through person-to-person contact than the relative parameters of such work. One problem is the difficulty in separating the various influences. For example, one early study of a local campaign found it nearly impossible to separate the effect of changing attitudes and encouraging voters to go to the polls.[23] A related problem is separating the influences on voters who would vote anyway, particularly in regard to turnout. An important aspect of direct-contact activities is finding and stimulating those voters who are committed or predisposed to a party or candidate, and making that extra effort to get them out to register and vote. Since it is difficult to find which registered voters need stimulation and which do not, undoubtedly much effort is wasted.[24]

Direct voter contact can be implemented to conduct virtually the same campaign appeals or implement any stratagem that media can. The committed, whether to party or to candidate, can be motivated to go to the polls and vote in a certain direction. Indeed, the bulk of the party efforts studied here are predicated on identifying and mobilizing the committed. Direct contact can activate more passive citizens. As was revealed in Chapters 2 and 3, conversion is also possible, particularly among the uncommitted and when the voter has little previous information or few preconceived notions. In a similar fashion, party, candidate, and issue appeals can be blended into direct-contact work. Although most of the research cited here refers to partisan activity, direct contact is increasingly organized by, and performed on behalf of candidates. The Kennedy campaign of 1960 was the first highly visible candidate-centered, direct-contact effort; it was a hallmark of Kennedy electioneering.[25] Other candidates, whether aspiring to city hall or to the White House, have similarly conducted their own efforts. Partisanship is very often incorporated in the effort and appeals, but increasingly, only candidate support and issue positions are gauged and pitched. This, again, reflects the declining party loyalties, the independence of candidates, and the weakness of constituency-party organizations.

THE EXTENT OF PARTY EFFORT

It has been maintained throughout that party effort (campaigning for the candidate as part of a party team) is ordinarily incorporated in a campaign on the basis of strategic impact and availability. That is, various settings require varying party strategies. Generally, the stronger the majority partisanship for the majority party candidate, the more valuable it is to make use of the party. The converse is true for a minority situation. This, of course, assumes that there is a party organization available to campaign. It has been suggested that their activity levels vary considerably, and now we focus on their direct contact activities.

County party organizations are considered to be the basic units of American political parties. William Crotty measured the relative campaign efforts of county parties in North Carolina, examining whether the organization expended some effort in each race faced by the party unit. As Table 15.1 suggests, the races listed at the top of the ballot—president, congress, and governor—received the greatest attention. Of those offices elected from the county, or where the county was the chief electoral unit, more county party organizations campaigned for the state representative office than for any other. County level offices were supported from only one-third to one-half of the county party organizations. Only about one in five organizations had anything to do with local races. Crotty's figures represent the average of 157 county organizations. Obviously, a wide range of activism and inactivity is masked here.[26] Nevertheless, it reveals that the relative performance of parties for some races is greater than for others, to the disadvantage of the less visible office campaigns. Crotty's data seem to confirm our suggestion in Chapter 1, that, even when parties are highly active, every candidate does not have a guarantee of equal treatment.

Eldersveld's Detroit study measured levels of partisan activism at the precinct level. He asked party workers to rate their organization's performance in eight different campaign activities. One can see from the data presented in Table 15.2 the campaign performance of party workers reveals a very mixed picture. Party leaders were spread somewhat evenly in their conduct of the three, critical, person-to-person-contact activities (registration, canvassing, and get-out-the-vote), with some performing all three tasks, some two tasks,

Table 15.1   Offices for Which County Party Organizations Campaigned*

| Office | Percent of County Organizations Campaigning | | |
	Dem.	Rep.	Total
Local	22.4%	19.4%	21.0%
County Commissioner	47.1	58.3	52.2
County Sheriff	41.2	30.6	36.3
Other County Offices	40.0	38.9	39.5
State Legislature	52.9	62.5	57.3
Judicial	22.4	5.6	14.6
U.S. Congress	69.4	68.1	68.8
Governor	84.7	76.4	80.9
President	85.9%	81.9%	84.1%
N	85	72	157

*Most county organizations campaigned for more than one office. Therefore, the total percentage does not equal 100.0%.

Source: William J. Crotty, Approaches to the Study of Party Organization (Boston: Allyn and Bacon, 1968), p. 278.

and some one task. Some performed no campaign tasks. Eldersveld also found many precinct organizations with teams of workers available, but the leaders did not use them. The percentage of precinct worker teams which did not engage in important campaign activities were:

	Democrats	Republicans
Election-day work	66%	20%
Registration	7%	20%
House-to-house canvassing	54%	68%[27]

Thus, even with party personnel available, precinct organizations did not live up to their potential. Significantly, Eldersveld's Detroit study examines a party organization more typical of parties than the folk literature on powerful urban party machines, implying that party organization always covers every door, mobilizing thousands of voters behind a party ticket. It is a situation that an increasing number of candidates are facing.

The Survey Research Center at the University of Michigan has attempted to measure the extent of all personal contact campaigning—party and candidate—in presidential election years. They have consistently asked respondents if

Table 15.2 Campaign Task Performed by Precinct Organizations

Task patterns	Reports by:	
	Democratic precinct leaders	Republican precinct leaders
All 3 critical tasks: registration, canvassing, election-day roundup	17%	25%
2 critical tasks Registration, plus one other	38	19
No registration, but other two	0	3
Only 1 critical task	31	23
No critical tasks, but did report other types of activities	4	12
None of the 8 tasks performed	10	18

Source: Samuel J. Eldersveld, *Political Parties: A Behavioral Analysis* (Chicago: Rand McNally, 1964), p. 350.

they recall whether or not personal contacts by parties or candidates have been made. Table 15.3 depicts the measures of this electioneering. Despite the increasing importance of television during this period and the declining importance of party organizations, the combined efforts of parties and candidates had resulted in a steady increase in voters contacted, from 11 percent in 1952 to 29 percent in 1972. Since party activism, as measured by Eldersveld and others, is seemingly declining, the increase apparently represents a large increase in effort by the candidate-centered groups, particularly since 1964. Measurement of personal contact in a presidental year represents an estimate of the "peak voter-contact effort," yet about three out of four citizens are not contacted. The rate is undoubtedly lower for other races and in other elections. For example, only 14 percent of Newark citizens reported a personal contact by a campaign worker in the 1970 mayoral election.[28] Obviously, there is unfulfilled potential for campaign work.

PLANNING
DIRECT-VOTER-CONTACT ACTIVITIES

Planning and organizing person-to-person contact activities require little of the technical expertise or previous experience that most media-related activities do. In fact, the most critical skills include the ability to think plans and steps through and the ability to apply campaign research about the setting to a concrete operation, particularly operations planning, the establishment of a plan, and estimation of volunteer resources.

Operations Planning

In Chapter 1 we presented the case of the muddled door-to-door work in a mayoral campaign. It was a case of poor planning, timing, and coordination. Management required that the campaigners involved pause at some early point

Table 15.3   The Extent of Personal Contact Campaigning by Parties and Candidate Groups in Presidential Election Years, 1952–1972

Contacted by	1952	1956	1960	1964	1968	1972
Democrats	3%	6%	7%	7%	7%	12%
Republicans	4	6	8	10	8	8
Both	3	6	4	8	9	8
Total % Contacted	11	17	20	26	25	29
Number of Cases	1899	1762	1954	1450	1345	1119

Source: Survey Research Center, University of Michigan. Made available through the Inter-University Consortium for Political Research.

and carefully think through the details of how far in advance of the target dates they would have to secure an adequate number of volunteers, canvass voters, register the unregistered supporters or neutrals, plan and arrange for printing of literature, organize a literature distribution, and then repeat similar plans for the election-day centered activities. Many person-to-person contacts formally unfold in the closing days of the campaign, but planning for them must begin almost immediately after the start of the campaign. Between the initial planning and research phases and the actual contact of voters, many steps must be followed.

In large campaigns, a separate voter-contact section or chairperson is designated in the early stages of the campaign. This operation either conducts its own research or works closely with the legal and research sections of the campaign. The specific research should include the following: voter eligibility, registration timetables, polling places, registration places and the legality of mobile registration or registrars, registration forms, the rules regarding election judges, campaigning at the polls, voter-assistance regulations, voter registration by various areas, estimates of eligible voters, and voter turnout rates. To this list would be added the voting habits research covered in Chapter 5. Much of this planning will have to be handled by a designated operative in smaller campaigns.

The next phase involves planning operations to fit into the research conducted earlier. Among the activities included in this phase are: recruiting volunteer leaders, recruiting volunteer workers, recruiting legal advisors, establishing a telephone bank if necessary, ordering supplies and equipment, arranging for necessary printing, setting priorities, planning written instructions and establishing volunteer kits, training volunteers, and dividing the constituency. As a more specific case, the steps involved in a voter-registration operation will be illustrated. After the aforementioned research is conducted, one must secure voter registration lists for each unit of the constituency; establish a file of voters by address (or alternatively computerized); check the files against a city or reverse directory; establish a file of unregistered voters; decide on a method of identifying and then identify unregistered voters who are likely to be supporters; establish priorities of unregistered voters in areas where support yield is likely to be greatest; secure precinct maps; organize recruitment, material preparation, and training of workers; begin house-to-house or telephone canvass; follow through, by mail reminder or with a registration form; a later telephone check to see if registrants require any voter assistance, such as absentee ballots; the organizational steps at the beginning of this paragraph; and, of course, conducting the specific tasks.[29] Practically every person-to-person activity requires a similar operations blend. Plans can only unfold if they are made, and they cannot be made without sufficient lead time.

Priority Systems

Direct voter contact is ordinarily organized and conducted by small areas, usually the precinct. Campaigning by small areas is based on the phenomenon that

Figure 15.1 Final Month Direct Voter-Contact Schedule for the 1972 Nixon Illinois Campaign

SUNDAY	MONDAY	TUESDAY	WEDNESDAY	THURSDAY	FRIDAY	SATURDAY
8 OCTOBER	9 • Begin hostess phone calls • Last day to register outside Cook County • Senior citizen visit report due	10 • Cook County precinct registration day — Last day to register!	11	12 —Transfer Canvass Information— —Mail Computer Sheets— —Continue Election-Day Recruitment—	13	14 • Last day to mail in computer sheets. • Hostess report due.
			—Phone & Door-to-Door Canvass Continues—			
15	16 • Phone center canvass update • Senior citizen visit report. • Chicago campaign meeting 6:30 pm.	17 • Springfield campaign meeting.	18	19 —Continue Election Day Recruitment—	20	21 • Hostess reports due.
			—Phone & Door-to-Door Canvass Continues—			
22	23 • Phone center canvass update • Senior citizen visit report.	24 • Advance absentee ballot voting begins	25 —Continue Election Day Recruitment and Organization—	26 —Continue Election Day Recruitment and Organization—	27	28 • National voter turnout kick off day. • Hostess reports due. • Last day for canvassing.
			—Phone & Door-to-Door Canvass Continues—			
29	30 • Start reminder calls: Phone centers & Hostess programs. • Senior citizen visit reports.	31	1 NOVEMBER	2 • Last day to get absentee ballot application.	3	4 • Last day to vote by absentee ballot.
		—Continue Election Day Recruitment & Organization—				
5	6 • Election Day check — all systems.	7 VOTE & WORK				

people who live in the same areas tend to have similar life patterns (according to various social indicators) and these lifestyles are likely to engender similar political outlooks and behavior. As a result of dividing into small areas, and the reporting of voting results by those areas, one is able to establish reasonable estimates, which can be used to establish priorities for area-based voter-contact activities. In Chapter 2 we examined various voting patterns and how the electorate can be stratified. Such stratifications—partisan, occupational, religious, ethnic, SES—are not evenly distributed throughout constituencies. They often concentrate and are, generally, the basis of planning area-based priority systems.

Chapters 4 and 5 covered the raw materials and information necessary to establish area-based priority systems. Each one must be tailored to the strategy and setting of the campaign. After establishing priority areas, they can be integrated with any of the direct-contact activities. Voter registration can begin in the greatest potential support areas containing the largest proportion of unregistered voters. Voter canvassing can proceed from the greatest potential yield areas to less important but significant areas, writing off the lowest priority areas. A similar plan can be followed with literature distribution. As voters are canvassed and their preferences are known, this information can be built into the system, shifting the priorities from area to individuals. Get-out-the-vote appeals and election-day checks can move from known supporters, to those who lean to the candidate to the undecided, ignoring opposition supporters or relegating them to the lowest priority. If individual voter information is unavailable, area-based, aggregate-data priority systems can be continued. In many campaigns without accurate canvasses, for example, all homes in areas of high party strength (60 to 67% base party vote) are called, on the assumption that it will do more good than harm. Every direct-contact plan should be based on a priority system, to maximize the implementation of strategic principles and to best use scarce campaign resources.

Estimation of Volunteer Resources

Earlier discussions of various strategic principles are likely to suggest that the two most contingent resources related to direct contact activities are money and workers. Other factors being equal, the more money one has, the less reliance on workers, through purchase of mass media and other means. If money and media are inaccessible, workers can be a valuable resource, compensating for such deficits. In actual practice, our investigation has revealed that other factors are rarely equal; money and workers tend to flow together. Most volunteer and party efforts gravitate toward the more visible candidacies at the top of the ticket, just as do the money resources. This and other organizational concerns lead to a need for campaigners to attempt a realistic assessment of the volunteer resources available to do the job planned.

Planning for direct-voter-contact activities should be placed in the context of available campaign resources. Chapter 7 revealed some realistic estimates and findings about the likely range of volunteers. It clearly is not enough to assume, for example, in a disadvantaged money situation or in a compact constituency, that volunteer, person-to-person work will be the mainstay of voter contact, and then, expect enough volunteers to come forth to implement plans. Planning includes a rough survey of the number of volunteers available and the means to acquire them. If the number estimated appears to be reasonably adequate, then workers can be regarded as a substitute for money. If the number falls short of this, but is still useful, plans can be altered. If volunteers are virtually nonexistent, then plans will have to be reformulated. Estimating the relative availability of workers further suggests the need for operations planning and priorities.

VOTER REGISTRATION

Most areas of the United States require a previous legal step to voting, enrollment of voters on an eligible list, voter registration. Although the trend has been to increasingly eliminate restrictive legal barriers to registration, such as poll taxes, literacy tests, and long residence requirements, there remain various legal regulations which condition both the voter registration of citizens and the operation of voter-registration campaign efforts in various areas. Of course, voter-registration efforts must also face the other two barriers to voting as well; non-registration because of lack of motivation or because of some accidental factor. Voter-registration campaigns can be important components of a campaign effort. Since most organized efforts make some attempt to locate supporters, or likely supporters, registration can add and reinforce increments of the committed, or activate latent supporters, and, perhaps, convert a few of the undecided. In many consitutencies, voter registration may be the most important means of gaining increments of voters.

Investigations of voter-registration efforts reveal that campaigners should be aware of some very important considerations regarding these undertakings. First, registration and the rules governing it are not strictly administrative, but are also political acts. They are often the product of a practicing politician's efforts to control the size and shape of the electorate. Stanley Kelley and his associates found a definite association, for example, between restrictive rules and procedures for registration and limited competition between the major parties in the states where their sample cities were located.[30] Under these circumstances, voter-registration efforts by certain campaigners can be regarded by others as highly political acts, and sometimes may meet with subtle political resistance. Second, since registration requires thorough organization, tedious and time-consuming work, and follow through, it usually requires high volunteer motivation to follow through. Penn Kimball found, in his investigation of registration, that the more successful registration efforts were those centered around a definable political goal, such as the election of a symbolic or charismatic candidate, a change in the balance of power within local political institutions, or the projected elimination of unfriendly incumbents.[31] Third, voter registration requires a broad range of skills, including technical organizing and administrative abilities, as well as the tedious work. Kimball thus found that voter registration drives among minority groups required broad coalitions of indigenous workers, middle class activists and other persons.[32]

The Legal-Organizational Context

The first step in voter registration is becoming familiar with the appropriate state and local legal regulations concerning voter registration. Many states publish special booklets about election laws, and, in others, they will have to be either secured from the officer in charge of registration or distilled from the statutes. The answers to a number of important questions should be ascertained:

1. In which areas is voter registration required? Some states do not require registration in the smaller towns and rural areas.
2. Who is the local officer in charge of voter registration? In large metropolitan areas often there is a separate commissioner of registration and election administration; in other areas it is often the city or county clerk.
3. What are the responsibilities of the voting registrar? In most states the registrar must supply the forms and is responsible for prescribing rules and regulations for registration hours in his office and for places and hours of registration outside of the office.
4. Who is entitled to register voters? In many states the local registrar is empowered to appoint extra registrars to take care of registration during peak periods. It can be done either by hiring additional employees or by deputizing volunteer registrars. In many states it is common to have party or campaign activists serve as volunteer registrars.
5. Where may registration take place? In some states and localities registration must take place in certain designated public buildings or offices. Others allow mobile registration or house to house (called in-precinct) registration. Absentee registration by mail is also legal in most states.
6. Who is elibible to register? The Twenty-sixth Amendment to the U.S. Constitution sets the minimum age at 18. States further set eligibility. Normally the requirements include a period of time as a U.S. Citizen, a specified time as a state resident and a shorter period of residence in the precinct. States also proscribe certain categories of persons, such as felons, persons under guardianship or persons judged mentally incompetent.
7. Is registration by party affiliation? Some states require the declaration of party, others do not require a declaration but make it difficult for registrants to switch primaries and others have no party registration.
8. When may persons register? In most states the registration period closes at at a specified number of days before the election. The trend has been to shorten the time between closing and the election, and some states have

enacted mail registration or are considering registration at the polls.

9. What circumstances require re-registration of citizens? Some states have permanent registration, whereas others require a citizen to vote at least once every two or four years to remain eligible. Re-registration is ordinarily required for persons who move to another municipality and for those who have undergone a name change. Regulations for re-registration for persons moving within a municipality or precinct vary considererably from state to state as do regulations for persons who move too close to the election day to re-register.

10. What are the circumstances for challenging a person's registration? States normally provide a specified time within which a person may be challenged, and allow for a hearing and court appeals.

Anwers to these questions represent the basic operating framework of the voter-registration operation.

This framework is then ordinarily expanded to include establishment of an organization. The size of the organization and degree of task differentiation depends on the setting. In very large campaigns voter registration is separated from other voter-contact activities; in smaller campaigns they are integrated. The organizational roles include: someone to coordinate the entire operation; a volunteer coordinator who will recruit, train, and deal with volunteers in various phases; a person to keep records and files; and various support roles such as transportation, legal, finance, and publicity. Some campaigners organize and coordinate with various nonpartisan voter-registration efforts. Election officials will often more readily cooperate with such groups as the League of Women Voters, the Youth Citizenship Fund, Frontlash, and so on, by deputizing them or extending hours and places of registration for them. Campaigners who link up with them ordinarily do so with discretion, and follow the conditions set by these groups, since any association with partisan efforts can jeopardize their legitimacy, their tax deductable status, or both.

Registration Priorities

As organizational arrangements are established, the organizers will also have to consider priorities. Registration campaigns can be conducted with various categories in mind—by area or by residence; by individuals who are identified as partisan or candidate supporters; or by group, such as age, ethnicity, or labor-union families. If registration is by groups, then the lists supplied by groups or names of residents taken from high residential concentrations (from the census or other means of identification) become the basis of checking information. Where the registration campaign is to be based on some prior canvassing of citizens for degree of support, those not registered are selected by survey. Canvassing (see the next section) then precedes voter-registration efforts. Priorities are relatively easy in these two cases. Since there is a rating system built into the canvass, or, since members of the list are judged to be prime prospects, only

Figure 15.2   Mail Voter Registration Form, Montgomery County, Maryland

INSTRUCTIONS

DO NOT USE THIS FORM if you are already registered to vote in Montgomery County, Maryland. If you are unsure of your registration status, call the elections office, 279-1507.

USE THIS FORM to Register to vote in Montgomery County if you are
* A citizen of the United States.
* At least 17 years old and will be 18 years old on or before the next General Election.
* A resident of Montgomery County.
* Not convicted of a disqualifying crime.
* Not under guardianship for mental disability.

GIVING FALSE INFORMATION TO PROCURE VOTER REGISTRATION IS PERJURY AND IS PUNISHABLE BY IMPRISONMENT FOR NOT MORE THAN TEN YEARS.

Telephone number (in the event we need clarifying information)_____

This application must be received by the elections office no later than 9 P. M. on the fifth Monday prior to an election in order for you to be registered to vote in that election.

If your application is received on time and if it is complete, it will be processed and a Voter Notification form mailed to you. **YOU ARE NOT A REGISTERED VOTER UNTIL YOU RECEIVE THAT NOTIFICATION.**

The Board of Supervisors of Elections is not responsible if application is late or registration information is incomplete or inaccurate.

BOARD OF SUPERVISORS OF ELECTIONS
for Montgomery County, Maryland

Box 333, Rockville, Md. 20850
Telephone: 279-1507

— — — — — — — — — — — — — — — — Fold here for mailing — — — — — — — — — — — — — — — — —

NAME: (PRINT)   LAST   FIRST   MIDDLE

RESIDENCE: (PRINT)   ST. NO. OR BOX NO.   STREET OR ROUTE   APT. NO.

POST OFFICE   DATE OF BIRTH   PARTY AFFILIATION CHOICE (CHECK ONE)

DEMOCRAT_____   REPUBLICAN_____

ZIP   SEX (M OR F)   PLACE OF BIRTH (STATE OR COUNTRY)   OTHER (SPECIFY)_____

DECLINES TO AFFILIATE _____

DO NOT WRITE IN SPACE BELOW

DATE OF REGISTRATION

I AM A CITIZEN OF THE UNITED STATES AND A RESIDENT OF MONTGOMERY COUNTY, MARYLAND. I HAVE NOT BEEN CONVICTED OF A DISQUALIFYING CRIME. I AM NOT UNDER GUARDIANSHIP FOR MENTAL DISABILITY.

I DO SOLEMNLY SWEAR (OR AFFIRM) THAT THE INFORMATION SET FORTH HEREON ABOUT MY PLACE OF RESIDENCE, NAME, PLACE OF BIRTH, CRIMINAL OFFENSES, QUALIFICATIONS AS A VOTER, AND MY RIGHT TO REGISTER AND VOTE UNDER THE LAWS OF THIS STATE IS TRUE.

DIST.   PREC.

ID NUMBER

SIGNATURE OF APPLICANT

lists or categories need be rated. Campaigners might integrate previously gathered voter information into their priorities, such as a party's or a comparable candidate's canvass.

When priority information on an individual's candidate or party support is not available, aggregate data must be put into priority systems. If party registration data are available, ratios of unregistered voters in areas of high party concentration can be used. Without such information, various aggregate indicators will have to be considered. For each small unit, a base race or some other index of likely strength will have to be calculated, and units put into priorities. (See Chapter 5.) Next, proportions of eligible but unregistered voters will have to be estimated by comparing the totals of registered voters against census estimates of residents 18 years and older. (See Chapter 5.) One could add to this information some special information which contains certain groups of transients with low registration rates. Among such targets are new housing units, trailer parks, apartment complexes, colleges, and new businesses. Identification of these units can come from the chamber of commerce, the zoning commision, planning commissions, or labor groups. Lists of individual names can be acquired from various sources such as realtors, high-school and college graduation lists, new telephone listings, property transfer records, welcome wagons, or newcomer groups. These groups contain highly mobile people, and they should either be combined with high priority areas or they should be given special treatment. Other information is also combined into a priority system, including: the total population of the unit being considered; population trends (growing, stable, or declining); potential number of people to be registered relative to the total population; if the campaign is by telephone, which areas can be reached from phone banks without toll charge; and availability of financial and personnel resources. Each of these items can be included in the priority system and assigned a relative weight. Areas are assigned a priority weighting such as *A, B, C, D,* etc., from high to low, in terms of the numbers of unregistered voters likely to become supporters.

Records Check

The next important step is the tedious registration records check. Here the list of citizens by address must be checked against registration rolls. The most common method is to match the list of registered voters against a listing by household. Most cities publish a city directory or reverse directory, that is, a listing by street address rather than by alphabet. Voter-registration lists are ordinarily alphabetical by precinct. Thus, the name of each registered voter will have to be looked up by address and checked off. Those names remaining are unregistered voters. A simplified version of a registration street listing would be:

District *43A*
  Precinct *6*
Street *HEMLOCK*
From No. *200–398*
Assigned to _____

House	Name	Tel.	No. Eligible	Regis.	Remarks
202	Doe, John	895-9124	3	+	
202	Doe, Jane	"		+	
202	Doe, Jan	"		−	just turned 18
206	Anderson, John	563-2142	1	−	new resident
210	Smith, James	863-2112	2	+	
210	Smith, Joan	"		+	

This process is often simplified by having volunteers list the name of each resident on 3 × 5 index cards, and then sort by different address sequences. Cards are often color coded for registered and unregistered, change of address, dwellings where no one is home, for those not on the poll list, or for deletion from poll list. In larger scale campaigns, data processing is employed to keep registration records, either by use of punched cards or automatic typewriter tapes. Ordinarily, conversion to data processing is not undertaken unless the volume of information is sufficiently large to warrant the effort, there is considerable time and manpower available to convert information, and it is cost effective.[33]

A list of registered and unregistered voters by area enables the assignment of specific names to go after for registration. Identifying specific unregistered voters is time-saving except in areas of extremely low registration, where there are outdated voter lists and reverse directories, or in places of high mobility.

Approaches to Registration

There are two basic approaches to registering the unregistered. The first is to identify the predisposition of the voter, either to party or candidate, and then only to register favorable voters. This method is often used in areas which are substantially for the opposition party, nominally for one's party, or where there are large blocks of questionable candidate supporters. The McGovern workers used the following door-to-door technique to screen out Nixon, or vehemently anti-McGovern, voters.

'Good afternoon, Mr. _____ . My name is _____ . I'm a volunteer for Senator George McGovern, the Democratic nominee for President. We'd like to know if you'd consider voting (Democratic this year) or (for Mc-Govern, the man who says what he thinks, etc.)'

If negative reply: ask if there are any other persons who might be interested. Thank them and go on.

If positive or undecided: canvass for registration and attempt to register. (Undecideds if registered by us will tend to be influenced by your visit and vote for McGovern.)[34]

This technique also adds valuable canvass information about individual voter predisposition, which can be added to information gathered on registered voters.

The second approach is to register everyone that is unregistered in an area without regard to leaning. This is ordinarily undertaken in areas where the overwhelming number of voters are likely to be supporters. Depending on the setting, this may be areas of 2 to 1, or higher, party strength, concentrations of minority groups, a college campus, high-income areas, or others. In some areas, the McGovern forces, going from door-to-door, used a conversation like this:

'Good afternoon, Mrs. _____ . My name is _____ . According to our records you are not registered to vote. When would you like to go down and register? We'll provide transportation.'[35]

This initial effort was buttressed by publicity and deputy registrars in the field where it was allowable. The most important assumption behind this method is that identifying and registering all unregistered voters is more productive than spending time trying to screen out an occasional hostile voter. Thus, the areas included must be selected carefully, ordinarily based on the established priority system. Information as to where and when to register should, of course, be included in both methods.

Either of these two approaches can be implemented by door-to-door visits or by telephone. Door-to-door contact is considered more effective because of the personal element involved. Ordinarily it is conducted by having a series of block workers cover priority-based assigned areas. Telephone surveys are increasingly used to bridge the manpower gap. A caller can cover from five to six times more names than a door knocker. Precincts are covered on the same priority basis as door-to-door. Often a series of two to three "call-throughs" are made through each precinct, between 9:30 A.M. and 9:30 P.M. (calling only in the evening is considered a waste of equipment, if rented), at different times of the day. Homes not contacted in the first series of calls through the precinct are contacted again in a few days, and again in a few days. Each succeeding wave will entail fewer calls and the number of waves can be determined from the priority system.

Following through unregistered voters is very important. Since unregistered voters are, for the most part, citizens with low political motivation, one cannot assume that persons contacted will automatically register. One method is follow-through phone calls after a period of time has passed since the initial contact, but before registration closes. Another method is a letter signed by a prominent public official, with an enclosure containing information *specific to the recipient* as to when and where registration is possible in the community. Other means that have been used include mass contacts, such as door hanger literature in areas of low registration, mass media public service announcements, or having registration parties or rallies.

Records

Keeping accurate records of individuals and of the registration effort is both a useful support system and management technique. The raw materials for records include the voter lists by precinct, area street maps divided by precinct, and index-card files. Lists and card files can be updated with records of phone calls made, time when registered, follow through, and other information. Since registration occurs while the legal registration period is open, new registrants will have to be checked at registration places and integrated with records. These records should be flexible enough so they can be integrated with voter canvass and get-out-the-vote activities. As a management technique, it may be useful to collect statistics by precinct, ward, town, or congressional district on the number of calls or contacts made; number of no answers, busy signals, and information refusals; number of Republicans, Democrats, Independents, candidate supporters, or opponents; and the number of times the information provided is unreliable. These data can be compiled into daily and weekly statistical reports, which can be used to test the priority system, checking an individual worker's performance against average performances or to give some estimate of the number of registered voters being added to the electorate. Accurate record keeping will not only give the campaigner continuous information about important operations, but transference to other campaigns can render future efforts more efficient.

VOTER IDENTIFICATION

The purpose of voter identification, or canvassing, is very fundamental in a political campaign. Its purpose is to designate, on an individual voter basis, those who are committed, those who are in various stages of indecision, and those who are opposed, for use in other campaign operations. Traditionally, canvassing was the province of the political parties, whose precinct workers covered their neighborhoods on foot to find Republicans, Democrats, and Independents. Contemporary voter identification includes canvassing by telephone as well as on a door-to-door basis, and it is used to tap candidate support as often as party support. It is organized by the party and the candidate organization. Ultimately, the results of voter canvassing are used to selectively appeal to individual voters, encouraging supporters to turn out and vote, activating the latent supporters, converting the undecided, and ignoring opposition support.

In forty-three states, voters are required to register by party affiliation, thus offering campaigners somewhat of a pre-existing canvass. In other areas, a particularly active party organization may have produced a relatively accurate and updated party canvass. While helpful, party registration or affiliation is not always a perfect predictor of party vote. California Democrats have held a steady 3 to 2 registration edge for nearly three decades, yet Republican candidates win quite often, and by large margins. Registration only locks voters into a party's primary election, and a different type of voter votes in primaries than in general elections.[36] Whether there is party registration or not, electronic media and candidate efforts offer alternative cues which make party support indicators less reliable. Thus, the candidate-centered campaign very often finds it necessary to conduct its own voter-identification effort to determine predispositions in the particular contest for which one is organizing.

Approaches to Canvassing

There are three approaches to voter identification: screen every voter, identify them on some basis of selection, or a random canvass of areas. The latter, sometimes called a Kennedy canvass, is predicated on starting with a small core of workers who fan out and recruit other canvassers. The core worker makes calls around a designated block, asking people for their views. When a favorable response is received the resident is asked if he or she would be willing to canvass, distribute literature, and conduct other activities. When a block worker is recruited, a packet of voter information, literature, buttons, and other material is forewarded to the local person and he or she handles the canvass. Obviously, this technique of recruitment and canvassing requires a visible candidate whose name readily attracts volunteers.[37] Selective identification is ordinarily conducted by some predetermined priority, such as lists of identified partisans, labor union members or members of some other organization, supporters of a previous candidate similar in character or some other criterion which is likely to generate a high ratio of supporters. This type of selection is ordinarily used when a small number of workers and high quality lists are available.

The most prevalent mode of canvassing is to screen every single voter within a designated area. Some campaigners attempt to cover every single area, whereas others set priorities and work within them. Most campaigners ideally would like to survey every eligible voter if possible, but his is an unrealistic goal in practically every campaign, so priorities are ordinarily established. Area-based priority systems can be established on the basis of likely vote yield (Chapter 5). The most important determinant is, of course, the availability of workers.

Voters can be screened by telephone or on a house-to-house basis. Telephoning is ordinarily undertaken where volunteers are not sufficient to go door-to-door. In telephone canvassing, one must, of course, establish the resident's name and telephone number before calling, ordinarily by transferring reverse directory information to voter lists. Unlisted numbers will be missed, and in some areas they can constitute a high proportion of the vote. House-to-house screening does not absolutely require the name and telephone number of each person, as it can be ascertained by asking persons as one goes from house to house. Ordinarily the worker is supplied with a precinct walking list containing the block name at the top, and columns for the street number, the resident's name and telephone number. The rest of the information is gathered by the worker.

The amount of information to be gathered during the canvass depends on whether or not it is combined with registration, how many times voters are to be contacted, and the number of follow-through activities that are to be undertaken. Generally, as much information regarding individuals and households as possible is gathered to make campaign worker efforts as efficient as possible. Above all, it must contain a ranking of the candidate sentiment or a measure of party support. The McGovern effort in Illinois and Wisconsin, directed by Eugene Pokorny, gathered the following information, as illustrated by their coding system:

1	-	definite McGovern supporter	CA	-	filed change of address
2	-	pro-McGovern	AB	-	filed absentee ballot request
3	-	undecided			
4	-	against McGovern or for Nixon	FD	-	filed physical disability request
NH	-	not home	*	-	wants to help
WS	-	won't say	Trans	-	transportation appt. with us
UR	-	unregistered			
R	-	registered	B	-	needs babysitter[38]

These code items illustrate the range of information that can be used. Pokorny had around 3000 McGovern volunteers working Wisconsin in the 1972 primaries. On primary day they pulled those coded as *1*'s and *2*'s, and used the same volunteers to telephone them, providing transportation and babysitters, among other activities.[39]

The specific door-to-door approach also depends on the extent of information desired. The following canvass conversation was used by the Nixon campaign in 1972:

Write in house number *BEFORE* knocking on the door.

"Hello, my name is _____ . I am a volunteer working for the re-election of President Nixon. We believe President Nixon is an outstanding President. May we count on your support and vote for President Nixon on November 7?" *PAUSE, WAIT FOR ANSWER*

IF NO: "Thank you for your time. Goodbye."
>MARK *AGAINST* COLUMN

IF UNDECIDED: "We think President Nixon is the best man for the job, and we hope you decide to join us in voting for him."
>OFFER THEM LITERATURE
>MARK *UNDECIDED* COLUMN

"We certainly thank you for your time. Goodbye."

IF YES: 1. "Do you usually vote Republican?"
>MARK *PARTY* COLUMN (R, D, or I)

2. "Are *all* Nixon supporters in your home registered to vote at this address?"
    IF NOT REGISTERED: "Could you give me (your/their) name(s)? Here is information on how to register to vote. *Please* register soon."
>RECORD *NAMES* ON CANVASS SHEET
>MARK *TO REGISTER* COLUMN
>GIVE *PINK* REGISTRATION PIECE

    IF REGISTERED: "Good."

3. "Would you volunteer to help us in President Nixon's campaign?"
    IF YES: "That's great. I'll be happy to have our volunteer chairman call you."
>MARK *WILL HELP* COLUMN

    IF NO: "I understand."

4. "Is there a chance that you may be away on November 7th and will need to vote absentee for President Nixon?"
    IF YES: "Here is complete information on how to vote absentee."
>MARK *ABSENTEE BALLOT* COLUMN
>GIVE *YELLOW* ABSENTEE BALLOTT PIECE
>GIVE *WHITE* APPLICATION FORM

    IF NO: Go on to closing statement.

5. "Thanks so much for your time. May we have your *name* and phone number for our records? Thanks again. Goodbye."
>PRINT *NAME* ON CANVASS SHEET
>RECORD *PHONE NUMBER*
>OFFER THEM LITERATURE

FOR NOT AT HOMES, MARK *NOT-AT-HOME COLUMN*[40]

The Nixon technique combined information gathering on party support, registration, and names and addresses, as well as identifying the degree of candidate

Figure 15.3 1972 Nixon Campaign Canvass Sheet

CANVASS SHEET

COUNTY OR CITY _____

PRECINCT _____

STREET NAME _____

NAME OF CANVASSER: _____

Canvasser Telephone _____

Party Code:
R = Republican
D = Democrat
O = Other Parties
  and Independents

VOTER I.D.

HOUSE NUMBER	APT.	TITLE	LAST NAME	FIRST NAME	TELEPHONE	PARTY	AGAINST REGISTERED	FOR REGISTERED	UNDECIDED ABSENTEE BALLOT	NOT AT HOME

Households this page _____

Households contacted _____

For _____

Against _____

Undecided _____

Need Registration _____

Need Absentee Ballot _____

Will Help _____

Paid for by the authority of the Finance Committee to Re-elect the President. Hugh W. Sloan, Jr., Treasurer, 1701 Pennsylvania Ave., N.W. Washington, D. C. 20006.

support, seeking volunteer help, and checking for possible absentee voters plus literature distribution. The party support information enabled them to make special mailings to Republicans, Democrats, and Independents for Nixon. The other information sought is standard. The McGovern forces used a similar door approach to canvassing:

> "Hello, Mrs. _____. (Sir). My name is _____ . I'm a volunteer for Senator George McGovern, the Democratic nominee for President. We'd like to know if you'd consider (voting Democratic this year) or (supporting George McGovern, the working man's candidate)."

> If negative: ask if there are any other people at home.

> "I'm sorry to hear that, Mrs. _____. Would Mr. _____ be at home?"

> "Are you the Mrs. _____ with a college age daughter, etc.?"

> Thank them and say goodbye.

> If undecided:

> "Well, Mr. _____, I realize voting for President is a tough decision. Could we leave some literature with you about George McGovern?"[41]

The McGovern people worked from a precinct list of names, but they tried to ascertain similar information. Obviously, different approaches can be made, depending on the various information sought, the setting, and the strategy.

Volunteers are almost always supplied with a canvass kit containing precinct maps, voter lists broken down by blocks, canvass forms, issue and background information sheets on the candidate so that canvassers can answer questions, literature to distribute, a set of duplicated instructions, and not-at-home cards. All of this material is placed in a file folder, a "hard card" in the argot of campaigners, with the map stapled to one inside cover and the block list to the other. The remainder of the materials go inside of the folder.

Integrating the Canvass

When the information is gathered, it is integrated into the campaign information systems. In many campaigns, volunteers are asked to tally the number of supporters, leaners, undecided, hostiles, and persons needing absentee ballots, transportation, and babysitters. As these reports are pooled and assessed over a period of weeks, it gives leaders an idea of how the campaign is moving. Also, the voter canvass is used to test the priority system, matching individual voter preference data against aggregate data. If an entire constituency, or large portions of it, is canvasssed, the individual data can be used to establish a new priority system, to supercede the one based on past voting habits.

It is most important to integrate individual information with campaign records so that further campaign operations can be undertaken. Ordinarily, this means entering individual voter preference and other information into the card file or a data processing system. A color-coded card system or coded data processing then will allow the campaigner to sort out, by area or priority, or both, supporters to turn out on election day, the undecided to whom a special appeal should be made, supporters to whom rides should be offered, solidify those leaning to the candidate, or any other contact targeted to the individual. Voter identification is only an intermediate step in the direct contact of individual voters.

ABSENTEE BALLOTS

The handling and stimulation of voter participation for those who are unable to be present at voting places on election day represents a significant means of implementing voter identification findings. There are important categories of absentee voters—college students, traveling workers, shut-ins, military personnel, vacationers, and foreign workers. Nationally, about 5 percent of all votes counted are absentee ballots. In a congressional district, this could mean that as many as 10,000 voters cast absentee ballots. Surveys indicate the actual number of registered voters who are absent and do not vote in a given election is higher than the number of voters who cast absentee ballots. Thus, the potential task for the campaigner is there; to find those supporters, or likely supporters, who are unable to get to the polls and to encourage them to vote by absentee ballots.

The Legal Web

Each state has its own legal regulations as to when and where to apply for and cast an absentee ballot. Ordinarily the voter must go through a series of steps to vote: a ballot must be applied for; the reasons for being absent ordinarily have to be stated; the voter receives a ballot in the mail; the voter must take the ballot to a notary public, who certifies the affidavit that accompanies the ballot; the voter marks the ballot with the notary present, but he cannot know how the elector voted; the ballot is sealed in a special envelope, and, the ballot is mailed or delivered personally to the appropriate election official. In some areas, voting machines are provided at the polling places, where the voter may appear within a designated time to vote.

The time for requesting a ballot ranges from state to state, ordinarily from 90 days prior to the election, to one day prior to the election. There are closing dates for ballot applications which range from "anytime prior to the election" in Maine, to 21 days before the election in Rhode Island. Deadlines for receiving ballots likewise range from noon the day before the election, to anytime before the polls close. The official to whom one applies is ordinarily the election administrator, although in a number of states it is to a county election board, and, in Alaska, it is to the Lieutenant Governor. An increasing number of states use a post-card application (Standard Form 76) for registration of citizens living abroad, adopted by congress as an amendment to the Federal Voting Assistance Act of 1955. Military voting regulations can be secured from the nearest military installation or recruiting station. With the variances in election laws and timing, it is obviously imperative that campaigners investigate relevant regulations and deadlines early, as a part of planning.

Absentee Ballot Operations

The planning phase may also involve the establishment of separate personnel. In the larger scale campaigns, an absentee ballot chairman or committee, which organizes the effort, becomes fimiliar with the regulations, works with publicity, and searches out any pockets or categories of absentee voters. Normally, the absentee voter efforts come after registration and canvassing but before other election day activities (since one must be registered). Also, a considerable amount of lead and follow-through time is required for application, certification, and delivery. For most of the categories of absentees, the individuals usually know in advance that they are not going to be able to appear at the polls on election day. If properly surveyed, only a few who will be absent for last minute accidental reasons will not be reached.

If the voter canvass includes an inquiry about the need for an absentee ballot, it becomes the basis for identifying potential voters. Normally, only identified supporters or those leaning to the candidate are stimulated. In some cases, undecided voters are also encouraged, combining the absentee ballot approach with another campaign appeal. In cases where there is no canvass, campaigners ordinarily proceed very carefully in selecting individual voters, looking for priority areas or possible pockets of strength. For example, Republican candidates sometimes seek out shut-in voters in retirement homes in small towns or in Republican communities. Democrats often seek out absentees on college campuses or in senior-citizen homes or housing projects for retired labor-union members.

Turning out the absenteee vote can be done through direct mail, door-to-door contact, or by telephone. If the campaign is organized well enough to have regular block workers in designated areas, a list of absentees can be supplied to them along with application instructions. The block worker can call on each one, leave instructions, and recheck. Normally, however, this is done by mail or telephone, or a combination of both. A mailing to absentees usually includes a letter containing an encouragement to support the candidate, instructions on application, and a telephone number to call for further information. In some states, a ballot or application can be mailed to the voter. Telephone conversations can include virtually the same information.

Two kinds of follow through are required after the initial contact. Not

Figure 15.4 Absentee Ballots

APPLICATION FOR A NEW YORK STATE MILITARY BALLOT

(MUST BE RECEIVED IN ALBANY, N.Y. NO LATER THAN THE 12TH DAY BEFORE THE NOVEMBER ELECTION)

I am a citizen of the United States and hereby apply for a military ballot.

I am ☐ a member of the armed forces;
OR
☐ the spouse ☐ parent ☐ child of ....
        (Name of member of Armed Forces)

My name is: ....
                    (Print your name)   (Social Security Number)   (Rank)

My residence in the State of New York is: ....
                                    (Number and Street or R.D.)   (ZIP Code)

in the (Borough) (City) (Town) (Village) of .... County of ....

My military address is: ....
                    (Regiment, Company, Troop or other Command)

located at ....
            (Name of Camp, Vessel or Base)   (Post Office Address of Camp)

My signature is: ....
                            (Sign Your Name)

Date of Birth: ....   Insert P.P.R. No.
                (Month) (Day) (Year)   (If Known)

FORM 1

---

1. List below the names of unregistered persons who are unable to go to the voting booth to register on registration days because of illness, away at college, in service, etc. State the reason why they cannot go to the voting booth, since this information determines what type of application the Board of Elections sends to the person.

2. Also list those persons who are registered but who will be unable to go to the voting booth, on Election Day, for such reasons as are listed above.

3. Return this form by Oct. 1st to Democratic Registration Committee, Genesee Bldg., Buffalo, N.Y. 14202.

HERE ARE A COUPLE OF EXAMPLES:

NAME	ADDRESS	APPLICATION FOR Registration	Voting Ballot	REASON
John Smith	500 Main St., Buffalo	X	X	SICK
Mary Jones	500 Delaware Ave., Buffalo		X	AT COLLEGE

PLEASE PRINT WHEN FILLING OUT BELOW

NAME	ADDRESS	APPLICATION FOR Registration	Voting Ballot	REASON

Return to: Democratic Registration Committee
        Genesee Bldg., Buffalo, N.Y. 14202

                                    _____
                                        Print Worker's Name

                    Election
Zone/Town _____ District _____   _____
                                                    Address

all voters will take the initial cue and make application, and then vote. Thus, a few weeks before the election (for military and overseas voters it could be a few months) ordinarily a series of follow-through phone calls are made to check (1) whether or not ballots have been applied for, and (2) whether or not the voter has voted.

The final stage comes with the absentee ballot count. Most absentee ballots are paper ballots which trickle into the election administration official's office over a long period of time. Ordinarily they are counted separately the day after the election and are allocated to the precincts. Candidates often find it useful to have someone on hand to oversee the counting of the ballots.

LITERATURE DISTRIBUTION

Campaigners use literature distribution activities in many different ways. It is primarily a means of making appeals, and, where volunteer labor is employed, it can enhance involvement and stretch scarce campaign resources by avoiding mailing costs. Also, literature distribution can give volunteers a chance to get out of the headquarters and meet people, it can supplement a canvass, and it can give the impression that the campaign is on the move. Three literature delivery systems are popular: direct-mail, house-to-house, and distribution at selected gatherings.

Direct-mail distribution allows the campaigner to make effective use of the canvass. As was indicated in Chapter 14, appeals can be based on virtually any information gathered on the individual; by degree of support, partisanship or strength of partisanship, occupational or issue interests. Ordinarily, more than one piece of literature is printed to appeal to various interests. If circumstances make it difficult to vary literature, appeals can be made selective with a cover letter. As more and more campaign efforts include information at the individual voter level, other means of literature distribution are giving way to direct mail.

House-to-house distribution is used when volunteers are relatively available to cover large areas of a constituency. Ordinarily, literature is delivered in areas of high supporter concentration, which can be determined either by an aggregate indicator priority system or by information gleaned from the canvass. In many campaigns, literature is distributed in waves. The earliest distribution is used to identify the candidate and to cue voters that an election is approaching. Another wave, closer to the election, is used to distribute more solid information about the candidate and issues, and to link the candidate with party, if it is deemed strategically wise. This is the distribution whereby a brochure, if there is one, would ordinarily be distributed. The last wave again would be a shorter message reminding voters to turn out and vote. The first and last pieces of literature are often inexpensively produced. Many different variations of this three-wave system can be and are employed, depending on the availability of volunteers, printing, money, and other factors of strategy and setting. In some areas it has become popular to "knock and drop," that is, to knock on the door and hand the literature to the resident, making only a very short appeal. Even though the individual voters who receive the literature are not identified as in direct mailings, a priority system can reduce the risks of appealing to non-supporters. It, also, is a more efficient use of resources, since workers can be employed where they are needed, rather than where they happen to live.

Distribution at gatherings of people is the most random method, because material is handed to anyone who happens to walk through. Many types of voters are likely to be present and receive leaflets at shopping centers, theaters, concerts, and sporting events. Chance can be reduced by selecting concentrations of perceived supporters, such as at plant gates, college dormitories, or lines outside of certain entertainment events, such as rock concerts and movies. Appeals can be tailored to the common interests of the recipients, for example, union issues, consumer affairs, or government support for the arts. Literature distribution at gatherings often requires permission of the owners or officials, and often there are established policies within which campaigners must work.

Like other phases of campaigning, literature distribution does not just happen; it requires planning, management, and awareness of and operation within legal and other regulations. Such tasks as recruitment, instructions, mapping, transportation, checking busy entrances and exits, coordinating with candidate appearances, and securing permissions must be considered when planning this activity.

GET-OUT-THE-VOTE
AND ELECTION DAY ACTIVITIES

Just as all of the planning, design, and media relations can pay off near the end of the media campaign, much of the planning, organization, registration, and voter identification activities can come to fruition in the final days of the campaign. Direct-voter-contact activities in a campaign are predicated on ensuring that one's supporters turn out to vote on election day and protecting the candidate's interests at the polls. The activities being referred to here include: in the few days immediately preceeding the election, urging supporters to turn out and vote; through the use of poll watchers and telephoners, checking the voting participation of supporters on election day and reminding those who have not voted to vote; providing voter support services, such as transportation and babysitters; and ensuring fair election administration through the use of challengers at the polls.

Organizing the Voter Mobilization

The conduct of so many different activities in such a short period of time, spread over a large number of voting districts, obviously requires considerable planning and management. First, considerable thought will have to be given to whether voter-contact activities can be organized within the framework of the existing organizational form. Those organizations resembling the generalist model, depicted in Chapter 7, will have to shift personnel to get-out-the-vote activities. Organizations with persons covering all activities in designated sub-units of the constituency similarly will have to get local people to gear up for the last few days to work in their home areas. The other more complex forms of organization are usually organized with separate leadership for each activity and are usually conducted according to some priority or target precinct system.

A second and critical managerial decision relates to the number and extent of election-day activities undertaken. Most campaign manuals suggest that every campaign effort requires urging every single favorable voter to vote, checking up on this with poll watchers and telephoners covering every precinct, having election judges in every precinct, plus providing transportation and babysitters. The data presented on the relative availability of campaign volunteers and on the extensiveness of party work make extensive coverage problemmatical in most campaigns. Thus, campaigners must often scale down their aspirations and per-form those activities most necessary, and must do so in those areas for which there are adequate resources, perhaps shifting available workers to higher priority areas.

An interrelated factor is obviously the priority system. By the latter stages of the campaign a great deal of campaign information can be available for the purposes of maximizing rational decision making. In addition to aggregate data indicators, there may now be up-to-date registration and canvass information. This allows one to pool the number of supporters, those leaning, those un-decided, and those needing babysitters and transportation, for the purpose of determining where and what kind of work is most essential. If polls have been taken, they can be used to identify key groupings of voters for which special efforts might have to be made. For example, if a Democratic candidate finds his support unusually low among union members, special efforts may have to be made to mobilize these voters.

Soft and judgmental data will also have to be included. For example, poll watchers and callers may not have to be used in the higher-income areas where practically every registered voter turns out. If certain areas are deemed trouble-some, challengers can be sent only to those precincts. Careful reflection on the past voting behavior of various groups may also be helpful. Certain groups tend to be low turnout groups, and if they are important strategically, extraordinary efforts will be important. In 1970, a massive voter registration drive was con-ducted among the Latino's of San Antonio, Texas. But recent registration was no guarantee of voting; in some precincts, as many as one-third of the new reg-istrants did not vote in the next election.[42]

Some of the methods one chooses to use are also interrelated managerial decisions. Chief among them are whether the major get-out-the-vote activity is to be by telephone or by door-to-door activities. If it is by telephone, is it to be con-ducted in private homes or by telephone banks? Is the door-to-door get-out-the-vote activity to be combined with the last literature distribution or any other activity?

A final set of managerial decisions relates to all of the important logistical and material tasks which must be carried out in order to implement election-day activities. The tasks which organizers might face are similar to those related to registration: recruitment of activity chairmen and workers; checking state and local regulations regarding such matters as providing voter assistance, campaigning near the polls, positioning of poll watchers, and regulations for poll challengers; training workers, the gathering of appropriate materials, and the preparation of instruction kits; establishing shifts and determining work assignments according to established priorities; maintaining records on election-day workers and election-day activities; arranging transportation for volunteers; securing lists of polling places; and relevant support activity, such as publicity. Each one of these activities involves considerable time and detail, but space prevents a detailed analysis here.

These activities require the same type of lead time, investigation, and follow through as other activities. The end product should be a matching of resources, capabilities, and techniques. It will almost always require that priorities be established and, inevitably mean that for some activities or areas, one will have to rely on the efforts of other candidates, the party organization, the work of interest groups, or that tasks will simply go undone.

Voter Contact

It is the realization that not all registered voters actually vote in a given election that gives impetus to get-out-the-vote drives. The most widely used and most rational plan is to make this effort a part of one's vote maximization effort by encouraging only citizens who will vote or who are likely to vote for one's candidate, leaving civic duty in this regard to more nonpartisan, non-candidate groups. In other words, one identifies one's supporters (either through canvassing or with priority systems) and then reinforces or activates them through mobilization. If the undecided are encouraged to vote (a decision based entirely on setting and strategy), the opportunity is taken for a final vote appeal. For example, following the rating system used by the McGovern forces in canvassing, all definite and leaning supporters (1s and 2s) were called; next, the undecided (3s) were called, and the pro-Nixon or definitely not McGovern (4s) were ignored. The Nixon forces used a similar system, only in reverse. When individual data are unavailable or not used, all voters in high priority areas are contacted, normally through the reverse directory or by the door-to-door method.

The telephone has become the most popular means of getting out the vote. With all of the activities undertaken in the final days of the campaign and with scarce volunteer worker problems, the telephone allows for many more contacts. Since the actual message is shorter than canvassing and is more informational than investigatory, calls are easier to make. The number of calls per hour usually ranges from 20 to 30, depending on the length of the message and the amount of information the caller already has. Telephones also make it easier to reach into homes and apartments, particularly after dark, when many will not open the door, or where security systems bar entrance. Some also suggest that the telephone lends itself well to activation, a major function of get-out-the-vote activity.[43]

The Minnesota Democrats (Democratic-Farmer-Labor) have conducted an extensive get-out-the-vote telephone effort for a number of years. It has been operated and financed jointly by the state party organization and by the major-office candidates. In its early phase they had a "Phonerama" program, which relied primarily on volunteers telephoning from their homes. The voter canvass was not very complete, and every registered voter was called who lived in high priority areas. They switched to centralized telephoning in 1970, to overcome the problems of lack of controls—no one was sure what was said, how much calling was actually done, or when the calling was done. Also, as of 1970, a substantial canvass which in this case contained party support information, was the basis of the system. Telephone banks were established in centralized locations in urban areas of the state. Every identified DFL'er and every independent in high DFL areas (60 percent or more were contacted and urged to vote). Phonerama was used in the rural areas to supplement telephone banks. The phone banks were organized over a six-day period, with paid supervisors. More than 200,000 calls were made in 1970, and more than 300,000 calls were made in 1972.

As in the case of other get-out-the-vote campaign efforts, the DFL effort is buttressed by various support activities. For example, in the 1970 campaign they distributed "door-hangers" the day before the election. A mass communication campaign included: stimulation of radio and TV public service announcements; prepared print advertising for local committees to put into local papers; and news releases on getting out to vote to newspapers, radio, and television. In other years they have supplemented these efforts with large hand-carried signs at busy intersections and plant-gate reminders the day before and on election day.[44]

Getting out the vote, door-to-door, operates in a similar fashion. If a canvass has been conducted, each worker is provided with a walking sheet containing names, addresses, partisan or candidate preference, and other relevant information. If the territory is strange, the volunteer will also need a map. As the workers walk along, they check the disposition of each voter (or household), and they remind those in the assigned categories to vote. If there is no canvass, door-to-door workers go from house-to-house in high priority areas. All door-to-door workers are normally supplied with identification badges, literature on the candidate, and a list to check off the households contacted, as well as with postage-paid envelopes to be sent to headquarters or, alternatively, a telephone number to call in the same information.

The specific message to be delivered, either by telephone or face-to-face, can be designed to be nonpartisan, candidate-oriented, party-oriented, or a

Table 15.4   Minnesota Telephone Operation Data

TELEPHONE OPERATIONS
METRO AREA DISTRICTS 3 - 4 - 5 Includes Hennepin, Ramsey, Anoka, Washington and Dakota Counties

Goal Total - Completed Calls	180,000
Number of Calling Days	6
Number of Calling Hours	64
Calls Per Day	30,000
Calls Per Hour	2,813
Number of Phones @25 calls per hour	115

Shifts Worked:

Thursday	9-9	12 hours	3 shifts
Friday	9-9	12 hours	3 shifts
Saturday	10-8	10 hours	3 shifts
Sunday	12-8	8 hours	2 shifts
Monday	9-9	12 hours	3 shifts
Tuesday	9-7	10 hours	3 shifts

Number of operators needed if each operator will work 2 shifts during operation—920

Number of supervisors @ 1 per 30 lines—4

Source: Minnesota Democratic-Farmer-Labor State Central Committee, *Get-Out-The Vote,* (Minneapolis, Minn.: 1970), p. 6.

combination. The first illustration, from the Rural Citizens Get Out The Vote Committee, is nonpartisan:

This is Mrs._____ calling for the Rural GET OUT THE VOTE COMMITTEE.

We want to remind you that today is ELECTION DAY.

Have you voted yet? You vote today at _____. (polling place)

(If they have voted, thank them. Suggest to them that they remind their neighbors to vote also.)

We want to urge you to vote as soon as possible. Is there anything we can do to help you get there? Do you need an automobile to take you to the polls?

(If so, check at what time and *verify* the address.)

Be sure to vote today. Many elections are very close. One vote can make a real difference in a close election.

Remember, you vote before _____ PM at _____ .

Goodbye.

NOTE: BE BRIEF, POLITE–DON'T TALK ISSUES, PARTIES OR CANDIDATES–AND NEVER ARGUE.[45]

The second message is candidate oriented:

"Hello, I'm calling on behalf of the _____ campaign committee. We want to remind you and everyone in your household to vote next Tuesday. Your vote will make a difference. Remember you vote at _____ between _____ and _____ . Thank you."

The third message was used in Minnesota in 1972 by the joint campaign effort. It reflects both party and candidate appeals:

Hello–I'm calling on behalf of the (McGovern for President/Mondale for Senate/____for Congress) campaign committee. We want to remind you and everyone in your household to vote next Tuesday and we urge you to support all of our Democratic candidates. This year we have the best chance ever to elect a DFL majority to the legislature. We hope you will be sure to vote for your DFL legislative candidates: _____ for the senate and _____ for state representative. Your vote will make the difference. Thank you.[46]

In some states, specific campaign appeals cannot be made on election day. Thus, the simple message:

Hello. Don't forget to vote. You're vote will make the difference. Please remind any other voters in your home to vote. Thank you.[47]

With the use of high volume centralized telephone banks the inclusion of polling-place information often slows down the operation, i.e., looking up polling places and entering them on calling lists. An alternative method, if a polling place inquiry is made, is to have the caller fill out an inquiry slip which is passed on to someone who looks up the polling place and calls the voter back with the information. If the canvass contains transportation or child care information, this is sometimes rechecked and arrangements are made, although separate lists are usually made so as not to slow down the calling. Door-to-door workers almost always have polling place and voter assistance referral capability, since the work is normally organized by precinct and call backs are rarely made to the door.

At the Polls

The next, significant step in getting-out-the-vote occurs on election day, with the use of poll watchers or poll checkers. Ordinarily, a worker is placed in each

Figure 15.5 Sample Calling Sheet of the Nixon Campaign Telephone Bank

State	12	OHIO
County	27	CUYAHOGA
City or TWP	3	
Ward or Dist	8	
Precinct	12	
Other		

PHONER'S TALLY BOX

	TIME OF CALL	DATE	TOTAL COMPLTD
1st Try	M A E		
2nd Try	M A E		
3rd Try	M A E		

Cum Total

CLERICAL BOX

	Names Transferred? (Check ✓)
Abs Ballot	
Will Help	

Fill in MAGIC NUMBER (1/3 Non-GOP Hshlds) 3

Tally	PTY	Phone Number	Title	Last Name	First Name	Suf.	VOTER I.D. FOR	AGAINST	UNDECIDED	WILL HELP CANVASS	PHONE	ELECT DAY	ABSENTEE BLT	REMINDER	ELECT DAY CALL 1	CALL 2	VOTED 7	Seq. Number	House No.	Street Name	Dir	Apt. No.	Zip Code
I * I	R	889-9160	MRS	SMITH	ADELLE		*F	A	U	C	P	E	B	R	1	2	V*	97591001-1	694	PLEASANT	NW		55970
I * I	R	889-5854	MR	SMITH	ALEX		*F	A	U	C	P	E	B	R	1	2	V*	97601001-1	369	RAVINE	NW		55970
I . . . I	D	889-7887	MRS	SMITH	ALICE		F	A	U				B	R	1	2	V	97611001-1	816	LOCUST	NW		55970
I . . . I	D	889-5854	MR	SMITH	BERT		F	A	U				B	R	1	2	V	97621001-1	369	RAVINE	NW	619	55970
	D			SMITH	SAM		F	A	U				B	R	1	2	V	97621001-2					
I . . . I	O	889-0678	MR	SMITH	CARROLL		F	A	U				B	R	1	2	V	97631001-1	786	NUECES	NW		55970
I * I	R	889-5854	MRS	SMITH	DELORES		*F	A	U	C	P	E	B	R	1	2	V*	97641001-1	369	RAVINE	NW	619	55970
I . . . I . . .		889-1342	MR	SMITH	HERBERT	JR	F	A	U	C	P	E	B	R	1	2	V	97651001-1	960	DANVILLE	NW		55970
. . .			MRS	SMITH	ADA		F	A	U	C	P	E	B	R	1	2	V	97651001-2					
I * I	R	889-2367	MRS	SMITH	KARLA		*F	A	U	C	P	E	B	R	1	2	V*	97661001-1	369	RAVINE	NW	207	55970
I * I	R	889-7887	MR	SMITH	LAMONT		*F	A	U	C	P	E	B	R	1	2	V*	97671001-1	816	LOCUST	NW		55970
I . . . I	O	889-9160	MR	SMITH	MELVILLE		F	A	U				B	R	1	2	V	97681001-1	694	PLEASANT	NW		55970
I * I	R	889-2367	MR	SMITH	MONTMORENCY		*F	A	U	C	P	E	B	R	1	2	V*	97691001-1	369	RAVINE	NW		55970
I * I	R	889-5854		SMITH	NANCY		*F	A	U	C	P	E	B	R	1	2	V*	97701001-1	369	RAVINE	NW		55970
I . . . I	O	889-8574	MR	SMITH	OSCAR		F	A	U				B	R	1	2	V	97711001-1	740	NUECES	NW		55970
	O		MRS	SMITH	BETTY		F	A	U				B	R	1	2	V	97711001-2					
I . . . I	D	889-2367		SMITH	PAULA		F	A	U				B	R	1	2	V	97721001-1	369	RAVINE	NW	207	55970

polling place with a precinct list. As each voter enters the polling place, if the worker does not know their name, the voter is asked for his or her name (in some states the election judges will give precinct workers access to their lists of those who have voted). Beginning about four or five hours before the polls close, the lists of those who have already voted are fed back to headquarters, either by a runner system or by telephoning them. The names of those who have not turned out are checked against the canvass lists and those supporters (some include names of the undecided) who have not voted are called and reminded to vote. If a card file system is used, the cards of those supporters who have not yet voted are pulled. If the voter reports a problem, such as transportation or babysitting, assistance is provided. This process is repeated at hourly intervals until the polls close, so that persons who have already voted are not unnecessarily contacted. Ordinarily, no more than two contacts are made to the same person, but persistance is stronger during the second contact.

Transportation and child care are the main support services for election-day get-out-the-vote activities. Many details need to be worked out, including organization, recruitment, worker shifts, worker assignments, assembly points, message centers, child-care centers, and emergency personnel. A very simple method of organization is to divide drivers and babysitters into groups by precinct. One of each kind of worker should be allowed for four precincts, coordinated out of a central headquarters. Drivers and babysitters are sometimes combined in a single driver-babysitter. Ordinarily the demand for such services rarely exceeds a reasonable supply. Some campaigns have been known to include the telephone number for this type of voter assistance in their advertising. In all cases, the legality of these support services should be investigated. In some states it is illegal to provide any type of assistance to voters.

There are also other types of activities at the polls. Many campaigns distribute leaflets at the polls, thus reaching the voter just before voting. Although not essential, it is desirable to employ workers who are from the precinct and likely to know many of the voters personally, similar to old style, party-machine methods. In areas where there is an extremely long ballot, or where the voter is faced with a complex voting machine, very often a sample ballot or a reproduction of the face of the voting machine, highlighting the position of the candidate, is offered. These leafleteers or poll workers, to appear official and to demonstrate the presence of the candidate's effort, are ordinarily identified with a sticker, pin, or ribbon. State and local regulations should be checked. Some states require that a certain distance from the polls be maintained, whereas others have no specific distance requirements but insist that poll workers not interfere with voters entering the polling place.[48]

Another activity frequently implemented at the polls is use of the challenger. This person (where law permits) is ordinarily certified by the election administrator or election board, stays close to but does not interfere with election officials to insure that no election fraud occurs during the balloting. The duties and legal powers of watchers vary from state to state. Their duties include checking the voting machines or ballot boxes before the polls are open to see that boxes are empty and machines are set at zero and to check the levers to be sure that they are working properly. During the voting, the poll watcher watches the proceedings near the election officials, but cannot talk to voters or campaign in any other way. Among the tasks a poll watcher might perform during this time are: checking to see that each voter is qualified; making sure voters do not return to the polling place after voting; if assistance in the booth is allowed, checking that it is given only under legally specified conditions; checking the total votes cast on the machines periodically against one's own total; where allowable by law, challenging the right to vote of anyone whose status is questionable; and, seeking arrest if any violations or fraud exists. During the counting, the watcher examines each ballot, watches to see that the proper officials are present when machines or boxes are opened, observes the counting of the ballots and ordinarily reports the results to campaign headquarters.[49] The poll watcher also checks any questionable practices with the voluntary legal counsel by telephone. (See Chapter 7.)

Obviously, such a detailed set of legally regulated duties requires considerable training and instruction. Most campaigns that seriously undertake challengers usually have legal counsel and campaign staff work out important information that challengers need, and write out detailed instructions. A two- to three-hour training session can then cover election law, the most frequent types of infractions, how they are discovered, and the rights and duties of challengers.[50]

If poll watching, challenging, and distributing leaflets are to be undertaken seriously in a large number of precincts, obviously, the personnel demands can be quite high. Moreover, it may be difficult to get workers to work an entire 12- to 14-hour shift at the polls. Some activities are broken down into two or three shifts, making it necessary to use more volunteers, but thereby avoiding fatigue. Since poll challengers are officially designated and the duties require more precision and training, it is more difficult to rotate them. Also, some states will not allow each candidate to have a challenger, but require that each party designate one person to represent all of its candidates. The duties of two of the three election-day precinct workers can often be combined. Challengers often check off the names of persons who have voted and hand them to runners. Leafleteers or poll workers sometimes check off the names of voters, although it is more difficult to catch up to voters, ask for their names, and hand them literature.

While not exhaustive, this account of the various election-day activities indicates that a process of assessment, information, planning, and implementation, similar to media or any other campaign activity, must go into election-day activities. Between the decision to undertake an activity and election day comes many hours of recruitment, checking laws, updating lists, developing forms, training, writing instructions, preparing kits, confirming volunteers, establishing schedules, arranging for worker transportation, and providing for refreshments.

DIRECT VOTER CONTACT AND THE CAMPAIGN

With the advent of mass-media campaigning and the decline of party activity, it was assumed by some that direct voter-contact activities would go the way of the party newspaper, the whistle stop, and the torchlight parade. This has not happened. Direct voter contact is as important as it always was, although as likely to be organized by the candidate or a coalition of candidates as by the party. Some activities, such as registration and getting out the vote, are better organized at the individual voter level than through mass-media appeals. In addition, limits being placed on the amounts of money spent in national and state campaigns will further encourage other types of campaign activities. The research presented at the beginning of the chapter indicated that direct contact can make a difference, albeit incremental, in many cases. But then most campaign efforts offer similar increments. Putting together such incremental efforts is what campaigning is all about.

Notes to Chapter 15

1. Richard Jensen, "Armies, Admen and Crusaders: Types of Presidential Election Campaigns," *The History Teacher* 2 (1969): 36.

2. Samuel J. Eldersveld, "Experimental Propaganda Techniques and Voting Behavior," *American Political Science Review* 50 (1956): 160.

3. Ibid., p. 161.

4. M. Margaret Conway, "Voter Information Sources in a Nonpartisan Local Election," *Western Political Quarterly* 21 (1968): 75.

5. Morris Janowitz and Dwaine Marvick, *Competitive Pressure and Democratic Consent* (Ann Arbor: Institute of Public Administration, Univ. of Michigan, 1956), pp. 79-80.

6. Gerald H. Kramer, "The Effects of Precinct-Level Canvassing on Voter Behavior," *Public Opinion Quarterly* 34 (1970-71): 567.

7. Ibid., p. 572.

8. Phillips Cutright and Peter H. Rossi, "Party Organization in Primary Elections," *American Journal of Sociology* 64 (1958): 268.

9. Phillips Cutright and Peter H. Rossi, "Grass Roots Politicians and the Vote," *American Sociological Review* 63 (1958): 175.

10. Ibid., pp. 176-77.

11. Ibid., p. 178.

12. Phillips Cutright, "Measuring the Impact of Local Party Activity on the General Election Vote," *Public Opinion Quarterly* 27 (1963): 384-85.

13. Daniel Katz and Samuel J. Eldersveld, "The Impact of Local Party Activity Upon the Local Electorate," *Public Opinion Quarterly* 25 (1961): 11-12.

14. Ibid., p. 24.

15. Raymond E. Wolfinger, "The Influence of Precinct Work on Voting Behavior," *Public Opinion Quarterly* 27 (1963): 396-97.

16. David E. Price and Michael Lupfer, "Volunteers for Gore: The Impact of a Precinct-Level Canvass in Three Tennessee Cities," *Journal of Politics* 35 (1973): 432-34.

17. William J. Crotty, "Party Effort and Its Impact on the Vote," *American Political Science Review* 65 (1971): 446-47.

18. John C. Blydenburgh, "A Controlled Experiment to Measure the Effects of Personal Contact Campaigning," *Midwest Journal of Political Science* 15 (1971): 376.

19. Ibid., p. 377.

20. Ibid., pp. 380-81.

21. Price and Lupfer, "Volunteers for Gore," pp. 436-37.

22. Ibid., p. 438.

23. Samuel J. Eldersveld and R. W. Dodge, "Personal Contact or Mail Propaganda? An Experiment in Voting Turnout and Attitude Change," in *Public Opinion and Propaganda* eds. Daniel Katz, et al., (New York: Holt, Rinehart and Winston, 1954), p. 540.

24. Janowitz and Marvick, *Competitive Pressure and Democratic Consent,* pp. 82-83.

25. Murray B. Levin, *Kennedy Campaigning* (Boston: Beacon Press, 1966), ch. 1.

26. William J. Crotty, "The Party Organization and Its Activities," *Approaches to the Study of Party Organization* ed. William J. Crotty (Boston: Allyn and Bacon, 1968), p. 255.

27. Samuel J. Eldersveld, *Political Parties: A Behavioral Analysis* (Chicago: Rand, McNally, 1964), p. 351.

28. Penn Kimball, *The Disconnected* (New York: Columbia Univ. Press, 1972), p. 77.

29. For details on these steps see Lee and Anne Edwards, *You Can Make the Difference* (New Rochelle, N.Y.: Arlington House, 1968), pp. 201-212.

30. Stanley Kelley, Jr., Richard E. Ayres and William G. Bowen, "Registration and Voting: Putting First Things First," *American Political Science Review* 61 (1967): 375.

31. Kimball, *The Disconnected,* p. 208.

32. Ibid.

33. Robert L. Chartrand, "Information Technology and the Political Campaigner," in *The New Style in Election Campaigns* ed. Robert Agranoff (Boston: Holbrook Press, 1972), p. 134.

34. Illinois McGovern for President, "Suggested Outline of Voter Registration," Chicago, Illinois, August, 1972, p. 5.

35. Ibid., p. 4.

36. Austin Ranney and Leon D. Epstein, "The Two Electorates: Voters and Non-voters in a Wisconsin Primary," *Journal of Politics* 28 (1966).

37. Sam Brown, Jr., *Storefront Organizing* (New York: Pyramid Books, 1972), p. 123.

38. Illinois McGovern for President, "Suggested Outline for Voter Registration," p. 6.

39. *National Journal,* 29 April 1972, p. 715.

40. Committee to Re-Elect the President, "60 Days to Victory," Washington, D.C., September, 1972.

41. Illinois McGovern for President, "Suggested Outline for Voter Registration," p. 6.

42. Kimball, *The Disconnected,* p. 242.

43. Ibid., p. 162.

44. Minnesota Democratic-Farmer-Labor Party State Central Committee, Get-Out-The-Vote (Minneapolis, Minn.: 1970), pp. 2-3.

45. Citizenship Department, National Farmers Union, "A Poor Man's Guide to Getting Involved in Campaigns for the State Legislature," (Denver, Colorado, 1971).

46. Minnesota Democratic-Farmer-Labor Party," Voter Turnout Program," (Minneapolis, Minnesota, 1972).

47. Ibid.

48. The most complete instructions are contained in the now famous "O'Brien Manual," Lawrence F. O'Brien, *Citizens for Johnson and Humphrey Campaign Manual* (Washington, D.C.: Citizens for Johnson and Humphrey, 1964), pp. 25-30.

49. Mary Meehan, "Canvassing and Election Day," (St. Louis, Mo.: New Democratic Coalition, 1970).

50. Dick Simpson, *Winning Elections* (Chicago: Swallow Press, 1972), pp. 139-42.

For Further Reading and Research

Alexander, Herbert E. and Molloy, J. Paul. *Model State Statute: Politics, Elections and Public Office.* Princeton, N.J.: Citizens Research Foundation, 1974.

Blydenburgh, John C. "A Controlled Experiment to Measure the Effects of Personal Contact Campaigning." *Midwest Journal of Political Science* 15 (1971): 365-81.

Carlson, Richard. *Modernizing Election Systems.* Lexington, Kentucky: Council of State Governments, 1974.

Crotty, William J. "Party Effort and Its Impact on the Vote." *American Political Science Review* 65(1971): 439-50.

Cutright, Phillips. "Measuring the Impact of Local Party Activity on the General Election Vote." *Public Opinion Quarterly* 27(1963): 372-86.

Edwards, Lee and Ann. *You Can Make the Difference.* New Rochelle, N.Y.: Arlington House, 1968.

Eldersveld, Samuel J. *Political Parties: A Behavioral Analysis.* Chicago: Rand McNally, 1964.

Katz, Daniel and Eldersveld, Samuel J. "The Impact of Local Party Activity Upon The Electorate." *Public Opinion Quarterly* 25(1961): 1-24.

Kelley, Jr., Stanley; Ayres, Richard E. and Bowen, William G. "Registration and Voting: Putting First Things First." *American Political Science Review* 61 (1967): 359-79.

Kimball, Penn. *The Disconnected.* New York: Columbia U. Press, 1972.

Kramer, Gerald H. "The Effects of Precinct-Level Canvassing on Voter Behavior." *Public Opinion Quarterly* 34(1970-71): 560-72.

League of Women Voters. *Making It Work: A Guide to Training Election Officials.* Washington: National League of Women Voters, 1973.

Polk Directory of Households. A directory organized by address rather than by name, also referred to as city directory or reverse directory.

Price, David E. and Lupfer, Michael. "Volunteers for Gore: The Impact of a Precinct-Level Canvass in Three Tennessee Cities." *Journal of Politics* 35 (1973):410-38.

Simpson, Dick. *Winning Elections: A Handbook in Participatory Politics.* Chicago: Swallow Press, 1972.

Toward the Management
of Election Campaigns

Throughout this book constant reference has been made to the lack of a managerial tradition in campaigning, as well as the reasons for this condition. Despite the emergence of managers, consultants, and other specialists for hire in campaigns over the past quarter-century, campaign management lacks many of the characteristics associated with a profession. In this final chapter we will break with the tradition of most "practical" campaign manuals and hope to use it as a vehicle to work toward a professional campaign-management tradition. Because of various conditions—the short-term nature of campaigns, the part-time involvement of most campaign managers, its state of infancy as a profession, the paucity of available information, and the relatively elementary nature of campaign management science—the effort will necessarily be crude. But we can take significant steps toward a professional managerial tradition if we begin to discuss, in addition to attention to application of scientifically gathered knowledge and strategic thinking, a concern for: the campaign enterprise as an ongoing entity, documentation, how various operations are connected, as well as accounting for its future prospects.

Ordinarily, practical books urge campaigners to gather the faithful together on election night to receive election returns and to hold a victory party. Soon after all volunteers and contributors are sent thank-you notes. It is presumed that these actions conclude a particular campaign. It is a truism to many successful campaigners that the post-election period is only the beginning of another phase of political activity. The job of campaign management is a continuous one. Politicians engage in political activities which are not specifically those of the campaign trail: they work in government; they are covered by the news; they communicate interpersonally; they mass communicate and their physical presence is noted. Meanwhile, someone is maintaining and nurturing a hibernating campaign organization. Campaign management has its own requirements of continuity, long-range planning, and phased activity, similar to other enterprises.

No self-respecting business firm would ignore market analysis, economic conditions, consumer demands, and activities of competitors, neither would it destroy sales records, lists of prospects and past customers, fail to take note of key contacts, ignore the most successful and efficient procedures, or in any other way fail to continue important documentation and information from one sales campaign to the next. No sales organization would ignore some form of postcampaign reconstruction, in which marketing successes and failures are fed back into future campaigns. Yet, this is a near universal occurrence in election campaigns. Adequate records are rarely kept; if there is some documentation, it is usually misplaced or destroyed; and, systematic postcampaign analysis is rare. Ordinarily, the campaign comes to a stop on election night. Some months later, some familiar and many unfamiliar faces begin the same type of activity, in the same constituency, working for the same office, on the same ticket, without much benefit from the information or the experiences of their predecessors.

The information presented in the preceding fifteen chapters should have revealed that campaign processes and the connecting operations related to them are quite complex and dynamic. Among the thousands that could have been presented, literally hundreds of concepts, contingencies, situations, and techniques have been offered for managerial consideration. Somehow these ideas have to be put into operation, and, somehow, continuity in the operations has to be conveyed and transmitted. Operationalism and continuity must begin in the course of the campaign and then be carried through the postelection period. It begins by connecting the operations.

CONNECTING OPERATIONS

Campaigning was defined in Chapter 1 as an attempt to coordinate or connect various operations. Strategic campaign planning was defined as an attempt to chart a path among the various operations and pathways. The task remains to illustrate how specific operations can be connected in a campaign management scheme. To this point, the various phases of the operation—information assessment, public relations, organizational development, media, voter-contact activities—have been presented as if they were activities which occur in isolation from each other. Obviously, they relate to each other in the real world of the campaign, and their interrelation depends on such factors as timing, premises, rescources, advantages, disadvantages, assets, liabilities, in short, setting and strategy. Somehow or another they have to be combined into a coherent operation.

The connecting of operations will be demonstrated in simplified form by selecting various campaign operations and illustrating them in a time sequence. Time is one of many means of sequencing operations. They may also be arranged in order of absolute strategic priority, or in terms of some vote yield scheme, or in terms of a sequence of operational steps based on a level of resources. Time appears to be especially suitable for sequencing operations in a campaign because they are so bound to a specific occurrence—an election. Events in a campaign are geared up to bracket a legally established election. Many campaign resources, such as the availability of money and workers are linked, to a considerable degree, to an election schedule. The attentiveness of groups and voters is also bound to an election time schedule. Campaign managers have many difficulties sequencing events in relation to available resources, or in terms of votes or strategies, but all of these issues seem to cut across the time problem. Thus, the management problem becomes not only what to do, but when to do it. Time sequencing will be demonstrated with illustrations from macroscopic and microscopic levels, and then by presenting a "slice" of the two, illustrating a time schedule for a single, campaign week.

One of the earliest tasks a manager must perform is to fit the many different kinds of activities discussed in this book into some coherent time frame. Some of these activities must be geared to a specifically prescribed period, such as the time surrounding the opening and closing of voter registration. Other activities, logically or practically, precede each other. Others have no exact time referent, but their performance is dictated by the pace of the campaign and or their distance from, or proximity to, the election. Figure 16.1 is meant to demonstrate the time sequence of various major activities in a hypothetical campaign. It is easiest to think of these activities as phases, or categories of activities which relate to each other. At the very earliest phase of the campaign informal soundings and contacts with party, political, and community leaders are made, core workers and campaign staff are recruited, and political-party relations are established. The second phase involves assessment of information and the solicitation of contributions by the candidate. The third phase involves actual strategic assessment of the information, and the setting of priorities. At about the same time, party activists and group leaders are lined up. The next phase, about eight months before the election, involves the development of specific plans based on the strategies planned and tactics derived. Here, specific finance plans, media plans, voter-contact activities, and organizational development plans are undertaken. The next phase, five to seven months before the election, involves operationalizing the soundings, strategies, and plans developed earlier. Leaders must be recruited, specific activities must be organized, and a core of volunteers must be identified, recruited, and trained. The last three to four months involve the unfolding of specific campaign activities: developing literature, scripts, releases, holding fund-raising events, preparing mailings, supervising volunteers, engaging in registration, canvassing, get-out-the-vote and election-day activities. Another phase begins as various postelection activities are undertaken. (See page 456). Notice that most, but not all, activities can fit

Figure 16.1   A Macroscopic Time-Scaled Activity Calendar

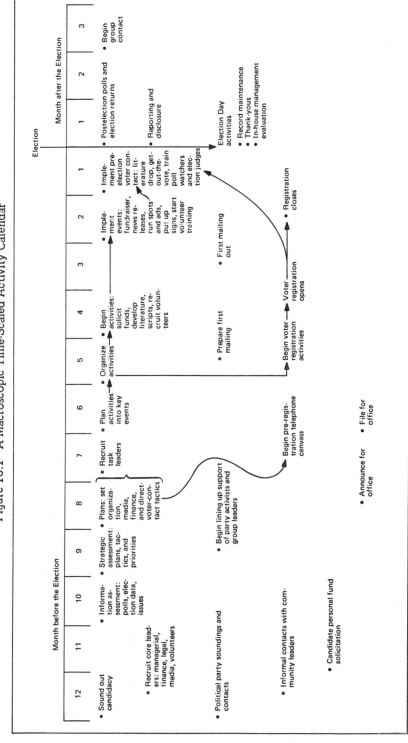

within these broadly conceived phases. There are always exceptions, such as canvassing and registration, which in this case must be sequenced to bracket the opening of registration, four and one-half months before the election, and its closing, six weeks before the election. Though not exhaustive, Figure 16.1 suggests that campaign activity flows in logical and practical phases, based on some rough time sequence surrounding the holding of elections.

The activities within every single one of these campaign management phases are based on a series of individualized events which in turn must be sequenced. In Chapter 5, the numerous and complicated steps involved in campaign polling were illustrated. The steps involved in voter identification, voter registration, and voter turnout were illustrated in Chapter 15. For each campaign activity, an integrated set of management events must occur before the final activity can ensue. Some of these events are essential to the activity involved, and some are related campaign events required to undertake a single campaign activity, such as an election-weekend literature blitz. Figure 16.2 makes it clear that someone in the campaign does not merely decide the week before the election that certain residents in the constituency will be greeted by a worker who gives them a short message and a piece of literature. Rather, the event must be preceded by certain staffing, precinct priority, fund availability, printing capability, and content decisions. Then, the dual tracks of volunteer development and literature production begin some four months before the activity. In each respective track, essential events such as recruitment, designing, checking, distributing, planning, and instruction are performed. The two tracks must meet at the same time when volunteers are handed literature to distribute and are instructed—just before they hit the streets. Every campaign activity requires a similar sequencing of events into a coherent pattern enabling it to unfold at the proper time.

The complexity of campaign management is compounded when one realizes that often hundreds of events support dozens of activities which are part of numerous phases. Just as phases overlap, some events and activities tend to occur at the same time. Indeed, campaigns resemble many other enterprises in that many different phases, activities, and events in an operation are designed to achieve a single goal (e.g., the construction of a super-highway). Thus, at any given point many events are occurring. To illustrate this, Figure 16.3 represents a hypothetical activity calendar for a single campaign week, the sixth week before the election. It is self-descriptive. The events listed obviously are designed to be supportive of many activities, which in this case are primarily part of two phases. Thus, one challenge of campaign management is to order many happenings into some time-sequenced interrelation.

The process of time sequencing must be understood as only a step toward the connecting of operations. The campaign process is a dynamic, interactive process. Any paper and pencil time sequencing is bound to be modified when plans meet people, the availability of resources, or other dimensions. There are many interconnections with other activities that will not become obvious until

Figure 16.2 A Microscopic Time-Scaled Activity/Event Calendar for an Election Weekend Literature Blitz

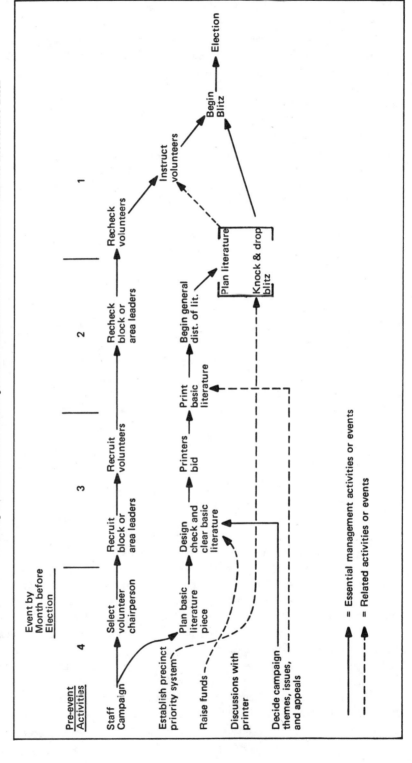

Figure 16.3 A Micro-Macroscopic Activity Calendar for a Single Campaign Week (Sixth week before the Election)

SUNDAY	MONDAY	TUESDAY	WEDNESDAY	THURSDAY	FRIDAY	SATURDAY
• Release pollution position paper from Sierra picnic	• 8:00 am Staff meeting	• 6:45 am General Merchants Trucking Gate	• 6:00 am Warner-Smith plant gate	• 7:30 am Party Leadership Breakfast	• Voter registration closes 5:00 pm	• 10:00 am Training session for canvassers
• 1:00 pm Candidate at Sierra picnic, 30 min. speech	• 9:30 Volunteers arrive to stuff teachers mailing	• Release on aid to blind	• 10:00 Review last week's TV spots at agency	• First weekly newspaper ad runs	• 9:00 am Candidate at WDIK radio call-in show	• Candidate door-to-door W_7P_2
• 5:00 pm Meet with Nolan Montgomery	• Last minute check of newspaper ads	• First radio spots to run	• Candidate lunch with Health Planning Board	• Elk River C of C luncheon, 15 min. talk	• Second financial statement due at Capitol by Monday	• 1:00 pm Weekly campaign liaison with other candidates
• Evening off for candidate	• Last week of voter registration	• Candidate at Lions luncheon	• 2:00 pm Plan canvasser training session	• Begin recruiting poll watchers	• 11:00 to 1:30 Candidate with Model Cities Action Board	• 4:00 Old Mill shopping center
	• Taxpayer Assn. luncheon	• 4:00 pm Accountant to enter fund-raiser receipts	• Begin preparing 2nd financial report	• Teachers mailing	• 2:00 Candidate at Lincoln sch.	• 5:00 Issue Forum Review with staff
	• Begin rechecking area block worker leaders	• Candidate at League of Women Voters Forum	• Re-check Fri. eve. volunteers	• 8:00 pm Candidate at Education assn.	• Lit. dist. at district high sch. football games	• 7:00 Tape Issue Forum
	• Continue dist. of lit. to groups		• Candidate at St. Anthony's fall festival and speaks at Peotone Grange	• Call reporters, release on state funding of schools	• Candidate at Monee game	• 9:00 Fund raiser at home of Smiths
	• 8:00 pm Candidate at Joint Labor Council					

events unfold. This sequencing assumes rigid adherence to an established strategy, logical tactical derivations, and operational priorities. In actual practice, sufficient flexibility is necessary to alter strategy as the campaign progresses, not to speak of certain non-strategic events which are "necessary" if not "proper." As the campaign begins to leave the control of the planners and is put into the hands of the implementors, a high degree of goal displacement occurs.

Moreover, a static, time-based sequencing of campaign events does not do proper justice to the dynamism of strategic premises and strategic thinking. It was demonstrated in Chapter 6 that strategists must consider many things interrelatedly, for example partisan strength, group support, one's own organization, and financial strength. To connect operations only by time is to treat the priorities among interrelated factors as unidimensional. Thus, it may become necessary to combine time, as a sequencing factor, with resource bases or other strategic priorities. In the 1974 congressional elections, the Democratic Senatorial Campaign Committee provided a time plus financial resource sequencing for its thirty-four candidates by time scaling hundreds of campaign events over a 15-month period for high, medium, and low-budget campaigns. While it is only a beginning, the Democratic Senate project suggests that dynamic aspects of campaign management can be tapped.

Despite the very real limitations involved in time sequencing, its use represents a significant step toward connecting the operations involved in managing a campaign. To paraphrase a popular colloquialism, its purpose is to let the right hand inform the left hand if it is doing it, what it is doing, and when it is doing it. Such exercises in planning and commitment to paper are bureaucratic functions too little used in American campaigns.

DOCUMENTATION

Any political scientist or historian who has made an attempt to systematically study a campaign, or some aspect of campaigning, will testify that they have found a dearth of written materials from which to gather evidence. A lack of professionalism has led to an almost non-exchange of information, little professional interchange among managers, great discontinuity between succeeding managers, and very little continuity in operational procedures. This low level of continuity and interchange is symbolized by the almost nonexistent level of records, files, written plans, and other forms of documentation. Such a dearth of written materials affects both theory and practice in campaigning. Scholarly studies have been largely reduced to sketchy historical accounts, single case studies, or the behavioral study of a narrow range of variables imposed by the researcher. Practice in campaign management has meant that each manager begins *de novo*, without benefit of reflection on, or reaction to, past plans, lists, documents, schedules, correspondence, or other written records.

It is suggested that a significant step toward campaign management could be taken by increasing the level of documentation therein. For the sake of continuity in management, it would be useful if all plans, voting reports, roll calls, issue papers, voter lists, media records and studies, election maps, priority systems, poll reports, volunteer lists, finance records and lists, meeting minutes, calendars, schedules, timetables, itineraries, correspondence, and other campaign documents and files were preserved. In the preservation of records, all steps and procedures developed for the purpose of supporting an event, such as instructions to poll watchers, the number of telephone calls per hour, or ideal sign locations, should be documented and preserved. All news releases, position papers, advertisements, literature, flyers, and other campaign materials should become archived. Because so many events occur over a relatively long period of time, it would be very useful to keep a daily log of campaign events, in which the principals involved enter a paragraph or two about that event. In the very largest scale campaigns, it even makes sense to appoint a campaign historian, responsible for collecting all materials and documenting events.

With the benefit of such written material, the succeeding campaign manager will begin to experience a starting point similar to that of the operating officers of any other organization, having histories, records, and files. As a new manager or executive takes up the reigns of an enterprise, it is always clear that while the present and future are to be faced, it is useful to account for the past. The written record never tells all, but it can suggest important insights and patterns of behavior. They can be the basis of asking the right questions, that is, a base point from which one can gather additional data to organize managerial perceptions. This practice is almost nonexistent in the campaign management enterprise.

POSTELECTION MAINTAINENCE

Modern campaign management requires that many of the types of tasks performed during the campaign period must be extended beyond the election. Postelection activity is necessary to decelerate rather than dismantle the operations of an organization which ordinarily self-destructs rather quickly, after a single occurrence. Certain operations, such as documentation, meeting legally prescribed requirements, information gathering, communication with voters, and other means of involving volunteers can serve the cause of organizational maintenance. A sustained organization, such as the continuing campaign organizations nurtured by many incumbent officials, offers numerous advantages: established lines of communication, tested and experienced leadership and workers, continuous information, regular voter contact, a means of feeding experiences back to the organization, and other organizational-maintenance functions.

One of the earliest postelection tasks that a campaign organization can undertake is to use loyal volunteers to get out a thank-you mailing to all who have worked in or contributed to the campaign. It would be useful to use such a mailing to ask workers if they would care to assist in the continuation of the campaign by working on future interelection projects, such as a fund-raising or mailing activity, or otherwise inform workers that the campaign is to continue. The postelection thank-you note is the first overt step toward organizational maintenance.

Many candidates hold postelection fund-raising parties or dinners, usually to pay any remaining campaign debts. These affairs usually take place during the time between the election and the taking of office, and for elected executives, sometimes in conjunction with that official's inauguration. Notice the emphasis here is on candidates who will take office, since these affairs are rarely successful for losing candidates. The winning candidate obviously has the advantage of drawing funds from those who bet wrong, or those who did not place a high enough bet, or those who forgot to bet, or from those who wish to further advance their own or the official's cause, or a combination. A postelection fund-raising event can be an important means of keeping the organization intact.

The previously mentioned files and records must also be put in order. Lists such as contributors, volunteers, locations of lawn signs, mailings, and media contacts should not only be preserved but evaluated. Some campaigners have been known to rate items on these lists, for example: easy to difficult contributors, superior to inferior workers, workers who can take on more responsibility next time, the fund-raising yield of various lists, high and low voter registration yield areas, and the ratio of campaign effort to turnout results in various areas. Other records, such as news releases, calendars, itineraries, literature, ad and spot samples, and correspondence should be put in order. If, in the hectic pace of the pre-election period, no one has recorded the steps involved in very useful techniques, methods and procedures should be recorded. It is not unusual for a group of campaigners to find themselves trying to remember how they put together a successful fund-raising operation or a public relations effort some two to six years earlier, and all they can remember are very sketchy outlines of the project.

The legally prescribed, postelection financial reports must also be handled. As a prior step, the internal campaign financial records will have to be completed, at least up to the date of the report. As financial reporting and limitations on contributions and spending become more stringent, it will become increasingly important for campaigners to seek outside auditing, accounting, and legal assistance, much the same as individuals and businesses seek tax-preparation assistance. If there are plans to continue activity beyond the date of the financial report, financial accounts must remain open with more than token funds available.

Perhaps more important than these housekeeping functions are attempts to gather and analyze systematic information, chiefly postelection polling and aggregate-data analysis. Such post-mortem analyses are very difficult to get campaigners or candidates to agree to. There usually is a feeling that the election is over, funds have already been overspent, and if "we won, who cares how we won," and if "we lost, who wants to go to great expense to reconstruct a painful experience." Yet, much valuable campaign management information can be captured at this point. The major survey organizations have found that postelection polls do a better job of revealing: last-minute vote switches; the turnout or stay-at-home reasons of citizens with low motivation; the electoral effect of various campaign techniques, appeals, and events; plus, a better recall (and therefore a more accurate measure) of actual voting patterns. Candidates have begun to take advantage of these factors by engaging in postelection polls themselves, often by use of the "tracking" method. Election data are available relatively soon after the election; the official totals usually are available within a month or two when the election board certifies the results. Analysis of these figures while the campaign is fresh in the analysts' minds allows one to check vote yields against priorities and special efforts made, as well as trying to explain patterns and any deviations from the expected, or any findings discernable in the light of recent events.

A major part of the postelection campaign organization effort is the various communication efforts on the part of the candidate and other campaigners. Basically, they are extensions of the support-gathering, public relations, and media efforts explained earlier in this book. First, there is ordinarily some continuing contact with political and community leaders. Incumbents use the pretense of discussing pending governmental issues and their involvement in problem solving, plus the usual organizational appearances. There are also continued contacts with the party organization and party leaders. Non-incumbents can, but rarely do, follow the same channels. It is not unusual to see an unsuccessful challenger who plans to run again "go on vacation" from public affairs until the next formal campaign. Political and community leaders make public affairs a continuing effort and interaction with them is a good way to continue the campaign.

A second form of contact is to maintain and utilize some of the core leadership group over a period of time. Candidates have been known to form a group of executive branch monitors, a sort of campaign organization "shadow cabinet." Such a group has responsibility for following the actions of various departments and department heads. Candidates for legislative office similarly have employed observers at legislative hearings and committee sessions to buttress research concerning the formal record of an opponent. Other forms of issue research can also be performed. Campaign leaders need not, however, restrict themselves to issue efforts. They too can maintain liason efforts with various groups, discuss future campaign strategies and tactics, plan and conduct fund-raising efforts, and assist in organizing any media efforts. Being active and attentive citizens, members of such a core leadership group represent continuous lines of effort to like-minded persons in the community; they signal the continuation of a campaign.

The third form of contact includes all of those means of mass citizen contact which we normally associate as the office holder "campaigning." They include: citizen questionnaires and surveys and their publication, speaking before groups, news releases, radio and TV interviews and "beepers," news and news program appearances, formal, open hearings, and mail communication with voters. The incumbent obviously has the advantage here because of his or her status as a governmental official. A forum is more easily provided under these auspices. The person out of office must carefully calculate the effect of appearing like a candidate when no formal campaign exists. The non-incumbent must therefore be more creative in developing organized vehicles for public attention and communication. It is often a special study commission, leadership in a community organization, the holding of a part-time appointed position to a board or commission, participation in a movement, rally, or demonstration, or any other vehicle that does not appear completely self-serving. Any of these means of mass citizen contact remains available as a tactic for any candidacy to extend the campaign.

The techniques outlined in this section, therefore, need not be restricted to incumbent officials. Losing candidates often run for the same or another office. Sometimes a candidacy is offered to further a cause, and an organized effort is necessary to continue the fight. Even if there is no desire on the part of the candidate and campaigners to run again, it becomes useful to hold onto an organization until a like-minded group of campaigners arrives on the scene.

THE FUTURE OF CAMPAIGN MANAGEMENT

Campaign management is a craft that will possibly become a profession. Some significant organizational, informational, and political trends are contributing to the development of a corps of campaign managers, whose applications appear to be similar and could develop into a recognized professional specialization.

Information Accessibility

The extent and quality of systematic information from voting, communications, and campaign processes is expanding at a very rapid pace. A substantial amount was incorporated into the body of this book; a great deal more is available as each set of campaigns and elections ensues. Two important trends are significant. Academic researchers have increasingly given attention to examining the impact of various campaign events on the vote. Papers and articles are now appearing on such topics as the impact of broadcast campaigning on the vote, the marginal advantage of newspaper endorsements, and the information advantages of commercials versus newscasts. A second trend is the development of research on various campaign operations by professional campaign managers. Examples of such research include: the use of operations research to plan, implement, and evaluate precinct work; postelection polling to test attentiveness to various media efforts, and the testing of various direct-mail-vote and fund-raising appeals. The latter type of operational research is obviously dependent on the theoretical nature of the former, but both appear to be coming together to begin to create a body of knowledge which someday will be applied by a corps of professional managers.

Technology

Along with knowledge, some increased technological application has already arrived in campaigns, increasing professionalism. Technological changes include: polling and market research; computers; films, radio, newspaper, and television; advertising; graphic design; systematic use of the telephone and telegraph; behavioral science applications; jet travel; and, industrial engineering and management science techniques. Each of these advances has brought new professionals to the campaign. In addition to some of the older campaigners, the younger breed, coming into activity, learned to combine their partisan zeal or their activism with a desire to learn and to use the new techniques to help advance their causes. One of the most interesting, recent phenomena was to see an idealistic Goldwaterite, McCarthyite or McGovernite rapidly adapt to polling, telephone canvassing, or the use of management techniques, yet maintain their idealism.

The blending of technical specialization with politics has served to enhance a new professionalism in campaigning. It could lead to the development of a new breed of politician, one whose skill is based on bringing a specialization to the campaign, other than mobilization of people within a limited geographic area.

Professional Managers

Throughout this book we have referred to the emergence of a corps of persons who consider themselves to be professional campaign managers. They come from a variety of backgrounds and function in a variety of ways. The most visible are the managerial consultants, who move from state to state and work in a variety of campaigns, overseeing the overall direction of the campaign. Next, are the specialty operators, who perform polling, advertising, public-relations, direct-mail, media-production, or other services, in a number of campaigns. There are also the less visible but emerging breed of "campaign handlers," in-house managers who do not necessarily live in the state or constituency where they are operating. They usually travel through party circles on their reputation for successfully putting together the complex strands of a modern campaign. Even less visible are the numerous experienced managers who are continually called upon to organize a campaign for their party within an area or a single state. Before the advent of "professional campaign management" as embodied in the three former types of manager, this latter group constituted the textbook definition of a professional campaign manager.

All four of these managerial types have brought more professionalism to campaigning. Some of it has come through the practice of applying techniques and practices from an earlier profession to campaigns. Some of it is because these managers are good at the older techniques of politics. Professionalism has also come because fewer managers are professional political party types or government workers. They tend to bring a managerial tradition with them from their regular occupation. Continuity tends to bring something in addition to experience—the desire to seek organizational development, systemization, procedures, and operationalism. Thus, professional managers are increasing the level of professional management in campaigns.

Political Parties

In the early stages of the development of modern campaign technology and management, political party organizations abrogated any leadership they had in running campaigns by largely ignoring technological advances, campaigning as usual. This nullification came at a time when there was a declining level of party activism and party loyalty, thus further leading to the displacement of parties in campaigns.

There is evidence that parties are beginning to make a comeback on the campaign scene by finding a new role in campaign management. Rather than serving as the guiding force in campaigns, parties around the country are beginning to serve as important technical and operational backup for candidate-centered campaigns. Parties are performing such valuable functions as maintaining data bases, developing address files, working on issue development, training, and systematically handling unified voter-contact activities. They are also beginning to provide technical assistance and consulting services on a wide range of subjects for those candidates who cannot afford the entreprenurial consultants. These new functions appear to begin the relinking of parties with campaigns and can only lead to increased levels of professional management in campaigns.

Legal Regulation

The 1970s are proving to be the decade of campaign regulation with meaning. Depending on the office to be sought, there are regulations on the amount of money that can be contributed, who can contribute it, what it can be spent for, and how much can be spent. All of this must now be carefully recorded and reported. The import for professional campaign management is obvious. For the first time campaign executives will be faced with operating within a legal web similar to executives of other enterprises. It is likely to bring on newer types of political consultants—the accountant and paid legal counsel. Regulation will *require* a more thorough and accurate level of documentation and record keeping. It will become much more difficult to keep fund sources and ledgers in the finance director's head or vest pocket, and expenditures will have to be documented beyond the checkbook recordings that are typical of campaign treasurers. Limitations on spending will stimulate the desire to more efficiently use resources and reduce waste. This will come not only through traditional comptrolling but through various means of cost-effectiveness testing. Finally, public disclosure regulations will dramatically increase the quantity and quality of public information available for the systematic study of campaign finance and other aspects of campaigning which, of course, will buttress theoretical and operational research.

Colleges and Universities

Perhaps it is because of the traditional connotation of partisan involvement, or, perhaps it is because campaign management was never considered to be a full-time occupation, or, perhaps because there has never been a real managerial tradition, but whatever the reason, American colleges and universities have virtually ignored professional campaign management. Most schools teach about campaigns, many schools have some sort of practical applications or field work in campaigns classes, and a few schools try to get their students to apply systematic techniques or social science findings to campaigns. But, there has been virtually no effort to academically train a corps of professional managers, similar to programs in school, hospital, public, or business administration. The John F. Kennedy School of Public Affairs at Harvard has made some efforts to offer courses and seminars in professional management, and other universities are beginning to offer campaign management courses through their evening or adult-education divisions. A number of the civic-minded have even called for a "West Point for Politics," and in the not-too-near future it is likely that a school of public affairs might be offering a master's degree with emphasis in campaign management.

Information Exchange

The continued advance of professional campaign management depends on a greater placement of campaign information in the public domain. Only by professional managers subjecting their ideas, methods, or research to peer evaluation will the enterprise be advanced beyond the level of alchemy. Too often professional managers have claimed "secret method," client confidence, or actually engaged in some form of covertness to withdraw their techniques from public scrutiny, when in actuality there are no secret methods or established codes of confidentiality. This reluctance, perhaps, reflects the desire of a new specialization to maintain a professional mystique or a myth of indispensability. Its effect is carried, however, from usage on an unsuspecting public and clients to professionally organized activities. As a result, the content of campaign consultants' educational vehicles have been indistinguishable from political discussions at the student union, the ward club, or the voters' league meeting. Many professional campaign management seminars and one unsuccessful attempt at a journal unfortunately have taken on the cast of high level citizenship forums rather than vehicles for examining professional developments.

Campaign management needs more avenues for true professional interchange. As a beginning, the Citizen's Research Foundation is sponsoring meaningful seminars on financing of campaigns and broadcast spending and its effects. Other seminars of a professional nature are being sponsored here and there, such as the four-year-old foundation-backed nonpartisan Institute of Politics in Arkansas, where professional consultants place their techniques and findings before budding candidates. Monthly newsletters on campaign techniques, election related legislation, and election administration now exist. Many experienced campaigners claim the time is ripe for a professional campaign management journal, in which academics and practitioners could have a common research forum. Also of use would be some readily accessible information sources, such as data banks and poll banks. More and more of these types of professional interchanges are occurring, and more are needed.

The need to regard campaign management as a serious enterprise depends on approaching it as a complex, interconnected series of operations which are based on a combination of expertise, information, and judgment. The end result of every campaign has serious consequences for the American system. It is time that those enterprises which lead to such results begin to receive serious attention.

Index